WINSTON CHURCHILL

THE YEARS OF ACHIEVEMENT

Companion Volume to

WINSTON CHURCHILL
THE YEARS OF PREPARATION
by Lewis Broad

WINSTON CHURCHILL

THE YEARS OF ACHIEVEMENT

A BIOGRAPHY

BY

Lewis Broad

HAWTHORN BOOKS, INC. *Publishers*

New York

Acknowledgments

Cartoons: © *Punch*, London, England
This volume contains some material which previously appeared in *The
War That Winston Waged*, published by Hutchinson & Co., Ltd.,
London, © 1960 by Lewis Broad.

H-9415

A C Silbert

CONTENTS

5

BOOK THREE

ALLIES IN CONFLICT

BOOK FOUR

ALLIES IN VICTORY

BOOK FIVE

ALLIES IN THE COLD WAR

LIST OF ILLUSTRATIONS

INTERLUDE

WHAT WE OWE TO
WINSTON CHURCHILL

M ORE than twenty years have passed since the opening of Sir Winston Churchill's premiership in the day when the survival of Britain, of freedom in Europe, and of much else in the world besides was in the balance. Under his leadership and inspiration, the peoples of Britain sustained the fight against Hitlerism until, by the contrivances of Providence and the folly of the enemies, allies to east and west were joined in the struggle, so that Hitlerism was swept away.

Never in Britain's history has such a premiership been known. It opened at the time of Britain's most grievous plight. His was the leadership of her finest hour.

We saw him in the plenitude of his powers when, in 1940, the world seemed to be falling to pieces. It was then that the diverse strands of his character were fused together and he emerged as the indomitable leader of the British people. It was then that his massive figure seemed to absorb in his own person the shock of successive calamities, breaking their force as the breakwater receives and breaks the force of the tempest.

His people, and the world's free people, drew comfort and inspiration from him at the time of peril. Without need to brace himself to meet the emergency of catastrophe, he stood there in his solid strength. By his bearing, resolute, unflinching, imperturbable, he gave an example for the hour of adversity, showing the way to survive and to prevail.

The qualities in the repertory of greatness were displayed by Winston Churchill in those days. The man and the hour were matched. His life, it seemed, had been directed to prepare him for the occasion of that supreme emergency. What he did could have been performed only by a man in whom strength of character was joined to vast capacity. When all was over and the record of his services made fully known it seemed

13

incredible that one man, in his single person, could have achieved so much.

Nothing that was done can compare in its effect with the influence he exerted by the force of his character. But much that he did do contributed to the war's result. Looking over the course of those years, I reckon the tally of his services stage by stage and make my acknowledgment of the debt I conceive we owe to Winston Churchill.

There was the order that called a halt to the superfluous sacrifice of British planes in the Battle of France and which, by the narrowest of margins, retained fighters in sufficient number to turn the scale in the Battle of Britain.

There was the strategic direction which averted the withdrawal of the Fleet from Alexandria that would have yielded the eastern Mediterranean to the enemy, with the inevitable loss of North Africa and of Egypt and the opening of the gates for a German drive to the east.

There followed the reinforcement of the Desert Armies by the dispatch of some of the few tanks available, which he was pressed to retain for home defense, and the dispatch of the hazardous convoys to Malta.

By these and other measures, and by his insistence on the strategy of the Mediterranean offensive, he gained the prize of the rout of Rommel, victory in "Torchland," the exposure of the "under-belly of the Axis" and the knocking out of Italy from the war.

These results were secured in the face of opposition from his own military advisers and much resistance by United States strategists. There was some niggling criticism over his meddling in military operations. In the perplexities, anxieties, and harassments of war that was understandable. It is less to be understood that there should have been a raking-over of the ashes of these old disputes in some recent memoirs (with some exposure of the fallibility of their authors), seeing that Churchill's "meddling" was proved by the event to have contributed successive winners on the course to victory.

Attention has been called to his regard ("meddling" again) over such matters of military details as the loading of ships engaged on the great assaults on enemy coasts. Reflecting on other enterprises, before and since—the tragic muddle of Gallipoli in Asquith's time, the flop of Suez in Eden's—we may arrive at a more just appreciation of the advantages that resulted from the "meddlings" of Churchill.

Against the pressure of the combined opinion of the American Chiefs of Staff, and of strong advocacy within his own Cabinet, he delayed the opening of the Second Front in France until it could be mounted in such strength as to ensure success, one of the vital decisions affecting the war in the west. By the tenacity of his resistance to the counsel of the over-hasty he spared the Allies the calamity of an assault prematurely undertaken with insufficient force in 1942 and 1943. For this he had to bear the opprobrium of reproach, supported by some vilification and much misrepresentation, although, in the light of after-knowledge, two who differed with him at the time, President Eisenhower and Admiral Leahy (President Roosevelt's Chief of Staff), acknowledged that he had been in the right.

Sustained by the conviction that the loss of thousands of Allied lives had been prevented by his intervention, he bore the burden of complaint with becoming fortitude. In truth he deserved not to be upbraided but to be saluted.

It was Winston Churchill's leadership that ensured large-spirited acceptance of the Russians as allies, providing for them, in conjunction with the United States, munitions of war to the limit of the capacity to supply them. It might have been otherwise, for there were those who looked askance at Stalin and his associates, and who would have left the Soviets to fight their fight alone and unassisted. It may well be that it was the aid from the West, thus afforded, that turned the scales, enabling Moscow and Leningrad to be precariously held until the winter brought to the Red armies the relief of the vital breathing space.

It was his leadership, again, that swung the great Republic of the West into line, transforming tepid American neutrality into warmhearted support for Britain and the cause. Half American by right of birth, he was gifted with the percipient understanding that kindled Roosevelt's friendship and inspired the splendid gesture of Lend-Lease, the backing for the British people begun when they alone were waging the fight for freedom.

In the later stages of the war his opinion did not always prevail with the great American ally. Difficulties and dangers resulted for the free peoples, but he sounded the alarm and he set out the policy that was to bring them through the perils of the Cold War. Without the rallying call at Fulton, what fatal concessions might not have been made to an intransigent Stalinism?

Recalling the push that he gave to the wheel at successive climacterics in affairs, I believe the world today would be a different and even less salubrious place to live in had it not been for the leadership of Winston Churchill. Others, less inclined than I to yield the amplitude of their commendation, have objected that I have not often displayed Churchill to be in the wrong. I cannot, in this volume, claim to have shown improvement in this respect. For as John Winant wrote of the days when Britain's survival was in doubt: "It would have taken so few mistakes to bring about defeat; the miracle was how few were made. . . ."

This present work is the result of my researches into the records of the many authors whose works I enumerate and to whom I acknowledge my indebtedness. From my former books I have incorporated passages on the politics of the premiership, a subject on which few additions have been made to our knowledge. Indeed, by comparison with the military men, the politicians have been singularly reticent and uncommunicative.

There was some perplexity over the references. Necessarily, I had to provide myself with a working catalogue by which I could check my sources. I notice that some authors, of late, have been chided for putting these in their books. Previously, I have been chided for leaving them out. I conclude on balance it is better to put them in. They seem to be essential where in their memoirs some have done damage to their own reputations.

There is scarcely a statement in these chapters for which an authority cannot be quoted. My purpose has been to state the facts so far as I have been able to ascertain them. Any misstatement that may appear results from the natural infirmity of authors, not from intention or design. At no point have I sought to rig the facts to suit a thesis, for the sufficient reason that I have no thesis to prove.

On the controversy of the Second Front I set out with no intention of taking sides, content to do no more than record the facts as I found them. Having set down what was found, the conclusion inevitably followed that Churchill had been flagrantly misrepresented by his critics. But argumentation is foreign to the design of what was conceived as a simple, straightforward account of events, a presentation in story fashion of the Churchill tale.

Already, Winston Churchill belongs to history. A generation is arising that must learn of his services from their fathers. It is for us who knew and saw him in the days of his leadership to testify to his achievements and his greatness.

When I was very young it was my delight to listen to the stories of England's worthies as I was seated on my father's knee. Are there still, in this later generation, those who read and those who listen by the fireside of a winter's evening? If such there be I should like to think that they may find some of my passages acceptable, for they have all been fashioned by ear as well as by sight, so that the words may come easily off the tongue and so that those who listen may comprehend.

It is upon the saga of the chroniclers that the fame of the heroes of history must ultimately depend. The storyteller, rather than the historian, creates the figures of a nation's folklore. The historian memorializes them in his books. The storyteller makes them live in the hearts of the people. Here for the storyteller of the future is the Churchill tale unfolded as a narrative of events as they occurred. The source notes should serve to attest the faithfulness of the record.

LEWIS BROAD

Podkin Farm,
  Biddenden, Kent, England

BOOK ONE

ALLIES IN CATASTROPHE

CHAPTER ONE

THE ADMIRALTY AGAIN

SEPTEMBER, 1939—MAY, 1940

A T SIX O'CLOCK on the evening of Sunday, September 3, 1939, Winston Churchill reported for duty at the Admiralty. The signal was thereupon flashed to the Fleet: WINSTON IS BACK.

He served as First Lord of the Admiralty and member of the War Cabinet, with ever-increasing responsibilities, until, at the first crisis of the war, eight months later, he was himself called to the premiership.

His return to the Admiralty was marked by the signs of uncertainty that attended Britain's entry into war. It was at dawn on Friday, September 1, that Hitler launched the Luftwaffe against the Poles. The Panzers followed the planes. The British Government lost no time in serving its warning—unless German forces were immediately withdrawn Britain would fulfill her pledge to support the Poles by force of arms.

That afternoon Churchill was summoned to 10 Downing Street and was invited to join the War Cabinet that Neville Chamberlain was proposing to set up. The two men talked of the measures that were needed and of the Ministers to undertake them. At midnight, in his study, Churchill set down some supplementary thoughts for the Prime Minister. "Aren't we," he began, "a very old team?" [1]

Saturday was a day of suspense. There was no further word from the Prime Minister to the First Lord designate. Churchill was puzzled. The House of Commons met that evening in anxious mood. For thirty-six hours the Poles had borne the German onslaught without sign of succor from the Allies pledged to their support. Still Britain was not committed to war.

The Prime Minister made a brief statement, temporizing and evasive. The Government was in communication with the French. The state of war was still delayed. The statement was heard in stony silence. Members were incredulous, apprehensive, hostile. Was there another Munich hatching?

Arthur Greenwood rose from the Labour benches to be encouraged by the shout "Speak for England." He made a short, robust speech that drew cheers from Tories who had heard their own leader in glum embarrassment. Members dispersed in an angry mood.

There was a gathering that night at Churchill's flat. Anthony Eden was there and Duff Cooper, Robert Boothby, Brendan Bracken and Duncan Sandys. All of them opponents of appeasement, they were in a state of bewildered rage.

Churchill shared their anxieties. He did not disguise that he felt himself to have been badly used by the Prime Minister.[2] He had agreed, the previous day, to join the Chamberlain Government and had consequently felt himself to be precluded from speaking out in the House of Commons, which otherwise it would have been his duty to do.

Late that night he wrote again to the Prime Minister to express his sense of misgiving. "I really do not know what has happened during the course of this agitated day, though it seems that entirely different ideas have ruled from those which you expressed to me when you said 'the die is cast.' "[3]

In Downing Street other Members of Parliament expressed their remonstrances to Ministers. That night there were urgent telephone conversations with Paris. The French pleaded for delay—their mobilization was proceeding; there was still a chance that the Italians might induce Hitler to negotiate. The British Cabinet would concede no more—war must be declared the following day. The reluctant French gave way.

Until the final minutes ran out, the Prime Minister held back from confirming Churchill's appointment. He was reluctant, to the last, to surrender the vestige of hope that he might be spared the searing agony of war. It seemed that he regarded the calling of Winston Churchill within the circle of his Cabinet as signalizing beyond the possibility of recall the declaration of Britain's purpose to accept the challenge of Hitler and the arbitrament of battle.

On the Sunday morning of gracious September sunshine, the nation waited expectantly on the Prime Minister. On wireless sets throughout the land the voice of the BBC was heard in the interminably repeated refrain of Sullivan's "Di Ballo." At last Neville Chamberlain came before the microphone to announce to the waiting world that Britain was at war.

After the suspense, the declaration came almost as an anticlimax. How different from the circumstances of 1914! Then there were the surging crowds in Downing Street, the drama of Edward Grey's speech in the House, the unforgettable tension of the last hours of peace. Now the announcement was made to listeners in the domesticity of their own parlors. The Prime Minister's statement was simple and brief. His hearers at the time—and readers of his words afterward—were left with the impression that he was concerned not so much to bid defiance to Britain's enemies as to justify himself at the bar of world opinion, and of history, for his own failure that he had not averted the catastrophe of hostilities.

"You can imagine what a bitter blow it was to me that all my long struggle to win peace has failed. Yet I cannot believe that there is anything more or anything different I could have done. . . . We have a clear conscience."

The words, appropriate as they might have been in 1914, when there were many who questioned the necessity for British intervention in a Continental war, were out of key in 1939 when doubt was scarcely entertained. Rarely have the British people been so united in going to war. The entire nation was resolved on resistance to Hitlerism.

The broadcast over, and after the warbling sirens had wailed their first warning in a false alarm, the House of Commons met to hear the Prime Minister. The doubts of the previous night had vanished and the M.P.s were in an exalted mood. Again Neville Chamberlain emphasized the personal note of his sense of regret. "It is a sad day for all of us and for none is it sadder than for me. Everything I wished for, everything I hoped for, everything I believed in during my public life has crashed in ruins." He pledged himself to spare nothing of his strength and powers in forwarding the cause of victory.

Churchill, in the last speech he was to make as a private M.P., gave expression to the nation's purpose in more vigorous terms. It was a consolation, in that solemn hour, to realize Britain's repeated efforts for peace. These had been of the highest moral value. Churchill went on:

> The Prime Minister said it was a sad day and that indeed is true. But it seems to me there is another note which may be present at this moment. There is a feeling of thankfulness that if these trials were to come upon our island, there is a generation of Britons here now, ready to prove that it is not unworthy of those great men, the fathers of our land. Here is no question of fighting for Danzig or fighting for Poland. We are fighting to save the world from the pestilence of Nazi tyranny and in defense of all that is most sacred to man. This

is no war for imperial aggrandizement or material gain. It is a war pure in its inherent quality, a war to establish on impregnable rocks the right of the individual. It is a war to establish and revive the stature of man.

The contrast in character and outlook between Chamberlain and Churchill was emphasized by their speeches. Where one could not forget his own personal sense of regret, the other spoke, as they had bidden Arthur Greenwood, "for England." A political observer noted presciently in his dairy: "Neville good, but not the speech of a war leader. I think I see Winston emerging as P.M. out of it all by the end of the year." [4]

As soon as the brief proceedings in the House had been concluded, Churchill conferred with the Prime Minister, who now offered him the Admiralty as well as the proffered seat in the War Cabinet. He accepted with jubilation. Nothing could have given him greater elation. Here was the place where best he could acquit himself. Here, too, was his vindication, the wiping out of the stain of his dismissal from that office a quarter of a century before.

Without waiting for the formalities to be completed, he inducted himself that evening at the Admiralty. Until late into the night he was in conference with the heads of the departments, taking into his capable hands the reins familiar to his grasp in the First World War. He called for the map on which he had plotted the movements of His Majesty's ships in 1914. It was still there. He remained at work until the early hours and he was back at his post at ten o'clock the following morning.

The first meeting of the full Board of Admiralty under the new First Lord was an occasion. As Churchill took his seat in the First Lord's chair, memories of the past came flooding back and he did not disguise his emotion. He was made welcome by the First Sea Lord, Admiral Dudley Pound, and he briefly acknowledged the greeting. It was a privilege and an honor for him to return to his old place.

Winston Churchill's recall was generally acclaimed. His fighting qualities, his dynamic energy, and his detestation of Hitlerism were known, and the fame of his anti-appeasement speeches made him the man of the hour. To those who doubted the capacity of Ministers—their sincerity was not in question—the fact that Winston Churchill had been brought back contributed something of the feelings of confidence the appointment of Kitchener to be War Secretary had imparted in 1914. For years Churchill had been out of office, his judgment questioned, mistrusted because of his very brilliance. Now there was scarcely a newspaper in the Empire that did not express satisfaction that he had returned to his old place. Friends, however, did not join in the general acclamation.

They were suspicious of Chamberlain's intentions in saddling him with the double duties of membership in the War Cabinet and departmental office. Was this a device to keep him occupied, to ensure that he would not have the opportunity to meddle in the affairs of his colleagues and take over the running of the war? [5]

On Monday afternoon Churchill resumed his place on the Treasury Bench. When he rose to speak he was given an ovation from all quarters of the House. Old parliamentary hands could not remember the appearance of a new Minister evoking so long and loud a burst of applause. It was noted that, after an absence of eleven years from the Treasury Bench, he seemed to find the dispatch-box * an unfamiliar place. Instead of resting his notes upon the box he held them in his hand in the manner of a back-bencher.

His first statement concerned the sinking of the liner *Athenia*, the outrage with which, in characteristic fashion, the Nazis opened their campaign at sea. The ship, with many Americans among her 1,400 passengers, was sent to the bottom 200 miles west of Ireland within a few hours of the opening of hostilities. "She was," said the First Lord, "torpedoed without the slightest warning in circumstances which the whole opinion of the world after the late war, in which Germany concurred, has stigmatized as inhuman."

Goebbels and his propagandists, in one of their most fantastic efforts, sought to put the blame for the *Athenia's* destruction on Winston Churchill himself, the suggestion being that he was seeking to inflame American opinion against the Nazis. There was no need to deny this stupid invention.

It was with characteristic thoroughness that Churchill took over his responsibilities. He made the personal acquaintance of the admirals in command, he made personal inspection of the naval stations, traveling to the North to join the Home Fleet in its anchorages amongst the Scottish lochs. By the end of September he could report himself as having qualified for the effective discharge of his duties.

Meanwhile the war had run through its first phase. The Poles, beyond the range of assistance from the Allies, had succumbed. History will note, with her customary appreciation of the ironic, that Polish independence, the immediate occasion of the war, was not conspicuously advanced by its outcome. The Russians joined in the carve-up of Poland, advancing their frontiers to meet the Germans from the west. There was an immediate outcry against the perfidious Bolsheviks.

With a shrewder appreciation of the realities, Churchill declined to

---

* The attaché case used by the Chancellor of the Exchequer—traditionally it remains to be used by successive holders of the office.

join in the chorus of reprobation. He came to the microphone on October 1, 1939 to deliver the first of his wartime surveys of operations. His analysis presented a conception of events that was startling to many of his hearers:

Russia has pursued a policy of cold self-interest. We could have wished the Russian armies should be standing on their present lines as the friends and allies of Poland instead of as invaders. But that the Russian armies should stand on this line was clearly necessary for the safety of Russia against the Nazi menace. At any rate the line is there and an Eastern Front has been created that Nazi Germany dare not assail. I cannot forecast to you the action of Russia. It is a riddle wrapped in a mystery inside an enigma, but perhaps there is a key. That key is Russian self-interest.

Thus, my friends, at the risk of being proved wrong by events, I will proclaim my conviction that the second great factor of the first month of the war is that Hitler, and all that Hitler stands for, is being warned off the East and Southeast of Europe.

How soundly based was this appreciation of the Soviet motives— though not of Russia's security—events were in due course to establish.

The war moved into its second and dormant phase—the twilight or the phony war. Hitler put forward peace feelers, which Lloyd George, of all men, recommended the Government consider. There was little other support.

Churchill, in his second wartime broadcast (November 12), was heard in scornful voice proclaiming the iniquities of the "Narzees":

The whole world is against Hitler and Hitlerism. Men of every race and clime feel that this monstrous apparition stands between them and the forward move which is their due and for which the age is ripe. Even in Germany itself there are millions who stand aloof from the seething mass of criminality and corruption constituted by the Nazi Party machine. Let them take courage amid perplexities and perils, for it may well be that the final extinction of a baleful domination will pave the way to a broader solidarity of men in all lands than we could ever have planned if we had not marched together through fire.

Churchill made use of the occasion of this speech to proclaim his unqualified support of the Prime Minister. He had now served for over two months in the Ministry, and there had been much public speculation as to the relations between Neville Chamberlain and the candid friend who had been his sternest critic. There was natural curiosity whether the First Minister of the Crown and the First Lord of the Admiralty worked harmoniously together. Doubts were set at rest. "You know," said Churchill, "I have not always agreed with Mr. Chamberlain, though we have always been personal friends. He is a man of very tough fiber and I can tell you he is going to fight as obstinately for victory as he did for peace."

During those opening weeks of the war Churchill gave the impression that he, a newcomer to the Ministry, was playing himself in. He had behind him the abundance of his experience of war. He was an old hand where his colleagues were beginners at the game. But he conducted himself with restraint and forbore from the veteran's odious habit of recalling, at every turn, what was done when he was there before.

His position was an anomalous one. He was younger, by five years, than the Prime Minister, but he belonged to an earlier generation of statesmen. He had been holding office before most of his colleagues had reached the House of Commons. He was a political contemporary of men who had passed on—of Asquith, Haldane, Grey, Morley, the last flowering of the Victorians. Now he was serving in a War Cabinet with colleagues of whom John Simon alone had reached Cabinet rank before the twenties opened.

He had been eleven years out of office. His colleagues had been closely associated in the day-to-day conduct of affairs. He came among them as one who had been a critic of their appeasings and he set himself to win them. Scrupulous to avoid the appearance of meddling, he immersed himself in the work of the Admiralty. When he addressed a paper to the Prime Minister it was with the disarming preface: "I hope you will not mind my sending you a few points privately."

His conduct was impeccable. The suggestions he had to make were put forward in personal communications. In council he was careful to avoid being drawn into controversy with his chief. He was conscious of a certain aloofness on the other's part that he found natural enough. He had castigated the policy of appeasement and its author, and it was hardly to be expected that the Prime Minister should immediately warm toward the critic whom he had taken as colleague under the pressure of outside opinion.

There was nothing halfhearted in Churchill's cooperation. He entered the Government not as a rival, to intrigue against his chief, but as the most loyal of colleagues. He was quick to defend his leader even against family critics in his home. In the end he wore down mistrust so that Chamberlain could write: "To me personally he is absolutely loyal." But it took some time for this sense of trust to be established.[6]

At first, Churchill was not admitted to the inner circle of the Prime Minister's associates. It was on Lord Halifax, his Foreign Secretary and closest of his friends in politics, that Chamberlain placed his reliance.

Halifax came of one of those families whose members, down the centuries, have done the State some service. As Lord Irwin he had been Viceroy of India. When Anthony Eden left the Foreign Office rather than truckle further to the dictators, Chamberlain appointed Halifax as likely to be more conformable. It was Halifax who accompanied the Prime Minister to Paris for meetings of the Supreme War Council. Lord Chatfield, Minister for Coordination of Defense, and little Kingsley Wood, Air Minister, were also called on to attend, but not Churchill: "I had not at that time reached the position where I should be invited." [7]

By the new year, Churchill had moved up. He was asked to join the party for the February meeting in Paris and arranged for the Channel crossing to be made in a destroyer. On the way over he was shown the reply Chamberlain had given to German peace feelers made through the United States. Having read the blunt terms of rejection, Churchill commented: "I am proud to serve in your Government." [8]

Churchill was still following his subordinate role. He was a silent onlooker at the Council meeting. Naval affairs did not come up for discussion, and he did not permit himself to contribute a word to the proceedings. Thereafter, he was a regular member of the Prime Minister's party. The final mark of trust came in April, 1940, when he was invited to preside over the Military Coordination Committee of the Cabinet, with his responsibilities vastly extended.

One contact was made in those times that was to have far-reaching consequences. Armistice Day brought a letter to the Admiralty from President Roosevelt. It bore friendly and encouraging greetings. Recalling that they had occupied similar positions in the First World War, Roosevelt congratulated Churchill on his return to the Admiralty. "What I want you and the Prime Minister to know," he wrote, "is that I shall at all times welcome it if you will keep me in touch personally with anything you want me to know about."

The two men had met once years before when Roosevelt was Assistant Secretary of the Navy. He was then the handsome, vigorous figure of his early manhood. Later he was crippled by paralysis, but rising above his physical disability he continued the political career that brought him to the White House. Like Churchill, he had been prompt to realize the menace of Hitlerism, but he was far in advance of American public opinion. The United States was officially committed to strict neutrality.

Churchill was heartened by the President's message. Across the Atlantic there was a kindling friendship. He replied at once, and so began the long correspondence between the "Naval Person" (as he signed himself) and the President that was to continue without a break. To have the ear of the President was a privilege of which the value was not to be overestimated. The letters they exchanged paved the way to the close understanding between White House and Whitehall that the two men were to extend later to their military advisers, with incalculable benefit to the Allied cause.

The twilight of hostilities of the phony war did not extend to the high seas. There hostilities opened in full intensity. There were the U-boats, which at this early stage were not numerous enough to be menacing. "The Royal Navy," said Churchill, "is hunting them night and day, I will not say without mercy—God forbid we should ever part company with that—but at any rate with zeal and not altogether without relish." There came thrilling deeds for the First Lord to announce and chronicle—the scuttling of the pocket battleship *Graf Spee* off Montevideo after the Battle of the River Plate; the attack by H.M.S. *Cossack* in a Norwegian fiord on the German prison ship *Altmark* and the freeing of 299 British prisoners.

At London's ancient Guildhall, in February, he was present when the City did honor to the men of the *Ajax* and *Exeter* for their part in the victory over the *Graf Spee*. "The Battle of the River Plate," he declared in one of his happiest and most homely phrases, "in a dark cold winter has warmed the cockles of our hearts." Of the achievement of the *Cossack* he remarked that to Nelson's own signal there had been added the not less proud words, "The Navy is here"—words with which the *Cossack* announced her arrival in the fiord.

The First Lord was not prepared to sit on the defensive while the Western Front waited on Hitler. The possibilities of action in the Baltic had been pressed by old Lord Fisher in the First World War and Churchill had not long been back at the Admiralty before he set the naval planners to work. The swiftly moving tide of war was to carry events forward too fast for the project to be developed, but the lure of the Baltic and the North was to remain teasingly in the background of Churchill's mind.

More immediately pressing was the German device of the magnetic mine, the first manifestation of Hitler's secret weapon. Heedlessly scattered from the air, the mines sank merchant shipping under neutral as well as the British flag. It was, as Churchill said, "about the lowest form of warfare that can be imagined," but the Germans were not to be moved by verbal protests against methods of barbarism. The Admiralty were not unprepared for the development; there were magnetic devices in their own armory. Once the mechanism of the German mine was available to them for inspection, British inventors were able to find the appropriate counter. But there were anxious days for the First Lord and his advisers until "degaussing" made shipping safe from the magnetic peril.

As a retaliation Churchill proposed that floating mines should be dropped into the waters of the Rhine, a waterway indispensable to the Germans.[9] Under his direction plans were prepared and Cabinet authority was obtained. But what of the French—would they agree? They certainly would not. The British, they represented, should drop their mines at sea to sink German shipping slipping southward off Norway's coast. Mines in German rivers and canals were too close home for French liking—the Germans might hit back at France.

Churchill, with 6,000 mines ready to use, was angered by French hesitations. He contacted Paris but was unable to bring the French Ministers to agree. He grew concerned at the lack of French spirit—it was so different from 1914.

The French leaders were forgetting their patriotism in their personal jealousies. The two leading generals, Gamelin and Georges, were disputing each other's authority. The two chief Ministers, Reynaud and Daladier, were scarcely on speaking terms. Behind each Minister was the figure of a woman. The ladies were jealous in their rivalry and each inflamed the animosity of her Minister.[10]

Operation "Royal Marine" had to be deferred until it was too late. Not till the Nazis struck in the West were mines dropped in the Rhine, with gratifying and destructive results, but the German advance made it impossible for the operation to be long continued.

There was another waterway essential to the Germans—the Leads, off the west coast of Norway. The First Lord pressed for action to deny to the Germans the use of these waters by which iron ore from the north was conveyed to the Reich. There were immediate objections. It would involve the mining of Norwegian waters. Were we to follow Hitler in breaking international law? It required four months of Cabinet discussions before the decision was taken and the mines were laid. By then it was April, and Hitler was ready with his projects for infringing the law of nations and the rights of neutrals on an immeasurably vaster scale.

With the mining of the Leads, the curtain rose on the somber drama that shattered the placidity of the phony war. German forces swept across the frontier into Denmark. Norway was invaded, and Quisling added a new term to the vocabulary of treachery.

Submarines took toll of German transports, half the cruisers of the German Fleet were sunk, but the Royal Navy could not hold off the

Nazi invaders. An expeditionary force, quickly assembled, was flung ashore on the Norwegian coast. It was too late—there were no landing grounds for Allied planes and without air cover the troops fought at an unsupportable disadvantage. The campaign had to be abandoned and the troops shipped home.

CHAPTER TWO

PRIME MINISTER
MAY 7—MAY 10, 1940

T HE first clinch of the war had gone against Britain. At Westminster it brought to a head the smoldering discontent that had been mounting through the months. On every hand there were mutterings of complaint—men engaged on useless jobs; men not employed at all when munitions were the screaming need; no sense of urgency; no drive, no initiative, no direction, no inspiration, no leadership—above all no leadership.

Discontent was focused on the Prime Minister. Munich was remembered against him. His latest indiscretion—"Hitler has missed the bus"— had been given the publicity of blazing headlines only a few days before the Nazi descent on Scandinavia. It could not have been more unfortunately timed and was seized on by those who looked on the replacement of Chamberlain as the first necessity if the country were to escape defeat.

And Churchill? His friends feared that his position must have been weakened by the Norwegian debacle. They had learned with misgiving of his appointment as head of the Military Coordinating Committee of the Cabinet. He had been saddled with full responsibility without effective authority. How could he bear this burden and direct, at the same time, the administration of his own department and operations at sea? Now that disaster had occurred, had he been compromised? Would he be made the scapegoat for Norway? Men were dismayed who looked on him as the sole hope as leader for Britain at war. Little Leo Amery reflected that it was all terrible: "It must mean the end of the Government and perhaps of Churchill as well. If so, what on earth have we left?" [1]

In the faultfinding of those questioning days, Churchill did not escape criticism. Some blamed him for decisions that he had not made, others for failing where it had not been in his power to act.

To these matters Churchill himself paid scant heed. His concern was with the conduct of operations, not the backwash of politics. But at that point it was the politicians who took control. There was to be a debate in the House of Commons, an inquest into the Norwegian failure. Ministers were to be called to account, and when the Ministry was arraigned there was no doubt that the First Lord would stand by his chief, formidable in defense.

The war debate (May 7-8, 1940) changed history's course. It is inconceivable that under Neville Chamberlain's leadership Britain could have found her way through the disasters that lay just around the corner. The debate was to establish Churchill in Chamberlain's place, but at the time this outcome was by no means the inevitable conclusion that in retrospect it came to appear.

The House met in a grave mood, anxious, apprehensive. The anti-Munich group scarcely dared to hope they would succeed in their object of displacing the Prime Minister. There were two principal contributions to Chamberlain's fall—his own further indiscretion and the speech of Leo Amery. In the chorus of criticism it was Amery's indictment that had the decisive influence upon the Tories.

Amery, short of stature, pugnacious of spirit, had been a member of Lloyd George's Secretariat in the First World War. He had served in Baldwin's Cabinet, but had not found a place in recent Ministries. His militancy had given spirit to the anti-Munich group. Now he was carried to the orator's heights. Point by point he challenged the Government and exposed its inadequacy, its failure to foresee the enemy's moves or to counter them when made. He began to a glum and uneasy House, but as he warmed to his indictment there came growls of support, notably from the Tory benches.

"We are fighting for our life, for our liberty, for our all," he cried. "We cannot go on being led as we are."

He ceased as though he had done, and then resumed with the crushing afterthought: "I have quoted certain words of Oliver Cromwell. I will quote other words. I do it with great reluctance, because I am speaking of those who are old friends and associates of mine, but they are words that are applicable to the present situation. This is what Cromwell said to the Long Parliament when he thought it was no longer fit to conduct the affairs of the nation: 'You have sat too long here for any good you have been doing. Depart, I say, and let us have done with you. In the name of God, go!' "

Amery had achieved his purpose. His speech, with its dramatic climax, had raised the temper of the debate to a new level of urgency, involving the question of the Government's survival. With an ineptitude not to be expected of so skilled a parliamentarian, Neville Chamberlain exposed himself to his opponents.

Herbert Morrison announced that the Labour Party would divide the House * at the end of the debate. This brought the Prime Minister to his feet to accept the challenge with an unfortunate reference to his "friends."

"I do not," he said, "seek to evade criticism, but I say to my friends in the House—and I have friends in the House—that no Government can prosecute the war efficiently unless it has public and parliamentary support. I accept the challenge and welcome it. I call upon my friends to support us in the lobbies tonight."

It was an ill-advised appeal, which the old parliamentary hand, Lloyd George, was quick to seize upon. The situation, he said, must not be treated as a personal issue. The Prime Minister was not in a position to make his personality separable from the interests of the country.

"What," asked the Prime Minister, "is the meaning of this observation? I took pains to say that personalities ought to have no place."

Lloyd George recalled the remark, "I have my friends." It was not a question of who were the Prime Minister's friends. There was a far graver issue. The Prime Minister should remember that he had met the formidable foe in peace and war and had always been worsted. He was not in a position to call for support on the grounds of friendship.

"I say solemnly," Lloyd George added, "that the Prime Minister should give an example of sacrifice, because I tell him that there is nothing which would contribute more to victory in this war than that he should sacrifice the seals of office."

When Churchill intervened to say that he, as First Lord, took complete responsibility for everything that was done by the Admiralty, Lloyd George waved him aside. "I hope," he said, "that my Right Honorable friend will not allow himself to be converted into an air-raid shelter to keep the splinters from hitting his colleagues."

Lloyd George's bitter attack was supplemented by A. V. Alexander.

* Voting in the House of Commons is accomplished by members passing through one or other of two "division" lobbies, or passages. When a division is called, the "ayes" and the "noes" file through the pertaining lobby to be counted by tellers.

Winding up for the Opposition, he remarked that since the Prime Minister's intervention he had had news of more than one neutral representative in London who felt that if these matters were to be dealt with on the basis of personal friendship, rather than the winning of the war, Britain should have done a great deal to alienate any sympathy she enjoyed in neutral spheres on the Continent.

Churchill received his share of criticism. His old friend, Admiral of the Fleet Sir Roger Keyes, attending in full-dress uniform, reproached the First Lord for not daring to sanction the hazard of a naval attempt to take Trondheim. "The iron of the Dardanelles," said the Admiral, mournfully, "has entered his soul."

It was Churchill's unenviable task, as final speaker, to address a House whose mind was already made up. Prejudice and personalities had done their work. It was too late to counter prejudice by reasoned argument. His examination of the strategic situation in Norway was exhaustive. He dealt in the frankest manner with the case for going into Trondheim and Bergen, points to which the critics had principally addressed themselves. The decisions taken had been reached on the unanimous advice of the Service experts, the Chiefs of Staff, and their deputies. The decision to abandon the attack on Trondheim saved Britain from a most disastrous entanglement; it would have been a forlorn operation.

"We must be careful," he warned the House, "not to exhaust our Air Force in view of other grave dangers which might open upon us at any time, and not to throw such strain on our flotillas and antiaircraft auxiliaries as might hamper the general mobility of the Fleet. There are other waters we have to think of."

He protested against the action of the Opposition in forcing from the Government statements in public which might be of benefit to the enemy and added: "A picture has been drawn of craven politicians hampering their admirals and generals in their bold designs and of myself personally overruling them. There is being suggested—for if truth is many-sided mendacity is many-tongued—that I have personally proposed violent action to the Prime Minister and the War Cabinet and they shrank from it and restrained me. There is not a word of truth in all that."

Toward the close of the First Lord's speech, members became impatient for the division and there was some interruption from the Opposition back benches. Churchill complained that one interrupter was "skulking in a corner," at which there were protests.

"On a point of order," Mr. Maclean intervened, "is 'skulk' a parliamentary word?"

"It depends," pronounced Mr. Speaker, "whether it applies accurately or not."

The vote was taken. The Government emerged with a majority of not more than 81 in a total of 481. On paper, in a full House, the Government majority should have been in the region of 200. Forty backbenchers normally supporting the Government went into the Opposition lobby. They included Admiral of the Fleet Sir Roger Keyes, Brigadier General Edward Spears, Duff Cooper, L. S. Amery, Harold Nicolson, Lord Wolmer, Lord Winterton, Leslie Hore-Belisha and Richard Law, son of the former Prime Minister. Many loyal Tories sat in their seats, unable to bring themselves to vote against the leader in whom they could no longer put their full trust.

After the hubbub of the division, a hush fell on the chamber as Neville Chamberlain was seen to rise. He passed, head erect, from the sight of the members who had dealt him so hard a blow.

A night of intense lobbying followed. It was accepted that the Ministry could not survive the vote. Would the Government be reconstructed, or would Chamberlain have to go? The claims of other men were canvassed—Halifax, Churchill, and little Amery. At that stage the majority of Conservative M.P.s would have given the preference to Halifax. Labour would have been similarly inclined.

Clearly, the Labour Party would now have to come in to serve in a national coalition. With appreciation of the needs of the hour, the faithful Brendan Bracken sought out the Socialist leader, Clement Attlee, to press Winston Churchill's claims. Attlee, mindful of incidents in Churchill's past, was inclined toward Halifax, whereupon Brendan Bracken did not hesitate to assert that Churchill would not serve as a subordinate to Halifax—for which assertion he had not a tittle of authority.[2]

Chamberlain himself was in a state of indecision. At midnight he felt that he could not go on, though Churchill pressed him not to be unduly dismayed by the vote. In the morning his mood had changed. He would lead an all-party government if the Socialists would agree to come in and serve under him.[3]

For a few hours the matter was poised in uncertainty. Late in the afternoon the Prime Minister summoned Halifax and Churchill to Downing Street, together with the Chief Whip, David Margesson, for a formal discussion of the possibilities.* He then announced his decision

---

* An account of this interview was written by Churchill in his war memoirs in which he antedated the occasion by a day. Halifax's account, restrained and factual, appeared in *Fullness of Days.* Churchill, more dramatic, but less accurate, conveyed the atmosphere of the occasion and the sense of his own feelings.

—a new Ministry must be formed, a coalition Government, with the Socialists taking part. He acknowledged that their participation was unlikely under his leadership. He was prepared to serve under either of the other men.

The Chief Whip agreed that the national unity was the first consideration. He did not think this was to be secured under Chamberlain. That narrowed the choice.

Lord Halifax then settled the matter. For him to succeed to the premiership, he said, would be to create an impossible personal position. As a peer he would be denied access to the House of Commons. He would be no more than an honorary Prime Minister living, as he put it, in a kind of twilight, responsible for everything but lacking the power to guide the assembly upon whose confidence the existence of the Ministry would depend. Churchill would have the effective authority in running defense.

When this was said, the question was in fact decided. The Prime Minister reluctantly acquiesced. So it was that Lord Halifax set the future moving in its new course. It was a high-minded decision. Had he permitted it, Chamberlain would have submitted his name to the King, who would have been well satisfied with his appointment. Halifax, indeed, "the obvious man" as he considered him to be, would have been King George's first choice and His Majesty would have been prepared to alter the Constitution so that, though a peer, he might have taken some part in the proceedings of the House of Commons. Halifax, with a splendid gesture of renunciation, stood aside.[4]

There was a break in the Downing Street discussions and a cup of tea was taken in the garden. Then the two Labour representatives, Clement Attlee and Arthur Greenwood, were called in to receive the formal invitation to their party to enter a Coalition Ministry. Attlee left it to his colleague to give the reply. It was fatal to Chamberlain. Without the evasion of soft words, Greenwood told him bluntly that the Labour Party neither liked nor trusted him, and would decline to cooperate with him. Churchill championed his leader, but Greenwood was not impressed.[5]

The decision rested with the Labour Party, then assembling in conference at Bournemouth. Chamberlain wrote down the brief alternatives—agreement to serve in a coalition under the present Prime Minister or under another leader. The Socialist leaders left to take instructions, Attlee with the warning that the first alternative would not be acceptable to his associates.

The official answer had to wait for the next day. Before the day came, Herr Hitler had intervened.

That night the air was heavy with rumors of dire events. Telephone communication with Holland was cut off. The Dutch Government ordered all canal locks to be closed. At dawn the blitzkrieg broke. Holland was invaded; the Germans burst across the frontiers of Belgium; they crossed into little Luxembourg.

Churchill was on duty at the Admiralty. Two of his colleagues, calling upon him at 4 a.m., found him breakfasting on fried eggs and bacon, to be followed by an early cigar. He was in the highest spirits, as fresh as if he had returned from an early-morning ride in the park. Later in the morning the Cabinet met. The Prime Minister then took the line that the German attack had changed the situation and made it necessary for him to remain at the head of affairs. To the last he could not escape the conviction common to men in high office that they are indispensable and irreplaceable.[6]

From the council chamber Churchill returned to the Admiralty to find Ministers from Holland awaiting him, tragedy in their bearing. Their country had been confounded. The Germans had streamed in. The dikes had been opened to the sea.

Meanwhile the decision was taken at Bournemouth. The National Executive of the Labour Party resolved to take their share of responsibility as full partners in a new Government under a new Prime Minister. Under Chamberlain they declined to serve. Indeed it was the general opinion at Bournemouth that he was lingering too long—"incorrigibly limpet," in Hugh Dalton's phrase. Chamberlain thereupon tendered his resignation to King George VI. The summons came to Winston Churchill to attend at Buckingham Palace, to be greeted with the lightly jesting words from the King: "I suppose you don't know why I have sent for you?" [7]

The Sovereign's commission to form a Ministry was given in brief and gracious audience and Churchill was soon on his way back to his room at the Admiralty. He had realized the crowning achievement in politics, but under the crush of events it passed as no more than an incident in a day that gave little pause for savoring its satisfaction. Not even the cheer of a spectator had marked the honor that had been done him. For once, at the climax of his career, the limelight had not been playing.

That evening he spent in the task of Cabinet-making. It was three o'clock in the morning before he went to bed. He passed from consciousness with a feeling of confidence and contentment. He felt equal to the task that had fallen on him. It was a relief to know that at last the authority was his to direct operations over the whole vast field of national endeavor.

CHAPTER THREE

DAYS OF DISASTER

MAY 10—JUNE 4, 1940

NEVER did a Prime Minister assume office in such an hour. The blitzkrieg had opened as a tornado. Every message gave tidings of disaster from Holland, from Belgium, and from France. The Germans were sweeping all before them. They had broken out at the Ardennes gap. It was on the shortest road to Paris.

Churchill lost no time in picking his team, but, quickly though the choice was made, the German advance moved faster. Before the new Lord Chancellor was on the woolsack,* the Panzers were charging into France. Before the Minister of Labor was at his desk, the Dutch Army had laid down its arms. Before the first full meeting of the Cabinet the Germans had reached the Channel ports.

It was in those days of crisis that the famous coalition took office. The fame of Churchill's Ministry will not soon be forgotten. From the Labour Party ranks there came Clement Attlee, Herbert Morrison, Arthur Greenwood and many more. They joined with Tories whom they had spent their political lives in denouncing, among them Neville Chamberlain, who served under his successor. Men who had resigned office in appeasement days were called back—Anthony Eden, Duff Cooper and Lord Cranborne. Ernest Bevin, of the Transport Workers, sturdy of figure and staunch in spirit, was made Minister of Labor. Lord Beaverbrook was summoned from Fleet Street to put vigor into the production

---

* The wool cushion on which the Lord Chancellor sits in the House of Lords.

of aircraft. As Secretary for Air there was the Liberal leader, Sir Archibald Sinclair, who had been Churchill's adjutant when he served in the trenches in the Kaiser's war. They made a splendid team.

Churchill presented himself and his Ministry to the House of Commons. In a single speech (May 15) he established himself. The House, listening to his words, recognized the accents of the nation's leader. He spoke simply and somberly. It was not an occasion for which he had had time to prepare. Without much premeditation he gave utterance to the faith that moved him. He felt himself to have been reserved by Providence for that hour of Britain's trial. It was this feeling of destiny's fulfillment that gave the undertone to his stark sentences. Members hearing him knew that the man and the hour were matched. The phrases remain forever memorable:

> I would say to the House, as I said to those who have joined this Government: I have nothing to offer but blood, toil, tears, and sweat.
>
> You ask, what is our policy? I will say: It is to wage war by sea, land, and air, with all our might and with all the strength that God can give us; to wage war against a monstrous tyranny, never surpassed in the dark, lamentable catalogue of human crime. That is our policy.
>
> You ask, what is our aim? I can answer in one word. It is victory, victory at all costs, victory in spite of all terror, victory, however long and hard the road may be—for without victory there is no survival. Let that be realized—no survival for the British Empire, no survival for all the British Empire has stood for, no survival for the urge and impulse of the ages, that mankind will move forward towards its goal.

He spoke as a man dedicated to a cause, and those whom he called to join him in an act of national dedication rendered their assent in a deep-throated roar.

Lloyd George, in the name of the friends of freedom, wished him Godspeed: "I congratulate him personally on his accession to the premiership. But that is a small matter. I congratulate the country upon his elevation to the premiership at this very, very critical and terrible moment."

James Maxton, the pacifist, found a phrase that did honor to the man and to the occasion. He could not join in the motion of support to the new Government, for that conflicted with all his pacifist beliefs. But, congratulating the new Prime Minister on his appointment, he observed: "His personality no one can deny and—I am getting more and more fatalist—it was written in the book of fate, say, perhaps, on the battlefield of Blenheim, that he would one day be Prime Minister of this country, and, perhaps, it will be a comfort to us now."

With the change in the premiership a new note of urgency was made manifest in the conduct of affairs, a new effectiveness in their direction. Churchill's widely ranging interest embraced the activities of all fields of endeavor. His directives began to flow out in never-ending stream. But the paramount preoccupation was the battle proceeding across the Channel. Here he was a spectator of operations, powerless to intervene. The stage had been set before he had taken over, and the drama had begun. The issue was with the soldiers. The outcome was not long in doubt.

With lamentable lack of consideration for the French strategists, the Germans struck through the difficult terrain of the Ardennes at the point where the defenses were weakest. The fortifications were neglected, the troops of second-line quality.[1] The name of Sedan, place of ill-omen, appeared in the communiqués. The catastrophe of 1870 was about to be repeated on a vaster scale.

With further inconsiderateness the Germans took advantage of their opponents' strategy. Through the twilight war, French and British forces entrenched themselves west of the Belgian frontier, but it was the best-shared secret of the war that were the Belgians to be attacked then the Allied forces would leap forward to their aid, abandoning their entrenchments.[2] It had all been arranged by the French staff and the German generals could rely upon it. It worked like pressing a button. Holland and Belgium were invaded. The Allied troops obligingly pushed with all speed to the east. With equal speed, and greater punch, the Germans struck in behind them. The gap made at Sedan, the Germans wheeled for the coast. There was no stopping them. The Allied armies of the north were encircled.

To sustain the assault the Germans were provided with three thousand armored vehicles, a thousand being heavy tanks. In England, where the tank had originated, only one armored division had been completed. The French, concentrating on defense, had spent millions on the Maginot Line, which the Germans contemptuously by-passed.

Early in the morning—it was May 15—Churchill was awakened by an urgent telephone call from Paris. It was Paul Reynaud, the French Premier, calling to tell of disaster.[3]

"The battle is lost," came the words in English.

Churchill was incredulous.

"Surely," he objected, "it can't have happened so soon."

"The front is broken," came Reynaud's reply.

Churchill could not believe things to be so serious. He would come over to Paris at once.

Certainly the news was bad, but so it had been bad in 1914. Often enough in the First World War the enemy had broken through. But after the breakthrough there was the counterattack and then the check. Reserves were thrown in and the enemy was pushed back. Churchill did not realize, as yet, the extent to which the tank—his contribution to that other war—had made his ideas out-of-date in 1940. He was soon to learn.

He arrived in Paris the following day to find the French gloomy and despondent.[4] Little Gamelin, the Generalissimo, told the tragic tale. The Germans, pouring through the Ardennes, had smashed the troops in front of them and had cut the Allied armies in two. The Panzers were unchecked and uncheckable.

Little Gamelin finished his recital. There was gloom on every French face. Churchill accepted the facts. The situation was worse than he had feared. But the day might yet be saved. Where were the reserves to be thrown in, where was the *masse de manœuvre?*

The reply came in one word.

"*Aucune*," said Gamelin. There were no reserves. There was nothing left. There was nothing to hold the Panzers.

The effect of that single word of confession was shattering. It blasted the reputation of the dapper Generalissimo. Gamelin passed from the stage of history. It shattered the Prime Minister's assurance, the most surprising statement he had ever heard.

With his sense of history, Churchill perhaps recalled the terms of another admission made of another French Army. Wellington was the questioner. A captured French colonel answered him about Napoleon's rout after Moscow.

"*Où était le quartier-général de l'Empereur?*"

"*Il n'y a plus de quartier-général,*" came the reply.

"*Comment, plus de quartier-général?*" inquired the Duke.

"*Monseigneur, il n'y a point de quartier-général, et point d'armée; l'affaire est finie.*"

Gamelin could well have added the final confession. "*L'affaire est finie*" applied in 1940 as in 1813.

Inside the conference room the gloom deepened. Outside, to be seen through the windows, there was the smoke of belching fires. The French civil servants were committing their secret papers to the flames. Official Paris was preparing even then to quit.

Churchill left for home with a sense of foreboding. His thoughts for a space were on the consequences that had followed from trusting the

French strategists. The British had relied on them absolutely. Never had confidence been so misplaced.

There was a press of problems to be faced. There were the men of the British Expeditionary Force cut off in Flanders. Let the Admiralty, he directed, prepare for the massing of small ships to be ready to take them off. If France were to capitulate, what were Britain's chances, standing alone? Let the Chiefs of Staff report. If Britain were to be invaded, what of the risk from quislings? Let the aliens be rounded up, Communists and Fascists placed under control. If Italy were to come into the war, what of our shipping in the Mediterranean? Our vessels from India and the Far East should be warned to sail the long route round the Cape.

There was the President to be informed of the gravity of the situation. Whatever might happen, the British in their island would fight on to the end. But if the Americans were able to render assistance—"if it is to play any part it must be available soon."

He was shocked by the supineness of the French [5] before the invading Panzers. He fired off a letter to Reynaud urging stronger countermeasures. In an effort to impart some of his spirit to the French he again crossed the Channel (May 22).

By then the veterans were back—Marshal Pétain in the Cabinet, the aged hero of Verdun. Weygand was Generalissimo, the general who had been Chief of Staff to Foch. Churchill was not impressed. Were these men going to put much stiffening into the fight?

Weygand outlined his plans. The encircling line of Germans must be broken. A new French Army was to strike northward from the Somme. At the same time the French and British in the north must thrust south to extricate themselves. It was all that could be contrived, and even that could not be executed. Churchill came home to prepare his colleagues for the worst.

The encircling Germans began to close in on Calais. The order was given to evacuate the town. Churchill protested—it would add to the peril of Dunkirk. The order was countermanded: evacuation must not take place. For the sake of the BEF, the British troops defending Calais must continue their heroic endeavor to the end. It was a heart-rending decision.

The splendid stand at Calais contributed to the escape of the BEF. Churchill paid tribute to the gallantry that was shown:

> The Rifle Brigade, the 60th Rifles, and the Queen Victoria's Rifles, with a battalion of British tanks and 1,000 Frenchmen, in all about 4,000 strong, defended Calais to the last.

The British brigadier was given an hour to surrender. He spurned the offer, and four days of intense street fighting passed before silence reigned over Calais, which marked the end of a memorable resistance. Only thirty unwounded survivors were brought off by the Navy, and we do not know the fate of their comrades. Their sacrifice, however, was not in vain. At least two armored divisions, which otherwise would have been turned against the British Expeditionary Force, had to be sent for to overcome them. They have added another page to the glories of light divisions, and the time gained enabled the Gravelines waterlines to be flooded and to be held by the French troops. Thus it was that the port of Dunkirk was kept open.

The position of the BEF grew ever more perilous. Lord Gort and his men had tried in vain to hack their way through the encircling lines and join up with the French to the south. It was not possible; the German corridor was too wide, the hold too strong. On the left, the Belgians threw in their hands in a capitulation of despair. The flank was terribly exposed. With admirable composure, the BEF re-formed to meet the new emergency and then began to fall back slowly toward the sea in fighting retreat. It was doubtful whether they could stave off the attacks on either flank and, even could they do so, their withdrawal along the corridor must end in disaster unless the men could be taken off.

Churchill warned the House of Commons to prepare for hard and heavy tidings. It was at that time of suspense that he summoned his full Cabinet to meet, the first time the Ministers had gathered collectively since the administration was formed. He addressed them, explaining the gravity of the dangers.

"Of course," he concluded, "whatever happens at Dunkirk we shall fight on."

He was surprised by the demonstration that followed. They shouted their approval and gathered round to thump him on the back. They were imbued with his own spirit, and he drew inspiration from the manifestation of their resolve.[6]

A cause of concern was the French demand for help in the air. Send all the fighter planes across the Channel, they cried, to drive the Luftwaffe from the skies. Churchill found it difficult not to yield to their appeal. Fighter Command grew alarmed. The force left for home defense was reduced to thirty-six squadrons, sixteen below what was considered to be the absolute minimum.

Churchill, with his warm sympathy for France in her hour of need, was faced with the demand for the dispatch of yet ten more squadrons. Air Marshal Dowding, chief of Fighter Command, appeared before the War Cabinet when the matter was considered. With cold passion he protested against the further whittling away of Britain's shield in the skies. He seemed to make little impression on the Prime Minister. Rising from his place he advanced to the table and planked down a graph of figures.

"Look," he said, "if the present rate continues for another fortnight we shall not have a single Hurricane left—neither in France, nor in this country."

His plea was effective. The Cabinet reluctantly decided against the French request. Dowding was vastly relieved. A few days later Churchill ruled that no more fighter squadrons were to leave the country.[7] Dowding's graph and gestures had done the trick. The fighter force had been saved from the vain sacrifice of squadrons that were to turn the scales in the battles that lay ahead. Churchill had been guided to give one of the decisive orders of the war.

The little ships began to make for Dunkirk. Operation "Dynamo" was begun. By Churchill's foresight and direction an armada of boats was available and they sailed across the North Sea—sailing boats, yachts, fishing boats, paddle steamers from the Thames—to join in taking off men of the BEF.

What was happening in France? Never was the fog of war so obscure. Churchill could obtain no satisfaction from Paris. Was nothing being done to check the roving tanks? Where was the spirit of 1914? Again he crossed to Paris (May 31). The Supreme Council met.[8] The French, with so heavy a burden to bear, could scarcely conceal their dejection. There were complaints from Reynaud. Were the French to be left behind at Dunkirk while the British took off their own men? Was the RAF being held back for defense of Britain?

Churchill waved aside the complaints. They were companions in misfortune; it was no time for recriminations. One of his main reasons for journeying to Paris was to ensure that at Dunkirk the French troops as well as British were taken off. Weygand should give the order to his commanders; there would be little time before the Germans closed in. He was distressed at the suggestion that in the embarkation of rear guards priority should be given to the British over the French. He would not countenance it—"*Non, bras dessus bras dessous*"—and he gestured his meaning. As to the RAF, Britain had thrown in all the planes available down to her last reserve, beyond what was essential for her own defense.

"It is impossible to run further risks," he said. A minimum of fighter squadrons must be retained in England. They were the last line of defense and nothing would induce him to give way.

As to furnishing new British divisions for France, scarcely anything remained to be offered. Britain had to prepare to resist an invasion and had only the merest nucleus of troops. Her resources had been exhausted to provide for the BEF. The men who returned home to England would be without arms or equipment.

Churchill closed the discussions with an eloquent harangue. He addressed the Council as if they were members of his own Cabinet. Words poured from him in a torrent and he spoke with an intensity that stirred the emotions of the French. The interpreter ceased to function, spellbound with the others. There was no need for an interpreter.

The peoples of Britain and France, Churchill said, were not born to slavery. They must be united in the common cause. They had only to fight on to conquer.

"We shall carry on," he declared, "if every building in France and Britain is destroyed. We are prepared to wage war from the New World if England is laid waste. Better that the last of us should fall fighting than to linger on as slaves."

His declaration of faith and of unconquerable resolution held the French Ministers under his spell. But, the meeting over, the magic faded before the stark realities of the battlefield.

He returned to London as the final stage was reached at Dunkirk. The little boats plied to and fro across the sea. Many were sunk, but the work went on. British soldiers were taken off the beaches, along with many of their French comrades in arms.

"Suddenly," said Churchill, reporting to the House, "suddenly the scene cleared. The crash and thunder for the moment, but only for the moment, died away. A miracle of deliverance, achieved by valor, by perseverance, by perfect discipline, by faultless service, is manifest.

"The enemy was hurled back by the retreating British and French troops. The Navy, using nearly a thousand ships of all kinds, carried over 335,000 men, French and British, out of the jaws of death and shame, back to their native land."

The men were back, but not their weapons. All their equipment, their guns, their tanks, all the paraphernalia of the Army, had to be abandoned. Britain had an armless Army to defend her shores. Some batteries on the coast had no more than a dozen shells for their guns.

The first great clash of the war had begun in a catastrophe. Worse was to follow. France's position was precarious, and if France fell— what then?

Churchill gave a hint to the House on June 4 that the French might not be able to continue the fight. The British in their home, he said, would continue to battle on, if necessary for years, if necessary alone. And if it were to be "alone," what then? He gave the answer in those famous words:

"We shall not flag or fail. We shall go on to the end. We shall fight in France, we shall fight on the oceans. We shall defend our island whatever the cost. We shall fight on the beaches, we shall fight in the fields and in the streets, we shall fight in the hills. We shall never surrender."

The speech in which Churchill gave an account of these events to the House of Commons was a story of heroic feats of arms, magnificently told. Members were gripped by the splendid narrative. It was a report of disaster of the first magnitude, despite the heartening news of the deliverance of Dunkirk—"we must be careful not to assign to this deliverance the attributes of victory." He had feared it would be his duty to report on an even greater catastrophe—that the whole root and core and brain of the British Army would have been lost, perished on the field or led into ignominious captivity. Now, with the Belgian Army gone, the French Army gravely weakened, and the Germans in possession of the Channel ports, Britons could expect the next blow to fall on their island citadel.

"We are told that Herr Hitler has plans for invading the British Isles. This has often been thought of before. When Napoleon lay at Boulogne for a year, with his flat-bottomed boats and his Grand Army, he was told by someone 'There are bitter weeds in England.' There are certainly a great many more of them since the British Expeditionary Force returned."

In such fashion did the Prime Minister draw inspiration from disaster and fire the people with his own resolution to enable them to rise above the further reverses that lay ahead and to join in the mighty endeavors that were needed of them.

CHAPTER FOUR

FOR FALLING FRANCE
JUNE 5–JUNE 18, 1940

THE pressure of events mounted. On the battlefields there was a pause as the Germans regrouped themselves for the final assault. There was no respite for Winston Churchill and his colleagues, facing the consequences of the initial catastrophe. There was double duty to be done—the French to sustain and the expected ordeal of invasion to prepare for.

These were conflicting claims, both of top priority. Britain's meager resources were not adequate to meet one of them, but even in their extremity of need the French were placed first. Two of the remaining British divisions were earmarked for France, and a lesser Expeditionary Force was formed under General Brooke (later Lord Alanbrooke and Chief of the Imperial General Staff).

In factories and workshops there was a prodigy of effort. Men and women labored so that the machines might be kept turning night and day to restock the depleted arsenals. No effort was spared to rearm, to re-equip and to reconstruct the shattered forces.

The pressing need was for arms. Churchill had appealed to Washington, but there came a warning note to the White House from the American Ambassador in Paris. He submitted to the President it might be that the British Government, holding back their planes from France, were contemplating peace talks, intending to use their Navy and RAF as eventual bargaining points in negotiations with Hitler. Here Churchill's character provided the answer, a guarantee of British purpose.

"The President and I," Secretary of State Cordell Hull testified later, "were convinced that, under Churchill's indomitable leadership, Britain intended to fight on. We believed that Mr. Churchill meant what he said. Had we had any doubt we would not have taken the steps we did." [1]

So the United States Army was deprived of all but the essentials so that rifles, machine guns and field guns with their appropriate ammunition might be shipped off to Britain. It was a magnificient gesture, made on the strength of Churchill's character.

With France stretched to breaking point, there were new urgencies for Churchill's widely ranging concern and his ever-flowing directives. If Spain should declare war, what of Gibraltar's position? Britain must be on her guard over Egypt and the Suez Canal. There were her interests in Turkey to sustain. And, above all, there was Italy.

He had been only a few days in office when he wrote to Mussolini in personal appeal and warning. Was it too late to stop a river of blood flowing between British and Italian peoples? There was a chilling response from Rome.

President Roosevelt was asked to use his good offices. He was abruptly repulsed by the Duce.

The French would have tried to buy off the Italians with concessions. Churchill, reckoning it to be useless to offer what, in the worst event, Mussolini would be able to grab for himself, directed preparations to begin in readiness for the bombing of Italian war industries in Milan and Turin.

On the fifth day of June the Germans opened the final assault—124 divisions against 65. By weight of armor alone they must prevail. Some French regiments fought with gallantry till they dropped with fatigue. Others, stunned by the disasters that had overwhelmed their country, began to disintegrate. Men cannot fight machines; the infantryman is at the mercy of the tank. The valor of the poilu could not make up for the omissions of his leaders who had neglected to provide him with the mechanized instruments of modern battle. He was commanded by men stupefied by the pace of mechanized war and a Generalissimo who was preparing for an armistice.

Encouraged by the weakness of the French, the jackal of Italy, scenting spoils from afar, declared war on June 10. The RAF bombers were ready. In the twilight of the summer evening the Wellingtons were seen in the English skies, setting out to deliver their loads on Turin, Milan and Genoa. Watching Londoners cheered them on their way.

There came warnings from France. Reynaud might be replaced by a Premier of capitulation. Churchill was distressed. General Spears, most able of liaison officers, was summoned from Paris to report. He confirmed the worst fears—Weygand was concerned only to stop the fighting; Pétain was urging capitulation; Reynaud was still stout of heart, but he could not stand indefinitely against defeatist pressure.

"We will go to Paris this afternoon," declared Churchill.

Paris was no longer a place for conferences. The Germans were at hand. Weygand had declared it to be an open city. The Government had moved out to the west toward Tours.

A rendezvous was made at last at Briare,[2] the new GHQ near Orléans. Churchill's plane, with its escorting Spitfires, was compelled to seek safety by a wide detour far down the Channel. At the château at Briare the bearing of the French told its own tale. Dejection was on every face. Churchill, in somber mood on the trip across, radiated confidence as he strode to meet Weygand and so he continued throughout the discussions. He felt infinite compassion for the French in the agony of their death struggle. No criticism or reproach was allowed to disturb his good will. He had come not to engage in recriminations but to consider how best they could contrive to carry on the struggle.

Weygand offered no hope. He could not guarantee his troops would hold for another hour.

Churchill would not yield to the all-pervading sense of calamity. Once more he sought to infect the French with his own resolution, exhorting them in phrases of fire to fight on. The tide would turn, as it had turned in the other war. Could not Paris be defended, the Germans made to fight street by street?

The French recoiled at the thought of the devastation to their capital, their national shrine. "To turn Paris into a city of ruins will not affect the issue," replied Weygand.

Then let France become one vast battleground for guerrillas. Weygand would have none of it. Pétain growled in protest: "It would mean the destruction of our land."

Reynaud asked for the canceling of the bombing raid on Italy; it would bring retaliation on Lyons and Marseilles, both unprotected. Churchill, not without grim satisfaction, replied that it was too late to intervene—already the bombers were on the way. It emerged later that other British bombers, based in the South of France, were to have joined in the raid, but the French placed obstacles on the airfield and prevented them from taking off.

Reynaud and the defeatists were at daggers-drawn, and, as the discussions of the Council proceeded, French tempers began to rise. Weygand spoke of the possibility of an armistice.

"That," snapped Reynaud, "is a political affair."

Churchill here broke in to say: "If it is best for your Army to capitulate, let there be no hesitation on our account. We shall fight on for ever and ever and ever."

What, asked Weygand, did the Prime Minister propose to do with invading Germans?

Churchill replied that his technical advisers held that the best method to deal with invaders was to drown as many as possible on the way over and to knock the survivors on the head as they crawled ashore in England.

"At any rate," commented Weygand dryly, "you have a very good antitank ditch."

The discussions were continued the following day. They remained inconclusive. Weygand proclaimed the hopelessness of the situation. Reynaud repeated his ceaseless call for more help from the RAF. Churchill maintained his chant of eventual victory. The meeting ended with Churchill's formal request: Before the French made any fundamental decision, would they inform the British Government so that a further conference might be held?

Before leaving for home, he had a parting word with Admiral Darlan, professional head of the French Navy.

"You must never let them get the French Fleet," he said.

Darlan gave his word. "There is no question of doing so," he replied. "It would be contrary to our naval traditions and honor." [3]

In the desperation of those days, Reynaud resolved, as a last resort, to continue the war from afar, withdrawing with his Government overseas. The Empire in Africa offered its refuge; there was the Fleet to give protection. General de Gaulle, recently appointed a junior minister, began working on the plans and was sent to London to discuss them. At first Churchill scented defeatism in the idea, but he came to realize the possibilities, if the plan could be carried out.[4] Any plan was acceptable that would keep the French still in the struggle, and it would impress the Americans.

Churchill and Reynaud now shared the common hope of American intervention. Must not the President be moved by France's plight to intervene in freedom's cause? Churchill wrote to the White House urging Roosevelt to do his utmost to strengthen Reynaud and so prolong French resistance.

Churchill stood, in those days, monumental in his strength and resolution. In the battle everything was crashing in ruin. Britain, it seemed, might go down in the common disaster. The failings of the French planners had brought about this catastrophe. He wasted no time on reproaches. Recrimination over the past and anxiety over future perils had no place for him. His stolidity impregnable, he concentrated his purpose on meeting the difficulties of the hour.

Moved by compassion for the French in their agony, his mind dwelt not on the mistakes of their strategists, but on the limitations of Britain's resources that made it possible to throw no more than a couple of divisions into the battle. When the French clamored for help in the air he had to harden his heart. In his sympathy he would have ordered every plane to support them, but there was a limit beyond which it was impossible to go. The fighter squadrons of the RAF were Britain's last line of defense. To deny them to the French was a bitter decision, but it was a vital one. Those squadrons, which would have been powerless to save the French then, were a few weeks later to turn the scale by the narrowest of margins in the Battle of Britain.

Hardly had Churchill returned to Downing Street than the summons came from Tours [5] for a further meeting. He set out on June 13 for the last visit he was to make to France for four years. Halifax and Beaverbrook were in his party.

This time the discussions were not prolonged. Reynaud had been instructed by his Cabinet to pose the question that lay at the heart of the future. Britain and France were bound by a solemn pledge to stand together, neither to make peace without the assent of the other. Would the British be prepared to release the French from their promise, since they had suffered so grievously and could continue no further? Could this be conceded while Anglo-French solidarity was still maintained?

The British Ministers had come prepared for bad tidings, but, even so, the words of the formal question fell on them with the force of drumbeats of doom. Churchill's answer was made in plain terms.

"Under no circumstances will Great Britain waste time in reproaches. The cause of France will always be dear to us and if we win the war we will one day restore her to her power. But that is a very different thing from asking Britain to consent to a departure from the solemn undertaking binding the two countries."

For all his sympathy, the Prime Minister spoke stern words of warning. Were France to fall out, she must abide by the consequences. The war would grow ever more terrible. "We are fast approaching a universal blockade. France, if she is occupied by the Germans, cannot hope to be spared."

Once again, with his passionate eloquence, he pleaded with the French to struggle on. France still had her fine Navy and her great Empire. At all costs time must be gained to enable the United States to rally to her side.

At the suggestion of General Spears, Churchill asked for a short adjournment, for consultation with his colleagues *"dans le jardin."* Into the garden they stepped. It was a dismal place, drab and ill-kept. As they walked the muddy paths they talked. There was little to discuss, for all agreed with their leader.

Beaverbrook voiced the common feeling: "Tell Reynaud there is nothing to say or discuss till Roosevelt's answer is received. Don't commit yourself to anything. We are doing no good here—in fact listening to Reynaud only does harm. Let's get along home."

Before the Council meeting was ended, Churchill raised the question of German pilots held in France as prisoners of war, many of them brought down by the RAF. Could not they be sent to England, out of harm's way? Otherwise there would be the trouble of shooting them down a second time. Reynaud undertook that this should be done, but despite his promise nothing came of it.

Without delay, for evening had now come, the British Ministers left for home. This was unfortunate, for the members of the French Cabinet were waiting, expecting to meet Churchill. His resolution might have stiffened the waverers, but their wishes were not made known to him and the chance was lost.

That night Reynaud broadcast his final appeal for aid to the President: "The sufferings and the pride of France must now be told. Everywhere on earth the free men must know what they owe to her. The hour has now come for them to pay to her their debts."

In London the "Former Naval Person" sat writing in reinforcement of the French Premier's pleading. Churchill did not scruple to employ the pressure he fancied might reside in the fate of the two Fleets, French and British. Had the President, he asked, considered that Hitler might bargain with the French after capitulation: "Surrender your Fleet intact and I will leave you Alsace-Lorraine." And the Royal Navy—were Britain to be beaten, another Government might come into being under another Prime Minister, who might fail to send the Fleet across the Atlantic. There might thus be a revolution in sea power, so sudden that there would be no time in America to prepare against it.

"I know well, Mr. President," added Churchill, "that your eye will have already searched these depths, but I feel that I have the right to place on record the vital manner in which American interests are at stake in our battle and that of France." [6]

This artless attempt at diplomatic blackmail shows the length to which, in the stress of the emergency, Churchill was prepared to go to secure succor for the French. It could produce no effect. Already Roosevelt had reached the limit of his presidential prerogatives. There was nothing further he could do. The President's sympathies were with the

French in their heart-rending hour, but the Congress alone could sanction what the French needed.

On June 14 the Germans entered Paris. Their tanks drove past the Arc de Triomphe, the Swastika flag fluttered above the Tour Eiffel. The Seine was crossed, the Maginot Line was pierced and more than 400,000 French troops were cut off in those useless fortifications.

It seemed, once again, that the BEF must be involved in the French disaster. Brooke, who had distinguished himself in the retreat from Dunkirk, had now the painful duty to seek authority to bring his troops home. Churchill was known to be adamant against withdrawal. The two men talked on the telephone. Braving the other's displeasure, Brooke pressed his case—to continue where they were would be to throw away good British troops for no useful purpose. For half an hour the argument went on. At last the soldier prevailed. Churchill was convinced, and the order for retirement was sanctioned. In a lesser Dunkirk, 150,000 men were brought back across the Channel.[7]

The inevitable end was not to be delayed. Churchill drew up a message to prepare the Commonwealth Prime Ministers for the shock of the French surrender. Evaluating the hazards to be faced, and British ability to meet them, he found reason for sober confidence. All should enter the life-and-death struggle in good heart, resolved not to allow themselves to be deterred by the fate of France from going on to the end.

At Tours, Reynaud was desperately engaged in a political rear-guard action. No waverer himself, he was ready to continue in Africa when resistance in France was no longer possible. Tentative orders were issued for organizing the struggle in the Empire but he was surrounded by intriguers and defeatists who were too strong for him. Mandel was resolutely backing him, and so were a few more. But the Generalissimo believed only in capitulation. Pétain, the aged Pétain, was of this mind, and so too were Chautemps and Bauduoin. From his Egeria, the intriguing Hélène de Portes, Reynaud, for days past, had listened to arguments for making peace. Her voice must have tended to undermine his confidence. He acted astutely as a politician, but he lacked the force to impose his will on events, to sack Weygand and, under a new Generalissimo, to make a fighting retreat south, across the Mediterranean to Algiers.[8]

Sunday, June 16, was the day of decision. In London the Cabinet agreed to release the French from their pledge were they to undertake that their warships should sail for British harbors.[9] Then came the dramatic proposal for the amalgamation of Britain and France in a solemn act of union—a union of Empire, Cabinets and Parliaments.

This bold proposal for an Anglo-French superstate owed its inspiration not to the Prime Minister but to officials of the French Embassy and the British Foreign Office. The War Cabinet endorsed it. De Gaulle, then in London, telephoned the terms to Bordeaux.[10]

Reynaud was impressed by the declaration: "Every citizen of France will enjoy immediately citizenship of Great Britain; every British subject will become a citizen of France."

Churchill's voice was heard on the line: "Hallo, Reynaud, you must hold out. Our proposal may have great consequences."

Reynaud was heartened by the encouragement. The two premiers then arranged to meet on the morrow, at sea if need be, in a warship.

"See you tomorrow," shouted Churchill, "at Concarneau." [11]

The day following Churchill boarded the train to begin the journey to the rendezvous, his staff with him. At the last minute there was a delay, and the trip was called off. Reynaud had fallen.

The declaration of union had been Reynaud's undoing. He had presented it to his Ministers and it had perished with his words, stillborn. The intriguers had forestalled him. He was spied upon, the telephone line tapped as he spoke to Churchill in London. The defeatists, forewarned, laid their plans. The project for liaison was dismissed with a couple of phrases.

"All it means is that we should become a British dominion," pronounced a hostile voice.

"Liaison with a corpse," added Pétain, contemptuously.

It was false, but it was shattering. It was addressed to French pride and it carried the day, weakening Reynaud's position.[12]

The point had been reached where the French had not the strength to fight on. What was it to be—surrender by the soldiers, or capitulation by the Ministers? Capitulation meant the end of all resistance—there could be no withdrawal to Africa. Reynaud recommended surrender in the field. Weygand would not hear of it.

"Never will I inflict such shame on our colors," he declared. Rather than agree he would have used military force in a coup against Reynaud.[13]

In this atmosphere of intrigue and defeatism the vote was taken. In the morning the Ministers, by the narrow margin of 13 to 11, were for continuing the war. At night the figures were reserved—13 to 11 in favor of asking for armistice terms. Reynaud fell, and with Reynaud the tattered flag of France came down. Pétain became Premier, the aged Pétain, veteran of eighty-four, admirer of the Fascist system.

The next day Pétain pronounced the fateful decision. "It is with a heavy heart," he said, broadcasting to the people of France, "that I say we must cease the fight. I have applied to our opponent to ask him if he is ready to sign with me, as between soldiers after the fight and in honor, a means to put an end to hostilities." It was the first step to the capitulation of Compiègne.

The defection of France was a calamity. The people of Britain were left to continue the struggle alone. The Prime Minister, in a speech to the House of Commons on June 18, summed up the chances of the future in words of the highest inspiration:

It seems clear that no invasion on a scale beyond the capacity of our land forces to crush speedily is likely to take place until our Air Force has been definitely overpowered. The great question is: Can we break Hitler's air weapon?

Of course [he went on, recalling the words once used by Baldwin], it is a great pity that we have not got an Air Force at least equal to that of the most powerful enemy within striking distance of these shores. But we have a very powerful Air Force which has proved itself far superior in quality, both in men and in many types of machine, to what we have met so far in the numerous fierce air battles which have been fought. In France, where we were at a considerable disadvantage and lost many machines on the ground, we were accustomed to inflict losses of as much as two to two-and-a-half to one. In the defense of this island the advantages of the defenders will be very great. We hope to improve on the rate of three or four to one which was realized at Dunkirk.

During the great battle in France we gave very powerful and continuous aid to the French Army, both fighters and bombers, but in spite of every kind of pressure we never would allow the entire metropolitan strength of the Air Force, in fighters, to be consumed. This decision was painful, but it was also right, because the fortunes of the battle in France could not have been decisively affected, even if we had thrown in our entire fighting force. The battle was lost by the unfortunate strategical opening, by the extraordinary and unforeseen power of the armored columns, and by the great preponderance of the German Army in numbers.

I do not at all underrate the severity of the ordeal which lies before us, but I believe our countrymen will show themselves capable of standing up to it. Every man and every woman will have the chance to show the finest qualities of their race and render the highest service to their cause. For all of us at this time, whatever our sphere, our station, our occupation, our duties, it will be a help to remember the famous lines:

He nothing common did or mean,
Upon that memorable scene.

Those were the lines that had come to his mind on the departure of the Duke of Windsor following his abdication.

Our professional advisers of the three Services unitedly advise that there are good and reasonable hopes of final victory. We have also consulted all the self-governing Dominions, and I have received from their Prime Ministers, messages, couched in the most moving terms, in which they endorse our decision and declare themselves ready to share our fortunes and to persevere to the end.

The Battle of France is over. The Battle of Britain is about to begin. Upon it depends our way of life. The whole fury and weight of the enemy must very soon be turned on us. If we fail, the whole world will sink into an abyss of a new dark age, made more sinister, and perhaps more protracted, by the lights of a perverted science.

Let us therefore brace ourselves to our duties, and so bear ourselves that, if the British Empire and Commonwealth last for a thousand years, men will still say: "This was their finest hour."

Churchill took pride in the fact that no formal decision to fight on, alone though Britain stood, was ever made. It was automatically accepted without question put to the Cabinet. It was inevitable, but there was precious little to fight with. There were no rifles for the soldiers, a beggarly 500 field guns for the artillery and not many shells for these. In the whole country there were fewer than 200 tanks.

The British people knew none of these things. The words of their Prime Minister filled them with confidence and resolution. It was their own war now. The shopkeeper in St. James's Street [14] voiced a common feeling: "Thank God we have no more allies: now we know where we are." Even King George felt relief that there were no allies left to pamper with politenesses.[15] Churchill would not have echoed the talk of the foolhardy, but he shared their spirit. It was their war now and it was his to run.

CHAPTER FIVE

RUNNING THE WAR

SUMMER, 1940

BEFORE proceeding further with the narrative of events, it is necessary to pause to consider the political basis of Winston Churchill's authority and the manner in which he exercised it for the direction of the war. As democratic Prime Minister he was dependent on the will of the House of Commons. It was his strength and his weakness. Hitler, an omnipotent despot, could dragoon the Germans. Churchill could persuade, convince, he could direct and he could lead, but he worked, subject to the approval of the House of Commons, on a twenty-four-hour contract.

Abundant trust came to be reposed in him, but the House was jealous of its rights, and when occasionally he transgressed he was sharply reminded that he was the servant, not the master, of Parliament. There were inconveniences when M.P.s were in a recalcitrant mood. Then he might be moved to protest that Hitler could not be called to account and suffer the embarrassment of the proddings of members whose criticisms could be met only at the risk of the disclosure of information to the enemy.

With his capacity for domination he might have made himself an autocrat, in the pattern of Cromwell, but forty years passed in the House had made him a faithful parliamentarian, upholder of the customs and traditions of the past. He came to glory in his vulnerability. Stalin, as he pointed out, was secure, Roosevelt impregnable during his term of office. He, Winston Churchill alone, was invested with no lease of office, but was subject, day by day, to dismissal at the hands of the Mother of Parliaments.

Even under the stress of war, politics and the claims of party were not to be ignored. His administration was based on the support of the three parties, and this determined the apportionment of offices. There were Liberals as well as Socialists to be accommodated in his Ministry. The Socialists filled rather more than a third of the ministerial posts. The Liberals, with their small representation in the Commons, were allotted more appointments than was their due on a strictly actuarial basis.

When the administration was formed, there was no time to be spent on the niceties of party bargaining. Subordinating personal feelings, all placed themselves at the Prime Minister's disposal, eager to serve in whatever capacity he might decide, and so they continued, a loyal and harmonious team. With Clement Attlee, Churchill worked with ease and confidence. Greenwood was sound and of a stout heart. Ernest Bevin was a man from the same mold as himself, of strong will, aggressive spirit and dauntless courage.

Men who had been opponents of appeasement were marked out for office. The Right Honorable Leopold Charles Maurice Stennett Amery became Secretary for India; Lord Lloyd was appointed to the Colonial Office; Duff Cooper was made Minister of Information; Sir Henry Page Croft, translated to the House of Lords, was appointed Under-Secretary to the War Office.

Of former members of the Chamberlain administration, Sir John Simon vacated the Treasury for the woolsack, no longer considering himself to have political prospects to be damaged by acceptance of a peerage; Sir Kingsley Wood took over the nation's finances; Sir Samuel Hoare (later Lord Templewood) was dispatched to the Embassy in Spain. Lord Halifax continued to direct the affairs of the Foreign Office until, on the death of Lord Lothian, he was selected to be His Majesty's Ambassador to Washington, whereupon Anthony Eden was transferred from the War Office to succeed as Foreign Secretary.

Two men were brought in from outside the ranks of the professional politicians whose services Churchill particularly required—Lord Beaverbrook and Ernest Bevin. Each was outstanding in his own sphere, one among the magnates of Fleet Street, the other among leaders of the Trades Unions. Each was a conspicuous success, one as Minister of Aircraft Production (and later as Minister of Production), the other as Minister of Labor. By his unorthodox methods Beaverbrook stepped up production of the fighter planes that were to win the Battle of Britain. Bevin, moving on orthodox lines, obtained authority over the nation's manpower to an extent never before exercised. It was unfortunate that these two men, outstanding for ability and strength of character, could not find it possible to work amicably together. They tried to get on terms, but their similarities in temperament and their differences in outlook made this impossible. Nor was Churchill—for whom both had the utmost admiration—able to prevent the clash between them that was to be the major disturbance in good relations within the Ministry.

Few of the men whose cooperation the Prime Minister sought refused to serve under him. The conspicuous exception was Lloyd George. Believing the inclusion of his old chief to be of supreme importance, Churchill spared no effort to bring him into the Government. There was opposition from Neville Chamberlain, who could not forget the humiliations of the past and who was dubious of the advantages to be gained from Lloyd George's presence in the Cabinet. He yielded, however, to Churchill's persistence. The office of Minister of Agriculture was offered. Lloyd George would not accept. Beaverbrook approached him with subtle persuasion, but Lloyd George rejected all entreaties—he was not going in with "that gang." He had held first place in the old war, and he would not bring himself to serve as a subordinate in this. Nor was it beyond his calculations that, if events were to go badly, there might come the time when a Minister would be needed to make terms with Hitler.[1]

When he formed his Ministry, Churchill was in the position of Lloyd George in the First World War—he was head of a Government, but not of a political party. Neville Chamberlain was the leader of the Tories, and still held by many followers in high esteem. It is customary for a Conservative Prime Minister to lead the party, but Churchill would not permit Chamberlain to surrender the position—found, indeed, compelling reasons why the other should continue in the leadership. He wrote:

MY DEAR NEVILLE,

You have been good enough to consult me about the leadership of the Conservative Party. I am, of course, a Conservative, but as Prime Minister of a National Government, formed on the widest basis and comprising the three parties, I feel that it would be better for me not to undertake the leadership of one political party.

I therefore express the hope that your own leadership of our party will remain undisturbed by the change of Government or premiership, and I feel sure that by this arrangement the cause of national unity will be best served.

The relations of perfect confidence which have grown up between us make the division of duties and responsibilities very agreeable to me.

Yours ever,
WINSTON CHURCHILL

Churchill was loyal to his colleagues, a quality that was often to be noted thereafter. The cynic, indeed, remarked that his loyalty was such that ministerial failures were promoted rather than dismissed. Certainly we were spared the unedifying spectacle of public recrimination which under Lloyd George had marked the supersession of the politically unfit.

Neville Chamberlain's position in the Government was the cause of some concern. The original intention had been that he should act as Leader of the House of Commons, and so relieve Churchill of the management of parliamentary business, but the antagonisms of the past cut deep and the Socialists would not agree to the arrangement. To persist would have caused ill-feeling and the proposal was dropped. Chamberlain took the post of Lord President, free of departmental responsibility, to serve in the War Cabinet. Churchill himself had the title of Leader of the House, but Clement Attlee, as his deputy, relieved him of the day-to-day conduct of parliamentary business.

Though he might yield over Chamberlain's case, Churchill set himself firmly against proscriptions arising from the past. Let the sorry days of appeasement be forgotten. How many, indeed, were there, Socialist or Tory, whose records would bear scrutiny? So the slate was wiped clean.

With the political basis of his administration secure, Churchill could devote himself to the supreme task of beating Hitler. For this he considered himself to be specially qualified. To this end he assigned himself the post of Minister of Defense.[2]

Prime Ministers, for the most part, have been satisfied to lead without taking the additional burden of a department, though occasionally the responsibility of the Foreign Office has been added to the premiership. Churchill allocated himself the Defense Ministry as a means to provide for his own special requirements. He had suffered in the past from trying to undertake major operations from a subordinate position. It had caused his fall over the Dardanelles. Now he established himself so that he could direct operations from a position of constitutional security. He had his own conception of how a war should be run. He was determined that decisions should be swiftly reached and orders promptly given. In Asquith's time the war had been managed in committee, with interminable discussion. Lloyd George had improved on this by establishing a small War Cabinet. Churchill set himself to improve on Lloyd

George. He, too, would have a small War Cabinet as the executive authority. But for the direction of affairs, the planning and control of operations, he would act through and in conjunction with the Chiefs of Staff, the professional heads of the three Services.

His powers and responsibilities as Defense Minister remained, like the British Constitution, undefined. Unspecified by royal patent or statutory enactment, they became very much what he wished them to be, as extensive as the exigencies of the war required. He was subject to the decisions of the War Cabinet and the overriding voice of the House of Commons. Winning the confidence of both, he was able to issue directions with discretion virtually unlimited over the whole of the vast field of operations, in conformity with the advice of the Service Chiefs.*

The Chiefs of Staff Committee was the operational authority for running the war. Churchill was the guiding force. As Defense Minister he presided over the meetings, as circumstances required, and to him the Chiefs of Staff were directly responsible. Authority and responsibility could not have been more concentrated. The three Service Ministers, First Lord of Admiralty, Secretary for War and Air Minister, were confined to the running of their departments. The Minister of Defense reported direct to the War Cabinet. He was punctilious in placing matters before his colleagues, but it was infrequently that the War Cabinet came to intervene in operational matters.

It was a procedure, evolved under the stress of emergency, that was successful to the highest degree. It might have been otherwise. Indeed, he exposed himself to political disaster, for his personal responsibility was unlimited. He functioned as a Chief of Staff in his own right. No Prime Minister before him had exercised such direct and intimate authority in the military sphere.

Lloyd George, leader of the First World War, did not and could not have played the same part. Lloyd George was always the civilian, with profound mistrust of the professional heads of the Services, intriguing against Robertson, the C.I.G.S. whom he removed, and against Haig, the commander in chief in the field whom, had he dared, he would have sacked. Churchill, by training, by experience of affairs, and by insight, moved on terms of equality with men of the Services. He had fought as a soldier, he had devoted himself to the administration of the Navy, he had served as Air Minister and Secretary for War. His perceptive understanding of war had been heightened by his contact with the professionals and by his study of the campaigns of his ancestor, the great Marlborough. He acquired a personal authority on military affairs that no Prime Minister, Wellington not excepted, ever possessed.

* See also Chapter Seven, Book Two.

"I thought I knew a great deal about it all," was his reflection as he took over the leadership.[3] From the outset he conducted himself as one who was entitled to make his voice heard on all major matters, operations as well as strategy, even down to the details of instruction on points of tactics.

So effective was this machinery for running the war that, when the United States came in, it was extended to the wider sphere of Allied operations. Thereafter it was through the Combined Chiefs of Staff, sitting in permanent session in Washington, that unified direction was exercised. Churchill had evolved the successful model, and he continued to play his part as member of the larger team.

"I cannot remember any major discussion with them in which he did not participate," was the testimony Eisenhower gave to his widely ranging influence on events.[4]

Churchill and the country were splendidly served by the professional Chiefs, the triumvirate of the Services, first Pound, Dill and Newall, and then Brooke, Cunningham and Portal, with "Pug" Ismay as indefatigable head of the secretariat. With their various subordinates they made a superb team, their cooperation founded on mutual esteem and good will.

They had their differences, which were freely and vigorously voiced. They worked subject to the pressure and proddings of the masterful Defense Minister, who at times exasperated them to the limits of their toleration.

In a score of memoirs, tribute has been paid to Churchill's leadership. The picture of the man has always been the same—magnificent in spirit, undismayed by reverses, fertile in resource, a man, like Odysseus, of many devices. But there are two sides to every medal, and two aspects to every character. Churchill was tenacious—never more so than over his own designs. He was gifted with strategic imagination, prolific in ideas; in argument he did not always distinguish between the practicable and the disastrous. He was matchless for his pugnacious spirit—his impish pugnacity could be harassing for his advisers. As orator of freedom's cause, his phrases were an inspiration; his discourses to colleagues and advisers in support of his opinions could be exhausting and, when provoked by opposition, his invective could be stinging. When the heat of the moment was over, he forgot, but some who felt the lash of his words remembered. With some of the lesser spirits the hurts festered, as wartime reminiscences have sometimes attested.

One source of strain was the timetable to which he worked. Men of the Services, who had to be early at their desks, found it difficult to adjust themselves to the requirements of a chief who came to later in the day and whose mental activity did not reach its peak until midnight.

In the morning, colleague or adviser would be summoned to the presence of a Prime Minister still abed, attired in a red and gold dressing gown decorated with dragons. Papers and dispatches would litter the bed around the mandarin propped up amidst the pillows. So reclining, he would deal with the affairs of the morning—dispatches, speeches, instructions, visitors. After the business of a Cabinet meeting, or a House of Commons debate in the afternoon, a siesta would restore his strength and he would be ready to continue with unflagging zest until the early hours. It was then the high-powered organ of his brain functioned as a dynamo, humming with activity, throwing off sparks that illumined the scene of war. It was then that he sought the company of advisers for the informal airing of his ideas. Early starters, exhausted by the labors of the day, found themselves required to sacrifice half their night's rest. They were kindled by his flow of ideas and at times they longed for bed.

All who gave counsel to him were required to conform. Some, who realized the weight of the burden he was shouldering, bore up with resignation. It was trying. Others, thinking more of their own responsibilities than his, doubted whether the immense additional effort was justified. Visitors from America—Eisenhower, Marshall, Harry Hopkins and the rest—were roped in for the midnight talks. When Churchill stayed at the White House, Roosevelt was tempted to stay up beyond his usual early hour of retirement. In the Kremlin there was a companion spirit in Stalin, who was prepared to talk in the dawn.[5]

The offensive spirit was Churchill's dominant contribution to running the war. His questing mind ranged the Continent for chances to strike a blow. Any action was desirable that offered stubborn resistance to the will of the enemy. That was the cardinal principle, the essential element in victory.

He demanded the offensive spirit in the men around him. He showed it against his advisers, he expected it from them in return. He challenged them in the battle of ideas and he demanded that they should fight back. Some, like the C.I.G.S., John Dill, could not maintain the conflict in dialectics.

Between the departments of state, conflict and the offensive spirit was encouraged. His Ministers did not share his taste. Beaverbrook would write to deplore the "crabbing" he as Minister of Aircraft Production received from the Air Ministry. He was recommended to accept that unusual stimulus. "It is more in the public interest," pronounced Churchill, "that there should be sharp criticism and counter-criticism between two departments than that they should be handing each other ceremonious bouquets."

The flow of Churchill's ideas presented problems for the military mind. The disciplined training of the soldier makes for rigidity of outlook. Generals are no more tolerant than bishops of the unorthodox, and here was a man brimming over with unorthodoxy, his strategic imagination seemingly inexhaustible, bubbling over with expedients, some sound, some merely ingenious, all of them needing to be sifted. Staff officers were kept busy and staff chiefs were vexatiously employed insisting on the rejection of the impracticable. But without him they might have run out of ideas and there were times when he was unquestionably, disconcertingly, in the right.

His interest ranged from the major operation to the minor detail. There was need to discourage him from running a battle from Downing Street and dictating tactics to the commander in the field. He would insist on seeing the loading tables for ships carrying supplies to the forces overseas, challenging items on the lists.[6] Some staff officers were disturbed by the meddling that placed extra strain on the war machine. They had not had his salutary lessons in the First World War, when the soldiers, left to themselves, made a bungling hash of transporting the Expeditionary Force to Gallipoli. He remembered. He would not permit similar operations to be marred for lack of his direction.

Churchill was dogmatic, domineering, provoking, infuriating, but he was an inspiration. He would play the termagant to the Chiefs of Staff, but he trusted them to the full, deferred invariably to their considered opinion, gave them immense authority, and spread over them the umbrella of his powerful protection. He would rate them as the anger of the moment moved him: "Have I to wage the war with ancient weapons?" But it was his sole prerogative. Anyone in his hearing who criticized the Chiefs of Staff would find the Prime Minister's guns brought powerfully to bear upon him.[7]

In recent years, with the multiplication of war memoirs, the curtains have been drawn aside and we have been made privy to some of the secrets concerning the direction of the war. We have been told of differences between the Minister and his advisers, and men whose counsel had been sometimes rejected have passed criticism on Churchill the strategist.

When he had given his account of affairs, Churchill, with characteristic magnanimity, had passed the sponge over many old controversies. What mattered the processes of discussion so long as the right decision was taken? The military mind, less accustomed to the conflict and acerbities of debate, had been more impressed by the differences. After the match is over the players are usually content to forget the rough handling of the game, but generals are not seen at their best in loose mauls. Resentment occasionally lingered and maybe a sense of pique. Doubtless it was galling to find that, often enough, when they had opposed their professional opinion to his, the event proved him, after all, to have been in the right.

Churchill, by nature and experience, was disinclined to bow to the infallibility of the expert. For nearly half a century he had watched generals in action. He had reported and criticized their shortcomings in the little wars of the nineties and in the Boer War. No one who had played his part in the First World War could have preserved intact his faith in the military expert. Under Asquith and Lloyd George the generals had had greater freedom to make their own mistakes in their own way. Any lingering illusions about their infallibility that might have survived the shambles of the Western Front, with the holocaust of Passchendaele, must have perished when the generals took up their pens to refight the battles they had lost. In a score of memoirs military reputations went down like ninepins as General X to establish his own soundness exposed the weakness of General Y. Nor, between the wars, had confidence been restored by the generals of a later generation. It was the Germans who had exploited the tank, to a great degree Churchill's contribution to the other war. In 1939 the British Army was only slightly mechanized.* Many campaigns were to be lost because the British tanks were outgunned, outranged, and outclassed, a deficiency for which the Minister of Defense was made to take some of the blame. Like the Army, the Royal Air Force had been kept short of funds in the thirties, but the air marshals had provided themselves with planes, Hurricanes and Spitfires that won the Battle of Britain. The generals had not kept pace with the progress of mechanization.

What would we not give to have been present at some of the more lively meetings between Defense Minister and Service Chiefs. They were the despair of precise minds, looking for nicely ordered proceedings, with decisions taken in the light of well-weighed expert opinion. Instead there would be exhortations and harangues, stimulating challenges, explosive expostulations. Disregarding the agenda, offering little encouragement to others to intervene, Churchill, often enough, would discourse till time had run out and no decision would be reached. The Staffs, frustrated though they might be, would disperse with the sense that they had participated in a historic occasion. Or, encountering persistent opposition to a pet project, the Minister would angrily exclaim against

---

* Churchill states in the first volume of his war memoirs: "The awful gap in our prewar arrangements was the absence of even one armored division in the BEF in 1939. Eight months after the declaration of war, when the hour of trial arrived, there was only [in Flanders] the 1st Army Tank Brigade comprising 17 light tanks and 100 infantry tanks."

advisers bent on frustrating him in all his offensive plans. Let there be doubts and questioning of his robust optimism. Then, the vials of his wrath opened, he would denounce defeatist generals with cold feet. Did none of his generals want to fight the "Narzees"? Or, though more rarely, it would be the boneheads of the Admiralty on whom he would pour out his scorn.

There was the occasion *, apocryphal maybe, when he was set on an assault on a Mediterranean island. He had received no support from his advisers and he brought up the question for formal decision at a Staffs meeting. Would the Navy undertake it? Prime Minister, we have no landing craft. Would the Army see it through? Prime Minister, we have the men, but there are insufficiently trained officers. The Air Force, could they provide cover? Prime Minister, our planes are already engaged.

Churchill, with a withering glance, surveyed his non-cooperative advisers.

"First Lord," he burst out, "do you mean to tell me that the Royal Navy is completely unable to see this through?"

The First Lord excused himself. "The tradition of the Navy——" he began, when Churchill broke in.

"The tradition of the Navy!" he exploded. "Do you know what is the tradition of the Navy? I will tell you. Rum, sodomy, and the lash—that is the tradition of the Navy."

The raking-over in the ashes of controversy has had the result of bringing out Churchill's strength as War Minister. We have been enabled to sit in at meetings of the Staff Chiefs—to perceive the skill with which that instrument of war was directed. He was the originator, the idea man of the team. Some of his notions were sound, others questionable. There were times when his advisers found it difficult to induce him to abandon the impracticable. At other times he had to exert himself to secure the adoption of measures that were to be justified by their success and in which those who had opposed him at the time came afterward to concur.

As Defense Minister, he was both advocate of his own measures and final arbiter on what was to be done. It is the measure of his judgment that they were so invariably guided to the proper decision. No matter how hot the dispute, how strong his personal opinions or how vehement the advocacy of his own project, he was able to pick his way to the right answer to the question debated. Never did he carry his persistence so far that any one of the professional advisers found it necessary to resign. For, dispute with them as he might, he had the utmost respect

---

* This anecdote has already been narrated in his reminiscences by Sir Ronald Wingate, whose version is less pungent than the one I received.

for the considered verdict of the Service Chiefs. Never when they were unanimous in opinion did he overrule them on a purely military matter.[8]

Some may remember the strains and stresses, as they hammered out their differences until reason in the end prevailed. But it was out of the crucible of these discussions and the combustion of these controversies that, under Churchill's leadership, the path to victory was found.

His personal contribution to running the war extended to maintaining top-level contacts overseas. In the leisured times of peace the Foreign Secretary conducts the Government's correspondence, suffering from time to time the intrusion of Prime Ministers. Even before he took over the premiership, Churchill was in touch with President Roosevelt. Direct contact was continued and the Prime Minister's communications became the channel for much vital business. He also composed, on important occasions, the messages to the heads of Dominion Governments and foreign states. At a later stage, direct correspondence developed into personal contact. Churchill became the peripatetic envoy of the Allies, ready to take off at a moment's notice for a meeting, east or west, as the necessity of the hour required, at any time, at any place, at any risk. But these things belonged to the future.

In the summer of 1940 there were no Allies to consult. Britain, standing alone against Hitlerism, was a beleaguered fortress. Churchill's immediate task was to prepare for the reception of the Nazi invaders, whose descent on England's shores seemed to be imminent.

CHAPTER SIX

BRITAIN ALONE
JUNE—JULY, 1940

THIS was the testing time of Winston Churchill's leadership. Alone, cut off in her island, saved from immediate conquest by the encircling seas, England was reduced to the lowest level of defense. For a space there was little she could do but hold grimly on, and take what came to her.

With France's fall the watching world waited for the end that, it was supposed, could not long be delayed. How could Britain stand where France had gone down? It was imagined she would anticipate destruction by surrender. And if she did not yield—then, as General Weygand pronounced: "The English will have their necks wrung in three weeks."

During the months that followed Britons accepted the blows that fell, covering up as best they could. In the dark days it was an encouragement to know that the solid figure of Churchill was at the head, radiating assurance and resolution. The voice came on the air, those tones never to be forgotten, ringing out, the bellman of freedom's cause, or harsh in scornful contempt for that wicked man Hitler and his jackal accomplice, Mussolini.

Churchill moved up and down the land, exhorting the defenders of the island citadel and, amidst the smoking ruins, manifesting his sympathy with the victims of the Blitz. His mind was fertile in improvising expedients for meeting the German invader, but, though

Britain was pushed back on her defenses, he would never suffer the defensive habit to become the paralysis that had been disastrous for the poor French. There was to be no sitting back behind the Maginot Line of the English Channel waiting for the blows to fall. "The habit of mind that ruined the French must not," he declared, "be allowed to ruin all our initiative."

At every turn he faced gaps in the defenses. The years the locusts had eaten had left the British pitifully exposed. In the air they were short of planes, on the seas there were not enough destroyers, and the Army—virtually it was an army without arms. It was fortunate Hitler held off while he went gallivanting in Paris, dancing a jig of joy for victory. Every hour of the respite was turned to advantage in the scramble to rearm and to replace the planes that had been lost.

Even in the days of adversity Churchill's mind went leaping forward to the future, planning for the time when they would be strong enough to carry back the war to the Continent from which they had been expelled. Rummaging among his papers he turned up his notes, from the old war, for the building of landing craft and set the inventors to work. The vessels that one day were to carry the tanks across the seas owed their development to the impetus he gave in 1940.

As the French threw in their hands, his immediate concern was with the French Fleet. Next to Britain's own it was the most powerful in Europe. At all costs the Germans must be prevented from possessing themselves of these fine warships. Churchill pressed Pétain, Premier of the capitulation, to send the ships to safety across the seas before the Germans moved in. To surrender them to the Nazis would be an act that would scarify the names of France's leaders for a thousand years of history. Pétain ignored the appeal. The heads of the Admiralty, First Lord and First Sea Lord, were sent to Bordeaux to meet Darlan, now become Minister of Marine. They were given vague assurances, but the warships remained in their ports.

Disquieting signs of French intentions came to hand. The defeatists were rounding up the men who had been Reynaud's supporters. Mandel was arrested. Darlan ordered the detention of the deputies and senators who had sailed by warship for North Africa. Churchill sought to release them from the trap, suggesting a cutting-out expedition to capture the *Massilia,* in which they were confined. The ship lay under the protection of the batteries at Casablanca and nothing could be contrived.

The trapping of this remnant of Reynaud's supporters pointed to one need of the times. Stout hearts were still beating in France and an escape route must be found. Churchill's thoughts moved on romantic lines. A "Scarlet Pimpernel" organization must be set going to extricate

Frenchmen with the will to fight. Romance was realistically applied and the Underground Movement came into being.[1]

Pétain might yield, but there is no France without a sword. Free France needed a leader. He was at hand in the person of de Gaulle, whom General Spears had smuggled out of Bordeaux.[2] With Churchill's support he became the standard-bearer of the Free French colors. Lanky de Gaulle was an angular man, staunch and resolute, but lacking the suppleness of politicians or the capacity for accommodation required of statesmen engaged as partners in an alliance. Blundering in his earnestness, he was called *maître gaffeur*. Unable to adjust himself to the requirements of the team, he was to be the source of much exasperation, so that the Cross of Lorraine was not the least burdensome that Churchill had to bear. But, according to his inflexible fashion, de Gaulle devoted himself to the cause of France and freedom.[3] As leader of the French National Committee, his words, broadcast by the BBC, were the rallying cry for his fellow countrymen when Pétain submitted to the Germans. De Gaulle gained the distinction of a death sentence, passed on him in his absence by one of Weygand's *conseils de guerre*.

The armistice terms caused dismay to Churchill and his colleagues. Under Article Eight the French were required to place the vessels of their Fleet under German and Italian control. An immediate British protest was sent to Vichy, seat of the Ministry of capitulation, but protests, however vigorous, could scarcely keep the warships from the Nazis. It was a sinister prospect. The British Cabinet met to take the most unpalatable decision of the war. There was only one way to ensure that the *Dunkerque* and the *Strasbourg* and the two great battleships nearing completion were not manned by the enemy. Failing all else, they must be immobilized or destroyed. It was a heart-rending decision, but the War Cabinet did not hesitate. Sentiment, however strong, could not be allowed to add to Britain's perils.[4]

The orders went out. French warships in British ports were taken under control. Those at Alexandria were ordered not to sail at peril of being sunk. At Oran drastic action was required against the French squadron at anchor at Mers-el-Kebir.

Vice Admiral Somerville, with a strong naval force, including the battle cruiser *Hood* and two battleships, sailed for Oran. He carried Churchill's instructions: "You are charged with the most disagreeable task a British admiral has faced: we rely on you to carry it out relentlessly."

The French admiral was presented with an ultimatum: he must sail his ships away or sink them—failing that, force would be used. The French refused to submit. Discussions were continued throughout the day. Churchill, in London, sat waiting, hopeful that persuasion would prevail but sternly resolved if it did not. The British commanders strove to persuade the French to give way and, when their arguments failed, they sought to induce their own superiors at the Admiralty to spare them the discharge of a melancholy duty. Churchill and the Cabinet were unyielding. The French must comply or their ships be sunk before dark.

Fire was opened and it was soon over. In the space of ten minutes the battleship *Bretagne* was blown up, the *Dunkerque* ran aground, the *Provence* was beached. The *Strasbourg* forced her way out and, though damaged by aerial torpedo, reached Toulon. At Dakar, later, the battleship *Richelieu* was hit by aerial torpedo. So the unhappy business was done, and many brave French sailors, till recently fighting as allies of Britain, perished.

The House of Commons met July 4, 1940, to receive a report on the episode. Churchill explained how the War Cabinet had been driven to its decision by the inexorable necessities of war. He paid tribute to the gallantry of the French sailors.

> I need hardly say that the French ships were fought, albeit in this unnatural cause, with the characteristic courage of the French Navy, and every allowance must be made for Admiral Gensoul and his officers who felt themselves obliged to obey orders they received from their Government and could not look behind that Government to see the German dictation. I fear the loss of life among the French and in the harbor must have been heavy, as we were compelled to use a severe measure of force and several immense explosions were heard. I have not yet received any reports of our casualties, but Admiral Somerville's Fleet is, in all military respects, intact and ready for further action. The Italian Navy, for whose reception we had also made arrangements and which is, of course, considerably stronger numerically than the fleet we used at Oran, kept prudently out of the way. However, we trust that their turn will come during the operations which we shall pursue to secure the effectual command of the Mediterranean.

The report made, he submitted himself to the verdict of opinion.

> I leave the judgment on our action with confidence to Parliament, I leave it to the nation, I leave it to the United States. I leave it to the world and history.

Parliament's answer was immediately given to him. The House might have been expected to respond with a subdued and sympathetic murmur. Instead, to his surprise, it cheered him to the echo, M.P.s rising to their feet to roar their approval. It was not (as General de Gaulle and many French patriots thought, in their distress) that the British gloried in what had been done. Members were moved by the demonstration of the Government's fixity of purpose, unmistakable in its tragic emphasis, to fight Hitlerism to the last.

Abroad, the same impression prevailed. Now the world could see beyond the peradventure of doubt that Britain would not haul down the flag, but that, under Churchill's leadership, the battle would be fought to the bitter end. World opinion was converted about Britain's intentions, but the estimate of the outcome still remained. How could the British be expected to prevail against the new masters of Europe, whose supremacy was unchallenged from the Mediterranean to the North Cape?

While Hitler passed the time sunning himself in the summer glow of victory, Churchill, in resolute mood, pressed forward the preparations for throwing back the invaders. The strategy was agreed. Beach defenses were contrived, command zones established. Antitank obstacles and barbed-wire entanglements were improvised with indefatigable zeal. The Home Guard sprang into being, nearly a million strong.

Churchill's directives poured out in never-ceasing flow. Vulnerable beaches must be blocked off. Creeks and harbors must be made secure. To man the defenses the troops must have their leavening of seasoned officers. Behind the first line there must be mobile brigades, "Leopards" as they were called, to spring at invading throats. Well-armed divisions should be held in reserve, with artillery to deal with the emergency of the capture of an English port. Churchill was not going to allow Britain to be defeated for lack of a *masse de manœuvre*. And never did he cease to urge that the first line of defense was the enemy ports and the surrounding seas.

With plans formed, he set out to see for himself how the work was progressing, touring the coast from the Tyne to North Foreland. There were a thousand miles of beaches to suit the invader, and no adequate armor to defend them. There were masses of men, but few of them armed, many untrained. All were in splendid spirit, an inspiration for their leader. He spent the summer days on the invasion coast. He was provided with his own special train that, like a circus caravan, gave him a home and an office. Shunted into a siding, he could sit at his papers, keeping in touch with Whitehall by telephone. His traveling quarters were complete with bath as well as bed.

He made the acquaintance of officers who were to lead the armies of the future, one of them a certain General Montgomery, commanding the 3rd Division. Montgomery's headquarters were near Brighton and they passed an evening of discussion at the Royal Albion Hotel. Churchill was favorably impressed. He spent a fruitful day with Alan Brooke, then heading the Southern Command. Brooke had been recommended for promotion to replace General Ironside in command of the Home Forces. As the two men drove along the Hampshire and Dorset coasts, Churchill was pleased to note that the General had the right ideas and the proper spirit. Two days later Brooke was appointed to the Supreme Command of Britain's defense, a post that brought him into closer contact with the Prime Minister.

Meanwhile prodigies of work in the factories were producing arms for the troops. The tank force was doubled. Under the vigor of Beaverbrook's direction, the output of aircraft leaped up. Everything was concentrated on turning out fighters—Hurricanes and Spitfires. Production spurted—325 new machines in May, 440 in June, 490 in July. Churchill's faith in Beaverbrook was justified. The new Minister of Aircraft Production was working wonders. The scandalous muddle of the past was ended. The methods of Beaverbrook the unorthodox were a nightmare for ordered planners, but they produced the results—just in time. The future rested with the young men of Fighter Command, the superb weapon fashioned by Dowding, pioneer of high-speed air combat.

CHAPTER SEVEN

INVADERS FOILED

AUGUST—SEPTEMBER, 1940

As JULY ran out Churchill received the first warnings from the Continent. After the junketings, the German war machine began to stir. Hitler had given the order for the onslaught on Britain, an operation "bold and daring," as he termed it, in face of the "utterly determined islanders." It was to be completed, he ordered, by mid-September. His generals began to assemble troops, a quarter of a million of them, and his admirals the shipping. Both generals and admirals waited on Goering and the Luftwaffe to clear the skies. Unless the British planes were kept out, the admirals could not hope to shut out the British warships from the Channel, and if the British ships were there, then the generals knew it would be suicide to attempt the crossing—"pouring men into a sausage machine."

The Battle of Britain commenced. It ended as it started, in the air. Churchill followed its course with anxious attention. The kills-and-losses chart was his chief concern. Britain was heavily outnumbered and to lose plane for plane would put her out of the fight. Day after day the Germans flew over, bombing airfields and radar stations, the magic eyes of the defense. At night Churchill scrutinized the returns. Heavy toll was taken of the enemy but, gratifying as were the figures, they were not his main interest. What was the price the RAF had been made to pay? It was considerable, and as the losses mounted apprehension grew.

The front-line airfields bore the brunt of the attack. Some, like

Manston and Lympne, in East Kent, were out of action until the damage could be repaired. Biggin Hill suffered severely. Churchill made visits to give encouragement to the men and sometimes to criticize. At Manston he complained of the delay in filling in bomb craters—it was feeble, far below the level of German performance.

In mid-August Churchill came to the microphone to report on the progress of the battle and to pay tribute to the young airmen in the words that register their fame—"The Few." Undaunted by odds, unwearied by constant challenge and mortal danger, the men of the RAF were turning the tide of war by their prowess and devotion. And then, the immortal phrase: "Never in the field of human conflict has so much been owed by so many to so few."

He gave words of praise to Beaverbrook for the astounding increase in the output and repair of machines achieved by an organization and drive "which looks like magic." But, magnificently as the Minister of Aircraft Production had labored, the handicap of years of neglect was not to be overcome in a couple of months. By sheer weight of numbers the Luftwaffe began to wear down the defense. Reserves of aircraft began to dwindle. The rate of loss was greater than factories and repair shops could replace and a shortage of trained pilots added to the anxieties of Dowding and the RAF Command. "The Few" were taxed to the uttermost limit.

As the fight went on, suspense mounted and anxiety grew. The attackers, regardless of their losses, pounded away at the airfields in southern England. Taking time off from Westminster, Churchill followed the engagements at close hand from air stations in Kent and Sussex. With everything at stake he had to be on the spot.

One afternoon in September he was present at Fighter Group headquarters, from which were controlled the squadrons in Kent, Essex, Sussex and Hampshire. In the operations room below ground he watched as battle was joined. Flashing bulbs marked the progress of operations. The Luftwaffe had fielded a full team that afternoon. The red lights soon showed that British fighters were up and after them. There were no more red signals to be flashed.

Churchill broke his silence. "What reserves have we left?" he asked.

"There are none," replied the Air Vice Marshal.

The defense had been stretched to the limit. The planes, their tanks empty, must begin to land to refuel. If more raiders came in they would catch Britain's pilots at a disadvantage. Happily, the Luftwaffe had been fully extended as well. The attacking planes flew off, save for the sixty that had paid the penalty.

There was relief in the operations room. Churchill had seen the turning point of the long contest. The Battle of Britain, though he did not know it at the time, had been won.

Goering, too, had been following the air battle with eager concern. He pronounced that the first phase had been won and that the RAF had been sufficiently weakened for raids on London to herald the invasion. His verdict was premature, his new directive providential for the defenders.

When the first bombs fell on London the Prime Minister ordered immediate retaliation to be made. The night following, 105 planes took off for a reprisal raid on Berlin.[1] That week the German capital experienced the first attentions of British bombers, puny affairs by comparison with the havoc that was to come, but they had a decisive influence on the course of the Battle of Britain. Hitler, too, called for immediate retaliation and the rubbing out of British cities. London was the first target. Churchill's order to attack Berlin had been instrumental in diverting the Luftwaffe at the critical moment from the vulnerable target of the airfields. Londoners had to pay the price for the respite that gave the RAF the breathing space to recover. The RAF, as Goering was informed, might be down to its last reserves of Hurricanes and Spitfires, but sufficient strength remained to punish the vast target of bombers displayed by daylight on the route to London.

Meanwhile, on both sides of the Channel, the opposing forces stood ready. Over there, four thousand ships of the Nazi invasion fleet lay huddled in the ports from Rotterdam to Le Havre. Von Rundstedt waited on the Grand Admiral; the Grand Admiral waited on Goering. Hitler hesitated. The day was fixed—it was postponed. The RAF played havoc with the invasion fleet and, with the RAF so destructively active in the air, the Germans had no stomach for the Channel crossing.

Back in England the long alert continued. Watchers on cliffs and downs peered into the night. The scouts of the Navy, vigilantly patrolling in their little craft, were ready to signal the alarm before being blasted from the sea. In the West Country the code word was flashed— "Cromwell!" The church bells rang from their steeples. A Home Guardsman's vision of phantom parachutists had sounded the tocsin of alarm. Rumor improved on what imagination had begun. Bodies of German soldiers were washed ashore from the Channel. Europe heard the tale and smirked at the thought of a Nazi defeat, though, in fact, the troops for the invasion had not begun to embark.

The days were passing, the storms of autumn grew near and with them respite till the spring. Churchill could for a few months strike out from his calculations the possibility of imminent invasion. When the weather improved it had to be restored to the calendar of risk, so to continue an ever-present menace for many months to come, always to be guarded against. For there was no knowledge in Britain that Hitler had called off Operation "Sea Lion." It was not one for which the Fuehrer ever had a liking and he accepted the failure of the Luftwaffe in the summer of 1940 as decisive. Never again were the barges to be massed in the invasion ports. The victory "The Few" won in the air was the defeat, in its opening phase, of the invasion of Britain.

Churchill, in passing, could note that the new team for the direction of the war had successfully played themselves in. They were an effective instrument for the conduct of operations, and they gained in mutual confidence and understanding. But the swiftly rolling tide of battle gave little opportunity for applauding the score of vantage points. Without a pause, the Battle of Britain was merged into the long drawn-out ordeal of the Blitz.

To "The Few" the glory of the Battle of Britain; to the many the credit for endurance in the Blitz. The civilians were in the front line and they stuck it out through the black winter of the bombing. The Londoners proclaimed that they could take it and proved the words to be no empty boast. Take it they did—for fifty-seven consecutive nights— and so did others up and down the country as their turn came.

Churchill shared in all the perils of the bombings. He was heedless of danger, a source of anxiety for his Ministers and his family. When the bombs began to fall he would insist on having a look and was not to be induced into the shelters.

"Busybodies," he called them, as they voiced their alarm. "You can't teach an old dog new tricks."

He shared the hazards with his Ministers and with Members of Parliament. Plans had been made for an exodus from Whitehall if the pace became too hot. Ministers were to have been given a retreat in Warwickshire, and Parliament would have met in Shakespeare's town of Stratford-on-Avon.

All the arrangements were complete and pink passes were issued. Some there were who thought it time to move, but Churchill would have none of it—he was not going to allow any Hitler to drive him out.

"It's unthinkable that the Government should leave the capital," he said. "I, for one, will not go." [2]

So they remained. Parliament sat in London throughout the war, despite everything that Hitler and his bombers could achieve. One move had, however, to be made.

Churchill's figure, dressed in a siren suit, became a familiar one after a raid. He would stand scowling at the wreckage of houses and offer words of sympathy to the homeless.

One morning he stood surveying the ruins of the House of Commons. An oil bomb had set the place in flames and a high explosive completed the destruction. As he looked on the rubble that had been the place of history and of his own parliamentary triumphs, the tears came. He made no attempt to hide them, but remained there, mourning in sympathy with the Mother of Parliaments. The House had to find alternative accommodation, the peers obligingly placing the Upper Chamber at their disposal.

Downing Street suffered its damage. The kitchen of Number Ten was shattered by blast when Churchill was dining in an adjacent room. By a fortunate hunch, he had ordered the kitchen staff into safety only a few moments previously.[3]

Had Churchill's view prevailed, the strident sirens that gave warning would have been silenced. "Banshee howlings" he called them, but not all were blessed with his fortitude under fire. The raid warnings had to be continued. He grew concerned over the interruption that was caused in the arms factories and the consequent fall in output. At his instigation a system of factory watchers was established, to give local warnings of danger overhead. In Government departments in Whitehall work fell behind during daylight raids till he put a check on the dugout routine. Departments, by his direction, were required to put in a daily return of dugout hours. Whitehall shelters thereafter were less frequented.[4]

The Blitz posed its own pressing problems, each to be accepted as a challenge and to be met by the improvisation of the moment—incendiary bombs, the threat of famine, the menace to London's sewage. Nothing was too trivial to escape Churchill's attention, no problem too great for some solution to be contrived. Moved by his sympathy for the distress of the homeless, he took steps for the inception of the national scheme of insurance against bomb damage.[5]

With the interest of a nonscientific mind, he followed the course of the battle of the laboratories. Where the RAF navigated by the stars, the Nazi pilots flew by radio beam. Churchill introduced one member of the research team to the Cabinet, to give an exposition of the device by which the beam could be bent and the bombers diverted from their course, to drop their cargoes in the empty spaces of the countryside. Bending the beam could give little relief to London, a target not to be missed, but it contributed to the escape of some provincial towns with their vital factories.

CHAPTER EIGHT

ORATOR OF FREE MEN

OCTOBER, 1940—JANUARY, 1941

IN THE DAYS when Britain stood alone, the people took heart from the speeches in which Winston Churchill chronicled the course of the conflict and declared Britain's inflexible purpose. He gave cause for confidence in the outcome of the struggle, strengthened the waverers, and imparted a new inspiration to the staunch of heart.

There was no propaganda in any way approaching the effectiveness of the addresses of this champion of the free peoples. He was the very embodiment of the national spirit. His manner was exquisitely adapted to the purposes of the leader of the nation at war, the voice firm and hard, incapable of the softer modulations, but not to be excelled for expressing the ideas he had to convey—iron resolution, trumpet calls of confidence in the people and their cause, rasping contempt for the "Narzees." The harsh tones brought out the fullness of his scorn for "that wicked man," and his accomplice, the guttersnipe of Italy. The language was rich and infinitely varied. No speaker could surpass him in extracting the last essence of drama from a situation; few equal him in his irony.

As pieces to be read, many of his speeches are assured of their place in literature as well as history—and of how many of our statesmen could the same be said? Of the men of his own time who served as Prime Minister none combined such a felicity of phrase with so dramatic an interest. Balfour, despite his dialectical skill, is not remembered for his speeches. Asquith, for all his vaunted style and stately diction, is scarcely read except by the students of politics. Bonar Law and Neville Chamberlain, Anthony Eden and Clement Attlee did not aspire to the same rank of orator. Ramsay MacDonald was diffuse and dull. Lloyd George made many speeches of scintillating raillery, and his perorations won him fame. Stanley Baldwin's somewhat wistful musings of the plain man with a delicate mind were never in Churchill's heroic mold.

Looking at the six fat volumes that were needed to record Churchill's public utterances during five years of war, it is impossible not to marvel at his output. Over half a million words are therein enshrined. Imagine the labor of composition that went to their preparation. Each of the major speeches was the result of much brooding thought. The ideas and the words that clothed them were elaborated in advance. He would need to wait at times for the mood of inspiration, and then he would dictate to one of his skilled and dedicated secretaries, in the manner of an orator, with appropriate gesticulations, but in a voice muffled by the rarely absent cigar or made indistinct by noise of car or train.[1]

Sometimes he would dictate from his place among the pillows, or he would pace the lawns at Chequers. At night his thoughts flowed freely and on the eve of a big speech, before dictation ceased, lark and cuckoo might be heralding the dawn. Alteration, revision and rephrasing continued until time permitted no more changes to be made. The throes of composition of the speeches in those six volumes would have been sufficient to tax professional writers. He took speechmaking in his stride, no more than part of the work of directing Britain's war effort.

As a broadcaster his ascendancy remained unchallenged. No man who appeared before the microphone ever attracted and retained so vast an audience, not merely in his own country but abroad, even in Nazi-dominated Europe where to tune in to the BBC was an offense heavily punishable. The Prime Minister's addresses to the nation were as much a contribution to the war effort as the arms and munitions for the fighting forces. These it was that kept the people in good heart throughout the anxious days.

While Londoners were "taking it," Churchill was pressing for the mounting of a heavier bomb offensive on Germany. The Cockneys who cried "Give it 'em back!" voiced what he demanded on strategic grounds. To win the war, German factories and arsenals must be pounded until, eclipsing the havoc wrought on Coventry, the RAF had paralyzed the enemy's industrial machine. This, in his reckoning, was the "only sure path" to victory. The supply of fighter planes had barely been assured before he was calling with growing insistence for more bombers and bigger bombs. He was deeply concerned at the stagnant state of the bomber force. The fighters were streaking ahead, a great comfort, but the bombers were lagging.[2]

In October of that year Churchill succeeded to the leadership of the Conservative Party on the resignation of Neville Chamberlain. Chamberlain, his health failing after a serious operation, had had to surrender his post as a member of the War Cabinet. Churchill, in accepting his resignation, expressed admiration for Chamberlain's "unshaken nerve and persevering will," adding: "The help you have given me since you ceased to be my chief tided us through what may well prove to be the turning point of the war. You did all you could for peace; you did all you could for victory." They were generous words.

On the motion of Lord Halifax, Churchill was elected leader of the party (October 9). In May, on becoming Prime Minister, he had found good reasons for not accepting the leadership. Now that Neville Chamberlain could no longer lead, he found reasons as cogent for taking the post. Conceding there were considerations for and against, he gave his decision for acceptance.

> Considering [he said] that I have to be in daily relation on matters of such domestic consequence with the leaders of the other two parties who are serving in the Government, I felt that it would be more convenient that I should be able to speak for the Conservative Party with direct and firsthand knowledge of the general position which they occupy upon fundamental issues and also to speak with their authority.

Balancing the negative of May with the affirmative of October it may be concluded that Churchill's original decision not to accept had been inspired by his consideration for Neville Chamberlain. He would not wound the man he had succeeded as Prime Minister by superseding him in the Party.

There was a further question which he had to consider and resolve upon: "Am I by temperament and conviction able sincerely to identify myself with the main historical conceptions of Toryism and can I do justice to them and give expression to them spontaneously in speech and action?" Had not the urgencies of war been so pressing, there would have been a wider appreciation of the full political flavor of the man who had distinguished himself as a Liberal Minister posing this question to himself. His reasoned answer gives his own explanation of the manner by which he found it possible in the course of his career to serve with enthusiasm the two political creeds of liberalism and conservatism:

> My life, such as it has been has been lived for forty years in the public eye, and very varying opinions are entertained about it— and about particular phases in it. I shall attempt no justification, but this I will venture most humbly to submit and also to declare, be-

cause it springs most deeply from the convictions of my heart, that at all times, according to my lights and throughout the changing scenes through which we are all hurried, I have always faithfully served two public causes which I think stand supreme—the maintenance of the enduring greatness of Britain and her Empire, and the historical continuity of our island life.

Alone among the nations of the world we have found the means to combine Empire and liberty. Alone among the peoples we have reconciled democracy and tradition; for long generations, nay, over several centuries, no mortal clash of religious or political gulf has opened in our midst. Alone we have found the way to carry forward the glories of the past through all the storms, domestic and foreign, that have surged about us and thus to bring the labors of our fore- bears as a splendid inheritance for modern, progressive democracy to enjoy.

It is this interplay and interweaving of past and present which, in this fearful ordeal, has revealed to a wondering world the uncon- querable strength of a united nation. It is that which has been the source of our strength. In that achievement, all living parties, Con- servative, Liberal, Labour, and other parties like the Whigs—who have passed away—all have borne a part and all today, at the moment of our sorest need, share the benefits which have resulted from it.

This is no time for partisanship or vaunting party claims, but this I will say—the Conservative Party will not allow any party to excel it in the sacrifice of party interests and party feelings which must be made by all, if we are to emerge safely and victoriously from the perils which compass us about. In no other way can we save our lives and, what is far more precious than life, the grand human causes which we, in our generation, have the supreme honor to defend. It is because I feel that these deep conceptions, lying far beneath the superficial current of party politics, have always been mine, that I accept solemnly, but also buoyantly, the trust and duty you wish now to confide in me.

In December, Churchill rose in the House to render his last tribute to his predecessor in office. Neville Chamberlain had not long survived his retirement. In his last days he had declined all honors, but one signal mark of respect was paid him. Churchill sought and obtained royal permission to have him supplied with Cabinet papers and documents of state so that to within a few days of his death on November 9 he was able to follow the course of affairs.

At the lychgate [Churchill said] we must all pass our own conduct and judgments under a searching review. It fell to Neville Chamber- lain, in one of the supreme crises of the world, to be contradicted by events, to be disappointed in his hopes and to be deceived and cheated by a wicked man. Those hopes, those wishes, that faith that was abused were surely among the most notable and benevolent instincts of the human heart—the love of peace, the toil for peace, the strife for peace, and the pursuit of peace even at great peril and certainly to the utter disdain of popularity or clamor.

Amidst the cares of war, Churchill found time to send a memorandum to the heads of the civil service departments, urging the need for simpler language in official papers and the cutting out of jargon. It was a salutary challenge to the masters of circumlocution from a master of particularly plain speech. Brevity and simplicity should, he urged, take the place of officialese jargon; paragraphs should be short and crisp. "Let us not," he pleaded, "shrink from the short expressive phrase, even if it is conversational." It demanded a minor revolution in Whitehall.

He was also responsible for some Constitutional experiments. One was the dispatch of Cabinet Ministers on service abroad while still retaining ministerial status—Lord Halifax as Ambassador to Washington, remaining a member of the War Cabinet; Oliver Lyttelton as Minister of State to the Middle East; and Duff Cooper who, as Chancellor of the Duchy, was sent out to the Far East. An Act of Parliament was necessary to enable some Members of Parliament to retain their seats while holding the posts to which they were appointed.

At this time Churchill had to deal with an unfortunate incident involving Admiral Muselier, the leading naval figure in de Gaulle's Free French movement.[3] According to reports submitted by secret agents, Muselier was working for the Vichy Government, to whom he had betrayed plans of impending British operations. On this information his arrest was ordered, and he was held incommunicado. No public announcement was made concerning his detention, but garbled accounts of the matter were soon in circulation. Imagination made good the lack of facts and, in the clubs, an explanation for the Admiral's arrest was put about that reflected on his morals rather than his loyalty.

De Gaulle at once rallied to his support. He had no doubts about the Admiral's innocence, and his inquiries established that the accusations were based on faked French papers, fabricated by men with a grudge. Thereupon, in his loftiest manner, de Gaulle threatened to break off relations between Free France and the British Government unless Muselier were restored to liberty in twenty-four hours.

Inquiries having confirmed that the authorities had been grossly deceived, Churchill spared no effort to put matters right. He was appalled that the honor of a gallant sailor should have been impugned by so egregious an error. De Gaulle was summoned to Number Ten to receive the Prime Minister's apologies and an undertaking that ample reparation should be made. So amply was this promise fulfilled that de Gaulle considered the measures to have been excessive. He, himself, benefited from the solicitude which, for some time, Churchill displayed toward the Free French.

Britain was now at the nadir of her prospects, hemmed in, alone. Churchill looked beyond the smoke and dust of bomb-pounded cities to the time when there would be others in the fight and Britain would be one partner in a great alliance. Already he had presciently calculated Hitler's intentions and the coming move against Russia: "If Hitler fails to beat us here, he will probably recoil eastwards—indeed, he may do this without trying invasion." And, in the west, there was America, vast in potential might. The day must surely come when the United States would be engaged side by side with the champions of freedom. Already American assistance was coming in growing volume, arms for the soldiers, destroyers for the Navy, traded for the use of British bases. But it was not enough. Britain's dollars had run out. Her holdings in American stock were disposed of, great businesses were sold for dollars, and gold bullion shipped by warship across the Atlantic. They had paid as long as they could, but the national pockets were empty.

Churchill sat down at his desk to importune the President. British necessities were set out in a begging letter of four thousand words, the longest he ever wrote and the most successful. The British Ambassador in Washington, in frequent interviews, had prepared the ground with hints from London to support his arguments. He was advised to dwell on the menace to America of an all-victorious Germany: "If we go down Hitler has a very good chance of conquering the world." [4]

Roosevelt was deeply moved, but how was he to meet Britain's needs? For a while he pondered the problem. He was still tied by the restraints of neutrality, but growing sympathy for Britain gave a backing to his policy of granting all possible material aid to those still resisting the aggressors. With new authority springing from his election for a third term, he was in a position to take action. Legal ingenuity devised the means within the limits of the Constitution. Arms could not be given to the British, but, under the terms of a half-forgotten statute, they could "for the public good" be leased. So the magnificent solution was announced.

Britain, he ordered, was to be supplied with everything she required. There would be no reckoning in terms of dollars. The defense of Britain was the best defense of the United States. It was the beginning of Lend-Lease, the most unsordid act, as Churchill called it, in the history of any nation. America would be the arsenal of democracy.

Not long afterward, an unofficial envoy arrived in London from the

United States, in the person of Wendell Willkie; who had been the Republican candidate in the presidential election. He came with a letter of introduction from the President, who, in his own handwriting, had written out a verse from the poet Longfellow with the comment: "It applies to your people as it does to us."

The verse was:

> Sail on, O Ship of State!
> Sail on, O Union, strong and great!
> Humanity with all its fears,
> With all the hopes of future years,
> Is hanging breathless on thy fate!

Churchill, too, at the suggestion of Brendan Bracken, offered a verse by Clough to suit the occasion, which he sent with a letter of thanks to the President.

> For while the tired waves, vainly breaking,
> Seem here no painful inch to gain,
> Far back, through creeks and inlets making,
> Comes silent, flooding in, the main.
>
> And not by eastern windows only,
> When daylight comes, comes in the light,
> In front, the sun climbs slow, how slowly,
> But westward, look, the land is bright.

That January there reached Downing Street an American who came as a personal token of New Year greetings from the President. Harry Hopkins had been sent over to bear Roosevelt's assurances of support and to report back on the true state of affairs in Britain. The information reaching the White House was contradictory. The President's own conviction was that Britain would fight and would prevail, but defeatist warnings had been sent by the two Ambassadors, Kennedy in Britain and Bullitt in France. They advised that it was purposeless for America to "hold the bag" while Britain was licked.[5] Roosevelt did not share their forebodings. He had faith in the British and had made up his mind to back them to the limit.

Harry Hopkins was ordered across the Atlantic to carry the tidings to 10 Downing Street. He was an unknown figure in England, but Churchill had been notified that the visitor was on the closest terms with the President. In America he had received the full play of the limelight as the presidential favorite, the adviser in the background, who was attacked as the sinister influence in the White House. Frail, so obviously a sick man, he did not in appearance suggest a Machiavellian influence.

He was now entering on his last phase of service as the President's peripatetic envoy and liaison officer in Europe, rendering services that were to win him the Distinguished Service Medal for his contributions to the war effort. Of "piercing understanding," a down-to-earth common sense and a breezy good fellowship, he immediately got on terms with Churchill, for whom he conceived an esteem second only to his admiration for F.D.R.

His words were his best introduction. "The President," he said, "has sent me here to tell you that no matter what happens he will see you through. He is determined we shall win the war together." [6]

The two men spent the weekend in the country. Churchill sent his thanks to the White House that the President should have chosen Hopkins as his envoy. Harry Hopkins sent back his report, expressing his faith in the British people and their leader. He ridiculed the suggestion that had gained currency that Churchill had no liking for America and the President—it just didn't make sense. As to the Prime Minister's place in the British war effort, he wrote:

> Churchill is the government in every sense of the word—he controls the grand strategy and often the details—labor trusts him—the army, navy and air force are behind him to a man. The politicians and the upper crust pretend to like him. I cannot emphasize too strongly that he is the one and only person over here with whom you need to have a full meeting of minds. [7]

The meeting, and the good impressions created, helped forward the understanding between Downing Street and the White House.

Cooperation was extended between British and Americans. American civil and military technicians crossed the Atlantic to exchange views with the British. British warships were repaired in American shipyards, and American warships took over the patrol of sea lanes in the West Atlantic. Preliminary meetings of staff officers developed into staff talks at a high level. The secret of this last development needed to be guarded, for the American isolationists were still influential and vociferous.

By these expedients, and the exertions of her people, Britain turned the winter of the Blitz to good account, and could face the hazards of 1941 with grounds for confidence more solidly based than they had been at midsummer. As the year of disaster ran out there came clashes of arms, the curtain raisers to the operations that were to carry hostilities forward in ever-widening circles across continents and oceans.

CHAPTER NINE

BATTLE OF THE MEDITERRANEAN

AUTUMN, 1940—FEBRUARY, 1941

THE scene changed and the clash of arms moved south. They had fought out the first engagements of the war on battlefields where for a thousand years commanders, kings and emperors had contested the supremacy of the North. Now, in the South, they were to engage amidst scenes made famous by the battles of antiquity. Greeks of a later day were to stand where, in a former age, they had fallen heroically in their passes in freedom's ancient cause. A new Salamis was to be added to the decisive battles of the Middle Sea. Lesser legions were to march from Rome's gates, a puppet Caesar play out his little day. On the burning sands of Africa, Desert Rats were to engage the invaders of the Nile Valley as the hosts of the Pharaohs had engaged the invaders at the dawn of history.

Winston Churchill was to concentrate his attention and his purpose on the battlegrounds of the Mediterranean. A modern Mercury, he was to descend from the skies to bring messages of direction and exhortation to the commanders. He was to stand amidst the ruins of the amphitheater, exultant, to address the modern victors assembled at ancient Carthage.

As the winter of the Blitz ran its course, the Battle of Britain was succeeded by the Battle of the Mediterranean. Continuing over many months, it was tenaciously contested. In its successive phases it involved all the lands that lie about the Middle Sea. Spain to the west and Turkey to the east escaped the ruin of the fighting but were embroiled in the battles of diplomacy.

Churchill, as biographer of the illustrious Marlborough, had studied and chronicled campaigns on land in which army was matched against army. As leader in war, he directed operations that followed the pattern of the struggles with Napoleon. It was sea power that enabled Britain to sustain the contest with an opponent supreme on land. Churchill had been schooled in the Service in which command of the sea is a tradition. In Napoleon's day, moving armies by ship, the British had popped in and out of Europe. The coasts of the Mediterranean in 1940 still offered extensive facilities for the hazards of amphibious warfare.

"What," asked Churchill of one of his generals, "is the use of having the command of the sea if it is not to pass troops to and fro with great rapidity from one theater to another?" To have amphibious power and fail to use it was, he pronounced, a crime.[1] It was not one of which he would be guilty.

But for his determination, the opportunities offered by control of the Mediterranean would have been forfeited at the outset.[2] On sea, as well as land, Britain was grievously exposed on Pétain's capitulation. In the apportionment of responsibilities, the French Fleet had been entrusted with the Mediterranean sphere. Admiral Cunningham was based on Alexandria with a comparatively small force. Responsibility had rested with the French to hold the Italians. With the French out of the fight, Cunningham's force was vastly inferior, on paper, to the Italian line of battle.

The position was reviewed at the Admiralty. Paramount importance was assigned to keeping open the sea lanes of the Atlantic. Unless the food ships plied back and forth Britain must starve, and to protect them, it was held, everything must be sacrificed. The western exit of the Mediterranean must be guarded lest the Italian battleships should slip out to the west to go commerce-raiding in the Atlantic. The Straits of Gibraltar, it was considered, could be held only by moving over Cunningham's Fleet from the eastern Mediterranean. Thus the Admiralty.

At this stage the Prime Minister intervened, to impose his veto. There would be no yielding in the Mediterranean. A brief and restrained account of this matter was given by Churchill in his war memoirs, but you may wager a battleship against a dinghy that he expressed himself with the force of a broadside. He fired an indignant expostulation at the First Sea Lord. Never again, he hoped, would he hear of this idea. Risks? Of course there were risks but, he tartly observed, "Warships are meant to go under fire." Then, with one of his infrequent reproaches for past neglect, he censured Admiralty experts who, vaunting the strength of warships against air attack, had neglected in prewar days to strengthen their decks against the falling bomb.

Cunningham and his Fleet stayed on at Alexandria, and a squadron under Admiral Somerville was stationed at Gibraltar. Steps were ordered to strengthen the defenses of Malta.

This was one of the critical decisions of the war, molding its course in the West. Had the Navy withdrawn, hard-pressed Malta could scarcely have held out. Egypt, as General Wavell foresaw, could not then have been defended much longer. The consequences would not have ended there, but, as Cunningham gave warning, there would have followed a landslide in territory and prestige. Cyprus and Palestine would have been forfeited and the neutrality of the Turks endangered. The result would have been the complete loss of the Middle East and all chance of beating Italy in the Mediterranean. From these consequences, the Allied cause was preserved by Churchill's intervention. He would not yield command of the sea that was the highway to North Africa and Egypt and that gave access to the back doors in Europe—"the soft underbelly of the Axis."

More than ships at sea were required. Hitler, also, had turned his gaze on the Mediterranean. He needed to feel secure on this southern flank before he launched himself against the Russians in the East. Expulsion of the British Fleet from the Mediterranean became for him an urgent priority. Gibraltar must be bolted against the British. It was a job for General Franco and the Spaniards, who must be brought into the war. A battle of diplomacy was fought over Spain. In the end Churchill was to prevail, but in the opening moves the advantages were with Hitler.

When France fell, General Franco was eager to join the victors, but, as the invasion of Britain was deferred, he began to have doubts and held back, being a cautious little man. The whisper was going around Europe that, perhaps, after all, the last word in the war had not yet been spoken. Hitler put on the pressure. Franco put up the price for his support. Fuehrer and Caudillo met. Hitler was submerged by the tedious Spanish rigmarole, being compelled, for once, to listen to another man's harangues. Rather than endure such an experience a second time he would have had four teeth taken out. He suffered in vain; Franco was not to be persuaded into action.[3]

This was one of the moments of destiny. Hitler was recommended by his advisers, notably Goering, to send his troops through Spain, with or without the Caudillo's cooperation, to seize Gibraltar and to spill over into North Africa. Had he done so, the course of war would have been decisively changed. Hitler declined to follow the advice. He would show that plaguy fellow Franco that the war could be won without

Spain's assistance. This, in Goering's reckoning, was Hitler's greatest error.

Churchill noted the signs from Madrid and applied his pressure. The Navy was ordered to cut down the flow of imports to Spain. President Roosevelt was approached. Spain, wrote Churchill, was not far from starvation, and, if the President offered continuance of food supplies as long as the Spaniards kept out of the war, it might have a decisive influence.[4] Cautious Franco was no longer to be induced into action. He would neither attack nor give the Germans passage through Spain to assault Gibraltar. And so Hitler's expectations of taking the rock fortress early in the new year remained unfulfilled.

Vichy France was another subject for concern. Pétain, like Franco, was under pressure from Hitler to join in the fighting on the side of the Germans. Egging him toward the Nazis was his Foreign Minister, Laval, that "dirty little politico" with a hatred for England.[5] Churchill was forced to take a tough line with the French to make them feel that "we have teeth as well as Hitler." Again he sought Roosevelt's support. The men of Vichy would pay great heed were the President to indicate his disapprobation of any French assistance for Hitler, "a betrayal of the cause of democracy and freedom." [6]

Meanwhile, there was Mussolini to attend to. To the south of the blue waters of the Mediterranean the Italians were massed in Libya for an attack on Egypt. There were 150,000 troops under Graziani. General Wavell's effective forces for the defense of the Delta numbered about 50,000. The Army of the Nile must be reinforced. Even while the menace of the invasion of Britain persisted, Churchill resolved to send out half the available tanks to the Middle East. It was a risk to run but, as he pronounced, "Safety first is ruin in war." [7] He secured the War Cabinet's approval. As the need was pressing he proposed that reinforcements should be sent by the short route through the Mediterranean. The Admiralty considered the hazards of air attack were too great and Churchill had to give way. The tanks were sent by the long sea route around the Cape. Still, they were in time. The Italians advanced from Libya into Egypt's approaches. There they remained, hesitant.

Surveying the dispositions in the Middle East Command, Churchill found cause for criticism. Prodding messages arrived for Wavell. Forces must be employed to their highest capacity. Fighting strength was not up to ration strength—why was this? There were troops standing idle in Kenya and in Palestine.

Malta was a cause for continuing apprehension. Churchill was dismayed by the neglect of prewar years and the weakness of the island's defenses. Hard pressed as Britain was at home, planes must be sent out, for there were but three fighters to defend the island. Troops must be dispatched, for the beaches were open to the invader. The risk of air attack on the convoy must be faced. The need was urgent—every day, every hour counted.

Men and equipment were sent with all possible speed to the Army of the Nile—70,000 troops, with tanks and artillery, in the space of a few months. As the build-up proceeded, and the Italians still delayed, Churchill's thoughts began to turn to the offensive. Was not Wavell in a position to strike? There were proddings through Anthony Eden, who had flown out to represent the War Cabinet in the Middle East. Eden was informed that a British attack was about to be launched, but Wavell, with a proper insistence on secrecy, did not permit his intentions to be disclosed, not even in the secrecy of code to Downing Street.

At this point Mussolini gave a new turn to events. Emboldened by German successes, jealous of Hitler's victories, he embarked on an adventure on his own account with an attack on Greece. Britain was pledged to give aid to the Greeks and Churchill immediately responded to their appeal. "We will give you all help in our power," was his reply.[8] Within a week a token British force had landed. The Navy took a hand to prevent an Italian descent on Crete. The Greeks were encouraged to repulse the invaders and to counterattack with spirit and effect.

Churchill called for divisions to be sent to Greece. It was a cause of embarrassment for Wavell. Forces for Greece could be supplied only by the Army of the Nile, and with an offensive in preparation how were they to be spared? London and Alexandria were at cross-purposes. Cables crossed and recrossed. Churchill became insistent. If the British did not keep their word with the Greeks, what would the effect be on the neutral Turks? There came the counter from Anthony Eden—to divert troops to Greece would imperil the operations of the Army of the Nile. Back went the Prime Minister's protest—loss of Athens might be more disastrous than injury to Kenya or Khartoum; it was no time for passive policies.[9]

Anthony Eden flew home to explain the situation and to give the welcome news that Wavell was about to launch his forces against Graziani. Churchill was delighted. His satisfaction was heightened by the success of air operations against the Italian Fleet. Bombed at their base at Taranto, three battleships and a cruiser were hit by aerial torpedo—half the Italian Navy disabled.

After the curtain raiser at sea there came victories ashore. Wavell smashed the Italians at Sidi Barrani. A few days later (December 19) the

Prime Minister had a gratifying report for the House of Commons. In the opening battle thousands of Italians had been captured at the cost of a thousand casualties.

"One cannot say that the Italians have shown a high fighting spirit," he said. "Perhaps their hearts are not in their work."

A few days later he broadcast, over the heads of their rulers, to the Italian people, urging that the time had come for their King and their Army to depose Mussolini and take charge of the country's future. One man and one alone had involved them in the deadly struggle with the British Empire—Mussolini, who was leading their country to the verge of ruin. "It is one man who has arrayed the trustees and inheritors of ancient Rome upon the side of the ferocious, pagan barbarians. There lies the tragedy of Italian history. There stands the criminal who has wrought the deed of folly and shame."

Success followed success in North Africa. Graziani was ignominiously defeated. Wavell advanced far into Libya. Churchill had a magnificent story to unfold on February 9:

> Abroad in October, a wonderful thing happened. One of the two dictators, the crafty, cold-blooded, black-hearted Italian, who had sought to gain an Empire on the cheap by stabbing fallen France in the back, got into trouble. Without the slightest provocation, spurred on by lust of power and brutish greed, Mussolini attacked and invaded Greece, only to be hurled back by the heroic Greek Army, who have revived before our eyes the glories that from the classic age gilded their native land.

> While Mussolini was writhing and smarting under the Greek lash in Albania, Generals Wavell and Wilson, who were charged with the defenses of Egypt and the Suez Canal in accordance with our treaty obligations, whose task at one time seemed to difficult, had received very powerful reinforcements of men, cannon, equipment, and above all, tanks, which we had sent from England in spite of the invasion threat. Large numbers of troops from India, Australia and New Zealand had also reached them.

> Forthwith began that series of victories in Libya which have broken irretrievably the Italian military power in Africa. We have all been entertained and I trust edified by the exposure and humiliation of another of what Byron called

> > Those Pagod things of sabre sway,
> > With fronts of brass, and feet of clay.

When the brilliant decisive victory at Sidi Barrani, with its tens of thousands of prisoners, proved that we had quality, maneuvering power, and weapons superior to the enemy, who had boasted so much of his virility and military virtues, it was evident that all the other Italian forces in eastern Libya were in great danger. They could not easily beat a retreat along the coastal road without running the risk of being caught in the open by our armored divisions and brigades ranging far out into the desert in tremendous swoops and scoops. They had to expose themselves to being attacked piecemeal.

General Wavell, nay, all our leaders and all their live, active, ardent men, British, Australian, Indian, in the Imperial Army saw their opportunity. At that time I ventured to draw General Wavell's attention to the seventh chapter of the Gospel of St. Matthew, at the seventh verse, where, as you all know, or ought to know, it is written: "Ask and it shall be given you, seek and ye shall find, knock and it shall be opened unto you."

The Army of the Nile has asked and it was given. They sought and they have found. They knocked and it has been opened unto them. In barely eight weeks, by a campaign which will long be studied as a model of military art, an advance of over 400 miles has been made. The whole Italian Army in the East, an army which was reputed to exceed 150,000 men, has been captured or destroyed.

The entire province of Cyrenaica, nearly as big as England and Wales, has been conquered. Egypt and the Suez Canal are safe, and the port, the base, and the airfields of Benghazi constitute a strategic point of high consequence to the whole of the war in the eastern Mediterranean.

The Libyan campaign would not have been possible if the British Mediterranean Fleet, under Admiral Cunningham, had not chased the Italian Navy into its harbors and sustained every forward surge of the Army with all the flexible resources of sea power.

How far-reaching these resources are, we may see from what happened at dawn this morning, when our Western Mediterranean Fleet, under Admiral Somerville, entered the Gulf of Genoa and bombarded in a shattering manner the naval base from which a Nazi expedition might soon have sailed to attack General Weygand in Algeria or Tunisia.

A few hundred miles to the east, other Imperial forces were beginning the campaign which was to cost the Italians the remainder of their African empire and which was to restore the Emperor of Ethiopia to the throne of his ancestors.

As yet it was premature to claim that Egypt and the Canal were safe. There had been easy successes over the Italians. Sterner tasks lay ahead. Churchill, with his ear to the ground, noted the portents and his warning went out to Wavell: prepare for the storm center to shift from Africa to the Balkans.

CHAPTER TEN

DEFEATS IN THE BALKANS

JANUARY—MAY, 1941

To THIS point, Churchill's conduct of affairs had met with universal approbation. Now, events in the Balkans opened the door of dissent at the time and the floodgates of controversy thereafter.

With the new year of 1941, reports from southeast Europe came to hand. A German attack on Greece was forecast for mid-March. The Greeks were holding their own against the Italians. They could not take on Hitler's Nazis as well. What, in that event, was Britain to do? Churchill was in no doubt. Britain was pledged to support Greece against attack; Britain would keep her word. After a discussion with the Chiefs of Staff, the order went out to Wavell: Greece must take precedence over all operations in the Middle East.[1] This was greatly disappointing for Wavell, who was hoping to make a clean sweep of the enemy in North Africa. He protested and set going an argument, long continued, that turned on the question of priorities.

Wavell's resources were not sufficient to sustain operations in Africa as well as in the Balkans. There was a strong case for completing the easier job and pushing west along the African coast from Benghazi to Tripoli. Churchill favored the other and more difficult course of full-scale intervention in Greece. At first the Chiefs of Staff were divided. For the Navy and Air Force, Pound and Newall supported the Prime Minister. Dill, Chief of the Imperial General Staff, took the contrary view [2]—and he had to bear the brunt of opposing the Prime Minister.

He was stiffened in his dissent by his Director of Military Operations, General Kennedy, an officer of decided opinions who looked with mistrust on political interventions in the realms of strategy. Dill and Kennedy persuaded themselves that the Prime Minister was forcing an unsound and dangerous policy on Wavell.

Churchill was attracted by the possibilities of forming a Balkans Front. At the War Office it was held that a political front was possible, but without military backing it would be ineffective, and Britain lacked the resources to equip the Balkans.

It was essential to explore the possibilities on the spot. Again Anthony Eden was sent out to represent the Government with the authority of a Cabinet Minister. He had recently been made Foreign Secretary and Churchill, in his absence, took over duty at the Foreign Office. Eden was accompanied on his mission by Dill and was joined by Wavell.

The Balkans Front was easier to visualize than to organize. Reports from Eden were not encouraging. The Greeks were reluctant, unless the Germans struck, for British troops to land in force; their presence might provoke Hitler into action. The Yugoslavs were fearful of the Germans. The Turks were not prepared to depart from their neutrality.

There was now a recasting of opinion.[3] In London the Chiefs of Staff became more impressed by the hazards of the operation. Churchill began to draw back, inclining to the opinion that it might be better to accept the loss of the Balkans rather than intervene with insufficient forces and be pushed ignominiously from Greece. The men on the spot, however, reported there was a fair chance of success for an expedition to Greece. Dill, too, changed his mind and, no less than Wavell and Eden, favored going ahead.

While the issue was poised in uncertainty, a cable from Eden turned the scale. Dismayed by the change of heart in London, he pressed strongly for the Greeks to be supported. He and Dill and the Service commanders had reviewed the situation; they were unanimous for proceeding in the Balkans. Better to stand by and suffer with the Greeks than submit to the calamity of leaving them to their fate. Churchill and his colleagues accepted Eden's recommendations. The Chiefs of Staff backed them. They advised that, in view of the steadfastly expressed opinion of the commanders in chief on the spot, of the Chief of the Imperial General Staff, and of the commanders of the forces to be employed, it would be right to go ahead. The Cabinet decided to authorize the operation. So the arrangements proceeded for transferring the greater part of the Army of the Nile across the Mediterranean to Greece.[4]

In any case, it was the Yugoslavs, not the Greeks, who brought the Germans into the Balkans. Incensed by their rulers, who had signed up with Hitler, the Belgrade patriots revolted and turned out their pro-Hitler Ministers.

"Better war than the Hitler pact," was the cry.

Hitler was roused to a fit of paranoic rage. Yugoslavia must be annihilated with unmerciful harshness.[5] The bombers were dispatched against Belgrade and 17,000 Yugoslavs perished amidst the ruins of their capital. Operation "Punishment" upset Hitler's time schedule. Descent on Greece was delayed.

At this point, the Germans complicated the situation by taking a hand in the fighting in North Africa under the command of the thrustful general, Rommel. Wavell, badly served by his Intelligence, was unaware of the extent of the build-up of German forces. Taken by surprise, the British advance posts at Benghazi were forced back. The British tanks were no match for Rommel's Panzers. The Desert Army, its resources depleted to provide for the expedition to Greece, was pushed back along the African coast road by which it had recently advanced. Tobruk, port of history, was held, an isolated advance post, a strategic thorn in the enemy's flank, but Rommel's thrust was not halted until the Army of the Nile was in its old positions at the gateway to Egypt.

"We seem to have had rather bad luck," commented Churchill in a message of sympathy to Wavell.

Churchill pressed for the dispatch from home of more tanks for the Desert Army. Alan Brooke, Commander of Home Defense, demurred. Invasion of Britain was still a danger that must be guarded against, and he had nothing to spare from "his orchard." Churchill was insistent: risk at home must be faced. The tanks were sent. It was as well, for Rommel was being reinforced.[6]

The appearance of the Germans in force on the North African Front called for new dispositions. The Battle of the Mediterranean was intensified at sea. Churchill ordered reinforcements to be sent out to Admiral Cunningham, and he exhorted Cunningham to new endeavors. Warships, submarines and aircraft must take toll of the Germans crossing to Africa by the narrows between Sicily and Tripoli. Every enemy convoy that got across must be ranked as a failure against the Navy.[7]

Cunningham scored a heartening success in the Battle of Matapan. Losing a battleship and three cruisers, the Italians were effectively discouraged from further part in naval operations in the Mediterranean, Mussolini's vaunted *mare nostrum*.

In April the Germans marched on Greece. Some British forces were occupying their positions, others were still disembarking, when the Greeks were overwhelmed by the weight of the divisions unloosed against them. The battle had scarcely begun before it was lost. Regarding the prospects as hopeless, the Greeks asked that the British troops should immediately be withdrawn as a means of saving their country from the devastation of purposeless resistance.

Once more a British Expeditionary Force was engaged in a fighting retreat. Famous names appeared in the news—Thermopylae and the Olympus Pass. Churchill, with memories of the heroic age, nourished hopes of new feats at Thermopylae, but the Greeks could not hold the flank and the retreat had to proceed. By the end of April the Battle of the Balkans had been lost and won. As Nazi troops entered Athens, another British evacuation was proceeding, harassed by incessant attacks from Nazi bombers. There were 50,000 British troops in Greece. By the skill and courage of the men of the Navy, 40,000 of them were taken off.

Again a swift revaluation in priorities had to be made. A short while since, Churchill had laid it down that Libya must be subordinate to Greece. Now he pronounced anew: Libya counted first, evacuation of troops from Greece second.[8] The loss of Egypt and the Middle East would have grave consequences. At all costs the Nile Valley must be held —half a million men were there and mountains of stores had been built up. Britain should fight to the last ditch and the last ounce of her strength.[9]

At home the double reverse caused the greater disappointment after the facile successes against the Italians. During his first six months as Prime Minister, Churchill had been required to give little of his attention to his parliamentary position. The voice of criticism had been hushed by the sense of national peril. He had addressed a House that had been eager to support him and execute his will. The disasters of 1940 had been borne with stoic resignation. The reverses of 1941 nerved a few critics to break the silence.

Some murmurs of criticism began to flow out from Service circles. Staff officers who had opposed the Greek operation did not conceal their view that it had cost the reverses in Libya. The Prime Minister was saddled with the blame. Once again the whispers went the rounds that he had overruled the Service Chiefs into adventuring upon a rash expedition in the Balkans. At the War Office, General Kennedy persuaded himself that the Prime Minister was an embarrassment to the war effort; the Chiefs of Staff were being browbeaten by the forceful Minister; if things continued in this fashion the war might well be lost in Whitehall.[10]

These views communicated themselves to various M.P.s and formed the basis of an attack by Lloyd George against the Prime Minister in House of Commons debate on May 7, 1941. The leader in the First

World War drew upon his experiences to instruct the leader in the Second how a war should be run. His strictures drew a sharp retort from the Prime Minister:

> It was the sort of speech with which, I imagine, the illustrious and venerable Marshal Pétain might well have enlivened the closing days of M. Reynaud's Cabinet.
>
> Mr. Lloyd George has spoken of the great importance of my being surrounded by people who will stand up to me and say, "No, no, no." He has no idea how strong is the negative principle in the constitution and working of the British war-making machinery. The difficulty is not to have more brakes put on the wheel, but to get more impetus and force behind it. We are asked to emulate the German vigor, and the next moment the Prime Minister is to be surrounded by "no-men" who are to resist at every point anything in the nature of speedy, rapid, and above all, positive, constructive decisions.

The critics found scant support in the House. Confidence in the Government was registered by 447 votes to 3. The Prime Minister walked from the chamber through a lane of cheering members. It was his last speech in the old House of Commons, which was destroyed by enemy bombers, as I have already described.

The tide of reverses continued. The Germans, following up from Greece, descended by parachute on Crete. With inadequate defenses and few fighter planes to counter the attack, the island fell to history's first airborne invasion. Only the sinking of the German battleship *Bismarck,* after a 1,700-mile chase across the Atlantic, afforded relief in those grey days.

The evacuation of Crete, following upon the withdrawal from Greece, caused a renewed murmur of anxiety. In Crete at least, some imagined, Britain should be meeting the foe on terms which were not so adverse as to make success impossible. The armchair critics in the clubs provided articles for the press, and, in the prevailing mood of uneasiness, they found ready readers. When Crete was debated (June 10) the Prime Minister had to face a House that was anxious. His appreciation of the strategical situation provided the answer to the critics. Against the suggestion that Britain should not have intervened in Greece at all, he made an emphatic protest.

> I see [he said] there are those who say that you should never fight without superior or at least ample air support, and they ask, "When will this lesson be learned?" But supposing you cannot have it? The questions that have to be settled are not questions between what is good and what is bad. They are very often the choice between two

terrible alternatives. If you cannot have this essential, this desirable air support, must you then yield one important key position after another?

There are others, also, who have said you should defend no place you cannot be sure you can hold. One would have to ask: Can you ever be sure how a battle will develop before it has been fought? If this principle of giving up without a fight any place you cannot be sure of holding were adopted, would not the enemy be able to make a vast number of valuable conquests without making a fight at all? And where would you make a stand and engage with resolution? The further question would arise: What would happen if you allowed the enemy to advance unopposed and to overrun without cost the most invaluable strategic points?

Suppose we had never gone to Greece, and suppose we had never attempted to defend Crete. Where would the Germans be now? Suppose we had simply resigned territory and strategic islands to them, without a fight, might they not at this early stage of the campaign of 1941 already be masters of Syria and Iraq, and preparing themselves for an advance into Persia?

The Germans in this war have gained many victories very easily. They have overrun great countries and beaten down strong powers with very little resistance being offered to them. It is not only a question of the time that is gained by fighting strongly even at a disadvantage for an important point, but there is also this vitally important principle of stubborn resistance to the will of the enemy. The whole history of war shows again and again that stubborn resistance, even against heavy odds, and even under exceptionally unfavorable conditions, is an essential element in victory.

The debate on Greece, hotly argued at the time, has persisted since. A narrative biography is not the place to reargue it at length, but the main points may be briefly stated.

Was the Greek expedition a justifiable risk? General Wilson, who commanded the operation, considered that it was. "I thought at the time it was politically and morally right. From the military point of view most of us concerned agreed it was a military gamble." [11]

Had it any immediate effect on events in the Middle East? It may be. The daring of Britain's offensive operations may have saved Turkey from invasion and conquest by inducing the Germans to consider Britain to be stronger than she actually was in that theater of the war.[12]

Did not the fights in the Balkans—although no such result was envisaged when they were launched—delay the German onslaught against the Russians, who were thus enabled to hold out in front of Leningrad until the winter snows gave them respite? Here the extreme view to the contrary is given in the curt assertion: "No postponement was caused." [13]

Alan Brooke considered intervention in Greece to have been a definite strategic blunder, but seems to have conceded that the start of the offensive against Russia was in fact delayed "though the forces involved [in the Balkans] were only a minute fraction of the immense German and satellite armies." [14]

The German divisions numbered twenty-seven. Ten of them, seven Panzer and three motorized, formed part of the spearhead of the attack in Russia. Two months were required to transport those divisions from the Balkans to the Eastern Front. Hitler was compelled to defer his attack and announce: "The beginning of Operation 'Barbarossa' will have to be postponed up to four weeks as a result of the Balkans operations." [15]

On this point, too, the opinion of Field Marshal Lord Wilson has been unequivocally given:

> Without the British–Imperial intervention in Greece, Yugoslavia would have adhered to the Tripartite Pact [with Hitler] and the *coup d'état* of April 25 would not have taken place: the breakaway of Yugoslavia threw Hitler into such a rage that he employed more troops than were necessary to ensure its complete liquidation, causing all 27 German field divisions (including seven Panzer) to become involved in those two countries: the complete upset of the railway timetable for concentration and the difficulty of extricating divisions from countries where terrain precluded rapidity of movement cannot but have caused a postponement of the original target date by some four or five weeks. In addition the period of re-equipment between the two campaigns was thereby so reduced that it cannot but have had a blunting effect on the arm on which the Germans relied to achieve rapid successes in Russia—their Panzer formations.[16]

Reckoning must also be taken of the effect in the United States of British efforts to succor the Greeks. The British people were applauded for action on behalf of a weaker country. The President cabled his appreciation of heroic work done for Greece.

At the time there was no consciousness of the ultimate advantages gained to soften the blow of defeat in Greece. Nor in Africa could any hint of silver be perceived in the skies. In retrospect it was possible to discern in Rommel an agent providentially assigned to provide exercises for the British troops and their commanders, so that they might qualify themselves in the craft of modern warfare upon the training grounds of the African desert.*

In the spring of 1941 Rommel and his Afrika Korps were a menace to Egypt and the Canal. Churchill called for drastic measures to strengthen Wavell's forces. The Desert Army had the men but they were short of weapons. Tanks must reach them forthwith. As time was the vital factor he pressed for a convoy to be sent out by the short route through the Mediterranean. Dill objected to the robbing of the Home Front as a means of reinforcing Wavell.

"We cannot risk sending any more units from here," he bluntly declared.[17]

Churchill countered that the loss of Egypt could not be risked. Rommel was being reinforced, and tanks must reach Wavell in time. The Chiefs of Staff were summoned. The proposal for running a convoy through the Mediterranean was put before them and was unfavorably received—the risks were too great. Churchill persisted. The discussion continued late into the night. Eventually Admiral Pound was convinced by the Prime Minister's arguments. He was prepared, on behalf of the Navy, to accept the risks of the Mediterranean passage.[18]

Churchill followed the course of the convoy with eager concern. He was in no doubt about the risk that was involved.

"Pray God it's the right decision," was his exclamation as he left the staff conference.

His reputation as Defense Minister was bound up in the convoy's fortunes. Were the worst forebodings to be fulfilled and a disaster to occur, he would have to bear ministerial responsibility.

From Gibraltar the ships were shepherded by Admiral Somerville. Off Malta Admiral Cunningham took over. Heavy air attacks were repulsed. The convoy was brought into Alexandria with the loss of one ship. Churchill was vindicated in his daring. He looked for impressive results as the reward.

Days of suspense followed before Wavell could bring his new tank forces into action. Churchill waited expectantly for the rout of the audacious Rommel. It was mid-June before Wavell was ready to launch Operation "Battleaxe." For two days the issue was in doubt, and then

---

* Some weeks after writing this passage I chanced on the following in *The White House Papers:*

"Another thought [Harry] Hopkins expressed when he had time for reflection was this: 'In trying to figure out whether we could have got across the Channel in 1942 or 1943 you have got to answer the unanswerable question as to whether Eisenhower, Bradley, Spaatz, Patton, Beedle Smith, and also Montgomery, Tedder and a lot of others could have handled the big show as they did if they hadn't had the experience of fighting Germans in North Africa and Sicily.' "

the unpalatable result had to be accepted. The offensive was a failure.

Churchill was disconsolate. His disappointment was the greater for the high hopes he had formed and for the exertions he had made to provide Wavell with the necessary reinforcements. He had been losing confidence in Wavell, a general who had great achievements to his credit, but who was nearing exhaustion as the result of the burden of his widely ranging responsibilities. He was a tired man, and Churchill decided on his dismissal. Wavell was instructed to exchange posts with the commander in chief in India and General Auchinleck took over in the Middle East.[19]

During these anxious weeks Churchill was dialectically engaged with his professional advisers over the proper strategy to be pursued. Opinions on either side were firmly held and strongly pressed, and the debate was complicated by the intervention of President Roosevelt, who at one stage supported the course to which Churchill was inflexibly opposed.

Against the weight of professional opinion Churchill had to exert himself to maintain the Desert Army in strength to continue the fight against Rommel. Losses in the Balkans and in Wavell's unsuccessful offensive made further heavy reinforcements necessary if Auchinleck was ever to be in a position to return to the attack. Already half Britain's war production was being sent out to the Middle East.[20] John Dill called for a halt, fearing that the drain on resources was imperiling security at home. Invasion of Britain was a danger still to be guarded against and Dill presented the Prime Minister with a memorandum he had circulated among his professional colleagues. It drew attention to the risks to which the island was being exposed: "We have gone to the limit and beyond it." After all, the loss of Egypt, calamitous as it might be, would not end the war, but the successful invasion of Britain could spell irreparable defeat. The defense of Singapore should, Dill submitted, have priority over Egypt.[21]

Opinion so emphatic, even backed by the authority of the Chief of the Imperial General Staff, did not prevail over Churchill's convictions. Such ideas were anathema to him. He confessed in his memoirs to being "astonished" by Dill's memorandum. It was an understatement. The mere suggestion of the possibility of the loss of Egypt drew his heaviest fire against "defeatist" generals with "cold feet." Some months before, the admirals had contemplated withdrawing from the Mediterranean. He had stopped that and now here were the generals prepared to let Egypt go, if need be, to save Singapore. He did not credit that any such choice of evils could arise, but he would be prepared to accept the forfeit in the Far East rather than lose the Nile, with the ruin and surrender of an army of half a million men.[22]

"Even the most expert opinion," he wrote tartly, rejecting Dill's sub-missions, "may sometimes err amidst the uncertainties of war."

He learned that Wavell had previously drawn up a plan of action providing for the evacuation of Egypt, should the worst occur. Copies had been circulated among senior officers. Churchill ordered them to be called in forthwith. No whisper of the existence of such a plan could be tolerated. There must be no thought of retreat, or withdrawal, on the part of the Army of the Nile. Surrenders by officers or men would not be accepted unless there had been fifty per cent casualties. Generals and staff officers were directed that, surprised by the enemy, they were to use their pistols in self-defense.[23]

It was while these differences prevailed that Roosevelt tried his hand at influencing British strategy. He, too, was becoming concerned at the resources that were needed to sustain the fight in North Africa. The Americans were suggesting to him that, instead of being lost in an un-availing struggle in the desert, tanks made in the United States would be better employed in England. The President sent a diplomatically phrased letter to the Prime Minister. Having paid tribute to the heroic work that had been done in Greece, he ventured his suggestion in ample verbal wrappings:

> I am satisfied that both here and in Britain public opinion is growing to realize that even if you have to withdraw further in the eastern Mediterranean you will not suffer any great debacle or sur-render, and that in the last analysis the naval control of the Indian Ocean and the Atlantic Ocean will in time win the war.[24]

This intrusion into the realm of strategy—which took on a strange appearance a few months later when the Americans and the British had lost control of the Pacific and the Indian Oceans—was coldly received by the Prime Minister. With becoming expressions of deference, he dissented from the view that the loss of Egypt and the Middle East would not have grave consequences, as being no more than the mere prelimi-nary to the successful maintenance of a prolonged oceanic war. If all Europe and the greater part of Asia and Africa became part of the Axis system, then

> A war maintained by the British Isles, the United States, Canada and Australasia against this mighty agglomeration would be a hard, long and bleak proposition. I adjure you, Mr. President, not to underrate the gravity of the consequences which may follow a Middle East collapse. In this war every post is a winning post and how many more are we going to lose?

This was plain speaking not well received at the White House. The

President, according to Harry Hopkins, "hit the roof" but, having ventilated his annoyance, he sent a friendly and understanding reply to London.[25] Churchill remained inflexible in his purpose to defend Egypt at all costs. He carried his ministerial colleagues with him, and the flow of reinforcements to the Middle East continued—and so too the controversy with the generals.

It made relations difficult with the C.I.G.S. The talents with which John Dill was endowed did not include the capacity to cope with the masterful Defense Minister. Dill was too sensitive to criticism, too orderly in his professional methods, to be able to adjust himself to the unorthodoxy of inspired intuition. But he was as firm in his opinions as was Churchill, and although receiving little support from the other Chiefs of Staff he continued to press his objections to the sending out of tanks and equipment needed at home.[26] He feared that in the effort to save Egypt the war might be lost.

Churchill, overruling him, averted the consequences of a policy that to preserve themselves at home against an invasion which never came would have involved the loss of Egypt and the Canal. What was seen afterward to be his farsighted determination was at the time deplored as his obstinacy. His interventions in the details of affairs caused disquiet in the Services. Mutterings of discontent reached the ears of the politicians. The professional mind rarely finds difficulty in discovering that dislikes can be aired if they can be seen to be grounded on matters of high principle. Men at the War Office who resented meddling and sharply phrased criticisms of "generals with cold feet" persuaded themselves that it would be impossible to win the war as long as Churchill was in a position to determine strategy.

The point was reached where Dill considered it necessary to write in warning to Auchinleck, bidding him "to be on his guard against" undue pressure from Downing Street, Auchinleck must be prepared to resist if need be and even "in the extreme case" to disassociate himself from the consequences.[27]

As advocate of his own stratagems, Churchill was a formidable proposition for minds unaccustomed to the conflict of debate. There were times when his advisers sighed for more balance and less brilliance in their leader. But, though he might harass and exhaust them, the stimulus of his proddings kept them on their toes. The differences between them over the claims of the Middle East persisted until the next turn in affairs added a new complication to the situation. It brought Britain the encouragement—and for many months the burden—of a fighting ally.

BOOK TWO

ALLIES FROM EAST AND WEST

CHAPTER ONE

RUSSIA AN ALLY

JUNE–JULY, 1941

A T MIDSUMMER the situation was transformed. Hitler launched his armies eastward on an 1,800-mile front against the Russians. Britain, having sustained the burden for a year, no longer stood alone.

It was, in Churchill's phrase, "the fourth climacteric of the war, one of the decisive moments in history." What course would Britain pursue? The choice was open. The decision rested with Churchill and his colleagues. They could accept the Russians as allies against the common foe. Or, holding aloof, they could follow the operations in the East with the concerned detachment the Russians had shown toward the fate of France and Britain. For Russian communism, its principles and its methods and its leaders (men he looked on as no less than "fiendish criminals"), Churchill's detestation was profound. But now, all was changed. There was no hesitation in accepting as allies the peoples whom Hitler had chosen to attack. So history was fashioned and the new pattern laid for the years ahead.

Churchill, that midsummer weekend, was out of London taking a few hours of relief at Chequers, his official country home in Buckinghamshire.[1] Anthony Eden was with him and Winant, the United States Ambassador. Throughout Saturday, Russia was uppermost in his thoughts, for, according to the intelligence reports, the German blow was imminent. It was struck at dawn on that Sunday morning (June 22, 1941) as he slept, and he was given the news on waking. Without comment he ordered the BBC to be prepared so that he might broadcast that evening.

His Cabinet colleagues had dispersed for the weekend. He made a few telephone calls, and two Ministers joined him for lunch, one of them Lord Beaverbrook, but no Cabinet council was summoned. Britain's course in the light of the attack on Russia was determined, as it had been when France dropped out, without the formality of a Cabinet meeting. It sprang from the temper of the time, and from the man whose spirit imparted so much to the temper that prevailed.

From Lord Beaverbook and Stafford Cripps contradictory advice was received. Cripps, recently returned from Moscow, had no faith in Russian ability to withstand the Germans—"They will go through them like a knife through butter." Beaverbrook, from the outset, had confidence in the Russians, with their enormous manpower. Churchill was encouraged by spirited opinions that matched his own.

Radio sets the world over were tuned in to London at nine o'clock that Sunday evening. Outside the inner circle of his colleagues there were few who knew what Churchill was going to say or how Britain was going to act. He had spent the day in preparing his speech, which was not completed until shortly before he was on the air. With the brief introduction of the announcer, the familiar voice was heard, firm and full, speaking in measured tones. He began—in the manner of a good journalist—putting the news first.

> At four o'clock this morning Hitler attacked and invaded Russia. All his usual formalities of perfidy were observed with scrupulous technique. All this was no surprise to me. In fact I gave clear and precise warnings to Stalin of what was coming. . . . I can only hope that these warnings did not fall unheeded.

For a moment, allowing suspense to mount, he held back the declaration of Britain's intentions in this new situation, while he spoke of Hitler, a monstrosity of wickedness, insatiable in his lust for blood and plunder, grinding human lives. The Nazi regime was indistinguishable in its worst features from communism—a statement seen to be a grim jest when the sequence of the words is reversed. It was a prelude to the explanation of his own personal position.

> No one has been a more consistent opponent of communism than I have been for the last twenty-five years. I will not unsay a word I have spoken about it. But all this fades away before the spectacle that is now unfolding. The past, with its crimes, even follies, and its tragedies, fades away.

Another passage followed, directing sympathy to the kindly Russian peoples, fathers, wives and mothers, in the sufferings they would endure at the hands of the brutish masses of the Hun. And then:

Now I have to declare the decision of the Government, and I feel sure it is a decision in which the great Dominions will in due course concur. But we must speak out now, at once, without a day's delay. I have to make the declaration. But can you doubt what our policy will be?

Any man or state who fights against Nazidom will have our aid. Any man or state who marches with Hitler is our foe. That is our policy. That is our declaration.

It follows, therefore, that we shall give whatever help we can to Russia and the Russian people. We shall appeal to all our friends and allies in every part of the world to take the same course.

Appeal to friends—the meaning, of course, was American friends. This was underlined in passages that followed. Churchill went as far as it was possible to associate the United States with his declaration.

Hitler hoped to accomplish his purpose before "the fleets and air power of the United States may intervene," he said, and again:

The Russian danger is therefore our danger and the danger of the United States, just as the cause of any Russian fighting for his hearth and home is the cause of free men and free peoples in every quarter of the globe.

In such a large-hearted fashion Churchill held out his arms in welcome to the Russians. His lead was acclaimed by the people, supported by the Governments of the Dominions and endorsed by the President. The free peoples of capitalist states joined hands with the communist advocates of the class war. A duster was passed over the slate and old differences were wiped away. There was much to forget, reason enough indeed for Britain to have stood aside while the Russians suffered the consequences of their trust in Hitler, the pact-breaker.

The deal Stalin had made with Hitler in 1939 had been the preliminary to the Nazi attack on Poland. The Russians had joined with the Nazis in sharing the spoils. The three Baltic states of Latvia, Estonia and Lithuania were absorbed, eastern Poland taken over, and for the Germans the Soviet furnished raw materials of war, continuing to send supplies down to the very eve of the attack. Since 1939 the Communist Party line had required their followers in Britain to oppose the war effort and stir up trouble in factory and workshop. From Soviet radio stations there had been ceaseless abuse of Fascist warmongers, British imperialists and Wall Street financiers. Stalin had proffered the unction of his congratulations on Hitler's victories. Molotov, negotiating in Berlin, had joined with Ribbentrop in arranging for the carve-up of the British Empire.* These last discussions were initiated by the Nazis with intent to deceive, so much dust thrown in Russian eyes.

Long before that date, Hitler and his generals had prepared for Operation "Barbarossa," the whirlwind campaign that was designed to eliminate Russia and leave the Nazis free to finish the reckoning with Britain.

With his instinct for divining the moves of his opponent on the other side of the hill, Churchill had some months previously accurately forecast Hitler's intentions—he would "probably recoil eastwards." [2] There came, in March, reports of German troop movements in eastern Europe.

The Balkans operations were then in progress, but Churchill could discern the shape of vaster designs. General Wilson was provided by Greek agents with the intelligence that the dispatch of German forces to the Balkans had upset the railway program for moving large German forces to Galicia. This pointed to one conclusion—an attack on Russia was impending.[3] Other reliable reports reached Downing Street of the dispatch of Panzer divisions to Cracow. They were a clear pointer to Hitler's intentions.

Churchill lost no time in sending a warning to the Kremlin. To make certain that it should arrest Stalin's attention he asked that it should be delivered in person by the British Ambassador, Stafford Cripps. Cripps failed to carry out the letter of his instructions. The warning was handed to Vyshinsky and was by him conveyed to Stalin. For Churchill it was to remain a source of regret that personal presentation was omitted— that might have underlined the gravity of the message and so enabled the Russians to take what precautions they could in the time remaining to them.[4]

It is to be doubted that anything Churchill could have contrived would have influenced the Soviet leaders. Stalin was as responsive as the steel of his name. In the land in which truth is no more than another argument, statements of fact are received as essays in propaganda. Any statement from British sources was doubly suspect. The British premier was regarded as serving his own ends, striving to foment dissension between Russians and Germans, his purpose to embroil the Soviet in war. British maneuvers drew a rebuke from the official Russian news agency

* This was the occasion on which Molotov grimly indulged in his one recorded jest. Ribbentrop had been holding forth on a defeated Britain, reduced to the verge of surrender, when the Berlin sirens gave warning of the approach of RAF bombers. When the discussions were resumed in the safety of the deep shelter, Molotov turned to Ribbentrop with the question: "You say, Your Excellency, that Britain is down and out. Then why have we taken refuge in this air-raid shelter?"

which, with childlike gullibility, protested at rumors of impending war with Hitler—these were propaganda maneuvers. So, to the last, Russian consignments of essential supplies continued to roll westward to Germany.[5]

Better informed about the Nazi divisions massed from Finland to Rumania, Churchill waited during the days of June for the signal that would unleash the Panzers on the credulous Russians. He and his colleagues were prepared. He sounded opinion in the White House. Britain proposed to give every encouragement to the Russians; he trusted that there would be no cause of embarrassment for the President. That weekend Ambassador Winant had journeyed down to Chequers to convey the assurance that any announcement of British aid for Russia would be endorsed by Roosevelt.[6]

Churchill's warnings had been fatally neglected. The Russians had not taken elementary precautions. Their aircraft were grounded, open to attack. They were destroyed in the opening German assaults and their airfields put out of action. With the Luftwaffe supreme in the air, the Panzers went lunging forward. Retreat across the illimitable plains alone saved the Russian armies from annihilation.

Operation "Barbarossa" (Hitler's code name) was the fulfillment of Churchill's hopes; Britain no longer stood alone, the exclusive object of Hitler's intentions. But the sequel did not match his expectations. He had looked to gain friends as well as allies, to establish with Stalin the terms of easy fraternity he had formed with Roosevelt. He had been warmhearted in his welcome, but Stalin remained chilly and aloof. Churchill, in his speech, promised to provide everything that Britain could spare. The Russians scarcely troubled to report him in their newspapers.[7]

Churchill wrote in cordial terms to Stalin. Two weeks passed before an answer came.[8] Stalin was mild in his appreciation of what was offered him and vigorous in his demands of what he required should be done. In this, his first letter to the Prime Minister, he began the call for the creation of a Second Front in the West, a demand that was to be continued with mounting insistence. He quaintly recommended a Second Front as being a step that would be popular with the British Army and with the whole population of southern England.

Despite the tone from the Kremlin, Churchill maintained his cordiality, though he did permit himself a pointed reference to the year during which Britain had stood alone. He renewed and extended the pledge of British aid. But on the subject of the Second Front he was brief and firm—it was beyond the range of possibilities. Anything "sensible and effective" would be undertaken and he referred in particular to the chance of naval operations in the North, to safeguard the sea routes to Archangel and Murmansk.

There was no hanging back in making arms and supplies generously available—fighter planes, the first demand of every British commander; rubber, consigned from the precious reserves; lead, wool, cloth.

Would the Russians hold out? Were they a good risk to underwrite? Churchill had no doubts—they would be hammered, but they would endure. His confident view was not generally shared. Professional opinion in the West did not rate the Russian military machine very high. When the war began the British and French staffs reckoned the Poles to have a stronger army than the Russians, and the Poles had lasted but eighteen days. Against the Finns the Russians had made a poor showing, so that Neville Chamberlain could say: "I cannot take the Russians seriously as an aggressive force." [9] Under the German flail the Red armies were driven back three hundred miles. Could they survive? If they were to be pulverized out of the fight, better to retain everything for Britain's defense. Churchill rejected such hesitation, springing from promptings of safety first and self-interest. Full backing must be given to the Soviet.

Stalin's demands multiplied. They were curtly pressed, in language to which his sense of peril gave a harsher tone. Maisky, Ambassador in London, was sent to Downing Street to plead the case for a Second Front. There was some plain speaking.[10] The Ambassador, following his instructions, used forceful words to Churchill, who listened in gloomy silence. It seemed not so much an appeal for aid as a warning, in menacing language, of what the result would be if Russian wishes were not met. Without the relief that would be afforded by a Second Front in the West, the Russians might find themselves unable to prolong their resistance, and then . . . ?

Churchill's resentment grew. He had suffered Russian ungraciousness without protest, but this was beyond his toleration. He reminded the Ambassador of the indifference Stalin had shown to Britain's fate. The Russians had not been concerned over Britain's survival; indeed, so close had been their association with the Germans, it had seemed likely that Stalin would join in on Hitler's side. These things being considered, it scarcely behooved Stalin to offer reproaches against Britain.

The Ambassador was surprised at the heat he had kindled. Let the Prime Minister calm himself, he urged. Churchill's anger subsided and he closed the interview on a more cordial note. He recognized, perhaps, with grim appreciation, that he was receiving from the Russians the blackmailing importuning he had himself employed in milder language against Roosevelt at the time of the French collapse.

The demand for a Second Front was impossible to meet, but the Russians continued to press for it. Their agents in Britain campaigned for it. On roadways, pavements and walls the slogan was chalked: "Open the Second Front Now." The sentimental British, moved by the spectacle of Russian fortitude and Russian losses, took up the cry. Churchill shared their feelings, but sentiment could not overcome the difficulties of geography.

He wrote again to Stalin: "Although we should shrink from no exertion, there is no possibility of any British action in the West, except air action."

Supplies for the hard-pressed Russians were sent north across the sea by way of Archangel, a route made perilous by the lurking U-boats. Searching for an alternative, Churchill was impressed by the advantages of communications through Persia. A military expedition was the necessary preliminary for the establishment of a base and for the occupation of the Persian oil fields. This aroused Soviet suspicions, although he had been scrupulous to propose a joint Anglo-Russian expedition, and he had to bear the reproach of scheming to gain advantages for Britain in Persia at the expense of the Russians.[11] Nonetheless he persevered, and the operation was successfully carried out. The Persian route ensured the flow of supplies to Russia. To silence suspicions, Churchill gave a personal undertaking to Stalin: "I pledge the faith of Britain that we will not seek any advantage for ourselves at the expense of any rightful Russian interest during the war or at the end."

The Persian operation completed the safeguarding of the flank in western Asia. In Iraq, British intervention was in time to suppress a Nazi-inspired revolt. In Syria action was taken in collaboration with de Gaulle for the occupation of that country. The gateway to Asia was no longer standing wide open to the enemy.

There were puckered brows among the Chiefs of Staff as they faced the new problems in priorities. Three conflicting claims for supplies—Home Defense, Middle East and Russia—had to be weighed and debated. Churchill, confident that by then there was little danger of the invasion of Britain, was prepared to make everything available for the armies actually engaged in action against the enemy. He pressed the claims of Auchinleck and insisted on the dispatch from England of the 1st Armored Brigade. Otherwise, everything that could be spared must go to the Russians.

Dill was not prepared to run the risk of denuding home defense, particularly where the Russians were to benefit. He did not find it easy to forget the past and accept Stalin and the Communists in the close association of allies—they were "so foul." It was hard to tolerate the man who had "ratted" to the Germans two years before.[12] He had had no confidence in the Red armies and, with the Nazi Panzers pressing toward Moscow and Leningrad, his apprehensions mounted. There was time, before September ran out, for the Germans to finish off the Russians and turn their strength against Britain. While the danger of invasion persisted, argued Dill, tanks must not be sent overseas regardless of the needs of home defense.

Churchill, in his own mind, had written off the danger of invasion, but between Russia and the war in the desert the choice was hard. The professionals of the Services could take the strictly military view and give their preference to reinforcing Auchinleck. Churchill had to take into his reckoning political as well as military considerations. Since the assistance of a Second Front was not possible, he felt himself under compulsion to give all possible aid to the Red armies even though it meant depriving Auchinleck of supplies.

Once again there was American intervention in this debate on priorities. By this time the President had modified his objections and was inclined to back the Prime Minister over the Middle East,[13] but the American Chiefs of Staff were alarmed. They held that the British position in North Africa was hopeless and that to send further reinforcements was "throwing snowballs into Hell." [14] Harry Hopkins had crossed the Atlantic with the warning that, unless the Americans were reassured about the Middle East, they might prefer to keep their equipment for themselves.

Churchill summoned (July 24) an Anglo-American conference at Number Ten that was equivalent to a meeting of joint Staffs.[15] The three British Chiefs were present and for the United States the three ranking officers in London—Admiral Ghormey, General James E. Chaney and General Raymond E. Lee. The Americans voiced their fears that Britain ran the risk of being overwhelmed at home and submitted that the defense of Singapore and the sea lanes for supplies should rank before the Middle East.

The Prime Minister and the Chiefs of Staff replied, contesting the American appraisal—John Dill finding it possible to support the case for the Middle East without yielding in any of his own firmly held opinions. American anxieties were in some measure allayed. It was agreed by all that the key to the future was with the Russians. In the allocation of supplies the determining factor was whether or not the Red armies could keep the field despite their enormous losses.

Churchill, contrary to military opinion on either side of the Atlantic, had confidence in the Russians. To enable them to fight on he was prepared to accept all hazards. For that end, what risk was not worth taking? In the desperate position of the Red armies, a dozen tanks or a squadron of planes might mean the difference between continuance in the war or Russian collapse.

He was gratified to note that Beaverbrook had constituted himself Russia's advocate in the War Cabinet, backing Stalin's claims for supplies with ingenuity and determination.[16] It was an unexpected development. Never could it have been predicted that this individualist and millionaire capitalist, antagonist of state control, who stood for the freest of free enterprise, would find himself anywhere but at the furthest pole from the men of the Kremlin. But there is no telling where lightning will strike. There was need for a mission to be sent to Moscow to report at first hand and make arrangements for the dispatch of supplies. Churchill nominated Beaverbrook as its head, an excellent choice as it proved. He was recommended to Stalin in a personal letter from the Prime Minister as "one of my oldest and most intimate friends," a man in whom the War Cabinet had the fullest confidence. The mission met with a cool reception, but the lively, go-ahead Beaverbrook, the Puck of the British Cabinet, thawed the icicles of the Kremlin. A formal agreement was reached and a basis of cordiality established with the Soviet leaders. Churchill sent Beaverbrook his heartiest congratulations.

It was an achievement to have made any advance toward an understanding with the men of the Kremlin. Coping with Stalin was not the least of the responsibilities brought by the burden of the new ally. It was Churchill's special problem. There were times when his forbearance was strained by the harsh language of Stalin's importunities and reproaches. It was so different from the terms of good companionship he had established with the head of the American republic.

CHAPTER TWO

ATLANTIC MEETING—ATLANTIC
CHARTER

AUGUST, 1941

THAT August, President and Prime Minister met aboard ship off the coast of Newfoundland as if their countries were already united in war against the common foe. Since then the highlights have faded from the Atlantic conference, its importance dwarfed by greater events, but at the time it was looked on as a landmark in the development of Anglo-American relations. For Winston Churchill it was a diplomatic and a personal success.

The cultivation of good relations with America was the cardinal point in his foreign policy, overshadowing all else. Under his touch good will flowered in the White House. To this result the correspondence he, as a "Former Naval Person," conducted with "P.O.T.U.S." was a major contribution. His letters to his pen-pal, the President, were worth more than a chancellery of ambassadors. They were propaganda in its most subtle form, intimate and more than faintly flattering. They were written on the basic assumption that F.D.R., so much shrewder and more percipient than his fellow countrymen, was already a partner in the fight for the democratic way of life, and as such was entitled to share in the plans and inner secrets of Great Britain.

With two strong characters, self-opinionated and determined, their meeting might easily have ended in repulsion. Harry Hopkins, who played a large part in arranging it, was aware of the risks. With two such temperamental persons—he thought of them as prima donnas—there was no telling what might happen when they were kept in close contact aboard ship. He feared there might be "terrible rows." His apprehensions were needless.[1] The meeting was an unmarred success, the two principals as friendly as could be. Their good opinions of each other survived the test of four days (August 9–12) spent in each other's company at sea. The good will of the two men at the top was to prove the inspiration of the Anglo-American alliance.

The support received from the United States had been an encouragement that sustained Winston Churchill during the darkest hours. The people of Britain had watched with admiration as Roosevelt, politician of surpassing skill and subtlety, had inched his way forward, leading his people to accept their responsibilities in the battle for freedom. As one observer expressed the matter: "Roosevelt is the greatest jockey the human race has known." His was a superior skill in riding public opinion, that tricky jade. His opponents, the isolationists, supported by German propagandists, clamored against the possibility that America might once again be involved in the quarrels of the Old World. "We did not raise our sons to fight in Europe" was a slogan that made a wide appeal among a peace-loving people.

Roosevelt had a keener appreciation of the perils of the times and the menace of the dictators to the American way of life. To him isolation was no better than appeasement as a means of holding off Hitler and the Nazis. The best immediate defense of the United States would be success for Britain in defending herself.[2]

When the war began the overwhelming majority of Americans were isolationist, their feelings no more than lukewarm toward Britain and France. The betrayal of Munich was remembered. Britain's solitary struggle kindled warmer sympathy. By the time Roosevelt had been elected for his third term, the American people were in the mood to respond to the more incisive leadership his re-election made possible.

The Lend-Lease Act followed. It was soon apparent it would be futile to dispatch arms and munitions to Britain if they were to be sunk by torpedoes in the Atlantic. Accordingly, American warships and flying boats were ordered to patrol the western Atlantic to warn shipping of the presence of U-boats. In time the zone was extended to cover the sea lanes from Iceland to the Azores, and the occupation of Iceland was taken over, thus providing the United States with a jumping-off ground halfway across the Atlantic.

"One of the most important things that has happened since the war began," was Churchill's comment on the arrival in Iceland of American forces.

In a more kindly sphere, two university ceremonies marked the growth of the ties across the Atlantic. First, at Harvard on June 19, President Roosevelt was made Doctor of Civil Law of Oxford University. Every effort was made to make the ceremony conform with Oxford tradition. A special Convocation of Oxford was held at Harvard, the Chancellor of the University being present in the person of the British Ambassador, Viscount Halifax, who was attended by six beadles.

A week later, on June 26, Churchill received the degree of Doctor of Laws of Rochester University, the presentation being made in a ceremony conducted across the ocean by radio telephone. Rochester, as Professor Valentine recalled, when presenting the degree, was the birthplace of Churchill's mother. So, when the professor declared, "Winston Churchill, America admires you," the people of the United States could feel that their admiration was directed to a son, or at least a half brother.

It was the sense of kinship which touched Churchill:

As I speak from Downing Street to Rochester University [he said], and through you to the people of the United States, I almost feel I have the right to do so because my mother, as you have stated, was born in your state, and here my grandfather, Leonard Jerome, lived for very many years, conducting, as a prominent and rising citizen, the newspaper with the excellent eighteenth-century title of *The Plain Dealer*.

The great Burke has truly said: "People will not look forward to posterity who never look backward to their ancestors," and I feel it most agreeable to recall to you that the Jeromes were rooted for many generations in American soil and fought in Washington's armies for the independence of the American colonies and the foundation of the United States. I expect I was on both sides then. And I must say I feel on both sides of the Atlantic Ocean now. I will make bold to say that here at least, in my mother's birth-city of Rochester, I hold a latchkey to American hearts.

As the two countries drew together, the leaders took thought of planning for the day when American cooperation should have developed into full belligerency. Staff talks were authorized. They had to proceed under a cloak of secrecy for the merest hint would have sparked a rumpus, with the isolationists already, in Harry Hopkins' phrase, "screaming bloody murder." In Washington, the British participants, wearing mufti instead of uniform, met their opposite numbers. They were introduced, for the benefit of observers, as "technical advisers to the British Purchasing Commission." In London, the American Embassy in Grosvenor Square was busy with military, naval and air attachés. American officers began to plan naval and air bases in Britain, the sites for which were marked out. The Service Chiefs were not going to permit events to find them unprepared. A grand strategy for war was evolved. A British Joint Staff Mission was permanently established in Washington, providing the basis from which the Joint Chiefs of Staff organization was eventually to be evolved.[3]

Both President and Prime Minister wished to complete the get-together moves by a summit meeting, but it was difficult to arrange a date. At first Bermuda, in the month of April, was proposed, but the exigencies of war made this impossible—to Churchill's disappointment, for after the stresses of the winter Bermuda had its attractions. The meeting was put off to the summer and then, with the press of problems arising over Russia, it was no longer to be postponed.

August was agreed upon. Then Roosevelt grew apprehensive about Churchill's safety—two voyages among the lurking U-boats in the Atlantic. Churchill brushed aside these fears.

"Damn the risk," he said to Harry Hopkins. "I'll telephone the President tonight."

The day was fixed. Churchill consulted the Cabinet. The King gave him leave of absence. He arranged to cross the Atlantic in the *Prince of Wales,* the Navy's latest battleship. Clement Attlee was concerned about the danger—perhaps the *Tirpitz* might put out to send Churchill and his party to the bottom of the ocean.

"I fear there will be no such luck," was Churchill's comment, as he thought of the possibilities of being engaged in person in battle at sea.

As the arrangements were proceeding the President was slightly piqued to learn that Churchill regarded this as their first meeting. Roosevelt recalled how, as a junior member of the Wilson administration in the First World War, he had shaken hands with Churchill, then a Cabinet Minister. Churchill might forget, but it was an occasion F.D.R. remembered.*

Placentia Bay, a landlocked anchorage on the Newfoundland coast, was chosen as the rendezvous. Churchill was accompanied by his professional advisers, the First Sea Lord and the Chief of the Imperial General Staff. The Chief of Air Staff was not able to join the party; he was left behind to "mind the shop."

There seems to be no consensus whether the meeting of President and Prime Minister, that August, was the best- or the worst-kept secret of the war. It was variously described in both terms. So far as the British

---

* Robert Sherwood, in *Roosevelt and Hopkins,* gives his authority for the statement that at the time Churchill asserted he had not previously met Roosevelt. In the second volume of his memoirs Churchill recalled that the occasion of their first meeting was in London at a dinner at Gray's Inn. Evidently, comments Sherwood, Churchill had "conducted searches through the voluminous files of his memory."

press was concerned the secret was preserved, although it was known in Fleet Street and in circles that are termed well-informed, that the Prime Minister was bound for America. He would have been not ungratified had he been aware of the intensity of the anxiety over his safety that was felt in the hearts of newspapermen who are supposed, by the exactions of their profession, to become superior to common hopes and fears.

No hint of the impending meeting was allowed to reach the newspaper readers of Britain, but in America the reticence was not so complete. There were reports in the United States press of a mystery surrounding the President's voyage in the yacht *Potomac* and these were coupled with the absence from London of the Prime Minister. American correspondents next established that, one by one, members of the President's Cabinet were leaving Washington for destinations on the Atlantic seaboard, along the route believed to have been taken by the *Potomac*. Sumner Welles, Undersecretary of State, Colonel Knox, Secretary of the Navy, and Averell Harriman, special expediter of the Lease-Lend Act, as well as General Marshall, Chief of the Army General Staff, General Arnold, Chief of the Army Air Staff, and Admiral Stark, Chief of Naval Operations, were among those whose absence was noted and commented on. There came reports of Presidential fishing from the *Potomac*. They were a blind. The fisherman had transshipped at sea to the cruiser *Augusta* which, under strong escort, was on her way north.

Meanwhile, Churchill, who had slipped away from London, was storm-tossed in the Atlantic. On the second day out from Scapa, the seas were so heavy that the attendant destroyers could not keep pace unless the battleship were to slow down. It was the hunting ground of the U-boat and several were known to be operating. Nevertheless, the order was given for the battleship to forfeit the protection of the destroyers and steam ahead.

So foul was the weather that for once Churchill found it impossible to sleep. He emerged from his quarters, deafened by a hellish racket, to demand to be taken to the admiral's sea cabin on the bridge. It was an eminence to be reached only by the ascent of many flights of ladders, but he disdained the assistance of a young officer's supporting arm.

"Young man," he protested, "do you suppose I have never climbed a ladder in my life?"

Having navigated ladders and manholes, he found the admiral's quarters so much to his liking that he established himself there for the rest of the trip.

To guard against the disclosure of the ship's whereabouts, a complete ban was placed on the sending out of radio messages. So, for a couple of days, Churchill was cut off, able to receive news but unable to transmit directions. He diverted himself with a novel he found to his taste, re-counting the exploits of the indomitable (and imaginary) Captain Horn-blower, R.N., in the wars with Napoleon. With an occasional zigzag, en-forced by a reported U-boat, the *Prince of Wales* made an uneventful crossing.

The arrival was ahead of schedule, for timings had not been adjusted to allow for the fact that by the reckoning of British double-summer-time the clocks of the *Prince of Wales* were ninety minutes ahead of those of the *Augusta*. So the warship patrolled the coast for a while before enter-ing Placentia Bay, a vast anchorage whose waters penetrate ninety miles into the land.

The last headland rounded, the party assembled on the bridge of the *Prince of Wales* saw the American ships at anchor in the lee of the fir-clad hills. The battleship passed down the line of American vessels, a strange contrast in her wartime camouflage with the natty, peacetime grey of the others. She swept slowly by the *Augusta,* and Churchill stood at salute as the band played "The Star-Spangled Banner." Aboard the *Augusta,* the President, supported by his son, could be seen with his hand raised in salute and down the wind came the sound of "God Save the King." A little later the President, in a Palm Beach suit, and the Prime Minister, wearing blue naval uniform, were shaking hands aboard the *Augusta*. Having saluted the quarter-deck, Churchill came forward, beaming.

"At long last, Mr. President," he said.

"Glad to see you aboard, Mr. Churchill," was the cordially given reply.

From his pocket the Prime Minister produced a letter from King George. Bowing stiffly, he presented it. The formalities concluded, a cigar was lighted, and the two leaders with their staffs went below. They soon got down to business, which went forward till dinner was served. That night the *Prince of Wales* lay in obscurity, blacked out, amidst the brilliantly lighted ships of the American Fleet.

The next day the President returned the visit. It was Sunday and, beneath the big guns, he attended church parade on the quarter-deck of the *Prince of Wales*. This was the emotional climax of the meeting. The two flags, Union Jack and Stars and Stripes, were draped together on the lectern. American and British chaplains conducted the service. British and American sailors joined their leaders in singing the sailors' hymn and that paraphrase of the great funeral psalm of the Church of all ages, "Lord, Thou hast been our refuge." Churchill was stirred by the occasion and the scene lives in the words in which he pictured it for his hearers at home:

On the quarter-deck of the *Prince of Wales* there were mingled together many hundreds of American and British sailors and marines. The sun shone bright and warm while we all sang the old hymns which are our common inheritance and which we learned as children in our homes.

We sang the hymn founded on the psalm which John Hampden's soldiers sang when they bore his body to the grave, and in which the brief, precarious span of human life is contrasted with the immutability of Him to whom a thousand ages are but as yesterday when it is past and as a watch in the night.

We sang the sailors' hymn, "For those"—and there are very many— "in peril on the sea." [This was by Roosevelt's choice.] We sang "Onward, Christian Soldiers," and, indeed, I felt that this was no vain presumption, but that we had the right to feel that we were serving a cause for the sake of which a trumpet has sounded from on high. When I looked upon that densely packed congregation of fighting men of the same language, of the same faith, of the same fundamental laws, of the same ideals, and now to a large extent of the same interests, and certainly, in different degrees, facing the same danger, it swept across me that here was the only hope, but also the sure hope, of saving the world from measureless degradation.

Churchill made no mention of the fraternal scene that followed the service as men of the two navies, cameras in hand, bore down upon President and Prime Minister, to snap them as they sat, beaming, side by side. Outraged officers, who would have intervened, capitulated and ran off for cameras so that they, too, might photograph the scene. No British quarter-deck had ever submitted to such an outrage.

The informalities were a relief for the two principals whose discussions ranged far and wide over the fields of war—the position in Africa, the chances of the Russians pulling through, the future of Lend-Lease. At Churchill's request Beaverbrook joined the party to provide the benefit of his advice on the dispatch of supplies to Russia. These matters were easily disposed of. Japan raised a problem of greater difficulty.

Churchill was looking for aid against Far East perils. With Russia engaged against the Germans, the Japanese were free to attack. They had been biding their time, and there were signs that the time was at hand. Already the ships of the Royal Navy were taxed to the limit to guard the sea lanes and hold the U-boats in check. To meet a new foe in the Far East would be beyond Britain's resources.

Churchill emphasized the dangers. Until the United States entered the war, Japanese cruisers would be able to range the seas at will. The life lines with Australia and New Zealand would be cut. British merchant shipping in the Indian Ocean would be destroyed. In these circumstances, he suggested, the Americans should join with Britain in issuing what he called parallel communications to the Japanese. He proposed that each Government should give a warning to Japan that any encroachment in the Southwest Pacific would be resisted, even though it involved hostilities. Were the Americans to join in such a declaration, it might serve to hold the Japanese in check.

The President was sympathetic, but he declined to commit himself very far. He would give a warning in some form to the Japanese Ambassador. It was something, but it fell short of what the Prime Minister had sought.

President Roosevelt had arrived for the conference with a fixed purpose. Whatever else might be achieved, the discussions, he was resolved, should be rounded off with a solemn declaration, a manifesto for the world to read. The result was the Atlantic Charter, the product of his inspiration and Churchill's literary endeavors, with some contributions by controversialists on either side.

Americans have a liking for the manifesto. It is tradition with them. The founding fathers of the republic declared themselves in terms of literary elegance. With the English it was different. Their rude forebears drew up their Magna Carta in the obscurity of lawyers' Latin. The later charters of their liberties were not set down in imperishable prose. Outside the classroom there are few Englishmen who could quote their Bill of Rights or the Habeas Corpus Act.

It would not, I think, have occurred to Churchill to produce a charter for the conference. The idea came naturally to the President, with the example, from the other war, of his predecessor's Fourteen Points. We have been reminded, often enough, that Roosevelt regarded himself as a second and greater Woodrow Wilson, one who, profiting by the example of the past, would crown his own policy with success. The Atlantic Charter was Roosevelt's equivalent to the Wilsonian Fourteen Points of World War I.

The President lost no time in putting the suggestion to the Prime Minister. There was an immediate response, sympathetic and eager. Only the bare bones of the declaration were presented by the President, the basic ideas. They were enough to fire the imagination of the author whom few have excelled in clothing ideas in sumptuous phrases. That night, when the talks of the day were done, Churchill devoted himself to composition. In the morning he produced his piece—the first five points of the Atlantic Charter. In after times he took pride in the fact that the Charter was largely a British production and his own work.[4]

There is the authentic Churchillian ring about the opening phrase, that they, President and Prime Minister "being met together to resolve and concert the means of providing for the safety of their respective countries in the face of Nazi and Fascist aggression and of the dangers to all peoples arising therefrom, deem it right to make known certain principles which they both accept for guidance in the framing of their policy and on which they base their hopes for a better future for the world." The first two clauses recorded that the signatories had no intention of extending their territories as a result of the war. The right of the free peoples to freedom of speech and thought and to the choice of their own form of government was declared in appropriate terms. There seemed to be no immediate difficulties here. The conflicts that would arise over the principle of self-determination were veiled with the other uncertainties of the future. Who, in those summer days of 1941, could have been expected to foresee the fate awaiting many of Europe's ancient kingdoms?

In the drawing up of the Charter differences arose over the declaration in favor of free trade and access to the world's raw materials. This was the equivalent of Wilson's third point. Churchill drafted the words: "Fourth, they will strive to bring about a fair and equitable distribution of essential produce, not only within their territorial boundaries, but between the nations of the world."

As an old free trader, he saw no difficulty there, but to Beaverbrook the words were an affront. The spirit of the Empire crusader was aroused. He had devoted his political life to championing the cause of Empire, with imperial trade and imperial preference. Nine years before, in Baldwin's time, the Empire Conference at Ottawa had resulted in some achievement, on which Beaverbrook looked at a meager return for the advocacy of a lifetime. Were they, off Newfoundland, to cancel what at Ottawa had been achieved? He gave Churchill a plain warning that the clause was at variance with the Ottawa agreements and could not be accepted without the consent of the Dominion Governments.

For a time the war was forgotten in the renewal of the old battle of tariffs, with representatives of America supporting the principles of free trade. To meet Beaverbrook's objections, Churchill proposed a modifying phrase making the clause subject to "the existing obligations" of the signatories. This drew objections from the Americans. Sumner Welles declared that for years past the State Department had striven for the ideal of free trade the world over.

To this Churchill retorted that for eighty years successive British Governments had enforced free trade against the discouragement of mounting American tariffs. This was not to be disputed and the qualifying phrase went in.[5]

The guarding of the world's peace after the war was another point for debate. Here it was Roosevelt who raised objections.

The seventh clause, in its first draft, was limited to the expression of pious hopes for disarmament. Churchill asked for the addition of a phrase foreshadowing the constitution of a reformed and more effective League of Nations—without some such provision British opinion would not be satisfied. He suggested the addition of words providing for the setting up of an international organization.

Roosevelt demurred, fearing the effect on the rampaging isolationists. Over the League of Nations Woodrow Wilson had suffered defeat. Roosevelt had no intention of exposing himself to the same humiliation. "International organization" would conjure up memories of the false hopes that, twenty years before, had been reposed in the League.

The matter remained for a while in suspense. Harry Hopkins came to Churchill's aid. Roosevelt was brought round to the view that the American people no less than the British would expect something to be done, in the future, to safeguard the world's peace. To meet his wishes a phrase was found—"the establishment of a wider and permanent system of general security." This eliminated the dangerous term "organization." It meant roughly the same thing, but how differently it was capable of being explained. F.D.R. was satisfied.[6]

With the text of the declaration agreed upon, it was necessary to obtain Cabinet approval from London, for Churchill was most punctilious, as his American friends noted with some surprise, to consult his colleagues on all major matters to be decided. With the text went the Prime Minister's admonition—the President was dead-set on the issue of the declaration; it would be impolitic to raise difficulties.

Time was now pressing, for the meeting was to end on the following day. The speed with which the business was handled won American admiration. By London time it was seven o'clock in the evening before the coding of the messages from the *Prince of Wales* began. It was midnight before the messages had been unscrambled and were ready for the Cabinet. Ministers were in session until four o'clock in the morning when, after a full discussion, approval was given and a new clause suggested. This, the fifth clause, concerned labor standards and social security.

Churchill was thus able to meet the President at noon to agree on the final version. Roosevelt welcomed the British Cabinet's addition and with some other minor amendments, "verbal flourishes" as Churchill termed them, the declaration was passed for publication to the world at large. Its authors were highly gratified. The President was delighted at the embodiment of the ideas of his Four Freedoms speech in the enduring form of a world proclamation. The Prime Minister drew deep satisfaction from the fact that the United States should be seen to stand beside Britain as partner in the planning of the postwar world. It was formal notification that Anglo-American association was already close, with identity of views so complete that already it fell little short of an alliance. For Britain and her leaders this, in August, 1941, was a great encouragement.

Finally there was Russia to be brought into the picture. A joint message was drawn up for dispatch to "dear old Joe." It paid tribute to the splendid resistance of the Red armies and gave promise of speedy and continuous assistance, the very maximum of supplies. The terms of this declaration had been drafted by Stafford Cripps, whom Harry Hopkins had met in Russia some weeks before.[7]

Business completed, President and Prime Minister could relax over lunch. They were in a mellow mood and, with Beaverbrook adding the graces of good fellowship, they settled themselves to enjoy each other's company. Each was stimulated by the other. Churchill showed the President the deference due from the head of a government to the head of a state, or, according to the percipient observer: "You'd have thought Churchill was being carried up into the heavens to meet God." Roosevelt paid the Prime Minister the compliment of listening with sustained attention to his appraisal of the war situation.[8]

Harry Hopkins was greatly relieved that his apprehensions had been groundless. He watched them as they talked with ease and frankness. He knew them well and felt an affectionate admiration for them both. He saw them as two eminent specialists in the same field, comparing notes and appraising each other's qualities. Their relations came as near to friendship as is possible between statesmen of different countries, but this shrewd observer noted that neither man for one moment forgot what he was and what he represented. The great thing was that they parted, as they had met, in good will.

"I am sure," Churchill cabled home to his colleagues, "I have established warm and deep personal relations with our great friend."

On Tuesday (August 12) Churchill began the return journey. As a precautionary measure the President remained afloat for a few days longer, so that no hint should be given to the Germans that the Prime Minister might be on the high seas. The *Prince of Wales* steamed from the landlocked bay under an escort of United States destroyers, the President's son Franklin serving aboard one of them as an ensign. The Americans had taken over patrol duties on the stretch from America to Iceland, and their destroyers were operating under battle conditions.

Only once was the voyage disturbed by the report of an operating

U-boat. With no papers to trouble him, Churchill was free to divert himself with a game of backgammon against Hopkins, in which he showed more zest than skill. The stakes were small, but by the end of the trip he had to pay thirty-two dollars. He was invited to try his luck at gin rummy, then the craze in America, but declined, though later he was to become "a demon" at the game.[9] A call was made at Iceland, recently occupied by American forces. It was too cold for Churchill's liking.

On the last stages of the homeward run, course was changed, so that Churchill might be gratified in his wish to see an Atlantic convoy on the high seas—seventy-two ships spread out across the ocean. The *Prince of Wales* steamed slowly down the lanes, passing some of the convoy vessels close enough for the figure of the Prime Minister to be seen as he stood on the bridge. The news spread from ship to ship. Sirens were sounded in salute and flags were hoisted.

"A delectable sight," pronounced Churchill, with pride.

At his suggestion the battleship retraced her course so that he might see it all over again. He was thrilled by the spectacle of the ships going about their business of bringing food and munitions to the island citadel of Britain. Thus fortified in spirit he reached Scapa Flow six days after leaving Newfoundland. He said goodbye to his sailor hosts, their parting undimmed by any premonition of the fate that before the year was out was to befall the *Prince of Wales* and her ship's company.

On reaching London he was surprised by the enthusiasm with which the crowds greeted him. The streets rang with their cheers. The newspapers had told the story of his mission, and the people were glad to know that "old Winnie" was safe among them once more.

Satisfied though they were that the Prime Minister was safely back among them, they were disappointed with the tangible results of his mission. This was evident on the faces of listeners when the official statements were first broadcast. Since President and Prime Minister had met, should not a declaration of war by America have followed? The Charter was received with the polite acceptance of an anticlimax. But the propaganda services made much of the occasion. The Charter no great achievement? But, surely! And it was implied that what had been announced was all that could be immediately disclosed, but. . . . Those claiming to be in the know conveyed that there was more to the meeting than the world had been told.

For the free peoples it was some encouragement to be assured that the head of the great republic of the West had participated in the Atlantic meeting. Broadcasting a few days after his return (August 24), the Prime Minister spoke of the results achieved:

The meeting symbolized the deep underlying unities that at decisive moments rule the English-speaking peoples throughout the world. Would it be presumptuous for me to say that it symbolizes something even more majestic—namely, the marshaling of the good forces of the world against the evil forces which are now so formidable and triumphant, and which have cast their cruel spell over the whole of Europe and a large part of Asia?

This was a meeting which marks forever in the pages of history the taking-up by the English-speaking nations, amid all this peril, tumult and confusion, of the guidance of the fortunes of the broad, toiling masses in all the continents; and our loyal effort, without any clog of selfish interest, to lead them forward out of the miseries into which they have been plunged, back to the broad high road of freedom and justice. This is the highest honor and the most glorious opportunity which could ever have come to any branch of the human race.

The question has been asked: How near is the United States to war? There is certainly one man who knows the answer to that question. If Hitler has not yet declared war upon the United States, it is surely not out of his love for American institutions; it is certainly not because he could not find pretext. He has murdered half a dozen countries for far less.

I rejoiced to find that the President saw in their true light and proportion the extreme dangers by which the American people, as well as the British people, are now beset. It was indeed by the mercy of God that he began eight years ago that revival of the strength of the American Navy, without which the New World today would have to take its orders from the European dictators, but with which the United States still retains the power to marshal her gigantic strength, and in saving herself to render an incomparable service to mankind.

That autumn the Americans moved appreciably onward from neutrality to belligerency. Roosevelt issued the order to his naval patrols to "shoot at sight." American merchant ships were armed to protect themselves against the rattlesnakes of the sea. But, though Churchill might declare that Hitler alone knew the date of the United States entry into the war, it was by other means, already in course of preparation, that the Americans were brought in as belligerents.

CHAPTER THREE

STRATEGY—BOMBS—ATOMS

SEPTEMBER—NOVEMBER, 1941

For the British Ministers and their advisers the autumn of 1941 was a time of suspense and of sustained argument. Spared for a space from the pressure of imminent disaster at home, they waited anxiously on the outcome of events abroad—Auchinleck's offensive in the desert, American participation in the war, the maneuverings of the Japanese, and the fighting in Russia.

The fate of the Russians hung as a cloud, dark and forbidding, over the scene of war. Were the Russians to go the way of the French and be battered out of the fight before the United States, as a fighting partner, could, in conjunction with Britain, bring its forces to bear in the battles on land? It was the universal question as the Red armies were forced back, Orel evacuated, Odessa lost, and Moscow threatened.

Watching the Russians, in admiration and anxiety, British people asked: "Are we to do nothing to help them in their desperate need?" It was a question raised on every hand—by the man in the street, the worker in the factory, the critic in the club, and the publicist in the press. Now, surely, they urged, was the time for a Second Front to be opened, and they began to exclaim against British inaction. While the Second Front was delayed, it was urged, the Russians would be defeated.

Public disquiet, added to his own concern, gave the spur to Churchill's impatience. While the Red armies strove and suffered, the only British forces opposing the Germans were inactive. He chafed at the delay in the launching of Auchinleck's desert offensive. Something, somewhere, must be done to engage the enemy in battle. His questing mind ranged the strategic scene from Sicily to the Azores, from Tunisia to Trondheim. His advisers were hard-driven as he pressed for action and attack. So fertile was he in projects that the Staffs could scarcely keep pace with his eager exploration of strategic chances. There was Sicily, an inviting target—let plans be made for Operation "Whipcord." When Auchinleck's attack succeeded the way would be opened for an advance across North Africa to Morocco—let the planners prepare for Operation "Gymnast." There was no possibility of a Second Front in France, but relief might be given to the Russians by an expedition to Norway—let plans be drawn up for an assault against Trondheim.

Military advisers grew anxious lest Britain's growing strength should be weakened by the dispersal of forces, frittered away on side shows. When they raised their objections, the Minister rated them for their obstruction. Did not the generals want to fight the Germans? He was not to be diverted from his purpose—some relief for the Russians must be provided somehow, somewhere.

By October the Germans had advanced to within forty miles of Moscow. Stalin proclaimed that the city would be defended to the last, although, as a precaution, the Soviet Government was transferred five hundred miles to the east. In the desert Auchinleck still delayed the assault and Churchill wrote in expostulation. Did Auchinleck not realize that, while the Russians were being battered, the Army of the Desert had been for four months immobile without engaging the enemy? It would be difficult to justify this to Parliament. So far the matter had not been raised in debate, but public discussion could not indefinitely be stifled.[1] It was essential to strike in Africa without delay.

Justify to Parliament—it was an aspect of the responsibilities of the Minister of Defense that did not directly concern the professional staffs. They estimated military situations, evaluated military hazards, calculated military possibilities by the application of military principles. As Minister of Defense, Churchill could apply the same military considerations and submit to the same conclusions. But as Minister of the Crown he was subject to other influences and had need to conform with other requirements. Never would he permit the politically desirable to prevail over the militarily impracticable, but he did not live in the professional vacuum of his military advisers. He was a politician, responsive to political opinion, subject to political pressures. There was no mistaking the rising temper of the British people. There were biting comments on the inactivity of British forces while the Russians, the gallant Russians, were suffering so grievously.

Churchill pressed for the mounting of the Norwegian expedition and the attack on Trondheim. This was a project that had been powerfully pressed upon him by Beaverbrook, who presented a memorandum forcefully contesting the policy of "inertia" favored by the Service Chiefs. Beaverbrook pressed for action to conform with the rising temper in the country. An attack on Trondheim was his recommendation.

Churchill was impressed. He was swift to calculate the advantages to be gained. A success in Norway would have a powerful influence on neutral Sweden. It might even induce the Swedes to join in the war! Professional opinion was against him on the difficulties of the operation, but he persevered in argument. The Chiefs of Staff would not yield—it was a project likely to end in disaster.[2] He did not accept their verdict but directed Alan Brooke, Commander of the Home Forces, to make an independent study and prepare a detailed plan for a Norwegian landing.

Brooke came to the same conclusion as his colleagues—it would be folly. He was summoned to attend a full conference at Number Ten. He had been instructed to prepare a plan; instead he had presented a reasoned rejection. Thereafter he was submitted to what in the courts is termed a grueling cross-examination. He met question with reasoned reply, rattling off his words in curt, incisive sentences. Unlike Dill he was not to be discomposed by the Prime Minister's probing. Finally Brooke succeeded in diverting the attack from himself onto the First Sea Lord—would the Navy undertake to ensure cover for the landings? Emerging from the doze in which he took refuge when naval affairs were not being discussed, Dudley Pound shook his head. He was not prepared to send in the Fleet to support the Trondheim landing.[3]

The Prime Minister had to accept the rejection of his scheme. He directed that Alan Brooke should not again be troubled with the preparation of reports, nor should he be invited to further staff conferences.[4] Churchill's displeasure was not long continued. Within a month Brooke had been summoned to Chequers to be offered the post of Chief of the Imperial General Staff.

For eighteen months John Dill had borne the burden and was exhausted by his labors. He was, strangely for a soldier, a man of unusual sensitivity. Coping with Churchill was not a task for which he was equipped. It had fallen on him, in the name of the Army, to oppose the Prime Minister and to state the objections to schemes that were considered to be militarily impracticable. He had sustained, in consequence, the assaults of that formidable controversialist, for whom he was no match in argument. He was worn down to the point of exhaustion. As head of the British Mission in Washington, Dill was to find a field for new and continuing service to the cause of the British Army to which he gave a lifetime of selfless devotion.

Conscious of the heavy responsibilities involved in the appointment proposed to him, Alan Brooke hesitated.

"Do you not think you will be able to work with me?" Churchill asked.

With the encouragement of the Minister's cordially expressed good wishes, Brooke accepted the charge. There had been hesitation on both sides over the appointment, for which other candidates had been considered.[5]

Brooke held the post till the war was won, making his contribution to victory by his soundness in strategy and his skill as chairman of the Chiefs of Staff.* He conceived himself to be specially equipped to cope with the Prime Minister, to whom he offered his loyalty and his inflexible opposition in military affairs as his judgment suggested. He looked upon his chief as an erratic being, unpredictable in his sudden intuitions, a spur, a danger and an inspiration. He conceived it to be his role to exert a restraining influence on this wayward genius, to which duty he brought a patience and understanding his predecessor lacked. John Dill was to be conspicuously successful with the Joint Staffs in Washington, winning the respect of the Americans with whom Alan Brooke, curiously enough, was handicapped by an imperfect understanding.

During the breathing space of those autumn months Churchill engaged in a stocktaking of the nation's resources and a re-examination of over-all strategy in the light of the war's developments. There was much revaluation to be done. No longer was it possible to accept earlier reckonings that had assigned to the members of the Royal Air Force the principal role in defeating Germany, in conjunction with the blockade at sea.

Under the powerful inspiration of Lord Trenchard, first Marshal of the RAF, unlimited confidence had been placed in the destructiveness of the bomb. More bombers and bigger bombs had been the accepted means for achieving ultimate victory.† With the Continental battle-

---

* As biographer of Winston Churchill it does not seem to fall to me to pronounce —even were I equipped to do so—on the controversy that has arisen over the contributions made to the war effort by Field Marshal Lord Alanbrooke following the publication of his diaries in Sir Arthur Bryant's two volumes. Alanbrooke's professional distinction is sufficiently attested by his period of service. The man whom Churchill appointed C.I.G.S. in 1941 and retained in that position until the end of the war must patently have been a master in his profession and one equipped with unusual qualities of character.

† Sir Arthur ("Bomber") Harris "had the conviction that bombers alone could win the war"—Alanbrooke, *Triumph in the West.*

grounds barred after the fall of France, and with the British Army put virtually out of business, it was natural enough in 1940 to subordinate the soldier to the airman. At that time Churchill was prepared to relegate the Army to the lesser role of guarding the home citadel while the bomber squadrons laid Germany waste. He did not then conceive that an amphibious striking force of more than eight or ten divisions could be needed for the West.

> There can be no question [he asserted, in a directive in March, 1941] of an advance in force against the German armies on the mainland of Europe. . . . It is impossible for the Army, except in resisting invasion, to play a primary role in the defeat of the enemy. That task can only be done by the staying power of the Navy and above all by the effect of air predominance.

At the War Office eyebrows were raised over the Minister's confidence in the ability of the airmen to win the war. The soldiers had no exaggerated respect for the airmen, who appeared to be assigned a place apart among the Services, privileged to go their own devastating way uncontrolled by the Chiefs of Staff. For some reason that the soldiers could not fathom, Churchill and Chief of Air Staff Portal settled bombing policy and targets between themselves.[6]

The advent of an ally in the Russians, and the spectacle of three hundred divisions locked in the struggle on the Eastern Front, demanded a strategic revaluation. By October there was a change in emphasis.

> We all hope [wrote Churchill to Portal] that the air offensive will realize the expectations of the Air Staff. Everything is being done to create the bombing force desired, and there is no intention of changing this policy. I deprecate, however, placing unbounded confidence in this means of attack and still more expressing that confidence in terms of arithmetic.

There had been hair-raising forecasts, before the war, of the havoc that would be wrought by the bombers. The Air Staff had fostered the idea that, with the enemy in the Low Countries, Britain's position would be rendered impossible by air raids. "However," commented Churchill, "by not paying too much attention to such ideas, we have found a good means of keeping going." From past experience, the conclusion was drawn that, though the RAF raiders would play a great part in causing German morale to crack, it would be an unwise man who thought there was any one certain method of winning the war.

In the light of these new considerations, he directed that it was necessary to provide for an Army of ninety-nine divisions, with a Home Field Army of forty-five divisions, including seven armored divisions, with eight tank brigades. The task for 1942 was to develop, equip and maintain these units. The program thus outlined provided the striking force that was to be the British contribution to the invasion of France two years later.[7]

As a step on the road to the Continent, Churchill appointed Lord Louis Mountbatten to succeed Keyes as Chief of Combined Operations. Mountbatten was told that his duty, apart from continuing commando raids, was to prepare for the great invasion. "For," declared Churchill, "unless we return to the Continent and beat the Germans on land we shall never win the war." At that time (October, 1941), as the United States had not joined in the fight, it might have seemed a visionary project, but the Prime Minister required a planner to be the embodiment of the fighting spirit—"to think offensively, to devise the technique, find the appliances and the landing craft, to organize bases from which the great organization can be launched." A year later there followed the appointment of Gen. F. E. Morgan to prepare the blueprints of the invasion. As Chief of Staff to a phantom command, he provided the bare bones of the skeleton for "Overlord."

Meanwhile, Churchill pressed for better bombs. The Germans had produced greater destruction by blast than by bomb splinters. Let the designers profit from this experience, gained at the receiving end. The enemy packed more explosive in a thinner casing. There was a double advantage to be gained by following their example—a more effective agent for the destruction of enemy cities and one that was cheaper to manufacture.

There was need to be prepared to retaliate if the Germans were to employ poison gas, perhaps on a tremendous scale. There must be no relaxation in preparations—the maximum possible gas must be produced and charged into suitable containers.[8]

Looking back, when the fighting was over, it was a matter for surprise to reflect how this aspect of frightfulness faded from public consciousness. Before the war began it had been the general expectation that the population would be exposed to the spraying of corrosive and asphyxiating mists. It was then a major problem for civil defense. When the war had run half its course the civil population, amidst their numerous perils, had forgotten poison gas. Gas masks, provided by the millions, had been thrown aside. By the time peace came it needed an effort of imagination to recall the anxieties with which the fighting had begun, when the war was a scare, not yet a reality, and when the shops sold out of cellophane, supplies exhausted by the demand for making rooms proof against mustard gas.

The strength of Britain's bomber force had been a continuing cause for disquiet. Twelve months previously production figures had been deplorable—everything had been sacrificed in the scramble for fighters. By September, 1941, Churchill had become deeply concerned at the slowness with which the output of heavy and medium bombers had been raised.

"If we are to win the war we cannot accept this position," he expostulated.

With Britain's war machine reaching toward full capacity, manpower was beginning to run out. Munitions works were competing with the Services. Under the direction of Ernest Bevin, at the Labor Ministry, Britain had mobilized men and women to an extent not reached in any other country. Still the demands of the insatiable war machine were unsatisfied. Forty was the age limit for national service. Churchill was prepared to extend the call-up to men of fifty and, at the other end of the scale, to youths of eighteen instead of nineteen. He favored the direction of women into the arms factories, but he was not prepared to conscript women for the Services—their menfolk objected.[9]

Some special sign, letters of flame or crimson capitals to proclaim "Danger to the human race," should have marked a report made to the Minister of Defense in August of that year (1941). Supercharged with illimitable possibilities of calamity, it should have been attended by such portents as occurred "a little ere the mightiest Julius fell."

As one of innumerable items put forward for Churchill's attention, the first reference to the investigations that were to result in the atom bomb slipped almost casually into the orbit of his consideration. It made, at that time, no particular impact upon his mind. There was nothing to indicate that he was being invited to pronounce on the work that, penetrating the secret of the basic force of the universe, was to arm mankind with the thunderbolt of the H-bomb. These conceptions came later.

Until 1941 atomic research had not reached the stage when the scientist seemed likely to provide the soldier with a new weapon for several years to come. The prize to be won was a lure to proceed, but the prospects were not ranked high. Even before the war Churchill had been alert to the possibilities and was kept informed by his scientific adviser, Professor Lindemann. He wrote on August 5, 1939, to the then Secretary for Air to reassure him against wild reports that seemed to invest Hitler with a secret weapon that could wipe out London. He submitted that the discovery that the uranium atom could be split, with the release of an immense amount of energy, must not be taken to be the herald of an explosive of revolutionary power. "It is essential to realize," wrote Churchill, on the strength of the information he had been given, "that there is no danger that this discovery, however great its scientific interest, and perhaps ultimately its scientific importance, will lead to results capable of being put into operation on a large scale for several years." [10]

Since then research had gone forward, speeded by the needs of war. While tanks careered the battlefields and bombs blasted the cities, the scientists in their laboratories were engaged in a sinister race that would give world supremacy to the victor. In Germany, indeed, the point had been reached where there were visions of the production of a war-winning agent of destruction. In Britain, when the Coalition Ministry was formed, Churchill placed atomic research under Beaverbrook's wing, and a committee was formed of leading scientists (Chairman, Sir George Thomson) to coordinate the work of inquiry.

In August, 1941, there was presented to the Prime Minister a sober, factual statement that the research workers had reason to believe they would, within the period of the war, be in a position to produce an atomic bomb. No spectacular claim was advanced for this agent of destruction. Churchill was satisfied to remit the matter to the Chiefs of Staff. His directive, with no mark of special urgency, recommended it to their attention with the opening phrase: "Although I personally am quite content with the existing explosives, I feel we must not stand in the path of improvement." With this historic understatement the matter of Tube Alloys, the code name for the research, passed for the moment from his consideration. [11]

This casualness, so incongruous as seen in retrospect, accorded well enough with what had gone before. Atomic research, the most scrupulously controlled of all state enterprises, began as an amateur effort, undertaken neither by state nor industry, but by men seeking after knowledge for its own sake. In 1939 they were not far advanced toward the control of the new agent of destruction that was going to revolutionize war. But the work was held to be important enough for the scientists to be encouraged to proceed. Research was carried out at the universities —at Cambridge, Oxford, London, Liverpool and Birmingham.

In America a team of investigators appointed by the President was discouraged by the seemingly insuperable obstacles to progress. [12] The British were inspired by the conviction that a chain reaction could be achieved, and by the summer of 1941 George Thomson reported that there was a reasonable chance of early success. The point had been reached where the facilities of university laboratories were no longer adequate. Resources were required on an industrial scale and for these developments the directing authority of the Prime Minister was needed. The Chiefs of Staff recommended that no time should be lost. [13]

Tube Alloys was accorded the ranking of top priority. A special division of the Department of Scientific and Industrial Research was formed. Sir John Anderson, Lord President of the Council, was given supervision of the work and a new council, the Tube Alloys Directorate, was set up.

During the late autumn of 1941, the matter of Tube Alloys was under discussion at the highest level, President and Prime Minister finding here a new field for cooperation. At Roosevelt's suggestion, some of the members of the British research team crossed the Atlantic to collaborate with the Americans.

The Prime Minister became impressed by the tremendous possibilities —so, too, the President. There was the appalling prospect that the enemy might get ahead of them. The progress made by the British workers gave a new fillip to the Americans. Further advances followed, and in May, 1942, Tube Alloys was the first subject discussed by Prime Minister and President when they met for the second Washington conference. Churchill then proposed that all information should be pooled on equal terms and all research combined, with the results shared equally. Where was the work to proceed? Concluding that the British were at least as far advanced as their allies, Churchill's preference would, naturally, have been for a site in Britain, but this was ruled out by the risk of a German invasion. Canada, with its supplies of uranium, a vitally important source of raw materials, was the obvious alternative. The President, however, suggested that it should be undertaken in the United States, and Churchill was well satisfied to close with an offer that placed the illimitable resources of American industry at the disposal of the Anglo-American investigators.

Thereafter Tube Alloys went underground. Under the cloak of secrecy the work was pushed ahead in laboratories, commercial plants, even in an abandoned squash court at the University of Chicago, and at Gumbo Gulch in Tennessee. At last, on a lonely table mountain at Los Alamos in New Mexico, the most secret place in the United States, the combined teams set about the final stage. Severed from the world, in a magnificently spacious laboratory, they began the building of the A-bomb.

Cooperation over Tube Alloys was an example of what the Anglo-American partnership could achieve. It was made possible only by the complete trust and understanding that existed between President and Prime Minister. With none of the paraphernalia of international agreements, they committed their countries by simple word of mouth to a scientific partnership that was to be magnificently rewarded.

In the early autumn of 1941, Churchill was still somewhat skeptical about remote and visionary speculations. His immediate concern was the battle for supremacy in North Africa. At last Auchinleck's offensive opened. Advances were made and the garrison of Tobruk sallied forth to join in the assault. Churchill was encouraged by the reports, but the Germans struck back. The position became critical and Auchinleck, by his personal intervention, saved the battle. Fighting continued, but there could be no early fulfillment of the hopes of an African victory that Churchill had fostered.

As the autumn moved toward winter, the news from the Russian fronts grew less disquieting. The weather had given the Red armies a respite. Churchill was encouraged in his expectations. The Russians, after all, would not collapse and a long struggle could be counted on, giving time for Britain's mounting strength to be brought to bear. There would be time, too, for the Americans to come into the war as full, fighting partners. By the dispensation of Providence and the Japanese that day was at hand.

CHAPTER FOUR

AMERICA IN THE SAME BOAT

DECEMBER, 1941

IT WAS in an unceremonious fashion that Winston Churchill received the first news of the dire happenings of the "date which will live in infamy," when the Japanese attacked the United States' Pacific Fleet at Pearl Harbor. With two American guests, John Winant and Averell Harriman, Churchill was at his country house in Buckinghamshire when they heard the news on the 9 p.m. newscast. A few minutes later Churchill was speaking by telephone to President Roosevelt, who confirmed the BBC report.

"It's quite true," F.D.R. said. "They have attacked us at Pearl Harbor."

Churchill made an appropriate comment and heard the President add, "We are all in the same boat now."

For a while Churchill stood talking in the hall at Chequers with his two visitors. The three of them adjusted themselves mentally to the new turn of events that had brought the Americans into the war as fighting partners. Having, as yet, no knowledge of the catastrophe that had befallen the Pacific Fleet, they shared a common satisfaction that America was, at last, a fighting ally in the battle for freedom.

The pause for talk was brief, for there was much business to be done. Churchill had undertaken that, were Japan to attack America, then Britain's declaration of war would follow "within the hour." A telephone call to the Foreign Office set this matter in process. Parliament was not due to meet until Tuesday. Telephone calls to Mr. Speaker and the Whips were needed. Directions were given for M.P.s to be recalled for a meeting the next day, notice, for the first time in history, being given by radio. There were telephone messages to the Chiefs of Staff and to Cabinet Ministers. A Cabinet meeting was called for the following day at noon.

After the bustle of those crowded hours Churchill went to his bed in a mood of supreme exultation. That evening had brought the realization of the expectations and hopes that had sustained him through the perils and uncertainties of the months of war. There had been moments in the past when, even for the stoutest hearts and most resolute of minds, misgivings for the future were not entirely to be banished. Now the outcome was assured. With the United States joined with Britain and Russia, the war could have but one end—victory. Had he been a poet he would have written a paean of praise and thanksgiving.[1]

The morning brought news of the full measure of the disaster of Pearl Harbor—seven American capital ships had been put out of commission in the first hour of hostilities. The Japanese had invaded Malaya. Singapore and Hong Kong had been bombed.

The first duty of the Cabinet was to authorize the declaration of war. With Anthony Eden absent, on his way to Russia, Churchill was doing duty at the Foreign Office, and it fell to him to send to the Japanese Ambassador the formal notification of the opening of hostilities, concluding with the high-flown subscription: "I have the honour to be with high consideration, sir, your obedient servant Winston S. Churchill." There were few official communications to which his signature was appended with greater satisfaction. He had been better than his word. Instead of following the Americans within the hour, he was ahead with the British declaration of war. The President had first to obtain the authorization of the Congress.

At the Cabinet session, Churchill had taken the first steps toward a meeting with the President. Having secured his colleagues' approval, he sought leave of absence from the King, which was readily given. Roosevelt shared his wish for a meeting, but was again concerned about the risks of the journey, with U-boats on the alert in the Atlantic. Churchill brushed aside the hazards. There would be greater danger in not having a meeting, so pressingly urgent, to settle problems of plans, supplies and priorities.

A full House of Commons met that afternoon to hear the Prime Minister. Having given a brief outline of events, he said:

It is worth while looking for a moment at the manner in which the Japanese have begun their assault upon the English-speaking world.

Every circumstance of calculated and characteristic Japanese treachery was employed against the United States. The Japanese envoys, Nomura and Kurusu, were ordered to prolong their mission in the United States, in order to keep the conversations going while a surprise attack was being prepared, to be made before a declaration of war could be delivered. The President's appeal to the Emperor, reminding him of their ancient friendship and of the importance of preserving the peace of the Pacific, has received only this base and brutal reply.

Now that the issue is joined in the most direct manner, it only remains for the two great democracies to face their task with whatever strength God may give them. We must hold ourselves very fortunate, and I think we may rate our affairs not wholly ill-guided, that we were not attacked, alone, by Japan in our period of weakness after Dunkirk, or at any time in 1940, before the United States had fully realized the dangers which threatened the whole world and had made such advance in its military preparation.

So precarious and narrow was the margin upon which we then lived that we did not dare to express the sympathy which we have all along felt for the heroic people of China. We were even forced for a short time, in the summer of 1940, to agree to closing the Burma Road. But later on, at the beginning of this year, as soon as we could regather our strength, we reversed that policy, and the House will remember that both I and the Foreign Secretary have felt able to make increasingly outspoken declarations of friendship for the Chinese people and their great leader, General Chiang Kai-shek.

When we think of the insane ambition and insatiable appetite which have caused this vast and melancholy extension of the war we can only feel that Hitler's madness has infected the Japanese mind. The root of the evil and its branch must be extirpated together.

That evening Churchill broadcast the speech he had made and added a postscript appeal for a special effort from all those engaged upon the making of munitions of war. Particularly was this effort essential for the production of aircraft, which would be more than ever necessary, since the war had spread over so many wide spaces of the earth.

In America a united nation was now behind the President. Pearl Harbor was a naval disaster, but the Japanese bombs had destroyed isolationism. Even the Hearst press fell into line—"all out to win."

A unanimous Senate endorsed the President's declaration of war. One Representative alone differed from 388 other members of the House —a woman pacifist who had voted in 1917 against war with Germany. Three days later the European partners to the Axis regularized their position by open declarations of war on the United States—an overt declaration made, presumably, because a prior act of aggression was no longer possible. The entire English-speaking world (apart from Eire) was now engaged and, as Churchill said to the House: "I know I speak for the United States as well as for the British Empire when I say that we would all rather perish than be conquered—and on this basis, putting it at its worst, there are quite a lot of us to be killed."

There were hard knocks ahead in the Far East. The first was suffered within a couple of days, a grievous blow. Two warships, the *Prince of Wales* and the *Repulse,* had been sent out in the autumn to fly the flag in the Pacific. Three days after Pearl Harbor they were sunk by Japanese aerial torpedoes. Churchill was sick at heart when he was given the bad tidings—in all the war he scarcely received a worse shock. Only a few months before he had himself crossed the Atlantic in the *Prince of Wales,* and on her quarter-deck he had stood beside the President singing the sailors' hymn, on the Sunday morning of their first meeting. Now she was a hulk on the ocean bottom and many of the gallant company aboard her had perished, among them Admiral Tom Phillips, commander of the squadron, who went down with his flagship.

With these ships lost, and the American Pacific Fleet crippled, there was nothing in eastern waters to oppose the Japanese Navy. Their ships could range the Pacific and Indian Oceans at will, transport their forces to attack at any point they chose. As Churchill reckoned the consequences he could see little hope of holding Hong Kong, Singapore or Malaya. India would be menaced, even Australia. The outlook gave an added urgency to the need for a full conference in Washington.

A few days later he slipped away from Westminster. From the Clyde he sailed in the latest addition to the Fleet, the battleship *Duke of York,* accompanied by his team of expert advisers and attended by his personal doctor, Sir Charles Wilson, who was to travel with him from conference to conference. Two of the Chiefs of Staff, Admiral Pound and Air Marshal Portal, were in the party, and there was Beaverbrook from the War Cabinet. Alan Brooke remaining behind to master the intricacies of his new duties as C.I.G.S., John Dill made the third member of the Staffs' team.

The Atlantic crossing was a repetition of the previous trip. As the attendant destroyers were reduced in speed by heavy seas, the *Duke of York* left her escort behind and, steaming at twenty knots, crossed the U-boat stream.

Churchill had been given the heartening send-off of good news from the battlefronts. At last, on the shifting sands of North Africa, the tide of battle seemed to have turned in Auchinleck's favor. Rommel's forces were being driven slowly back toward Agheila and expectations of a conclusive success appeared to be well founded. But, even as his hopes began to rise, events in the Middle Sea were taking a new and adverse turn. The crippling of a couple of warships at Alexandria, the sinking of the Malta patrol in a mine field, gave the Germans their chance to send heavy reinforcements across the Sicilian narrows. Rommel was preparing to hit back, but that was hidden by the veil of the future.

On the Eastern Front the Germans had at last been held. Hitler's all-out autumn offensive had failed in its purpose. Moscow survived. The German armies were exposed to the rigors of weather for which they were ill prepared. Hitler, like Napoleon, had calculated without the Russian winter. The German soldiers had to pay the price as they suffered in cold so intense that their guns would not fire and their motors would not start.

There were pressing problems in the Far East requiring immediate decisions—reinforcements for India, planes for Burma, troops for Singapore. Confined aboard ship, Churchill fretted that he was not at hand in London to ensure that proper provision was made for the defense of the fortress of Singapore. As soon as it could be contrived in safety, he radioed his directions to London, urging that nothing must be allowed to impede Singapore's defense.

Confined below by the heavy weather, Churchill was able to sit back and review the war situation. At last he was in position to form long-term plans for the future. Until then events had been in control, and it had been necessary to swing like a weathercock to face each emergency as it arose. The end of this hand-to-mouth strategy was approaching. With the might of the United States and its vast resources waiting only to be mobilized, the time was near for the orderly planning of future operations. He could afford to smile at his former evaluations, in which the soldier had been relegated to a very minor role. Now his mind played with the ideas of sending vast armies into Hitler's citadel. His thoughts raced ahead into the future—ten million Americans under arms; forty armored divisions, half of them British, storming the beaches of the Continent; Germany crumpling under bombs rained down in unprecedented intensity.

His imagination lighted by the glow of his expectations, he visualized the invading Allied armies going into action. They were landing not at ports but on the open beaches. Specially designed craft were enabling them to emerge into action from the seas. There was a gigantic spearhead of armor, forty armored divisions of 15,000 men apiece, and in their wake armies of a million men advancing to liberate the peoples under the Nazi yoke. Fired by the exuberance of his imaginings, he could see the prospect of victory before another three years had run their course.

The ideas came tumbling from the crucible of his imagination. He disciplined them, reduced them to coherent form, and presented them in the well-regulated ranks of sentences and paragraphs appropriate to a state paper. It was his design for Allied operations. He submitted it for comment to his advisers, so that all might be agreed upon the program for Washington.[2]

The statesman's dream was to become the blueprint of victory.* The steps were set out in numbered sequence: victory over Rommel in Libya and advance through Tripoli to Tunis; a campaign to conquer the whole of North Africa, thus restoring free passage through the Mediterranean; a footing established in Sicily and Italy; and finally the descent on Europe in force, for he had no doubt that only by the defeat of the German armies could the war be brought to an end. In the timetable, 1943 was the year appointed for the climax of the invasion. In the event, it was too soon. Rommel was to delay the initial steps, but once begun the victory march was to conform closely with the design.

As he contemplated the possibilities of the future, one doubt alone arose. What would be the effect of the Japanese attack on American intentions? Hitherto it had been agreed at Anglo-American consultations that accounts must first be settled with Hitler in Europe. But might not the disaster of Pearl Harbor have wrought a change in American policy and priorities? Might not the President now insist on defeating Japan first, with Hitler left to be dealt with later? It was the vital question and the possibilities were anxiously canvassed by Churchill and his colleagues.

As the Atlantic crossing neared its end, preoccupation with the strategy of the war was broken by reports from Anthony Eden,[3] then negotiating with the Russians. Stalin, he reported, was raising a variety of issues that were difficult and delicate. Eden had traveled to Moscow to discuss current questions—the signing of an Anglo-Soviet agreement and the possibility of the Russians joining in against Japan.

Stalin, coolly calculating, was taking advantage of the Foreign Secretary's presence to advance Russian interests in the postwar world. Abroad, his allies might debate Russian chances of survival. In the Kremlin they were already preparing their moves for the day when victory had been won, seeking to exploit to their own advantage the good will for Russia then prevailing in the democracies. Churchill and Roosevelt might be satisfied to plan ahead for victory. Stalin raised his sights to a target more distant in time. For him, war aims and peace aims were

* This paper, dated December 18, 1941, written some months before the Second Front became the subject of urgent controversy, testifies to Churchill's soundness on a point on which he was to be assailed by his critics. In the third volume of his memoirs he recommended it to the reading of those disposed to attribute to him a rooted aversion to large-scale invasion of the Continent.

one and indivisible—the advancement of the cause of Soviet communism. In the West they might be satisfied to fight in the name of justice to overthrow the dictators, without thought of gain for their own peoples. The rulers of the Kremlin were not so high-principled. They intended that victory in the war should further their ambitions to make the world safe for communism.

Eden, then and there, was invited to underwrite Russia's postwar frontiers, which would have involved British assent to vast appropriations of territory. The Russians had grabbed the Baltic states of Latvia, Lithuania and Estonia; they intended to retain them. They proposed to move their frontiers westward, incorporating areas of Poland up to the old Curzon Line; the Poles, they suggested, should be permitted, as compensation, to take over East Prussia. Bases in Rumania were sought, with compensation from the Rumanians at the expense of Hungary. As backing for these and his other requirements, Stalin let it be known that his price for signing an Anglo-Soviet agreement was British acquiescence in his postwar designs.

Accustomed as he was to Stalin's importunities, Churchill was scandalized. Of what value was a Soviet pledge? The Russians had subscribed to the Atlantic Charter, with its declarations against territorial gains: Stalin's proposals were at variance with the Charter in three of its articles. As soon as could be, the instruction was sent to Eden—Britain could not acquiesce. Politely but firmly Eden must decline. Let Stalin be told that the peace conference when the war was won was the time and place for these matters. For the present there could be no secret commitments —Britain was pledged to the Americans against the conclusion of any separate pacts.[4]

As he reflected upon Stalin's enormities, Churchill was distressed by the possible consequences on American opinion. The President had a parent's concern for the Charter. To disclose to him how lightly its pledges were esteemed by Stalin would surely be highly injudicious. Even to mention the wretched business would be inexpedient—it might be the cause of lasting trouble.

Stalin pursuing Soviet aims was not more resolute than the Prime Minister in his devotion to the cause of the grand alliance against Hitler. Nothing must be allowed to jeopardize the alliance by causing ill will between Stalin and the President. So from the outset Churchill took on his self-appointed part of middleman and conciliator, between Kremlin and White House, ironing out differences. In this he anticipated the role Roosevelt was disposed to assume as mediator between Russia and Britain. Churchill's was a fruitful contribution to the smooth functioning of the alliance.

The counsel of wisdom was given centuries ago: Rehearse not unto another that which was told thee and thou shalt never fare the worse. From this salutary rule, affairs involving Stalin and his associates should, perhaps, have been excluded as a special case. Later Churchill was to suffer a handicap from the fact that he had not immediately rehearsed to the President all that Eden had reported.

We have lived for so long under acute consciousness of Soviet designs that a mental effort is needed to recapture the wartime atmosphere. There was little general appreciation in 1942 of the part the rulers of Russia were intending to play on the world stage. In the thirties the Bolsheviks had been cold-shouldered by the West, viewed with mistrust and alarm. Stalin had been watched with detestation as with cold-blooded ruthlessness he had gone about the business of liquidating the rivals in his path. Hitler, by his attack, transformed democratic opinion about the Russians. Mistrust gave way to admiration of the valor of the Red armies, and Stalin the liquidator was lost to sight in the figure of the gallant Generalissimo.

Across the Atlantic the Americans shared with the British in admiration and surpassed them in their ignorance of the truth about the rulers of the Kremlin. Churchill could have informed them. He had a shrewder appreciation of the nature and aims of the masters of the Kremlin. For the past six months he had dealt with Stalin and had experienced at first hand the importunities and the grasping ungraciousness of the Russian. Eden's report had added new and somber tints to the picture of the dictator.

Roosevelt was less knowledgeable about the men of the Kremlin. Even the most eminent of statesmen have to take many of their opinions on trust—there is not the time to become informed about all the questions that agitate the world. Outside the range of his particular studies, the statesman is reduced to the prejudice level of the man in the street, and he comes to accept as truths the opinions he learned as a child with his alphabet. F.D.R. had absorbed the views against British imperialism that were commonly held in the days of his youth, when so many patches on the world's map were marked red for British. This colored his outlook, although the old British imperialism had faded with the passing of the old-style British Empire. The Russians, F.D.R. could approach without the prejudice of preformed opinion. He continued, and the State Department shared his views, to reserve his mistrust for the British, while holding that patient reasonableness and the display of good intentions might lead the Soviet rulers to adopt and apply the principles of the Atlantic Charter.

The Prime Minister's diplomacy, by concealing the worst about Stalin and his associates, tended to sustain Roosevelt's illusions. At the outset of their discussions as allies he might, to his own advantage, have stimulated the President's prejudices against Stalin, with his designs to carve up postwar Europe. He was more concerned to keep the Americans on good terms with their Russian allies and Roosevelt's illusions persisted to the time of the Yalta conference, with its fateful decisions for the Western democracies.

In due course, Churchill was to inform the President of Stalin's demands. He then received Presidential approbation for the firm line he had taken.[5] Managed less diplomatically, the matter could have been used to set Russian designs in perspective, so that Stalin's moves thereafter would have been followed by the President with alert and mistrustful scrutiny. It was an opportunity that did not recur. The omission was to have fateful consequences for the postwar world.

After eight days at sea, it was with relief that Churchill escaped from cabined life aboard the *Duke of York* and stepped ashore on American soil. A short flight brought the party to Washington airport where Prime Minister and President clasped hands. Soon afterward Churchill was entering the White House, the first Prime Minister ever to visit Washington in time of war. It was three days before Christmas and he made his way through passages lined with parcels. Despite the season no time was lost in getting down to the business of the Arcadia conference.

CHAPTER FIVE

ARCADIA

DECEMBER, 1941–JANUARY, 1942

O F THE several meetings of the war, summit talks, discussions of the Big Three, and the rest, the first Washington conference should have precedence by reason of its achievements. It was the founding meeting of a copartnership that was without parallel in modern war.

Many decisions were reached. Common strategy was agreed, the blueprint of operations was accepted, an organization of command was set up, the association of the United Nations was declared to the world. But these were minor matters when seen against the basic decision that, henceforth, Britain and America were to run the war as one, with staffs combined to give single direction. It was reached by the inspiration of President and Prime Minister, their outstanding joint contribution to eventual victory.

As far as sovereign states may do so, they did away with national barriers. Resources and manpower were combined in a common pool. Over all was set up a common command. Armies, navies, and air forces were to be directed as though they were drawn from a single state.

It might well have been otherwise. The history of war tells of many alliances that were marred by the ambitions and jealousies of generals and of politicians. With the Russians it still was otherwise. Despite Churchill's striving for more cordial relations, the rulers of the Kremlin continued in wary aloofness, demanding to share in what their allies could provide, but offering to impart little of the secrets of their own operations. On the other side, the Axis powers eyed each other with the mistrust of gangsters engaged in a conspiracy of crime.

With Churchill and Roosevelt kindling the partnership spirit, Britons and Americans came closer together than they had been since the War of Independence. To this result both men made their contributions. The Atlantic meeting had paved the way and they resumed where they had left off. Churchill was in what his friends called his benign mood and so he continued, it being noted that he "did not take anybody's head off." He told his colleagues that concessions must be made by both sides and American views deferred to, for "we are no longer single but married." [1] Cooperation was the easier since on matters of strategy the thoughts of the two men tended to flow in the same direction.

Churchill showed to his host the consideration of the strong man for the weak. He was to be seen in the White House, posted behind the invalid chair, pushing it from room to room. The two men were together at all hours, F.D.R. breaking his early-to-bed rule so that he might join in Churchill's talks into the small hours.

There is the story, so informal were the terms of the visit, that one morning Churchill was surprised by his host as he stood, pink and steaming, on emerging from his bath. He waved aside Presidential apologies with the assurance that "the Prime Minister of Great Britain has nothing to conceal from the President of the United States." To the strict accuracy of the account Churchill demurred—he had never been without a bath towel.[2]

For some reason this first Washington conference was assigned the code name of Arcadia. The chroniclers have failed to find any reason to give point to the name. *Arcades ambo*—it was a farfetched allusion. Nor could the White House be easily identified with Arcadia.

Two days after his arrival Churchill was invited to join in the ceremony of lighting the Christmas tree on the White House lawn.

The folks at home in Britain heard the familiar voice over the radio sending them Christmas greetings. "Let the children," it said, "have their night of fun and laughter."

On Christmas day, President and Prime Minister attended services at the Foundry Methodist Church. Churchill took particular pleasure in one of the hymns—"O Little Town of Bethlehem," a carol unknown to him, with its verse:

> Yet in thy dark streets shineth
> The everlasting Light;
> The hopes and fears of all the years
> Are met in thee tonight.

The Prime Minister made his debut before that most critical of assemblies—the American newspaper correspondents. At the President's invitation he took the chair at the weekly press conference at the White House. To make himself visible to all the assembled journalists, Churchill had to mount the chair, and there he stood delighted and delighting. The newsmen cheered themselves hoarse. He submitted himself to questioning by the correspondents and acquitted himself with adroitness. One correspondent reminded him of his remark about certain "climacteric periods of the war," and asked whether he ranked the entry of the United States as one of these. "I sure do!" was the response in the American vernacular that the audience appreciated.

On the day after Christmas came the public appearance that was the highlight of the visit—the address to the two Houses of Congress assembled in joint session. The American legislators had hurried back from their vacation to hear the Prime Minister. It was an occasion without precedent in Congressional history. Every seat was filled. Members of the Cabinet were there, judges of the Supreme Court, a full attendance of the diplomatic corps. A conspicuous absentee among the notables was the President, who remained in his study to listen by radio. Churchill was heavily guarded as he drove to the Capitol. A roar of cheering went up as he was seen entering the House chamber escorted by Senator Barkley.

With happy inspiration, he began by reminding his hearers of his kinship with them as descendant through his mother of five generations of Americans.

> I cannot [he said] help reflecting that if my father had been American and my mother British, instead of the other way round, I might have got here on my own. In that case this would not have been the first occasion on which you would have heard my voice. In that event I should not have needed any invitation, but, if I had, it is hardly likely that it would have been unanimous, so perhaps things are better as they are.

At this there were roars of laughter and cheers from Republicans and Democrats alike. Churchill had won his audience and he held them.

Having spoken of the Olympian fortitude he had found in America, mask of inflexible purpose and proof of well-grounded confidence in the final outcome, he spoke in warning of the severity of the ordeals ahead. The enemy had the advantage of preparedness; only a portion of American resources was as yet mobilized.

> For the best part of twenty years the youth of Britain and America

have been taught that war is evil, which is true, and that it would never come again, which has been proved false. For the best part of twenty years the youth of Germany, Japan and Italy have been taught that aggressive war is the noblest duty of the citizen. . . . We have performed the duties and tasks of peace. They have plotted and planned for war. This has naturally placed us, in Britain, and now places you, in the United States, at a disadvantage.

Surveying the position of the Allied forces, Churchill answered in advance criticisms which were to be passed in the weeks ahead, of American as well as British lack of preparedness in the Far East.

If people ask me—as they have a right to ask me in England—why it is that you have not got ample equipment of modern aircraft and army weapons of all kinds in Malaya and in the East Indies, I can only point to the victories General Auchinleck has gained in the Libyan campaign. Had we diverted and dispersed our gradually growing resources between Libya and Malaya, we should have been found wanting in both theatres.

If the United States has been found at a disadvantage at various points in the Pacific Ocean, we know well that it is to no small extent because of the aid you have been giving us in munitions for the defense of the British Isles, and for the Libyan campaign, and, above all, because of your help in the Battle of the Atlantic, upon which all depends, and which has in consequence been successfully and prosperously maintained. . . .

Japan's decision to plunge into war in a single day against the United States and the British Empire appeared to be an irrational act.

They have certainly embarked upon a very considerable undertaking, for, after the outrages they have committed, they must know that the stakes for which they have decided to play are mortal.

Here the speaker's voice assumed a tone of scorn that will never be forgotten by those privileged to hear him, as he asked his historic question: "What kind of people do they think we are?" We were a people, did they not realize, who would never cease to persevere, until the Japanese had been taught a lesson they and the world would never forget.

Finally, the Prime Minister touched on the problems of maintaining the world's peace when victory had been won:

Prodigious hammerstrokes have been needed to bring us together again—or, if you will allow me to use other language, I will say that he must indeed have a blind soul who cannot see that some great purpose and design is being worked out here below, of which we have the honor to be faithful servants. It is not given to us to peer into the mysteries of the future. Still, I avow my hope and faith, sure and inviolate, that in the days to come the British and American peoples will, for their own safety and for the good of all, walk together, side by side in majesty, in justice, and in peace.

This was a declaration of faith on a matter that Churchill considered to be of paramount concern. The cooperation of Britain and the United States in an association of continuing and increasing intimacy was one of the fundamental clauses in his creed. Never was he to waver in pursuit of its realization despite the discouragements he received. For it was an aspiration not shared by his friend, the President, who, animated by his conception of British imperialism, looked for the establishment of closer relations with the Russians.

From Washington, Churchill journeyed to Canada to consult with the Prime Minister, Mackenzie King. Arriving at Ottawa on December 29, he took part in the deliberations of the Canadian War Cabinet, and the following day he addressed the two Houses of the Dominion legislature. He allowed himself much greater freedom of speech than he had used in his address in Washington.

Having paid tribute to what the Canadians had achieved and the contributions they had made to the Empire's cause, he said:

> I should like to point out to you that we have not, at any time, asked for any mitigation in the fury or malice of the enemy. The peoples of the British Empire may love peace. They do not seek the lands or wealth of any country. But they are a tough and hardy lot. We have not journeyed across the centuries, across the oceans, across the mountains, across the prairies, because we are made of sugar candy.
>
> Look at the Londoners, the Cockneys, look at what they have stood up to, grim and gay with their cry: "We can take it," and their wartime mood of "what is good enough for anybody is good enough for us." We have not asked that the rules of the game should be modified. We shall never descend to the German and Japanese level. But if anybody likes to play rough, we can play rough, too. Hitler and his Nazi gang have sown the wind. Let them reap the whirlwind.
>
> I have been all this week with the President of the United States, that great man whom destiny has marked for this climax of human fortune. We have been concerting the united pacts and resolves of more than thirty states and nations to fight on in unity together, and in fidelity one to another, without one thought except the total and final extirpation of the Hitler tyranny, the Japanese frenzy, and the Mussolini flop. The enemies coalesced and combined against us have asked for total war. Let us make sure they get it.

Canada has a large French-speaking population and close ties with France, and Churchill spoke of the fate that had befallen the French people. At the time of the collapse of French resistance, it was the duty of the French Government and it was also in their interest to have gone to North Africa, where they would have been at the head of the French Empire.

If they had done this, Italy might have been driven out of the war before the end of 1940, and France would have held her place as a nation in the counsels of the Allies and at the conference table of the victors. But their generals misled them. When I warned them that Britain would fight on alone whatever they did, their generals told their Prime Minister and his divided Cabinet: "In three weeks England will have her neck wrung like a chicken." Some chicken! Some neck!

To the delight of his hearers, and of French-speaking Canada, Churchill broke into French to greet the French national resurrection:

Et partout dans la France occupée et inoccupée (car leur sort est égal), ces honnêtes gens, ce grand peuple, la nation française, se redresse. L'espoir se rallume dans les cœurs d'une race guerrière, même désarmée, berceau de la liberté révolutionnaire et terrible aux vainqueurs esclaves. Et partout, on voit la pointe du jour et la lumière grandit, rougeâtre, mais claire. Nous ne perdrons jamais, la confiance que la France jouera le rôle des hommes libres et qu'elle reprendra par des voies dures sa place dans la grande compagnie des nations libératrices et victorieuses. Ici, au Canada, où la langue française est honorée et parlée, nous tenons prêts et armés pour aider et pour saluer cette résurrection nationale.

With these two speeches Churchill caught the ear of the peoples of North America. They heard the authentic note of leadership and they responded to him as his people at home had responded in the dark days. His words had a steadying influence on the newcomers to the war. The first shock of Pearl Harbor had sent ripples of alarm through the forty-eight states. On the West Coast, citizens, watching the skies with apprehension, had made hourly reports of approaching enemy bombers, phantoms that left no trace of ruin behind them.[3] The breadth of a continent away from the Pacific there was some jittering in the eastern states. Government officials in Washington prepared their minds for a line of battle in the Rockies, and Congressmen pressed for the latest antiaircraft batteries to be placed for the defense of Capitol Hill.[4] Despite these initial tremors, the people of America were to emerge from the war without experience at first hand of the hazards that had become accepted as the normal incidents of existence in Europe's bomb-scarred cities.

In the conference rooms, progress was rapid. No meeting of allies could have been more harmonious. It could scarcely have proved otherwise, since the Americans conceded at the outset, on their own initiative, the one major point which, for Churchill and his colleagues, was fundamental—the war in Europe was to have number one priority, taking precedence over operations against the Japanese. Churchill had gone into conference prepared to exert himself to gain this decision against what he had imagined would be American opposition. Instead, he found that Pearl Harbor had made no difference in the reckoning. The Americans recognized that they might beat Japan and lose the war, but that once Hitler was defeated total victory was assured. Only a minimum of forces, it was then agreed, were to be diverted to the Eastern theatres of war until victory in Europe was won.

With this unanimity on fundamentals, there was little difficulty in agreeing to the items in the program. Churchill's blueprints were adopted, with a descent on French North Africa as the first operation for the partnership. The preference of the American military staffs would have been for an attack on German land power and production centers, but on Africa President and Prime Minister thought as one.[5] Gone, now, were Roosevelt's doubts about Churchill's strategy in the Middle East. It was clear beyond questioning that the British bastion in the desert was of paramount importance. Were Egypt to fall, there would be no obstacle to the link-up of the Germans with the Japanese, commanding the Indian Ocean. On the other hand, were the Germans to be driven from Africa, the Mediterranean would be reopened to Allied shipping. The staffs were directed to prepare for a North African expedition (Operation "Gymnast," later renamed "Torch").

The appointment of a supreme commander for the Pacific zone of the war—from the Bay of Bengal to Australia—caused some misgivings on the British side. To mark the British contribution to the war effort, Roosevelt proposed that the appointment should go to a British general and he nominated Wavell.

It was an unenviable command to take, with disasters so plainly looming ahead. The British Chiefs of Staff protested that this was no post for a British general to be assigned. The Americans, they suggested, were seeking to evade the odium for the defeats to come; let the Americans provide the commander.

Churchill would listen to no aspersions against the Americans. To have doubts about your ally was no way to run an alliance. The suspicions entertained of Roosevelt were unworthy of them—Roosevelt was making a friendly gesture, intending a compliment to Wavell.[6]

The appointment was made. It was a short-lived office, for Wavell had not established himself before his command had fallen to pieces. But the incident had its influence on the future of the alliance. Churchill's remonstrances to his colleagues, like Roosevelt's friendly gesture, helped to set the tone for the partnership in its earlier stages.

The idea of a supreme commander in the field was followed, naturally, by the conception of unity of staffs for the direction of the war. Various proposals were put forward. The first was for a supreme council for all the Allied powers, including the Russians, but this was held to be too cumbersome. A liaison council between the Staffs in Washington and London—this would scarcely be effective. So the British model was taken for the wider sphere. To run the war from day to day it was decided to set up the Combined Chiefs of Staff. It was a revolutionary idea and it was tentatively adopted for a trial run to see if it would work. The trial lasted until victory was won. Where were the headquarters to be? The British, having fought the Germans for a couple of years, had their claims for London. The Americans, with their vast potentials of man-power and resources, stood out for Washington. In the interests of the partnership Churchill gave way and Washington was agreed to.[7]

There had been no Chiefs of Staff organization in the United States until Roosevelt established a higher command on the British pattern, with Gen. Marshall as Chief of Army Staff. An expert in supply and logistics, he was to prove himself a master of global war. Sir John Dill was appointed head of the British Mission in Washington, a post in which he served with distinction till his death, "on active service," in 1944.

By these simple steps there was created the instrument that made possible the continuous coordination of Anglo-American strategy throughout the war. The Combined Staffs met almost daily. Dill and his two colleagues for Navy and Air Force kept the closest contact with their chiefs in London. Major decisions were taken at conferences in which President and Prime Minister took part, giving their final approval to agreed plans or bringing their influence to bear when the Staffs were deadlocked in disagreement.

Churchill sat with the Combined Staffs on level terms with the Service members; Roosevelt held rather aloof from staff discussions, deferring to the judgment of his professionals. As the President was not be induced to overrule his advisers, Churchill had to address his arguments to them when he wished to influence the decisions. There were few discussions in which he did not intervene. The Americans came to experience at first hand the qualities, already legendary, of Churchill the controversialist—the eloquence, the ingenuity and the stubbornness with which he pressed his point of view. Where he disagreed he maintained his opposition with tenacity to the last, but once action was begun his loyal support was generously accorded to whatever project had been decided on.[8]

"I support a supreme command in supplies as well as in strategy." Beaverbrook's recommendation was the logical sequel to what had gone before, but it was hotly debated. As the Americans were to provide munitions and supplies in vast measure, they insisted that control should be exercised from Washington. Churchill, supported by Beaverbrook, raised objections, but they had finally to bow before American insistence and conceded that the allocation should be controlled by an Assignment Board under the Combined Staffs.[9]

Again, as with the Atlantic meeting, there was a declaration for the world. As this did not impinge upon the realm of strategy, the President was able to make it the subject of his special concern. The declaration represented the articles of association of the coalition of Allies, the grand alliance against Hitlerism. It was to receive the signature of all the nations at war with the Axis, the Associated Powers or, in Roosevelt's happier phrase, the United Nations. Churchill took a hand in the drafting of this document by which twenty-six sovereign states pledged themselves to devote their resources and coordinate their military operations to the advancement of victory, undertaking to make no separate peace.

A point over religion arose from the preamble to this simple declaration. As it was first drafted, it read: "Being convinced that the complete and world-wide victory of all the Governments is essential to defend and preserve life, liberty and independence, as well as the righteous possibilities of human freedom and. . . ." The President was disturbed by the omission of any specific reference to religious freedom, one of his Four Freedoms. In the autumn there had been sharp criticism that religion had been left out of the Atlantic Charter, and he did not wish to incur further reproach, but there was felt to be difficulty over Russia, godless Russia. Was not Stalin likely to jib at being asked to subscribe to religious freedom?[10]

Prime Minister and President considered the problem. They broached the matter with Litvinov, the Soviet representative, who doubted whether his masters would agree to religion going in. Other questions were put aside while Prime Minister and President set themselves to convert Litvinov, who was eventually persuaded into conceding that the Kremlin might accept the phrase "freedom of conscience."

With his elasticity of outlook Roosevelt agreed that freedom of conscience and freedom of religion added up to the same thing. After all, the traditional American conception of freedom was so broadly democratic that it included the right to have any god or no god at all. But, for the sake of its associations, the President preferred the word "religion." Could not this be accepted?

Churchill himself, in a brush with Litvinov on another matter, had told the Russian that he wasn't much of an ambassador if he had not the power to add a word to a declaration. Litvinov, however, was not risking anything, and insisted on taking instructions from the Kremlin.

It was unfortunate that there is no record of the reactions of Stalin when, amidst his preoccupations with the strategy and fate of the Red armies, he found himself invited to consider this problem. Eventually the word religion found its way into the preamble. Stalin had not considered himself any more strained by subscribing to religious freedom than he had been by the giving of the pledge in the Atlantic Charter against seeking territorial gains. Pledges and declarations and charters were all the same to him if they contributed to the essential business of beating Hitler. Churchill was so impressed by the President's zeal and skill in religious persuasion that he undertook to put forward his name for the post of Archbishop of Canterbury should a vacancy occur.

A fortnight of the new year had gone before the work of the conference was ended. After dinner on January 14, the President escorted his guest to the railway station where a special train was waiting. The two men shook hands and parted with their liking for each other strengthened by their work together. They had a common satisfaction in a good job well done, and they shared memories of hours of pleasant informality at the White House.

The battleship *Duke of York* was waiting among the coral reefs of Bermuda for the Prime Minister and his party. And at large in the Atlantic were twenty U-boats, their commanders alerted, no doubt, about the imminence of a special target for their torpedoes. The President had been anxious about the risks of the trip home, seeing that his guest's presence in Washington had been publicized the world over.

On the way to Bermuda, Churchill took over the controls of the Boeing flying boat in which he was traveling. He was impressed. Would the plane be capable of the Atlantic crossing? Of course. Then what about it?

In those earlier days, flying the Atlantic was still in its pioneer stage, an enterprise of hazard, not lightly to be undertaken. At first the two Service Chiefs would not think of consenting to their charge exposing himself to the risks of an air crossing. He might be in a hurry to be back in London, but, as motorists are told, better be late and safe. Churchill reminded them that the ocean, with the U-boat packs on the alert, was no more free from hazards than the air. After some debate they yielded to his persuasions. The return trip would be made by air.

Bermuda did not suffer the visit of the Prime Minister to pass unmarked. The Legislative Assembly was hurriedly convened and there, in the Sessions House at Hamilton, the leader of the Mother of Parliaments addressed the oldest parliament in the New World, with a continuity unbroken since 1620.

As he waited in his seat for the Boeing to take off, Churchill had a pang of misgiving. Perhaps, after all, he should have journeyed back by warship. Once airborne, he was satisfied, and that night slept soundly in the bridal suite of the plane. The flight was uneventful until the final stage, when the course had hurriedly to be changed. They had been making directly for the French coast, and the German guns had been no more than a few minutes' flying time ahead.[11]

Members of the Cabinet assembled to greet their leader on his return. He was heartened by the cheer they gave him, but he soon discovered that politically it was a cheerless home-coming.

THE
WORLD

CHAPTER SIX

THE CRITICS

JANUARY, 1942

O N HIS mission to America, Winston Churchill had been engaged in concerting plans for the winning of battles. Back at Westminster he was obliged to exercise the arts that win debates. His return from the United States was made the occasion for the release of the feelings of dissatisfaction that had been generated during his absence.

In December he had left a country exhilarated by the acquisition of a new ally. In January he returned to find that spirits were flagging under the chilling influence of bad news from the Far East. Every day, it seemed, a new bit of the Empire was being lost. There was concern at the range and speed of the advance of the Japanese. Their conquests fanned out eastward to the mid-Pacific, southward toward Australia, westward toward India. They reached the tip of the Malay Peninsula, they bombed Rangoon, they landed in Borneo, Celebes, New Guinea and the Solomons.

The harvest was being reaped of the years the locusts had eaten. Until the deficiencies had been made good and munitions, planes, tanks, the ships to transport them, and the warships to guard them became available, the Japanese could (in Churchill's phrase) "make hell while the sun shines."

With discontent in the air of Westminster, the back-bench critic, who had been as extinct as the dodo, began once more to raise his voice. There were proddings in the press. The backstairs intriguers found a situation to their liking. Whispers were set going about the Prime Minister and his colleagues—Churchill was too powerful, Beaverbrook meddlesome, there were the shortcomings of Margesson, the pomposity of Dalton, Attlee's want of courage, and Greenwood's lack of drive.[1]

Had he not been otherwise informed, the columns of the London press would have brought home to the Prime Minister the change in the political temper. A leading article in *The Times* would have completed his enlightenment. While proclaiming the utmost confidence in Winston Churchill's leadership, *The Times* expressed a very considerable lack of confidence in his administration and called, in particular, for the appointment of a Minister of Production. The Prime Minister was exhorted to consider how his Ministry might be recruited from its lower ranks, or even from outside Parliament.

In the House the critics fired their first shots on the minor issue of the broadcasting of the speech the Prime Minister was to make. On his return it was made known that, in opening a three-day debate, he would deliver one of his periodic war reviews, and would broadcast to the nation. On his first reappearance in the House Churchill invited members to sanction the recording of his speech, so that it might be available for subsequent broadcasting, thus sparing him the labor of repeating it before the microphone. It had been represented, he said, that large numbers of persons, in the Dominions as well as at home, would like to listen to the actual speech, or parts of it, rather than to a news summary, and he hoped that the House would be disposed from time to time to grant this indulgence to him "or any successor I may have in the war."

The House being jealous of its rights, there was opposition to the indulgence. Hore-Belisha found reasons for objection. While recognizing the desire of the public to hear the speech, he frigidly invited the Prime Minister to bear in mind that Parliament was not a platform but a representative assembly, and he suggested that a small committee of M.P.s should consider the matter. The argument was elaborated in the newspapers. The Prime Minister was bluntly told that he must not regard his position as being analogous with that of the President of the United States.

At the next sitting of the House, Churchill withdrew his request. Doubtless the champions of parliamentary privilege had by their objections saved the ancient seat of government from grave consequences. The infection of the insidious microphone is incalculable in its influence. But the jealous champions of the rights of the House might have spared a thought for the wishes for the electors, whose preference could scarcely have been in doubt.

The three-day debate on the war situation opened on January 27. Churchill's temper had been roused by the pinprickers, and in opening the debate he invited them to come into the open. Let them carry their criticisms to their logical conclusion, into the division lobby.

"If an Honorable Member dislikes the Government very much and feels it to be in the public interest that it should be broken up he ought to have the manhood to testify his convictions in the lobby. There is no need to be mealymouthed in debate and no one should be chicken-hearted in voting."

He claimed the verdict of a division as his right. Hostile sections of the press had proclaimed that the credit of the Government was broken. It was flashed over the world that the Prime Minister had no authority to speak for the nation, and that the Government was about to collapse. "Whoever," he declared, "speaks for Britain at this moment must be known to speak not only in the name of the people—and I feel pretty sure I may—but in the name of Parliament, and above all of the House of Commons. It is because things have gone badly and worse is to come that I demand a vote of confidence."

Having invited the critics to come at him, he entered upon a strategic survey. In Churchillian phrases he posed to the House the dilemma that at every new crisis of the war had had to be faced by the Government. Manpower and munitions of war were not sufficient for all the fronts in every part of the world; where should they be employed?

Having survived thus far, by a small margin, where would Britain have been had the Government yielded to the clamor for invasion of France and the Low Countries? On the walls could still be seen the inscription "Second Front Now." Let them imagine what the position would have been had Britain yielded to that vehement temptation. Every ton of shipping, every flotilla, every airplane, the whole strength of the Army would have been committed, and Britain would be fighting for life on the French shores or on the shores of the Low Countries. All the troubles of the Far East and the Middle East would have sunk into insignificance compared with the question of another and far worse Dunkirk.

> I suppose there are some of those who were vocal and voluble and even clamant for a Second Front to be opened in France, who are now going to come up bland and smiling and ask why it is that we have not ample forces in Malaya, Burma, Borneo and Celebes.
>
> When I was called upon to be Prime Minister, now nearly two years ago, there were not many applicants for the job. In spite of the shameful negligence, gross muddles, blatant incompetence, com-

placency, and lack of organizing which are daily attributed to us—
and from which chidings we endeavor to profit—we are beginning to
see our way through. . . .

While facing Germany and Italy here, and in the Nile Valley, we
have never had any power to provide effectively for the defense of the
Far East. Had we started to scatter our forces over those immense
areas in the Far East, we should have been ruined.

From strategy, Churchill turned to personalities and the demand for
ministerial scapegoats. For the broad strategic decisions he took, he said,
the fullest responsibility:

If we have handled our resources wrongly, no one is so much to
blame as I. Why then should I be called upon to pick out scapegoats,
to throw blame on generals, or airmen, or soldiers? Why should I be
called upon to drive away loyal and trusted colleagues and friends,
to appease the clamor of certain sections of the British and Australian press, or to take the edge off our reverses? I should be ashamed
to do such a thing at such a time and if I were capable of doing it,
believe me, I should be incapable of rendering the country or this
House any further service. . . .

A variety of attacks are made upon the composition of the Government. It is said that it is formed upon a party and political basis.
But so is the House of Commons. It is silly to extol the parliamentary
system and then in the next breath to say, "Away with party and
with politics."

From one quarter I am told that the leaders of the Labour Party
ought to be dismissed from the Cabinet. This would be a return to
party government pure and simple. From opposite quarters it is said
that no one who approved of Munich should be allowed to hold
office. To do that would be to cast reflection upon the great majority
of the nation at that time and also to deny the strongest party in the
House any proportionate share in the national Government, which
again might cause inconvenience.

The speech brought about a considerable change of feeling at Westminster. It was conceded that the Prime Minister had provided yet one
more example of the quality that had given him his commanding ascendancy in the people's confidence. M.P.s, generally, were relieved to
have their anxieties reduced, if not allayed.

A wide range of topics was touched upon by the speakers in the extended and rambling debate that followed. No fewer than 618 columns
of the official report were needed to record the three days of speechmaking. For Churchill there was more praise than criticism—indeed the
customary formula was to preface attacks on the Ministry with professions of confidence in its head. The chief reproach against him was that

he took too much responsibility upon himself and erected too effective an umbrella over his colleagues. Few M.P.s challenged his arguments on strategy, but complaints were general about the deficiencies in production and there were powerful appeals for the appointment of a Production Minister.

Interest in the other speeches could scarcely survive the debate. Emanuel Shinwell's contribution is worth recalling for the parallel he drew between Churchill and Pitt the Younger. Victor of a once famous election fight with Ramsay MacDonald at Seaham Harbour, Shinwell ranged himself with the critics of the Government, but he prefaced his criticisms with a tribute to the Prime Minister for his heartening speeches in America and for his magnificent contribution in cementing the relations between the two great English-speaking peoples. Having urged Churchill to abandon his stubborn attitude over the appointment of Production Minister, he quoted a celebrated passage from Macaulay:

"It may seem paradoxical to say that the incapacity which Pitt showed in all that related to the conduct of the war is, in some sense, the most decisive proof that he was a man of very extraordinary abilities. Yet this is the simple truth. For assuredly one-tenth part of his errors and disasters would have been fatal to the power and influence of any minister who had not possessed in the highest degree the talents of a parliamentary leader. While his schemes were confounded, while his predictions were falsified, while the coalitions which he had laboured to form were falling to pieces, his authority over the House of Commons was constantly becoming more and more absolute. If some great misfortune had spread dismay through the ranks of his majority, that dismay lasted only till he rose from the Treasury Bench, drew up his haughty head, stretched his arm with commanding gesture and poured forth in deep and sonorous tones the lofty language of inexhaustible hope and inflexible resolution. Thus, through a long and calamitous period, every disaster that happened without the walls of Parliament was regularly followed by a triumph within them."

Does my Right Honorable friend [Shinwell asked] recognize himself in that vivid and colorful description?

After three days of debate, Churchill wound up in a conciliatory speech that suited the temper of a House bent on conciliation. Almost at the outset he made a concession that was more welcome to his supporters, perhaps, than to his critics, who were thereby robbed of one of their targets. The decision was made known in well-turned Churchillian phrases. He would, he assured the House, be ready to profit by helpful lines of thought, even though they came from the most hostile quarter, and he went on:

I shall not be like that saint to whom I have before referred in this House, but whose name I have unhappily forgotten, who refused to do right because the devil prompted him. Neither shall I be deterred from doing what I am convinced is right by the fact that I have thought differently about it in some distant or even in some recent past.

So, he came to his point—the creation of a Ministry of Production, a development to which he had been converted by the appointment of Donald Nelson to a similar post in the United States. For harmonious working, the equivalent office was necessary in England. "I have been for some weeks," he said, "carefully considering this, and the strong opinions which have been expressed in the House—even though I do not share their reasoning in all respects—have reinforced the conclusion with which I returned from the United States."

But for the Independent Labour Party members, bent on an antiwar demonstration, Churchill would have been deprived of the satisfaction of a division. James Maxton entered the division lobby against the Government, the solitary bag for his two tellers. In the other lobby 464 members supported the Government. It was a convincing demonstration to any doubters at home or abroad that the House, as well as the people, was behind the Prime Minister.

The result of the division brought Churchill hearty congratulations from his friends across the Atlantic. "It is fun to be in the same decade as you," ran a message from Roosevelt.[2]

Within two weeks, Churchill announced the choice of Lord Beaverbrook to fill the new post of Minister of Production. The creation of the post met with unqualified acclaim, but the choice of Minister with scarcely universal approval. Throughout his career the qualities of Beaverbrook had been consistently underestimated by the public. Opinion on his previous achievements was divided between the extremes of admiration and detraction. It was agreed that he was a man to expend the last ounce of a dynamic personality in time of emergency, but there was no unanimity that his talents were those needed for a sustained task of planning. By his critics his influence on affairs was likened to a badly mixed cocktail—highly stimulating for an hour or two, but productive of a virulent hangover.[3] But it was Beaverbrook who conjured into existence the fighter planes that turned the scale in the Battle of Britain. As Hugh Dalton said of him: "No man who stayed on the ground did more to win that battle."

Churchill knew his qualities, his courage and his drive, and made him his closest confidant. He recognized a companion spirit, formed for a crisis, for the perpetual crisis of war. No man served the state so well and his own interests so ill. To attain his objects Beaverbrook rode roughshod over lesser men. Unscrupulous in his resourcefulness, the great disorganizer, he was the nightmare of civil servant orthodoxy.

Beaverbrook's colleagues complained of "poaching." They alleged that when their trucks went to the docks to collect supplies from America they found that his transport had got in first.[4] The generals protested that he had tried to form his own private army to protect his aircraft factories in the event of invasion, cornering armor plating to provide his troops with "Beaverettes"—small armored cars.[5]

Poaching for labor, as well as supplies for his factories, he was brought into conflict with Ernest Bevin. The masterful Minister of Labor was not the man to tolerate the breaking of his rules by the wayward genius of the M.A.P. A public scandal seemed likely to break when Bevin threatened to prosecute Beaverbrook and his Ministry for breach of the labor regulations, but the affair was settled out of court.[6]

Bevin's hostility was a source of difficulty when Beaverbrook was made Minister of Production. A conflict of authority was clearly imminent over the allocation of labor. The line of demarcation between the rival chiefs was not easy to fix, but it had to be settled if the two determined Ministers were not forever to be contesting each other's authority.

It was the more difficult for Churchill to find a solution since he held both in high esteem, the two outstandingly successful members of the administration. Bevin at the Labor Ministry was as near as could be irreplaceable. For the "old sea raider" from Fleet Street Churchill's respect was no less, though he and Beaverbrook were forever falling out and making up their differences. Bevin had hitherto been chairman of the War Cabinet's Production Executive, a body now become redundant. He was not likely to permit the power of the Production Minister to extend far into the field of labor.

Beaverbrook had demanded a dictator's powers in his new position. Churchill had gone far to meet him, to the alarm of other departments. To allay those apprehensions, and define the limits of authority of the new Minister, Churchill devoted a weekend of consideration. The results of his cogitations were received with curiosity by those aware of the delicacy of the personal issues involved.

A White Paper ten paragraphs long set out the fruits of the Prime Minister's deliberations. It recorded that under the new arrangement Lord Beaverbrook, with the authority of a member of the War Cabinet, was to be vested with the prime responsibility for all the business of war production. The Ministers of Labor and Production were to work in the closest cooperation. The Minister of Labor would find and supply the labor and would follow it up to see that it was not used uneconomically. To make the position clear, Churchill added the explanation: "That is exactly what the Minister of Labor does at the present time. He does that in the way that the Chancellor of the Exchequer, under the direction of the Cabinet, supplies money, follows it up and sees that it is not used uneconomically."

Public curiosity was intrigued rather than satisfied by these explanations. Clearly, it was concluded, the problem had been delicate in the extreme since it had resulted in so evasive a compromise. Clearly, too, Beaverbrook's authority, if it ran at all in the realm of labor, did not extend very far. Churchill, indeed, had feared that Beaverbrook would not accept the delimitation of his powers, and he warned him, in blunt terms, that he could go no further. Were Beaverbrook to decline the offered post he would be harshly judged by the nation, striking a blow at his own reputation. Thus exhorted, Beaverbrook accepted.[7]

The appointment brought to a close the first phase of the period of discontent. The debate had cleared the air. The Prime Minister had received a conclusive majority. The critics could look upon the production appointment as a concession to their views. In politics, however, satisfaction fades like a snowdrop in the desert. The Minister of Production had scarcely had time to get his brass plate upon the door before the future of the Government was again in question.

CHAPTER SEVEN

CABINET CHANGES

FEBRUARY, 1942

B Y MID-FEBRUARY there had been ample fulfillment of Churchill's prediction of reverses ahead. Withdrawals in the Far East were reported daily. British forces were pushed out of Malaya. It was the Prime Minister's melancholy duty (February 15) to announce the fall of Singapore —"the greatest disaster to British arms which our history records." The Germans rubbed salt into the wound to British pride.

Three German warships, the *Gneisenau, Scharnhorst* and *Prinz Eugen,* had for some weeks been confined to the harbor at Brest, where they had been the object of nightly attention by the bombers of the RAF. Watch was kept lest they should make for the open sea to go commerce-raiding in the Atlantic. Brest was no place of safety for a German ship, and one February morning, under cover of sea mist, the trio steamed up-Channel to make for the refuge of the German ports. Though winged on the way, they ran the gauntlet. There was a gasp of national stupefaction when it became known that the three ships had slipped through the Straits of Dover and reached their home ports, despite the RAF and the Royal Navy. It was reckoned a greater mortification than the loss of Singapore, the most humiliating episode in Britain's naval history since van Tromp had sailed his Dutch ships up the Thames in the reign of Charles II.

It was a black weekend. There was a surge of discontent. The critics were once again in full cry. The back-bench intriguers were busy.

Whispers were sent on their rounds—Churchill was failing. Churchill had served his turn, Churchill was a national Jonah. The whispers spread among the ragtag and bobtail of politics.

The talk had no effect upon the nation at large. The robust common sense of the people was not to be disturbed by the slanders of small minds. But among the hangers-on the whisperers created quite a stir. The political hacks were impressed by the echoes of their own malignancy. They were encouraged to search for a candidate for the highest post if that post should fall vacant—and they persuaded themselves a vacancy would occur. Bets were laid, substantial bets, that Churchill would not last out the war. There was some preening of feathers among the lesser lights of near-ministerial rank, who fancied they had prospects. At least one man, who some time afterward was selected by Churchill for office, began to let it be known in the clubs that he had his qualifications for the highest place—and his followers.

Criticisms of the previous month were renewed. Those who had called for ministerial changes remarked that remodeling of the Cabinet had not gone far enough and that the appointment of a Minister of Production fell short of what had been expected. Sir William Beveridge burst into print to protest that the Government conducting the present war bore little likeness to the administration which conducted the nation to victory in 1918. In the Churchill administration, it was declared, all the dominant personalities from the Prime Minister down were absorbed in executive duties, whereas the essence of the Lloyd George War Cabinet was that it consisted of Ministers without departments.

When the House met on February 17, the atmosphere of tension was unmistakable. The Prime Minister rose to make a brief statement on events. While regretting the escape of the German warships, he found some cause for satisfaction that they had abandoned their positions at Brest; thereby they had relieved Britain of a threat to her convoy routes. "Whatever smart of disappointment or annoyance may remain in our breasts," said Churchill, "that the final forfeit was not exacted, there is no doubt that the naval position on the Atlantic, so far from being worsened, is definitely eased." That was not a consideration to temper the prevailing dissatisfaction.

As for the fall of Singapore, he spoke but to administer a caution. "It would ill become the dignity of the Government and the House," he said, "and would render poor service to the alliance of which we are a part, if we were to be drawn into agitated or excited recriminations at a time when all our minds are oppressed with a sense of tragedy and with the sorrow of so lamentable a misfortune." While he could not take part in any debate, he would provide members with the occasion for expressing their opinions.

The House was far from satisfied with the statement. Feelings were running high. Since they were denied a debate there and then, M.P.s debated when the debate should be, and found some vent for their dissatisfaction by demanding a grand inquest into all that had occurred— "calamitous things" as Winterton termed them.

Wardlaw-Milne had come into the House expecting an immediate debate and was disturbed to find he would have to wait for the opportunity to express his views. Hugh O'Neill considered that the Prime Minister had failed to realize the immense amount of public anxiety caused by the escape of the German ships. Bellenger of Bassetlaw reported a feeling in the country that the right kind of persons were not directing the war.

Churchill rose again, plainly disturbed by the temper of the House. They should have their debate, he told them; there was not the slightest reason why they should not have it; he would give every facility for it. The House was absolute master. If its confidence were not extended to the Government, and it considered it could make better arrangements for the conduct of the war, then it was its right, indeed it was its duty, to make known its opinion in the proper constitutional manner. What he deprecated was that the debate should take place in "a mood of panic," an observation that drew a chorus of protesting "Noes" from all quarters.

When the House adjourned, members were in the mood to go to any lengths in their insistence on changes in the War Cabinet. Conservative M.P.s from the Midlands, by formal resolution, recorded their conviction that there should be reconstruction of the War Cabinet to free its members from departmental duties.

Politicians sought to profit by the occasion. The whisperings from the political fringes were intensified. Some sought a leader for the malcontents; the Government did not want the services of Stafford Cripps, let him lead His Majesty's patriotic Opposition. Some went so far as to ask why Cripps should not captain the Government team.[1]

The crisis was resolved before the debate took place. There was no mistaking the mood of the House, and the Prime Minister was persuaded to anticipate further expression of its will. By the following weekend a major reconstruction of the War Cabinet and the Ministry had been announced. In terms of personnel, Lord Beaverbrook and Arthur Greenwood were omitted and two recruits, Stafford Cripps and Oliver Lyttelton, were brought in. The War Cabinets old and new were constituted:

OLD	NEW
Winston Churchill, Prime Minister and Minister of Defense	Winston Churchill, Prime Minister and Minister of Defense
Clement Attlee, Lord Privy Seal	Clement Attlee, Dominions Secretary and Deputy Prime Minister
Sir John Anderson, Lord President	Sir Stafford Cripps, Lord Privy Seal and Leader of the House
Anthony Eden, Foreign Secretary	Sir John Anderson, Lord President
Lord Beaverbrook, Minister of Production	Anthony Eden, Foreign Secretary
Ernest Bevin, Minister of Labor and National Service	Oliver Lyttelton, Minister of State (for Production)
Sir Kingsley Wood, Chancellor of the Exchequer	Ernest Bevin, Minister of Labor and National Service
Arthur Greenwood, Minister without Portfolio	

Public interest was focused chiefly on the omission of Lord Beaverbrook and the inclusion of Stafford Cripps—changes which the politically informed hinted were not unrelated. It was a matter of surprise that the man who had been appointed to the new post of Minister of Production should within two weeks leave the War Cabinet and the Government. The fact that Beaverbrook was to undertake special duties in Washington concerned with the pooling and allocation of munitions was not accepted as the explanation.

Oliver Lyttelton was recalled from the Middle East, where he had been Resident Minister, to take over the production post, though at first without the full title and lacking, too, the ten-point White Paper to define and delimit his responsibilities. Here, again, the politically informed let it be known that certain difficulties over manpower which had arisen when Beaverbrook was appointed were likely to prove of easier solution now that Lyttleton was to hold the office. So, though the politically informed discreetly stopped short of naming names, the not-so-discreet suggested that Ernest Bevin, as Minister of Labor, had been concerned in those delicate problems over the powers of the Minister of Production which previously had given the Prime Minister concern.

In fact the political gossips were wide of their mark. Bad health was the reason officially assigned to Beaverbrook's withdrawal from the Ministry, but this was no more than a contributory factor. It was true enough that he had been afflicted for years by the scourge of asthma from which he sought in vain for relief. By 1942 he had reached the point of breakdown, and was overcome by a profound weariness. The strain of his work as Minister had accentuated the consequences of his affliction. But it was Russia and the Second Front that were the immediate reason for his resignation.

For months past strong feelings had been aroused among his Cabinet colleagues by his advocacy of Russian claims. So thoroughgoing was his acceptance of the Soviet point of view, so complete his faith in Stalin and his "pulsating power," that Beaverbrook backed all demands from the Kremlin—supplies, frontiers, Second Front. His was the voice of Stalin within the Cabinet. By sponsoring the case for the absorption by Russia of the Baltic States and Polish territories, he aroused the opposition of his leading colleagues—Ernest Bevin, Clement Attlee, who would resign rather than give way to the Soviet—and the Prime Minister himself. There was further dissent over a "Tanks for Russia" week. This aroused Bevin's heated protest, though the tanks were obtained.

Over the Second Front Beaverbrook came into direct conflict with the Prime Minister. The point was reached where he must give way or go out. He chose to go, so that he might be free to campaign for the Second Front. His final word to the Prime Minister was a formal demand asking for a Cabinet decision in favor of the Soviet claims on frontiers: "The British Government will not be fulfilling the Prime Minister's pledge unless it concedes the rightful frontier claims put forward by the Russians." [2]

It was with sincere regret that Churchill accepted the withdrawal of this old friend, with whom he had shared the burdens of the First World War and from whom he had received encouragement in the dark years of appeasement. Beaverbrook's friendship and admiration for his leader gave a shining quality to the words of his resignation letter, beginning: "I must tell you about the twenty-one months of high adventure, the like of which has never been known . . . everything that has been done by me has been due to your holding me up." He concluded with the offer of his devotion to "the saviour of our people, the symbol of resistance in the free world." [3] So highly did Churchill value Beaverbrook's judgment and driving force that he was resolved to bring him back into the Government as soon as his health permitted. Beaverbrook's return, after an interval in which he campaigned on both sides of the Atlantic for the opening of the Second Front, was delayed until the autumn of 1943, when he took office as Lord Privy Seal.

On all sides the appointment of Stafford Cripps was welcomed. It seemed long ago that Sir Stafford had aroused the wrath alike of right wing and of left—of the right because he was so leftish, and of the left because he was so independent a Socialist that the party expelled him for flouting their decisions. As Ambassador to Moscow during a period of extreme delicacy he had rendered great service and the Prime Minister was complimented on choosing him as Leader of the House of Commons, in the manner that Bonar Law had acted in the First World War under Lloyd George.

Among Cabinet Ministers below the salt, a precedent was created by the appointment of a civil servant as Secretary for War, Sir James Grigg being promoted to take charge of the department in which he had been Permanent Under-Secretary of State. Never before in the history of the civil service had a permanent official been promoted to succeed his political chief. Only a day or two previously the Army budget had been introduced by David Margesson, with whom his friends now sympathized on paying the penalty for having been too efficient a Chief Whip under Neville Chamberlain.

The completion of the Cabinet was attended by a minor incident. In response to suggestions from Australia that the voice of the Commonwealth should be heard, Churchill invited R. G. Casey, Australian Minister in Washington, to become a member of the Cabinet and to proceed to Cairo as Minister of State in the Middle East. The Prime Minister had sought to secure the consent of John Curtin, Prime Minister of the Commonwealth, but by some mischance in timing a broadcast announcement of the appointment was made before the request was received in Australia. It seemed that Curtin would pay Casey the compliment of insisting that he was irreplaceable at Washington, but the matter was put to rights. Churchill gained a valuable colleague, but he failed in his other purpose of pleasing Commonwealth opinion by selecting an Australian for the post.

Before the promised war debate took place there was ample time for the House to weigh the chief changes that had been made. They were commended on a variety of grounds. The Prime Minister was complimented for showing himself responsive to parliamentary opinion. He was praised for having replaced a War Cabinet that had become unwieldly with a superior instrument that should give a new impetus to the war effort. Critics of the old administration were assured that the main points for which they contended had been conceded to them. Members of the House were given the further assurance that they had strengthened the Prime Minister's hands.

Certainly there was general satisfaction, though hardly for the reasons so ingeniously assigned. Democracy from time to time appreciates a political shake-up. Loyalty in politics is a quality not rated so highly by the many as by Winston Churchill. In the old days it might not have been edifying when Lloyd George had parted company with ministerial failures, but the multitude had been diverted by the fireworks that so frequently enlivened their departure.

There was no mistaking the alteration in the mood of the House when the debate began on February 25. It was made manifest in the cordial cheer that greeted the Prime Minister as he rose to make his statement on events. He gave the House his own view of the merits of the changes he had effected, reiterating his opinion that a War Cabinet composed entirely of Ministers without departments was neither practicable nor convenient. In other respects the similarity with the Lloyd regime was fairly close.

> It is now the fashion [he went on] to speak of the Lloyd George War Cabinet as if it gave universal satisfaction and conducted the war with unerring judgment and unbroken success. On the contrary, complaints were loud and clamant. Immense disasters, such as the slaughter of Passchendaele, the disaster at Caporetto in 1917, the destruction of the Fifth Army after March 21, 1918—all these and others befell that rightly famous administration. It made numerous serious mistakes. No one was more surprised than its members when the end of the war came suddenly, in 1918, and there have even been criticisms about the character of the peace which was signed and celebrated in 1919. Therefore we, in this difficult period, have other calls upon us besides that of living up slavishly to the standards and methods of the past, instructive and on the whole encouraging as they unquestionably are.

By the time of this debate echoes of the controversies in which Churchill had been engaged with his military advisers had reached the outer fringe of politics. Differing from normal experience, the sound grew with the distance traveled. No one ventured to say that he personally had spoken to a general who made complaint, but the political hacks had their own methods of propaganda. To remove misunderstandings Churchill devoted much of his speech to clarifying his position as Minister of Defense:

> At the time when I was called upon by the King to form the present Government, we were in the throes of the German invasion of France and the Low Countries. I did not expect to be called upon to act as Leader of the House of Commons. I therefore sought His Majesty's permission to create and assume the style or title of Minister of Defense, because obviously the position of Prime Minister in war is inseparable from the general supervision of its conduct and the final responsibility for its result. I intended at that time that Mr. Neville Chamberlain should become Leader of the House and take the whole of the House of Commons work off my hands. This proposal was not found to be acceptable. I had myself to take the leadership of the House as well as my other duties.

I must admit that this parliamentary task has weighed upon me heavily. During the period for which I have been responsible I find, to my horror, that I have made more than twenty-five lengthy speeches to Parliament, in public or in secret session, to say nothing of answering a great number of questions and dealing with many current emergencies. I have greatly valued the honor of leading the House, which my father led before me, and in which my public life has been spent for so long; and I have always taken the greatest trouble to give it the best possible service, and even in very rough periods I have taken most particular care of its rights and interest. Although I feel a great sense of relief in laying down this burden, I cannot say that I do so without sorrow. I am sure, however, it is in the public interest.

Let me now speak of the office, or title, which I hold as Minister of Defense. First of all, there is nothing which I do or have done as Minister of Defense which I could not do as Prime Minister.

There is, of course, no Ministry of Defense, and the three Service departments remain autonomous. For the purpose of maintaining general supervision over the conduct of the war—which I do under the authority of the War Cabinet and the Defense Committee—I have at my disposal a small staff, headed by Major General Ismay, which works under the long-established procedure and machinery of the prewar Committee of Imperial Defense and forms a part of the War Cabinet secretariat.

While I take constitutional responsibility for everything that is done or not done, and am quite ready to take the blame when things go wrong—as they very often do, and as they are very likely to do in future, in many ways—I do not, of course, conduct this war from day to day myself. It is conducted from day to day, and in its future outlook, by the Chiefs of Staff Committee, namely the First Sea Lord, the Chief of the Imperial General Staff and the Chief of the Air Staff. These officers sit together every day, and often twice a day. They give executive directions and orders to the commanders in chief in the various theatres. They advise me, they advise the Defense Committee and the War Cabinet, on large questions of war strategy and war policy.

Each of the three Chiefs of Staff has the professional executive control of the Service he represents. When, therefore, they meet together, they are not talking in a vacuum, or in theory. They meet togther in a position to take immediate and responsible action, in which each can carry out his share, either singly or in combination. I do not think there has ever been a system in which the professional heads of the fighting Services have had a freer hand or a greater or more direct influence, or have received more constant and harmonious support from the Prime Minister and the Cabinet under which they serve.

It is my practice to leave the Chiefs of Staff alone to do their own work, subject to my general supervision, suggestion, and guidance. For instance, in 1941, out of 462 meetings of the Chiefs of Staff Committee, most of them lasting over two hours, I presided at only forty-four myself. In addition, however, there are, of course, the meetings of the Defense Committee, at which the Service Ministers are present, as well as other ministerial members, and there are the Cabinet meetings at which the Chiefs of Staff are present when military matters are discussed. In my absence from this country, or should I be at any time incapacitated, my deputy has acted and will act for me.

Such is the machinery which, as Prime Minister and Minister of Defense, I have partly elaborated and partly brought into existence. I am satisfied that it is the best that can be devised to meet the extraordinary difficulties and dangers through which we are passing. There is absolutely no question of making any change in it of a serious or fundamental character as long as I retain the confidence of the House and of the country.

The debate that followed the Prime Minister's statement was different in tone and temper from what had been expected during the crisis of seven days before. Then, tension almost reached the point of a quarrel between the House and the Prime Minister as to the structure of the Cabinet and the functions of its members. Reconstitution of the Government had taken the sting out of the Westminster air.

The pages of *Hansard* with their full record of two days of speeches well repay study for the light they shed on the work of a parliamentary assembly under the stress of war. The responsibilities of the M.P.s in time of national crisis are heavy. In the final reckoning theirs is the responsibility for the proper discharge of affairs. Elected by the nation, it is their corporate will that makes and unmakes Ministries.

As Robert Denman observed, the House stood very high in the list of forces capable of losing the war. The regrettable ill feeling of the previous week, were it to become general, would endanger the success of the war effort. The House should, he advised, show less willingness to reflect immediately the agitations outside it, and the Government should show greater rapidity in understanding what House members were seeking.

The debate was discursive. Some M.P.s talked strategy and some spoke of the reconstruction. The widely ranging choice of subjects passed from civil defense to India, scientists in wartime, propaganda, the shortcomings of the BBC, an Empire going to the dogs, and working men to dog races. Many speakers drew attention to faults and failures in various parts of the national machine, but criticism for the most part was constructive. The speeches of which the sole intent was to vilify the Prime

Minister and his colleagues stood out by contrast with the general tone.

James Maxton, half a party in his own person, welcomed the appointment of Stafford Cripps but doubted whether he could make good the loss in the Cabinet of the two capable but differing personalities of Beaverbrook and Greenwood. This double duty was the task for a giant. Maxton also had doubts about the choice of James Grigg for the War Office. It seemed to be bringing a new element into the civil service which the British had prided themselves on keeping out.

Other speakers took up the point. Sir Alfred Knox, with the rank of Major General, did not appear to be able to bring himself to give Grigg the title of his new office. "I ask the new official in charge of the War Office," was the Major General's periphrasis.

Hore-Belisha deplored Margesson's departure from the War Office ("he loved the Army and served it with a genuine faith") and regretted the passing of Beaverbrook ("at the time of the Battle of Britain his genius manifested itself in an infinite capacity for making planes").

Garfield Weston devoted a maiden speech to regretting the departure from the Ministry of his fellow countryman and great Canadian, Lord Beaverbrook, whose courage, tenacity and drive would be missed. "We are told," he said, "that he has gone because he has asthma. He has had asthma for twenty years and, if asthma does to a man what it has done to him, I would enjoy the experience of hearing every Honorable Member coughing so vigorously that no one would hear a word I am saying."

Vernon Bartlett would have liked to see Lloyd George in the War Cabinet—an omission, as I have explained, that was due to the refusal of the veteran of World War I to accept the invitation extended to him by the leader in World War II.

Major Vyvyan Adams protested that the war would not be won by periodic explosions against the Prime Minister. No one was indispensable, least of all in a democracy, but Winston Churchill was as nearly irreplaceable as any man had ever been. "Whereas," said the Major, "it was our duty to displace his predecessor, our present leader is to the Allies the epitome of British determination. He is a terror to our enemies. It is a crime to seek to weaken the authority of the Prime Minister."

With this expression of opinion Winston Churchill was in cordial agreement. One thing was certain. He would suffer no abridgment of his authority. Rather than accept the separation of the Defense Ministry from his office as Prime Minister he would resign within the hour.

Criticism of the Government's failures was at this time to be read on every bookstall. The field for faultfinding was so wide. The urgencies of war threw up the shortcomings in national affairs. Men of patriotic purpose thought it their duty to protest so that the wrong might be put right. Ministers with the burden of responsibility to bear grew resentful of perpetual prodding.

Churchill in those days developed a sensitiveness to criticism scarcely to have been expected of one outspoken in his criticism of others. It was understandable that he should be strained by the burden of his responsibilities, his endurance taxed by continuing tension on the rack of anxiety, living, as he did, with the daily knowledge of how small was the margin of national survival.

Devoting himself with consecrated purpose to the cause, he looked for support unqualified and unlimited not merely for himself but for members of his team. To him in person it was given. In the popular mind the hero's aura was about him. But not even his standing with the people could confer any immunity from reproach upon his Ministers.

The people conceived of Winston Churchill as the embodiment of England. He spoke with the voice of England, expressed England's hopes and resolves. But by no stretch of imagination could his colleagues be regarded as coming within this magic circle.

There was restiveness because some of the foremost appeasers were Ministers of the Crown. There were elements of the old gang, signs of the old complacence. The survival of old failures gave an acid touch to criticism of muddle and mismanagement.

Churchill took it badly. Attacks on the way the Services were run were undermining the confidence the nation should place in its leaders. Criticism of Ministers was vicious and malignant. He expected men of good will to rally round as a patriotic duty. Some of the offenders were hauled before him from Fleet Street to be lectured on their iniquities— magnifying grievances, vilifying Ministers, creating distrust and generally "rocking the boat."

Executives of the *Daily Mirror* were singled out for a tirade of remonstrance. As the Prime Minister strode up and down the Cabinet Room at Number Ten, they heard themselves denounced as fifth columnists. They were threatened with prosecution or closing down. They thought it very hard to be thus attacked. They were one hundred per cent Churchill's men. In appeasement days the *Mirror* had provided Churchill with a newspaper platform, publishing his articles and endorsing his policy. Was this onslaught of reproach to be suffered because the paper urged the removal from the Ministry of appeasers and muddlers? Churchill was reminded of his own words in *The World Crisis:*

> There is no place for compromise in war. Clear leadership, violent action, rigid decisions one way or the other form the only path not only of victory, but of safety. The state cannot afford division or

hesitation at the executive center. To humor a distinguished man, to avoid a fierce dispute—nay, even to preserve the governing instrument itself cannot, except as an alternative to sheer anarchy, be held to justify half measures.

The publication of this passage beneath the heading CHURCHILL, YOU HAVE WARNED YOURSELF did nothing to reduce the Prime Minister's displeasure.[4] Dedicated as he was to encompassing the defeat of Hitler, he found it difficult to conceive that there could be any path to victory but the one he proposed to follow. He looked for complete unanimity among the people. That this unanimity did not always prevail perplexed and pained him.

CHAPTER EIGHT

DIFFERENCES OVER INDIA

1942

A S HE looked out upon the battlefronts, Winston Churchill was conscious, in those days, of being baffled by the turn events had taken. His ebullient spirits would rise in face of peril, no matter how menacing, but the series of reverses that had followed Pearl Harbor were harder to bear than danger's sudden challenge. The advent of the United States as a fighting ally, for which he had prayed with such earnestness, had been attended by calamities. Britain's position had deteriorated, and still misfortunes multiplied.

In the Atlantic the U-boat packs were ranging to within sight of the American coast, sinking ship after ship, the loss of oil tankers being so severe that the war effort was imperiled. It was a massacre by the U-boats, whose operations offshore were assisted by the lights of cities against which ships were silhouetted in clear profile. When the United States authorities ordered lights to be dimmed (the "brownout"), there were protests from Atlantic City to Florida that the tourist season would be ruined.[1]

In North Africa there had been a disastrous change of fortunes. Auchinleck had been driven back three hundred miles, with vast losses of tanks, stores and equipment. Churchill saw the ruin of his hopes and an end, for the time being, of his dream of ridding Africa of the enemy.

In the Far East the Japanese were sweeping on. The Dutch East Indies, Siam and British Malaya were engulfed, and the invaders were advancing from southern Burma. Japanese warships operated in the Indian

Ocean. Ceylon was bombed and India was menaced. The consequences would be incalculable were India to be cut off.

India proved a double problem—in defense and in politics. Hard pressed though they were with competing claims upon their resources, the members of the War Cabinet had by some means to provide men and munitions. And, many as were their preoccupations, they had to contrive a settlement of the political question. With the Japanese on the frontiers, the Indian peoples must be united behind the King-Emperor in resistance to the enemy. But there could be no unity while the politicians of the Congress Party were campaigning for release from the British yoke. Concerned only to advance their cause, the Congress leaders were ready to stand aside from the war, following the example of Gandhi. The extremists looked for Britain's defeat by the Axis powers. The masses were fertile soil for Japanese propaganda, with its specious advocacy of the New Order in the Far East. India's fighting races were magnificently loyal, but they needed to be backed by the masses in their millions.

Winston Churchill, a decade before, had devoted his implacable opposition to the Indian constitutional reforms. Now, under compelling pressure, he was constrained to submit proposals for self-government for an India already accorded the pledge of Dominion status. A new constitution had to be worked out, which was no task to be accomplished in a week, but, with the Japanese advancing, some interim arrangement must quickly be concluded. Indian opinion must for the present be satisfied with pledges that could be fully carried out only when peace came. Churchill had need to rise above his own past and to assure Indian opinion that his word and Britain's pledges were to be relied upon.

It was necessary that a prominent member of the Government should travel east to conduct the negotiations. No man could be more acceptable to the Indians, carrying the guarantee of personal sympathy with their aspirations, than the Lord Privy Seal, Stafford Cripps. He was asked to undertake the mission and, with habitual disdain of his own interests, he accepted without hesitation. In his position an ambitious, self-seeking politician would not have run the risk of undertaking a mission little likely to be attended with success or to advance him in public estimation.

Stafford Cripps then held an outstanding place among the politicians. Having been British Ambassador in Moscow, he was identified in popular opinion with the fighting Russians. There was no special achievement to his credit, but some of the reflected glory of the Red armies fell on him. He had the appearance of his qualities—austere, uncompromising, high-principled. Had he chosen to ride on the tide of his popularity he could have emerged as Churchill's rival, leader of a patriotic Opposition, as Edward Carson had been in the First World War, and potential Prime Minister. There were politicians who noted the way the wind was blowing and whispers were circulated. Churchill, it was hinted, had served his turn. He had done good service when Britain stood alone but no man was irreplaceable. Past achievements gave him no title to remain. Cripps would be a suitable successor.

It is not to be supposed that Sir Stafford was unconscious of these possibilities, but he gave no encouragement to those who might have backed him. He cared for none of these things, and it was with a contemptuous disregard for personal considerations that he volunteered to undertake the mission.

When he reached India on March 23, hopes ran high. The First World War had been followed by a settlement in Ireland. Would the Second World War bring a solution to India? The terms Cripps was empowered to offer provided for the setting up of a self-governing Dominion of India immediately upon the ending of the war. The future constitution would be evolved by a specially appointed body elected by the Indians themselves on the principle of proportional representation. The British Government would, by treaty with this constitution-making body, provide for the complete transfer of responsibility from British to Indian hands. Provinces of British India would have the right to contract out of the new Dominion and retain their existing status. For the immediate future the British declaration provided:

> During the critical period which now faces India and until the new constitution can be formed, His Majesty's Government must inevitably bear responsibility for and retain control and direction of the defense of India as part of their world war effort, but the task of organizing to the full the military, naval and material resources of India must be the responsibility of the Government of India with the cooperation of the peoples of India. His Majesty's Government desire and invite the immediate and effective participation of the leaders of the principal sections of the Indian peoples in the councils of their country, of the Commonwealth and of the United Nations. Thus they will be enabled to give their active and constructive help in the discharge of a task which is vital and essential for the future freedom of India.

It was this concluding passage of the declaration which formed the chief subject of the Cripps negotiations. The Congress leaders were not interested in self-government at some date in the future; that had been pledged to them in 1940. The immediate present was their concern. Were the Indian leaders asked to enter the Viceroy's Council, would they have the responsibility and powers of Ministers? And if that were accorded, then would an Indian Minister of Defense have authority over the war machine in India and over the commander in chief?

The Indian negotiators were by no means satisfied with the assurances they received on these points. Nevertheless they came near to acceptance of the British plan. Then, at the eleventh hour, when a successful outcome of the negotiations seemed assured, the Congress Working Committee rejected the declaration, a decision resulting from the intervention of Gandhi. The Committee had, by resolution, agreed to accept, but Gandhi pronounced otherwise and the Committee thereupon reversed its decision.

Negotiation is difficult against non-cooperation and non-compromise. To have granted Gandhi's demands as voiced by Congress would have brought chaos to India, a result of which Gandhi was himself desirous. "I tell the British to give us chaos," he proclaimed.

In his report on the failure of his mission, Stafford Cripps testified: "The action which Gandhi was threatening was calculated to endanger the Allied war effort and to bring the greatest aid and comfort to our common enemies. Mr. Gandhi was not prepared to wait. He would rather jeopardize freedom and the whole cause of the United Nations."

India was a subject on which American opinion was involved. It cast a shadow over the good relations between Prime Minister and President. Sharing the American feeling that British rule in India was a lamentable instance of British imperialism, Roosevelt had started to voice tendentious views on this matter at the Arcadia conference. He was discouraged from proceeding by the vigor of the Churchillian dissent and the subject was dropped.[2] But the claims of the Congress Party leaders were widely supported in the American newspapers and Churchill was in no position to ignore the effect on the harmony of Anglo-American relations. He was careful to keep the President posted about the moves he proposed and the progress of the Cripps mission. He received in return advice, suggestions and admonitions that taxed his forbearance.

Over their other differences Prime Minister and President preserved a good-humored give-and-take, but Churchill's feelings on India were deep-rooted. When Roosevelt suggested that the Indians might solve their problems on the lines of the American Constitution—this was recommended as being in line with half a century of democratic progress—Churchill exploded wrathfully. Did they imagine in Washington that their position as ally entitled them to handle this matter over the heads of the British Prime Minister and his colleagues?[3]

The war was bringing Americans into touch with affairs on which they had strong opinions but limited knowledge.[4] Churchill reflected ruefully on the gap between the limitations of his critics and his own knowledge of the diversity of creatures and conditions in the subcontinent. He thought of the India he knew, but which few of his American friends did, with its millions outnumbering the population of the United States, with peoples separated by race, creed and caste, by gulfs that were ancient and unbridgeable. He thought of the various Indians for which the noisy politicians of the Congress Party did not and could never speak—the India of the Moslems, of the Untouchables, and the Native States. There was the India of the politicians who for their own purpose were ready to encourage disorder and looting, bring transport to a standstill and hamper the country's defense. And there was the India he had known as a young officer, with its fighting races, on whom the defense of the land depended, races who were providing loyal troops for the King-Emperor, men whose bravery had already been shown on many battlefields.

When the Cripps negotiations broke down, the President intervened to press for a further attempt with an insistence that was coldly received in Downing Street. Churchill had submitted that everything had been done that tenacity and perseverance could contrive; it must be apparent that the British Government had been sincere in its professions for a settlement. Roosevelt bluntly commented that Americans would not be satisfied; the breakdown of the negotiations would have a prejudicial effect on opinion in the United States with which, it was apparent, he identified himself. He urged that forthwith a nationalist government should be constituted for India on the American model.[5]

To Churchill this was madness. To hand over India on those terms would be the way to anarchy and civil war, a betrayal of Britain's responsibilities. Here was a matter of duty on which there could be no wavering, not even to meet opinion in the United States. He wrote to the White House in terms of regret deploring the argument that had arisen —"anything like a serious difference between us would break my heart and would surely deeply injure both our countries." [6] So Prime Minister and President had to agree to disagree.

It was a melancholy ending to the Indian negotiations. Even the flicker of good will in Congress Party circles faded and non-cooperation degenerated into civil disobedience. The British Government declined Gandhi's invitation to walk out of India, which then, on the Mahatma's advice, would have offered no more than passive resistance to the Japanese. By the end of the summer the situation had so far deteriorated that for the preservation of order Gandhi and the Congress Party leaders were arrested and interned.

In his final message to the Indian people, before leaving for home, Stafford Cripps lamented the critical and unconstructive attitude which he had met—"natural enough for the law courts or the market place." He could feel, in common with the Prime Minister, the War Cabinet and the people at home, that all that could be done had been done.

Churchill, in a message of appreciation of the Lord Privy Seal's perseverance, observed: "Even though your hopes have not been fulfilled, you have rendered a very important service to the common cause, and the foundations have been laid for the future progress of the Indian people."

Churchill made a statement to the House of Commons on the Government's policy. In point of time it comes at a later date (September 10), but it is convenient to complete the record. His main purpose was to reassure Indian opinion that the British offer still held good despite the failure of the Cripps mission. He was also concerned to state the Government case in answer to American critics, who had deplored the internment of Gandhi and the Indian leaders. He said:

The Congress Party abandoned, in many respects, the policy of non-violence which Mr. Gandhi so long inculcated in theory, and has come into the open as a revolutionary movement, designed to paralyze communications and generally to promote disorder, the looting of shops and sporadic attacks upon the Indian police, accompanied, from time to time, by revolting atrocities—the whole having the intention or, at any rate, the effect of hampering the defense of India against the Japanese invaders who stand on the frontiers of Assam and also upon the eastern side of the Bay of Bengal. It may well be that these activities of the Congress Party have been aided by Japanese fifth-column work on a widely extended scale, and with special direction to strategic points. It is noteworthy, for instance, that the communications of the Indian forces defending Bengal on the Assam frontier have been specially attacked.

It is fortunate, indeed, that the Congress Party has no influence whatever with the martial races, on whom the defense of India, apart from British forces, largely depends. Many of these races are divided by unbridgeable religious gulfs from the Hindu Congress, and would never consent to be ruled by them. Nor shall they ever be against their will so subjugated.

India was to prove a continuing difference. While Churchill was nettled by Roosevelt's critical attitude, American opinion was exasperated by the Prime Minister's refusal to surrender British sovereignty. Senators told the President that he had a "Churchill complex"—he ought to turn on the heat, inform the Prime Minister that India was no longer Britain's exclusive business, and order the withdrawal of American support from that sector unless a reasonable measure of independence were conceded.[7]

Not until the war was over was the problem of India solved by the elaborate processes of partition—and the loss of half a million lives. These were no matters to have been embarked upon in the spring of 1942, with the Japanese penetrating through Burma. With their warships at large in the Indian Ocean, it seemed that Ceylon might be lost— and where then would the British warships be based? Already the sea lanes to India were in danger and communications threatened with the armies of the Nile.

Churchill's attention was directed to the island of Madagascar,[8] lightly held by the French. Were the Japanese to install themselves at this strategic point, establishing a base for their submarines, they would be able to paralyze the convoys proceeding off the coast of East Africa. He proposed that an expedition should be mounted to forestall the Japanese. The admirals supported him, the generals did not—it was a diversion that would delay the building up of land and air forces for the defense of India. From Field Marshal Smuts of South Africa, there came an urgent demand for action—Madagascar was the key to the Indian Ocean. It was decided to go ahead.

The operation, carefully planned and boldly executed, was immediately successful. After two days' resistance Diego Suarez, with its fine port, was occupied. Churchill could find satisfaction in the fact that he had initiated the first large-scale amphibious assault since the attack on Gallipoli a quarter of a century before. The torpedoing of the battleship *Ramillies* underlined the dangers to Allied shipping in those waters and the advantages gained from the occupation of Madagascar. Once again the Service advisers had reason to be satisfied that the Minister of Defense had overborne their objections.[9]

After the initial success, the expedition was able to deal with resistance at other centers in the island at their leisurely convenience, and several months passed before the final surrender of the French Governor General. This occupation of a French possession involved Churchill in one of his periodic clashes with de Gaulle. Like so many of his countrymen, the Free French leader was sensitive about his personal position and prestige, ceaselessly looking over his shoulder to see if he were accorded the recognition he demanded, wounded by the rebuffs he suffered, particularly at the hands of the Americans. Deeply offended at his exclusion from the Madagascar show, he poured out expostulations.[10]

Churchill devoted an hour to answering his accusations. The British, he said, had no ulterior motive in Madagascar. As to the future of the

French Empire: "I am the friend of France," he cried. "I have always wanted a great France with a great army."

When de Gaulle protested that Free French troops had not been engaged, Churchill used a phrase that had its appeal.

"You," he said, "are not my only ally."

For his hearer this was a most acceptable ranking, and it conveyed an explanation of the exclusion of his Free Frenchmen that conformed with de Gaulle's own conceptions. There was, as he was aware, no liking for him and his movement in Washington, where his activities had affronted the Secretary of State, Cordell Hull.[11] American views, he suspected, had had their influence on the Prime Minister. As de Gaulle saw it, Churchill, bowing "to the imperious necessities of the American alliance," had made it a rule never to do anything without Roosevelt's agreement.[12]

It was a mollified general who was escorted to the door of Number Ten. He left Downing Street to the sound of the cheering words: "I shan't desert you, you can count on me."

India was a new complication in the allocation of supplies. Russian needs must be met, and Churchill would not hear of cutting down consignments. Auchinleck required a continual flow of men, munitions and tanks to hold Rommel. Wavell was clamoring for planes for India— there were only a dozen squadrons in that country where seventy were needed.[13] Churchill had consistently vetoed proposals to strengthen the Far East at the expense of the Desert Army but, with Calcutta and the plains of Bengal naked to the enemy, forces for Wavell had to be found. They could be provided only from North Africa and some weakening of Egypt's defenses had to be accepted. With these problems to face, Churchill was required to be in almost permanent session with the Chiefs of Staff. Since Dill's departure for Washington there had been a lowering of the previous tension and Alan Brooke, having proved his capacity, was advanced to be chairman of the Chiefs of Staff Committee.

The burdens borne by the Minister of Defense did not earn for him remission from the attention of his political opponents. From their columns in the press and their chairs in the clubs the critics kept up their fire. The political sharpshooters were busy in the House. From the background of the War Office an occasional general slyly dipped his oar into the troubled waters of politics.

The central direction of the war was now the target for debate. When the constitution of the Cabinet had been under attack, the technique had been to applaud the captain and to assail the team. Now the method was changed—the captain had too great a burden upon his shoulders and therefore he should divest himself of some of his responsibilities. Two arguments were advanced—that the post of Defense Minister should be divorced from that of Prime Minister and that the Prime Minister should no longer preside over the Chiefs of Staff Committee.

It might be suspected that the critics had been turning up their histories of the previous war to find their inspiration for this line of attack on the Prime Minister. It was on this very issue that Asquith fell from power in 1916. There had then been acute dissatisfaction over the manner in which the War Committee had been functioning. Lloyd George finally presented Asquith with the demand that the conduct of the war should be assigned to a committee of three, including L. G. himself, but excluding the Prime Minister, who would have been left with the titular role while Lloyd George had the power and responsibility. Asquith, declining to agree, lost power and title.

Lord Chatfield, former First Sea Lord and Minister for the Coordination of Defense, drew attention to Churchill's constitutional responsibilities as Minister of Defense. Thereby he provided the critics with a target for their attacks on what was termed Churchill's irresponsibility. Addressing his fellow peers, Chatfield remarked that, having removed the Service Ministers from the War Cabinet, the Prime Minister could have technical consultations on strategy with the Chiefs of Staff and Service Ministers outside the Cabinet and could then go to the War Cabinet with his determined mind made up. He would become not only the advocate of his own decisions but, as Prime Minister, the final arbiter on whether a decision was to be agreed to or not. How could they expect others in the Cabinet to criticize what was recommended by the powerful advocacy of that wonderful man? Julius Caesar at his best and Napoleon could never have attempted to run a war of such magnitude, to conduct armies, navies and air force as well. There should be a separate Defense Minister.

The case for the establishment of what its supporters termed a Great (or Combined) General Staff was presented in the House of Commons by Sir Edward Grigg (later Lord Altrincham). He argued that the elaborate machinery of the Chiefs of Staff was not producing the balanced strategy or coordination of strength by sea, land, and in the air, which the exacting task ahead demanded.

As a means of removing misapprehensions about the functions of the Chiefs of Staff and of his own part in the planning of war strategy, the Prime Minister issued a White Paper on "The Organization for Joint Planning." It repeated the information he had given to the House in the recent debate and enlarged upon it. After the White Paper came the debates, from which it emerged that the misapprehensions had not been removed from some minds; or alternatively that the White Paper had furnished new ammunition for the critics.

The peers led the way. Lord Denman opened a debate calling for the setting up of a high command which could "plan the war as a whole." Lord Addison considered the White Paper arrangements to be "cumbrous and complicated." Lord Hankey, who had been primed by inside information, asserted that the chief weakness in the War Cabinet's machinery was over-centralization at the top. He also voiced the complaint against the hours kept by the Defense Minister.

The point was taken up by Chatfield. "I have had representations made to me by those who work in Whitehall," he said, "that the hours they are made to keep are perfectly intolerable. It does not lead to efficiency. Nobody is at his best in the Middle Watch."

The generals were delighted. They did not expect there would be a change of habits, but at least the grievance had been aired. Churchill did bring one meeting to an early close with the remark that otherwise "Lord Hankey will be after us," but he continued to draw guidance from nocturnal consultations with colleagues and advisers.[14]

A few days later the Commons gave their opinions. Some critics attacked the machinery and some, with less evasion and more courage, the man in charge of the machine. It is difficult now—it was difficult enough at the time—to understand how some of the opinions expressed could have passed as serious contributions to a national debate. The simple fact was that the means to defend what were once called Britain's "far-flung possessions" had not in the years before the war been provided. Britain had tried to run an Empire on the cheap and the forfeit had been claimed. Overlooking omissions for which they shared the responsibility, the captious, the envious, the office-seekers, and the ragtag and bobtail of politics found a stick conveniently at hand for belaboring the Defense Minister.

Neither setbacks in the field nor pinpricks in the House could now disturb the Prime Minister in his confident expectations of the future. With Allies to the west and east he was clothed in an assurance of ultimate success that was proof against the slings of passing misfortune. The second anniversary of his premiership gave him the opportunity, in a broadcast talk, to count the gains in the national balance sheet (May 10, 1942). He dwelt with pride on the honor that had befallen him:

> It fell to me in those days to express the sentiments and resolves of the British nation in that supreme crisis of its life; that was to me an

honor far beyond any dreams or ambitions I had ever nursed, and it is one that cannot be taken away.

All the world, even our best friends, thought that the end had come and we, united in that majestic hour, prepared to conquer or perish. Then it was that the tyrant made a fatal blunder, for dictators as well as democracies and parliamentary governments make mistakes sometimes.

Hitler's first mistake was the invasion of Russia. His second grand blunder was that he forgot about the winter. There is a winter, you know, in Russia. Hitler forgot. He must have been very loosely educated. I have never made such a bad mistake as that.

He added that no one could say how many ill-clad Germans perished in Russia and its snows and the valiant Russian counterattacks. Certainly more perished than were killed in the whole four and a quarter years of the last war—a statement that sent many to the history books to find that the total German losses from 1914 to 1918 were two million killed and four million wounded.

He spoke of the toll that the RAF was inflicting on the Germans. The raids were still on a modest scale compared with the blows that were to come (the first 1,000-bomber raid on Cologne in that month of May taxed the capacity of Bomber Command), but they were mounting in strength—a form of warfare which, as the Prime Minister put it, should, according to the German view, be the strict monopoly of the *Herrenvolk*. In September, 1940, Hitler had boasted that he would "rub out" British towns and villages. Now the boot was on the other foot and Hitler had even called in question the humanity of these grim developments of war. It was a pity that his conversion had not taken place before he bombed Warsaw, or massacred twenty thousand Dutch folk in defenseless Rotterdam, or wreaked his cruel vengeance on the open city of Belgrade. Now it was the other way round.

> Though the mills of God grind slowly yet they grind exceeding small. And for my part I hail it as an example of sublime and poetic justice that those who have loosed these horrors upon mankind will now in their homes and persons feel the shattering strokes of just retribution.

The civil population of Germany had an easy way to escape from these severities. All they needed to do was to leave the cities where munitions work was being carried on—abandon their work, go out into the fields, and watch their home-fires burning from a distance. Churchill suggested grimly:

> In this way, they may find time for meditation and repentance.

There, they may remember the millions of Russian women and children they have driven out to perish in the snows, and the mass executions of peasantry and prisoners of war which, on varying scales, they are inflicting upon so many of the ancient and famous peoples of Europe.

He warned the Germans against resorting to the use of poison gas as they had done in the First World War. The Soviet Government had suggested that the Germans, in their desperation, might employ gas against the armies and people of Russia.

> We ourselves [he said] are firmly resolved not to use this odious weapon unless it is first used by the Germans. Knowing our Hun, however, we have not neglected to make preparations on a formidable scale. I wish to make it plain that we shall treat the unprovoked use of poison gas against our Russian ally exactly as if it were used against ourselves. If we are satisfied that this new outrage has been committed by Hitler we shall use our great and growing air superiority in the West to carry gas warfare on the largest possible scale far and wide against military objectives in Germany.

This warning, inspired by Russia's fears, drew a message of appreciation from Stalin. It was also the cause of some mutterings in Service circles. Did not the Prime Minister realize that the cities of the United Kingdom, with their dense population, were a more vulnerable target than anything in Germany?[15] To assist his ally, Churchill would have faced the consequences.

CHAPTER NINE

SECOND FRONT—THE DEBATE

MARCH–JUNE, 1942

Wᴵᴛʜ the Americans belligerent in their own right, the pressure was intensified to get to grips with the Germans on the battlefronts. Here the Washington planners were at one with Churchill in his impatience to engage the enemy. The problem was: Where?

It was a fundamental question, and, receiving two answers, it set going a sharp debate, with British and American staffs at odds, their opinions stoutly pressed. Prime Minister and President were involved and there would have been a rift in the alliance had not reasonableness in time prevailed.

Is there to be a Second Front in Europe in 1942? That was the question posed. Churchill, replying, "No, we are not yet strong enough," provoked American reproaches and resentment. Later, when the fighting was over and the arguments of history began, he was attacked, exposed to much misrepresentation and some vilification. He was accused of being reluctant (even fearful) to invade France at any time. Echoes of these imaginary tales linger yet.

The first Washington conference was not long ended before the American strategists got busy. It seemed that the original plan of campaign for 1942 had fallen through. At the Arcadia conference a joint expedition to North Africa had been agreed (Operation "Gymnast"), but this was lapsing for lack of ships.[1] With "Gymnast" out there would be no target for attack. The blank in the program was filled by an Army officer then almost unknown—Dwight D. Eisenhower. A plan for an American line-up in favor of France as the immediate field for operations in the West was the first impact on Allied affairs that Eisenhower produced. Summoned to the War Department, to take charge of the newly created Operations Division, his appointed task was to find the means for bringing to bear the maximum American force against the Germans.

Having taken a pasting at the hands of the Japanese, and being conscious of their reserves of strength, the Americans sought the chance to prove themselves, to restore their reputation and their self-confidence. They wished to engage the enemy in Europe at the earliest practicable moment. Eisenhower soon reached decisive conclusions. American resources must not be frittered away on side shows and diversions. They must concentrate on slugging the Germans in their own land, first from the air and, as quickly as could be, by invasion.

The shortest way from America was to northern Europe with Britain as the front-line base. The map showed the route across the Channel for subsequent operations in the general area of Calais–Arras–Paris, and a port at Antwerp. The strategic outline prepared by Eisenhower and his group was considered by General Marshall.[2] He was impressed by the design and the vision of Allied invaders supported by fleets of aircraft engaged in their thousands in battering down German resistance. These aircraft in overpowering numbers (but still nonexistent) were an essential feature of the Eisenhower plan.

"This," pronounced Marshall, "this is it. I approve."

At first the President was dubious. He was still held by the idea of the Mediterranean operation,[3] but under the influence of his advisers, notably Henry Stimson,[4] Secretary of War, he came to give the Eisenhower scheme his support.

Churchill was informed of the change of views in Washington. "I am becoming more and more interested," read a cable from F.D.R., "in the establishment of a new front this summer." General Marshall and Harry Hopkins came bustling to London to secure British approval, a preliminary, as the President wrote, to informing Stalin of what was afoot: "It is my hope that the Russians will greet these plans with enthusiasm."

Marshall and Hopkins presented a memorandum of the design for an invasion early in 1943 by a force of 48 divisions (three armored), supported by 5,800 aircraft and transported by 7,000 landing craft. This project came to be known as "Roundup." An emergency landing might be required in 1942 to avert a Russian collapse; it would be on a smaller but still substantial scale. In the guise of an attack on Cherbourg[5] or Brest this was called "Sledgehammer."

Churchill spoke in ready acceptance of the ideas that were put before him. It was gratifying that the Allies were intending to strike against the Germans with their total strength. With the American staffs present, a full meeting of the Defense Committee was held on April 14, at which the Prime Minister welcomed what he termed a momentous proposal. It was the framework; the details remained to be filled in. But the defense of India and the Middle East called for the employment of Britain's immediate resources. Indeed, it would require all available resources from both sides of the Atlantic to prevent a link-up between Japanese and Germans. There was also Australia needing yet further protection, that only the United States could accord, against invasion by the Japanese. Meanwhile, in principle, he agreed that preparations for the joint invasion in 1943 should proceed.

Roosevelt was delighted to learn that unanimity of opinion prevailed and he hurried off a cable to Stalin: "I have in mind very important military proposal involving the mobilization of our armed forces in a manner to relieve your critical front; this objective carries great weight with me." Stalin must have been more than gratified to receive the assurance.

American enthusiasm was not shared by the British Staffs. Alan Brooke was apprehensive about the calamitous chances, and his fears grew on discovering that American planning had scarcely advanced beyond the landing stage. What was then to be done when the troops were ashore, whether to aim east or south, had scarcely been considered. The future problems of maintaining the expedition, against an enemy able to reinforce with double the speed, did not seem to have been studied.[6] The chances of success were small, of defeat illimitable.

Harry Hopkins, sensing that British backing for the scheme was less than wholehearted, pressed upon the Prime Minister that the President was ready to take great risks to bring relief to the Red armies. It would be a mistake for approbation to be given on the assumption that the assault was not possible for at least a year. President and American people were at one—"our men must fight"—and northwest Europe was the one immediate battleground available.[7]

On this point the Nazi propaganda services made an ironical comment. Deducing from the presence of high-ranking Americans in London that an invasion of the Continent was being considered, they issued a radio invitation to the British to come over in the greatest possible numbers. The Fuehrer was ready to evacuate any part of the Continent to permit them to get ashore without difficulty! [8]

The American visitors had not long returned across the Atlantic before it was seen that the London agreement had been based on differences in outlook and emphasis. Churchill, thinking of landings in Europe at a later date, looked for the North African operation "Gymnast") to be undertaken in 1942. The Americans required all-out concentration on landings in Europe, with a beginning in 1942.

The more "Sledgehammer" came under scrutiny the less did Churchill like it—it was beyond Allied capacity to carry out. His doubts, however, needed to be diplomatically conveyed. Already he was at loggerheads with the President over India and he did not wish to enlarge the field of their differences.

While matters were poised in uncertainty, the Russians brought the urgency of their pressure to bear. Public opinion at home strongly supported the call—"Second Front Now." Clamorous crowds in Albert Hall and Trafalgar Square demanded action. At Westminster, many M.P.s were infected by the aid-Russia spirit. Once again Churchill pressed on his reluctant Staffs his idea for a Norwegian landing. A successful operation among the northern fiords would at least reduce the dangers for British convoys to Murmansk.

Supplies for Russia were transported by the Arctic route at the price of losses that were appalling. Each convoy was a major naval operation, with the battleship *Tirpitz* to be guarded against, as well as the marauding U-boats. Losses mounted to as high as twenty-two ships in a convoy of thirty-three, their crews exposed to death by freezing in those icy waters. Lend-Lease deliveries fell inevitably behind. Churchill had to face a double barrage of protest—from Stalin direct, and from Stalin via the President.

Roosevelt urged that, despite the risks, additional escorts should be provided to force the convoys through. It was more than could be undertaken. "I can assure you, Mr. President, that we are absolutely extended," Churchill replied. "With very great respect what you suggest, is beyond our power to fulfill." [9]

In May, Churchill experienced Russian entreaties at first hand when Soviet Foreign Minister Molotov arrived in London (May 20). He was received as an honored guest, the Prime Minister's country home being placed at his disposal. Chequers is a haunt of quiet peace in the heart of Buckinghamshire, but the Soviet visitors regarded it as a potential danger spot, deeming it necessary to sleep with pistols beneath their pillows.[10]

Molotov had come over to sign an Anglo-Soviet agreement that, he hoped, would accord British recognition for postwar Russian frontiers. This was refused him. Instead he was offered a twenty-year treaty of alliance with Britain, and this was concluded. Molotov was also charged to obtain a decision on the Second Front. In what manner, he demanded, did the British propose to aid the Red armies by drawing off at least forty German divisions from the East?

Sympathetic as he was, Churchill would enter into no firm commitment. Instead, he gave the Russian a lecture on strategy, trying to bring him to an understanding of the difficulties of a cross-Channel invasion.[11] Trained troops and shipping were insufficient for a landing in 1942 in such strength as to draw back German divisions from the Eastern Front.

Since Russian expectations had been aroused by Roosevelt's cables to the Kremlin, the Prime Minister's statements came as a damper. It was agreed that Molotov should cross the Atlantic to explore possibilities in Washington. Thereafter, he would return to London for final discussions.

There is no record of Molotov having been in a jocund mood, but during his stay in America he unbent with rarely displayed cordiality. He set himself to please and flatter his host. In the Soviet Union, he said, the President was popular because of his clear understanding of the interests and needs of his people and the farsightedness with which he pursued them. The President's statesmanship in the handling of international affairs was another subject for praise. Stalin was represented as sharing Roosevelt's ideas for the postwar world and disarmament.[12]

Good will having thus been fostered, Molotov posed his crucial inquiry: "What is the President's answer with respect to the Second Front? What reply shall I take back to Moscow?"

To this the President gave the answer that he expected a Second Front to be established in 1942. British staff officers were imminently due in Washington, with whom it was planned to arrive at an agreement on the creation of a Second Front. With this assurance, several times repeated, Molotov seemed to be content. He left with all the appearances of cordiality and a presentation copy of the Presidential photograph.[13]

Molotov's satisfaction would have been substantially less had Roosevelt added the information that the British visitors, headed by Admiral Mountbatten, had been sent across the Atlantic to express Churchill's sense of doubt. "Dickie will explain to you the difficulties for 1942 when he arrives"—such was the heralding cable Churchill had sent to the President six days before Molotov reached the United States. In it Churchill brought up once more the subject of North Africa: "We must never let 'Gymnast' pass from our minds." The cable made its mark in Washington. It provided, according to White House observers, "the first danger signal" to Roosevelt and his associates that the British were "veering away from the attack across the Channel."[14]

The discussions with Molotov, made expectant by the encouragement he had received in Washington, had now to be completed in London.

His expectations were again disappointed. British staff discussions on "Sledgehammer" had produced nothing but difficulties. Less than ever was Churchill prepared to commit himself. It was finally agreed (June 11) to issue a communiqué recording that, "In the course of the conversations full understanding was reached with regard to the urgent task of creating a Second Front in Europe in 1942." But "understanding" fell short of agreement. To establish the British position beyond doubt, Churchill handed to the Russians, then in the Cabinet Room at Number Ten, an *aide-mémoire* stating: "It is impossible to say in advance whether the situation will be such as to make the operation feasible when the time comes. We can therefore give no promise in the matter, but provided it appears sound and sensible we shall not hesitate to put our plans into effect." It was not encouraging for the Russians, but it could not mislead them.[15]

There followed a further stiffening of the Prime Minister's objections to cross-Channel adventures in 1942. He was much disturbed by the report brought back from Washington by Mountbatten. The President had spoken of a "sacrifice" landing, meaning by "sacrifice" an emergency operation made necessary to aid the Russians, a life-saver for a drowning ally. The idea of sacrificing British and American lives in an unavailing effort roused Churchill's indignation.[16] Even were there a cry of despair from Russia, what would it serve to throw some few divisions on to the French shores only to re-embark them? It would entail the loss of valuable lives for no better purpose than to make the Allies and their capacity for waging war ridiculous throughout the world. Were the Russians in dire straits it would not help them "for us to come a cropper on our own." He set down two guiding principles:

No substantial landing in France unless we are going to stay.

No substantial landing in France [in 1942] unless the Germans are demoralized by another failure in Russia.

So important did he conceive the matter to be that, having secured the concurrence of the Chiefs of Staff, he placed his guiding principles before members of the War Cabinet, who endorsed them.[17]

Churchill ruled out Operation "Sledgehammer" for 1942 because it was not possible to mount it. There were neither the trained men nor the ships to transport them. At the most there could be in 1942 no more than ten British divisions trained to invasion pitch and two American—twelve divisions against which the Germans could oppose the twenty-five divisions permanently stationed in France.[18] As for shipping, movement at sea was already constricted by shortages. Construction was not keeping pace with sinkings, losses at one time exceeding replacements by as much as 2½ to 1. Of landing craft there were sufficient to put no more than 4,000 troops ashore in one wave. How was it possible to make good these deficiencies before the weather broke in the autumn? There was, in Churchill's view, no need to argue against "Sledgehammer" in 1942; it fell by its own weakness.[19]

Meanwhile, for the guidance of the planners, he set down (June 15) his own ideas for the invasion of Europe in the year 1943.[20] His purpose was not to provide a blueprint for the assault, but rather to indicate the scale and spirit of the operation. No lightweight engagement, it would be backed within a week by 400,000 men and, within two weeks, by 700,000. In the magnitude of the operation, and the strength to strike the sledgehammer blows, he reached to a realization of the resources ultimately to be employed against Hitler's citadel. The way to burst into France was not to match twelve divisions against twenty-five, but to employ an army prodigious in strength that would submerge resistance. Unless immense forces were committed, then this operation should not, he pronounced, be attempted.[21]

It was in these days that Churchill issued his celebrated directive that was the genesis of the floating harbors for the Normandy beaches. Addressed to the Chief of Combined Operations and dated May 30, 1942, it concluded:

PIERS FOR USE ON BEACHES

They must float up and down with the tide. The anchor problem must be mastered. Let me have the best solution worked out. Don't argue the matter. The difficulties will argue for themselves.

From the researches thus inspired there resulted the "Mulberry" (in its code name), the floating landing stage, fabricated at home and ferried across the Channel for use on the Normandy coast on the occasion of the invasion.[22]

With the program for 1942 still undecided, and the President tending to get "off the rails," Churchill concluded that he must once again cross the Atlantic. In his own mind he had dismissed "Sledgehammer" for 1942 and was looking for action in Africa. Among his allies different notions prevailed. With the Germans threatening the Caucasus, the Russians were buoyed by their expectations of a Second Front. Neither had the American Staffs yielded in their opinions—after all, they were not as they asserted, training their men to play tiddlywinks. "A second front?" asked Hopkins rhetorically. "Yes, and if necessary a third and fourth front." [23] This was no time for disputes at a distance and Churchill prepared for a second ocean crossing by air. Before leaving it was thought necessary that he should name his successor, against the possibility of his being killed. It was a constitutional innovation.

The appointment of First Minister of the Crown rests with the Sovereign, who does not necessarily consult an outgoing Prime Minister concerning the choice of his successor. There was no precedent for a Minister still serving in office to offer advice on this delicate question, but war breaks with tradition and makes its own precedents. Better that than the evils of a disputed political succession. So, in accordance with the royal suggestion, Churchill wrote to King George VI advising that "in case of my death on this journey I am about to undertake," Anthony Eden should be invited to form a government. Eden was recommended as the outstanding Minister in the largest political party in the House of Commons, one "with the resolution, experience, and capacity which these grievous times require." Anthony Eden was the colleague with whom Churchill had formed the closest association, a man whose judgment on affairs he considered to be close to his own. They were to continue in harmonious partnership until the mantle fell on Eden's shoulders thirteen years after he had been named Churchill's political heir presumptive.[24]

Departure for Washington was delayed by bad news from the desert. Rommel had beaten Auchinleck to the attack, outfighting the British in the battles of Gazala, Knightsbridge, and Acroma. The 30th Armored Corps lost 230 out of its 300 medium tanks, and Auchinleck had fallen back on Egypt. Churchill was relieved to know that the frontier fortifications were held and that, at all costs, it was intended to retain Tobruk, with its well-tested defenses.[25] Thus assured, he left by flying boat (June 17) with a small party that included Alan Brooke, who was savoring the satisfaction of his initiation in summit discussions. Twenty-seven hours later the plane landed on the Potomac, the pilot, pursuant to Churchill's reminder, scrupulously avoiding the Washington Monument as he came down.

A short flight the following morning brought Churchill to the Roosevelt family home at Hyde Park. The two men got down straightway to business in the car. F.D.R. drove an apprehensive passenger on the heights above the Hudson River, for the President, by reason of his disability, was unable to employ more than his arms for driving.[26] The question of atomic research was the first to be tackled. It was soon disposed of. Prime Minister and President, with Harry Hopkins assisting, reached the agreement to pool research and share results. It was a hush-hush agreement, the top secret of the war.

After a meeting of minds, extending over a day in the isolation of Hyde Park, the two principals were ready to proceed with the business at Washington. Their arrival was awaited in nervous expectation by the Joint Staffs, American and British alike. They were two men whose moves were incalculable. When they got together there was no telling what they might be brewing. The Americans feared the President might be going to "jump the traces." Alan Brooke was disposed to expect the worst, though his anxieties for the moment were divided between strategy and his own sartorial shortcomings.[27] Caught off his guard, he had to present himself to the President in mufti instead of in his newly ordered uniform, but F.D.R. was so charming about it that all was well.

"Sledgehammer," or Second Front, was the chief item on the agenda for their Joint Staffs. It produced some sharp speaking on both sides, "a good deal of powwow, and a rumpus," with Churchill contributing to the rumpus.

Even before the Prime Minister reached their shores the American advocates of "Sledgehammer" had been prepared for a tussle. They had noted the portents from Downing Street, the emphasis on the difficulties of 1942, the references to "Gymnast." These were taken as danger signals —the Prime Minister was veering away from France toward diversionary landings.

There were signs that the President was not to be relied upon and that he might go off on "a wild kind of dispersion debauch." Henry Stimson, Secretary of War, sought to infuse the President with some of his own enthusiasm for "Sledgehammer," the "brain child of the United States Army." This essentially American project had been brought forward as the "vitalizing contribution of our fresh unwearied leaders and forces," and Stimson was shocked to detect any Presidential weakening.[28]

"The only hope I have about it all," he reflected, rather despairingly, "is that I think the President may be doing it in his foxy way to forestall trouble that is now on the ocean coming toward us in the shape of the British visitor." To stiffen the President's resolution, Stimson provided him with a sharp memorandum. It asserted that the war would be won only by a cross-Channel campaign, and deplored so risky an undertaking as a landing in North Africa. The cross-Channel plan had already been adopted at the London meeting, and, Stimson urged, "when one is engaged in a tug of war it is highly risky to spit on one's hands even for the purpose of getting a better grip." [29]

Not long after the time Stimson was seated at his desk, Churchill was preparing his memorandum for the President. It set out the case against landings in France as early as that autumn. No responsible British authority had been able to draw up a plan that had a chance of succeeding, unless the Germans were by then utterly demoralized, and that was unlikely enough. Questions were pertinently put that went to the heart of the American project. At what points was it proposed to strike, what landing craft were available, what officer was to command, what British forces were needed? If a reasonable plan could be evolved, Britain would share the risks and sacrifices to the full. Otherwise they should look elsewhere for the employment of their forces that autumn. Churchill ended his paper with a reference to the landing in French North Africa. This, the original proposition agreed on at the Arcadia meeting, was shrewdly recalled. It was one to which the President was inclined—it was his secret baby.[30]

On his arrival at Washington from Hyde Park, Churchill was disturbed by decisions that had been taken in his absence. The Combined Staffs had been discussing the invasion projects. An agreement had been tentatively reached that the build-up of American forces in Britain was to proceed in readiness for invading the Continent. The possibilities for a landing in France were to be further studied, with a landing in 1942 "in case of necessity." This hankering after the impracticabilities of 1942 was disturbing.[31]

When the Combined Staffs met, Churchill stated his objections with no punches pulled. In the reckoning of one of his American hearers, General Marshall, it was a "terrific attack." [32] Marshall was not accustomed to such interventions in the realm of strategy, for on military affairs F.D.R. deferred to, rather than directed, his experts.

There is no doubting the effect Churchill produced on the Americans. In his own memoirs he passed over the argument, nor was Brooke sufficiently impressed to note the matter in his diaries. But from American sources we learn that Churchill "poured out his matchless prose" in opposition to the trans-Channel operation in 1942. He dramatized the possible cost of such an adventure in lurid figures of speech, describing the Channel as flowing with "rivers of blood." [33]

Marshall and Hopkins stood firm in resistance to his arguments. They were supported by the President, despite his own predilection for North Africa.

The debate was at its height when there came a sudden interruption. The President was handed a pink slip, a telegram that could be read at a single glance. Without a remark he handed it to the Prime Minister, who saw the words: TOBRUK HAS SURRENDERED WITH 25,000 MEN TAKEN PRISONERS.

It was a staggering reverse.* Churchill would not accept a report so

---

* Precisely when this incident took place is obscure. Churchill placed it in the morning not long after breakfast. It was also timed in the morning by the Hopkins papers. Alan Brooke, however, set the time as the middle of the afternoon, and he kept a day by day diary. The morning of that day stood out for him as the occasion when he was presented to the President in his old coat. Churchill, on the other hand, noted the afternoon as the time he first met Eisenhower.

grievous and so unexpected. A telephone call to London gave confirmation and added the further intelligence that the situation had so far deteriorated that Alexandria was open to air attack. As a precaution, the Fleet had been moved from Alexandria south of the Suez Canal.[34]

This was one of the heaviest blows the war inflicted on the Prime Minister, whose British pride was wounded sorely. In the previous year Tobruk had withstood siege for thirty-three weeks. Now, the garrison had yielded almost at the first assault. It was not defeat but disgrace that confounded him. His hosts rallied to him. No one could have been more understanding than the President in his sympathy, or more helpful than General Marshall.

"What," asked F.D.R., "can we do to help?"

Tanks shipped at once to the Middle East was the reply. At that time the Sherman tanks were beginning to come from the United States factories. Without a thought for their own troops the order was given. The first of these new machines had only then been issued to American divisions. As Marshall said, it was a terrible thing to deprive a soldier of his weapons, but, since the need was great, it was done. Without delay the tanks were loaded in six ships, with a hundred guns added for good measure, and were shortly on their way to the Army of the Nile. The ship conveying the tank engines was sunk by torpedo. At once replacements were sent off to catch up with the convoy.

Tobruk was a disaster, but it enabled the Americans to prove themselves staunch and true as allies. Talks on strategy had to give way to the more urgent needs of plugging the holes in the Middle East. At first the Americans proposed to send out an armored division, but the men were only partly trained, and other measures were ordered.

At home in Britain the Tobruk disaster touched off a new political storm. The critics once more were in full cry, and the headlines in the American newspapers told Churchill of the rough handling he must expect on his return: TOBRUK ANGER; CHURCHILL TO BE CENSURED; GOVERNMENT MAY CHANGE. Readers imperfectly informed about British politics would have imagined Churchill's fate to be in the balance. With nicer calculation of the prospects, he reckoned that twenty or thirty M.P.s might vote against him, but it was no time to linger while feeling mounted at home. His stay at Washington was, accordingly, cut short.

At General Marshall's insistence, Churchill delayed for a day so that the new armies in training at Fort Jackson might show off their paces before the British visitor. He had questioned the "battleworthiness" of American infantry and the Army chiefs were keen to show the quality of their men. He was astonished that so much had been done in so short a time under Marshall's mass training methods. "But," he said, "to make a fine professional army on a great scale from recruits requires at least two years." All the same he thought highly of them and would not permit his colleagues to criticize. The Americans had wonderful material—they would learn quickly.[35] Of necessity there were gaps in their training; they would be remedied in the hard school of war.

As Churchill's plane took off for England on June 25, the best wishes of his friends went with him for his encounter with his critics. But he left behind doubts about the question that had been the main object of his visit. According to the formal decision, consideration of a landing in France in 1942 was still to proceed, but the Americans began to doubt whether Churchill meant business, even for 1943. This was to give rise to questioning and resentment in the future.

CHAPTER TEN

THE CRITICS ROUTED

JULY, 1942

WINSTON CHURCHILL returned from Washington depressed by an accumulation of anxieties. Tobruk's fall had broken his composure. The defeat of France, the reverses in the Balkans, the catastrophes in the Far East—these he had taken in his stride. But the capitulation of the Tobruk garrison, with scarcely token resistance, had for a time unnerved him.

He gave the appearance of bearing in his own person the loss of Britain's reputation, reckoning himself to have fallen in the estimation of his allies. In this he was sensitive beyond his rights. The loss of Tobruk gave Britain no particular pre-eminence in disaster. It was an experience common to them all. The Americans were well to the fore in sharing in war's reverses. The Russians were enduring calamity on a yet vaster scale.

While the Prime Minister's critics were planning their attack on his leadership, Rommel was sweeping all before him. One barrier remained and, that broken, Egypt would be open to him. Mussolini began to preen himself. He was encouraged to cross the waters of his *mare nostrum* and strut, a blue and gold peacock, on the Tobruk promenade. A white horse was provided to bear him forward and he waited for the summons to play the conquering hero, just as he had waited, years before, at a safe distance while his fellow Fascists marched on Rome. Among the Egyptians panic prevailed.

So menacing were appearances that Churchill prepared to fly immediately to Egypt, and it was with difficulty that he was persuaded to delay his departure. His exhortations flew out to Auchinleck. "You are," he cabled, "in the same kind of situation as we should be if England were invaded, and the same intense, drastic spirit should reign. The men in the fighting line should be reinforced by bringing in administrative personnel—every fit male should fight and, if need be, die to win the battle of Egypt."

Rommel, created Field Marshal for his victories, delayed his attack. He had outrun his supplies. Away on the Russian fronts the Germans were pushing ever eastward toward the Caucasus and the oil fields. Allied fortunes were at their lowest, although at that time there was still no assurance that rock bottom had been reached.

Churchill the parliamentarian had now to take the center of the stage. His critics presented the direct challenge of a motion of censure. Upon his skill in reply his ministerial existence might depend. This was no attack by political lightweights. The critics were men of courage and principle, powerful in their influence, their leader Sir John Wardlaw-Milne, respected Tory member for Kidderminster and chairman of an important parliamentary committee.

In the country a feeling of frustration prevailed. The crowds still cheered "Good old Winnie" whenever he appeared. But the succession of reverses was damping national spirits.

It was on the first day of July that the House met for a two-day debate on the censure motion. The main armored forces, British and German, were then known to be engaged to the west of El Alamein in the preliminary encounters of the Battle of Egypt.

Commander King-Hall rose to ask Wardlaw-Milne to defer his motion until the battle had been concluded. It was a suggestion that found favor in all quarters of the House, where the extreme step of a censure resolution at such a time was generally deplored.

The Prime Minister would have no delay. "After all, this vote of censure has been on the Order Paper for some time. When I was in the United States I can testify to the lively excitement which was created by its appearance. Although we in this country may have our own knowledge of the stability of our institutions, and of the strength of the Government of the day, yet that is by no means the opinion that is shared or felt in other countries. Now that this has gone so far, and this matter has been for more than a week the subject of comment in every part of the world, it would be, in my opinion, even more injurious to delay a decision than to go forward with the issue."

So the debate proceeded. Churchill was in a fighting mood. The Government welcomed the challenge. An out-and-out censure had its advantages by comparison with the covert criticisms of the past months from candid and professing friends. The motion was to the following effect:

> That the House, while paying tribute to the heroism and endurance of the Forces of the Crown in circumstances of exceptional difficulty, has no confidence in the central direction of the war.

The critics had first say, the Prime Minister reserving his reply till the close of the debate. There was a full House when Wardlaw-Milne launched his attack. He began, defensively, by answering the critics of his action—that he had chosen his time badly. On the contrary, he claimed, he had given the Government the longest possible notice and, by so doing, had afforded the Government Whips every possible opportunity in which to make their influence felt. To their work in the past week he paid tribute and added: "It would be interesting, if time permitted, to deal with the extraordinary exhibition of human nature with which I have been treated during the past seven days. I realize how true it is that the 'tinker out of Bedford' [John Bunyan] was 'not of an age but for all time.' I have seen Mr. Steadfast and Mr. Valiant-for-Truth, but how often have I also seen Mr. Timorous and Mr. Pliable. They are all represented in this House."

A vital mistake, he submitted, had been made in allowing Mr. Churchill to combine the office of Prime Minister and Minister of Defense. Until recently, production had suffered from the want of a single head and from the lack of direction which would be obtained from a Minister of Defense, apart from the Prime Minister, in charge of the armed forces.

At this point Wardlaw-Milne made the suggestion that the Duke of Gloucester, youngest brother of the King, should be appointed Commander in Chief of the British Army. This was so far outside the range of practical possibilities that it was fatal to the speaker, who lost the ear of the House.

There followed the minor comedy of the intervention of Sir Roger Keyes, Admiral of the Fleet, whose eminence as a sailor was of a different degree from his abilities as a politician. His speech, seconding the censure motion, had not long been under way before doubts arose whether the objective of the attack was the Prime Minister or the Prime Minister's critics. Speaking from his own experience of affairs—he had been Director of Combined Operations—he protested against the supposition that the Prime Minister was a man who, riding roughshod over his Service advisers, took the entire direction of the war into his own hands. "It simply is untrue. Of course, he is masterful, dislikes criticism and, like every great man who is confident in his own judgment, prefers people who agree with him. But I assure the House that he could never be induced to override the advice of the Chiefs of Staff Committee or to undertake any enterprise unless they were prepared to share fully with him in the responsibility."

A member, confused at the course the debate was taking, sought enlightenment. He understood that the vote of censure was moved on the ground that the Prime Minister had interfered unduly with the direction of the war. The seconder seemed to be seconding because the Prime Minister had not interfered sufficiently.

Sir Roger: "I do not think that the mover ever suggested that the Prime Minister had unduly interfered with the naval direction of the war. [Interruption.] Well, if so, I submit I have dispelled the suggestion. We look to the Prime Minister to put his house in order and rally the country once again to its task."

Mr. Tinker: "If the motion is carried the Prime Minister has to go; but the gallant member is appealing to us to keep the Prime Minister there."

Sir Roger: "It would be a deplorable disaster if the Prime Minister had to go."

Once the occasion has gone by, there is little interest left in debates in Parliament. There is no breathing life into the bare, verbatim record of the words a speaker has said. *Hansard* reports are more dead than yesterday's cold mutton. Nonetheless it is worth the while to follow the course of this debate.

Already Winston Churchill has become a legend. His figure looms so large that it casts a shadow over the actual happenings of his career. The diversity of criticism he had to bear in the censure debate will serve as a corrective for those with exaggerated notions of the admiration accorded to him during his wartime premiership.

For the greater part of two debating days the House was given over to the discussion of his qualities—his merits, which were not conspicuously asserted, and his failings, which were abundantly exposed. When all had been said there was scarcely an aspect of his deficiencies that had not come under the microscope of scrutiny. If you wish to know how variously different observers can view the same person, here are illustrations almost without parallel, for, though the central direction of the war was the ostensible theme, it was Winston Churchill that was the subject discussed.

The debate again followed a discursive course. Most of the supporters of the censure motion rose to explain their reasons. Others would not go so far as to support the motion—neither would they vote for the Government.

Herbert Williams found peril lurking in Churchill's skill as a speaker. His amazing capacity was a dangerous weapon. Hitler had created his power by this same facility, but even Hitler delegated authority to other people. Churchill would not delegate and it was delegation of authority that was required.

Flight Lieutenant Boothby thought there was no reason for the House or the country to lose spirits over a tactical reverse in North Africa. The British Empire had not been created by those who were miserable and melancholy but by men who were merry. There were limits to the value of purposeless austerity. Rather say with "the greatest modern poet," A. E. Housman:

> The troubles of our proud and angry dust
>   Are from eternity and shall not fail.
> Bear them we can, and if we can we must.
>   Shoulder the sky, my lad, and drink your ale!

Earl Winterton argued the question of ministerial responsibility. They were told when things went wrong not to blame the Prime Minister, which was getting close to the moral position of the German people—"the Fuehrer is always right." In normal times, what happened in high places? "It may be an admiral, it may be a general, it may be a Prime Minister himself—he may be an excellent man—but if the results are bad it is he who is held responsible, constitutionally, for those results. The admiral or general is removed by the Cabinet Minister, the Cabinet Minister by the Prime Minister, or the Prime Minister by the vote of this House. I therefore ask the House: Are you prepared, if these disasters continue, whatever happens, to say that right up to the end of the war, however long it lasts, we must never have another Defense Minister or Prime Minister, that he is the only man who can win the war? I hope that is not the attitude." In a new Government Mr. Churchill might become Foreign Secretary because "his management of our relations with Russia and the United States has been perfect."

Colonel Colville suggested that the fall of the Churchill Government would be a greater victory for Hitler than the capture of any of the objectives he was at present attacking.

Major Gluckstein had no liking for the second team which he saw in the offing, the shadow Cabinet that had obtruded itself. It was unlikely that "Charles would be dethroned to make James king."

Communism's representative, Willie Gallacher, found ideological and sinister reasons for the attacks on the Prime Minister made by a tatter-demalion group. Their purpose was to weaken the Anglo-Russian alliance. Churchill had given great offense to them by linking Britain's fate to that of the Soviet Union. "Behind this campaign against the Prime Minister is the desire to prevent a Second Front in Europe, and an attempt to weaken our alliance with the Soviet Union."

Hely Hutchinson invited members to join with him in a general confession and act of contrition for their own past offenses. In the years before the war, when Winston Churchill had been urging the building of guns, ships and tanks, they in their foolishness had preferred to vote for social security or any security other than that form of security which alone could give security. "I find great difficulty in believing that the Prime Minister, who all those years before the war foresaw our chiefest need, is now the man I am not to trust in the central direction of the war."

James McGovern suggested that, because of his great capabilities as orator, a false assessment had been made of the Prime Minister's other abilities. "From my experience he is the most arrogant and intolerable member of this House. . . . So far as I am concerned, if I had to choose between Hitler and the Prime Minister, I should not know exactly on which the choice had to fall."

As one of the original signatories and drafters of the motion, Commander Bower deplored the attitude of those who had represented that there was something wrong in putting forward, in a proper constitutional manner, a vote of censure on a Government. He complained that the Prime Minister indulged in an extraordinary game of musical chairs if Parliament became troublesome. Once a certain stage had been reached in the hierarchy, people never got the sack. He quoted from Churchill's sketch of Lord Oxford and Asquith in *Great Contemporaries:*

> In affairs Asquith had that ruthless side without which great matters cannot be handled. When offering me Cabinet office, in 1908, he repeated to me Mr. Gladstone's saying: "The first essential for a Prime Minister is to be a good butcher," and, he added, "There are several who must be axed now." They were.

The Prime Minister, unlike Mr. Gladstone and Mr. Asquith, allowed his friendship for men who had failed him to prevent him from wielding the poleaxe.

Aneurin Bevan, fiery and ambitious Welshman, based his attack on the Prime Minister's shortcomings as strategist. In his view these things were wrong: the main strategy of the war; wrong weapons being produced; the weapons being used by men untrained in the use of them, who had not studied modern tactics. The Government had conceived the war wrongly from the very beginning, no one more so than the Prime Minister himself, than whom no man was more Maginot-minded. Absence of the dive bomber showed that the Prime Minister and his Government had not gone to the heart of modern war-making: "And I say it is disgraceful that the lives of British soldiers should be lost because of the absence of this elementary knowledge at the top." Strategy was wrong because the Prime Minister, although possessing many other qualities, sometimes conceived of the war in medieval terms. The Army needed to be purged at the top. Generals of Allied forces now in Britain, experienced in the use of modern weapons, should be placed in command of the men in the field. A Second Front should be opened in Europe; Stalin expected it.

Captain Profumo, as an active officer, told the House that there was great concern in the forces about the present situation, but there was far greater concern about the habitual critics "who, after every reverse, like lean and hungry dogs smell around for a bone to pick."

Hore Belisha wound up for the critics in a speech in which his main line of attack was that the Prime Minister had used unjustifiably optimistic phrases in referring to the Allied prospects in the Battle of Libya.

Churchill's turn came. Point by point he answered the case that had been made and carried the attack against his assailants. It was a debating speech to which he had given much care in preparation, but it did not stir his hearers as they had been roused by his inspired orations. He was considered to protest too much against the offense of attacking the Government and its head. If such were an offense, then in the past no man had offended more than he, against the heads of other Governments.

As he may be read in full in his collected speeches, I do no more here than give the highlights of what he said. He described, with a warmth of personal feeling, how he received the news of the latest disaster in North Africa.

When on the morning of Sunday, the 21st, I went into the President's room, I was greatly shocked to be confronted with a report that Tobruk had fallen. I hope the House will realize what a bitter pang this was to me. What made it worse was being on an important mission in the country of one of our great Allies. Some people assume too readily that, because a Government keeps cool and has steady nerves under reverses, its members do not feel the public misfortunes as keenly as do independent critics. On the contrary, I doubt whether anyone feels greater sorrow or pain than those who are responsible for the general conduct of our affairs.

It was an aggravation in the days that followed to read distorted accounts of the feeling in Britain and in the House of Commons. The House can have no idea how its proceedings are represented across the ocean. Lobby gossip, echoes from the smoking room, and talk in Fleet Street are worked up into serious articles, seeming to represent that the whole basis of British political life is shaken, or is tottering. That these rumors coming from home did not prejudice the work I had to do was due solely to the fact that our American friends are not fair-weather friends. Indeed, the bonds of comradeship between all the men at the top were actually strengthened.

All the same, I must say I do not think any public man charged with a high mission from this country ever seemed to be barracked from his homeland in his absence—unintentionally, I can well believe—to the extent that befell me while on this visit to the United States. Only my unshakable confidence in the ties which bind me to the mass of the British people upheld me through those days of trial.

Here, I will turn aside to meet a complaint which I have noticed, that the Minister of Defense should have been in Washington when the disaster at Tobruk occurred. But Washington was the very place where he should have been. It was there that the most urgent future business of the war was being transacted, not only in regard to the general scene but also in regard to the particular matters that were passing.

Churchill willingly accepted what Lord Winterton had termed the "constitutional responsibility" for everything that had happened. He had, he claimed, discharged the responsibility by not interfering with the technical handling of armies in contact with the enemy. He could not pretend to form a judgment upon what had happened in this battle.

I like commanders on land and sea and in the air to feel that between them and all forms of public criticism the Government stands like a strong bulkhead. They ought to have a fair chance, and more than one chance.

Men may make mistakes and learn from their mistakes. Men may have bad luck, and their luck may change. But anyhow you will not get generals to run risks unless they feel they have behind them a strong Government. They will not run risks unless they feel they need not look over their shoulders, or worry about what is happening at home, unless they feel they can concentrate their gaze upon the enemy. And you will not, I may add, get a Government to run risks unless they feel that they have got behind them a loyal, solid majority.

He had been reproached for having predicted that Singapore would hold out, to which he retorted:

What a fool and a knave I should have been to say it would fall.

I have not made any arrogant, confident, boasting predictions at all. On the contrary I have stuck hard to my "blood, toil, tears, and sweat," to which I have added muddle and mismanagement, and that to some extent, I must admit, is what you have got out of it.

I do not know what my critics would like me to say now. If I predict success and speak in buoyant terms, and misfortune continues, their pens and tongues will be able to dilate upon my words. On the other hand, if I predict failure and paint the picture in darkest hues, I might safeguard myself against one danger, but only at the expense of a struggling Army. Also I might be wrong. So I will say nothing about the future except to invite the House and the nation to face with courage whatever it may unfold.

He rejected in the strongest terms the suggestion that he should continue as Prime Minister but not as Minister of Defense.

I wish [he said] to speak a few words "of great truth and respect"—as they say in the diplomatic documents.

This Parliament has a peculiar responsibility. It presided over the beginning of the evils which have come on the world. I owe much to the House, and it is my hope that it may see the end of them in triumph. This it can only do if, in the long period which may yet have to be traveled, the House affords a solid foundation to the responsible Executive Government. If democracy and parliamentary institutions are to triumph in this war, it is absolutely necessary that Governments resting upon them shall be able to act and dare, that the servants of the Crown shall not be harassed by nagging and snarling, that enemy propaganda shall not be fed needlessly out of our own hands, and our reputation disparaged and undermined throughout the world.

Sober and constructive criticism, or criticism in secret session, has its high virtue. But the duty of the House of Commons is to sustain the Government, or to change the Government. There is no working middle course in wartime.

There is an agitation in the press, which has found its echo in a number of hostile speeches, to deprive me of the function which I exercise in the general conduct and supervision of the war.

I ask no favors either for myself or for His Majesty's Government. I undertook the office of Prime Minister and Minister of Defense, after defending my predecessor to the best of my ability, in times when the life of the Empire hung upon a thread. I am your servant, and you have the right to dismiss me when you please. What you have no right to do is to ask me to bear the responsibilities without the power of effective action, to bear the responsibilities of Prime Minister but clamped on each side by strong men, as one Honorable Member said. If today, or at any future time, the House were to exercise its undoubted right, I could walk out with a good conscience and the feeling that I have done my duty according to such light as has been granted to me. There is only one thing I would ask of you in that event. It would be to give my successor the modest powers which would have been denied to me.

The setting down of this vote of censure by members of all parties is a considerable event. Do not, I beg you, let the House underrate the gravity of what has been done. It has been trumpeted all round the world to our disparagement, and when every nation, friend and foe, is waiting to see what is the true resolve and conviction of the House of Commons, it must go forward to the end. All over the world, throughout the United States, as I can testify, in Russia, far away in China, and throughout every subjugated country, all our friends are waiting to know whether there is a strong, solid government in Britain.

The House divided and voted 27 for the censure action and 475 against. The opponents were drawn from all parties—eight Conservatives, eight Labour, six Independents, three I.L.P. members, and two Liberals.

The censure debate marked the end of effective attacks on Winston Churchill. With the turn of the tide of battle later in the year the times became less and less opportune for criticism of the central direction of the war. Looking back, one cannot but wonder at the vast measure of blame with which the Prime Minister was saddled in the days of Britain's reverses.

CHAPTER ELEVEN

SECOND FRONT—THE DECISION

JULY, 1942

THE Anglo-American alliance was now put to the test of its greatest strain. Divided over strategy, British and Americans were pulling in contrary directions. Like two satellites in space, they might have parted company and gone off on independent and divergent orbits. There was pressure enough to part them, and there was a day when it seemed to Harry Hopkins that Allied unity was in immediate peril.[1] That they continued together in harmonious association was due to the two men at the top. Prime Minister and President might have chosen to follow separate paths or they could have followed the wrong path in company. That they decided to continue in partnership on the right course was the result of their combined wisdom—of Churchill's in strategy, of Roosevelt's in statesmanship.

Midsummer had gone by, and the Americans were restive—indeed, flaming mad. Seven months since Pearl Harbor and still they were no nearer to carrying the war to the Germans. Eisenhower had gone to Britain as Commanding General of the European Theater. Back in Washington it began to appear that he was to remain a commander without a theater of battle.

It was not long after returning from his American visit that Churchill had had the pleasure of welcoming Eisenhower at Chequers. The two men struck up a liking for each other that was to hold them as friends despite their several professional differences.

Eisenhower, with his deputy, General Mark Clark, was made welcome by a host attired in siren suit and carpet slippers.[2] The generals were escorted through the Buckinghamshire woodlands, talking war, and they were still talking war in the early hours of the morning. Between times, for the benefit of his visitors, Churchill produced his ancient rifle and gave a hearthrug exhibition of how drill had been done in Queen Victoria's army, nearly half a century before. As they ranged over the battle-fronts, their discussions brought them inevitably to the blank on the war charts. It was marked by a question mark. The Second Front, was it to be in France this year, next year, some time . . . ?

Since Eisenhower had moved into London he had done some recasting in his ideas. The logic of facts had produced changes in his outlook. With British manpower already taxed almost to the limit, it became clear to him that the major invasion of Europe would have to wait until the United States was able to contribute substantial forces and, no less important, until American factories could produce the special equipment that would be needed. The conclusion was forced unpalatably on Eisenhower's staff that the invasion of France could not be mounted before late in 1943 or in the spring of 1944. Warnings to this effect were sent back to Washington. Indubitably, no landing on a substantial scale was possible in France in 1942.[3]

On the British side the strategists had been busy. Churchill and his advisers had again gone over the ground. Every conceivable offensive project in Europe was explored. All were rejected. A landing on the Continent could be made, but it would be impossible to hang on. The Germans in France would be able to push the invaders back into the sea without the need to call to their aid any assistance from elsewhere. Certainly no divisions would be summoned from the Eastern Front, thus affording the relief to the Russians that was the main object of the Allies. The time had come to write off "Sledgehammer" and prepare to attack elsewhere before the year ran out. North Africa—there, pronounced Churchill, was the true Second Front for 1942. A cable to this effect sent to the President touched off a new rumpus in Washington.[4]

Stimson was indignant, Marshall very stirred. The Prime Minister had gone back, once more, on what had been agreed. They were tired of these changes and reversed decisions. Stimson deemed it time for a showdown with the British. Marshall agreed. Since the British would not go through with the plan, it was time for the Americans to turn their back on Europe and settle the score with Japan.[5]

This was a move that would have been in line with the feelings of the American people. There was a strong inclination toward the Far East among the professional hierarchy. General MacArthur, quite naturally, pressed the claims of his own command. He had a powerful ally at headquarters in the person of Admiral King, the newly appointed Commander in Chief of the United States Fleet. King was assertively in favor of the Pacific first. Stimson was ready to give his vigorous backing to any measures that would "get through the hides of the British." Marshall, receptive of other men's arguments, came into line. A memorandum was drawn up for the President by Marshall, King and Arnold (Commanding General of the U.S. Air Force), stating the case for the Far East.

For a moment the future of the war and much besides was poised in uncertainty. Had the President shared the exasperation of his Staffs, hostilities in Europe might have been prolonged while the Japanese were disposed of, in which case Berlin, and not Hiroshima, might have been blasted by the first atom bomb. But Roosevelt took the statesman's course. To follow the promptings of his advisers would be "taking up your dishes and walking away." Stimson still urged that the threat should be used as a bluff to impress the British.[6]

The President talked over the position with Hopkins. Once again, he pronounced that defeat of Japan would not mean defeat of Germany but, if Germany were knocked out, then Japan might collapse, perhaps without need to fire a shot or lose a life.[7] The upshot was that Hopkins received orders to leave at once for London with General Marshall and Admiral King. Military action before the year was out must be agreed, and if it were not to be in Europe then they must look to Africa. But, first of all, the possibilities of "Sledgehammer" must be carefully probed, for F.D.R. was still of the opinion that "such an operation would definitely sustain Russia this year."

There was a lively opening to the London visit. The Prime Minister was awaiting his visitors at Chequers, where he expected them for the weekend. Their special train had had orders to stop at the local station, but these were countermanded by the Americans, who insisted on traveling direct to London. They wished to defer meeting the great diversionist, with his arguments for North Africa, until they had conferred with Eisenhower and his colleagues.[8]

Churchill waited at Chequers in vain. As soon as he learned of the change of plans, he was on the telephone to Harry Hopkins, furious in indignation. Hopkins had to sustain the force of the expostulations. Having done his unavailing best to excuse what seemed an affront to the Prime Minister, Hopkins left for Chequers to explain in person.

"The Prime Minister," he reported later, "threw the British Constitution at me with some vehemence. It is an unwritten document, so no damage was done."

The occasion must have been unforgettable as Churchill strode up and down the room, declaiming that, as Prime Minister, with the Staffs under his authority, he was the person with whom negotiations should be opened. As he declaimed with emphasis, he seemed to his hearer to tear out each page of the Constitution and throw it on the floor.[9] His anger exhausted, he was soon in the best of spirits.

There followed a week of intense argumentation. The old ground was once again traversed. Dill had given warning that the Americans had spoken of withdrawing to the Pacific, but Churchill was not impressed. "I cannot think," he wrote, "such an attitude could be adopted."

It was beyond his comprehension. Afterwards, when he related these matters in his memoirs, he still did not credit Marshall or King with having harbored such ideas. Therein he was in error.

The Americans strove earnestly for the execution of "Sledgehammer." After some frank speaking, Marshall was at last brought to concede that with July so far advanced there was no possibility by mid-September of staging an offensive in Europe on a scale to give relief to the Russians.[10] The admission was tantamount to ruling out 1942, for after September the weather and the tides would preclude cross-Channel adventures. On this subject officers of the United States Navy respected British opinion with warnings against the perils of a lee shore.[11] Nor was General Mark Clark encouraging as to the participation of American ground forces for an assault in mid-September. One of his divisions alone could be counted upon, but this had had little amphibious training, lacked anti-aircraft support, and was not equipped with tanks.[12] American arms and equipment needed for invasion had been sent to the Desert Army, tanks in particular. American troops to the number of several thousands had been dispatched south for the defense of Australia. As yet demands for Europe could not be met.

In the last stage of the discussions the Americans pressed for the seizing of the Cherbourg (or Cotentin) peninsula, to be held as a bridgehead until the time of a stronger invasion in the spring. On the map it seemed to be a favorable proposition, but British expert opinion was unanimous that the Germans would have no difficulty in brushing off any invaders who might succeed in getting ashore.

Deadlock was reached. It was made complete when the War Cabinet formally decided against the Cherbourg plan. "Sledgehammer" was ruled out. Eisenhower, in his chagrin, declared that it was a black day in American history, though later he came to see that those who opposed "Sledgehammer" had, in fact, reached the correct evaluation.[13]

Roosevelt was neither surprised nor disappointed. Since "Sledgehammer" was out, he cabled, agreement must be reached on some other project to bring American ground forces into battle with the Germans.

Thus exhorted, Marshall and Eisenhower set to work amidst the wreckage of their plans to contrive an alternative. There was only one effective design—the invasion of French North Africa, Operation "Gymnast." Without a pause for lunch, Eisenhower roughed out the plans to be cabled to Washington for endorsement. The President's "full steam ahead" was not long in coming. He was delighted with the decision. Stimson and his War Department staff might growl in disapproval, with mutterings of "heading for disaster." [14] The President was ready to back his judgment against theirs. The Mediterranean expedition had, throughout, been his preference. It was his secret war-baby.

Churchill did not disguise his gratification. The final decision gave him, in the main, what he had been seeking. He was thankful, and wrote to the President to salute the agreement and the cordial comradeship formed between the men on either side by whom it had been negotiated. Now it was to be full steam ahead in Africa and full blast with the build-up in Britain for the eventual invasion of the Continent. Twice within the month the Prime Minister had pledged himself to all-out backing for the assault on France when the time came.[15]

The President put the event in perspective. "It represented," he wrote, "a turning point in the whole war." [16] It was no less. To Roosevelt was due the guidance that made agreement possible when his Staffs were in no mood to compromise.

The Prime Minister received from John Dill, in Washington, a message of congratulation: "May I express my admiration of the way in which you have steered these difficult negotiations to so successful a conclusion?" Churchill had earned the commendation. By an insistence that never flagged, maintained at meeting after meeting, against the weight of American professional opinion, he had secured the rejection of plans which he, in common with the British strategists, conceived to be disastrous. His resistance had been grounded on his strategic understanding, backed by lessons from the past. He remembered the beaches of Gallipoli. He remembered how, after Russian disasters in that other war, British manhood had been flung on the battlefields of Flanders to perish, 400,000 men, in the mud of Passchendaele.

"More is expected of the High Command than determination in thrusting men to their doom," he had once written. It was a principle founded upon the experience of old butcheries that he was never going to flout.

Looking back, is there any doubting that his opinions and his apprehensions were solidly based? Any landing in France within the capacity of British and Americans in 1942—or early 1943 for that matter—would have ended in disaster. Estimating the possibilities amidst the shifting chances of war, he pronounced that calamity must be the result. After-knowledge compels the conclusion that he was right.

We remember the vast accumulations of forces and matériel ultimately employed on D-Day, the armada of ships and landing craft at sea, and the myriad planes that dominated the skies—6,000 seacraft and 15,000 aircraft.[17] In 1942 there were not enough ships to go round, landing craft sufficient only to put ashore one wave of 4,000 men,[18] and as for aircraft, Wavell was crying aloud for planes to defend India that could not be supplied him. On D-Day, 2,800,000 men were assigned to the expeditionary forces, with forty-one divisions ready to sail from the United States. In 1942 a couple of American and a dozen British divisions were available.

We recall the resistance that even against Allied strength in 1944 was offered by the Germans. Reflecting on these things, we may deem it providential that, under Winston Churchill's guidance, the Allies in their weakness were saved from undertaking the hazard of opening the Second Front in Europe prematurely in 1942. His stand was to draw upon him bitter reproaches from Generalissimo Stalin, but he was impenitent. The greatest comfort on such occasions, as he once pronounced, is to have no doubts, and about the Second Front in 1942 his mind was clear. It was an operation that, launched without the necessary strength and preparation, could cause "rivers of blood to flow"—Allied blood. It might, in the worst reckoning, lead to the loss of the war.

It was a conclusion in which Admiral Leahy, Roosevelt's Chief of Staff, came to concur. Repudiating the views of the grumblers who attacked Churchill, he wrote in his memoirs:

> The Prime Minister was convinced that England was not ready to undertake such a major effort and I did not think we were either. I, personally, was interested in the safety of the United States. A cross-Channel operation could have failed and we still would have been safe. But England would have been lost.[19]

We may be satisfied to know that Winston Churchill, advised by his Staffs and supported by his Cabinet colleagues, in conjunction with President Roosevelt, directed the Allied course away from calamitous hazards to the strategy that gave the surer path to victory. The results were soon to become apparent. At midsummer, 1942, the Japanese at the door of India and the Germans at the gateway to Egypt were threatening to link up. With an Axis front extending from the Atlas Mountains of Africa to the Himalayas of Asia, the war might have been indefinitely prolonged. At Christmas, six months later, the position had been transformed. The danger of the link-up was past, and Rommel was exposed to the pressure of Allied pincers that were to grip him to destruction.

While preparations for Operation "Gymnast" (now renamed, by Churchill's choice, Operation "Torch") were hustled forward, there was the problem of "Uncle Joe" in Moscow. Stalin was not going to take kindly to the change that would deprive him of the front in Europe the President had led him to expect. Churchill decided to undertake in person a mission to the Kremlin. Stalin must be made to realize that the North African expedition was the only practicable means of realizing a Second Front in 1942.

CHAPTER TWELVE

CHANGES TO SAVE EGYPT

AUGUST—NOVEMBER, 1942

W ITH the worsening of the situation in North Africa the Prime Minister's impatience mounted. The riddle of the desert must be solved. Only on the spot could he determine why it was that the Army of the Nile had been beaten back and was standing, baffled and depressed, with a victorious Rommel knocking at the gates of Egypt. Was responsibility for the reverses to be placed on the Desert Command? Churchill concluded that such was the case. Certainly, unless wrong things were righted, final disaster would involve the loss of Egypt. He was heavy with foreboding.

In other wars, under other Prime Ministers, the Secretary for War or the C.I.G.S. would have been sent out to report. But the missions across the Atlantic had given Churchill the taste for intervening personally as the man on the spot. The plane had given premiers no less than armies a new mobility. Colleagues might protest that at sixty-seven he was too old for capering round in the air. He was not to be deterred. The King's consent obtained, the Cabinet could not refuse assent, and he took off on August 1.

It was no feather-cushioned flight. The plane was an American bomber from which the racks had been removed. The sleeping shelf was hard, the drafts blew razor-keen. The journey over enemy territory had its hazards, making night flying imperative. The first hop to Gibraltar was without incident (August 2). From there the Liberator drove far to the south over the Sahara to avoid the battlefields. A wheel to the north and they came toward the Nile as the dawn was breaking. From his seat beside the pilot, Churchill perceived the silver thread against the dark background (August 3). Over forty years had passed since he had ridden across the Nile sands in the charge at Omdurman. A lifetime of history had intervened and still he was engaged on history in the making.

A full conference of advisers assembled at Cairo. Field Marshal Smuts of South Africa, rich in experience, wise in counsel, a vigorous septuagenarian who impressed those he met with the clarity of his thinking, had journeyed up from the south. Wavell had crossed from India. Casey was there, the Minister in Residence, and Alan Brooke, who had flown out by way of Malta. After meeting his advisers and having probed Army opinion, Churchill was confirmed in his view that Auchinleck must be replaced. It was no pleasant task, but . . . "Rommel! Rommel! What else matters but beating him?" [1]

There was much discussion over the succession. First offer of the Middle East Command was made to Alan Brooke, who was greatly tempted by the prospect. Commendably he declined, considering that he could render greater service as C.I.G.S. and Churchill's brake: "I would not suggest I could exercise any real control over him—I never met anybody who could—but I found he was listening more and more to any advice I gave." [2]

Finally it was resolved to refashion the military setup. The vast responsibilities that had fallen on the Middle East Command were too burdensome for a general with a campaign on his hands. As Churchill said later: "When you have a wild beast in your back garden like Rommel, you don't want to be worried about happenings a thousand miles away." Accordingly, "Jumbo" Wilson of the Middle East Command was appointed to have charge of Persia and Iraq. The Near East Command, as it was renamed, was entrusted to General Alexander, to whom the Prime Minister gave the following directive:

1. Your prime and main duty will be to take and destroy at the earliest opportunity the German–Italian army, commanded by Field Marshal Rommel, together with all its supplies and establishments in Egypt and Libya.
2. You will discharge, or cause to be discharged such other duties as appertain to your command without prejudice to the task described in Paragraph 1, which must be considered paramount in His Majesty's interests. [3]

A new leader was also needed to fight the desert battles as commander of the Eighth Army. Here, as the world knows, a certain General Montgomery first blazoned his name on history's roll, but he was not the

Prime Minister's original choice. It was Alan Brooke who pressed for Montgomery. Churchill considered the post should go to a man of the Desert Army and nominated "Strafer" Gott, commanding the 13th Corps, who had fought brilliantly with the Desert Rats. Twenty-four hours later Gott was killed by a Nazi airman when flying over the desert (August 7). It seemed that Montgomery was predestined for the position. One day he was called from the Southeastern Command in England to work with Eisenhower in preparing for the invasion of Northwest Africa; the day following he was ordered off to Egypt. By the time "Monty" arrived the Prime Minister had flown east to undertake the second phase of his mission.

With the Germans sweeping on toward the Volga and the Caspian, Russian demands had grown more insistent for the opening of the Second Front. It was necessary to inform Stalin that there could be no Second Front in Europe in 1942. Churchill resolved that, "raw job" as it was, he must himself tell Stalin of what was proposed. So while Montgomery flying to Cairo, was brooding over the problems and possibilities of his new command, Churchill was headed over the Persian mountains for Moscow, pondering the unpalatable duty he had allotted himself.*

Once his Moscow duties were discharged, Churchill returned to Cairo in a lighter mood. He was heartened by a message of congratulation from the King: "Your long journey has been well worth while: I hope that you are not too tired." Smuts, sending his felicitations on a really great achievement, urged the need for relaxation after Herculean labors: "You cannot continue at the present pace."

Churchill so far complied with the advice as to pass a few days in holiday spirit among the troops in the desert. In Alexander's car he drove out from Cairo beyond the Pyramids to Montgomery's headquarters (August 19). It was his first view of the celebrated Montgomery caravan drawn up amid the sand dunes. He celebrated the occasion by bathing in the Mediterranean, to the entertainment of the troops on the beaches, who watched with delight unconcealed as his figure, unclothed and untanned, was seen advancing into the sea. There was fun in the mess that night and, despite Montgomery's abstentions, the guest was suitably provided for with brandy and cigars.

Churchill had never met a military commander addicted to such austerity—non-drinking, non-smoking, accustomed to retire for the night at ten o'clock. Montgomery was to win his respect and his friendship, but Churchill never quite reconciled himself to the tastes of a man who washed down his sandwich with lemonade while the mess was mag-

* An account of this initial confrontation of Prime Minister and dictator is given in the next chapter.

nificently regaled. And the milkmaid's hours for bedtime! At ten in the evening Churchill was accustomed to settle down for his nocturnal confabulations. It was accepted that sailors, soldiers and airmen, advisers and visitors, should stay up to keep the talks going into the early hours. There were no nocturnes for Montgomery. Dedicated to his task, he followed a regimen to keep his brains in trim. Loss of sleep might mean a lost battle. Not even for the Prime Minister would he risk fatigue that might mar his judgment.

Only a week had passed since the changes in command but already, Churchill was gratified to note, there was a difference in the atmosphere. He could feel the rising spirits in the Army. There was a new sense of activity and alacrity. No longer were men looking over their shoulders toward the safety of the Delta. Rommel, they knew, was about to attack and the Desert Army, confidence reborn, was preparing to receive him.[4]

"Electrifying" was the word Churchill used to describe the transformation in the morale of the Army. The new Commander proceeded to exert the same influence upon the Prime Minister himself.

In his thin, sharp voice Montgomery delivered an appraisal of the military situation that was a model of clarity and confidence, forecasting with an accuracy borne out by the event the moves that Rommel would make. How those moves would be countered by measures already in train was expounded. By the time he was done Montgomery, from the abundance of his own assurance, had convinced his hearer that things would go according to plan, his plan. It was a remarkable *tour de force*. He spoke as one guided by inspired divination of what was being planned on the other side of the hill. There followed a forecast of the battle that would follow when Montgomery and the Eighth Army passed over to the attack. It was an exposition in advance of the Battle of El Alamein.[5]

The next day there was a conducted tour of the battlefield, with Montgomery as guide. Churchill was taken through the key positions to the Ruweisat Ridge, where the heaviest fighting was shortly to be staged. He was given the satisfaction of meeting men of his own regiment, the Fourth Hussars. He was uplifted by all he saw and returned to the caravan among the sand dunes reassured by the reviving confidence of the troops. Before withdrawing at ten o'clock, Montgomery asked for the favor of an entry in his autograph book. The Prime Minister complied with an apt Churchillian allusion:

> May the anniversary of Blenheim (August 13), which marks the opening of the new Command, bring to the Commander of the Eighth Army and his troops the fame and fortune they will surely deserve.

Back in Cairo, Churchill took a hand in the preparation of a new Nile front—a last line of defense in case of emergency. Every man from the rearward services was called on exactly as would be done in England, in case of invasion. Provision for the building of defense works along the line of the Nile having been set in operation, there was no reason for the Prime Minister to prolong his stay on the spot. He cabled home to his colleagues a full report on the measures taken: "Everything has been done and is being done that is possible and it is now my duty to return home as I have no part to play in the battle which must be left to those in whom we place our trust." There must have been a naughty glint in his eye as he emitted those words of virtuous resolve, so unctuously correct. Never was he less inclined to separate himself from the scene of action. Alan Brooke had the greatest difficulty in heading him off for home. Churchill hated to concede he must miss the coming show.[6]

Twelve RAF fighters formed an escort for the Prime Minister's plane as the return flight was begun, for the Germans were aware of his presence in Egypt. The first hop to Gibraltar was made without risk except that, at the last, fog shrouded the Rock, making landing hazardous. For security reasons Churchill was not allowed to leave the shelter of Government House, not even in his suggested disguise of an Armenian suffering from a toothache.[7] A few hours later the plane passed over Trafalgar Point and England was reached with nothing more disturbing than thunderstorms (August 24).

A week later Rommel came around the southern flank of the Desert Army to be repulsed according to Montgomery's forecast. There followed a pause as the counterblow was mounted. Churchill was in a fever of impatience, demanding that the attack be expedited.[8] Montgomery was not to be prodded into premature action. Rather would he resign his command than ruin his chances by striking before his time. Alan Brooke was taxed to cope with a Prime Minister fuming against the procrastination of generals, concerned about their own reputations, who lost their chances by waiting for a certainty. At length (October 23) the signal came, terse and dramatic: C. IN C. TO PRIME MINISTER AND C.I.G.S. ZIP.

It was the code word. The Battle of El Alamein had begun. For three days all went according to forecast. Then, as the troops were engaged in the slogging match on the desert ridges, there was a hold-up. There were anxious watchers in London. Events began to fall behind Montgomery's schedule. Doubts began to form. Had Montgomery been deluded by his own self-confidence? There came tidings that divisions were being pulled out of the line. There was alarm in Downing Street. Alan Brooke was summoned to explain. What was his "Monty" doing? Was this attack to be allowed to peter out in the manner of its predecessors? [9]

Churchill did not know then, as we do now, that Montgomery was regrouping for the final blow, forming the reserve that was to smash Rommel's Army. At last came the news that Montgomery had breached the enemy line and that his armor had broken through the gap. Hitler, to hearten Rommel's men, bade them choose between victory or death. Many were slain, many were made captive, but Rommel, ignoring Hitler's heroics, scuttled off with the remnants of his Army toward the west.

A delighted Prime Minister showered congratulations on the victors. Alexander and Montgomery had not merely rent Rommel. They had put an end to the disasters that had befallen Britain in unbroken succession. Churchill saluted this new experience when he attended the Lord Mayor's Day celebrations in the City of London, a luncheon replacing the traditional banquet. With caution born of persistent disappointments he greeted "not the end, not even the beginning of the end, but, perhaps, the end of the beginning." A little later he proclaimed his imperial purpose so that none might have uncertainty on that point:

> Let me make this clear, lest there should be any doubts about it in any quarter, we mean to hold our own. I have not become King's First Minister in order to preside over the liquidation of the British Empire.

In any quarter—and where might that be? Across in Washington they had no doubts. They knew how in the anxious past the Prime Minister had suffered over the President's promptings about relinquishing Hong Kong and establishing a federated and independent India. Here, at his first opportunity, was his proudly delivered reply.

To the House of Commons, on the twenty-fourth anniversary of Armistice Day, the Prime Minister did justice to the successes. As he said, it was the valid reply to the recent censure motion, which he cast behind him with a shrug of the shoulders.

Guided by the exposition he had been given in the caravan among the sand dunes, he was able to give the House a strategic appraisal of the Battle of El Alamein. The tale was splendidly ended:

> The skill of the commanders was rivaled by the conduct of their troops. Everyone testifies to the electrifying effect which the new Command had upon the Army. This noble Desert Army, which has never doubted its power to beat the enemy, and whose pride had suffered cruelly from retreats and disasters which they could not understand, regained in a week its ardor and self-confidence. Historians may explain Tobruk. The Eighth Army has done better—it has avenged it.
> From the moment that the seaward flank of the enemy was broken,

FIGHTING THE WARS

Ever a soldier at heart, Churchill is shown trying his hand with an automatic gun early in the war

The Bazooka, a tank destroying armored field piece, also had to be thoroughly checked out

And, of course, when Britain produced a new heavy tank called the "Churchill" it needed a first-hand test

His famous "siren" suit
Wide World

In the ribbon and garter of the Order of the Garter
Wide World

Inspecting coastal defenses
Wide World

Chancellor of Bristol University

In the robes of the Order of the Garter

Lord Warden of the Cinque Ports

THE TRAVELER

An autograph for a fan en route to
Quebec by train, 1943
Wide World

Churchill bites hard on his cigar as
he makes a triumphant entry into
Fontaine, France, astride a donkey
Wide World

Piloting a 74-passenger flying boat en
route from Bermuda to England, 1942
Wide World

CHURCHILL AND FRIENDS

Feeding time in the kangaroo cage

Kitten on the *Prince of Wales*

The gift of a lion cub

A pat of approval for his horse,
Colonist II, after a winning race

His poodle, Fluffy, swims with him
in the Mediterranean

In July, 1945, Churchill went to Berlin and toured the ruins of the German capital. Here he is seen gingerly sitting on a rickety chair outside Hitler's demolished bunker
Wide World

Wide World
Forbidden to watch the D-Day invasion, Churchill watched later landings on the Southern coast of France, from the H.M.S. *Kimberly*

Prime Minister with Mrs. Churchill and daughter Mary inspect air defenses in the south of England
Wide World

AND OFFENSES

The Prime Minister looks sadly at the bombed-out House of Commons on May 12, 1941

Wide World

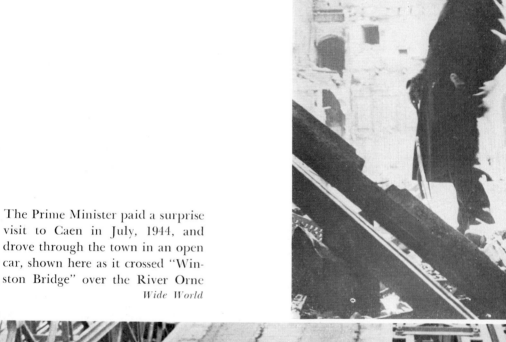

The Prime Minister paid a surprise visit to Caen in July, 1944, and drove through the town in an open car, shown here as it crossed "Winston Bridge" over the River Orne

Wide World

THE PAINTER AND THE PAINTED

This painting, w h i c h Churchill ridiculed, was presented to him as a tribute by members of both Houses of Parliament on his eightieth birthday

Wide World

Two famous amateur painters — Churchill and Eisenhower—discuss a portrait which the American President painted

Wide World

The war over, Churchill went back to his hobby with renewed vigor

Wide World

and the great mass of our armor flowed forward and successfully engaged the Panzer divisions, the fate of the Axis troops to the southward, amounting to six Italian divisions, largely motorized, was sealed. As our advance reached El Daba, and later Fuka, their lines of supply and of retreat were equally severed. They were left in a waterless desert to perish or surrender. At Fuka a grim action was fought on a smaller scale, but with unexampled ardor on both sides, between the British armor and the remnants of the German Panzer Army. In this action, particularly, the British and Germans had it all to themselves. The Germans were almost entirely destroyed, only remnants escaping to Mersa Matruh, where again no halting place was found.

It is impossible to give a final estimate of the enemy's casualties. General Alexander's present estimate, which reached me late last night, is that 60,000 Germans and Italians have been killed, wounded or taken prisoner. Of these, 34,000 are Germans, and 25,000 Italians. Of course, there are many more Italians who may be wandering about in the desert, and every effort is being made to bring them in. The enemy also lost irretrievably about 500 tanks and not fewer than 1,000 guns of all types, from 47 mm. upward. Our losses, though severe and painful, have not been unexpectedly high, having regard to the task our troops were called upon to face. They amount to 13,600 officers and men.

The pursuit has now reached far to the west, and I cannot pretend to forecast where it will stop, or what will be left of the enemy at the end of it. The speed of advance of our pursuing troops exceeds anything yet seen in the several ebbs and flows of the Libyan battlefields. Egypt is already clear of the enemy; we are advancing into Cyrenaica. Taken by itself, the Battle of Egypt must be regarded as an historic British victory.

The curtain went down on El Alamein to rise on Africa's northwestern coast with an Anglo-American force engaged on the high adventure of Operation "Torch."

CHAPTER THIRTEEN

FACING UP TO STALIN

AUGUST 11–17, 1942

For the first time a British Prime Minister met the Dictator of all the Russias. I do not know that diplomatically or strategically the occasion was of the first importance. But as an encounter of antagonists turned allies it was unmatched for the quality of its personal drama. For a quarter of a century Churchill had poured out the vials of his invective against Bolshevism and its authors. He had denounced Stalin as a force of unparalleled evil, mortal foe of freedom and civilization. Stalin, in the short honeymoon with the Hitlerites, had directed the venom of Soviet propaganda against Churchill, the Fascist and capitalist warmonger.

For the space of four days (August 12–16) the Master of the Kremlin was the Prime Minister's host. It was a meeting charged with explosive possibilities. Clashes were not to be avoided, but both men kept within the danger limits. By the time the visit was ended they had reached an appreciation of each other's qualities.

Churchill had broken into his mission in Africa in order to make this visit to Moscow. His trip east was made in two stages, with a break at Teheran, where the Prime Minister and his party were the guests of the young Shah. Over the mountains the flight was resumed. The Caspian was crossed, Baku with its oil fields came into view, and then the vast expanses of the Russian plain, broken by the Volga's course. At last spires and domes marked journey's end. Molotov was waiting to give the visitors a ceremonial reception. The band of the Soviet guard blared out the strange, capitalistic chords of "God Save the King." "The Star-Spangled Banner" followed to greet America's representative, Averell Harriman.

When first the arrangements had been discussed, Roosevelt had not proposed to be represented. He was quite disposed, according to Washington opinion, to leave it to Churchill to make the explanations to Stalin and to bear Russian displeasure over the Second Front. Harriman, however, deemed it better that Stalin should be left in no doubt about the solidarity of views that prevailed between the western Allies. Churchill agreed it would be an advantage—things would be "easier with Joe" if it were clearly demonstrated that President and Prime Minister were united in their policy. Roosevelt concurring, Harriman took the plane to Cairo to join Churchill's party.[1]

Churchill did not permit himself to be delayed by the ardors of Russian hospitality. Without lingering over the delicacies provided, he hurried off and, a couple of hours after landing, he was entering the Kremlin. No man was ever less inclined to doubts and hesitations, but for once he had no particular liking for what lay ahead. He felt, he confessed, like a man carrying ice to the North Pole.

At seven o'clock on the evening of August 12, 1942, the British Prime Minister and the Russian dictator stood face to face. Harriman was present, and Molotov, together with the interpreters without whose assistance conversation would have been impossible.[2]

No time was wasted over preliminaries. Stalin opened the discussions with an account of the situation on the Eastern Front and of the pulverizing the Red armies were enduring. There was no assurance that they could hold out indefinitely, he said, for it suited him to paint the picture as dark as he could make it.

It was Churchill's turn. With no beating about the bush he made his announcement. In 1943 the Allies would take the offensive in the West, but in 1942 there could be no Second Front in Europe. He was heard in somber silence.

When he had done he braced himself to suffer Russian reproaches. Stalin did not spare him. Were the British afraid of suffering the inevitable consequences of war? Difficulties in the Channel crossing? Stalin brushed them aside. The atmosphere grew more glum. Stalin would accept none of the explanations for British inaction. Surely it would be possible to land a small force in France, of, say, six divisions?

To what purpose, he was asked, to be repulsed and driven into the sea? "War," pronounced Churchill, "is war, not folly."

Hitler, he recalled, in all his strength had been unable to cross the

Channel. Stalin did not admit the parallel. The British would have fought the invader—the French people would welcome the British to their land. There was a pause in the discussions. The silence grew oppressive. It was broken by Churchill, who switched to the subject of the air attack on Germany. With the assistance of American bombers, this would shortly be intensified with mounting destruction.

Stalin was interested. Let German homes be destroyed, he urged, as well as factories.

As the interchanges continued, dictator and Prime Minister were shortly engaged in destroying Germany's industrial centers one by one. This devastation being accomplished, there was some lifting of the gloom, and Churchill was encouraged to speak of the preparations for the invasion that was intended, not in France but in North Africa.

Stalin was impressed. It was, he was told, to be on a large scale and there was a gleam of appreciation as Churchill ended his exposition with the suggestion that they would be hitting at "the soft under-belly of the Axis." He drew a picture of a crocodile bellied in the Mediterranean, with northern France as its snout. Where, Stalin asked, would such an operation eventually lead? The prime target, he was assured, was the Continent in the West.

"May God help this enterprise to succeed," exclaimed the Russian, his phrase, often on his lips, a reminder that he had passed his youth in a seminary under religious instructors.

As they stood before a globe, he was quick to point to the strategic possibilities of knocking out the Italians and attacking the Germans in the rear. The gloom had lifted long before the meeting ended after three hours and forty minutes.

Churchill was vastly relieved at the way things had gone and cabled his satisfaction to his friend in Washington. The reply soon came: "The cordiality shown by Mr. Stalin and his understanding of our difficult problems make me very happy. Give him my warm regards. . . . I wish I could be with you."

Gloom had again descended when talks were resumed the next day. Stalin, in the interval, had doubtless had to listen to the expostulations of his subordinates and associates over the failure of the British and Americans to open the expected front in the West. Russian reproaches were formally expressed on paper in a document Stalin handed over. It charged the Prime Minister with breaking his word over the Second Front, thereby inflicting "a mortal blow to the whole of the Soviet public opinion" and complicating and prejudicing the plans of the Soviet Command.

Stalin followed up his *aide-mémoire* with criticism and reproaches. He grew abusive.

"When," he asked, "are you going to start fighting? Are you going to let us do all the work?" With a purring sneer he added: "You will not find it too bad once you start."

That was the cue Churchill needed. He had kept his temper in hand, though hard tried, but at these taunts he broke forth in his most forceful style. Words poured from him in a torrent, and his fist crashed on the table as his wrath broke his restraints. Only on account of the bravery of the Russian soldiers did he pardon the unpardonable things that had been said. What purpose was there in the talks? He had traveled to Moscow to make friends, but not comradeship had he found. For a year Britain had fought alone against the Hitlerites. Now, with Russia joined with Britain and the United States, victory was certain, but . . .

The words flowed on as he gathered speed. The interpreter was baffled. The official note-taker, spellbound, put down his pen to listen. Churchill paused to chide him and then started off anew.

Stalin threw back his head and roared with laughter. "I do not know what you are saying," he broke in, "but, by God, I like your sentiment."

This was the climacteric of the conference. Thereafter tension declined. Stalin dropped his offensiveness and cordiality grew. According to Alan Brooke, who was a witness, Stalin's insults had been a deliberate provocation to test Churchill's reactions. They were immediate. There was no doubting the metal of which he was made.[3]

A retinue of British Service chiefs and advisers had journeyed to Moscow, among them Alan Brooke, Wavell (who spoke Russian), and Tedder for the Air Force. They passed uneasy days. Alan Brooke had the oppressive sense of being a prisoner in the custody of the armed guards who were always in attendance. Nor was his unease lessened by the warning of a Polish general that his sitting room was wired for microphones to enable the Russians to listen in.[4]

A ceremonial banquet was the social climax of the visit. In the state apartments, once made brilliant by the czars and their court, the elite of the Soviets were gathered, the dictator surrounded by his marshals, ministers and commissars. It was a new regime, but the old standards of lavishness prevailed, the tables burdened with viands for nineteen courses and the vodka flowing freely. Churchill sipped with caution, but others, not so well advised, drank to their own undoing. Stalin, under the influence of the occasion, mellowed into affability. His stumpy figure, with short, lilac-colored tunic, was seen here and there about the room as he trotted round to clink glasses with those he honored with a toast.

Through interpreters, he and his chief guest chatted over the past, and the Lloyd George days when the British had intervened in Russia against the Bolsheviks. Churchill confessed that he, too, had been active against the Leninists. Had he been forgiven?

"All that," came the reply, "is past and the past belongs to God."

In such fashion the evening passed off well. Stalin, proposing the Prime Minister's health, made a complimentary reference to the famous Dardanelles operations of a quarter of a century before. When Churchill, confessing for once to a sense of fatigue, took his leave at one-thirty in the morning, his host accompanied him through the interminable corridors and staircases to the front door of the Kremlin. A cordial handshake and they parted for the night.

One point raised that evening was for a meeting between Stalin and the President. Roosevelt was eager to make the Russian's acquaintance, confident that he could achieve more than Churchill. "Stalin hates the guts of all your top people," he had written not long before. "He thinks he likes me better." [5]

When Harriman put the proposal to him, Stalin readily assented. He did not rule out Iceland as a possible meeting place. Nor did he dissent from the suggestion that Churchill should also be present—indeed a meeting of the three would be the best solution.

Again there was a drop in cordiality on the third day. The military discussions were particularly unrewarding. Brooke and his colleagues found the Russians uncooperative and suspicious, not prepared to make their allies a party to their plans, not interested in any subject but the Second Front. It scarcely seemed worth their while to have traveled so far to such little purpose.[6]

Churchill shared the general sense of frustration and his spirits were low when he attended at the Kremlin to bid goodbye to his host. They talked of the fighting and the German thrust towards the Caspian. Stalin was quietly confident—"we shall stop them; they will not cross the mountains." Churchill was reassured.

At eight o'clock, after an hour's stay, he rose to leave, for the return flight was timed to begin at dawn. Stalin pressed him to stay—they could make a night of it. "Come to my apartment and have some drinks," he said.

They made their way through the maze of corridors to a flat of four rooms. Stalin was most affable as he set about uncorking the bottles. "Let's call in Molotov," he suggested. "He's a good drinker, and we can settle the communiqué."

A red-haired girl entered and gave Stalin a kiss. It was his daughter, who began to lay the table for dinner. Churchill noted that even a steel-fronted dictator had his softer side.

The conversation was informal and friendly, though not without its dangerous turns. There were some slighting references to the failure of British convoys to reach Russia—had the British Navy no sense of glory? Churchill, determined to take no offense, suggested that on war at sea he spoke as one completely informed. Meaning that Stalin was not? The Russian, he replied, was a land animal, the British sea animals.

Again the ice was thin when the subject of Soviet agriculture came up. Had it not been difficult to carry through the policy of collective farms? It was a terrible struggle, agreed Stalin, fearful. Churchill breathed the word "kulaks" and thought of the millions who were liquidated so that Russian farming could be Sovietized. But though memories came flooding from the past he said no more. It was safer to join in the game of chaffing Molotov, butt of Stalin's wit.

What of a return visit by Stalin? He was assured of a magnificent reception were he to journey to England. He appreciated the invitation but for the present he must decline; receptions were not so important when victory or defeat was in the balance.

Finally the wording of the official communiqué was settled. It was two-thirty in the morning when Churchill left the Kremlin. Three hours later he was in the air, the plane headed south for the Caspian and the mountains. Again the flight was broken at Teheran, where the visitors were entertained by the Persians in a tent beside a goldfish pool. The day following they were back in Egypt.

The tedium of the long flight gave the chance to reflect on the results. Had the journey been worth the making? Churchill was in no doubt that it had been justified. He had set himself to build up the same relations of cordiality he had established in America and in this, he was persuaded, he had succeeded to a considerable extent ("despite the accident of the Tower of Babel, which persists as a very serious barrier"). His military advisers were disposed to doubt whether it was possible to reach friendly terms with so cold and calculating a person as Stalin—it was like making friends with a python, as one of them phrased it.[7]

Churchill's impressions of his host provided matter for a personal picture of Stalin when he gave the House of Commons an account of his trip.

"It is very fortunate," he said, "for Russia in her agony to have this great, rugged war chief at her head. He is a man of massive, outstanding personality, suited to the somber and stormy times in which his life has been cast; a man of inexhaustible courage and will power, and a man direct and even blunt in speech, which, having been brought up in the

House of Commons, I do not mind at all, especially when I have something to say of my own. . . . He also left in me the impression of a deep, cool wisdom and complete absence of illusions of any kind. I believe I made him feel we are good and faithful comrades."

The rugged war chief—it was an inspired phrase in which to recommend the dictator to a democracy. The sentimental British took Stalin to their hearts. In the man of inexhaustible courage they forgot the sinister revolutionary who had liquidated opponents and associates as he advanced himself to the supreme dictatorship.

At the appraisal meeting Prime Minister and dictator took each other's measure. It was the Russian who profited the more. He sensed Churchill's weakness—his uneasy conscience that no greater aid in the field was being rendered to the Red armies—and set himself to exploit it. Soviet demands for matériel and equipment were importunately pressed. In return, as Alan Brooke deplored, the Russians were required neither to promise nor to give.

Churchill, in the discussions, suffered the handicap of being placed on the defensive over the Second Front. Before the autumn was out Stalin, for purposes of propaganda, made capital out of the Allied refusal. If the British and the Americans failed him in fighting, at least he would have the benefit of letting the rest of the world know. Through an interviewer, whom he summoned to the Kremlin, he publicly complained how little the Russians were being assisted in their struggle.

"As compared with the aid which the Soviet Union is giving to the Allies by drawing upon itself the main forces of the German Fascist armies the aid of the Allies to the Soviet Union has so far been little effective," he said.

Prime Minister and President disdained to publish to the world their complaints against the Russians, thereby leaving a void for the Communist propagandists to fill. World respect for the Russian armies was magnified accordingly. With farsighted calculation Stalin even then was engaged in the battle for postwar opinion.

BOOK THREE

ALLIES IN CONFLICT

CHAPTER ONE

TORCH FOR AFRICA

AUGUST, 1942—MAY, 1943

O PERATION "TORCH" was well named. It lighted the skies with a new hope. In the glow of its brightness it was to throw up the words: One Continent Redeemed.

It was the first essay in Anglo-American planning, the first test of the machinery for concerting action between the armies, navies, and air forces of the two nations. It was the first experience in command of that little-known United States officer, General Dwight Eisenhower.

The planners, the staff machinery, and the general were proved by the test. The amphibious operation that brought 90,000 Allied troops across the oceans in conformity with the requirements of a timetable of infinite complexity was meticulously planned and magnificently executed. But there had been uncertainty, some confusion, and much anxiety in the earlier stages. In the deliberations of the planners Winston Churchill took his substantial part. It was his strategic conception that was adopted and it was by his insistence that the operation was mounted on a scale sufficient to ensure success.

I. STRATEGISTS AT VARIANCE

Fresh from his meeting with Stalin, the Prime Minister returned home with bustling eagerness to get the operations going in Africa that were to expose the "under-belly of the Axis." He wrote to Washington demanding early and decisive action. To his dismay he found that indecisiveness prevailed, planning was confused, and action delayed by differences between the strategists.

In Washington there were doubts and hesitations. Apprehension about the risks involved were such that the American Staffs proposed that the operation should be whittled down to a degree that moved Churchill to vigorous protest.

"Torch" had been designed to clear the Germans out of Africa. Simultaneous landings had been projected in the three territories of Morocco, Algeria and Tunisia, but President Roosevelt, expressing the opinion of his advisers, wrote that this was "far too hazardous in the light of our limited resources." [1]

Landings in Morocco were still acceptable, but there was reluctance to adventure into the Mediterranean far to the east of the Gibraltar Straits. Hitler might send his armies into Spain; Gibraltar might fall; it was unwise to venture east of Oran, certainly not as far as Algiers and Bône. Rommel might switch his armor to the west and advance into French Africa.

The Prime Minister was not prepared to accept any whittling down of the operation as it had been originally planned. He was not minded to yield to apprehended perils. "This," he told Ambassador Kennedy, "is a soft job," and he set about infusing the planners with his own sense of confidence. In emphatic language he cabled his protests to the President against the disconcerting suggestions received from Washington. The whole pith of Operation "Torch" would be lost if Algiers as well as Oran were not to be taken: "Algiers is the key." Its occupation was essential to the advance on Tunis and Bizerte, the port through which Rommel was supplied and reinforced.

The British Staffs were in agreement with the Prime Minister. They contrasted the American reluctance to face risks in French Africa with the readiness with which, earlier in the year, they had been pressing for a landing in northern France in the face of German opposition. The interest of the American Staffs seemed to be directed away from Africa to the Pacific. There were difficulties about United States naval participation in "Torch." Was Admiral King committing, against the Japanese, naval resources needed against the Germans? [2]

Churchill could not understand what was at the back of all the evasions. He thought there had been agreement with General Marshall and that Admiral King had been paid off with what he needed for his Pacific war. But it seemed there was a bad comeback from professional circles in the American Army. He began to fear that the President's enterprise would, bit by bit, be wrecked. [3]

Cables passed to and fro across the Atlantic. There was a sharp reminder for the President of the undertakings that at Moscow had been given in his name: "I hope, Mr. President, you will bear in mind the language I have held to Stalin supported by Harriman with your approval." [4]

Matters were reconsidered at Washington. Churchill's remonstrances proved effective. The President signaled acceptance of the original plan, but on the understanding that the British would provide the additional troops and much of the shipping.

There the politics of the operation were involved, for, as Churchill had insisted from the outset, "Torch" was "primarily political." The first victory to be won was to avoid having to fight a battle with the French. If the Allies had to force their way ashore against the resistance of 200,000 French troops, casualties must be heavy. But could not unopposed landings be contrived? The French colonists owed their allegiance to Vichy and Marshal Pétain, but would they fight to oppose the Anglo-French forces.

The President had his views about the political aspect. There was, he was convinced, a far greater chance of winning over the French colonists if the landings were given the appearance of being not a British but a United States operation. The British had caused the spilling of much French blood—there had been Syria and Madagascar. To American forces they were likely to offer only token resistance, or so at least the President argued. For which reason he suggested that it should be an American enterprise, supported by the British, but under American command and with Americans very much in evidence.[5]

Churchill did not accept the President's theorizing, but he did not challenge the idea of emphasizing the American character of the expedition. If need be, British soldiers could wear American uniforms—they would be proud to do so. As long as the job was done, what did it matter who got the credit. After all: "We have no need to be anxious about the place which Britain will occupy in the history of this war." [6]

There was need of a French figurehead, a man with prestige and authority, who might be able to prevail upon the authorities in Casablanca, Oran and Algiers to admit the invaders. There were two candidates for the place, both generals, each as insistent as a prima donna on taking the leading role. One was supported by Whitehall, the other by Washington.

With the fall of France, Churchill had given his backing to de Gaulle as leader of the Fighting French. Washington would have none of him. The President was peremptory in his insistence that not so much as a hint must be given to de Gaulle that the landings were intended. American trust was placed in General Giraud, who was assigned the code title of "Kingpin." With a couple of escapes from the Germans to his credit, Giraud was a romantic figure. He was ferried over to Gibraltar by British submarine. There was much explaining to be done before he could be induced to accept that Eisenhower and not Giraud was to be the Supreme Commander for North Africa.

At last, under the stimulus of the Prime Minister's insistence, the planning was completed. In fourteen convoys, four hundred ships in all sailed from ports on either side of the Atlantic, timed to arrive off Northwest Africa for synchronized landings at Casablanca, Oran and Algiers. The movements had been splendidly concerted. The pieces of the amphibious jigsaw fitted "like a jeweled bracelet," as Churchill had postulated. Despite the U-boats, 90,000 fighting men were safely brought to their appointed destinations.

Politically, expectations were not fulfilled. Eisenhower, indeed, was surprised to find how badly he had been misled over French opinion in Africa; it did not remotely resemble the predictions that had been made. There was no disposition on the part of the French to welcome the invaders; the Americans in Morocco were met with such stiff resistance that after three days' hard fighting General Patton failed to take Casablanca. "Kingpin" Giraud was not welcomed as a conquering hero; he had no perceptible influence on his countrymen, who ignored him.[7]

It was at Algiers that events were decided. There, on a visit, was Darlan, head of the French Navy, one of Pétain's most influential Ministers in the Vichy Government. He was induced to side with the invaders. Eisenhower agreed to recognize him as head of the French state in North Africa and Darlan, accorded this position of authority, gave the orders for resistance to cease throughout the African colonies. Unlike Giraud, he carried the appearance of lawful authority among his fellow countrymen. He was obeyed and resistance ceased.

The invading forces were ashore, the military problem for the moment solved. Thereupon Eisenhower's political troubles began. While the troops set off toward Tunis, the Supreme Commander was engaged in a rear-guard action with the critics, in Britain and in the United States. Progressive opinion had been outraged by the deal made with a Vichy collaborator. There, at the first test, was seen to be a betrayal of the principles for which the war was being fought. If the Allies began by a sordid deal with so contaminated a personality as Darlan, they would be accepting Goering by the time they reached Berlin. So fierce blew the storm that it seemed Eisenhower must be ruined. It was useless for him to plead that through Darlan alone could resistance to the landings have been called off. The critics were not to be placated. It was one of those occasions when the high-minded, conscious of their own rectitude, were ready to enforce their principles at the cost of other people's lives.[8]

Goebbels and his propagandists did not fail to profit from the affair. Here, they proclaimed, was an example of the ineptitude to be expected when the Americans took a hand in Europe's affairs.

In Washington it was surmised that the Prime Minister might be deriving quiet satisfaction from American embarrassments. This supposition was wide of the mark. Churchill gave Eisenhower his full support. For him the saving of Allied lives was decisive. He wrote, however, to inform the President of the deep currents of feeling that had been stirred in Britain, stressing the political injury that would be caused were the arrangements more than temporary, for they conveyed the impression that "we are ready to make terms with local quislings; Darlan has an odious record." [9]

Mounting indignation in Britain made an explanation essential, but, with illimitable scope for giving offense, Churchill deemed it unwise to embark in public on these delicate matters. Accordingly a secret session of the House of Commons was held on December 10, at which he was able to speak with frankness.

"Torch," he emphasized, was regarded in the United States as an American expedition under the ultimate command of President Roosevelt—and it was to be borne in mind that since 1776 Britain had not been responsible for the policy of the United States. Some passages of raillery followed about the French and their conceptions of loyalty, prefaced by the reminder that "the Almighty in His infinite wisdom did not see fit to create Frenchmen in the image of Englishmen."

On the main point at issue there was no equivocation. The Prime Minister declared: "I must say that, personally, I consider, in the circumstances prevailing, that General Eisenhower was right, and, even if he was not quite right, I should have been very reluctant to hamper or impede his action when so many lives and such vitally important issues hung in the balance."

The speech had an influence on British opinion, for though it could not be reported the arguments soon reached a circle larger than the M.P.s who had heard them. The clamor over the affair was dying down when, on Christmas Eve, the unfortunate Admiral Darlan fell to the bullet of a French assassin.

For Churchill it was a greater cause for anxiety that Eisenhower, preoccupied with the politics of the situation, was neglecting to push on with military operations. Tunisia was the goal, a glittering prize. Hampered by the rains and faulty organization, and sparingly reinforced, the invaders moved slowly east.

Montgomery, meanwhile, was careering on to the west in the wake of the fleeing Rommel. Churchill, in his mental reckoning, was soon several moves ahead of the Eighth Army. Writing off the operations in Africa as successfully concluded, he was already envisaging the next objective. With one of those changes of front that surprised and embarrassed his advisers, he was calling for a Second Front in Europe for 1943.[10]

The Americans, Churchill noted, were slowing the pace of the buildup of their forces in Britain. Did this imply they had decided to abandon the idea of an early invasion of Europe? Again he protested to the President. It would be a most grievous decision. In the talks with Stalin it had never been suggested that "Torch" ruled out a Second Front in Europe. Even in 1943 a chance might come to get to grips with the main strength of the enemy.[11]

Here was a development little to have been expected from the man who at midsummer had been resolutely opposed to a premature assault in Europe. For Alan Brooke and his Service colleagues it was disconcerting. Resources did not exist to carry out an operation of this magnitude at so early a date.

The reason for Churchill's change of mind was not far to seek. Since he had left Moscow the Red army had suffered new and shattering reverses. There was no holding the Nazis, driving eastward toward the Caucasus and the oil fields. Stalingrad was invested, and there was fighting in the streets. In Washington the city was written off. Among British Staffs doubts grew whether the Russians could hold out. Churchill, remembering Stalin's assured confidence, was less disturbed. His concern was over the failure to keep the Arctic convoys going, bearing to Russia the supplies, arms and aircraft so urgently required, so vehemently demanded. From Moscow there came hints of what might happen were the Soviets not to be sustained by their allies. Russia, it was conveyed, might be forced to conclude a separate peace.

These were the circumstances that kept the Prime Minister on the tenterhooks of anxiety over the fulfillment of undertakings to Stalin. With emphasis he pressed for action across the Channel in 1943.

"The Russians have been led to believe that we were going to open a front in 1943. 'Roundup' [invasion of Northern France in 1943] was explained to them by me in the presence of the United States representative, Mr. Harriman. These conversations were duly reported to the President. I feel that Premier Stalin would have grave reasons to complain if our land offensive against Germany and Italy in 1943 were reduced to the scale of thirteen divisions, instead of nearly fifty which had been mentioned to him. Moreover, apart from any Russian obligations, I feel that our offensive plans for 1943 are on altogether too small a scale compared with the resources and power of Britain and the United States." [12]

For which reason, Churchill urged, the strategic position must be resurveyed with the object of finding means for engaging Allied armies directly upon the Continent.

The President sent a reassuring reply. Of course there was no intention of abandoning the plans for "Roundup." But whether or not the opportunity would be afforded to strike across the Channel in 1943 "no one could say." [13]

The battle of the strategists was now resumed. General Marshall, who had never had any liking for the Mediterranean adventures, was strongly in favor of the early assault on France. The British Staff Chiefs maintained their former objections. They recommended pushing on in the Mediterranean and knocking out Italy—Alan Brooke's fundamental strategy. They feared that were Churchill to line up with the Americans the refusal of midsummer would be reversed and a decision taken for a Second Front in France. Alan Brooke used his arguments and diplomacy. Churchill was induced to modify his views about the possibility of invading France before 1944.[14]

The time had come for high-level talks on strategy. Churchill and the President realized the need and each desired that Stalin should take part. The Russian was agreeable, replying almost cordially, but not omitting a reminder about "your promise in Moscow to establish a Second Front in 1943"; he hoped there had been no change of mind. When it was suggested that the meeting should be held in Africa Stalin declined; his constant concern with developments on the Eastern Front made it impossible for him to leave Russia.

To meet Stalin's convenience, Roosevelt had been prepared to travel as far east as Khartoum. But, with Stalin dropping out, Prime Minister and President might, as before, have met in the West Atlantic. Roosevelt, however, was not to be balked of a trip overseas. He was tired of learning from others about the world elsewhere; for once he was going off to see through his own eyes. He would savor the drama and the mystery of a secret mission in wartime.[15] After much canvassing of the possibilities Casablanca was chosen as the rendezvous.

By the time the conference had begun, Hitler had anticipated Allied strategists. While Eisenhower's forces were moving on through the African mountains, Germans in mounting numbers were being flown into

Tunisia. Hitler was going to fight it out in Africa. The British outposts, within twelve miles of Tunis, were pushed back. Fighting was to be hard and prolonged before that glittering prize was taken. By then the year was too far advanced for a Second Front to be opened in France in 1943. In Tunisia, no less than at Stalingrad, Hitler had imposed the strategy for the ensuing phases of the war.

II. CASABLANCA: UNCONDITIONAL SURRENDER

One January day in 1943, "Mr. P" stepped from his plane at the town of Casablanca. Two days later (January 14) he was joined by "Admiral Q" and the Casablanca conference opened with a historic pun.

A few months earlier Churchill had visited Africa in the disguise of "Mr. Bullfinch." Now, in Morocco, he was to be "Mr. P" to the President's "Admiral Q." Impenetrable disguises both and, as Churchill remarked: "We must mind our Ps and Qs."

Security precautions required, further, that the trip from England should not be made by cruiser as had been proposed. There were too many U-boats lurking to prey on the convoys for "Torch," and the risk was held to be too great. Again his plane took off for a flight by night. It was cold in the bunk as Churchill turned in, but in the early hours he awakened to find the special heating apparatus to be glowing red-hot. He decided it was better to freeze than burn.

There were risks at Casablanca. The place was within range of enemy bombers, and there were fanatics among the people. As a safeguard, a suburb, cleared of its inhabitants, was fenced off and there, in Anfa camp, two villas were assigned to Messrs. P and Q, picturesque and comfortable, with views over the blue expanse of the Atlantic below the green palms and red soil.

All were in high spirits. Churchill, arriving ahead of the President, had time to explore and admire the rocky coast. Watching the waves come pounding in he marveled it had been found possible for Patton's force to have landed.

Roosevelt was in a lighthearted mood, elated to have escaped from the burdens of state. He, too, had made the crossing by air, his first flight since becoming President, and to Harry Hopkins he appeared to be a sixteen-year-old schoolboy on a holiday.

The staffs were infected by the good spirits of their principals. It was as well, for on the strategy to be pursued they were greatly at variance. For a week they argued out their differences, but though they clashed in their ideas good temper throughout prevailed.

All the old ground was once again disputed over, starting from the scratch point: Which first, war in Europe or the Pacific? In fighting the Germans, was it to be in the Mediterranean or in northern France? In the Mediterranean, was the next move to Sicily or Sardinia?

Admiral King concentrated his thoughts on the Pacific war to which his professional training had been directed. General Marshall was for the assault in France. Arnold pressed for his bombers to be given the chance of blacking Germany out of the war. The British were in favor of exploiting successes in the Mediterranean, but were divided among themselves. Brooke plumped for Sicily as the next target, while others, including Mountbatten, were set on Sardinia. Apart from their strategic objections, the Americans were disinclined to accept the Mediterranean on political grounds, suspecting British intentions. Had they not imperialist designs?

By self-denying ordinance, Churchill did not sit in at the meetings of the Joint Staffs. He and Roosevelt were content to await the outcome of the deliberations. Strategic problems had been handed over to the Staffs, and the principals had their problems in attempting to induce the two French generals to cooperate in rallying their compatriots to the Allied cause.

The onlookers were diverted by the comedy of a reluctant marriage. The President reported that the bridegroom, Giraud, was ready to go through with the nuptials, but the Prime Minister was unable to produce de Gaulle, the temperamental bride, who was high-hat about the affair and for some days refused to leave London. When he arrived at Casablanca, de Gaulle still hung back, demanding recognition as the predominant partner. At length the two generals were brought together for the shotgun marriage. They shook hands and, because the photographers had not had their cameras ready, they shook hands again. Prime Minister and President looked on approvingly.

"We have met," the generals afterward announced, "we have talked. We have registered our entire agreement on the end to be achieved. This end will be attained by the union in war of all Frenchmen fighting side by side with their allies." But, somehow, the unity of Free Frenchmen was never to embrace the union of the two generals.

By this time the Joint Staffs had settled their differences. An agreed program was drawn up conforming, to Alan Brooke's surprise and relief, with British ideas. Sicily was to be the next target, the steppingstone to Italy. In preparation for the Second Front in France, the build-up of American forces in Britain (Operation "Bolero") was to proceed.

It was not to those operations ashore, however, that was assigned first place in the plans for the war in 1943. The defeat of the U-boat, the Staffs emphasized, must be the first charge on the resources of the United

Nations. No fewer than a thousand ships had been sent to the bottom in 1942. Until the sinkings were reduced, the U-boat must continue to impose a strangle hold on Allied efforts and offensive operations, supplies for Russia, and the Second Front in Europe.

While the British provided the strategic plan, the Americans were to furnish the commander. Churchill made no greater contribution to Anglo-American cooperation. Eisenhower had expected that he would be sacked over the Darlan business. Instead, with the Prime Minister's concurrence, he was nominated to be the Supreme Commander of Allied Forces in Africa, to take over once Montgomery and the Eighth Army had linked up with the forces in Tunisia. The Americans had anticipated that the British would seek to provide the generalissimo, for their forces outnumbered the Americans by twelve divisions to three and they viewed the Prime Minister's attitude with appreciative surprise. Churchill saw no particular merit in what he had done; it was his concept of cooperation. He had the highest regard for Eisenhower and his qualities as captain of the Allied team. Alexander was to be deputy chief and it was he who was in operational command.[16]

Churchill was gratified to report back to the War Cabinet that Allied strategy had been so satisfactorily decided. The plan was all right, but it was "not enough." Compared with the great resources of Britain and the United States, and the gigantic efforts of the Russians, the scale of operations was small. But Casablanca, he pronounced, stood out among all Allied conferences he had known for the thoroughgoing professional examination that had surveyed, in detail, the entire scene of the war.

At the last, almost with the appearance of an afterthought, there came the interjection of "unconditional surrender." It was President Roosevelt's special contribution to the proceedings and it was the cause of a barrage of criticism thereafter.

The occasion was the final press conference. The President was supplementing the official communiqué with a background talk. "Suddenly," as F.D.R. was to relate, "the press conference was on, and Winston and I had had no time to prepare for it, and the thought popped into my mind that they had called Grant 'Old Unconditional Surrender,' and the next thing I knew, I had said it." And, following him, the Prime Minister endorsed it, being as he said "unprepared and taken by surprise." [17]

In such fashion, according to the earliest accounts, was "unconditional surrender" given to the world. Later, when the controversy blazed up, it emerged that memory had played both these statesmen false. The President had not spoken with such casual unpremeditation; the fateful phrase was found to be included in the notes he had written beforehand.

Nor did the Prime Minister's surprise spring from complete lack of prior consultation. When he came to check up among his papers, Churchill found that four days previously he had reported to his colleagues in London: "I should be glad to know what the War Cabinet would think of our including in this statement [on the close of the conference] a declaration of the firm intention of the United States and the British Empire to continue the war relentlessly until we have brought about the 'unconditional surrender' of Germany and Japan." [18]

To complete the record of matters imperfectly recollected, it should be stated that six years later Ernest Bevin, when Foreign Secretary in the Labour Government, indignantly complained that the phrase had never been submitted to the War Cabinet. In fact, three days before F.D.R. dropped the words upon the press correspondents, a message was sent from London expressing the concern of the Cabinet, not at the projected employment of the phrase, but at the omission of Italians from those, German and Japanese, to whom it was intended to apply.

Many minds were exercised to discover the precise meaning of the phrase. The Prime Minister in his first statement on the subject to the House of Commons made no attempt to define it, but he placed a limitation on its interpretation. "It does not mean," he said (February 11, 1943), "that we shall stain our victorious Army by any cruel treatment of whole populations. But justice must be done upon the wicked and guilty. No vestige of Nazi or Fascist power, no vestige of the Japanese war-plotting machine will be left by us when our work is done."

Quantities of ink were later to be spilled in condemnation of the authors of "unconditional surrender," who learned from their critics that they would be causing (or had already caused) the needless prolongation of German resistance. That is an exploded fiction. Not a phrase, but Hitler, the paranoiac, was the obstacle to German capitulation so long as a Nazi remained to fight under the Fuehrer's direction.

The conference concluded, the President, after the briefest of visits to Marrakech, took off for home, but not so the Prime Minister. He had traveled with his painting kit, but the beauties of Marrakech, the Paris of the Sahara, did not hold him long. His restless vision had been ranging eastward and to the possibilities in Turkey. Were the Turks to be won over to the Allies, it would turn the German flank and open a short route for supplies to Russia. In November he had canvassed the Kremlin on this point and had found Stalin to share his views. What a chance was now presented! He would himself meet the Turks—did not the War Cabinet agree? The War Cabinet did not: were he to propose a meeting he would expose himself to rebuff or failure. The Prime Minister was piqued; he recommended his colleagues review the matter. The

Cabinet was obdurate. He grew more insistent and with mounting emphasis he restated his arguments. His colleagues thought it best to capitulate in unconditional surrender to their chief.[19]

The Turks cabled a cordial welcome—they would be delighted to receive him. Churchill was jubilant. "This is great stuff," he exclaimed. He sent a parting chortle to his Ministers as the plane flew over the Atlas Mountains, their snowy peaks gleaming in the sunshine. "How much," he cabled, "I wish I were going to be with you on the bench tomorrow, but duty calls."

The Cabinet had been concerned about the flying risks. He virtuously conceded that he would restrict his flights purely for trips that duty required. Flights just for pleasure he would cut out. The military advisers accompanying him, including the C.I.G.S., were concerned about risks of another sort. The Turks had provided him with a special train as his headquarters. It stood for two days in an open plain. Churchill's presence was a secret that all in Turkey shared, including the Germans and their agents. The cordon of sentries posted around the train was grotesquely ineffective. Alan Brooke was perturbed. The Prime Minister might be blown sky-high as he slept.[20]

The visit was a thoroughgoing social success. After dinner—served in the railway-coach apartments—Churchill addressed the company in his own particular brand of French, much anglicized in phrase. But, though President Inonu was most affable, he was not to be tempted to join the combatants. The Turk had backed the losers in one war: he was not going to risk a second embroilment. The Prime Minister was able to leave with a feeling of limited gratification at the results he had achieved, assured that henceforward the Turks would prove not belligerent but benevolent neutrals.

While his satisfaction was still aglow, he cabled a report to Stalin. He suggested that, before the year was out, Turkey would be in; a gesture of friendship from the Soviet would be helpful toward that end.

The reply from the Kremlin was coldly skeptical. There had been Soviet gestures in the past but, three days before the Nazis invaded Russia, the Turks had signed a treaty of friendship with the Germans. How did the Turks propose to combine obligations vis-à-vis Germany with new obligations toward Britain and Russia? More heartening from Moscow was the news that the Red armies had routed the Germans in their first shattering victory of the war. Stalingrad had been relieved, the German Sixth Army routed and 90,000 prisoners taken, including the commander, Field Marshal Paulus.

Tripoli gave the Prime Minister a magnificent conclusion to his tour. Montgomery and the Eighth Army had recently arrived, a victorious march of 1,500 miles behind them. Tripoli was the first Italian city to be delivered by British arms from German occupation, and the Prime Minister was mobbed by effusive Italians. He received the salutes and greetings of 40,000 British troops. Escorted and introduced by Montgomery, he inspected two divisions—the 51st (Highland) Division and the New Zealanders—and expressed to them the nation's admiration and gratitude. When the war was over and a man was asked what service he had done, it would be sufficient for him to say: "I marched and fought with the Desert Army."

There were tears in Churchill's eyes as the Highlanders marched past, with the pipers playing their wild, traditional airs. The men were turned out with the bearing of victors and the style of troops on ceremonial parade. "Talk about spit and polish," said Churchill, "the Highlanders and New Zealanders, after their immense ordeal in the desert, looked as if they had come out of Wellington Barracks."

There was a final security scare before he left for home. Algiers was his last call and to Algiers, according to the Intelligence Service, a noted enemy agent had been dispatched with orders to remove him. It was by an anxious Eisenhower that Churchill was received. Installed in the general's half-armored car, its windows smeared with oil and mud, he was hustled from the airport and driven by a roundabout route to the house provided for him within the military enclosure.[21]

The Prime Minister, finding the accommodation to his liking and wishing to prolong his talks with Eisenhower, shattered his host's peace of mind by proposing to extend his stay. Nor was he to be talked into leaving according to plan because of the danger from the enemy agent. Accordingly, for the benefit of any alien observers, a fake take-off was arranged, and a fictitious Prime Minister was escorted by military caravan to the airfield. At Gibraltar another fictitious VIP, arriving by plane, was met by the governor and ushered into Government House.

Having gained a twenty-four extension the Prime Minister was still reluctant to leave, but he allowed himself to be conveyed to the airfield. To his satisfaction the plane, having developed engine trouble, did not take off. Back he went for the further night's stay he had wanted. His hosts were inclined to attribute the engine failure to his machinations and the cooperation of his detective in removing an essential part.

The delays brought remonstrances from London. His colleagues wished him home and so, too, did Eisenhower. In London Churchill was worth an army; in Algiers he was a target and a responsibility.

At breakfast time on February 7 the Prime Minister landed at Lyneham airfield in Wiltshire. He had been absent for four weeks and had traveled about 10,000 miles. The strain of the journey, with its fluctuations in height and extremes of temperature, would have taxed a man twenty years younger than sixty-nine. Churchill, not surprisingly, contracted pneumonia. It was, his doctor told him, the "old man's friend." Why? Because it took them off so quietly. It was a well-contrived warning, and it was needed, for Churchill could scarcely be prevailed upon to put aside his official papers. The world's worst patient, restive and cantankerous, he clamored for forbidden cigars. His friends supported the doctor. Smuts wrote. The President cabled: "Please, please, for the sake of the world don't overdo it these days." King George ordered him to rest.

He obeyed. For six days, feeling a very sick man, he gave up work to devote himself to getting well. In this, with the aid of the recently discovered sulfa drugs, he was successful.

III. ONE CONTINENT REDEEMED

The scene was Washington, the date May, 1943. Once again President and Prime Minister met, and on this occasion the bells of the English churches had been ringing to peal in the victory of Tunis.

Operation "Torch" had ended in a triumph. For the Germans and Italians in North Africa there had been no deliverance of Dunkirk. A hundred alone succeeded in escaping, and nearly a quarter of a million were made prisoners.

There had been some hard fighting before success was won. The Allies had hoped to take Tunis and Bizerte "on the run," but the weather and German reinforcements thwarted them.

Churchill had to bear reproaches from Moscow over the delay and Stalin, with the assurance of Russian victories gained at Stalingrad, turned sharp phrases in letters to London: "I hardly need tell you how disappointing. . . ." "It is evident that Anglo-American operations have not only not been expedited, but have been postponed. . . ." [22]

As Churchill was shaking off the effects of his sickness, the advance in Africa was speeded. From east and west the Allied pincers began to close. Montgomery and his men drove on through the Mareth Line and the Gabès Gap. After the victory of Akarit, contact was made with the U.S. Second Corps, advancing from Gafsa.

"Hullo, Limey," was the greeting from an American to an Indian Army patrol that had fought its way across the deserts from the Nile.

In the final phases of the operations, the over-all Anglo-American command took control. All forces in North Africa, including Montgomery and the Eighth Army, came under Eisenhower. Alexander became Deputy Commander in Chief and was responsible for the conduct of the battles. Air Chief Marshal Tedder had authority under Eisenhower for all air operations in the Mediterranean area, while to Admiral Sir Andrew Cunningham was assigned the command of all naval forces. It was a great experiment in military cooperation. In the First World War, four years of fighting and the imminence of defeat had been needed to establish Foch as Allied generalissimo. Profiting from the lesson of the past, Prime Minister and President imposed unity of command almost from the outset.

Churchill exerted his influence to ensure that the arrangements were accepted. It needed his authority to recommend the subordination of British forces to an American C. in C., for the British Army had been fighting in Africa for a couple of years before the United States came to be engaged. There were over thirty British divisions and fewer than ten American.

From his place in the House of Commons, Churchill appealed for loyal acceptance of the new combination. It was, he said (February 11, 1943), completely in accord with modern ideas of unity of command. Members of the House and organs of the press should be careful not to criticize. "If they do, I trust it will not be on personal lines, to run one general against another, to the derangement of the smooth and harmonious relations which now prevail among this band of brothers. In General Eisenhower and General Alexander you have two men remarkable for selflessness of character and disdain of purely personal advantage. Let them alone, give them a chance."

The appeal was honored. Eisenhower proved himself to be a military diplomat, possessed of the qualities needed to run a mixed and spirited team in the same harness. Before the war was won he had established himself as second only to Churchill as champion of Allied cooperation. As strategist he was to be criticized by Montgomery and Alan Brooke, but all paid tribute to him as the great coordinator of the alliance.

After the link-up of the troops that closed the pincers on the Germans, the end was not long to be delayed. The Eighth Army swept on beyond Sfax and Enfidaville fell. On May 6 the final offensive was launched, Tunis and Bizerte were taken. The last stand of the Germans in Cape Bon was brought to an end on May 12.

Nothing could have been more fitting than that the Prime Minister should then have been in Washington. It was there, at the previous midsummer, that in his own person he had suffered the anguish of Tobruk's fall. Since General Burgoyne surrendered at Saratoga, no Englishman in the United States had ever been so unhappy as was he that day. Tunis was the avenging of Tobruk.

It was with a proud story to relate that Churchill stood before the United States Congress for the second time (May 19). The American legislators received the strategic appreciation that otherwise would have been delivered to the House of Commons.

> Mr. President [he said, for on this occasion Roosevelt was present at the Joint Session], the African war is over. Mussolini's African empire and Corporal Hitler's strategy are alike exploded. It is interesting to compute what these performances have cost these two wicked men and those who have been their tools, or their dupes. The Emperor of Abyssinia sits again upon the throne from which he was driven by Mussolini's poison gas. All the vast territories from Madagascar to Morocco, from Cairo to Casablanca, from Aden to Dakar, are under British, American or French control. One continent at least has been cleansed and purged forever from Fascist or Nazi tyranny.
>
> The African excursions of the two dictators have cost their countries in killed-and-captured 950,000 soldiers. In addition, nearly 2,400,000 gross tons of shipping have been sunk and nearly 8,000 aircraft destroyed, both of these figures being exclusive of large numbers of ships and aircraft damaged. There have also been lost to the enemy 6,200 guns, 2,550 tanks, and 70,000 trucks, which is the American name for lorries, and which, I understand, has been adopted by the Combined Staffs in Northwest Africa in exchange for the use of the word petrol in place of gasoline.
>
> These are the losses of the enemy in three years of war, and at the end of it all what is it that they have to show? The proud German Army has, by its sudden collapse, sudden crumbling, and breaking up, unexpected to all of us, the proud German Army has once again proved the truth of the saying, "The Hun is always either at your throat or your feet." That is a point which may have its bearing upon the future. But for us, arrived at this milestone in the war, we can say: "One continent redeemed." [23]

Amidst the anxieties of war, the British people paused, for a while, to rejoice. Parliament greeted the occasion with appropriate congratulations. Even from the frosty Kremlin there came a word of praise. King George VI, with acute perception, paid his Minister the tribute that was his due:

> Now that the campaign in Africa has reached a glorious conclusion, I wish to tell you how profoundly I appreciate the fact that its initial perception and successful prosecution are largely due to your vision, and to your unflinching determination in the face of

early difficulties. The African campaign has immeasurably increased the debt that this country, and indeed all the United Nations, owe to you.

GEORGE, R.I.

North Africa was, in a special sense, Winston Churchill's domain, the victory his contribution to the Allied cause. In strategy and in execution he had been the inspiration. At every turn his was the dominant influence.

It was by his original order that the command of the Middle Sea was contested. He overrode the admirals when they proposed to withdraw the Fleet from Alexandria to Gibraltar. He had denuded Britain to send tanks to the Army of the Nile. He had prevailed upon the admirals to run the risks to keep Malta and the Desert Army supplied. In days of defeat he had rejected the President's advice to cut the losses in North Africa by a timely withdrawal. He had obtained the decision to launch the first Allied landing in Africa rather than France. He had, in the final phase, insisted upon the mounting of Operation "Torch" in the strength needed to ensure success.

It was on land, in North Africa, that victory was won; but it was the larger operation, the Battle of the Mediterranean, that had been decided. With ironclads replacing Nelson's walls of oak, the British Navy had repeated the strategy of the wars with Napoleon. Sea power once again had proved decisive.

Many advantages came as the reward for Churchill's persistence. Freedom of the Mediterranean was restored, the "under-belly of the Axis" was exposed. British and American forces, by Hitler's special dispensation, had been enabled on the battlegrounds of the desert to become proficient in the craft of modern war. Montgomery and Alexander had proved themselves and the Anglo-American joint command had established itself under Eisenhower.

With the confidence springing from the first decisive victory in the West, Churchill (as is related in Chapter 3) could engage with the Joint Staffs in Washington on concerting those further measures needed to impose upon the enemy the terms of unconditional surrender proclaimed at Casablanca. The immediate matter, as he told members of the American press on May 25, was "to operate on the Italian donkey at both ends, with a carrot and with a stick."

CHAPTER TWO

PLANNING THE WELFARE STATE

1942—1943

T HERE was no escape from politics, not even in wartime, for the most
dedicated of War Ministers. Franklin Roosevelt had to win elections,
Winston Churchill divisions in Parliament. Churchill regretted the intrusion of affairs which interfered with what to him was the only business that truly mattered.

To encompassing the defeat of the dictators he would exclusively
have devoted himself, but the Prime Minister must needs ensure the
survival of his Ministry. Here Churchill was fortunately circumstanced.
His position was more securely based than those of his predecessors in
the First World War, Asquith and Lloyd George. Asquith fell because
of intrigue in his Cabinet. Churchill was supported by as loyal a team as
ever served a Prime Minister. Clement Attlee, leader of the Labour
Party, gave him wholehearted backing, and so too the strong man from
the Trades Unions, Ernest Bevin. Never was there the whisper of an
intrigue from within the Ministry. Churchill was aware of his good
fortune.

"I have been given loyalty and support," he said, "such as no Prime
Minister has ever received."

In the House of Commons he was more substantially established than
ever Lloyd George had been. Members had been elected in 1935 on a
League of Nations policy and they had voted for appeasement and
Munich. But when the hour struck they poked appeasement away in

the cupboard and transformed themselves into an efficient instrument of war. Having outlived their constitutional span of life by 1940 they voted themselves successive extensions of their existence.

They showed their confidence in the Prime Minister by defeating attacks upon his leadership by conclusive majorities. Had they failed to do so, it was in his power, as he more than once reminded them, to have swept them away in a general election, for the people gave him their unlimited trust.

When he appeared in the streets or when his picture was flashed on cinema screen the cheers and cries of "Good old Winnie!" testified to the nation's regard. As he put it himself: "My unshakeable confidence in the ties that bind me to the mass of the British people upheld me in those days of trial." Their trust in him was, in the last reckoning, his source of strength.

Once established, Churchill held undisputed place in the hearts of the nation. But there were passing phases when, for a time, the glitter of some other star caught the public eye. There was Stafford Cripps, the long, lean intellectual of the left wing of socialism. He enjoyed a following in the country that, as I have explained, could have made him a political rival to the Prime Minister had he chosen to exploit it. In the autumn of 1943, Churchill had reason to believe that Cripps would be the cause of a major political crisis. In the afterlight of history this may seem unimportant, but in those days it was the source of anxiety to both Churchill and his fellow Ministers.

Although a member of the Government, Cripps came to share some of the doubts of those outside who criticized the central direction of the war. He was disturbed by the sense of weariness in the country—of businessmen who complained of delays; of scientists whose ideas were not adopted; of workers who conceived that the weapons of war they had labored to produce were ineffective on the battlefield. He called for reform in the way the business of war was conducted and the setting up of a War Planning Directorate. Churchill regarded his ideas as unworkable, "a planner's dream." Each sought to prevail upon the other. Finally, having failed to carry his points, Cripps persuaded himself that he should retire from the Cabinet.[1]

The resignation of so prominent a member of the Government as the Lord Privy Seal and Leader of the House of Commons would have been an acute embarrassment, an attack on the Prime Minister's citadel from within. Coming after the succession of reverses in the field, the loss of one of the major members of the Cabinet would have caused a ministerial crisis. It is not to be supposed that the fate of the Government would have been involved, but it would have suffered in reputation.

These anxieties were added to the strain of waiting on the outcome of events in North Africa and, as Churchill expressed it: "I myself find waiting more trying than action." However, Cripps was prevailed upon by fellow Ministers not to push his complaints to the extremity of resignation at so critical a juncture. With patriotic spirit he held his hand and with the turn of the Allied tide found it possible to continue in office in the post of Minister of Aircraft Production, without membership in the War Cabinet. In that post his abilities found scope and he served with conspicuous success.

Rumors of these dissensions reached the outer fringes of politics to the diversion of the hangers-on. The political hacks were vastly intrigued. They put it about that Cripps' "demotion" from the War Cabinet was the penalty he had to pay for being too independent for the taste of the Prime Minister. But none then sought to weave any of their webs around Stafford Cripps in the role of successor-elect for Winston Churchill.

Embarrassment next arose over Sir William Beveridge, another figure to capture the imagination of the electors, as the author of the celebrated report that was the blueprint for the "welfare state."

It was to the credit of Churchill and his colleagues that amidst their preoccupations with the war they could find time to look ahead and consider the necessities of peace. The unimaginative plodded on from day to day carrying out their wartime responsibilities. To the question, "What are we fighting for?" the reply of the majority would have been: "Survival." So they had striven from 1914 to 1918 with the result that the old ways had survived and the promised land "fit for heroes" remained the promise of a dream. In the Second World War this mistake was not repeated. It was as well, for in the brave new world that lay ahead the Communists and their system were to be an ever-spurring reminder that the needs and longings of the proletariat were not lightly to be overlooked.

It was in 1942 that attention began seriously to be given by the Government to problems of the postwar world. The basic planning was initiated in those anxious days. There is a splendid confidence about this, a gesture of assurance that the British were going to be there when the fighting was done, to mold their existence according to their liking.

Churchill was one of the pioneers in social developments, the oldest living champion, as he once said, of state insurance. It was he who, in 1909, had spread throughout Britain a network of labor exchanges, the operating centers of unemployment insurance. To assist in that work a young man named William Beveridge had been brought into the public service.

It was this same Sir William, since promoted head of an Oxford college, who was appointed to report on how the system of state insurance should be extended when the war was over. The Beveridge Report, with the backing of the Prime Minister, received Government benediction and formed the basis for legislation that was eventually to bring into being the welfare state.

A team of civil servants assisted Sir William in his inquiry, but, though they cooperated in the examination, they did not do so in the conclusions reached. The Beveridge Report, presented on December 4, 1942, was Sir William's exclusive responsibility.

Few Government papers have reached such best-selling success. Overnight its author achieved the fame of the most popular person of the moment. His report became the focus of uncritical hopes.

The more critical, counting the most, asked where the £858,000,000 a year was to come from. To this the uncritical replied in the words of the Socialist M.P., Arthur Greenwood, "£ s. d. have become meaningless symbols." The popular demand was for the Beveridge plan, the whole plan and nothing but the plan. In the House there were protests from Socialist back-benchers because the Government did not pledge itself forthwith to accept Beveridge without qualification.

The Government rejected only one of the twenty-three Beveridge proposals. Of the others, sixteen were accepted and six were left open for further consideration. This was not sufficient for the critics, and in the House division 121 votes were registered against the Government. Political capital was then, and thereafter, made out of Beveridge. Socialists fostered the view that Churchill and the Tories were lukewarm and were standing between the people and the millennium that the Beveridge scheme was to establish. The Socialists implied that they had taken out the patent rights in the Beveridge scheme so that, despite the Tories, the millennium would be realized.

Churchill, still an impatient patient, was incapacitated from taking part in the first debates. On his recovery it was announced that he would broadcast one of his periodic speeches. It was not one of the most acceptable. I remember the occasion very well.

The loud-speaker—almost the only one in the village—was turned on. Half the villagers were grouped expectantly around the bar. There was the usual keen expectancy for the Prime Minister's words.

It was his first speech since his illness and he began, appropriately enough, with acknowledgments for the solicitous feelings his fever had inspired. But it soon became apparent that no major announcement or fighting speech was in prospect. Interest began to cool. Remarks about a new League of Nations were coldly received, and by the time the Prime Minister was proclaiming his Four-Year Plan for peace his audience had begun to dwindle. The local farmers trooped out in a body—they were in no mood to hear about schemes for transition and reconstruction.

Churchill spoke of postwar opportunities with his customary turn of phrase: "There is no finer investment for the country than putting milk into babies." He commended the Beveridge Report, recalled his own contribution to social progress, and proclaimed himself to be a "follower of the larger hope." But somehow the spirit of the speech seemed never to be kindled.

It may be that the marked "no-enthusiasm" of those farmers, unseen though they were, communicated itself to the speaker, for he closed almost with an apology, and an admission of a possible unseemliness that attention in Britain should seem to be diverted to peace when the Russians were fighting so dearly for life and honor.

The passages in the broadcast on which the attention of politicians was riveted were those concerned with the future of the parties once the war was over and the emergency was passed that had brought the Coalition Government into existence. The Prime Minister's Four-Year Plan gave rise to speculation about the ministerial team that would put those postwar schemes into operation. Since Ministers of all parties were engaged on planning ahead in so much detail, did it not mean that they contemplated working together to meet the difficulties of peace as they were mastering the perils of war? There was careful scrutiny of the words Churchill used: "When this [Four-Year] Plan has been shaped, it will have to be presented to the country either by a national Government formally representative, as this one is, of the three parties in the state, or by a national Government comprising the best men in all parties who are willing to serve. I cannot tell how these matters will settle themselves."

By no politicians were these passages given more anxious scrutiny than by the Socialists. The political truce, though observed, was irksome to them. Its extension into the days of peace was not to be tolerated and yet it appeared almost as if their leaders in the Government, planning now for postwar times, might be engaging themselves to continue the coalition indefinitely. Emanuel Shinwell put a direct question in the House to the Prime Minister.

"Did the broadcast statement," he asked, "about a Four-Year Plan, based on a coalition Ministry, represent the policy of the Government?"

To this the Prime Minister replied: "The answer about a Four-Year Plan is in the affirmative, but whether it will be put forward by a coalition Government or not depends on what the various parties decide to do."

From this it was inferential that Attlee, Bevin and Morrison had so far entered into no arrangement for a four-year coalition for the Four-Year Plan. To gain assurances on this point, the Socialist leaders were cross-questioned at the next meeting of their parliamentary followers. Clement Attlee specifically stated that he and his fellow Ministers had made no arrangements. They were instructed not to enter into any binding commitments about the future. Socialist M.P.s resolved to break with their wartime political associates the moment the military situation should permit.

The Prime Minister would readily have accepted the continuance of the Coalition Government to undertake the tasks of peace. Among the men of his time—and that is equivalent to three parliamentary generations—he stood out as a "party man." Yet no parliamentarian was more disposed to enter into arrangements with the other side. Even before the 1914-18 war, in the days when political affairs were in a state of perpetual crisis, when civil war was threatening over Ireland, and when the First World War was imminent, Churchill (Lloyd George also) was disposed to come to terms with the Opposition and approaches to the Conservatives were made, though they came to naught. It is the verdict of history that Britain hates coalitions, but the experience of coalition Ministries in two wars has proved the advantage of sinking party differences and cooperating for the national cause in time of emergency.

Churchill made his position clear in a speech to the House on the coal situation on December 13, 1943. A demand had been made for nationalization of the mines and the Prime Minister was giving the Government's decision against it. He could not, he said, be responsible for undertaking this great change in time of war, because he considered that it would need to be ratified or preceded by a national mandate. He went on:

> In time of war, or great public stress or danger, a national coalition, with all parties officially represented in it as parties, not as individuals, gives great strength and unity to the country, as it is doing now. Anyone, or any body of men, who succeeded in breaking it up in time of war would, I am sure, receive the censure of the vast majority of the people. But in time of peace conditions are different.
>
> I earnestly hope it may be possible to preserve national unity after the war. But I say quite frankly that I should not be alarmed for the future of this country if we had to return to party government. But this I will say—and the House will pardon me, I am sure, for saying it—that whatever differences, bitternesses, or party fighting may have to take place among us, each representing our constituencies and our

convictions, things can never be quite the same again. Friendships have been established and ties have been made between the two parties, minglings have taken place, understandings have been established which, without any prejudice to each man's public duty, will undoubtedly have a mellowing effect on a great deal of our relations in the future. For my part I must say that I feel I owe a great debt to the Labour Party, who were a most stalwart support to me at the time when I first undertook the burdens I am still being permitted to bear.

When the time came, Churchill was to be disappointed in his earnest hope. It was not found possible to preserve national unity when the war in Europe was over.

Here I feel compelled to make a short digression for a record of Churchill's speech on the place of the House of Commons in the national life.

For four decades, with their ins and outs, he had been a member of the House. He had advanced himself to first place by the speeches he had delivered within its walls. Hitler's bombs had left the House chamber in ruins and it was necessary to provide for its reconstruction. What model was to be followed? There were those who thought of a larger building to give each member a seat of his own. Churchill would have no break with tradition, and he found cogent reasons for restoring the place as it had been, with its occasional inconveniences. His speech was his confession of faith in parliamentary democracy and his declaration of love for the Mother of Parliaments.

"We shape our dwellings and afterward our buildings shape us," he began epigrammatically. "Having dwelt and served for more than forty years in the late chamber, and having derived very great pleasure and advantage therefrom, I should naturally like to see it restored in all essentials to its old form, convenience and dignity."

Two main characteristics of the old House commanded the approval and support of reflecting and experienced M.P.s. The first was that its shape was oblong and not semicircular. This was a very potent factor in Britain's political life. The semicircular assembly, which appealed to political theorists, enabled every individual or every group to move round the center, adopting various shades of pink as the political weather changed.

"I am," said the Prime Minister, "a convinced supporter of the party system in preference to the group system. I have seen many earnest and ardent Parliaments destroyed by the group system. The party system is much favored by the oblong form of chamber. It is easy for an individual to move through those insensible gradations from left to right, but the act of crossing the floor is one that requires serious consideration. I am well informed on the matter for I have accomplished that difficult process not once only, but twice.

"Were this House large enough to contain all its members, nine-tenths of its debates would be conducted in the depressing atmosphere of an almost-empty or half-empty chamber." The essence of good House of Commons speaking was the conversational style, the facility for quiet, informal interruptions and interchanges. Harangue from a rostrum would be a bad substitute. If Parliament was to be a strong, easy, flexible instrument of free debate, a small chamber and a sense of intimacy were indispensable.

He spoke of the place the House had won among the institutions of the nation. "It thrives," he said, "upon criticism. It is perfectly impervious to newspaper abuse or taunts from any quarter, and it is capable of digesting almost anything, or almost any body of gentlemen, whatever may be their views with which they arrive. There is no situation to which it cannot address itself with vigor and ingenuity. It is the citadel of British liberty. It is the foundation of our laws.

"In this war the House of Commons has proved itself to be a rock upon which an administration, without losing the confidence of the House, has been able to confront the most terrible emergencies. The House has shown itself able to face the possibility of national destruction with classical composure. I do not know how else this country can be governed than by the House of Commons playing its part in all its broad freedom in British public life."

Before the speech many Members of Parliament had been in favor of enlargement of the House chamber. When the division was taken there were only three votes against the course the Prime Minister advocated.

The war, by 1943, was going well and there was little but praise for the once-challenged central direction. Confidence in Winston Churchill, the leader of the people at war, was unqualified and universal. Nevertheless, even with the political truce in operation, Conservative seats were in jeopardy. Politicians grew concerned. There were no whisperings now about changing the captain. There was no doubt that the Prime Minister was the Tory Party's greatest political asset.

Feeling at Westminster was inevitably influenced by events in the constituencies. There was a restiveness in the House. Where war unity was not involved, back-benchers became more assertive, both Socialists and Tory reformers. On the education bill, for example, Mrs. Cazalet Keir and some of the progressive Tories caused the Government to suffer its first and only defeat by carrying an amendment in favor of equal pay for men and women teachers. Under the Prime Minister's direction, members had to reverse their vote (not, of course, their views) the following day.

Back-benchers of all parties were critical of the Government for what they termed its neglect of the problems of peace. There was no neglect of planning, but where party differences were involved preparation had to stop short of legislation. Planning was not likely to disturb the political peace. Legislation might have brought about a clash in which compromise would have been impossible. The Prime Minister would permit nothing to jeopardize political unity. It was a contribution to the national cause but, politically, the consequences were unfortunate for him. The impression was fostered that right-wing members of the Government were obstructing left-wingers from carrying out progressive measures.

The tide of politics was running strongly against the Government. An electoral truce was in operation. When vacancies occurred in the Commons, Socialists did not, officially, contest a Conservative seat and, in their turn, were not opposed in constituencies previously represented by Labour M.P.s. The Tories retained their seats only with difficulty. In a run of seven by-elections, for example, three duly resulted in the return of Labour candidates. But in four constituencies previously held by Tories only two were retained by the official Party nominees. In the other cases independent candidates presented themselves, attacked the Government, and reached Westminster on the rising tide of dissatisfaction.

Churchill might protest at the idea that the way to win the war was to knock the Government about and harry them from side to side. It was hard to bear with charity, but his protests were in vain. Not even his prestige and popularity could prevail against anti-Tory feeling. But the day of reckoning lay two years ahead. For the present the need continued for all to bend their efforts to the "ever more vigorous prosecution of the supreme task."

CHAPTER THREE

TRAVELS OF A STRATEGIST

MAY, 1943

I N THE first week of May in the year 1943, Winston Churchill was once
again running the hazards of an Atlantic crossing on his way to the
third Washington conference. It marked the turning point of the war.

Just three years had passed since he had taken office. Precariously he
and his people had survived the perils that had seemed about to engulf
them. Now the initiative was passing from Hitler and, at the conference
the Prime Minister was about to attend, the date was to be fixed for the
assault across the Channel on the citadel of Europe.

Stalingrad, El Alamein, the Battle of the Coral Sea—on every front
there were portents. But, in war, the future remains uncertain and incalculable till the last gun is fired. In 1943 all was still to play for. The
Germans had been contained and repulsed, the Italians were despondent,
but Hitler's hopes were undimmed. Secret weapons in the Nazi armory
would yet, he was confident, batter Britain into capitulation.

Churchill, with three years of reverses behind him, had cause for
measured satisfaction. Even as he made the Atlantic crossing the final
roundup (as I have described) was proceeding in North Africa. And,
from beyond the curtain of Germany's extended frontiers, came reports
of the mounting damage to the enemy centers of war production inflicted
by "Bomber" Harris's men by night and by the American Flying Fortresses by day. Systematically the Reich was being pounded into ruins.
Londoners learned, not without an occasional spurt of sympathy, that

their sufferings throughout the black winter of the Blitz were being requited. As Churchill remarked, "Though the mills of God grind slowly yet they grind exceeding small. And for my part I take it as an example of sublime and poetic justice that those who have loosed these horrors upon mankind will now in their homes and persons feel shattering strokes of just retribution."

From the rain of bombs there was no escape. Hitler drew his own grim conclusions from the evidence his own devastated cities provided. If such destruction could be caused by piloted planes, what must be the havoc from fleets of pilotless bombers? There was Hitler's secret weapon on which he placed his final hopes.

The flying bomb was nearing completion in German workshops. It was to be manufactured on a vast scale. A prodigious armada of flying bombs would be rained from the skies upon the towns of Britain. And after the flying bomb would come the rocket bomb, the explosive warhead that could be sent up into space to descend unheralded upon London.

While German ingenuity was devoted to buzz bombs and rockets, Allied scientists were pressing on with atomic research. Already the problem of chain reaction had been solved. It was the halfway mark to the atom bomb. Encouraged by this progress, the research workers pushed on with fanatical zeal, believing themselves to be matched in a life-and-death race with the Germans.[1]

Churchill's voyage to the United States for the conference called Trident was the fifth mission overseas he had undertaken since Pearl Harbor had brought the Americans into the war. In this, the final phase of his war leadership, he was the peripatetic envoy and liaison officer in chief to the United Nations.

At a moment's notice he was prepared to travel, now east, now west, as the urgencies of the time demanded. It was a contribution to the cause he reckoned himself to be specially circumstanced to undertake. Geography, as he put it, was the great obstacle to the preservation of Allied unity. Distance made it difficult for the three leaders to meet.

Because of his physical handicaps it was not easy for the President to undertake long-distance travel. Stalin was reluctant, even for a day, to leave his post in the Kremlin. Churchill had neither physical nor political obstacles to journeys abroad. The attacks on his leadership had petered out with the change in Allied fortunes. His colleagues murmured against the dangers he ran, but gradually he was educating them into accepting these as occupational hazards of wartime premiership.

There was, in this later phase, a change in channels of the Prime

Minister's contribution to the war effort. His direct interventions in the conduct of operations were necessarily curtailed.

In the early days as Defense Minister of the only state resisting Hitler in the field, he had been accustomed to dealing personally with commanders on land and at sea, exhorting, rebuking and directing—prodding, to use his own word. As fighting allies were added, an alteration was inevitable. What had been permissible from a premier to the heads of his own armies was obviously not to be tolerated when combined forces were involved, no matter how close the alliance.

Thereafter he had to deal with the Joint Chiefs of Staff, which separated him, as it did the President, from direct contact with the commanders. He accepted the new position without demur, giving to that organization his complete trust and backing it with his authority. He sat in at the decisive deliberations of the Joint Chiefs as strategist in his own right, and engaged in their discussion when he thought fit. To them he delivered many impassioned exhortations, disputing some projects and advocating others with unflagging persistence. Decisions once taken he accepted with characteristic loyalty.

For the Trident conference, Churchill so far submitted to doctor's orders as to abandon the idea of an air crossing. As he was not considered to be sufficiently recovered to stand the strain of flying at great heights, he agreed to travel by sea, and a suite was prepared for him aboard the liner *Queen Mary*. For the benefit of spying eyes, notices in the Dutch language were posted to give credence to the pretense that the VIP about to make the trip was the Queen of the Netherlands.

On May 5 Churchill took up his quarters in the *Queen Mary,* which had on board five thousand German prisoners of war. A full conclave of advisers made up his party—Chiefs of Staff and their staffs, Wavell from India, Somerville from the Mediterranean, and many more. This attendance was deemed necessary because of the clash on strategy that was in prospect. Victory in Torchland had not simplified Allied problems. Americans and British were at variance over the next steps to be taken.

For the maintenance of the team spirit it was as well that Churchill was available for good-will missions overseas. In the spring of 1943 good will between Whitehall and Washington was at a low ebb. The professionals on either side of the Atlantic were bedeviling relations with their jealousies and suspicions. The Americans, on the alert against imperialism, looked askance on moves in the Mediterranean. The British were no less mistrustful of their American friends.

Churchill, with growing concern, had noticed the signs. There were mutterings among his own advisers about the shortcomings of the Americans. They were not, it was pressed upon him, living up to the Casablanca agreements; they were seemingly more interested in settling accounts with the Japanese than with the Italians. Admiral King was diverting to the Far East naval craft that were essential for the assaults on Europe. Never were divergencies in strategy more acute.

For the British it was axiomatic that from Africa the advance should be against the "under-belly of the Axis." American opinion was set against further adventuring in the Mediterranean. Long-range exchanges by cable intensified differences. Discord was in the air, disheartening and disconcerting. If a rift in Allied good-fellowship was to be averted, then, Churchill concluded, it was imperative for the Joint Staffs to meet face to face and hammer out an agreement.

A week after leaving the Clyde, Churchill was welcomed by the President to the White House (May 11). The Joint Staffs at once got down to business. Inaugural speeches from the two leaders left no doubt about the conflict that was impending. The Prime Minister led off the debate by enlarging on the opportunities that had opened up in the Mediterranean, and the great prize of knocking Italy out of the war. The President argued to the contrary, questioning whether much advantage was to be gained from the occupation of Italy. In his view, the best way to fight the Germans was to engage them from across the English Channel on the old battlefields of France.

Having set the problem, President and Prime Minister withdrew. The teams of rival theorists were left to their disputations. There was no more vigorous engagement in military dialectics.

From the Churchill memoirs you will gain little idea of the intensity of the rumpus. Churchill was always reluctant to parade domestic difference in the Allied household. In the diaries of Alan Brooke, curtains were drawn aside and we were made privy to secrets of the conference chamber. We learned how sharply pressed were the differences between the opposing strategists—how the Americans demanded the closing down of operations in the Mediterranean once Sicily had been taken; how Admiral King resisted any suggestion that would direct forces from the Pacific theater of war; and how "Vinegar Joe" Stilwell added to the tension of the debates by his antagonism toward the "Limeys" and all their doings.[2]

Brooke and his colleagues were driven almost to despair as they contemplated the rejection of their carefully planned, step-by-step measures for carrying the war back into Europe. Unless the Americans could be prevailed upon, the Italians, on the verge of collapse, would be given a respite, and the Middle Sea would not be ridded once and for all of the nuisance of the Italian warships.

In these disputations Churchill, like F.D.R., took little part at first hand. Once more Churchill met the leading journalists of the United States, the President turning over to him his weekly press conference. He submitted himself to the interrogations of one hundred and fifty inquiring minds, answering or evading them with impromptus in his best parliamentary manner. Prime Minister and newsmen enjoyed themselves. The Americans greeted with applause a quotation from one of their own great generals, the successful Confederate leader, Nathan Bedford Forrest, who, when asked about the secret of his success, replied: "I get thar fustest with the mostest men." [3]

There was also Mme. Chiang Kai-shek to engage Churchill's attention. This lady was applying a woman's attractiveness to pleading the cause of her husband and Nationalist China. This was a task for which she was well equipped, for General Dill remarked that, meeting her, he received a very definite impression that the Chinese were not lacking in she-power.

A meeting with the Prime Minister was proposed and to that end the President invited her to stay at the White House. Madame, however, was prepared to do no more than make herself available for a meeting in New York, then her center of operations. As a gesture of good will, Churchill offered to travel half the distance to New York, but this did not accord with the lady's notions of the respect due to her, and she frowned at his levity. Churchill, without complaint, sustained the weight of her displeasure and the lost opportunity of meeting her. [4]

To the President, Churchill voiced his concern over atom-bomb developments. The British, he said, were being excluded from sharing in the results of the experiments at Chicago, where the first atomic pile had been made to function.

Churchill had, with regret, to submit that as the research advanced, the reserve of the Americans increased. At the outset of cooperation, everything was to be thrown into the common pool on the basis of sharing results as equal partners. But some months since a change had come over the Americans. The War Department had asked to be kept informed about any British experiments, but were refusing information regarding their own. British concern reached the point where the Prime Minister had cabled a warning to Harry Hopkins that, if the sharing of information were not resumed, Britain would be compelled to go ahead separately, and "that would be a very sombre decision."

The President gave sympathetic attention to these submissions. It was not by his intention the partnership had been breached. The War Department chiefs had their own ideas about this work. Their policy was to furnish information to those and those alone who could use it in furtherance of the war effort. In the interests of security they had proposed to restrict the interchange of information to this definite objective. To do otherwise, in their view, would be to decrease security without advancing the war effort.

There was no need for vigorous protest to be made against this policy of exclusiveness. The President confirmed that the original share-all pact should be honored. Churchill cabled home that the exchange of information was to be resumed henceforth. The Tube Alloys project was in the future to be considered a joint one to which both countries would contribute their best endeavors.

"I understood," Churchill added, "that the President's ruling would be based upon the fact that this weapon may well be developed in time for the present war, and that it thus falls within the general agreement covering the interchange of research and invention secrets."

Sir John Anderson, Lord President of the Council, to whom this cable was addressed, was agreeably impressed by the information it gave. He was the member of the War Cabinet charged with responsibility for atomic research. His knowledge of developments in America was a secret few in Britain were privileged to share, even among his Cabinet colleagues. "In time for the present war"—that was a prospect few would have thought possible when work on Tube Alloys had been started.[5]

At length the strategists in Washington completed their business. After twelve days of dispute, an agreed program was arrived at. The date was fixed for the invasion of France as May 1, 1944—and a compromise was accepted over Mediterranean strategy.

Churchill was relieved that agreement had been reached, for divergences at one time had been most serious, threatening to wreck the conference. He was, however, far from satisfied with the compromise on Italy. The utmost that could be wrung from the Americans was the issuing of instructions to prepare for the possibility of extending the Italian campaign.

"Husky," the assault on Sicily, was to be carried out. Eisenhower, as a matter of urgency, was to draw up plans for operations in exploitation of "Husky," "as are best calculated to eliminate Italy from the war, and to contain the maximum number of German forces." Whether, in fact, any such plan would be adopted was left for future decision by the Joint Chiefs of Staff.

Churchill voiced his protest at this compromise. For an hour he harangued the Joint Chiefs, pressing the urgency of the need to go ahead with the invasion of Italy, with the possible extension of operations into Yugoslavia and Greece. His arguments made no impression on the Americans, who had already spent themselves in resisting the same proposals from the British side at the Joint Staff meetings. They were in-flexibly opposed to any operations that would draw off forces earmarked already for the all-out assault in France.

Churchill left Washington for North Africa to bring his persuasive-ness to bear on Eisenhower. Since the decision on future operations in the Mediterranean was to rest so largely with the man on the spot, then on the spot the Prime Minister must be. The two Chiefs of Staff, Alan Brooke and General Marshall, traveled with him.

Churchill was by then sufficiently recovered in his health to permit the crossing to be made by air. The nonstop flight of three thousand miles to Gibraltar was still, in those earlier days, a considerable under-taking. He was comfortably asleep in his double bed in the bridal suite of the Boeing when a sudden jolt brought him to consciousness. He made his way to the control room and was told that the plane had been struck by lightning. No damage had been done, which was as well, for they were a thousand miles from anywhere in particular. The trip was com-pleted without further incident.

A short hop from Gibraltar brought the party to Algiers, where Churchill stepped from the plane cheered by the thought of a few days to relax in the bright African sunshine. After the labors of Washington he felt himself entitled to a break. But first there was business to be done, and he lost no time in getting down to it. As soon as he landed he was trundling along with Eisenhower. He made no secret about it that his purpose was to secure the decision he wanted for knocking Italy out of the war. Three times that evening, with three different approaches, he stated his case. Eisenhower was relieved that General Marshall was at his side to sustain the United States point of view.[6]

On the second evening there was a reiteration of the arguments used on the first. The listener might think the ground had been covered, re-covered, and uncovered. Churchill insisted on a recapitulation. To back his arguments he offered British shipping to carry the war into Italy. The British people would be proud to halve their rations if need be to release ships for use against the Italians.

The atmosphere at Algiers was several shades more sympathetic than it had been in Washington. As a good commander, Eisenhower sought the maximum exploitation of the victory that had been won. After Sicily fell he was ready to push across into Italy. But he, too, was suspi-cious of diversionary operations in the Mediterranean, and any measure tending to weaken "Overlord" (invasion of France) met with his prompt and rocklike opposition.

It was in these days that Eisenhower came to experience the Churchillian persistence in any matter involving strongly held convictions. Eisenhower found that Churchill would return again and again to the attack; at times he would become intensely oratorical, using humor and pathos with equal facility, drawing on every source for his quotations from Greek classics to Donald Duck.[7]

A staff conference was called of the men on the spot. Eisenhower was in the chair, supported by his staff and General Marshall. In addition to Alan Brooke, Alexander was there, Cunningham for the Navy, Tedder for the Air Force, and Montgomery, to whom the Sicily operation was to be entrusted.

To this audience Churchill spoke eloquently of the prospects that the capture of Sicily would open up. Eisenhower responded with a declaration that, if Sicily were polished off easily, then he would cross the Strait of Messina and establish a bridgehead on the Italian mainland.

Churchill was satisfied with the generally expressed desire of the leaders to go boldly forward, and for their guidance in further deliberations he presented some background notes. To compel or induce Italy to quit the war was, he submitted, "the only objective in the Mediterranean worthy of the famous campaign already begun."

As a relief from high strategy he took a hand in promoting good will between the two wings of the Fighting French. Anthony Eden was summoned from Downing Street to lend a hand in these delicate negotiations—"he is a much better fellow than I to be best man at the Giraud —de Gaulle wedding."

The proudest moment of the visit came when the Prime Minister stood in the Roman amphitheater at Carthage amidst soldiers of the Desert Armies. He was delighted to address the modern invaders in this ancient setting.

"I was speaking," he said afterward to Alan Brooke, "from where the cries of Christian virgins rent the air whilst the devouring lions consumed them. And yet [the quaint afterthought] I am no lion and certainly no virgin." [8]

When the departure time came, the invasion of the island of Pantelleria was about to be staged. Churchill wanted to remain to see the show from the grandstand of a destroyer. He was, he submitted, entitled to be in attendance seeing that he had a financial interest in the result. Differing from Eisenhower over the number of prisoners to be taken, he wagered that the haul would be no more than 3,000. In the end he had to pay out on a difference of 8,000—for the final figure was 11,000 prisoners. Despite these matters of high finance, Churchill's claim to see the Pantelleria operation was disallowed on security grounds.

There was apprehension over the return flight to Britain. The 500-mile hop to Gibraltar was no difficulty, but the last lap home was perilous. The Germans were on the watch, for the North African visit had been widely reported. The enemy patrols were eluded, but the perils were brought home by the fate of another aircraft boarded at Lisbon by a stoutish passenger smoking a cigar. This plane was shot down and among the thirteen passengers who perished was the actor, Leslie Howard.

Churchill could travel home with the assurance that he had left nothing unsaid to prompt Eisenhower and his men to drive on against the Italians. His fellow countrymen would have been surprised to learn of the nature of the discussions in which he had been engaged. The vast majority of them accepted it as a matter of course, requiring no argument, that Italy was to be next on the Allied list. They would have been startled to know that their Prime Minister had been faced with the suggestion that, after going into Sicily, the cease-fire should be sounded in the Mediterranean. A political crisis would have erupted at the mere idea that the successes achieved were not to be followed up, and that thirty Allied divisions in the Mediterranean should be rested from summer to spring while the assault on France was being mounted.

Not a breath of the American objections was allowed to reach the British public. In British minds the only doubt was whether the assault on Hitler's citadel immediately expected was to be made northward from Italy or across the Channel in France.

Back in England the Prime Minister lost no time in making his report to the House of Commons. It was one of his shorter surveys and, by way of excuse, he remarked that he had given to the joint session of Congress the statement which he would otherwise have made to the House on the victory in Tunisia:

> That is I think a valid explanation. Certainly, when I found myself walking into that august assembly, the free Congress of the most powerful community in the world, and when I gave them, as I would do in this House, a businesslike stocktaking survey of the war and of our joint interest, even touching upon controversial matters or matters of domestic controversy over there, and when I thought of all our common history and of the hopes that lie before us, I felt that this was an age of memorable importance to mankind. For there can be no doubt that, whatever world organization is brought into being after this war, that organization must be richer and stronger if it is founded on the friendship and fraternal relations and the deep understanding prevailing, and now growing, between the British Commonwealth of Nations and the United States of America.

Enemy resistance in Tunisia ceased on May 12. There was a lull for some weeks. Europe waited in suspense for the next Allied move. The school of thought that predicted a Second Front in France professed support for its views in Churchill's guarded phrase: "It is evident that amphibious operations of peculiar complexity and hazard on a large scale are approaching." The next-blow-against-Italy school, however, pointed in June to the taking of Pantelleria, the island fortress which hoisted the white flag without a struggle after days of air and sea bombardment. Here, it was claimed, an assault in Italy was assuredly betokened.

At the end of June, Churchill drove through the Blitz-scarred London streets to Guildhall to be made a Freeman of the City. In the Guildhall ruins he received the scroll of freedom in a casket of oak salvaged from the ancient roof. His speech was scrutinized for any clue it might yield to future operations. The phrase was there, impressive but inscrutable: "I cannot go further today than to say that it is very probable that there will be heavy fighting in the Mediterranean and elsewhere before the leaves of autumn fall. For the rest we must leave the unhappy Italians and their German tempters and taskmasters to anxieties which will aggravate from week to week and from month to month."

On July 12 doubts were resolved. Sicily was invaded. The Allies gained a footing on an outpost of Europe. The Italian forces had no will to fight. In the towns of Sicily the Allied armies were greeted as liberators, rather than as conquerors. German resistance was stiffer, and British troops on the east of the island had to overcome strong opposition.

A tremor of alarm spread throughout Italy when, on July 19, American bombers attacked military targets in the area of Rome. Allied propaganda supplemented the effects of Allied bombs. President and Prime Minister addressed a joint message to the Italian people, its terms attuned to their hopes and their hates. The war now being carried into their territories was "the direct consequence of the shameful leadership to which you have been subjected by Mussolini and the Fascist regime." The Italians were of the same way of thinking. Italian soldiers had been "betrayed and abandoned by the Germans on the Russian Front and on every battlefield in Africa, from Alamein to Cape Bon." The Italians were conscious of the shame. "The sole hope for Italy's survival lies in honorable capitulation." It was an expression of Italian hopes.

On July 19, Mussolini hurried north to meet his Nazi master. He came back to Rome and his fall. On the evening of Sunday, July 25, at about eleven o'clock, people in Britain heard with grim satisfaction that he had been cast out by his Fascist associates. In the House, two days later, Churchill pronounced, with relish, his downfall and the close of a twenty-one-year epoch in the history of Italy:

The end of Mussolini's long and severe reign over the Italian people undoubtedly marks the close of an epoch in the life of Italy.

The keystone of the Fascist arch has crumbled. The guilt and folly of Mussolini have cost the Italian people dear. It looked so safe and easy in May, 1940, to stab falling France in the back and advance to appropriate the Mediterranean interests and possessions of what Mussolini no doubt sincerely believed was a decadent and ruined Britain. It looked so safe and easy to fall upon the much smaller state of Greece. However there have been interruptions. Events have taken a different course.

And what of the future? A decision by the new Italian Government of General Badoglio to continue under the German yoke would not seriously affect the course of the war, still less alter its ultimate result. The only consequence would result in the land of Italy being seared and scarred and blackened from one end to the other. The choice was open to the Italians and the Prime Minister's counsel was to allow them to "stew in their own juice for a bit and hot up the fire a bit to accelerate the process."

So the Italians were suffered to sizzle. Air raids on their cities, Milan and Turin, heated the fires. In Sicily their German allies fought on, the ravages of war adding to the ages-old destruction of Etna, on whose slopes the last engagements were fought. The inevitable end came on August 17. The island had been taken in thirty-eight days with a loss to the enemy of 165,000 in killed, wounded, and prisoners.

By this time Churchill was again on his travels, for staff differences persisted. Quadrant was convened to settle what Trident had failed to solve.

CHAPTER FOUR

CONFLICTS AT QUEBEC
JULY–SEPTEMBER, 1943

M USSOLINI's fall found the Allies somewhat unprepared. Vast opportunities had been opened up in the field, but they could not
readily be exploited, for Eisenhower's hands had been tied by the decisions reached at the recent Washington conference. Political problems
arose that had in no way been provided for. There was an immediate
scurry to evolve a common policy.

For months past Churchill had watched the Italians expectantly. In a
note to the War Cabinet the previous November he had speculated on
the possibility that they might suddenly be faced with peace moves from
Rome. As recently as June he had exchanged cables with the President
on the terms of the propaganda leaflet to be rained down on Rome from
the skies.[1]

As originally designed by Roosevelt this was to have been an all-
American appeal. Churchill submitted that the message should be ad-
dressed not by Roosevelt alone, but jointly by Prime Minister and
President, for after all "we have been longer in the quarrel or war with
Italy than you," and there should not, in the alliance, be "any senior
partner." To those submissions F.D.R. readily responded.

As soon as the news came of the Duce's downfall, Prime Minister and
President set about taking the practical steps they had previously
neglected. Messages crossed in cable. "Let us," urged Churchill, "consult

together so as to take joint action." "Let me," appealed F.D.R., "have your thoughts."

Churchill drew up for the War Cabinet a memorandum of policy should the newly formed Badoglio Government seek peace. He listed the military requirements—the surrender of the Italian Fleet, the withdrawal of Italian troops from Greece and the Balkans, and the release of 74,000 British prisoners of war who must be spared the "measureless horrors of incarceration in Germany." The handing over of the "head devil," as F.D.R. had named Mussolini, and his partners in crime would be required.[2]

As to military action in Italy, Churchill submitted that it was "a time to dare"; they should push to the north forthwith. The President, in his cable, had referred to the use of all Italian territory and transportation against the Germans in the north, and against the whole Balkan peninsula. The Prime Minister endorsed this approvingly. It would be of the highest urgency to get agents, commandos, and supplies by sea across the Adriatic into Albania and Yugoslavia.

Approved by the War Cabinet, the Prime Minister's memorandum was accepted by the President, to whom it was immediately cabled. "It expressed generally," he commented, "my thoughts of today on prospects and methods."

Other complications shortly appeared. Churchill was prepared to deal with any non-Fascist government—"we should not be too particular." The President was dubious; he had memories of the trouble over Darlan in North Africa. The same voices in America would again raise a chorus of protest: "Contentious people here, getting ready to make a row if we seem to recognize the House of Savoy or Badoglio." [3]

Churchill was not prepared to defer to the political moralists: "We have no right to lay undue burdens on our troops." Herein he was supported by Eisenhower and the Chiefs of Staff. From hard, cold military calculation they were ready to avail themselves of the enormous advantage to be gained from dealing with any Italian government that had the authority to deliver an immediate surrender.[4]

There was concern in Washington over the future of the Italian state. How could the House of Savoy be identified with democratic government? Churchill, an avowed monarchist, who recommended the blessings of constitutional monarchy for Europe's ancient states, did not share all the misgivings felt in Washington. In any event, that was no time for constitutional chaos—"we must be careful not to throw everything in Italy into the melting pot."

After these preliminaries there were surrender terms to agree upon, in preparation for the peace approaches that were imminently expected.

For such complicated matters cabled exchanges were inadequate. It was time for the principals to meet. Arrangements were quickly concluded for a full conference to be held by invitation of the Canadians in the citadel of Quebec.[5]

Italy was the immediate occasion, but the Quadrant (code name) conference ranged discursively over the entire world scene. With the Chinese represented for the first time, prolonged consideration was given to the Far East. Blueprints for the coming assault on Normandy (Operation "Overlord") were for the first time considered in some detail. The old clashes on strategy in the Mediterranean were inevitably renewed and, having gained a new urgency, they were debated with an added asperity.

Churchill's expectations had mounted with the progress of operations in Sicily. He looked for bold moves in Italy. "Why crawl up Italy's leg like a harvest bug?" he asked. Let them strike at the knee, Rome itself. His flaming hopes were fanned by Roosevelt's phrase about "the whole Balkan peninsula."

He boarded the *Queen Mary* with his customary optimism and buoyancy, looking for a successful outcome of all the discussions. There was a "lot of fretfulness" on the other side of the Atlantic but, as he cabled back to King George, he was confident it would be removed.[6]

He had been delighted by the President's inspiration that had appointed Quebec as the meeting place. He looked forward to standing once more at the gateway to Canada and looking down from the citadel on the St. Lawrence waterway. There would be the opportunity for relaxation amidst the cares of state. Mrs. Churchill traveled with him, and their daughter Mary, then a subaltern in an antiaircraft battery, did duty as aide-de-camp. All the Warden family—Colonel Warden was Churchill's *nom de guerre*—set out across the Atlantic with the liveliest expectations.

There was a staff team of two hundred on this occasion. A last-minute recruit was Orde Wingate, newly summoned home to report on his achievements in the jungle of Burma. At a moment's notice he was conscripted into the Prime Minister's party and Mrs. Wingate, with even less ceremony, was bundled aboard the *Queen Mary,* a delighted participant in her husband's trip.

In approaching the conference, the Allies could count on one advantage they had not previously enjoyed—mastery at last over the U-boat. Patrols by sea and air, and the discerning eye of radar, had, for the time, won ascendency in the Battle of the Atlantic. To provide the vessels for the North Africa landings in 1942 it had been necessary to make a 45 per cent cut in the transport of rations for Britain. In 1943, plans for "Overlord" could go forward without overanxiety about where the ships were to come from.

There was a memorable moment on the crossing. Before Churchill's eyes, as he lay in his cabin, a large-scale map of Northern Europe was unfurled. It illustrated the scheme for the invasion of France timed for the following May, and he listened to the unfolding of the secrets of D-Day. For many months past detailed plans for Operation "Overlord" had been prepared under the direction of General Morgan, Chief of Staff to an Allied Commander still to be designated.[7]

The Prime Minister was impressed by the design for "Overlord"—it was majestic. The Normandy beaches had been selected for the grand assault. Here, from the English south coast, it is more than double the distance of the shortest crossing, to the Pas de Calais. It represented the range of the effective air umbrella for the attackers, for in those days the fighter plane was limited in its flight. The open beaches of Normandy were considered to offer better chances than the shortest crossing, since the French cliffs at Calais were formidably guarded by the enemy as the obvious point for attack. For Normandy the absence of a suitable port seemed to be an insuperable obstacle; if there was no port in existence then the invaders would need to bring one along.

Here Churchill's forethought contributed to the solution. Over twelve months earlier he had directed inquiry into the feasibility of making piers to float with the tides.

Now, in his cabin, he learned that the seed of inventiveness had borne fruit. Plans were complete for making two steel and concrete harbors to be towed across the English Channel, two "Mulberries" as they were styled in code, together with floating breakwaters. Another and more visionary project was for the creation of floating airfields to be anchored off the Normandy coast. Modeled on the iceberg, they were to be fashioned out of a mixture of ice and wood pulp—reinforced ice remarkable in its hardness.

The Prime Minister's satisfaction grew as he listened to the exposition of the blueprints for "Overlord." Here outlined was the fulfillment of the vision that had been his eighteen months before on an earlier Atlantic crossing. Then, on his way to the first Washington Conference, his imagination had kindled the conception of Allied troops in their many thousands landing on the open beaches of the Continent. Now, in the Morgan plans, the ideas were given the embodiment of facts and figures. No longer were they the fabric of a dream. There was a report in detail to present to F.D.R., one that would bring conviction to the Americans that the Prime Minister and his men were not hanging back over the invasion of France.

In this expectation the Prime Minister was to be disappointed. The suspicions he had engendered in Washington had struck deeper than he had conceived.

The American Staffs in no way shared the Prime Minister's anxieties over the assault on France. There was no realization that his opposition to a premature attack in 1942 had saved the Allies from disaster. When he spoke of rivers of blood flowing in the Channel they thought of cold feet. Nor did they, in the manner of their British colleagues, indulge in calculations of the advantages to be gained in France as the result of operations in the South pinning down German divisions in Italy and the Balkans. The Americans, conscious of their might, favored the method from World War I of the head-on assault, all strength packed behind it. They were not to be converted to the strategy of the indirect approach.

Personal pique gave an added spur to American suspicions. It rankled with General Marshall that in the previous year his project for a premature invasion had been rejected. At Quebec there was to be no repetition of this reverse. The Americans traveled to Canada firmly determined. Their country would be providing in large measure the men, the arms and the ships that would make the invasion of Europe possible. In their earnestness, their minds admitted of no doubts that theirs was the best plan. By all means at their disposal they would make their opinions prevail. To this end they packed their Quebec team with planners instructed to counter British arguments. There was to be an end of the disadvantages they had suffered in the past. Previously, according to General Marshall, the British had gone into conferences with their policy developed to the last degree and completely integrated. Hitherto American spokesmanship had not been integrated nor had Staff Chiefs and President spoken with a common voice.[8]

For Quadrant, the precaution was taken of priming the President. Before joining their Staffs at Quebec, the two principals had arranged to meet in the retreat of F.D.R.'s country place at Hyde Park. There, above the Hudson River, they were to be free for a couple of days to talk to each other in complete frankness. The President's advisers viewed the prospect with concern. There was no telling the lengths to which he might commit them—for he had a weakness for snap decisions—when exposed to the beguilements of the great diversionist. Sore memories persisted of the results of the previous occasion of a Hyde Park tête-à-tête.

Accordingly, Stimson provided in advance against these strategic hazards. The American Secretary of War, recently returned from a visit to Europe, was able to present his firsthand impressions of the British attitude. During his talks in London he had found evidence to support the apprehensions of his fellow Americans. The chief planner of "Overlord," General Morgan himself, had spoken of his fears of the effect on the invasion of too deep commitments in the Mediterranean.

Back home, Stimson gave the President the benefit of his guidance in a personal interview. He followed it up with a memorandum, vigorously phrased, so that Roosevelt might "see to the root of things" through the fog of successive discussions with the Prime Minister and his advisers. First and foremost the invasion of France must not, Stimson advised, be entrusted to a British commander. The British believed in "pinprick warfare" in the Balkans; only disappointing results in France could be expected from their halfhearted leadership.[9]

"The shadows of Passchendaele and Dunkirk," counseled Stimson, his apprehensions giving color to his prose, "still hang too heavily over the imagination of the leaders of his [Churchill's] Government. Though they have rendered lip service to the operation their hearts are not in it."

Thus primed, Roosevelt made his Staffs' policy his own. To their relief he went "whole hog" on the invasion of France.

"If he can only hold to it in his conferences with the Prime Minister, it will greatly clear up the situation," reflected Stimson. The President held to it.

It proved, indeed, unnecessary for Roosevelt to brace himself to the holding, for the Prime Minister was found to be unexpectedly accommodating. With one of those sudden turns, springing from his divination of the motions of other men's minds, he brought up the question of the command of "Overlord." He proposed that the post should be given to General Marshall,[10] an offer the more generous since the President had previously agreed that a British general should receive the appointment.

To promote American good will over the command, Churchill was going back on the offer he had already made to Alan Brooke, to whom he had promised the post. It was a crushing disappointment for the C.I.G.S., who accepted the change with a soldier's resignation to the unpalatable, but he was the most bitterly injured general in the Army, overcome by despair at the loss of the professional prize that had been snatched from his grasp.

The Prime Minister had made the initial contribution to bridging the gulf of mutual suspicion. He followed it up at a full session of the conference by a declaration in favor of the invasion of France. Far from opposing "Overlord" for 1944, he called for greater force to support the opening punches. The initial lodgment must be strong—25 per cent stronger than the plan provided for. To this end more landing craft must be made available.[11]

The Americans received the Prime Minister's statement with restrained enthusiasm. His declaration in support of "Overlord" did not remove their doubts concerning the earnestness of British intentions, doubts that grew with every mention of the Balkans. Nor did they concede the need for a 25 per cent increase in the weight of the initial assault, for that would involve additional landing craft, to be obtained only at the expense of American operations in the Pacific.

Churchill was alarmed. His forebodings were renewed. To attempt the invasion with the resources the Americans were prepared to make available would be courting disaster. He was determined that British troops—and American for that matter—should not be flung against the defenses of the Atlantic wall unless they were given the backing of adequate strength. He spoke, as he had often done before, of rivers of blood flowing in the Channel. Pointing to the map of France he showed the advantages the Germans possessed in the roads and railroads that would enable them to convey their reserves swiftly to the point of danger. The experience in Sicily had indicated what tough resistance the Germans would offer.[12]

These arguments were advanced to prove the need to pack greater punch into "Overlord." They produced no such immediate result. Instead, they gave rise to a renewal of the cry that Churchill was unsound about "Overlord." It is the fate of the man who knows more than his fellows frequently to be misunderstood and misrepresented. Churchill had the consolation that his insistence was a contribution to the final success. The failure of premature invasion had been averted. The hazard of an assault below strength was not to be run. The Morgan plan presented at Quebec was for an assault by three seaborne divisions and two airborne brigades, with two divisions in support. When the time came, it was enlarged into the D-Day plan,* employing three airborne divisions, with landings by seven American and six British divisions.

As a means of pinning down German forces, General Marshall recommended that landings in southern France should also be made. The operation (code name "Anvil") could be staged, he suggested, by switching Allied divisions from Italy. This project was thereafter to draw the Prime Minister's strenuous and sustained opposition.

Throughout the Staff talks the British side met stone-wall resistance from the Americans to any extension of operations against Italy. They would concede nothing but the landing Eisenhower projected at Salerno,

* See Chapter Seven, Book Three.

and beyond this they adamantly refused to move. Alan Brooke enlarged on the advantages to be derived in France from tying down Germans in the Balkans. His expositions on the elements of strategy were coldly received. The Americans were resolved not to be led up what they conceived to be the Mediterranean garden path. Churchill might dwell on its beauties, the peaches and the nectarines to be gathered there; they were not to be tempted into abandoning their position that diversions would weaken "Overlord." The British mourned over chances to be lost in the Aegean and the Balkans, and the starving of operations in Italy. Brooke grew discouraged and railed in his dairy against stupidity, pettiness, and pigheadedness that were stultifying his long-matured schemes.[13]

The Prime Minister, aloof from the arena of dispute, could take the larger view. Between allies give-and-take was inevitable. Two nations fighting a war were bound to have their quarrels, but they were the quarrels of brothers-in-arms.

The turn of events forced some concessions from the reluctant strategists. Eisenhower reported complete success in Sicily. The island was taken, though the bulk of the German forces had been permitted to slip away. At the same time a peace envoy from Badoglio had made contact. The peach was ripe for the picking, the Italians ready to leave the losing for the winning side.

Orders at once went out to Eisenhower. He was to accept Italy's capitulation. The greatest possible military advantage was to be forced out of it. There was to be unrelenting pressure against the Germans in North Italy. The instructions were unexceptional. It was unfortunate that previous decisions of the Allied Staffs had made their execution impossible. Eisenhower had been denied the forces by which the greatest military advantage could be derived.

Admiral King would not permit the Italian show to draw away ships he had earmarked for the Pacific. Nor was the President inclined to permit any interference with MacArthur's advance against the Japanese. F.D.R. was not in a position to consider the competing claims of the European and Pacific wars in a political vacuum. Churchill's position was so strong politically that he could ignore the clamor in Britain for a Second Front. F.D.R., with an election approaching, could not dismiss the pressure of American opinion about the Pacific Front, and the hopes of the voters were concentrated on knocking hell out of the Japanese. Nor could MacArthur's demands for men, munitions and craft be cavalierly treated, for MacArthur, a Republican, was a possible contender for the Presidency.

The Prime Minister intervened in the Far East discussions to stake

Britain's claim for reserved seats in the Pacific war. Once Germany had been counted out, there must be a share of airfields, bases and duties for the British forces. There was American resistance to these demands which were, however, conceded in principle. Churchill was satisfied to have established that Great Britain would not quit the fight until Japan was defeated. He was also gratified to secure approval for the appointment of Lord Louis Mountbatten as Allied Commander in Chief, Southeast Asia Command. Mountbatten had served as Chief of Combined Operations and was, according to the Prime Minister, a "complete triphibian," equally at home in the three elements—earth, water and air.

Mountbatten figured in a diversionary incident in the Quebec conference chamber. After a heated Staff's meeting, listeners in the room adjoining were alarmed by the sound of revolver shots and a cry of pain.

Within, Mountbatten had been given leave to report on "Habakkuk," the floating airport project. Large blocks of specially prepared ice were exhibited to the Chiefs of Staff. To demonstrate their quality, Mountbatten pulled out his revolver and fired a volley. The ice mixture was supposed to be splinter-proof. Its quality was shown. It was proof against the bullets which rebounded from its surface back among the watchers. Admiral King's trousers were pierced; Portal was a near miss. General Arnold, who showed his strength with a chopper, gave a cry of pain as he struck the reinforced ice.

It was those sounds that alarmed the party in the anteroom. "The shooting has started," shouted one. There was relief when, the "Habakkuk" demonstration over, the Staffs emerged unscathed, Churchill among them, laughing heartily.[14]

There was scarcely an Allied gathering at which the French question did not provoke discussion. The differences between de Gaulle and Giraud were mirrored in the divergencies between Whitehall and Washington. Cordell Hull, Secretary of State, was implacable in his opposition to de Gaulle. Churchill, though sorely tried by the burden of the Cross of Lorraine, championed the leader of the Fighting French.

At Quebec consideration was required for the results of the maneuverings at Algiers, and the new arrangement between the rival French factions. The original two-headed committee had been supplanted by a Committee of Liberation, of which de Gaulle was made political head, while Giraud was appointed Commander in Chief of Free French Forces. De Gaulle was soliciting from the Allied powers recognition that would be tantamount to underwriting the claim of the Committee to be the Provisional Government of France. Churchill was able to secure partial recognition of the Committee as a provisional instrument—"trustees of France during the time of her incapacity," as he phrased it. By this limitation it was sought to preserve the freedom of the French people to choose their ultimate government for themselves. By according partial recognition it was hoped to put an end to the embarrassment of sustained solicitation.

Recognition accorded, the de Gaullists continued their maneuvers to obtain the ascendancy. A few weeks later the Committee was again reformed, with de Gaulle as President and the Commander in Chief excluded from membership. The following year the post of Commander in Chief was abolished and Giraud, refusing the titular office of Inspector General, went into retirement.

Before the Quebec discussions closed, the Prime Minister had secured a declaration in writing on the sharing of the results of atomic research. Once again it had been his unpleasant duty to protest at the breakdown in the exchange of information. Despite what had been agreed at Washington earlier in the year, the Americans were continuing to withhold information from the British.[15]

Churchill had raised the matter during Stimson's recent visit to London. The Secretary of War was responsible to the President for the atomic undertaking and was directly connected with all policy decisions. In reply to the Prime Minister's complaints, he represented it was the impression in America that the British were interested in atom research primarily for the economic advantages they could gain when industry restarted after the war. The Americans balked at the idea of spending billions of dollars on financing research, and handing over the results for trade rivals to exploit. An expenditure of no less than $2,000,000,000 had been authorized by the President for this work.

You may imagine how the Prime Minister repudiated these insinuations. John Anderson was called in to add his contravention to the American assertions. Stimson did not withdraw them. To close an unhappy business Churchill suggested that full collaboration should be resumed, and that the question of the peacetime application of any discoveries made should be left to the discretion of the American President. It was a characteristic Churchillian gesture. It drew no response. After Stimson's return home there was no resumption of cooperation.

Once again, as men of good will, Prime Minister and President found no difficulty about the restoration of the old position. Their original agreement, unwritten and unwitnessed, had been for full collaboration, with the sharing of information as equal partners. Before the Quadrant conference ended the agreement was put into writing in a document entitled: "Articles of Agreement covering collaboration between the authorities of the U.S.A. and the U.K. in the matter of Tube Alloys." It began with a preamble stating that:

Whereas it is vital to our common safety in the present war to bring the Tube Alloys project to fruition at the earliest moment, and whereas this may be more easily achieved if all available British and American brains and resources are pooled; and whereas owing to war conditions it would be an improvident use of war resources to duplicate plants on a large scale on both sides of the Atlantic, and therefore a far greater expense has fallen upon the United States. . . .

The first clause solemnly affirmed, "we will never use this agency against each other." The second pledged the two states "never to use it against third parties without each other's consent." * Under the third clause there was to be no communication of information to third parties except by mutual consent. By the fourth clause it was left to the American President to specify the terms on which Britain would enjoy postwar advantages of an industrial or economic character.

On behalf of Britain the Prime Minister expressly disclaimed any interest in these commercial aspects "beyond what may be considered by the President to be fair and just and in harmony with the economic welfare of the world."

An agreement based to such a degree on personal good will and a sense of fair dealing is, so far as I know, without parallel in international affairs. Winston Churchill's large-minded spirit shines through words that are plainly his. They met with large-minded acceptance.

These Articles of Agreement were the war's top-level secret. Few were privileged to share it. Not all the members of the War Cabinet were made privy to it, for their authority was not sought for the conclusion of an agreement personally reached by President and Prime Minister. No reference to the matter will be found in the Churchill war memoirs. Not until eleven years after it was drawn up was the existence of the agreement made public, during the controversy over the working of the McMahon Act, forbidding the imparting of atomic secrets outside the United States.[16]

Churchill could consider the outcome of the Quebec disputations to be reasonably acceptable. Business concluded, he relaxed for a while, indulging his fancy for dips back into history as he paced the ramparts

* This power of veto survived until 1948 when, by the insistence of Senator Vandenberg, the Attlee Government was induced to agree to the cancellation of the undertaking. The Senator, as chairman of the Senate Foreign Relations Committee, had become aware of the terms of the Quebec agreement, and was astounded to learn that the United States had no freedom of action in the employment of the A-bomb. With the passing of the McMahon Act, banning the disclosure of atomic information outside the United States, Britain lost the right to share in the results of research secured by Churchill's Quebec pact.

above the St. Lawrence, and enjoying an angler's satisfaction as he fished in the Lake of Snows. With proper pride he sent off his biggest catch to F.D.R., already back at his post in Washington.

Attending a meeting of the Canadian Cabinet he was sworn a Privy Councilor of the Dominion. His Quebec visit was brought to a close with a broadcast to the Canadian people (August 31), who were commended for the indispensable part they had played in the war, one that had deeply touched the heart of the mother country. The Prime Minister's immediate task was to press for a more vigorous application of the Allied potential against the enemy in Italy and the Mediterranean.

CHAPTER FIVE

THIRD FRONT OPENED

SEPTEMBER, 1943

FROM Quebec Churchill traveled south to Washington, wishing, in view of developments in Italy, to be at hand for personal discussion with the President. As he entered the White House on September 1, news was received that Badoglio had accepted Eisenhower's surrender terms. One prop had been knocked out of the Axis.

Opinion was divided on what should follow. Churchill throughout the discussions argued emphatically, as he had contended at Quebec, that the all-important matter was to convert the Italians into active agents against the Germans. If they were ready to fight against the Axis, he was prepared for them to work their passage as co-belligerents. A similarly practical view of the situation was taken by Eisenhower. At Churchill's suggestion, Eisenhower was directed to press King Victor Emmanuel for a formal declaration of war.

While these arrangements proceeded Montgomery, crossing the Strait of Messina, began his advance north from the toe of Italy. Landings were prepared on the Salerno beaches to secure the port of Naples. Plans were laid for seizing Rome by an American airborne division.

Churchill was particularly concerned about the capture of Italy's Fleet. The ships would not only be a welcome accretion of strength, but British warships in the Mediterranean would be released for service elsewhere. Engaged in the Pacific they would be proof positive that Great Britain would fight to the end for Japan's defeat.

To a meeting of the Joint Staffs in the White House (September 9), the Prime Minister stated his strategy for Italy. He did not favor an advance beyond the narrow neck of the Italian peninsula, to the north of Fiume, seeing that Allied divisions had to be brought back to England in preparation for the assault in North France—"there can be no question of whittling down 'Overlord.'" Nevertheless the Balkans must not be neglected, with their far-reaching possibilities. Munitions and supplies should be sent to the aid of patriot forces and guerrillas. Then there were the islands in the eastern Mediterranean, notably Rhodes.[1]

Rhodes was a prize that particularly attracted him. It was coldly regarded by the Americans, and for many meetings to come they were harangued at length on the chance that was being neglected. They remained unresponsive and unrepentant.

Developments in Italy called for a second meeting of the Joint Staffs. Roosevelt had left Washington for a break, and in his absence the meeting was convened by the Prime Minister. Here was a demonstration of Allied solidarity—the Prime Minister of Great Britain taking the initiative in his host's absence and presiding over the proceedings in the council chamber of the President of the United States.

Churchill was perturbed over the slowness of the build-up of Allied forces on Italian soil—no more than twelve divisions to be provided by the month of December. He told the Joint Chiefs that he was horrified by the lamentably inadequate plans. General Marshall, agreeing in some measure with these criticisms, pledged that everything possible should be done.[2]

In the result, the Germans moved with greater speed to meet the emergency of Italy's defection. Hitler hurried another twenty divisions into the Peninsula, some withdrawn from reserve on the Russian Front. Rome was invested, to the frustration of Allied designs for airborne occupation.

Italy's surrender was made known to the world as Eisenhower launched the attack by British and American forces in the Bay of Naples. For a time the hold was precarious, and it seemed they might be pushed back into the sea, but supporting planes and naval gunnery turned the scale. The foothold was secured and five days later Montgomery's men, pushing up from the south, linked up with the Fifth Army.

At sea, ships of the British Navy steamed into the port of Taranto to land 6,000 picked men. In later years Churchill was fond of displaying in his Kentish home a memento of that daring operation—the Union Jack that flew over Taranto after its capture, presented to him by Alexander.[3]

A naval harvest was reaped with the surrender of the Italian Navy. Five battleships and six cruisers steamed from their refuges to come under the orders of Admiral Cunningham. It was heartening news, an event that "altered the naval balance of the world."

While Churchill had been pressing for a more vigorous initiative, he had to bear with complaints from Field Marshal Smuts that were the echo of his own criticisms. Surveying the scene with the detachment of an observer in South Africa, Smuts pronounced that the strategic program agreed to at Quebec was disappointing and inadequate. As for the steps taken to exploit the Italian collapse: "I sense a slackening and tardiness." [4]

It was hard to be made the target for such reproaches when he was himself making similar protests and pressing for greater speed in action. Churchill was content to reply that were they together he would be in a position to remove Smuts's anxieties apart from "inherent inexorable facts."

One contribution to this correspondence is of particular interest as establishing the sincerity and reality of the Prime Minister's belief in and support for the invasion of France. Smuts had advocated a full-scale attack on the Balkans, and received the reply that resources did not permit of this, seeing that troops and ships were needed for the invasion of France. Smuts countered: "I suggest our victories in the Mediterranean should be followed up in Italy and the Balkans, instead of adopting a cross-Channel plan . . . involving grave risks—preparations for which should be slowed down."

Here expressed were the views which Stimson, Marshall, and most of the American staff attributed to the Prime Minister. Had he shared them, Churchill would have acknowledged it in the confidence of private correspondence with Smuts, a close friend, on whose judgment he set great store. Instead, he replied with an emphatic rejection of the Field Marshal's suggestions. The cable must be given in full:

PRIME MINISTER TO FIELD MARSHAL SMUTS.

11th September, 1943.

There can be no question whatever of breaking arrangements we have made with the United States over "Overlord." The extra shipping available in consequence of U-boat warfare slackening, and of Italian windfalls will probably enable us to increase build-up of "Avalanche" (expedition to Italy). I hope you realize that British loyalty to "Overlord" is the keystone of arch of Anglo-American cooperation. Personally, I think enough forces exist for both hands to be played, and I believe this to be the right strategy.

This declaration, made in confidence to a friend he had no reason for deceiving, is clinching testimony to dispose of the theorists who deemed Churchill to be unsound on "Overlord." [5]

Amidst the pressure of affairs, the Prime Minister found some relaxation in wandering into America's academic groves. He traveled (September 6) to Cambridge, Massachusetts, to receive the honorary degree of Doctor of Law in Harvard University.

The ceremony, long planned, was one in which the President was closely interested as a member of the 1904 class. He suggested that it should be staged with pageantry and color, to which end the Harvard President scoured the United States for the scarlet hood of an Oxford LL.D. to replace the austere cap and gown of Harvard. To the audience assembled for the occasion Dr. Churchill delivered an earnest appeal for the development and preservation of Anglo-American friendship and cooperation.

"Our gift of a common tongue," he said, "is a priceless inheritance. It may well some day become the basis of a common citizenship."

Venturing into American domestic controversy he spoke of the perils of isolationism, so that he was accused of political indiscretion. If it was indiscreet it was so by calculation and committed with Roosevelt's assent, for the Prime Minister made no speech on American soil without previously discussing its terms with the President.

It was of no use, he argued, for the United States to say they did not want to be involved in future wars. The long arm of battle reached out remorselessly. The price of greatness was responsibility. Common action between the United States and Britain had reached the point where they used British and American troops, ships, aircraft, and munitions as if they were the resources of a single nation. It was a wonderful system. There had been nothing like it in the last war, never, in fact, anything like it between two allies.

"In my opinion," Churchill declared, "it would be a most foolish and improvident act on the part of our two governments, or either of them, to break up the smooth-running and immensely powerful machinery the moment the war is over. For our own safety, as well as for the security of the rest of the world, we are bound to keep it working and in running order after the war, not only until we have set up some world arrangement to keep the peace, but until all know it is an arrangement which will really give us the protection we must have from danger and aggression. We must not let go the securities we have found necessary to preserve our lives and liberties until we are sure we have something to put in their place."

Back at home, the Prime Minister presented his report to the House of Commons, unfolding a tale of high drama and of feats of daring crowned by success (September 21). But, though the highlights were picked out with the skill of the practiced narrator, the speech was pitched

in quite another key. The purpose was not merely to chronicle achievements, but to explain why progress in Italy had not been more swift and
far-reaching.

Once again he had to receive from others criticisms that in the privacy
of the conference room he had himself advanced. Nor, once again, did
he permit himself by so much as a covert phrase, barbed with double
meaning, to make reference to the hampering effect on operations that
flowed from the decisions of the conferences with the Americans.

Complaint was made that the plans of the Supreme Command had
not been flexible enough to take advantage of the situation; that the
Nazis had been swifter in their reactions; that there had been too much
direction from Quebec—meaning Churchill—and too little initiative left
to the men on the spot. There were, inevitably, objections that the
Italian landings had been made at the wrong place and at the wrong
time, and attacks on the Allied Commander for making a deal with the
Italians and on the Prime Minister for permitting it.

Churchill's reply to this catalogue of grievances is a model of parliamentary effectiveness. His hands tied by the necessity for withholding
many of the essential facts, he yet contrived to present an argument
that countered the complaints. The House responded to the admirable
spirit of the speeches. I give the salient passages of the reply made to the
charges of delay between the fall of Mussolini (July 25), the signing of
the armistice at Syracuse (September 3), and the landings at Salerno
(September 8).

I have seen it said that forty days of precious time were lost in
these negotiations and that in consequence British and American
blood was needlessly shed near Salerno. This criticism is as ill-
founded in fact as it is wounding to those who are bereaved. The
time of our main attack upon Italy was fixed without the slightest
reference to the attitude of the Italian Government, and the actual
provisional date of the operation was settled long before any negotiations had taken place, and even before the fall of Mussolini. That
date depended upon the time necessary to disengage our landing
craft from the beaches of southern Sicily, across which, up to the
first week in August, the major part of our armies actually engaged
had to be supplied from day to day. These landing craft had then to
be taken back to Africa. Those that had been damaged, and they
were many, had to be repaired and then reloaded.

When I hear people talking in an airy way of throwing modern
armies ashore here and there, as if they were bales of goods to be
dumped on a beach and forgotten, I really marvel at the lack of
knowledge which still prevails of the conditions of modern war.
Thus the whole of this operation—this is my answer to the charge

of delay, to the word "slothful" which I have seen used in one quarter—the whole of this operation was planned as a result of decisions taken before the fall of Mussolini. The Italian surrender was a windfall, but it had nothing to do with the date fixed for harvesting the orchard. The truth is that the Italian armistice was delayed to fit in with the attack, not the attack delayed to fit in with the announcement.

The invasion in the Naples area was the most daring amphibious operation the Allies had so far launched, or which had ever been launched on a similar scale in war.

The approach and the landing were successfully effected, but the battle which developed was most severe and critical. The British and American divisions fought side by side, with their backs to the sea, with only a few miles of depth behind them, with their equipment coming in painfully over the beaches, and their landing craft and supporting squadrons under recurrent enemy air attack.

The battle swayed to and fro, and the Germans' hopes of driving us into the sea, after a bloody battle on the beaches, must at times have risen high. We thought we had their measure, and so it turned out. The British battle squadron, some of the finest battleships, joined the inshore squadron in a heavy bombardment, running a great risk, within close range and in narrow waters, from the enemy's aircraft, U-boats, if any, and the glider bombs which inflicted damage on some of the ships—they came straight in and stood up to it at close range, and equalized and restored the artillery battle.

Meanwhile the Eighth Army—whose operations had been considered from the beginning as complementary to the blow we were striking with the Fifth Army—the Eighth Army, which had become master in the Toe, the Ball, and the Heel of Italy, advanced with giant strides, and on the tenth day of the struggle began to intervene, as it was meant to do, on the enemy's southern flank and rear. Reports from the battlefield leave no doubt that the enemy has been worsted, that our main forces are firmly ashore. We must, I think, consider this episode—the landing on the beaches of Salerno—as an important and pregnant victory, one deserving of a definite place in the records of the British and United States armies fighting together and shedding their blood in a generous cause.

Later a member interjected, "You will not get Italian people to rise behind the barrier of turncoats"—a line of criticism that had previously arisen over Darlan in North Africa. The Prime Minister retorted:

I think that the Honorable Gentleman may not be thinking quite sufficiently of the importance of diminishing the burden which our soldiers have to bear. In my view it is a duty, in a situation of this kind, for all forces who will make head against the scourge of their nation—the Fascist quisling government of Mussolini supported by the German invaders—to rally and get together to make the best stand they can.

On October 1, the Allied forces had won the first phase of the Battle of Italy and entered Naples. Thirteen days later the Badoglio Government declared war on the Germans, and the Allies accepted Italy as co-belligerent. Operations had successfully begun on what the Prime Minister termed the Third Front.

To round off the parliamentary record mention must be made of the occasion (October 12) when Churchill, with a broad grin, rose in the House to make the quaintly phrased statement:

"I have an announcement to make arising out of the Treaty signed in this country and Portugal in the year 1373 between His Majesty King Edward III and King Ferdinand and Queen Eleanor of Portugal." Without disclosing the substance of the communication, Churchill went on to quote the terms of this ancient undertaking:

In the first place we settle and covenant that there shall be from this day forward, true, faithful, constant, mutual and perpetual friendships, unions, alliances, and needs of sincere affection and that as true and faithful friends we shall henceforth, reciprocally, be friends to friends and enemies to enemies and shall assist, maintain and uphold each other mutually by sea and by land against all men that may live or die.

This engagement had lasted for six hundred years and was without parallel in world history. "I have now," proceeded the Prime Minister, coming at length to the subject of his announcement, "to announce its latest application. The British Government, basing themselves on the ancient alliance, requested the Portuguese to accord them facilities in the Azores to enable better protection to be provided for merchant shipping in the Atlantic. This request has been agreed to by Dr. Salazar, thus providing an additional guarantee for the development of Anglo-Portuguese friendship in the future."

This was one of the decisive measures in countering the ubiquitous U-boat. The year 1943 was the numerical climax of the U-boat war. Never were so many submarines in operation, never were so many sunk. Admiral Doenitz, believing that he had devised the answer to Allied methods of detection, intensified his efforts. The result was stated by Churchill in an account of what he termed the "May massacre":

"There are so many U-boats employed now that it is impossible not to run into one or other of these great screens of them which are spread out—therefore you have to fight your way through. There is no reason why we should regret that. On the contrary, it is around the convoys that the U-boats can best be destroyed. New weapons and new methods and the close coordination of effort between surface and air escort have enabled us to inflict casualties which have surpassed all previous records. In May, for the first time, our killings of U-boats substantially outnumbered the U-boat output. That may be a fateful milestone."

The new methods were the result of the adaptation of the magic eye of radar to the needs of the submarine chasers. When shipping losses on the Atlantic were at their peak in 1942, and Hitler was raising German hopes, the Prime Minister reconstituted the Battle of Atlantic Committee. He invited Stafford Cripps ("on account of the special aptitude which he possesses in forming a sound lay opinion upon these highly technical issues") to become his deputy on the committee, which was charged with the duty of finding still more effective methods of combating the menace to the ocean life lines. Under this direction research was pressed, and the results were vigorously applied to put the Allies again ahead of Admiral Doenitz.

The use of bases in the Azores was the final link in the chain enabling Allied airmen to close the Atlantic gap, which distance had previously imposed between the air patrols flying westward from Britain and eastward from America. Thereafter, night or day, fair weather or foul, the U-boat could not elude the destroyer. The Azores bases and radar had won the Battle of the Atlantic. So perilous was it for the submarines to surface that the Germans were driven to the invention of the "snorkel" air tube, to enable them to recharge their batteries while under water. The war ended before the Navy had had full opportunity to test its retort to this riposte.

Throughout the autumn Churchill continued his pressure for action in the eastern Mediterranean and the capture of island fortresses in German hands. They were prizes to be had for the little effort required to take them. "Storm Rhodes!" was his urgent call. It met with no response from the Americans. He disputed the matter with Eisenhower, the only acute difference that ever persisted between them. It was in vain. He exhorted the President. All was useless. He could not pierce the stone wall of opposition. To his remonstrances the stock reply was made: "No diversion of forces or equipment should prejudice 'Overlord.'" He was distressed at the rigid adherence to priorities for "Overlord." His opponents, he felt, were losing all sense of proportion, and he proposed to fly out to Tunis for a conference with the men on the spot. The President coldly, but understandably, replied that he was not in sympathy with this procedure.[6]

It quenched his hopes, but he would not press his case further—he could not risk any jar in his relations with F.D.R. His disappointment inspired one of his few criticisms of his Washington friends—the American staff had enforced its view: the price had now to be paid by the British in the loss of the islands of Leros and Samos, where the British garrisons could not hold out against the weight of German assaults.

It was a bitter blow. The Dodecanese were forfeited. The Turks, with the Germans on their flank, were not to be tempted from the safety of neutrality into the hazards of belligerency. There was no decision throughout the war which Churchill so keenly regretted: "Surely I was entitled to the very small aid which I required."

I make no attempt at a strategic evaluation of what losses the Allies suffered, or alternatively what disadvantages they escaped, by the rejection of the Rhodes project. In another sphere, what the Prime Minister lost is plain to see. Wearying his opponents by his importunity, he added to their suspicions, already strongly formed, about his political intentions in the Mediterranean. The President concluded that since they were so urgently pressed there must be some ulterior motive behind these designs; he was not going to jeopardize the lives of American soldiers to further British imperialist interests. Even Eisenhower, least suspicious of the American leaders, was of the opinion that the Prime Minister had political motives in advocating measures that seemed to lie outside the scope of the immediate military problem.

The seeds of mistrust yielded an unfortunate crop. They had their effect on the President, when he came to confer with Stalin, serving to add to the strength of his sympathies with the Russians. At a later stage they accentuated American disapproval when Churchill came to intervene to save Greece from the Communists. They strengthened the barrier of American opposition when, in the war's later stages, he sought concerted action to reduce the area of communist domination in Europe.

Lament as he might chances lost, Churchill could survey with satisfaction the gains in the battles of the Middle Sea, the arena he had once been counseled to abandon. The Americans, persuaded to advance beyond the successive limits of their intentions, had cooperated in the thrusts into the Axis under-belly. Beyond Sicily, which General Marshall had regarded as a final place to close down in the Mediterranean, the fight had been carried on to the mainland. The Axis had been ruptured. Badoglio's Government had declared war on the Nazis. German divisions in the Balkans, exposed to the attentions of patriots and guerrillas, were tied down by the expectation of Allied landings.

Italian warships had been added to the Allied fleets, and the routes of the Middle Sea had been reopened to Allied shipping. The Third

Front had been opened and a more strongly backed offensive would have swept the Germans back towards the Alps. But, even as it was, eleven Allied divisions held double the number of Germans. It was a continuing drain on Hitler's reserves at a time when they were urgently needed on the Russian Front.

Meanwhile the Prime Minister had turned his attention to preparing for the conference with Roosevelt and Stalin, the first meeting of the Big Three, that was to be held at Teheran.

CHAPTER SIX

TRIUMVIRS AT TEHERAN

NOVEMBER–DECEMBER, 1943

THAT autumn the Prime Minister set off on his travels once again, eastward bound for the first meeting of the Allied leaders, the Big Three. For long enough the Prime Minister and President had been seeking a meeting with Stalin and at last it had been arranged at the Persian capital of Teheran.

It was on the afternoon of November 12 that Churchill sailed from Plymouth aboard the battle cruiser *Renown*. Two months were to pass before he returned, having fulfilled an exhausting program. So various were the activities in which he engaged that for convenience the chronicle is presented in three parts.

I. THE PRELIMINARIES

There were difficulties to surmount before the way was clear for the summit talks at Teheran. Both Stalin and Roosevelt demurred over the place. The Russian suggested Teheran. The President thought of Basra. Stalin was unable to detach himself for long from his responsibilities in guiding the Russian armies—Basra was too far. Roosevelt was unable to detach himself from his constitutional responsibilities—Teheran was too inaccessible. Stalin's colleagues demanded his personal contact with the Supreme Command. Roosevelt begged the other to remember that he had his obligations to fulfill in maintaining the full American war effort.[1]

Churchill, for his part, would have preferred Cyprus or Khartoum, but he made no difficulties: "I will come anywhere, at any time, at any risk."

It was of greater concern to Churchill that he and Roosevelt should hold a preliminary meeting to evolve a common policy before the conference with the Russians. In the fifties this would be reckoned no more than routine procedure, but Roosevelt had not come to an understanding of Soviet communism and its designs. Churchill pressed his point: "My dear friend, this is much the greatest thing we have ever attempted and I am not satisfied that we have taken the measures necessary to give it the best chance of success. I feel very much in the dark at present and unable to think or act in the forward manner that is needed." [2]

So he submitted the case was "solid" for a preliminary get-together at Cairo before meeting "U.J." The President was reluctant to agree. "It would be a terrible mistake," he suggested, "if Uncle J. thought we had ganged up on him in military action." [3]

He was persuaded that the coming conference was to be "a genuine beginning of British-Russian-United States collaboration." As a gesture to impress the Kremlin, he suggested the Russians be invited to send a representative to sit in at British-American Staff conferences, with freedom to join in the discussion. Churchill was prompt to object. A Russian representative would "simply bay for an earlier Second Front and block all other discussions." [4]

Churchill was surprised to learn that the American Ambassador at Moscow had invited Stalin to send Molotov with a military representative for the Cairo talks. In the end, this proposal fell through, but Churchill was troubled by this wooing of the Russians. He was forced to the conclusion that there was a strong disposition in Washington to win the confidence of the Russians even at the price of jeopardizing Anglo-American collaboration.[5]

He made protest in one of the few strongly worded remonstrances he addressed to the President. The British Chiefs of Staff were very apprehensive about the presence of Russians and he shared their misgivings. A Soviet observer could not be admitted to intimate Staff conversations. He pressed for a preliminary Anglo-American exchange of views. "His Majesty's Government," he pronounced, "cannot abandon their rights to full and frank discussions with you and your officers about the vital business of our intermingled armies." [6]

President Roosevelt still lingered in a state of naïve innocence regarding the Soviets. There were, for him, two allies, British and Russian, and he was inclined to look with greater suspicion on the imperial-minded British than on the communist-minded Russians. As to negotiating, he had no doubt that he would be much more successful than Churchill in coming to terms with "Uncle Joe."

"Stalin," he had written long before to Churchill, "hates the guts of all your top people. He thinks he likes me better and I hope will continue to do so." [7]

Roosevelt's preference had always been for a meeting with Stalin on his own account, without the presence of Churchill. In a tête-à-tête he might be able to break the Russian ice more readily. The idea had been placed before Stalin, who had tentatively agreed, but it fell through. At least the approach had been made and the suggestion conveyed that the President was not merely trailing behind the British Prime Minister.[8]

The preparatory spadework for Teheran had been well done by the Foreign Ministers. Anthony Eden had traveled to Moscow to negotiate with Molotov and so, too, had Cordell Hull, who undertook the journey by air despite his seventy-two years—"a gallant eagle, who flew far on a strong wing," in Churchill's phrase. The Foreign Ministers covered a wide field and reached agreement on many matters. One of them was for the division of defeated Germany into zones of occupation, a decision that was to set up new tensions as final victory was being won. The Foreign Ministers of the West returned home to report a friendly atmosphere in Moscow.[9]

Churchill was nursing a heavy cold when he set out to join the President at Cairo, and was glad of the relief of a few days' rest at sea. At Malta, where he landed, a telegram of warning was received that the President's security officers considered Cairo unsafe as a meeting place. Churchill proposed Malta as an alternative and staff officers were hurriedly sent out to secure the necessary quarters for the two entourages. They returned to report that the bomb-scarred island could provide little better than ruins and cellars. The Cairo plan must be allowed to proceed, and the Prime Minister chose a Biblical reference to reassure the President, sending this laconic message: "See St. John, Chapter XIV, verses 1 to 4"—a reference to the passage containing the familiar phrases, "Let not your heart be troubled," and, "I go to prepare a place for you." Afterward his conscience was troubled that he might be suspected of profanity by this use of Holy Writ, but F.D.R. was in no way disturbed.[10]

The Cairo conference hall stood in the shadow of the Pyramids in an area cordoned off by barbed-wire fences, bristling with troops, guns, and searchlights. Ahead of the other principals the Chiang Kai-sheks had arrived with attendant advance publicity; Madame, indeed, sent a shiver of apprehension through the security forces by publicizing her presence with a visit to a Cairo hairdresser. But there are dues that must be paid to fashion and she was rewarded by mention in memoirs for her chic appearance by two American observers, Hopkins and Leahy. She and Churchill laughed off their previous contretemps, agreeing that no undue formalities should impede their future meetings.[11] Her husband, Churchill noted, had the appearance of an efficient personality.

Chiang's presence evoked no particular enthusiasm, for Churchill wanted the chance to discuss Allied strategy with the President, not Chinese affairs. These proved to be distracting. The President received Chiang with the respect due to the man who, in American eyes, was the champion of the New Asia. Regarding him with more critical appraisal, Churchill made no overestimate of Chiang's standing and strength. He deplored the intrusion of the Chinese discussions—"lengthy, complicated, and minor." [12]

In deference to the Chinese, the President promised that an amphibious operation should be undertaken across the Bay of Bengal in conjunction with land operations in Burma against the Japanese. The Prime Minister argued against this project, one of those cutting-a-dash gestures to which F.D.R. was occasionally inclined. It was one that would have taken essential landing craft from the Mediterranean and hampered the launching of "Overlord." Eventually Churchill was to prevail upon the President to retract his promise.[13]

As a consequence of the Chinese diversions, Churchill found that there was little time to consider the matters of greater importance. Perhaps it was as well, for he had drawn up an indictment of mismanagement in the Mediterranean. It was an up-to-the-minute recapitulation of his argument that the campaign in Italy was being allowed to flag for lack of support; that no real measure of assistance was being given to the patriots and guerrillas in the Balkans; and that, generally, the hampering influence of "Overlord" was enfeebling action. His conclusions were incontestable, but the preliminary talk before Moscow would not have been an occasion ideally chosen for their development.

The Americans, for their part, had come prepared. Anticipating trouble, they had brushed up their arguments. On one point above all they were ready for battle—the appointment of an over-all commander for all operations in Europe. Their belief in establishing this unity of command was so strong that they were prepared to accept a British super-commander in the person of John Dill.[14]

The Prime Minister offered immediate and uncompromising objection to this plan, in which he was supported by his Chiefs of Staff. Such a supreme figure would be an extra and unnecessary link in the chain of command, with responsibilities exceeding those reasonably to be delegated to a single soldier. But his clinching point was that the new Commander in Chief would make the Joint Chiefs of Staff redundant. Faced with the prospect of the extinction of their own authority, the American Chiefs dropped the proposal.[15]

Churchill had pressed for get-together talks. Despite F.D.R.'s reluctance to gang up, the Joint Staffs met to survey their strategy. They failed once again to reach unity of outlook. Churchill might declare his support for "Overlord"—the British were committed, he said, "up to the hilt." The Americans gave more heed to his attachment to other enterprises in Italy and strategic diversions in Southeast Europe, away from northern France. They prepared for battles at Teheran at which they and the Russians would form a united front. It was a poor preliminary for the summit. So far from ganging up against Stalin, the ganging up was to be done against the British. I find it difficult to conceive of circumstances in which Churchill would have entered a conference with the intention of ganging up with the Russians against Roosevelt.[16]

II. AT THE SUMMIT

The triumvirs met at Teheran on November 27. Stalin, who arrived a day ahead of the others, was absent from Russia for the first time since 1912.

The conference setting amidst the Persian mountains, the snow-capped peaks of Elburz, was like a scene from the *Arabian Nights* or, according to Roosevelt on his first awakening there, a landscape from Arizona. For a security officer it was a nightmare. There were rumors of plots against the visitors. German saboteurs were known to have been parachuted into the country not long previously. As precautions the Persian Government ordered the closing of the frontiers, suspended radio transmissions, and placed a stop on mails and telegraphs for the duration of the conference.

The Prime Minister arrived in splendid insecurity. The three-mile route to the British Legation was sparsely lined with cavalry—sufficient to indicate the imminence of a VIP, insufficient to provide protection. In the center of the city, so haphazard were the arrangements, crowds pressed round the car as it came to a standstill. It was a situation ideally contrived for the assassin, but nothing other than his thoughts disturbed the Prime Minister's journey.

Safety was assured within the British enclave, with its guard furnished by the Buffs and Sikh troops. Adjoining were the grounds of the Soviet Embassy, with men of the secret police, revolvers at their hips, and tommy gunners conspicuously placed. The United States Legation, machine gunners on the walls, was some distance removed on the far side of the city.

For greater safety the President was invited to stay at the British Legation, but he declined on the ground that as head of a sovereign state he could not be a guest on foreign soil. The Russians made a similar offer and this, too, was at first declined. But this invitation was backed by the report that the Russians had arrested three suspects, potential assassins. Thus persuaded of the perils to which he was exposed, F.D.R. accepted the hospitality offered him and moved within the Soviet enclave. Here a villa was placed at his disposal to his own comfort, but to the discomfiture of his Secret Service men, who had to watch the household chores being done by Russian guards armed with revolvers.[17]

As host it was quite natural that Stalin should go tripping along the gravel path to the villa fifteen minutes after the President had arrived. It was natural, too, that the President should make use of the occasion to break the ice in the tête-à-tête he had hoped for. As a gesture he threw out the suggestion that the American-British merchant fleets would shortly be reaching such strength that some vessels might be made available to the Soviet. Stalin responded with the appropriate sentiment that this would contribute to the development, for which he hoped, of good will between the two countries.[18]

The light flow of words touched on China (Stalin had a poor opinion of the Chinese as fighters), Burma, Malaya, and the arts of self-government. The President cautioned the Russian about bringing up India with Churchill. Stalin recognized that this would be a sore subject. When F.D.R., with proper democratic feeling, hazarded that reform in India should begin from the bottom, Stalin commented that reform from the bottom would mean revolution. The record does not indicate whether a glint was to be noted in the eye of the speaker.[19]

These exchanges lasted for forty-five minutes. The President was well satisfied. "I'm sure we will hit it off, Stalin and I," he confided to his son. "A great deal of the misunderstandings and mistrusts of the past are going to be cleared away, I hope once and for all." [20]

When the Big Three met for the first time, Stalin was sufficient of the diplomat to move that Roosevelt should take the conference chair. The President reciprocated by welcoming the Russians as "new members of the family circle." Thereafter he and the Prime Minister initiated a full and frank survey of Allied strategy in the West. This took Stalin by surprise. He was unaccompanied by his team of military experts, for he had not foreseen that the others would submit their strategic projects and invite him to pronounce as to which of the various enterprises would be most helpful to the Red armies. The question posed, he had no hesitation in replying that it would be unwise to disperse forces in various operations throughout the eastern Mediterranean.[21]

Roosevelt caused some surprise to his own advisers by proffering the idea of a drive across the Adriatic to link up in Rumania with Russians advancing from the east.

"Who's promoting the Adriatic business?" inquired Hopkins, suspecting Churchill's influence.

"As far as I know it is his own idea," replied Admiral King.

The Prime Minister was quick enough to associate himself with this project, but nothing came of it.[22]

There was much discussion of the way to induce the Turks to enter the war. Churchill suggested that they would be mad not to join the United Nations. On this Stalin dryly commented that some people preferred to be mad.

Thereafter, there was a discursive discussion on Mediterranean strategy, with the argument and counterargument that British and Americans had used to exhaust each other for several conferences past. It had the attraction of novelty for Stalin, who put pertinent questions not on strategic generalities but on the concrete facts of how many divisions. He was made privy to the plans and strengths of his allies, but the record in no place indicates that he offered corresponding information regarding the Red armies.

Of all the statements made, the most important was that contributed by Stalin, pledging Russian participation in the war in the Far East once the Nazis had been disposed of.

"We shall be able," he observed, "by our common front to beat Japan."

This was the first formal pledge of participation that Stalin had offered, although Molotov had informed the Foreign Ministers of Russian intentions. It was received with the greatest satisfaction by the President and his colleagues. Churchill, too, was relieved and he sought to turn the circumstances to his advantage by asking for the release from the Pacific of landing craft needed to support operations in Europe. The stronger the assaults in Europe the sooner would all be free, Russians as well, to dispose of the Japanese.[23]

At dinner that evening, Stalin was the host. In his humor he indulged his taste for raillery. At the Kremlin party Molotov had been the butt of his witticisms. At Teheran he set himself to tease Churchill. Nothing more was intended than to indulge the jester's sardonic sense, and it was accepted as such, though it was persistent throughout the evening. When, however, the Generalissimo's joking extended to the punishment to be exacted on the Germans, once defeated, there was an awkward moment.[24]

The Nazi core, Stalin asserted, consisted of fifty thousand zealots and these must be liquidated—shot, the lot of them. Churchill protested at this idea, even if made in jest. The British would never tolerate such butchery. "Fifty thousand," insisted Stalin, "must be shot." Churchill protested, with heat, that rather would he be led out into the garden and shot there and then than tolerate such an infamy.

To relieve the tension that had developed, Roosevelt intervened with a compromise—not fifty, but forty-nine thousand would suffice. His son Elliott, with more ponderous wit, rose to say he was sure the United States Army would support Stalin's idea.

Churchill could tolerate no more of this jesting that was too near the grim truth about Russian methods. Rising from the table he withdrew from the room. He was followed by Stalin and Molotov, grinning broadly, who clapped him on the shoulder with the assurance that they were speaking in play. Stalin assumed his most captivating manner, and Churchill suffered himself to be led back to his place.

The incident appears to have given Roosevelt the idea that he too should play the jester. Despite the first impressions he had created he was not satisfied with his relations with Stalin. They remained correct but not cordial. Determined to succeed by any means in thawing the Russian ice, F.D.R. resorted to badinage at the Prime Minister's expense. At the next conference session he began to poke fun at Churchill about his John Bull Britishness and about his cigars. Stalin appreciated the raillery. First he smirked and then he guffawed. The Prime Minister, we are told, scowled his disapproval. Stalin laughed. Roosevelt, thus encouraged, addressed him as "Uncle Joe." He felt that the Russian's friendship had been won.[25]

The ceremonial highlight at Teheran was the presentation to Generalissimo Stalin of the Sword of Honor, gift of King George VI, which had been specially forged to do honor to the defenders of Stalingrad. It was borne by a lieutenant of the Buffs. Premier Stalin and the Prime Minister stood while the "Internationale" and "God Save the King" were played. Then Churchill said: "Marshal Stalin, I have the command of His Majesty, King George VI, to present to you for transmission to the city of Stalingrad this sword of honor of which His Majesty has himself approved the design."

The blade bore upon it the inscription:

To the steel-hearted citizens of Stalingrad, the gift of King George VI, in token of the homage of the British people.

Stalin, himself the man of steel, was deeply moved as he briefly expressed the appreciation of the Russian people. Then the lieutenant of the Buffs placed the sword across the Prime Minister's outstretched arms. Stalin received it and kissed the blade below the hilt, thereafter passing it to Marshal Voroshilov, who fumbled and dropped it. The sword was entrusted to a Russian guard of honor.

When the full conference was resumed, Stalin fired off the question: "Who will command 'Overlord'?"

For Roosevelt it was an embarrassing inquiry. The choice rested with him and he was still dithering over the decision that had been troubling him for weeks past. There was no evading the admission that the nomination had yet to be deferred. Stalin thereupon remarked that until the Supreme Commander was named he could not believe in the reality of the operation. Churchill intervened to break the uneasy pause that followed with the suggestion that this was no matter for a large conference, but was appropriate for heads of governments. Stalin very properly disavowed any claim to have a voice in the appointment. All he asked was to know who was to be the man.[26]

There followed a recapitulation for Stalin's benefit of the familiar pros and cons of operations in the Mediterranean during the five months while the stage was being set for the assault in northern France. Churchill stated his case against sacrificing gains they had already made. He could not agree that the large British forces in the Mediterranean should stand idle for six months.

Stalin brought the proceedings to a close, as he had begun, with a question. This was bluntly put to the Prime Minister. "I wish," he said, "to pose a very direct question. Do the Prime Minister and the British Staffs really believe in 'Overlord'? Or do you support it to reassure the Russians?" [27]

To this Churchill gave the simple and emphatic reply: "Provided the conditions we have stated are established, when the time comes it will be our stern duty to hurl across the Channel against the Germans every sinew of our strength."

Stalin's judgment was that "Overlord" was so much the decisive business that by comparison Turkey, Rhodes, Yugoslavia, and even the capture of Rome, were not important.[28] This was accepted by the Americans as the final endorsement of the strategy they had advocated, the rejection of the designs of British imperialism. They were able to assign to Stalin that disinterested judgment on a matter of military strategy which they denied to Churchill, and do not seem to have considered the possibility that the political designs in the Balkans which they attributed to Churchill were motives powerfully influencing the Russian.

Stalin pressed for the date of "Overlord" to be firmly fixed, under the appointed Commander, so that he might concert an offensive on the Eastern Front. This would tie down German divisions and so rule out the need for diversionary operations in the Balkans.

Between the formal sessions of the conference, Roosevelt held aloof from contact with the Prime Minister. Churchill, knowing of meetings between Roosevelt and Stalin, suggested that he and the President should lunch together. Roosevelt declined. He did not wish the Russians to know that he was meeting the Prime Minister privately, "hatching their own schemes." To Harriman, who was sent to express F.D.R.'s regrets, Churchill remarked that he could accept rebuffs as well as the next one.[29]

"I shall," he added, "insist on one thing—that I be host at dinner tomorrow evening, and I think I have one or two claims to precedence. To begin with, I come first both in seniority and alphabetically. In the second place, I represent the longest established of the three governments. And in the third place tomorrow happens to be my birthday."

There was yet another claim of senior participation in the war by length of combatant service, but this was not mentioned.

So Roosevelt lunched with his own household and spent the afternoon with Stalin. He had his own ideas as to how the triumvirs should treat each other. They were not Churchill's, who considered that each should treat the others with equal confidence.

At the informal discussions with both Prime Minister and President, Stalin exchanged views on the postwar world. It was all very tentative and, on the Russian side, noncommittal. When Germany was discussed Stalin was downright in his assertion that the measures proposed by Churchill or Roosevelt were inadequate for ensuring continuing control once victory was won. Churchill, he protested, was too optimistic in assuming that Germany would not be able to rise again; unless forcibly prevented the Germans would have recovered their power for evil in twenty years. Consideration was also given to the postwar frontiers of Poland—a discussion to which Anthony Eden contributed with an exactness of knowledge on the intricacies of the Curzon Line and such technicalities.[30]

Winston Churchill's sixty-ninth birthday was appropriately celebrated in the town out of the *Arabian Nights*. From British forces on duty at Teheran he received Eastern gifts—a silver cigar-box of Isfahan work from all ranks of the Persia-Iraq Command, an Isfahan silver tray from the Buffs, and from the Sikhs an Imami miniature in a silver frame. The President presented a Persian porcelain vase of fine design. It was broken on the journey home, but was restored with patient craftsmanship. There must, I feel, have been something symbolic in this.

As the President continued in isolation from the Prime Minister, but in easy contact with the Russian, it was inevitable that Churchill should have felt uneasiness. With men of lesser minds there would have been resentment at being cold-shouldered and suspicion at what might be hatching between the two within the Soviet enclave. Churchill admitted to nothing more than apprehension that the Russian leader might be receiving an imperfect, because one-sided, impression of British policy and intentions. Accordingly he sought a personal interview with the Generalissimo to correct any false impression that might have been created about his attitude to "Overlord." [31]

So, the major business for the birthday was a tête-à-tête with Stalin. Churchill prefaced his exposition with the remark that he was half American by birth, and must accordingly not be suspected over what he would say of intending any disloyalty to his American allies and their leader. Thereafter he delivered a strategic survey from the British standpoint, emphasizing the preponderance of the British contributions to the Mediterranean operations, and of the equality in contribution to the launching of "Overlord."

He explained the differences in strategic outlook—that, while the Americans were content to hamstring operations in Italy to ensure the success of "Overlord," the British considered that there were sufficient resources for both these theaters of war. The landing craft position, in particular, had been made easier by Stalin's momentous declaration pledging the Russians' participation against Japan.

" 'Overlord,' " said Churchill with emphatic insistence, "will certainly take place." As to the date, for which Stalin pressed him, he insisted out of loyalty to his friend to leave the President to satisfy Russian curiosity.

This was duly performed at the lunch table. Roosevelt named May as the month for D-Day, and he and the Prime Minister gave solemn pledges to Stalin, who accepted them as the termination of his doubts. Later, at the final plenary session, the formal decision went on the record. Operations on Eastern, Western, and Mediterranean Fronts—that is First Front, Second Front, and Third Front—were to be concerted so that the Allies would close in upon "the wild beast of Europe" from all sides.

Churchill made a concluding appeal for more landing craft to be made available so that "Overlord" should be carried out with smashing force. A statement, tersely phrased, was drawn up, sounding the knell of

Germany's impending doom: "We have reached complete agreement as to the scope and timing of operations which will be undertaken from East, West, and South."

Consideration was given at this final session to postwar Europe. Stalin was prevailed upon to deal leniently with the Finns. The frontiers of an independent Poland were tentatively outlined.[32]

What to do with the Germans was debated. Stalin wanted the Reich to be split up. Roosevelt agreed. Churchill did not object in principle.

The President had a plan for a five-fold partition into self-governing sections. Two territories would be handed over to the United Nations—Kiel, the Canal and Hamburg; the Ruhr and the Saar.

Having heard these ideas outlined, Churchill remarked that the President had "said a mouthful." Stalin was prepared to support any project for weakening Germany by dividing it.

Churchill was of the opinion that the Prussians should be singled out for stern treatment, with easier conditions for the other German principalities.

Stalin thought that all Germans, apart from Austrians, were the same; the Prussian officers provided the cement, but North Germans and South Germans alike fought like wild beasts.

Roosevelt warmly agreed there was no difference between Germans, as American troops had already discovered.

Churchill raised the objection to partition that the dismembered parts would always seek to reunite unless independent life were given to the cut-off bits. For that reason he favored what he called a "Danubian confederation."

Stalin reiterated that it would be better to break up and scatter the German tribes.

Did Stalin contemplate a Europe of little states? Churchill asked.

Apart from Poland and France it seemed that he did. At all costs Germany must be broken up so that the parts could not reunite.

Roosevelt submitted that his plan provided for this result.

In such fashion the triumvirs took a preliminary ramble around Europe of the future.

The Prime Minister's birthday dinner party at the British Legation was also the celebration of the success of the Teheran meeting. Even the tedium of thirty toasts, formally observed, did not mar the proceedings. Stalin gave "My fighting friend, Winston Churchill," and the Prime Minister lifted his glass to "Stalin the Great," and "Roosevelt the Man."

It was one of the memorable occasions in Churchill's career. He sat with the President of the United States on his right and the master of

Russia on his left. Between them, he reflected, the triumvirs controlled the bulk of the world's navies, a preponderance of air fleets and armies of twenty million men.

Speeches around the table reflected the genial mood. Harry Hopkins raised a laugh by his epitome of the British Constitution, that unwritten charter. The provisions, Hopkins had discovered, were just what Winston Churchill wished them to be at any given moment.

To this the Prime Minister replied that he alone of the triumvirs held his job subject to dismissal at a moment's notice by members of the House of Commons.

The visitors left Teheran with their satisfaction undimmed, on the best of terms with each other. "We came here," attested the official statement, "with hope and determination. We leave friends, in fact, in spirit and in purpose." There is a Churchillian ring about the words and I am the more satisfied to ascribe them to him as a mark of his large-minded loyalty to his fellows. There were moments at Teheran when he must have been sorely tried by the diplomatic excursions of his friend, the President. And, with his consciousness of the compelling need for unity between the two great democracies, there were causes for dismay. As at home he was pained by any falling-short from the complete national unanimity he expected, so in his relations with the head of America's republic he was troubled by any crack in the fabric of their friendship. Beyond the disputations in which he vigorously engaged, he looked to Roosevelt for sympathy, understanding, and common purpose. Teheran brought bewildering disappointments.

Roosevelt was in the highest spirits. Teheran, according to Harry Hopkins, was the high peak of his career. He found it a pleasure to be working with Stalin. Concentrating on the cultivation of Russian friendship, and on winning Stalin's good will, he lost his native caution. He courted the Generalissimo with a wooer's uncritical scrutiny. He was prepared for sacrifices to dispel Soviet suspicions. He left on the return flight with the conviction that he had established in the Russian's eyes that Great Britain and the United States were not allied in one common bloc against the Soviet Union.[33]

"The one thing," he assured his son, "that could upset the applecart after the war, is if the world is divided, Russia against England and us. That's our big job now, making sure that we continue to act as intermediary between Russia and England." [34]

The Prime Minister was satisfied with the achievements at Teheran in the military sphere. Politically, he considered the results were "more remote and speculative." Nebulous, I suppose, would equally well describe them, wherein the consistent quality of summit conferences was maintained. Nor was Teheran outside the common experience down the centuries that no exaggerated expectations of permanence must be assigned to the agreements of triumvirs.

III. THE AFTERMATH

After the summit meeting there was clearing up to be done. For five days (December 2–7) President and Prime Minister, with their staffs, were engaged at Cairo. The one pressed for the operation against the Japanese in Burma which he had promised to Chiang Kai-shek, the other for an assault on Rhodes. Neither was allowed to have his way.

The British Chiefs of Staff had been concerned at the pledge Roosevelt had given for an amphibious operation across the Bay of Bengal. Churchill shared their objections. He now exploited the argument that nothing must be permitted to hinder "Overlord," turning their own phrases against the Americans. The President discovered a moral obligation to do something for Chiang; he would not be prepared to forgo the operation save for a very good reason. Churchill had no doubt that "Overlord" was a very good reason indeed.[35]

The Joint Chiefs were instructed to go into details of the operation. Deadlock persisted. The Americans were surprised by the force of British objections. Never before had they encountered such vigorous opposition as was given to Operation "Buccaneer"—its code name.

At this impasse, a cable was received from Mountbatten asking for 50,000 men to carry out the enterprise. This was decisive. On such a scale it could not be mounted. " 'Buccaneer' is off," came the message from the President, who was very much distressed. There was some bitterness among the American Staffs. Admiral Leahy, Chief of Staff to the President, considered that Chiang had every right to feel he had been let down. Churchill had no reason to consider himself involved, for he had not been consulted before Roosevelt, off his own bat, had given his promise to Chiang.

The Prime Minister could make no impression by his renewed pleas for assaulting Rhodes. The idea was raised by the British side, but the American Staff Chiefs refused even to consider it. The President had taken his decision against it and that, for them, was conclusive. Churchill continued to press for the adoption of his pet scheme. The Americans were wearied by his tireless advocacy. He deplored their unyielding obstinacy.[36]

No greater success attended the negotiations with Turkey. President Inonu traveled with his colleagues to Cairo. Churchill brought his verbal batteries to bear. The Turks were sympathetic and they were uncompliant. They were only too willing to enter the war; they must defer doing so until the Allies had ensured that there would be no quick destruction of their country.

The Americans were less concerned about what the Turks might do. Indeed, were they to come into the war it would mean, as General Marshall put it, that the American Staffs would need "to burn up our logistics right down the line." But they listened in admiration as the Prime Minister employed all his various resources—pleading, cajoling, even threatening the Turkish President. He knew, however, that his exhortations must fail so long as Rhodes remained in enemy hands on the Turkish flank. He was scarcely inclined to blame the Turks for their caution.[37]

The last major matter to be disposed of was the appointment of the commander for "Overlord." Roosevelt could delay no longer. He had been exposed to strong and contradictory influences. There were those who urged that General Marshall was the only man for the job, and there were those who objected that the job was not big enough for Marshall, who would suffer demotion by taking it.[38]

When the Cairo proceedings were nearing their close, Prime Minister and President drove together to the Pyramids. It was then that F.D.R. made known his choice. Eisenhower was to command in Europe; Marshall could not be spared from Washington—"I could not sleep o' nights with George out of Washington." So the expert in supply and logistics, the master of the global war, was, like Alan Brooke, denied the chance of winning renown in battle.

Churchill was surprised. He had been led to expect, in common with many of the President's advisers, that the choice would fall on Marshall. For Eisenhower the Prime Minister had the warmest regard; to him he was ready to entrust Allied fortunes with hearty good will.

So Roosevelt set going the new chain of circumstances that was to lead to the succession to the White House, at one remove, of General Dwight Eisenhower.

From the Pyramids to the Sphinx. Prime Minister and President stood before the grotesque stone, once the confidant of the Pharaohs, couchant in the sand, who had seen

> Chariots and horsemen in their dread array—
> Cambyses, Alexander, Antony.

Caesar too had stood where Churchill and Roosevelt for a time remained contemplating the sculptured features, brooding, inscrutable. She returned their gaze with the indifference of the ages. The scene dissolved.

Statesmen and advisers dispersed. A little later Churchill gazed in the skies as his great friend disappeared from sight, his plane winging westward. Soon it was lost to view in the desert haze.

From Cairo the Prime Minister had planned to visit headquarters in Italy, but pneumonia intervened and he was unable to make the journey. From December 13 he was kept to his bed, a very sick man, amidst the ruins of Carthage. Two days after Christmas he was sufficiently recovered to fly across the Atlas Mountains to Marrakech, his "beloved" Marrakech. He was exhausted beyond belief, scarcely able to totter around, and for once he surrendered himself to doctor's orders to rest and relax. The attack was a severe one and, though the pneumonia was checked, there was concern about the heart. There was always the possibility that heart flutter might cause clotting of the blood, with incalculable consequences to the brain.

The patient was far tougher than they thought. He was proud to affirm afterward that despite the fever and weakness he never relinquished the direction of affairs, nor delayed giving the decisions required of him. One matter to which he devoted such strength as he possessed was the mounting of the landings in Italy, at Anzio, for which purpose it was necessary to retain in the Mediterranean landing craft due to leave for England in preparation for "Overlord."

On Christmas Day he insisted on taking part in a conference with Eisenhower and leading commanders at Carthage. Would the Americans agree to delay over the landing craft? He was anxious as the matter was thrashed out at long range by cables exchanged with Washington. The eventual assent from the President delighted him, and he sent his thanks for a decision that "engages us once again in wholehearted unity upon a great enterprise."

Arrangements for the landings at Anzio could proceed on the fullest scale. To be at hand in London, at the center of things, when the new assault was launched, he cut short his recuperation. With members of the party that had assembled at Marrakech to help him through his convalescence—in addition to Mrs. Churchill they had included Beaverbrook, Duff Cooper and Lady Diana Cooper—he left for Gibraltar on January 15.

Arriving at Plymouth aboard the battleship *King George V* he was welcomed ashore by the Cabinet and Staff Chiefs, who were sincerely relieved to see him back among them once again. They noted with concern that his illness had left its mark. He looked tired and older, lacking his usual buoyancy. His recovery was slow. More than ever he was difficult to deal with. He confessed to tiredness, a weakness never before admitted. At times he seemed lacking in vitality and in the power to concentrate, and Alan Brooke grew convinced that he was failing. Considering the burden of his responsibilities it was no matter for surprise that even his constitution, robust as it was, should be strained by the exertions of four taxing years.[39]

The Staffs and advisers were similarly affected, in their varying degrees, by duties arduous and long sustained. None was more sorely tried than the Chief of the Imperial General Staff. As chairman of the Chiefs of Staff, Brooke carried the executive burden for Britain's war effort. There were days when the strain seemed insupportable. Only the solace of the birds it was his hobby to watch, an eagle soaring in the hills or a marsh tit near its nest, enabled him to find distraction and relief. His diary entries in those days were marked by an acerbity not previously displayed and he found the difficulties of coping with "that unique old man," the masterful Defense Minister, more than ever wearying. It was an encouragement for him to receive the baton of Field Marshall, betokening the value placed upon his services.

It was the accumulated strains on those bearing the supreme responsibility that exacerbated the differences between the Prime Minister and his professional advisers over the deployment of Britain's forces in the Far East. This was their most hotly contested dispute throughout the course of the war.[40]

Churchill had been hankering for the chance to strike a blow against the Japanese. His advisers favored a waiting policy, with British forces based on Australia to operate in conjunction with the Americans. He was not prepared to accept so passive and subordinate a role. It was time to do something to restore prestige, forfeited by the long line of British defeats since the loss of the *Prince of Wales* had opened the Indian Ocean to the enemy. He called for a forward strategy in the Bay of Bengal and an attack on Sumatra, with its tip pushing northward into the Indian Ocean.[41]

Mountbatten produced a plan. Churchill endorsed it. His Cabinet colleagues accepted it. The Foreign Office looked on it with favor. It would give the British a role of their own in the Far East instead of being the mere appendages of the Americans, making a minor contribution to their operations. A blow might result that would hasten Japan's defeat.[42]

The Chiefs of Staff were opposed to the scheme, unanimous and unyielding. They could not find the forces and the craft to carry out the operation. And even were they able to do so and the tip of Sumatra were taken, the results, they submitted, would fall far short of those the Prime Minister envisaged.

Differences hardened into deadlock. Churchill was not impressed by the contrary opinions of his advisers. He had differed with them before. They had been against the running of the convoy to Malta. They had opposed the assault on Madagascar. The event had proved him right in the past and he was not inclined to yield to them now, even though Alan Brooke might get heated up and Cunningham become "wild with rage." [43]

He lined up his Ministers against the obdurate Staff Chiefs. It was in vain. The professionals were not impressed by the politicians and their front remained unbroken. Brooke was not going to be browbeaten and there were mutterings of resignation. Churchill added to the ructions by proposing to cross the Atlantic for a conference with the President. The Staffs were dismayed at the idea that their differences might be aired before their allies. Sir Charles Wilson, now Lord Moran, was alarmed at the consequences for his patient. Churchill was in no condition to undertake an Atlantic mission. The C.I.G.S. grew apprehensive that his master might be verging toward collapse.[44]

The dispute was still unresolved when the Japanese sent their fleet to the base of Singapore. This was conclusive. For the time being, Churchill conceded, a stop had been put to amphibious projects in Indian waters.[45]

It was providential that the Japanese had imposed their veto. The conflict between the Defense Minister and his Staffs—"distressing," he termed it—had got out of hand. They had all allowed themselves to be exasperated by their own arguments. It was the measure of the strains to which their responsibilities subjected them.

With the vexations of the Sumatra dispute removed for the time being —Churchill never entirely abandoned the project—they were free to give their attention without distraction to the perfection of the plans for the adventure of D-Day that was then approaching.

CHAPTER SEVEN

D-DAY AND AFTER

MAY–NOVEMBER, 1944

O N THE sixth day of June in the year 1944, the Prime Minister rose in his place in the House of Commons to make his first announcement on the opening of the Second Front. Four years before (June 4, 1940) he had sat down, having imparted to the House the heavy tidings of calamity that had ended in the evacuation at Dunkirk. D-Day was the requital for the disaster from which Dunkirk had been the deliverance.

An armada of little ships had brought the men back from Dunkirk in 1940. In 1944 the English Channel magnificently displayed another and vaster armada converging on the Normandy coast for the most complicated military operation ever to have been staged.

In the setting of the pieces for that grand assault, Winston Churchill played his part with the Service Chiefs. He had his post in the midst of things as Operation "Bolero," the build-up in the marshaling yards of Britain, proceeded at last in full strength. In the preliminaries of planning he was adviser and supervisor. He remembered the lessons learned in World War I—how the arrangements for Gallipoli had been muddled, how supplies were wrongly loaded aboard ship, so that the essentials needed by the fighting men were not available on the Gallipoli beaches. Not for lack of his supervision were such defaults to ruin the Normandy enterprise.

He set up a supervising committee and himself took the chair at the weekly meetings. If there were obstacles to progress he brought his authority to bear to sweep them aside. If knowledge was required about the Normandy coast, orders would be given and a party would be sent across to find out. Under the cover of darkness there would be a silent approach. Without a sound the investigation would be made—the depth of water taken, or the whereabouts of enemy mines discovered. Then the stealthy raiders would slip away, unseen, undetected.

It was essential that they should give no clue. The Germans must not be made to think about Normandy. Every trick was tried to induce them to believe the blow would fall elsewhere—near Calais, by the shortest Channel crossing.

The invasion had been fixed for May, but delay arose from the enlargement of the scope of the operation. Here Churchill's opinion, given at the Quebec conference, was endorsed by the commanders. In the Joint Staff discussions he had consistently argued that greater force must be packed into the opening punch, but the Americans had resisted his arguments, preferring to consider them to be the objections of a man raising obstacles to an operation he disliked. Eisenhower and Montgomery, however, came individually to the same conclusion. Having taken a look at the plans, each pronounced there was need to widen the invasion front. D-Day was put back from May to June, so that the area of assault might be extended from the Normandy beaches to the cliffs of the Cherbourg peninsula. The change involved a host of new problems concerning beaches, booby traps, tides, and the moon's phases.[1]

The Prime Minister was encouraged by his contact with arrangements to report favorably on progress made. "I have presided at a series of meetings," he wrote to General Marshall in March, "and I am satisfied that everything is going on very well. . . . I am hardening very much on this operation as the time approaches in the sense of wishing to strike, if humanly possible, even if the limiting conditions we laid down at Moscow are not exactly fulfilled." [2]

The postponement of the Second Front yielded advantages in the air. Round-the-clock bombing of workshop and factory slowed down German production. During the final weeks before D-Day, a new phase of air attack was begun to seal off the invasion area of France and to create a railway desert, with tracks and bridges destroyed, through which enemy reserves could be moved only with difficulty.

Bombing of railroad centers in France on this scale of intensity aroused the War Cabinet's alarm. The Prime Minister voiced his anxieties to General Eisenhower; scores of thousands of French people, men, women and children, would become casualties, he feared. Eisenhower dismissed these estimates as grossly **exaggerated**. Churchill appealed to the President in the War Cabinet's name; the slaughter of civilian life would cause a revulsion of feeling among the French. The President shared his distress but regretted that he could not intervene. In any event, casualties among the French fell short of the 100,000 that had been feared.[3]

Strategic bombing, following the pattern of careful design, contributed powerfully to the success of "Overlord." In the final month of May, attacks were speeded up. More than 15,000 missions were flown, and 150,000 tons of bombs delivered on selected targets. Railways were blocked, the Seine bridges were destroyed. The strategic desert was created.

In that final month of May, as he journeyed about the country, Churchill moved through an England that had been transformed into a vast military camp. Under the concealing shelter of the trees, the woods of the southern counties were vast munition dumps. The railroads grew congested under the strain of transporting supplies from the northern ports to the troops awaiting them around the southern beaches. Opposite the cliffs of Calais congestion seemed to be on the greatest scale, but this was a fake to deceive the enemy, a deception supported by the provision of dummy ships.[4]

As D-Day came nearer, Churchill ordered secrecy precautions to be doubled. Coastal areas were sealed off. Restrictions were placed on foreign diplomats in London. Telegrams in code were barred. He was still fearful of the price that would be paid in men's lives, and uncertain about the result. He could not bring himself to share the supreme confidence of General Eisenhower.

"Ike," he said on one occasion, "if by the coming winter you have established yourself with thirty-six Allied divisions firmly on the Continent I will proclaim this operation to the world as one of the most successful of the war." [5]

The general was in no doubt that this would be fulfilled. "By the winter," he replied, "we shall be on the borders of Germany itself."

Churchill smiled at this confidence in the outcome of battles still to be fought.

"My dear general," he answered, "it is always fine for a leader to be optimistic. I applaud your enthusiasm. Liberate Paris by Christmas and I will assert the victory to be the greatest of modern times."

Midway through May all the military leaders met in conclave for the last once-over, the final review of the plans. Eisenhower and Montgomery were accompanied by their staffs, the Joint Chiefs were present, the Prime Minister, and members of the War Cabinet. King George VI attended and made a short address. Then Churchill spoke. It was a typical fighting speech.

"Gentlemen," he declared, "I am hardening toward this enterprise."

Under the influence of their old suspicions his American hearers regarded this as the Prime Minister's belated recantation, the abandonment of what they conceived to be his long-sustained opposition to the Second Front. As we know from the use of the phrase in his letter to General Marshall, he intended something quite other than this. Suspicions once formed are poisonous weeds, deep-rooted, infinitely difficult to eradicate.[6]

It is incontestable that Churchill's words at the meeting, packed with dramatic significance, gave unmeasured confidence to every commander present in the outcome of an enterprise that had been planned with scrupulous attention to the minutest details. It was the formal take-over of the operation by the soldiers who were to execute it from the planners who had prepared it. Thereafter, as Eisenhower and Montgomery fought the battles, the Prime Minister and his colleagues could sit back, spectators of events otherwise controlled, with the assurance that their share in the task had been well performed.

> 'Tis not in mortals to command success,
> But we'll do more, Sempronius,—we'll deserve it.

As D-Day drew near the air grew tense with anxiety. All the hopes and fears of the long weeks of preparation were centered in the hazards of the assault. Montgomery, who was to fight the battle, and his men had the fortunes of the Allies in their keeping. If they failed, the setback must be calamitous and the war indefinitely prolonged. But could they fail?

There were moments when the stoutest hearts beat faster at the thought of what D-Day might bring. Eisenhower, for all his vaunted confidence, had his moments of doubt. He prepared the terms of an announcement in readiness against the worst contingency—that he would have to order the withdrawal of the assaulting armies. For Alan Brooke the long drawn-out suspense was nerve-racking and agonizing. Churchill was sustained by buoyant spirits and by then doubted not of the outcome, but even he was reported to be highly strung during the final hours of waiting.

The meeting between Prime Minister and Commander of the Expeditionary Force was one of the enlivening moments before D-Day. Churchill had been making complaint that the paraphernalia of the invasion had grown excessive—too many trucks, radio vehicles, and the like, not enough men with rifles and bayonets. He arrived at Montgomery's headquarters near Portsmouth determined, so it was understood, to probe the matter on the spot. Montgomery received and disarmed him with some plain words. It was in the study before dinner, with members of Montgomery's staff waiting in the room next door. The general tells us that he met the Prime Minister with a cold appraisal of the situation.[7]

"I could never," he said, "allow you to harass my staff at this time, and possibly shake their confidence in me. You can argue with me, but in any case it is too late to change anything. I consider what we have done is right. If you think it is wrong it can only mean you have lost confidence in me."

The silence that followed is described as "awkward." Then Montgomery led the way into the room adjoining. The presentations were made, and the Prime Minister offered the appropriate comment: "Gentlemen, I was not allowed to have any discussion with you." The dinner that followed is described as having been a cordial success. Before leaving, Churchill made amends with a handsomely phrased entry in Montgomery's testimonial book:

> On the verge of the greatest adventure with which these pages have dealt, I record my confidence that all will be well, and that the organization and equipment of the Army will be worthy of the valor of the soldiers and the genius of their chiefs.

From which point was Churchill to watch the progress of the assault? In the front row, he asserted, from a warship in the Channel. This claim touched off one of the minor rumpuses of the war. Eisenhower, as Supreme Commander, refused his permission; the Prime Minister was too essential to the war effort for such a risk to be run. Churchill acknowledged Eisenhower's authority over Allied forces. "But," he objected, "it is not part of your responsibility to determine the exact composition of any ship's company in His Majesty's Fleet. By shipping myself as a member of a ship's complement it would be beyond your authority to prevent my going." [8]

Eisenhower could do no more than regret that the Prime Minister should choose to add to the anxieties of D-Day.

After the Supreme Commander, the King entered his caveat. At first, King George had proposed that he and his First Minister should share the excitement of the day from one of the bombarding cruisers. But second thoughts prompted him to the conclusion it would not be right for either of them to run the risk; the right thing for both of them would be to stay at home and wait.

The direction to the path of duty was unpalatable. Churchill was disposed to have his way. His Majesty's anxieties would be increased, it was represented, were his Prime Minister to be sent to the bottom of the Channel. The risk, came the reply, was negligible.

The King wrote urging that his Minister should not fall below his own standard of duty to the state. If it was not permissible for the King to lead his troops in battle, it was not right that his Prime Minister, an older man, should take his place.

The royal wishes, so graciously expressed, were not to be flouted. With a parting declaration of his right to go where he conceived his duty as Defense Minister required, Churchill gave way. It was a comfort for him to know that his Sovereign's wishes "arise from a desire to continue me in Your Majesty's service."

Deprived of what he termed the "refreshment of adventure," Churchill went cruising in *The Solent* to visit ship after ship as they lay awaiting the final signal to slip off with troops aboard, bound for Normandy and the grand assault. In those final hours, landing stages and beaches from Felixstowe to the Bristol Channel had been crowded with the expectant forces. Many had to undergo the ordeal of twenty-four hours cooped up aboard their landing craft when D-Day was postponed because of bad weather. Half a gale had been blowing in the Channel.

The weather was still stormy on June 5, but Eisenhower decided to go ahead. So, on that short summer's night, the opening blows were struck. The night bombers pulverized German batteries. Parachute troops, three divisions of them, were descending on France. Under cover of the short summer darkness, the armada of ships came steaming toward Normandy. As the June dawn broke, the battleships were in position to take up the hammering of German defenses. The barges moved in. The invasion had begun. Allied armies were returning to the French soil from which they had been driven four years before. The bad weather aided them. The Germans had also studied the forecasts. Their generals had gone to bed comforted by the belief it was too stormy for an attack to be started. The weather gave the invaders the advantage of a tactical surprise.

As a curtain raiser to Normandy, Alexander had gone over to the attack in Italy. The Gustav line was broken. The Fifth Army struck out from Anzio; the Eighth breached the Hitler line. On June 5 Rome was entered. It was a propitious overture to "Overlord."

At Westminster on D-Day, the House reassembled after their Whitsun break. They met expectantly. The P.M. was to give them the news from the front on events across the Channel. He was not in his place at question time. Questions disposed of, Mr. Speaker announced an interval, an innovation almost unprecedented in the proceedings where no check is permitted in the flow of speech. There arose a hum of conversation, for the chamber was crowded.

Then Churchill was seen and there was a burst of cheering. He rose at once to offer his apologies that pressure of business had made him keep the members waiting. Thereafter he kept them waiting longer as he digressed on the achievements in Italy. He invited the House to take formal cognizance of the liberation of Rome.

He went on, coming to the subject of his and the members' main preoccupation:

> I have also to announce that during the night and the early hours of this morning the first of the series of landings in force upon the European continent has taken place. In this case the liberating assault fell upon the coast of France.
>
> An immense armada of upward of 4,000 ships, together with several thousand smaller craft, crossed the Channel. Massed airborne landings have been successfully effected behind the enemy lines, and landings on the beaches are proceeding at various points at the present time.
>
> The fire of the shore batteries has been largely quelled. The obstacles that were constructed in the sea have not proved so difficult as was apprehended. The Anglo-American Allies are sustained by about 1,000 first-line aircraft.
>
> So far the commanders who are engaged report that everything is proceeding according to plan. And what a plan!
>
> This vast operation is undoubtedly the most complicated and difficult that has ever taken place. It involves tides, wind, waves, visibility, both from the air and the sea standpoint, and the combined employment of land, air, and sea forces in the highest degree of intimacy, and in contact with conditions which could not and cannot be fully foreseen.
>
> There are already hopes that actual tactical surprise has been attained, and we hope to furnish the enemy with a succession of surprises during the course of the fighting.
>
> Complete unity prevails throughout the Allied armies. There is a brotherhood in arms between us and our friends of the United States. There is complete confidence in the Supreme Commander, General Eisenhower, and his lieutenants, and also in the Commander of the Expeditionary Force, General Montgomery. The ardor and spirit of the troops, as I saw myself, embarking in these last few days was splendid to witness.

Having made his statement, Churchill was off posthaste to the South of England, to get as close as possible to the fighting front. General

Eisenhower's headquarters in Hampshire was the nearest he could contrive, and there he spent several hours, reading the reports from Normandy as they came to hand. They were all of them reassuring.

Before the House rose that night, he again entered the chamber to make a further brief but encouraging statement.

> Many dangers and difficulties which at this time last night appeared extremely formidable are behind us. The passage of the sea has been made with far less loss than we apprehended. Our troops have penetrated, in some cases, several miles inland. Lodgments exist on a broad front.
>
> The outstanding feature has been the landings of the airborne troops, which were on a scale far larger than anything that has been seen so far in the world. These landings took place with extremely little loss and with great accuracy.
>
> Heavy fighting will soon begin and will continue without end, as we can push troops in and the enemy can bring other troops up. It is, therefore, a most serious time that we enter upon. Thank God we enter upon it with our great Allies all in good heart and all in good friendship.

It was an auspicious beginning. Even Churchill's statement did not convey the fullness of the success. So surely had the plans been laid, and so well had they been executed, that at the end of twenty-four hours over a quarter of a million Allied troops were ashore in France. By D-Day+3 Spitfires had their own airfields across the Channel. On D-Day+4 the Allied Front was fifty-one miles wide and fifteen miles deep.

Churchill was eager to cross to France. On the fifth day after D-Day, he took off by plane, intending to visit the battlefront. They crossed the French coast and then it was reported that the plane must return—it was too foggy for a landing. Churchill remonstrated. There were consultations. The decision was repeated and so too the remonstrance. Thereupon the pilot reported: "I am instructed, sir, to inform you that the Dakota ahead of us crashed when trying to land, with the loss of everybody on board."

"I suppose that does make a difference," conceded the Prime Minister, as the plane turned for England.[9]

There was better luck the next day when the Channel was crossed by destroyer. Montgomery was waiting when the Prime Minister came scrambling ashore from a landing craft. Lunch was taken at Supreme Headquarters, and Churchill toured the territory that had been gained.

On the way back he watched from the destroyer as battleships and cruisers fired salvos at the German positions on the Allied left flank. Couldn't the destroyer join in?

"Certainly," agreed the admiral. The destroyer's guns obliged with a broadside. Churchill was highly gratified. It closed a "jolly day."

"We had a fling at the Hun," he reported afterward, adding with a tinge of regret, "although the range was 6,000 yards he did not honor us with a reply."

The battle and the build-up proceeded. Every day the Allies pushed farther into France. Every day brought more men ashore to strengthen the attack. Cherbourg was taken. Caen fell.

In July Churchill was in France again, and Montgomery took him around the ruins of Caen. In an observation plane he flew over the British line. He watched the work of "Mulberry." He inspected a site from which the Germans would have launched their buzz bombs on London.

He gained firsthand material for his next report to the House, with a wonderful tale of achievements in the field and of the planning that had made such progress possible.

It was heartening for Londoners, pestered by the affliction of the buzz bomb, the first of Hitler's secret weapons. The air defenses did what they could to stem the flow. But, said Churchill: "There can be no question of allowing the slightest weakening of the battle in order to diminish the injuries of these bombs. It may be a comfort to some to feel that they are sharing in no small degree in the perils of the soldiers overseas."

Churchill knew his Londoners. They justified his faith in them.

Differences arose over the employment of troops assigned to Operation "Anvil," the landings in southern France designed to assist operations in the North by drawing off German reserves. The Prime Minister and the British Staffs considered that "Anvil" was rendered superfluous by the successes achieved in Normandy. Far better, they urged, to employ some of the troops to dispose of the Germans in Italy and to penetrate into Austria. The American Staffs took the contrary view, maintaining their opposition to any adventuring in the direction of the Balkans.[10]

The Staffs being deadlocked in disagreement, Churchill invited the President's opinion. Roosevelt supported the agreed strategy of Teheran, with assaults in southern France to give added force to the drive into the heart of Germany. His views were strengthened by his early excursions in geometry and the axiom, "A straight line is the shortest distance between two points." If differences persisted he suggested that the question should be remitted to Stalin for decision. This would have made the devil arbiter in his own cause.[11]

The Prime Minister saw no reason for bringing in the Russians. He was preparing to accept the inevitable when the accumulation of successes in France gave him ground for a renewed appeal. He canvassed

Eisenhower, who was inflexible. He appealed to Washington, but the President declined to revise his views.[12]

Churchill was grieved that the splendid victories achieved together did not bring them into closer accord on strategy. His military advisers were not surprised. They had come to realize, as he had not, that his strategic cables served to rally against him the opinion of the American professionals. They imagined him to be forever dominating the British Chiefs of Staff, compelling their reluctant consent to his ideas on strategy.

There were complaints from the American side that had to be met, mutterings against Montgomery's conduct of the battle. The lodgment in France had been successfully made, the build-up had proceeded, and then there followed a hold-up, a slowing down, it appeared, in the tempo of the attack. Wasn't Montgomery at fault? Wasn't he playing for safety, one of those generals who wouldn't move till they knew the last shoelace had been supplied? There were criticisms in the New York press that the British divisions were not taking their fair share of the fighting—"dragging their feet" was the phrase—while the United States forces were bearing more than their share of casualties.[13]

Eisenhower, at lunch, reported some of these matters to the Prime Minister. Couldn't Montgomery be persuaded to "get on his bicycle and start moving"? Churchill was confident that Montgomery understood the necessity for "keeping the front aflame," words that Eisenhower dutifully passed on by letter to the General.

The plain truth was that the Supreme Commander had a limited appreciation of Montgomery's strategic purpose. Eisenhower's preference was for the frontal attack in force rather than for strategy and stratagems. There was no interference, however, from Supreme Headquarters. Montgomery, pursuing his master plan, put on the pressure. Two weeks later the great encirclement began. The Allied line began to wheel on the pivot of the British divisions on the left. The tempo of the wheel increased. The British were containing the enemy armor. The Americans carried all before them as they wheeled east and then to the north. The pincers began to close. Some 100,000 Germans were netted in the Falaise pocket. Half of them got away before the gap was closed, but 30,000 were made prisoner and 15,000 were left dead on the battlefield. The German rout was complete. France was open to the liberators. The battle that had begun to gain a foothold on the beaches had ended in Montgomery's strategic triumph. It was saluted in the House of Commons by the Prime Minister. "I no longer feel bound to deny," he said, "that final victory may come, perhaps soon."

In Downing Street—and at Montgomery's headquarters—glittering hopes began to form of a smash-through that might end the war as the autumn leaves began to fall. They were disappointed in their expectations. The smash-through on one sector of the front was replaced by a push on all sectors, and there was not the strength to pack the blows in force.

Since then the rival strategists have disputed over the methods that Eisenhower followed and the strategy Montgomery advocated. The refighting of the second Battle of France is scarcely part of the Winston Churchill story.

Some months of fighting still lay ahead in France. At home in Britain there were the final attacks to be borne from Hitler's secret weapon. The Prime Minister's words had been an encouragement to the people to sustain the casualties from buzz bombs. They had to bear the further infliction of the V2s, the rocket bombs that were to cause 9,000 casualties before the advancing Allied armies occupied their launching grounds.

By September the position on the Western Front had been transformed. The major part of France had been liberated, the Belgians had been set free, districts of Holland were in Allied hands. At various points Allied forces had reached and crossed the German frontier and had penetrated the Siegfried Line. In Germany an attempt had been made to assassinate Hitler who, no more than injured, took savage vengeance on the generals and their accomplices in the plot.

The Prime Minister was much engaged abroad in those days, journeying from battlefront to battlefront and from ally to ally. In August he traveled to Italy, arriving at Allied headquarters (August 11) in time to watch the setting-off of troops who were to take part in the invasion of southern France.

The politics of liberation claimed his attention. First he had conversations with the Yugoslavs, Dr. Subasitch and Marshal Tito. For a week he toured the Italian front, inspecting British, Canadian, Indian and New Zealand units. Having discussed plans for future operations, he left for Rome. At the British Embassy he met the new Italian Premier, Bonomi, and Prince Umberto who, on King Victor Emmanuel's retirement from public life, had been appointed Lieutenant General of the Realm.

Having entertained Badoglio at lunch, he received the entire Italian Cabinet, and rounded off the business of the day by a meeting with the Greek Premier, Papandreou. On August 23 he went to the Vatican to be received in audience by the Pope, with whom he had a forty-five-minute conversation, characterized, according to the Vatican announcement, by "affable cordiality."

"What impressed and touched me most in my journey through Italy," he said afterward in the Commons (September 28), "was the extraordinary good will to the British and American troops everywhere displayed by the Italian people. As I drove through the small towns and villages behind the line of armies, day after day, the friendliness and even enthusiasm of the peasants, workmen, and shopkeepers, indeed of all classes, was spontaneous and convincing. I cannot feel—I make my confession—any sentiments of hostility toward the mass of the misled or coerced Italian people."

The Italian tour was exhausting and Churchill yet again fell a victim to pneumonia, a fact that was not made public until a year afterward. The strain was exhausting him. Each mission abroad was taking its toll and the interval between attacks appeared to become successively shortened. His close associates—none others were admitted to the secret of his illness—were anxious. Once again, however, sulfa drugs worked their wonders for him and he allowed himself no prolonged convalescence. A meeting with Roosevelt had been arranged, and a trifle such as pneumonia was not going to prevent him from keeping the appointment. On September 10 he was in Canada for the conference. There was much to be discussed.

The second Quebec conference (September 11–16) opened, in Churchill's phrase, in a blaze of friendship. It was the least exacting meeting in which Prime Minister and President engaged. It was as well, for both men were in need of a chance to relax. Churchill was still suffering the aftereffects of the pneumonia. Ill health was plain to see in F.D.R. There were times when he appeared haggard and glassy-eyed. Those who had not met him for a time were perturbed to note his ravaged face and emaciated neck. Only by painful effort was it now possible for him to stand. Nevertheless, he had considered it to be his duty to go to nomination for a fourth term, with Harry Truman as his running mate.[14]

There were no differences on strategy to disturb the good-fellowship at Quebec. The main discussions turned on the Prime Minister's claim for Britain to be given an adequate share in the Pacific war once Germany had gone down in defeat. There was some hesitation over enlisting units of the British Navy. The Americans gave the appearance of coveting for themselves all the glory to be won from victories in the Far East.[15]

"The offer of the British Fleet has been made," insisted Churchill. "Is it accepted?"

"Yes," replied Roosevelt.

Over participation by the RAF, acceptance was not so readily forthcoming.

No difficulty was experienced over drawing up the strategic program for the Western Front, nor over Italy were there differences. The Americans, in a responsive mood, accorded the use of landing craft for the proposed attack on the Istrian peninsula. But so long as the battle in Italy was to continue there would, it was recognized, be only meager forces available to employ in the Balkans. In Egypt two British brigades were being held in readiness to occupy Athens, thus paving the way for the commencement of relief and the establishment of law and order. This fact, recorded in the strategic program, was passed over at Quebec without comment. It was shortly to have discordant consequences.

One feature of the conference Churchill noticed with regret—the absence of Harry Hopkins, who had suffered some decline in the President's favor. From Canada Churchill moved south to join F.D.R. at his country home at Hyde Park. Hopkins was made one of the party, and Churchill sensed an immediate improvement in his relations with the President. Affairs moved quicker as Hopkins regained his old influence.[16]

So Prime Minister and President passed pleasant hours together, unconscious that they were meeting, relaxed and at ease, for the last time on American soil.

In the autumn Churchill crossed to France to take part in the Armistice Day celebrations of France's liberation. There were thunderous cheers as he drove through the Paris streets. For security reasons, his coming had not been announced but the news spread fast. He walked on foot down the Champs Elysées. The crowds greeted him as liberator. Their cheers bore the message that de Gaulle put into words: "We should not have seen a day like this but for our brave ally, Britain, under Winston Churchill's leadership."

France had emerged from her ordeal by occupation. The problems of liberation were less difficult than had been feared. The Committee of Liberation, under de Gaulle, had evolved at Algiers into a fairly representative executive, embracing representatives of the Maquis, who had been resisting the Germans from within, as well as of the de Gaullists, who had been operating from without.

On the eve of the invasion there had been renewed pressure on the British Government to accord recognition to the Committee, but this Churchill refused to grant. He was reluctant, in the uncertain state of French political opinion, to give this endorsement to the Committee as Provisional Government of France. "We are not sure," he said, "that it represents the French nation."

Opinion in Washington was firm against according recognition. Relations between de Gaulle and the President remained cool. With Churchill, de Gaulle had had his differences, but though these had found vigorous expression, they had left no bitterness.

"I have never forgotten," said Churchill (August 2, 1944), "and can never forget that he stood forth as the first eminent Frenchman to face the common foe in what seemed to be the hour of ruin of his country. It is only fair and becoming that he should stand first and foremost in the days when France shall again be raised and raise herself to her rightful place among the powers."

With the expulsion of the invader from France and the liberation of Paris, the de Gaulle administration established itself in Paris, taking over responsibility for the affairs of the larger part of the country. The French Consultative Assembly was enlarged to include representatives of the resistance movements and the old political parties. There was no longer valid reason for delay. On October 23 the French Foreign Minister was informed by Britain's Ambassador, Duff Cooper, that it had been decided to accord recognition to the de Gaulle Committee as the Provisional Government of France. Recognition was simultaneously accorded by the United States and the Soviet Union. De Gaulle was invited to appoint a representative to the European Advisory Commission of the Allies on the basis of full equality.

On the day following the celebrations, the Prime Minister and Mr. Secretary Eden met members of the Paris Liberation Committee at the *hôtel de ville*. There Churchill was made a Freeman of the City, and was presented with the German flag which during the occupation had flown above the *préfecture de police*. He marked the occasion by addressing his hosts in French: "Be on your guard," he advised them, "because I am going to speak, or try to speak, in French, a formidable undertaking and one which will put great demands on your friendship for Great Britain." He told them that he had never lost his faith in them, in the citizens of Paris, or in the French Army.

The visit was not all vivas and felicitations. Between the courtesies there was serious business to transact. Prime Minister and Foreign Secretary had long discussions with de Gaulle and Bidault, the French Foreign Minister, on military, economic and diplomatic affairs—rearmament of the French fighting forces, help in French industrial reconstruction, and the delicate problems of Syria and Lebanon, which were to result in tension some months later. Nevertheless, the felicitations were of greater moment. Good will between Britain and France in the spirit of the old alliance was needed in the postwar world. Winston Churchill's visit as ambassador of good will helped towards the rekindling of the flame of the Entente.

CHAPTER EIGHT

LIBERATION FEUDS

FEBRUARY–SEPTEMBER, 1944

A s FINAL victory came nearer there were political complications for the Prime Minister. Hitherto he had been preoccupied with military matters—to face the hazards of the moment when survival had been in doubt, to debate strategy when the initiative passed to the Allies. With these urgencies to fill his mind it had not been possible for him to embark upon planning for the peace. The future of Europe could be shrugged off—when the war was won would be time enough, or, as he phrased it to Anthony Eden, "unfortunately the war has prior claim on your attention and mine."

By the autumn of 1944 the claims of the postwar world were not to be ignored. The ancient states of Europe were emerging from their bondage. The problems of liberation were pressing with an urgency not to be denied.

Henceforth Churchill was to be engaged on two levels in conflicts brought on by the challenges of the future. At home there were the opposites of politics, right wing and left wing, vigorously assertive over the interests of right-wing and left-wing parties in the liberated territories. Abroad there were the scheming Russians to hold in check lest Europe should be liberated from the Nazis only to pass under the ideological despotism of the Soviets. It was the specter of the Bolshevization of Europe that darkened the days as Churchill sought to rouse the President and his advisers to a realization of the "Red peril." As the months of the war ran out he labored, with a mounting sense of frustration, to break down the barrier across the Atlantic that was fatal to his purpose. He strove without success. Never was he to establish a common policy between Britain and the United States in resistance to Soviet designs. And so the war, with the Allies victorious on the battlefields, was to end in diplomatic defeat for the Western Allies at the hands of the Russians.

Leaving, for a moment, the chronicle of difficulties abroad, consider first the reactions in Britain. As the pressure of peril relaxed the political resentments of the prewar years began to release themselves. There was an accumulation of pent-up animosities in Britain. Abyssinia, war in Spain, Munich—these were bitter memories from the years of appeasement made manifest in mistrust between right wing and left wing in British politics. As the Prime Minister faced the problems of peace it was an added complication that he could not rely upon the solid support of a united people. Instead, he had to labor to reconcile the irreconcilables at home, the champions of the left wing, vociferous in their demands. "Confusion," he lamented, "is caused in some minds by mixing ideology with idealism."

Controversy was certain to arise from the basic divisions among the countries struggling to be free. Resistance to the Nazis was organized on dual lines by rivals in politics. In the occupied countries were the devoted patriots, members of underground movements that were leftish in politics. There were also the sovereigns and governments in exile, mainly right-wing, maintaining the constitutional existence of the various states. As the lawfully constituted authorities, they claimed and received recognition by the Government of Britain. The inevitable consequence, when differences arose between patriots and exiles, was that the Prime Minister came to be charged with backing reactionary governments against progressive democrats.

British Socialists professed to find evidence of reaction on all hands. Britain had entered the war, they protested, to remove the menace of Fascism, but, as the conflict developed, great popular movements had emerged in the various countries of Europe which had been in conflict, not only with the Germans, but with the forces in their own countries imbued with similar Fascist ideas. The Prime Minister's policy was represented as inclined to the support of many of the "worn-out regimes in Europe against the popular forces." There had been events in Belgium. There had been Darlan in North Africa, and in Italy there had been Badoglio and British opposition to Count Sforza.

Said James McGovern in one of the foreign policy debates: "The Prime Minister says Count Sforza will not do because he is a dishonorable man. Badoglio will do for the Prime Minister although he helped to gas the Abyssinians, took the oath of allegiance to Mussolini, took filthy Fascist lucre from the coffers of Rome and, like the rat he is, turned against his master when he saw Mussolini going down in the sinking ship."

Churchill was given a sharp reminder of the force of left-wing opinion on affairs abroad when he made some commendatory references to Spain in a survey of world affairs in the House (May 12, 1944). He introduced the subject by protesting against the idea that British policy toward Spain was best expressed by drawing comical or even rude caricatures of General Franco. There had been a time after the fall of France when it had appeared that the Spaniards might enter the war on the side of Germany. Had they yielded to Nazi blandishments the Allied task would have been harder, but already they had had enough of war.

"I must say I shall always consider a service was rendered by Spain, not only to the British Empire and Commonwealth, but to the cause of the United Nations," Churchill declared. "I have no sympathy therefore with those who think it is clever and even funny to insult and abuse the Government of Spain whenever occasion serves."

Haden Guest immediately challenged the tribute. Was not a Fascist government anywhere, he asked, a preparation for attack? Pethick Lawrence expressed the hope that the Government would not connive in the future for the destruction of democratic government in Spain as had been done in the past. Outside the House there were protests in the left-wing press. Labour Party opinion was shocked that the Prime Minister should have praised a man "whose hands are reeking with the warm blood of his own countrymen, thousands of whom are still in prison."

Churchill was not allowed to forget how deeply the critics were offended. The Spaniards might be required to stop exporting wolfram to Germany, or to turn the Nazi agents out of Tangier—the leftists were not appeased. Yet, though he had incurred their censure, Churchill was not of a different mind from Labour M.P.s about the Franco regime. He expressed himself with pungency when Franco wrote suggesting that Britain should join in an anti-Russian bloc. The Prime Minister replied:

> I should let your Excellency fall into serious error if I did not remove from your mind the idea that H. M. Government would be ready to consider any bloc of powers based on hostility to our Russian Allies or on any assumed need of defense against them. H. M. Government's policy is firmly based on the Anglo-Soviet Treaty of 1942 and considers permanent Anglo-Russian collaboration within the frame of the future world organization as essential, not only to her own interests, but also to the future peace and prosperity of Europe as a whole.

To complete the record on Spain, it should be added that one of Churchill's last acts as Prime Minister was to participate at the Potsdam conference in the drawing-up of the declaration excluding the Spanish Government from admission to the United Nations Organization.

Events in Yugoslavia were the cause of concern in London. Here there was a double problem, military and political in its aspects. Two organizations in Yugoslavia had proclaimed themselves resistance movements— one, Marshal Tito's Liberation Committee and his army of Partisans; the other, General Mihailovitch's organization and his Chetniks. Professing to pursue the same end of liberation for Yugoslavia, they were bitter rivals, engaged in civil war within their own land and competing for Allied support without. Mihailovitch was Defense Minister in the Royal Yugoslav Government. Tito made complaint that he and his subordinates were cooperating with the Germans, and these allegations were backed by vigorous denunciations of the Chetniks from Moscow. The British Government discontinued supplies to Mihailovitch, who was removed from his place as Defense Minister.

It was arranged that Tito should send a military representative to London to maintain contact. Among the members of the British mission at the Marshal's headquarters was the Prime Minister's son, Randolph, who on one occasion narrowly escaped capture by the Germans. Recognition of Tito failed to dispose of Yugoslav differences.

Poland provided the most vexatious of the problems of liberation. By the autumn of 1944 a Polish settlement had become imperative. In this case, the existence of rival governments was complicated by the backing given by the Russians to their protégés, the Lublin Poles.

The Polish government-in-exile had its headquarters in London. Mikolajczyk, its head, had the confidence of the British Government and the support in Parliament of the British Tories. It had been the natural expectation in Britain that the war would end with the restoration of the prewar Poland. This was natural enough, since it was on behalf of Polish independence that the fight had begun. The Russians, for their part, never had any intention of restoring Mikolajczyk's right-wing Ministry. It was a fundamental of Kremlin policy that a friendly—that is Communist—government should rule in Warsaw.

As the Red armies advanced eastward in 1944, freeing vast areas of Poland, Stalin was placed in a position to impose his requirements. Mikolajczyk and his Ministers were alarmed for the future. Tories pressed their claims. The Prime Minister and the Foreign Secretary backed the government-in-exile. Stalin offered to conclude an alliance with the Poles and Churchill was encouraged to hope that a settlement would be reached, but the government-in-exile would not accept Stalin's demands over frontiers. There were acrimonious exchanges between the Poles and Moscow, charges and countercharges. Diplomatic relations were broken off.

The Prime Minister was placed in a dilemma. The British had gone to war in support of Poland's frontiers in the west. Were they now to fall out with their Russian allies because Russia required the cession of Polish territory—or territory that had been Polish in 1939? Even the offer of compensation for the Poles by the grant of German lands did not induce the London Poles to agree to relinquish territories in the east. What had been Polish, they insisted, Polish should remain.

Following his talks with Stalin at Teheran, the Prime Minister gave his views on the Polish question in a statement to the House (February 22, 1944):

> I have an intense sympathy with the Poles, that heroic race whose national spirit centuries of misfortune cannot quench, but I also have sympathy with the Russian standpoint. Twice in our lifetime Russia has been violently assaulted by Germany. Many millions of Russians have been slain and vast tracts of Russian soil devastated as a result of repeated German aggression. Russia has the right of re-assurance against future attacks from the west, and we are going all the way with her to see that she gets it, not only by the might of her arms but by the approval and assent of the United Nations.
>
> The liberation of Poland may presently be achieved by the Russian armies, after these armies have suffered millions of casualties in breaking the German military machine. I cannot feel that the Russian demand for a reassurance about her western frontiers goes beyond the limit of what is reasonable or just. Marshal Stalin and I also spoke [at Teheran] and agreed upon the need for Poland to obtain compensation at the expense of Germany both in the north and west.

A compromise between Poles and Russians had somehow to be contrived. Churchill began to think of a personal discussion with Stalin as the only means of ending the dispute. He had other reasons for seeking a meeting, other matters to clear up. He had had promptings from the Dominions about the Russians and their intentions. His fellow Prime Ministers from the Dominions had met in London for the Empire Conference on the eve of D-Day. Their questions had prompted him to ask Anthony Eden for a paper to be drafted on the issues developing with the Soviet Government.

"Are we," he asked, "going to acquiesce in communization of the Balkans and perhaps of Italy?" Evidently the time was approaching for a clash with the Russians about Communist intrigues.[1]

Events began to move toward the showdown over Rumania and Greece. Anthony Eden took the opportunity of raising the question with the Soviet Ambassador. He made the proposal that, as a temporary expedient, the Russians should be regarded as having the main concern with Rumanian affairs, leaving Greece, still in German occupation, as a concern for Britain. Subject to United States approval the Russians agreed.

The Prime Minister placed the proposal before the President. He was careful to emphasize that the arrangement was a natural development of the existing military situation. There was no suggestion of a carve-up of the Balkans into spheres of influence.[2]

There was a cold acknowledgment from the State Department. The President emphasized the undesirability of spheres of influence, despite the assurances Churchill had given on this point. Roosevelt suggested that a consultative committee should be set up to deal with these problems.[3]

This brought a sharp rejoinder from the Prime Minister. Action would be paralyzed if everybody always had first to consult with everybody else. Someone must have the power to act, and, if an agreement were not reached with the Russians, civil war would ruin Greece. As to the Rumanians, it might be accepted that they should follow Soviet leadership seeing that "neither you nor we have any troops there at all."

A three-month trial run was suggested for the Eden idea. Washington opinion was not mollified. The real ground for complaint, confessed after ten days of correspondence, was that "your people took this matter up only after it had been put to the Russians." The words were the President's; their inspiration was Cordell Hull in the State Department.

Here the American record was impeachable as Churchill was quick to point out:

> I cannot admit [he wrote] I have done anything wrong. . . . It would not be possible for three people in different parts of the world to work effectively together if no one of them may make any suggestion to either of the others without simultaneously keeping the third informed. A recent example of this is the message you have sent quite properly to Uncle Joe about your conversation with the Poles, of which as yet I have heard nothing from you. . . .

The President perforce agreed that both of them had sinned. He advised that "it is essential that we should always be in agreement in matters bearing on our allied war effort." The sentiment was unexceptionable. The words came tripping out, but who was to defer to whom to make agreement possible?

The Joint Staffs set an example of solidarity in running military operations as a joint enterprise. In the more difficult sphere of political relationships, the gap in cooperation was wide. Had the Foreign Office and State Department been forced to pull aside their professional shutters and pool their principles, agreement "in matters bearing on our allied war effort" could have been achieved. The shutters were not to be removed. Misunderstanding and dissension were to follow from the neglect to plan policy, as well as strategy, as one.

With the preoccupations of D-Day, the Russian problem was shelved, but later in the year the Prime Minister's concern was sharpened by notes of warning from Smuts, man of sage counsel. "Knowing her power," he cabled, "Russia may become more grasping than ever." And again: "The more firmly Russia can establish herself in the saddle now, the further she will ride in the future and the more precarious our holdfast will become." It seemed advisable for the British to intervene in Greece if that country was not to come under the heel of the Communists. As to Prussia, her destiny under Russian occupation seemed to be "a Bolshevized Soviet province." Thus Smuts, with shrewd forecast of a future in which the Russians would be "drunk with new-won power." [4]

These soundings of alarm were passed on to Roosevelt who, Churchill considered, was "impressed" by Smuts's views. Reading the brief note of acknowledgment it may be doubted whether the impression on the Presidential mind went very deep. "I think," was the comment, "that we are all in agreement with him [Smuts] as to the necessity of having the U.S.S.R. as a fully accepted and equal member of any association of the Great Powers formed for the purpose of preventing international war." This was rather beside the point that Smuts was raising.[5]

Churchill was many steps ahead of the President in his evaluation of Soviet intentions. The United States, he reflected, was "very slow in realizing the upsurge of Communist influence, sliding on before as well as following the onward march of the mighty armies directed from the Kremlin." [6]

With these contingencies to provide against, Churchill concluded that something should be done. What better than have it out, face to face, with "Uncle Joe"? He would undertake a second mission to Moscow. He sounded the President, who at first viewed the idea with detached unconcern. F.D.R. was critically engaged on the political front, conducting his last campaign for the Presidency, and he needed prompting from Harry Hopkins to safeguard his own position. It would not do, submitted Hopkins, for the Prime Minister to appear to be speaking in the Kremlin for the United States as well as Britain. Accordingly, Averell Harriman was detailed to attend the Moscow meetings as American observer. F.D.R. wrote off to Stalin in a deprecatory fashion. It had been his hope, he stated, that no summit meeting should be held until he was free to join in. While he appreciated the necessity for Moscow discussions, "I choose to consider your forthcoming talks with Mr. Churchill as a preliminary conference of the three of us, to take place after the American elections." To Harriman, the President laid it down that he "retained complete freedom of action after this [Moscow] conference is over." [7]

Stalin acknowledged the President's note with appreciation. Otherwise, he explained, he would have fallen into the error of conceiving Churchill to be speaking for Roosevelt as well as for Britain.

CHAPTER NINE

BARGAIN-MAKING IN MOSCOW

SEPTEMBER–DECEMBER, 1944

T HE Prime Minister, who was accompanied by Anthony Eden, the
Foreign Secretary, was received in Russia with full ceremony when
he alighted from his plane on October 9. Molotov was there to greet
him, and for the next ten days he was lavishly entertained. It was one
of those cordial occasions that the Russians, when they set out to please,
can render delightful.

"Extraordinary atmosphere of good will here," reported Churchill on
arrival. "The atmosphere is extremely cordial," he cabled to King
George a week later. Was this a spurious bonhomie, the Russians smiling but to deceive? Or had they, dropping their political designs for
the occasion, surrendered themselves to the good spirits appropriate to
the meeting of Allies whose partnership in war was being crowned by
victories. These, on the Russian side, were celebrated by nightly salvos
of red, green, and yellow stars cascading down on the rejoicing Mus-
covites.

There was a command performance at the Bolshoi Theater. The two
leaders stood side by side in the privileged box, to be acclaimed by the
audience with a show of enthusiasm that was passionate in its intensity.
Always responsive to the atmosphere about him, the Prime Minister
was encouraged to the pitch of affability. In frank talks, overflowing
with hospitality, he and his host reveled in amiability. They allocated
the Balkans to zones of interest on a percentage basis, and even discussed

the business of the Poles and their frontiers without checking the effervescence of good will.

The men of Lublin were paraded for the occasion. So well had they been drilled that their leader could deliver himself of the demand that the ancient Polish city of Lvov should belong in the future to Russia—"it is the will of the Polish people." Even Stalin could not conceal the twinkle in his eye as this was chanted. It was not to be disguised that the men of Lublin were no more than Soviet stooges. Anthony Eden was disgusted at the performance. "Quisling" Poles, Churchill termed them.

Mikolajczyk was summoned to Moscow and was pressed by Churchill to agree to a compromise with Stalin. There were long talks but little progress. Mikolajczyk declined to recognize the men of Lublin, "arbitrarily chosen by a foreign power." He rejected the Curzon Line as the eastern frontier of his country; to accept it would mean abandoning five million Poles and forty per cent of Polish territory. He had not traveled to Moscow to submit to a new partition of Poland. No offer could induce him to change his mind. It was suggested that in the west Poland should be compensated by the grant of Prussian territory, with the City of Danzig and Stettin added for good measure. Mikolajczyk was not to be tempted.[1]

For the Balkans, the Prime Minister proposed making a deal with the Soviet, adopting for this purpose the idea Anthony Eden had put forward earlier in the year. To avoid being at cross-purposes, let it be agreed between them that Rumania was a sphere of special concern to the Russians, and Greece to Britain; Bulgaria of little less interest to the Russians, with interest at parity elsewhere. Churchill gave a mathematical expression to his intentions:

Rumania—Russian interest	90 per cent
Bulgaria—Russian interest	75 " "
Greece—British interest (in accord with U.S.A.)	90 " "
Yugoslavia & Hungary—Russian interest	50 " "
Other States—Russian interest	50 " "

The paper was passed to Stalin, who marked it with a blue tick of approval. It was settled, to Churchill's surprise, in no more time than it took to write down. Perhaps the evidence of so cynical an agreement had better be destroyed? Not at all, objected Stalin, let the Prime Minister preserve it.

But what had been settled? To what extent had Stalin committed himself by that blue-penciled tick? Would he have condescended so much as a tick had he been given the explanation of what Churchill was intending? The percentages might, he confessed, be reckoned crude and callous if exposed to the public scrutiny, but the Prime Minister's purpose was unexceptionable in its democratic correctitude.[2] The interest accorded to Britain and Russia by the percentages was to be subject, in his conception, to the overriding principle that each of the states should be free on liberation to choose the government it desired.

> We certainly do not wish to force any Balkan state into monarchic or republican institutions.
> We are very glad you have declared yourselves against trying to change by force or by Communist propaganda established systems in the Balkan countries.
> We feel we were right in interpreting your dissolution of the Comintern * as a decision by the Soviet Government not to interfere in the internal affairs of other countries.

These passages were included in a memorandum on the percentages drawn up for presentation to Stalin, but Churchill changed his mind and did not hand it over. Maybe it was all to the good. Under the effervescence of hospitality things could be said that in writing would read rather curiously when the glow had faded. The memorandum is of interest as showing the Prime Minister's lingering aspirations for "a long, stable friendship and cooperation with Russia," which in conjunction with the United States would keep the world engine on the rails.

Harriman raised with Stalin the question of Russia's participation in the war in the Far East. Stalin clarified his intentions, giving promise of a substantial contribution; the Red armies in the East would be raised from thirty to sixty divisions. He made it known that he expected recompense for his support, but he did not then name his price.

There was satisfaction in Washington when an account of these talks was received. No objection was raised to paying the price; it was sufficient that Stalin was proposing to join the fight on so considerable a scale.

Churchill's stay in Moscow was of undisturbed cordiality. It seemed that he had at length dissolved mistrust and reached an amicable understanding with Stalin. They talked with an ease and freedom never previously attained, taking their meals together and sitting over their drinks until the early hours. Stalin was impressed (as he testified in public speech) by the atmosphere of friendship.

Churchill left for home with hopes pitched high. He could persuade

* The Comintern, international organization of the Communist Party, was dissolved in 1943. In 1947 it was replaced by the Cominform, established with the avowed purpose of fighting the capitalist imperialism of Britain, France and the United States.

himself that some progress had been made over Poland. It might even be that the London Poles could eventually join in a government with the Lublin people on a percentage basis: "I do not think the composition of the government will prove an insuperable obstacle if all else is settled." [3]

In contact with the Russians in pleasant mood it was possible to take the impressions of the moment as realities that would endure, and to accept Stalin as a Russian counterpart of Roosevelt. But there was so much that perforce had to be forgotten in the actual day-to-day experience of Russian methods. Not long before the Moscow visit, the Prime Minister had been disturbed by the shattering incident of the agony of Warsaw.

As the Red armies in their advance to the west approached toward the Polish capital, the patriots within the city were given the signal to rise in revolt against the German oppressors. Their rising was conducted with gallantry and fortitude. It ended in massacre. Having touched off the rising, the Red armies permitted the Polish patriots to be overcome —they were patriots, not Communists—and Russia was well content that the Germans should rid the city of troublemakers for the future. The patriots were liquidated by the Germans, calling Heaven to witness the barbarity of their treatment.

The Prime Minister and the War Cabinet were horrified at this villainy. Representations were made to Stalin. He dissociated himself from the Warsaw "adventure," as he termed the uprising, which he attributed to a "group of criminals." Churchill appealed to the President to join in an emphatic protest. Roosevelt did not consider it "advantageous." Deepest anger prevailed among members of the British Government and the stopping of convoys to Russia was contemplated by way of protest. Nothing was possible to bring relief to the patriots of Warsaw. The incident had to be passed over, one of those "humbling submissions," as Churchill termed it, that must be accepted in time of war. But what faith could be reposed in Russian allies whose actions were governed by such cynical and calculating self-interest? It was a question that was forever arising. If the alliance was to endure till victory was won there was much to be overlooked and forgotten. Outraged as he had been in September, Churchill in October was able to persuade himself that "new links" were arising with Stalin. [4]

It was not long, however, before the Moscow mission was proved to have been fruitless over Poland. It had been Churchill's expectation that Mikolajczyk, after consulting his colleagues in London, would journey to Moscow with authority to negotiate a settlement of the future frontier. The difficulties of forming a Polish government with the Lublin

HATS

Wide World

There were many wartime conferences with Franklin D. Roosevelt

Marshal Tito of Yugoslavia visited England in 1953 (below left)
Wide World

After a luncheon party at the White House, June 26, 1954. Among those surrounding the Prime Minister and President are House Speaker Joseph Martin, Chief Justice Earl Warren, Senate Minority Leader Lyndon Johnson, and Senate Majority leader William Knowland

ere were smiling moments of
axation when the Big Three
t at Yalta (left)

Harry S. Truman and Churchill moved side by side from hot war into cold war (right)

A birthday gift from the people of Malta, 1955 (above) *Wide World*

A Dutch study that Churchill said gave him more character than he had (left) *Wide World*

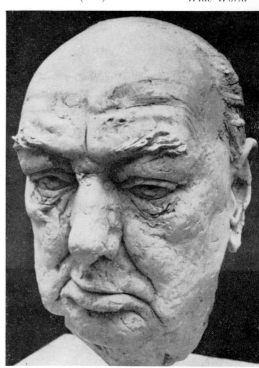

Head for a controversial nine-foot statue erected at Woodford, Churchill's last constituency (above) *Wide World*

A slightly larger-than-life likeness in London's ancient Guildhall (left) *Wide World*

Laying a cornerstone in London,
1956 (above)   *Wide World*

A medal from de Gaulle, 1958
(right)   *Wide World*

Wide World
A global cake on his eighty-fifth
birthday, 1959 (above)

Wide World
Victory Torch from Canada,
1941 (right)

His strong face more belligerent than ever, Churchill waited to speak, March 5, 1946, at Westminster College, Fulton, Mo. A few moments later he spoke the words "Iron Curtain" which rang through the college gym and, soon after, around the world

Wide World

Swedish Ambassador Gunnar Hagglof informs Churchill he has been awarded the 1953 Nobel Prize For Literature   *Wide World*

Campaigning in the rain, 1945, with the ever-present Mrs. Churchill holding an umbrella over his head and listening attentively *Wide World*

With Bernard Baruch and John Cashmore, President of the Borough of Brooklyn, Churchill visited 426 Henry Street in Brooklyn where his mother, Jennie Jerome, was born in January, 1850 *Wide World*

At 82, Churchill showed his sharp eye by winning a bottle of beer at a carnival-type game during a Conservative Party garden fete in his constituency at Woodford

NO MORE PICTURES, PLEASE!

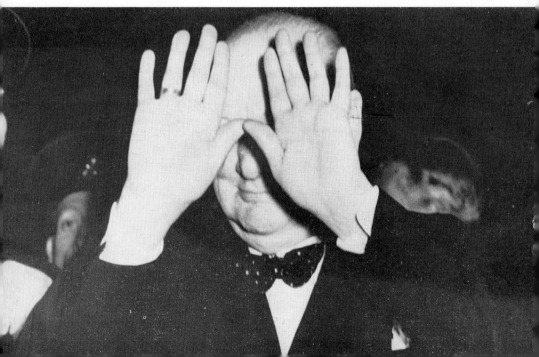

committee might be overcome were Mikolajczyk to be installed as head of a Polish government on Polish soil, recognized by the United Nations and assured of the friendship of Stalin. These hopes were disappointed. Mikolajczyk, after interminable discussions, failed to secure the assent of his colleagues in London. He resigned, a development regretted by Churchill, who regarded him and his friends as the "only light which burns for Poland in the immediate future." The prospects of a settlement vanished.

"One is reminded," commented Churchill, in his account to the House of Commons on October 27, "of the story of Sibylline Books for which, on every occasion, the price remained the same and the number of volumes decreased, until at last they had to be bought on the most unfavorable terms." As the Russians moved forward and the Germans were expelled from further tracts of Poland, the area administered by the Lublin committee would grow and its contacts with the Soviet Government would become more intimate and strong. "I do not know," lamented Churchill, "what misfortunes will attend such a development."

In the debate that followed there was criticism of the Prime Minister for making concessions to the Russians over the frontiers. Mr. Petherick, of Falmouth, protested against acceptance of the Soviet claim for territory as a means of obtaining military security and defense in depth for the Soviet Union. "We, whose armies are engaged in defense of the Low Countries," he argued, "might just as well say that we, who have experienced war at the gate of our country, will remain in occupation there after the war, because we require defense in depth for London!"

The Prime Minister was informed that his speech had been received without a cheer, "in a sort of awful, ugly, apprehensive, cold silence." Poland, it was asserted, was a test case for Europe; were the British to desert the Poles, Europe would desert the British, and that would be their ruin. As to the Lublin committee, that was "bogus," "a stalking-horse of Moscow," "child of the Ogpu and Russian bayonets."

From the other benches Churchill heard that Mikolajczyk and his associates were "apologetical hirelings," "political stooges," and reactionaries. The Polish Government in London was reactionary—"the spirit of Pilsudski broods over it." What title had the Poles to the lands the Russians claimed? As to territorial compensation for Poland in the west, there members saw dragons' teeth in the proposal, the seed of future wars.

That autumn the Prime Minister suffered some dejection at the slowing down of Allied progress when the weather broke. The armies were not keeping pace with his expectations. In the West they had to await the spring offensive. In Italy, where Alexander's forces had been weakened to provide divisions for France, bad weather was hampering movement and the armies were bogged down in the valley of the Po. In Burma, he complained, "we seem condemned to wallow at half-speed through the jungles." His dissatisfaction was increased by the realization that under the chain of command "it is not so easy as it used to be for me to get things done." [5]

Representations from France added to his disquiet. Montgomery was urging a change in the organization of command. Attributing the fading out of the Allied advance to the faulty strategy that had been pursued, Montgomery proposed that Eisenhower should be relieved of some of his burden of responsibility by the appointment of a Land Forces Commander. In North Africa, Alexander had exercised such operational control; it would be advantageous if he were similarly employed in France. There were moments when his suggestions, tersely explained, made Eisenhower "hot under the collar."

Churchill was informed of Montgomery's views. They were outlined by the C.I.G.S., and made their impression on a Prime Minister already persuaded that there was something wrong on the battlefront. Alan Brooke reinforced Montgomery's opinions, representing that the Allied armies had suffered nothing less than a strategic reverse. He urged that operational control should be "taken out of Eisenhower's hands," a more drastic proposition than Churchill was prepared to accept. Something, however, must be done, and the Prime Minister cabled off to Washington. The delays and frustrations, he submitted, made it essential for a full Staffs conference to be summoned. If the President could not attend then the American Chiefs of Staff might cross over and, in cooperation with Eisenhower, study the stormy scene close at hand and concert action for 1945.[6]

Roosevelt did not share Churchill's sense of disappointment. Having, as he recalled, once bicycled over most of the terrain, he had reason to conclude that the crossing of the Rhine would be no easy job. He dismissed the idea of a Staffs conference in Europe.

> My Chiefs of Staff are now devoting all their abilities and energies in directing their organizations toward carrying out the plans already made. . . . I do not feel my Chiefs should leave their posts at this time since no requirement exists for broad strategic decisions to guide our field commanders.

Assuredly Roosevelt was not in favor of staff talks, but was well satisfied with the course of operations. Complacency was shattered in December when the Germans attacked on the Western Front. Exploiting the faulty dispositions of the Allied armies, von Rundstedt struck in the Ardennes. The assault took Eisenhower by surprise and there were days of anxiety before General Omar Bradley and General Montgomery, assigned an extended command for the emergency, had countered the offensive. It was the last expiring assault of the German armies in the West.

There was much discussion that autumn of postwar possibilities. The Prime Minister began to show growing interest in the setting up of an organization for dealing with world affairs, to replace the defunct League of Nations. Suspected by his American friends of harboring imperialist designs, he was the least concerned of the Big Three about the realizing of ambitions in the postwar world. To his Foreign Secretary he sent a cautionary note against taking too much of a hand in the affairs of the Continent: "We must be careful not to involve ourselves in liabilities." There would be helpless nations, but Britain was not in a position to maintain armies to protect them.[7]

"The first thing," counseled Churchill, "is to set up the world organization on which all depends."

Beyond settling accounts with the Germans, the Prime Minister had no avowed war aims to pursue. He and the British people would have been well content for Europe, Germany apart, to have resumed after the war at the point where the clocks stopped in 1939.

Stalin made no disguise of his postwar aspirations. He was going to exact recompense for Russian sacrifices, including the extension of territory. His demands for frontier adjustments had been tabled even as the Red armies went into the fight. From the outset his purpose had been not merely to win the final battle of the war, but to achieve military success in the way calculated to achieve his political and territorial ambitions.

Roosevelt, sharing American liberal opinion, was not content for the war to end in the restoration of the Europe that once had been, with its monarchical and reactionary regimes. As to the Far East, Washington opinions were firmly set against the colonial powers, Britain and France. The President looked forward to applying sound democratic principles when the peace conference was held. Here he visualized an assembly such as drew up the peace in 1918, with himself playing Woodrow Wilson's part in the Big Three of a later generation. Knotty problems could be remitted to that future conference, particularly those concerning the Russians, for Roosevelt was not going to risk antagonizing "Uncle Joe" until the Japanese had been disposed of. To ensure Soviet assistance against Japan was the cardinal point in the President's policy.

Here United States idealists were placed on the horns of a dilemma. They had been disturbed since Teheran by reports of concessions made to the Soviets—making a deal with Stalin. Despite the Atlantic Charter it seemed he was to be suffered to retain the lesser states he had picked up—Lithuania, Latvia, and Estonia. And, further, was there not to be a carve-up of Poland on the pretext of Russian security? Was not Roosevelt—and Churchill, too, for that matter—leaning toward Stalin in a way outrageous to men sound in their democratic American principles? [8] Indignant Senators roused themselves to make formal protest only to discover the dilemma in which they were placed. If they proclaimed their principles they would antagonize the Soviets; they would disunite the war effort by attempting prematurely to determine the peace effort. Winning the war, they reluctantly concluded, must be placed before principles. Russia's premature withdrawal from the war might cost a million needless American casualties in the Far East.

Among the President's advisers there was at this date scarcely a ripple of mistrust over Russian intentions. His views were shared by Eisenhower, who considered there was a special bond between the United States and Russia, and that his fellow countrymen were "free from the stigma of colonial empire-building by force." Let the following top-level estimate suffice to indicate the opinion prevailing in Washington in 1944:

> Since Russia is the decisive factor in the war she must be given every assistance and every effort must be made to obtain her friendship. Since without question she will dominate Europe on the defeat of the Axis, it is even more essential to develop and maintain the most friendly relations with Russia.[9]

A new turn in affairs was given by events in Greece, and Winston Churchill's intervention to forestall the Communists. It was a development for which United States opinion was unprepared.

The Prime Minister's mind had been agitated for some months past over Soviet infiltration in eastern and central Europe, and the need for forestalling the Russians in certain regions. There were, for instance, the Hungarians. They would continue to fight the Russians, but were prepared to yield to British forces.[10] Churchill explored the military possibilities with Alan Brooke, but nothing could be contrived. Over Greece, swift and effective action was undertaken.

CHAPTER TEN

UNDER FIRE IN GREECE

DECEMBER, 1944–JANUARY, 1945

CHRISTMAS DAY of the year 1944—the sixth and last Christmas of the war—found Churchill on a bleak, snow-covered airfield outside Athens. The weather, according to those who had to endure it, was witheringly cold. He sat in conference in the plane in which he had recently arrived. The wind howled, rocking the aircraft in its gusts, and the sound of rifle-fire in the distance was occasionally broken by the heavier note of the guns.

Churchill, by then turned seventy, was engaged on the most hazardous mission of his premiership. On that inhospitable airfield there was physical danger, with Greek fighting Greek at no great distance, regardless of where their bullets might fall. There was the refreshment of adventure that he craved, in a form more personally perilous than had been denied to him on D-Day. Politically, also, he was exposing himself.

Already his intervention in the affairs of Greece had set a hornets' nest of critics about him on two continents. There had been strident manifestations of dissent from across the Atlantic and it seemed that a string or two must be lost in the lute of Anglo-American friendship. Convinced of his own rectitude Churchill held to his course, undeflected and undismayed.

In after times, when the ructions were past and events could be seen in perspective, it was clear beyond a peradventure that by his intervention he had preserved Greece from the Communists, and had found the way to save the country, newly liberated from the Germans, from the desolations of civil war. In the storms of his career, the Greek incident stood out for the fierceness of the denunciations that assailed him at the time and the conclusiveness of his vindication thereafter.

In preparation for the day of liberation in Greece, the British Government had taken steps to provide that the Greek people should be able to resume responsibility for the conduct of their own affairs. From King George of the Hellenes, Papandreou received a commission to form a government-in-exile. While Papandreou might have been acceptable to many of the Greeks, the King was unacceptable to any but the royalists, for he was held by the republicans to be personally responsible for the excesses and repressions of the prewar dictatorship under General Metaxas.

Throughout the war the British Government had had dealings with King George as the sovereign-in-exile. As affairs were viewed in Whitehall, that appeared to be the constitutional course, but in Greece it fostered the belief that the British were determined to impose an unwanted king upon an unwilling people.

Republican suspicions were intensified by the omission from the Papandreou Ministry, as first constituted, of representatives of the resistance movements of the left. The feuds between royalists and republicans in Greece had their counterpart among the forces of Free Greeks stationed in the Near East. Mutiny broke out in both Army and Navy, in which republican sympathies were strong. Papandreou invited leaders of E.A.M. (a Communist-inspired organization) to join the Ministry, but, though its basis was thus broadened, the ministerial façade scarcely concealed the political animosities within. With the departure of the Germans from Greece the façade collapsed.

On taking over in Athens when the Germans pulled out, the Papandreou Government ordered members of the various resistance movements to lay down their arms. The forces of E.L.A.S. (the military organization of the Communist-controlled E.A.M.) refused to comply. Left-wing Ministers resigned from the Government. Street fighting broke out in Athens, developing into civil war. This involved the British forces in Greece under General Scobie.

Churchill, some weeks previously, had issued a warning on the need for prompt action to forestall the Greek Communists. Having paid to Stalin the price for freedom of action in Greece, he had no hesitation about intervening in Greek affairs. British troops should be used to suppress lawlessness and to maintain the all-party Government of Papandreou. General Wilson, in Italy, was alerted that Scobie might be needing reinforcements.[1]

Reports reached the Prime Minister in London that the Athens police stations had been seized, their occupants murdered. It was late at night. The Cabinet was not available. Churchill took what he termed direct control of affairs. Sending to bed his solitary adviser, the Foreign Secretary, he remained on duty until the early hours. At three in the morning he cabled a vigorously phrased directive to General Scobie:

> You are responsible. . . . Do not hesitate to act as if you were in a conquered city where a local rebellion is in progress. . . . You may count on my support in all reasonable and sensible action. We have to hold and dominate Athens. It would be a great thing for you to succeed in this without bloodshed, but also with bloodshed if necessary.[2]

Churchill must have discharged the phrases with relish, and he confessed afterward that they were "somewhat strident in tone." A crisis in the early hours, giving him scope for the personal direction of affairs, was an occasion to fire his spirit.

The following day he pressed for reinforcements to be dispatched, at the same time sending a steadying message to Scobie: "Firmness and sobriety are what are needed now."

A crisis on the political front swiftly developed. There were criticisms of British action in *The Times* and *Manchester Guardian*. Left-wing opinion at Westminster identified itself with the cause of the left-wing Greeks. The employment of British forces was denounced. The Prime Minister was accused of seeking to install a government of Greek reactionaries and to suppress the republicans and progressives. Passages were quoted from a dispatch in *The Times* that the turn of events had made it appear "the British Government and the British Army were prepared to support M. Papandreou against his former partners in the coalition" and had "associated Britain with what is everywhere condemned as Fascist action."

The tale was taken up in the United States with further embroidery. Here, proclaimed American correspondents, was a flagrant instance of power politics; Britain's imperialist designs were at the root of it all. These views were re-echoed by critics at home. British left-wingers, who had taken a starkly realist line over the Polish question, were swept off their emotional balance by events in Greece. Members of E.L.A.S. could not more forcibly have maintained the inalienable right of Greek to cut the throat of Greek. British soldiers, who had looked upon the painful duty of intervention as the sole and timely means by which Athens was being spared the horrors of massacre, were pained to find themselves depicted as instruments for the oppression of Greek democrats.

A motion of censure on the Government was introduced, regretting that no assurance had been given that His Majesty's forces "will not be used to disarm the friends of democracy in Greece and in other parts of Europe, or to suppress those popular movements which have valorously assisted in the defeat of the enemy and upon whose success we must rely for future friendly cooperation in Europe."

The debate (December 8–9) was lively. Tempers were strained. The Prime Minister came down to the House spoiling for the fight.

Seymour Cocks, moving the censure, declared he would rather his right hand were burned off at the wrist, leaving a twisted and blackened stump, than that he should sign an order to the British Army to fire on the workers of Greece. Richard Acland, seconding, asked: "Are we to commit ourselves to a stark, slogging struggle, policing, arresting, confiscating and imprisoning and burning villages in order to stamp out a popular movement?"

The Prime Minister replied that he stood for democracy, but not for a swindle democracy. The last thing that resembled democracy was mob law, with bands of gangsters, armed with deadly weapons, forcing their way into great cities, endeavoring to introduce a totalitarian regime.

Here there were cries of dissent and interruption from the Socialist benches. "I am sorry," commented Churchill, "to be causing so much distress. I have plenty of time and if any outcries are wrung from members opposite, I can always take a little longer time over what I have to say."

Democracy was no harlot to be picked up in the street by a man with a machine gun. When countries were liberated, it did not follow that those who had received weapons from Britain should use them to engross power to themselves by violence, murder and bloodshed. Valorous elements might have done good service, but it was for the state and not for them to judge what should be their reward.

Tracing the course of events, Churchill said that for two years forces of E.L.A.S. had been planning the seizure of power. During the German occupation, E.L.A.S. had devoted far more attention to beating up and destroying right-wing Greeks than to attacking Germans. The British came to Greece, with American and Russian consent, at the invitation of the Greek Government of all parties, bearing such good gifts as liberty, order, food, and the assurance of an absolute right for the Greeks to determine their own future as soon as conditions of normal tranquillity were regained. . . .

However, events began to move. The carefully prepared forces of E.L.A.S. began to infiltrate into Athens and into the Piraeus. Other bodies began to move down from the northern hills towards the city. The six E.A.M. Ministers resigned from the Government at this timely moment. One gentleman, I believe, was a little slow, but, on being rung upon the telephone and told he would be killed if he did not come out, he made haste to follow the general practice. The intention of the friends of democracy, who now entered the city, was to overthrow by violence the constitutional Government of Greece and install themselves, without anything in the nature of an election, as the violent expression of the people's will.

I directed General Scobie, who has shown very great qualities of sobriety, poise, and at the same time of martial vigor, to assume complete control of Athens and the district. He was to use whatever force might be necessary to drive out and extirpate the E.L.A.S. bands by which the capital had by then become infested. If I am blamed for this action I will gladly accept my dismissal at the hands of the House. But, if I am not so dismissed, make no mistake about it, we shall persist in this policy of clearing Athens of all who are rebels against the authority of the constitutional Government of Greece, and of mutineers against the Supreme Commander in the Mediterranean, under whom all the guerrillas have undertaken to serve.

In the debate that followed the charges against the Prime Minister were amplified and extended. It was variously asserted that he was encouraging counter-revolution on the Continent as a matter of policy; that under the guise of disarming the guerrillas he was attempting to foist on the Greeks an unwanted and discredited monarch and the old unwanted and discredited politicians with the old totalitarian discipline.

When the division was taken the censure motion was defeated by 270 to 30. Churchill had the better of the division and the fighting honors of the debate. It was a limited satisfaction. The situation in Greece remained. Greek was killing Greek in civil war, and British forces were suffering casualties from the guerrillas. More damage was being inflicted on Athens, it was reported, than had been caused by the Germans throughout their occupation.

The Prime Minister was profoundly disturbed by reactions in Washington where Secretary of State Stettinius, recent successor to Cordell Hull, issued a condemnatory statement. He protested to Harry Hopkins; the statement reflected not merely on action in Greece but on British policy in Belgium.[3]

"I consider," Churchill submitted, "that we have a right to the President's support. . . . It grieves me much to see signs of our drifting apart at a time when unity becomes even more important."

In Washington opinion was cool and critical. It was considered that the British Government had messed up the Greek business pretty thoroughly. Roosevelt sent a message with soothing purpose. He professed

himself a loyal friend who was guided by the conviction that nothing
could shake the unity and association of the two countries. But, he explained, mounting adverse reaction of public opinion made it impossible
for the United States Government to stand along with Britain over
Greece.[4]

The sentiments might be unexceptional but, as Churchill was pained
to reflect, the letter was of no practical help. Meanwhile the position in
Athens was growing worse. The British forces were almost cut off. The
harbor of the Piraeus was not held, so that arms and supplies could
not be landed. Until reinforcements arrived order could not be restored.
General Alexander, leaving his headquarters in Italy to investigate on
the spot, recommended stern measures. The War Cabinet gave him a
free hand.[5]

The Cabinet, its Labour members included, was solidly behind the
Prime Minister. Ernest Bevin gained an overwhelming majority for the
Government when he addressed the conference of the Trades Union
Congress. Beyond these indications of support, the Prime Minister was
gratified to note that Stalin had observed the Moscow bargain. No word
of criticism had come from Moscow, nor of support for the Communists
in Greece.

Street fighting continued in Athens, and Alexander sent warning that
a political settlement must be reached. This was no easy matter. The
Papandreou Cabinet was discredited, the King was unpopular. A regency
under the Archbishop of Athens was favored by the Greeks, but their
King was opposed to it.

It was to resolve the deadlock that Churchill undertook his journey
to Athens. On Christmas Eve he was with his family at Chequers. From
his great friend in Washington a tree had arrived and the festivities
were in preparation.[6]

Throughout the day the possibility of a journey to Athens had been
canvassed. In the evening the decision was taken—he would go. The fireside scene was abandoned. Order was given for the plane to be prepared.
Anthony Eden was summoned from his home. Deaf to family reproaches,
Churchill bustled off.

At breakfast time he was at Naples. Before noon he was looking down
on the famous cities of Greece. The opening conference was held in his
plane on the airfield. Cold and fatigue gave Churchill a feverish appearance, to the anxiety of his attendants. Was he going to fall sick in that
bleak, inhospitable city of snow and bullets? Where was he to find refuge?
The Embassy, under siege, was scarcely suitable. The cruiser *Ajax* offered hospitality that was gratefully accepted. Christmas celebrations
were in progress when the Prime Minister and Foreign Secretary were

piped aboard. During the evening bombs from trench mortars began to fall near the warship. A move was made to a safer distance from the shore.

That night a new gunpowder plot was discovered. Had it succeeded, the Prime Minister, his Foreign Secretary, British generals, and Greek leaders would have been blown to the skies. In a sewer below an Athens hotel, guards found a ton of dynamite. It was placed in position with wire affixed for the detonator. Had it exploded the floor of the hotel would have gone up through the roof. The hotel was British HQ in Athens, and the seat of the Greek Government. Precautions were re-doubled. When Churchill went ashore in the morning he carried a revolver in his pocket.

"Where is your pistol?" he asked his private secretary, who, being unarmed, was chided for his neglect.

Armored cars escorted the British party as they drove through the Athens streets. They went into conference in a bare room, ill-lit and cold. The Archbishop Damaskinos was in the chair, a massive figure in a heavy cloak. In his youth he had been a champion wrestler and he still looked an athlete, all seven feet of him. Delegates in overcoats shivered as they waited in the conference hall for the arrival of the E.L.A.S. representatives, who, with safe conducts, had been conveyed to the meeting place by armored car.

The venerable Archbishop opened the proceedings and then Churchill spoke. If a settlement were not reached, he said, the British would discharge their part of the duty of rescuing Athens from anarchy. Apart from that there was no intention of interfering in Greek affairs. Whether Greece was to be a monarchy or a republic was a matter for Greeks alone. It was the British Government's hope that there might be established a broad-based government, possessed of sufficient armed power to preserve itself in Athens until a free general election could be held.

"All we want from the Greeks," declared Churchill, "is our ancient friendship. I exhort you to believe that I speak on behalf of my Government and that I speak the truth from my heart. My hope is that this conference will restore Greece once again to her former state and power among the Allies."

When the British Ministers withdrew, the Greeks, by the light of flickering hurricane lamps, and to the sound of intermittent and not very distant firing, began the discussion of their differences. It was the first time they had met since hostilities had broken out between them. Passions were inflamed. Four hours of discussion produced little more than expressions of recrimination. The conference was resumed the following day and, the heat of anger being exhausted, tentative steps were taken toward a settlement. Archbishop Damaskinos was able to report to the Prime Minister that on one point opinion was overwhelmingly clear—the establishment of a regency was the essential preliminary to the ending of Greece's troubles.

Churchill, with his party, left for home. He undertook to urge King George of the Hellenes to agree to the appointment of a regent. The conference was adjourned indefinitely. Suspicions between the rival parties were by no means allayed. The leftists regarded the order for the laying down of arms as the preliminary to a dictatorship of the right. The Government parties looked on the demands of E.L.A.S. as the means for bringing about a communist regime. Fighting still proceeded as General Scobie continued the process of clearing Athens and the Piraeus of insurgent forces.

Nevertheless the Prime Minister's mission brought peace to Greece. King George of the Hellenes was induced to issue a proclamation of his resolve not to return to Athens, unless summoned by a free expression of the national will, and appointing Archbishop Damaskinos as Regent. A new Government was formed under General Plastiras, a lifelong republican. On January 11 the final agreement was signed for the ending of the civil war.

When the House met in the new year, a second debate was devoted to events in Greece. The Prime Minister contributed to it one of the outstanding polemic speeches of his premiership. To most of his hearers he suceeded in bringing home the difficulties of the Greek political situation and the extreme bitterness and hatreds that were obstacles to the formation and functioning of an all-party government in Athens.

> At home it is hard to keep a coalition together, even between men who, although divided by party, have a supreme object and so much else in common. But imagine what the difficulties are in countries racked by civil war, past or impending, and where clusters of petty parties have each their own set of appetites, misdeeds, or revenges.
> If I had driven the wife of the Deputy Prime Minister out to die in the snow, if the Minister of Labor had kept the Foreign Secretary in exile for a great many years, if the Chancellor of the Exchequer had shot at and wounded the Secretary for War, if we who sit here together had back-bitten and double-crossed each other, while pretending to work together, and had all put our own group or party first and the country nowhere, and all set ideologies, slogans, and labels in front of comprehensions, comradeship, and duty, we should certainly, to put it at the mildest, have come to a general election much sooner than we shall. When men have wished very much to kill each other, and have feared very much that they will be killed quite soon, it is not possible, the next day, for them to work together as

friends. We must recognize the difference between our affairs and those which prevailed in Athens.

There was no case in his experience, he summed up, where a British Government had been so maligned and its motives so traduced in its own country by important organs of the press or among its own people:

> How can we wonder at, still less complain, of the attitude of hostile or indifferent newspapers in the United States of America, when we have in this country witnessed such a melancholy exhibition as that provided by some of our time-honored and most responsible journals and others to which such epithets would hardly apply?

Richard Acland moved a vote of censure on the Government and portrayed the Prime Minister as an atrocity-monger. In yet more extravagant language Aneurin Bevan described the Prime Minister's statement about forces marching on Athens to massacre the population as a "grotesque piece of Churchillian rubbish," and his speech as that of a "swashbuckler."

Only seven members could be found to support the censure motion on this second time of asking. The Government vote was 340.

To round off this record of the storm over Greece, it may be fitting to record the judgment on events passed by investigators of the left wing, who made the journey to Greece to find out for themselves where the truth lay. First there was the testimony of Gerald Barry, editor of the *News Chronicle,* who, when the controversy was at its height, himself left his editorial chair to make an inquiry on the spot. He did not agree with the Government for its handling of the long series of events that led up to the crisis, but as to the actual incidents of December he wrote:

> Given the situation with which the British authorities and Greek Government found themselves confronted on December 5, they acted in the only possible way. What is more, it deserves to be recorded that the British Army, under General Scobie's command, is performing a highly exacting task with imagination, discretion and brilliant efficiency. . . . The shootings and the taking of hostages are now admitted by responsible E.A.M.-ites themselves to have been unpardonable. They explain them but do not attempt to excuse them. . . . The majority of British soldiers like and respect the Greeks, but detest E.L.A.S. The exhumed corpses, the ill-treatment of hostages and some prisoners have soured their gall. There is no doubt about the reality of the corpses, nor about the means by which most of them met their death, nor about the ill-treatment of hostages.

From Liberal, I turn to Labour testimony. Under its secretary, Sir

Walter Citrine, a Trades Union Congress delegation went out to Greece. Members found the truth not easily to be ascertainable and, so far as the Greek labor movement was concerned, they were told that some of the blanks in the record were to be attributed to the fact that 114 trade-union officers had been killed by the Red fascists who, by force of arms, had taken possession of the trade-union offices when the Germans retreated from Athens.

As to atrocities, the delegation reported that horrible accounts were given to them of terrorism by a section of E.L.A.S. named O.P.L.A. The delegates themselves saw the bodies of 250 persons ("there were still many trenches to be opened"), practically all, if not all, of whom had been the victims of organized murder. Delegates were informed by the Regent that "as far as they could estimate, the number of persons murdered was at least 10,000." The treatment of hostages by E.L.A.S. was rigorous and cruel.

Finally, there was the information given to the delegation by members of the British forces and 500 troops of the Parachute Division: "The answers given by the soldiers confirmed beyond any doubt whatever that there was a deep sense of grievance against certain sections of the British press and particular Members of Parliament; that it was grotesque to describe what had taken place in Greece as that of reluctant troops on the side of reaction against a democratic people. . . . We were impressed with the universal opinion of these British troops and of many others whom we consulted that had they not been ordered into action there would have been wholesale massacre in Athens."

Summing up on this point, the T.U.C. delegates declared their opinion that "when the full history of this struggle has been written the people of our country will be proud of the courage, cheerfulness, restraint and steadfast behavior of our forces in Greece in circumstances of the greatest difficulty."

It took longer for the truth of the affair to become acceptable across the Atlantic. The revaluation of Soviet Russia after the fall of the Iron Curtain brought a realization of the service that had been rendered by preserving Greece among the free peoples, but that was later. In 1945 the lessons of Greece were not applied and the anti-British sentiment fostered across the Atlantic had its influence on American policy.

CHAPTER ELEVEN

SUMMIT AT YALTA

FEBRUARY, 1945

ON FEBRUARY 3, 1945, Winston Churchill arrived in the Crimea where for the ensuing week he was to engage in the Yalta conference, the last summit meeting in which President Roosevelt took part.

The secrets of Yalta have long since been revealed, the best documented and most debated of the war's conferences. It has been the fashion to saddle Yalta with the burden for the ills of the postwar world, but this is too great a measure of blame.

In what was done at Yalta, Winston Churchill's record is clear. He was, throughout the week's discussions, fiercely controversial. Stalin and Roosevelt had their reasons for avoiding disputes, for each was resolved to strike a bargain with the other. Churchill, with no such special interest to serve, labored in freedom's cause, championing the French "like a tiger," pleading the rights of the smaller nations and striving with unfaltering resolve on behalf of Poland. Any proposal affecting the interests of Britain placed him intensely and vigorously on the defensive, so that even the American observer could not forbear to applaud his devotion to the Empire, so complete and wholehearted.[1]

Once again a feat of imagination is required to recapture the atmosphere of the Yalta meeting, so different from the climate of opinion since the Iron Curtain descended. In 1945, while the war was yet to be won, British, Americans, and Russians were still fighting as allies, their relations not soured by suspicion and mistrust. In the West there was universal admiration for the spirit of the Red armies.

"My heart," declared Churchill, "goes out to Russia, bleeding from her wounds while beating down the tyrants."

As for the President, his trust was reposed in the Russians and his mistrust reserved for the British and their imperialism: "They would take land anywhere, even if it were only a rock or a sand bar." In contrast, he thought of the high-minded Russians, with their new outlook. "Winston," he said, "this is something you just are not able to see, that a country might not want to acquire land somewhere even if they can get it." Nevertheless, before the Yalta conference was done, the Russians, with the President's compliance, had arranged to pick up a territory or two in the Far East.[2]

The disturbing influences of the Greek incident had not died away when the arrangements for Yalta were made. Harry Hopkins, visiting London, reported the Prime Minister to be in a dangerous and explosive mood.[3]

With the Presidential election concluded and Roosevelt's fourth term inaugurated, the way was clear for a summit approach. It was becoming urgent for the Big Three to meet to settle the problems that lay just around the corner. Any day the Germans might quit the fight, and the Allies would have no plans made for what must follow—the treatment of Germany, the trial of war criminals, reparations, Poland, and all the myriad questions to arise when the guns ceased to fire.

There was the war in the Far East to provide for, of paramount importance for the Americans. There were tricky points arising from the setting up of the new world organization, the United Nations, that had been left over from the founding meetings at Dumbarton Oaks.

Yalta was not accepted as a meeting place before many cables marked "top secret" had passed between the three capitals. Scotland was Roosevelt's original suggestion. Stalin objected. Cyprus was named, and Athens, Rome, Alexandria, Istanbul, and Jerusalem. Stalin rejected them all—the reason given was that his health did not permit him to travel even to the warm shores of the Mediterranean. It may be, too, that he did not care to risk the complications that might arise at home in his absence. Whichever motive it was, he was firm in his determination not to leave Russian soil, and so Yalta it had to be, the resort in the Crimea that once had been the playground of the later czars and their court.[4]

I. PRELIMINARIES AT MALTA

On their way east, President and Prime Minister broke their journey at Malta for a preliminary meeting. This was by Churchill's insistence and he pleaded for a stay of two or three days. Roosevelt, had it been decently possible, would have avoided a meeting at all. With a bargain to fix with Moscow, he was more than ever concerned not to arouse any resentment of the touchy Russians, forever suspicious that the British and Americans might be uniting against them in a common front. He sought to excuse himself on the ground that his limited time did not permit a halt of two or three days at Malta.[5]

Churchill pressed for an opportunity for preliminary discussions on political questions. It was of the highest importance that the Staffs should get together before Yalta, a fateful conference, to be held "when the Allies are so divided, and the shadow of war lengthens out before us. . . . The end of this war may well prove more disappointing than was the last."

Roosevelt so far gave way as to agree to a meeting of the Staffs, but his Secretary of State, he insisted, could not arrange to be present, an effectual bar to discussion of political matters. So, once again, Churchill was deprived of the chance for concerting Anglo-American policy. He found, too, that even at Yalta the President was not prepared for protracted discussions, to which he would allot no more than five or six days. The Prime Minister made further protest. In that time it would scarcely be possible to complete plans for a new organization for the world. "Even the Almighty," he objected, "took seven days."

When Roosevelt stepped ashore at Malta, his appearance caused concern to those who had not seen him since the Quebec meeting four months earlier. His figure was frail. Despite his relaxation during the crossing, made aboard a cruiser, he was haggard and worn. In his family circle there had been anxiety over his condition, for it was not to be concealed that he was far from well, no longer the calm, imperturbable person his wife had known. But he was determined to make the journey to Yalta, for a meeting that he accepted as a challenge. He had enjoyed his first contact with Stalin at Teheran and was determined to complete an understanding with the Russians and to remove all grounds for mistrust.[6]

At Malta the Staffs went into joint session to settle differences over strategy. The old problem was presented once more in a new form. According to plan three divisions were due for withdrawal from the front in Italy to reinforce the armies on the Rhine.

Churchill, backed by the British Staffs, claimed that these divisions would be better employed from Italy to occupy a region in Austria. It was, he submitted, essential to move into Austria as the Germans were driven out; it was undesirable that more of western Europe than necessary should be occupied by the Russians. The President, being anxious to placate, not to offend, Stalin, backed his Staffs. The original arrangements were confirmed and the divisions were withdrawn to France.[7]

The last lap to Yalta was made by air, planes leaving at ten-minute intervals to fly the leaders and advisers to the landing ground in the Crimea, 1,400 miles away. The final ninety miles took six hours' traveling by car over winding mountain roads heavily guarded by Russian women troops armed with rifles.

Twice, in recent months, the tide of war had flown over the Crimea, reducing towns to shambles, and Churchill regretfully protested: "We could not have found a worse place for a meeting if we had spent ten years in search." By the time the conference met the Russians had carried out a transformation.

Thousands of soldiers were set to work to fill in bomb holes. Trains from Moscow brought furniture, bedding, and supplies. With seven hundred visitors to house, as well as the Russian delegation, accommodation fell far short. Generals had to share rooms with generals, and colonels were tightly packed. Admiral King, being assigned the Czarina's boudoir, was the butt of conference wits.[8]

For the leaders spacious provision was made. The President was accommodated in the Livadia Palace, where the Czar-of-all-the-Russias had once found summer relaxation, and Stalin in the palace of Prince Yusupov, assassin of the notorious Rasputin. Churchill was lodged in the Vorontsov Palace, once the home of a Russian Ambassador to England and since become a museum. The arrangements, it so happened, placed Prime Minister and President twelve miles apart, with Stalin between them at the halfway distance. Churchill was impressed by the efforts the Russians had made to render their visitors comfortable. Plumbing and road making had been carried out without regard to cost, and in hospitality Soviet prodigality was beyond belief.

II. CARVING UP GERMANY AND POLAND

Roosevelt, by Stalin's nomination, was the conference chairman. It was acceptable to him in the role he intended to play. He would be mediator while Stalin and Churchill fought out their differences, which they proceeded to do over seven days of strenuously conducted negotiations. The conference was no less exhausting on its social side, with banqueting on the grand scale, four hours at the table and forty toasts a night.[9]

The future of Germany was the first main problem to be faced. Here the Big Three were unanimous in principle. Twice in a generation the Germans had disturbed the world's peace. It must be placed beyond their power to repeat their crimes, and so the dismemberment of the Reich was unanimously accepted. There were differences over the method of the carve-up. Roosevelt favored division of Germany into five parts and Stalin supported him.

Churchill was inclined to division in two parts, Prussia and Austria-Bavaria, with international control of both the Ruhr and Westphalia. So involved, he said, were the issues that the details should be remitted to experts for report. So it was agreed, the Foreign Ministers being directed to produce a scheme for dismemberment.[10]

The military occupation of Germany was debated at length. It is to be noted that no differences arose over the zones allotted to the three powers. The plans had been worked out by the European Advisory Commission the previous September and were accepted without debate. There were divergences when the Prime Minister championed the right of France to join in as an occupying power.

Stalin objected, having no high opinion of the French: "I cannot forget that in this war France opened the gates to the enemy." He was prepared to concede the French a zone of occupation, provided it was allotted out of the area assigned to the British and Americans. He opposed the representation of France on the Allied Control Council to be set up in Germany.

Churchill claimed that British opinion would scarcely accept the position that the French should be excluded from joining in the discussion of French affairs when they came before the Council.

Stalin parried with the objection that the concession would lead to de Gaulle claiming admission to the Big Three. The Prime Minister doubted this—after all, the Big Three conference was a very exclusive club, with an entrance fee of at least five million troops. Britain wished to see the French grow in strength so that they might help to keep down the Germans. "They have had a long experience of occupying Germany. They do it very well and will not be lenient."

His insistence was strengthened by the President's intimation that United States troops were likely to be withdrawn from the Continent two years after the war was over.[11] Without French assistance Britain would not be able to contain the Germans in the west. "We must provide for France to stand guard on the left hand of Germany, otherwise Great Britain might again be confronted with the specter of Germany at the Channel ports. We have suffered badly from robot bombs and should the Germans ever get near the Channel ports we should suffer again. After the Americans have gone home we must think seriously of the future." *

As to what the Russians might proceed to do in the military vacuum of Germany, no word was forthcoming.

The President suggested that a zone be accorded to France without a seat on the Control Council. Anthony Eden objected; if they had a zone how was it to be controlled save through the Council?

Stalin: By the power through which they obtain the zone.

Churchill: We cannot agree to do it and the French would never submit to it.

On representations from his advisers, the President changed sides on this issue and Stalin was induced to accept France on the Control Council.

The sum to be extorted from the Germans as reparations brought the Prime Minister and Stalin into further conflict. With the experiences of the First World War as a guide, Churchill took a restrained view of the possibilities. Let them exact what they could, but let them take a sensible, realistic line.

The Russians were plainly greedy for reparations, which was understandable in view of the devastation that had been wrought on their cities and countryside. They proposed the confiscation of eighty per cent of Germany's industry. All possessions should be removed, factories, machinery, rolling stock, investments—everything removable should go. Money payments should be made by Germany for ten years, a sum of twenty billion dollars to be fixed, of which amount Russia should draw half.

Churchill questioned whether the figure was within the range of the practicable. With difficulty £1,000,000,000 was extracted after 1918 and that only because the United States supplied the Germans with a larger sum by way of loans. Never would they be able to get from a ruined Germany £250,000,000 a year for Russia alone.

"There also arises in my mind," he added, "the specter of a starving Germany. If our treatment is such as to leave eighty million people starving, are we to sit still and say: 'It serves you right?' Or will we be required to keep them alive, and who will pay for that? If you wish a horse to pull the wagon you should at least give it fodder."

---

* On this point Churchill had been forewarned. The previous November the President had informed him: "You know, of course, that after Germany's collapse I must bring American troops home as rapidly as transportation will permit." Churchill had protested that if the French had no postwar army then the British could not hold down western Germany. Without American cooperation and that of the French "all would disintegrate as rapidly as it did last time in 1918."

Stalin: But take care the horse does not turn round and kick you while you are not looking.

It was decided to remit reparations to the experts of a commission to be set up. In the days that followed the Prime Minister's doubts were proved to have been well founded; it was beyond the capacity of the Germans fully to pay for the damage they had done to others. As far as the complete dismantlement of the country could contribute, the Russians reimbursed themselves to the maximum.

Voting rights and the power of the veto in the proceedings of the United Nations were questions the Big Three debated at length. Trusteeships touched on matters affecting Britain's interests, with Hong Kong and rights in the Suez Canal cited in the discussions. Churchill made vehement protest against any interference with the concerns of the Commonwealth.

Never, he declared, would he consent to forty nations "thrusting fumbling fingers" into the British Empire. As long as he was Prime Minister there would be no yielding one scrap of Britain's heritage. How, he asked, would Stalin like to have the Crimea internationalized for use as a summer resort?

Stalin replied he would be glad to make a gift of the Crimea as a permanent meeting place for the three powers.

The trusteeship proposals were accepted on the explanation that the territories concerned were Japanese islands in the Pacific held under the old League of Nations mandates. The British Empire and its possessions were in no way involved.

All these were differences of a minor order by comparison with the dissensions over Poland. At seven out of the eight plenary sessions the Polish wrangle proceeded. Stalin was insistent that frontiers should be drawn and a government formed favorable to the Soviet.

The Prime Minister, with Anthony Eden's support, pleaded the Polish case. Britain would concede the Curzon Line * as the boundary in the east. But let there be a counter-concession by the Russians, according to the Poles their ancient city of Lvov and the adjacent oil fields. A magnanimous gesture here would win admiration for the Soviet.

Stalin made an impassioned reply. Lvov, he argued, had been assigned to Russia by Curzon. "Now some people urge that we should be less

* The Curzon Line was an eastern frontier demarcation that was proposed in 1919 during the Russo-Polish dispute. It came to bear the name of Lord Curzon, then Foreign Secretary, although he had little to do with it, Lloyd George being the author of the Curzon Line. It excluded from Poland territories in which the majority of the inhabitants were Ukrainians, White Russians and Lithuanians. It was not accepted by the Poles who, with French assistance, defeated the Russians and pushed their frontier many miles to the east.

Russian than was Curzon. You would drive me into shame. What will be said by the White Russians and Ukrainians? I could not return to Moscow with an open face. Rather let the Poles be given compensation in the west and advance their frontier into Germany as far as the Neisse River."

Churchill objected. It would be unwise to stuff the Polish goose so full of German food that he would die of indigestion. Besides, a frontier advanced to the Neisse would push out six million Germans.

Stalin thought the number would be much lower, for as the Red armies moved in the Germans ran away.

To avoid deadlock, the problem of Poland's western frontier was left over to the peace conference.

There remained the question: Who should govern the Poles? Stalin, on the ground of Russian security, demanded a friendly government, meaning the men of Lublin. Churchill insisted on the right of the Polish people to make unfettered choice in free elections.

"Britain," he said, "declared war on Germany so that Poland should be free and sovereign. Everyone knows what a terrible risk we took and how it nearly cost us our life as a nation and empire. Our interest in Poland is one of honor."

To this Stalin countered: "For the Russian people the question of Poland is not only one of honor but of security. Throughout history Poland has been the corridor through which the enemy has pressed into Russia. It is in Russia's interest that Poland should be strong enough to shut the door of the corridor. It is not only honor but life and death for the Soviet state."

When the method of elections in Poland was raised, the President urged that they must be free beyond question like Caesar's wife: "I did not know Caesar's wife but she was believed to have been pure." On which Stalin, smiling, commented: "It was said so about Caesar's wife but in fact she had certain sins."

Churchill suggested that representatives of the three great powers should supervise the voting in Poland. This roused Stalin to protest indignantly. Speaking at unusual length he declared that this would be offensive to the Polish people and their honor—"you cannot do that, the Poles are an independent people."

Stalin proclaiming the independent nature of the Poles was Yalta's grimmest jest.

Roosevelt provided the basis for a settlement of this aspect of the Polish question. A declaration was drawn up for the reorganizing of the Lublin committee on a "broad democratic basis," and its recognition as the Provisional Polish Government. Free and unfettered elections by secret ballot were pledged as soon as they could be held. To this declaration Stalin gave his assent. The betrayal of the Poles that followed arose not from the Yalta declaration but from the Russian violation of its terms.

III. PAYING STALIN'S PRICE

For a week of meetings Churchill played the debater's part, delivering impromptu speeches on a variety of subjects, their terms unrehearsed and unpremeditated. In this cut and thrust of verbal exchanges, he was perfectly at home; it was as if he were dealing with opponents in the committee stage of a bill before the House of Commons, except that there was translating to be done.

The President took on another role. He made his contributions to the discussion, but his place as chairman gave him the chance to follow his preference and act as mediator between the other two. For Roosevelt had not traveled to Yalta to debate and oppose the Russians, but to strike a bargain with them. He was one who had the reputation of being at his best in fixing things, and he had set out for Yalta determined to fix things with Stalin over the war in the Far East. For Russian participation against the Japanese he was prepared to pay a price. This he had ascertained beforehand through Ambassador Harriman, who had had several discussions with the Russian representative. Military opinion in Washington was pessimistic about the outlook in the Far East, holding that the Japanese in a fanatical fight to the death might cause a million casualties. In a memorandum the view was expressed that the most important factor the United States had to consider in relation to Russia was the prosecution of the war in the Far East. Throughout the Yalta meeting the military leaders put on the pressure to ensure the President would secure Russian cooperation against the Japanese at the earliest date.[12]

From the manner in which this matter was so assiduously pursued Stalin could have drawn his own conclusions. He was left in no doubt that the Americans would be inclined to side with him and that there would be the minimum of resistance to the realizing of his ambitions. Czarist Russia had lost the war against the Japanese in 1904. Stalin was resolved to regain the possessions that had then been forfeited.

The Prime Minister took no part in the talks in which Roosevelt and Stalin made their deal. The bargain struck was of the kind governments have concluded down the ages. Stalin pledged himself to join in the war against the Japanese within a short time after victory in Europe. In return he required the restoration to Russia of South Sakhalin and the islands adjacent, lost by the Russians in the war of 1904; the internationalization of the port of Dairen and the lease of Port Arthur as a naval base; and the acquisition of the Kurile Islands.

Roosevelt conceded the terms. He agreed to secure the concurrence of Chiang Kai-shek, whose acquiescence was essential to the carrying out of the bargain. Stalin further required that the terms should be put in writing with the specific pledge: "The heads of the three Great Powers have agreed that these claims of the Soviet Union shall be unquestionably fulfilled after Japan has been defeated."

Roosevelt had no objection, but what of the Prime Minister? He was no party to the striking of the bargain and Anthony Eden advised him not to put his signature to the agreement. Churchill, however, considered that he could not afford to abstain; if he failed to sign he might be excluded from future discussions over the Far East. Accordingly he complied.[13]

The pact was labeled top secret, and only the President's closest advisers knew of its existence. It was preserved in the Presidential safe at the White House, its contents undisclosed even to State Department officials. Some months after Roosevelt's death a startled Secretary of State learned of the existence of this agreement from a Russian newspaper report. With other agreements reached with foreign governments, the document was then transferred, by President Truman's orders, to the custody of the State Department. Before Stalin could fulfill his undertakings, Soviet participation in the Far East war had been rendered superfluous by the atom bombs that caused the Japanese to capitulate, but fulfillment of the pact was still required by the Russians —it contained no escape clause.[14]

Yalta had its lighter side, or at least its social side, for there was nothing light in the nature of the Russian hospitality. There were arduous hours in the banqueting halls, but there the differences of the conference were put aside and all was genial harmony. The Big Three did honor to each other in their toasts. Stalin raised his glass to Churchill as the bravest government figure in the world, the leader who fought against Germany when the rest of Europe was falling flat on its face before Hitler. There were few examples in history where the courage of one man had been so important to the world's history.

Churchill responded. Stalin was the mighty leader of a people who had broken the back of the Nazis. Both men paid their tribute to the President.

In their off-duty moments the three indulged their humor in jests. Churchill jokingly complained that he was always being "beaten up" as a Tory reactionary. Yet, of the three, he alone could at any time be thrown from office by the votes of the people.

Stalin dryly remarked that he preferred the one-party system; evidently Mr. Churchill feared the result of the next election.

"I glory in the danger," replied Churchill. "I am proud of the people's right to change their government whenever they wish."

There was a moment's anxiety when Stalin was told the secret of his nickname. They called him, Roosevelt disclosed, "Uncle Joe." The Marshal was annoyed. He moved to leave the table at which they were lunching. One of the Americans hastily intervened.

"You don't mind talking about Uncle Sam," he said. "Why should 'Uncle Joe' be so bad?"

With this explanation of the jest "Uncle Joe" was satisfied. The conference ended in all-round cordiality. Before he left for home, Churchill visited a famous battlefield of the past—Balaklava. There, a hundred years before, a British army had fought the Russians. He stood on the spot (February 13) and marked where the Light Brigade had ridden in their charge into the mouths of the Russian guns:

> Into the gates of death,
> Into the jaws of hell
> Rode the six hundred.

Greece was visited on the homeward journey, the plane being flown over the island of Skyros by way of tribute to Rupert Brooke, lying in his "corner of a foreign field." In Athens the Prime Minister was greeted by cheering crowds whom he addressed in Constitution Square.

"Let the future of Greece," he declared, "shine brightly in the eyes of every man and woman. Greece for all! Greece forever!"

He was voted the Freedom of Athens and a street was renamed in his honor.

At Alexandria he caught up with Roosevelt, who was engaged in the curious incident of the three Kings of Orient. These sovereigns, King Farouk, Haile Selassie of Abyssinia, and Ibn Saud of Saudi Arabia, were received by the President aboard the cruiser *Quincy*. Farouk was entertained at lunch, a social occasion. The "Lion of Judah" was invited to discuss territories on the borders of Abyssinia held by the Italians. From the sagacious ruler of Saudi Arabia the President received a discourse on Arab objections to the increase of Jewish immigration into Palestine.[15]

The fact that F.D.R. had arranged to meet these potentates from what was a sphere of British interest was slightly disconcerting, although the President had made no secret of his intentions. Churchill approached Harry Hopkins to discover the purpose of the meetings, leaving the feeling on that impressionable mind that he suspected an attempt to undermine British influence. Harry Hopkins surmised that Roosevelt had no serious purpose beyond satisfying his personal curiosity about the colorful potentates who held lands of the romantic East in fee.

The *Quincy* having steamed through the Suez Canal to Alexandria, Churchill came aboard to lunch (February 15). It was a family gathering. The President's daughter, Anna Boettiger, was present and the Prime Minister's two children, Randolph and Sarah. It was a lighthearted occasion, both leaders still upheld by the buoyancy of spirit in which they had left Yalta. They bade each other affectionate farewell on parting. Churchill thought his friend to be frail, with no more than a slender contact with life. It was their final meeting.[16]

Churchill remained in the East to have interviews in his turn with Ibn Saud, the "Lion of Judah," and Farouk, and with the President of Syria. Churchill showed his ready wit over a minor social emergency.

Exchange of gifts marks the meeting of rulers in the East and he had made the necessary provisions for the reception of Ibn Saud. The case of choice perfumes he had chosen was, however, completely outclassed by the King's munificence—jeweled swords, robes, perfumes, and gems. Having proffered his small offering, Churchill with astute improvisation made the explanation that it was no more than a token for the occasion; the British Government's gift would follow, the finest automobile in the world. He arranged for its dispatch on his return, the purchase price being provided by the sale of the jewels Ibn Saud had himself presented.

IV. YALTA BALANCE SHEET

Commendation was general for Prime Minister and President on their return home. On both sides of the Atlantic there was praise for the statesmen who had contributed, so it was said of them, to a landmark in human history and the dawn of a new era. Exaltation was soon to fade, but it was agreeable for the returning Argonauts, as Churchill termed them, Argonaut being Yalta's code name.

Emphatic endorsement of the decisions announced was given by the House of Commons. Over Poland, Tory doubts persisted, but the Prime Minister had no difficulty in persuading Members of Parliament that a sound course was being followed. All depended, of course, on the sincerity of Stalin and the Russians in carrying out the undertakings to which they had subscribed. Churchill declared his faith in their honesty of purpose:

I feel that their word is their bond. I know of no government which stands to its obligations, even in its own despite, more solidly than the Russian Government. I decline absolutely to embark upon a discussion about Russian good faith. It is quite evident that these matters touch the whole future of the world. Somber indeed would be the fortunes of mankind if some awful situation arose between the Western democracies and the Soviet Union, if the future world organization were rent asunder and a new cataclysm of inconceivable violence destroyed all that is left of the treasures and liberties of mankind.

For three days the debate proceeded, the Polish settlement being the subject to which criticism was principally addressed. The Tory irreconcilables divided the House on this issue, but mustered only twenty-five votes against the Government. The motion of approval of the Crimea decisions was carried by 413 to nil. There were some thirty abstentions, among them a Conservative Junior Minister, H. G. Strauss, who, finding it impossible to approve the treatment of the Polish people, resigned his post in the Government.

To his French friends, Churchill recommended the Yalta decisions in a manner to soothe injured national pride. Exclusion from Yalta had caused a hangover of resentment in Paris. Roosevelt had invited de Gaulle to meet him at Algiers, but the General tartly replied that pressure of affairs necessitated his presence in Paris, "particularly on the morrow of the Three Power conference at which France is not represented." So Churchill sent an invitation to Paris for the Foreign Minister, Georges Bidault, to come to London. From the Prime Minister and Anthony Eden, Bidault received an account in detail of the matters dealt with at Yalta. It was another contribution to the promotion of Anglo-French friendship, reinforced by the fact that it was to the Prime Minister that the French owed the allocation of a zone of Germany and a seat on the Control Council.

In Washington, Roosevelt commended Yalta to the Congress in an address that for the first time in his fourteen-year Presidency he delivered seated in his wheel-chair. He hailed the decisions on the new world organization as marking the end of the old system of power politics—of unilateral action, exclusive alliances, spheres of influence, balances of power, and all the other expedients the nations had for centuries tried, without avail, for the preservation of the world's peace. How pathetically extravagant the language seems today!

It was not long before criticisms followed, pitched only a little less extravagantly. Yalta was saddled with the blame for most of the troubles that were to follow the dropping of the Iron Curtain. Prime Minister and President were held to have betrayed the Poles. Roosevelt was charged with appeasing the Russians and buying Stalin's support at the expense of pledges he had given to Chiang Kai-shek.

The President's case has been ably presented in reply. My concern is with the Prime Minister. Churchill dissociated himself from the American deal with Stalin. That was the President's concern and he declined responsibility for anything beyond his signature. As to Poland, Churchill made answer: What would have happened had they quarreled with the Russians while the Germans had two or three hundred divisions still engaged on the fighting fronts?

For him two matters were paramount—to preserve the full alliance, including Russia, to win the war; to preserve the alliance with the Americans to ensure the peace. By standing out at Yalta with unyielding obstinacy he might have wrecked the alliance, antagonized the Russians, and ruined the future of cooperation with the Americans. He could not, neither alone nor in concert with Roosevelt, have saved the Poles. It would have required force, not negotiation, to have preserved their frontiers and independence. As Molotov said over the case of Hungary —the Soviets had no need to conclude an armistice with that country; they were master of the place and could do as they liked. They were masters equally of Poland.[17]

With Roosevelt's full backing, Churchill's championship of the Poles could have been pressed to the utmost limit, and some concessions might have been wrung out of Stalin, but that support was not accorded. The American policy was for conciliation, not opposition. Churchill did not share the President's faith in the good-neighbor policy, and the facile optimism that the wild Russian would be won by kindness. Neville Chamberlain had nourished a similar delusion about Hitler.

But, for all his knowledge of the Soviet past, Churchill was prepared to give Stalin the benefit of the doubt and to trust to his good intentions. It was difficult for him to do other than believe in the essential probity of those in high station with whom he did business. Great men in great places did not, in his conception, fall below the standards of greatness.

A lesser man could have acted otherwise. When Hitler attacked in the east in 1941, a lesser man, regarding the Russians with coolness and calculation, would have treated them with suspicion and reserve. Churchill, in his large-minded fashion, welcomed the Soviets as allies. When he negotiated with them at Teheran and Yalta he was not re-endowed with the qualities of coolness, calculation, suspicion, and reserve. So it was that he accepted Stalin's assurances.

The negotiators were not completely unmindful of the risks they were taking. As Admiral Leahy, his Chief of Staff, said to the President over the terms on Poland: "Mr. President, this is so elastic that the Russians can stretch it all the way from Yalta to Washington without ever technically breaking it." [18]

"I know, Bill, I know it," replied F.D.R., "but it's the best I can do for the Poles for the time."

There has been no solemn undertaking yet that an ingenious mind cannot twist to his own purposes. Every negotiator must credit the other side with good faith; otherwise, negotiation is a superfluous formality. Yalta was a failure because the Russians did not keep faith. There were no penalty clauses for nonfulfillment in the Yalta agreements. International diplomacy is not so conducted at the summit.

Not all eastern Europe could have been preserved from Russian domination and for that no blame is to be credited to Prime Minister, President, or Yalta. It arose from the military fact that the Red armies defeated and drove out the Germans. Lamentable results followed for the Poles and other liberated peoples. But, deplore the consequences as you may, you should not confound the causes. The Russians sustained the war in Europe before ever British and Americans opened the Second Front. Having done some, shall we say, of the fighting they expected some results for themselves. The liberated areas of France, Italy, Greece, Holland, Belgium, Norway, Denmark, and the West of Germany were dominated on liberation by the Western powers. The Russians dominated the rest. The West kept out communism, which they loathed. The Russians kept out capitalism, which they detested. To the Russian mind it was a logical result.

Militarily it was inevitable—at least in central Europe. During the remaining weeks of the war, Winston Churchill strove with insistent purpose to concert action with the United States in an endeavor to circumscribe the area of Soviet penetration.

BOOK FOUR

ALLIES IN VICTORY

CHAPTER ONE

HIATUS UNDER ROOSEVELT

MARCH–APRIL, 1945

THAT spring the tide of Allied success flowed unbroken upon the battlefields, but nevertheless the spirit of cordiality among the Allies began to fade. The Prime Minister, looking out upon the world from his windows in Downing Street, viewed the future with apprehension. Did he recall the warning that his old friend, Lloyd George, had expressed when the fighting in Europe was about to begin? [1]

"If," pronounced Lloyd George, "you simply crush Germany, what about Russia afterward? She may become the next enemy."

Now in the fullness of time the prophecy was being fulfilled. The Russians, it seemed, had emerged as Europe's menace for the future.

Lloyd George himself passed on as his forecast was seen to be coming true. He had suffered a brief decline in his powers before his tempestuous career was ended. He was laid to rest in the Wales of his ancestors in a copse overlooking the River Dwyfor.

With fitting tribute in the House of Commons, Churchill marked the passing of his oldest friend in political life, recalling how in former times they had worked together for great causes in peace as well as in war.

"I was his lieutenant in those bygone days and shared in a minor way in his work. Lloyd George was the greatest Welshman his unconquerable race has produced since the age of the Tudors. At his zenith, as a man of action, resource, and creative energy, he was without a rival."

Old friends drop out, leaving a gap in our lives no newly made friendship can fill. New friends do come and they in their turn are borne away. In Lloyd George, Churchill mourned the man with whom he had collaborated in the First World War. Death was shortly to rob him of the friend of the Second World War with whom he worked in the closest association, affording advantages beyond computation to the Allied cause.

President Roosevelt had been a sick man at Yalta, but the extent to which his powers were failing was concealed by his own fortitude and by the support of his devoted entourage. When they parted, the Prime Minister was conscious of his frailty. The tide of his life was beginning to run out, but how progressive was the deterioration in his condition was not to be judged in Downing Street.

Roosevelt returned to the White House exhausted by the burden of his labors. The strain of Yalta sapped his last resources of energy. There were times when he lay almost comatose, unable to answer simple questions, but between these crests of exhaustion he rallied, his spirit and determination enabling him to carry on.[2]

It was a tragic circumstance for the Allies of the West that at this time, when there was need for clear thinking and resolute action, the President of the United States should have been passing into a decline. Over a succession of incidents with the Russians the Prime Minister addressed cables urging upon the President the necessity for intervention. By then the task of replying was almost beyond the sick man of the White House, and his advisers had to undertake the responsibility.

Afterward, when all was done, and these things had passed with their consequences into history, Churchill wrote in his memoirs deploring the hiatus that had occurred in Washington during Roosevelt's decline and the novitiate of his successor, Harry S. Truman. It was the final impediment to the Prime Minister's endeavors to bring about a showdown with the Russians and the adoption of a concerted Anglo-American policy to meet their designs in Europe.

I. POLAND'S FATE

After Yalta, Poland provided the first test of Soviet sincerity. Churchill grew concerned to note that the Russians were making no attempt to carry out their promises. Poles from London were to have been given a place with the men of Lublin in the Provisional Government; they were not so invited. Free elections had been pledged "within a month"; no arrangements were made to hold them. Observers from the West were to have been sent to Poland; Molotov made difficulties about their reception.

The Russians, Churchill concluded, were going about the systematic business of setting up a communist regime, and had no wish for outsiders to observe their repressions and tyrannies. As if to give point to their intentions, the Russians took action in Rumania. With troops and tanks in the Bucharest streets they forced upon King Michael a Soviet-dominated administration.

These events removed all doubts from Churchill's mind. Yalta, it seemed, had been no more than a smoke screen of professions and he considered the time had come for a determined stand to be made against the Russians. Over Rumania his hands were tied, for under the percentages agreement with Stalin that country had been ranked as a Soviet sphere. Stalin, who had not intervened in Greece, would scarcely accept remonstrances about Rumania. But over Poland the case was clear beyond dispute. In conjunction with the Americans, pressure must be brought to bear on Stalin so that he would be forced to honor the Yalta agreements.[3]

Whether the Russians would at that stage have deferred to firm and concerted pressure from Britain and the United States it is not possible to say. Certainly, nothing less would have been effective, and the Russians were acting as if they could reckon on American compliance—as if, since Yalta, they had the President in their pocket.

Roosevelt declined Churchill's invitation to join in a joint protest to Stalin. "I feel certain," came the reply from the White House, "that the text you propose might produce a reaction quite contrary to your intent." It was better that they should hold their hands and delay personal intervention with "Uncle Joe" until all other means had failed.[4] With this Churchill could not agree. Time was playing into the hands of the Russians. While ambassadors exchanged their views and Soviet dialectics were exhaustively pursued, the Bolshevization of Poland was proceeding. In a cable of stark phrases, he asked for something more forceful to be done:

> Poland has lost her frontiers. Is she now to lose her freedom?
> It will have to be fought out in Parliament and in public here.
> I do not wish to reveal a divergence between the British and American Governments.
> It would be necessary for me to reveal we are in the presence of a great failure and an utter breakdown of what we settled at Yalta.
> The moment Molotov sees that he has beaten us away from the whole process of consultations among the Poles to form a new government, he will know we will put up with anything.[5]

This drew from Washington a reply that was stilted in its phrasing and uncharacteristic in its spirit. Not in this distant manner had the

"Former Naval Person" been accustomed to conduct his correspondence with Roosevelt. The clauses running from "a" to "e" were enfolded in a blanket of departmentalese. Churchill concluded that, despite the customary signature, it was by another hand. The President, he deduced, must be a very sick man, no longer possessed of the strength to dictate his own official letters. Was it beyond his strength to cope with a purely personal message? Churchill decided to be very personal indeed, using terms in his next cable that must bring a personal reply if it was still possible for one to be made. So, starting off with an apology for the boring nature of his recent telegrams, he proceeded:

> Our friendship is the rock on which I build for the future of the world so long as I am one of the builders. I always think of the tremendous days when you devised Lend-Lease. . . .[6]

Rambling on, he touched on his wife's coming visit to Russia, and ended, "The advantage of this telegram is that it has nothing to do with shop." It drew a response acknowledging the "very pleasing message," but nothing more. Churchill drew his own conclusions about Roosevelt's condition.

The days brought no improvement over Poland. Plainly the Communists were consolidating their position, so once again Churchill cabled to Washington urging the strongest of representations to Stalin.

> If we fail altogether to get a satisfactory solution on Poland and are in fact defrauded by Russia, both Eden and I are pledged to report the fact openly to the House of Commons. There I advised critics of the Yalta settlement to trust Stalin. If I have to make a statement of the facts to the House the whole world will draw the deduction that such advice was wrong; all the more so that our failure in Poland will result in a set-up there on the new Rumanian model. . . .
>
> Surely we must not be maneuvered into becoming parties to imposing on Poland—and on how much more of eastern Europe—the Russian version of democracy. . . .[7]

The President (or was it his entourage on his behalf?) allowed himself to be persuaded that the time had come for a direct approach to Stalin. The terms of the mild American remonstrance were far from what Churchill would have chosen, but he agreed that it was a "grave and weighty document," and backed it up with his own more forcible expressions. No one, he urged upon Stalin, had pleaded the cause of Russia with more fervor and conviction, and it was as a sincere friend of Russia that he made his personal appeal for a good understanding.[8]

Stalin replied, blaming the British and American ambassadors for what he termed the blind alley that had been reached over the Polish dispute. It was an answer closely argued in the Russian manner, cordial enough in tone, conveying the prospect of possible advances by negotiation. As to the dispatch of observers to Poland, he reiterated his old objection: "The Poles would regard this as an insult to their dignity," bearing in mind the fact, moreover, that the attitude of the British Government to the Provisional Polish Government "is regarded as unfriendly by the latter." [9]

In the matter of argument, there is no besting Russians trained in Marxian dialectics. Churchill, with faint hopes, set about the difficult task of inducing the London Poles to accept the Yalta terms on frontiers. This was a condition on which Stalin insisted were any of the London group to be included in the Lublin Government.

II. OVER THE RHINE

From these controversies it was a relief to savor the refreshment of adventure among the fighting troops. Churchill crossed to France on March 23, to be present with Montgomery at his headquarters as Operation "Plunder" was to be launched—the crossing of the Rhine. As Eisenhower reflected, Churchill always found it possible to be near the scene of action when any important attack was to begin.[10]

Churchill was given an exposition of the plans for the assault by eighty thousand men on a river front of twenty miles, on the edge of the Ruhr. All went to bed before ten o'clock so as to be up early to witness the drop of two airborne divisions.

From a vantage point, in the light that follows dawn, Churchill was able to follow the great fly-in. He judged from what he could observe that the operation was a success. A tour of HQ along the front confirmed his impression. By nightfall the four assaulting divisions, two British, two American, had established bridgeheads that in some sectors were nearly two miles deep.

The day following, he lunched with Eisenhower, who escorted the party to a strongpoint below which the Rhine flowed in broad expanse. Churchill voiced the common expectation as he said with elation, "My dear General, the German is whipped. We've got him; he is all through."

Eisenhower could not but agree. Shortly afterward he was called away, which was fortunate for the visitor, for he would otherwise have forbidden the escapade that followed. Having gazed his full at the country beyond the river, Churchill suggested: "Why don't we go across and look at the other side?"

Montgomery, to his surprise, assented. A launch took them across the Rhine, and they walked the German shore for half an hour unmolested. For Churchill there was a particular savor of satisfaction in that promenade. It was symbolic of Germany's defeat. The long trail had borne him and Montgomery from Dunkirk to El Alamein, from Africa to the Rhine. The task had been accomplished. Only the formalities of capitulation remained, for Allied troops were now far within the Reich. How long was it since British troops had fought on German soil? Montgomery put the question, and Churchill gave the answer. It was in 1813, when the Rocket Brigade participated in the Battle of Leipzig.[11]

The promenade concluded, they recrossed the Rhine and drove along the western bank to a bridge still within range of enemy guns. They had not long been watching before a salvo of shells came plunging into the water, sending up a cascade of spray no more than a hundred yards away. It was judged to be time for a discreet withdrawal.

That evening, from headquarters, Churchill sent a message of congratulation to the soldiers of the 21st Army Group. A further entry was made in Montgomery's autograph book to mark the occasion:

> The Rhine and all its fortresses lie behind the 21st Group of Armies. Once again they have been the hinge on which massive gates revolved. A beaten army, not long ago masters of Europe, retreats before its pursuers.

Churchill returned home with encouraging news from the American armies to the south. Progress was astonishing in its rapidity. The Western Front was collapsing. Germany's fate was sealed.

III. DOES BERLIN MATTER?

The Prime Minister's gratification at the advance beyond the Rhine was tempered by Eisenhower's announcement of his strategic intentions. He was proposing to drive east and south to join hands with the Russians, or to attain the general line of the Elbe—"It will not involve us in the crossing of the Elbe." Berlin, as a glance at the map will show, lies many miles to the east of the Elbe and was not, therefore, within the ambit of the Supreme Commander's ambitions. This was highly disturbing.[12]

Montgomery, at his headquarters, was also perturbed to receive similar information. Montgomery had placed Berlin, the political center, as a primary objective, one it would be advantageous to reach ahead of the Russians. In the previous September Eisenhower had agreed with this view. "Clearly," he had said, "Berlin is the main prize." But by March his opinion had changed and he informed Montgomery: ". . . You will note that in none of this do I mention Berlin. That place has become, so far as I am concerned, nothing but a geographical location and I have never been interested in these. My purpose is to destroy the enemy's forces and his power to resist." [13]

There spoke the plain soldier, a man directing military forces for a military objective. He was one who believed that military plans should be devised with the single aim of speeding victory in the battlefield. Montgomery threw up his hands; it was useless to pursue the matter further. The Americans could not understand that it was of little avail to win the war strategically and to lose it politically. "War," pronounced Montgomery, "is a political instrument; once it is clear you are going to win, political considerations must influence its further course." [14]

It was an expression of Churchill's own convictions. He had no doubt that, while the German flag waved over the city, Berlin continued to be the most decisive point in Germany. His concern mounted when he learned that Eisenhower had been in direct communication with Stalin, whom he had informed of his plans to thrust southward in Germany, to strike at the redoubt in Bavaria in which Hitler was supposed to be planning his final resistance. Eisenhower and the American Staffs gave credit to these reports concerning the last stand of the Hitlerites; the British Chiefs of Staff did not.[15]

Stalin was entirely in agreement with Eisenhower's purpose; it conformed with the intentions of the Soviet Command. "Berlin," agreed Stalin, "has lost its former strategic importance. The Soviet High Command plans to allot secondary forces in the direction of Berlin." [16]

Thus the man of political wiles to the Supreme Commander—politically innocent. It is almost superfluous to add that, in fact, the Soviet High Command displayed emphatic and persistent interest in Berlin until the city had fallen to the Red armies.

Eisenhower's contact with Stalin touched off a major rumpus that was conducted on two planes. There was the question whether he had acted within his rights or whether, as the British Chiefs of Staff contended, he had transcended his authority in communicating directly with Moscow. He had taken his decision and informed Stalin of his plans without reference to Tedder, his deputy, and without informing the British or American Staff Chiefs. Naturally, as Churchill wrote, the British were concerned over a procedure that left the fortunes of a

British Army, which, though only a third the size of the Americans', still amounted to over a million men, "to be settled without the slightest reference to any British authority." *

The point seems well taken. Churchill argued it out with Eisenhower and the American Chiefs of Staff, who backed their general, the Supreme Commander. Eisenhower continued to be blandly innocent, surprised that his procedure had been called in question, and naïvely puzzled by the political aspects. So far as he was concerned, communicating with Stalin was a "purely military move." The wrangle over the point of procedure has long since dwindled in interest. The question of the strategy remained, and still remains. Was it soundly conceived?

The Prime Minister expressed his dissent in a letter to the President that is conspicuous in his correspondence.[17] He was never accustomed to write as one who would "hint a fault and hesitate dislike." For the most part his wartime letters were short, his directives curt. Even his communications with the President were to the point. On this occasion he wrote with a restraint that is plain to note. His purpose was to express his profound sense of disagreement with Eisenhower on one particular point, and he sought to do so without causing offense to his American friends, to Eisenhower himself, or to F.D.R. He wrapped up his criticism in phrases testifying to his utter satisfaction with the Supreme Commander in every other respect. Having dealt with the matter of procedure, he wrote of the importance of Berlin in the eyes of the Germans, and of how the capital animated the resistance of all Germans under arms. Another aspect of the matter was proper to be considered.

> The Russian armies will no doubt overrun all Austria and enter Vienna. If they also take Berlin, will not their impression that they have been the overwhelming contributor to our common victory be unduly imprinted on their minds, and may not this lead them into a mood which will raise grave and formidable difficulties in the future? I therefore consider that from a political standpoint we should march as far east into Germany as possible and that should Berlin be in our grasp we should certainly take it. This also appears sound on military grounds.

Or, as he phrased it in a more vigorous message direct to Eisenhower: "I deem it highly important that we should shake hands with the Russians as far to the east as possible." [18]

There was no yielding in Washington to these representations. The President, by then, had grown so weak that the task of replying was en-

* Eisenhower's account of the incident written in his memoirs after a lapse of some years reflects his state of mind at the time, uninfluenced by the political knowledge that came later.

trusted to General Marshall. With his colleagues Marshall rejected the idea of pressing on to Berlin; the psychological and political advantages that might result should not be allowed to override the military essential —the destruction of the German armies.

So Churchill was able to achieve nothing. There could be no persuading the President to another point of view, for such matters were beyond Roosevelt's physical ability. What he, in the maturity of his strength, would have decided it is impossible now to determine. What is established is that one of the great issues of the war and the peace had been raised. It called for the penetration and direction of a vigorous mind. It fell for decision to an enfeebled President, dependent upon advisers who had their minds principally directed to affairs outside Europe. Accordingly a change in policy was beyond the range of possibilities in Washington. No political guidance or directive was furnished for the Supreme Commander in Europe.

Whether, at that date, the Russians could have been anticipated in Berlin is a matter of conjecture. It was a circumstance influencing Eisenhower's judgment that when he stood on the Rhine, in March, he was three hundred miles from Berlin, whereas the Russians, on the Oder, were no more than thirty miles distant. It was Montgomery's view that it was then too late, or almost too late. But not all the Allied forces were so far removed from Berlin, for United States troops, under General Simpson, reached the Elbe near Magdeburg on April 11 and crossed the river the following day. Zhukov was not then over the Oder. The Americans, had they been willing to accept the challenge, could have pushed on to Berlin.[19]

The Prime Minister was disappointed in his hopes. Later, in his memoirs, he drew a picture of himself at this time glooming amidst the cheers of approaching victory, sitting at a table adorned with congratulations "with an aching heart and a mind oppressed with foreboding." It was his final discomfiture that in his apprehensions he was powerless to rouse his great friend in Washington to share a sense of alarm or to secure his support.[20]

IV. STALIN'S INSULTS

While the Prime Minister was being constrained to soften his remonstrances to the Russians, Stalin, under no similar compulsion, was expressing himself with particular offensiveness. The Red armies, faced with sustained German resistance to the last, were slow in their advances by comparison with their Western Allies. The men of the Kremlin were surprised. They had so consistently belittled the war effort of British and Americans—major victories on the Western Front were no more than back-page news in the Soviet press—that they fell victims to their own propaganda. They could scarcely credit that Anglo-American armies were carrying all before them by virtue of their military strength or skill.

Soviet suspicions so born gave rise to complaints directed by Molotov to Downing Street. There had been unofficial peace approaches on the Italian Front. The Russians demanded to be admitted to the negotiations. It was explained to them there was nothing to be represented at; there were no negotiations, only a preliminary examination into credentials. These explanations were summarily rejected by Molotov, who asserted that for two weeks negotiations had been proceeding behind the backs of the Russians. He protested at what he termed "incomprehensible behavior." [21]

Churchill disdained to reply to these discreditable charges.

Molotov also made protest to Washington, through Ambassador Harriman, who reported his impression that since Yalta the Soviet leaders believed they could force their will on the United States on any issue. "Molotov's arrogant language," he cabled, "brings out into the open a domineering attitude toward the United States which hitherto we have only suspected." [22]

Harriman assured Molotov there had been no negotiations. Molotov rejected the denial. A cable from the White House was dispatched to Stalin in conciliatory terms, suggesting that the Russian misapprehensions arose from a misunderstanding; a categorical denial was given that surrender negotiations had taken place. Stalin brushed this aside with the assertion:

> The German Commander on the Western Front, Marshal Kesselring, has agreed to open the front and permit the Anglo-American troops to advance to the east, and the Anglo-Americans have promised in return to make it easy for the German peace terms. . . . As a result the Germans on the Western Front have ceased the war against Britain and the United States. . . . [23]

This was more than even Washington was prepared to tolerate. A stiff retort was sent, ending with the phrase: "I cannot avoid a bitter feeling of resentment toward your informers, whoever they are, for such vile misrepresentations of my actions and those of my trusted subordinates." [24]

Churchill sent his own message to Moscow, backing the American protest. To preserve good relations, he explained, he had previously considered it best to make no reply to the "most wounding and insulting charges." Stalin did not withdraw, but he rephrased his accusation in a form slightly less offensive.[25]

"About as much as we shall get out of them and certainly as near as they can get to an apology," was Churchill's comment.

The President insisted that this was no more than a minor incident in their relations with Stalin. He cabled his views to London on April 12, in the last communication he was to make to the Prime Minister.

"I would minimize the general Soviet problem as much as possible because these problems in one form or another seem to arise every day and most of them straighten out. . . . We must be firm, however."

The message was dispatched in the morning. By the evening Roosevelt was dead. Before the news of his passing had reached the Prime Minister in Downing Street, Harry S. Truman had taken the oath and assumed the responsibilities of chief executive and commander in chief of the United States.

V. ROOSEVELT'S PASSING

It was early on the morning of April 13 that Winston Churchill was told of Franklin Roosevelt's death. The news was not unexpected; nevertheless it was with the sense of receiving a physical blow that he learned of the loss of his cherished friend. At his suggestion the House of Commons adjourned its sitting immediately, a step without precedent as an act of sympathy and respect on the death of the head of a foreign state.

Winston Churchill had to mourn the breaking of an association without precedent for its closeness between the chief executives of two states. For five years the two men had corresponded in the frankest fashion on every aspect of affairs. The messages they exchanged numbered over 1,700. Nine times during the war they had met in person—off the coast of Newfoundland, at Washington (on three occasions), at Quebec (twice), at Casablanca, Teheran, and Yalta. Churchill calculated that they spent 120 days in close personal contact.

No one on that side of the Atlantic could have experienced a more grievous sense of personal loss. But President Roosevelt had won universal admiration among the British people and there were many that morning, who, on reading the black headlines in the newspapers, felt a sharp quiver of distress at the removal from the scene of a man who had given to the British people a sense of sustaining strength to uphold them in troublous days.

The Prime Minister's first intention was to leave immediately by air for Washington to pay his personal respects by attending the funeral service. He was pressed by his colleagues not to leave the country at so critical a time, and canceled the journey, for which a plane had been ordered to stand by. He was to regret that he missed the opportunity for such an early meeting with Harry Truman. He realized how totally unprepared, under the workings of the American Constitution, the new President must be for the responsibilities suddenly placed upon him. An immediate exchange of views between them would have been of the utmost value.[26]

In the House on April 17, he paid tribute to the statesman whose passing was a bitter loss to humanity. The President's physical affliction, Churchill said, had lain heavily upon him and it was a marvel that he bore up against it through the years of storm and tumult. Not one man in ten million would have tried, not one in a generation would have succeeded, not only in entering the sphere of political life, but in becoming an indisputable master of the scene.

Once again testimony was paid to the splendid contribution the President had made to the British war effort by devising the extraordinary measure of assistance called Lend-Lease:

> This [commented Churchill] will stand forth as the most unselfish and unsordid act of any country in all history. . . .
> When death came suddenly upon him, he had finished his mail. That portion of his day's work was done. He died, as the saying goes, in harness, and we may well say in battle harness, like his soldiers, sailors and airmen who, side by side with ours, are carrying on their task to the end all over the world.
> What an enviable death his was. He had brought his country through the worst of its troubles and through the heaviest of its toils. Victory had cast its sure and steady beam upon him. . . . For us it remains only to say that in Franklin Roosevelt there died the greatest American friend we have ever known and the greatest champion of freedom who has ever brought help and comfort from the New World to the Old.

The President's passing left a question mark at the termination of his administration. Would he, unaffected by the malady that struck him down, have continued, in the face of Russian provocations, to pursue his good-neighbor policy? To the very end he had shown a large tolerance for the Soviets, their rebuffs and their maneuvers. It may be that this sprang from a sick man's acquiescence and that in his normal strength he would have responded to the challenges from the Kremlin.

There is the contrary opinion that Roosevelt would have persisted in good will and in so doing would have won Stalin's trust and secured his continuing cooperation to the avoidance of the Cold War. Stalin, it is represented, had only to be sufficiently placated. That was Neville Chamberlain's method with Hitler, and there were those in Britain who clung to it until Munich had shattered the illusions of the credulous. Where was the ground for deeming the Russian to have been less unscrupulous or less treacherous than the German dictator? Only in the shades of refinement do there seem to have been distinctions in the perfidy of these gangsters who had, by merit, been raised to their bad eminence like Satan before them. Both had forsworn themselves, tricked and liquidated accomplices, engaged in orgies of murder, mass purges, and nights of knives. Negotiation they employed to deceive their opponents, pledges they uttered as false coins are used by counterfeiters to dupe those simple enough to accept them. Hitler at least had no creed for export. It was Stalin who believed in world revolution with the ultimate aim of replacing capitalism with communism—"mankind's only way out, for it alone can abolish the contradictions of the capitalist system."

Would Roosevelt have been content to persist in treading the path Neville Chamberlain had taken? It is difficult to credit. Certainly Winston Churchill harbored no illusions about Stalinism. The limit, in his view, had been reached in yielding to placate Soviet imperialism. He saw no reason for being pushed around everywhere, "especially by people we have helped." The perils of the future he now braced himself to face in conjunction with Harry Truman, the unknown and untested occupant of the White House.

CHAPTER TWO

HIATUS TO VE-DAY

APRIL–MAY, 1945

A s the days of the war ran out the Communist specter, in the Prime
Minister's vision, loomed over Europe, casting ever-deepening shadows. The people, growing expectant, awaited VE-Day with jubilation
scarcely restrained. Churchill was torn between the conflicting emotions
of elation and apprehension.

At the time we must suppose elation to have been uppermost. How
could it have been otherwise? Over a period of forty years in public life
he had devoted himself, in two world wars, to encompassing the defeat
of Germany, the Kaiser's Germany and Hitler's Germany. Under his
leadership the people had emerged from the catastrophe of 1940 to
achieve the victory of 1945. The Teuton power broken, Germany was
moving toward calamity and chaos. Thankfulness and elation must have
been his, or he would have been less than human.

Nevertheless, looking back afterward, he presented himself in his war
memoirs as one who in those final days was obsessed with anxieties that
dulled his satisfaction. Surely there was cause enough for black care to
be riding at his shoulder. In the First World War the Russians had
gone down, vanquished by the Germans, stricken by the Bolsheviks, so
that they were reduced to the level of the feeblest of Europe's powers.
From the Second World War the Soviet Union was about to emerge as
the dominating force in the Old World.

As Churchill's thoughts ranged over the future, he foresaw vast areas of Europe becoming Sovietized and police-governed. In mid-Europe the disappearance of Germany must leave a gap, a military vacuum. Nothing would remain to check the advance of the victorious Red armies. Already terrible things had been happening as they had driven across Germany to the Elbe.

He brooded over the future consequences. The fate of eastern Europe under the plans that had been agreed upon was melancholy indeed. The tide of Russian domination must sweep forward as the Red armies took up their position within the occupation lines that had been marked out and accepted by the Big Three. All the great capitals of Middle Europe would pass to the Soviets—Berlin, Vienna, Budapest, Belgrade, Bucharest, Sofia. It would be a catastrophe for which Europe's history could furnish no parallel. Poland would be engulfed, other states would be Sovietized, Russian occupation of a vast zone of Germany would indefinitely continue.[1]

He set down the grim probabilities (May 4) in a memorandum for Anthony Eden, gone across the Atlantic on business of the United Nations. His conclusion was that there must be an immediate showdown with Stalin. If matters in dispute were not settled with the Russians before the United States armies withdrew from Europe, and the Western World had folded up its war machines, then "there are no prospects of a satisfactory solution and very little chance of preventing a third world war."

The future was foretold with inspired prescience. As the course of events was charted so it befell, with the calamity of that third war narrowly averted. But what purpose can wisdom serve without the power to control events? Churchill, as he himself had lamented, was no longer in that position. Action must be concerted with the United States and that meant with the new President. With time running out could he induce Truman to follow the course Roosevelt had declined?

By April 18, less than a week after Roosevelt's death, Churchill was raising with Truman the question of Eisenhower's strategy. Would it not be advantageous that the Anglo-American drive into the center of Germany should be continued into territory allotted to Russian occupation? The advance, he urged, should not be stopped until the Soviets had given an undertaking to share with the rest of Germany (largely industrial) the food supplies of eastern Germany (largely agricultural).[2]

To this Truman replied that how troops in the field were to be employed was a military question and must be left to the determination of the military commander.

Truman was fettered to the policy of the past. The men around him, General Marshall, Admiral Leahy, and Secretary Stimson, were convinced of the need to humor the Soviet. It was a serious matter to risk a breach while there was fighting in the East still to be done. Reaching the White House by way of the Vice-Presidency, Truman was lacking in the authority of a man newly elected by the people. It was not to be expected that at the opening of his Presidency he would renege on Roosevelt.[3]

The Prime Minister did not submit to the discouragement of his first failure. He next urged that action should be taken in Czechoslovakia to forestall the Russians. If the Allied armies, he cabled to Truman (April 30), were to liberate Prague and as much as possible of the western districts of the country, it would have profound results in the future. If, on the other hand, the Western Allies were to play no significant part in the liberation, then Czechoslovakia might well go the way of Yugoslavia.[4]

On this point the State Department showed itself to be sympathetic toward Churchill's views. By that time, doubtless, the recurrent warnings of Ambassador Harriman from Moscow were having effect. The Ambassador had sounded the alarm over Soviet designs in eastern Europe and their intention to undermine the influence of the Western Allies: "The Soviet program is the establishment of totalitarianism and the ending of personal liberty and democracy as we know it."[5] These strong words were not to be ignored. The State Department endorsed the Prime Minister's proposal.

Truman took Eisenhower's opinion, passing on the State Department's recommendation. Eisenhower, at that stage, was more concerned with coordinating his movements with the Red armies than forestalling them. True to his soldier's creed he replied that he would not "attempt any move which I deem militarily unwise."[6]

Truman remitted the Supreme Commander's statement to Downing Street with the brief endorsement: "This meets with my approval." For Churchill the reply seemed decisive against the possibility of reversing Allied policy. Nevertheless he appealed directly to Eisenhower. "I am hoping," he cabled, "that your plan does not inhibit you to advance to Prague if you have the troops and do not meet the Russians earlier." The appeal met with no response.

These affairs were side issues by comparison with the major matter of the carrying out of arrangements for the Allied occupation of Germany. When the guns had ceased to fire the Russians would expect that, under the agreed plan, the various armies would advance up to or retire behind the appointed lines of demarcation.

Churchill had reached the opinion that there should be no immediate and automatic compliance with the occupation plan. He did not contemplate breaking faith with the Russians and throwing the scheme overboard. What had been agreed should be carried out, but, he urged, it should be done with discretion, and advantage should first be taken of the circumstances as a means of inducing the Soviets to fulfill engagements they had so far declined to honor.[7]

As Churchill recognized, a bargaining counter of weight had been placed in the hands of the West. When the zone scheme had been drawn up it had not been foreseen that the Red armies would have been greatly outdistanced in their advance into central Germany. In fact the Anglo-Americans had penetrated to the east far beyond the zones allotted to them. It would be necessary for them to withdraw to permit the Russians to take over their allotted territories.

First on the President, and then on the Chiefs of Staff, the Prime Minister urged that, when the surrender came, the Allied armies should not straightway be hustled back. Truman was not prepared to depart from the arrangements Roosevelt had concluded either in Germany or in Austria. Churchill demurred. An enormous territory would be handed over to the Russians. There were still details to be settled over Berlin and arrangements for Austria's occupation had yet to be made.

Austria had been omitted from the original occupation plan. Later a provisional scheme was drawn up but the Russians had delayed their acceptance of its terms. When they took Vienna they went about the business of setting up a provisional government to their own liking.

The Prime Minister recommended a joint protest to Stalin. Unless a firm stand were taken it would be difficult to exercise any influence over the future of Austria. Here Truman was sympathetic. Cables were sent to Stalin demanding the admission of Allied missions to Vienna. Nothing came of them. Austria was passing behind the Iron Curtain.[8]

On the South German Front and in the Balkans nothing was done to forestall the Soviets. To the north matters were differently contrived. Berlin had been lost, but there remained Denmark, a country that carried control of the Baltic.[9] The Prime Minister urged Montgomery forward and faster, anxious to move into Schleswig-Holstein before the Russians. Montgomery, fully conscious of the political implications, was irritated by the proddings. When Eisenhower added his urgings, Montgomery riposted that the tempo of his advance would have been quicker had not the U.S. 9th Army been removed from his command.

Churchill watched with anxiety as the thrusting columns, by-passing pockets of enemy resistance, drove on. Great was his relief when the report came to hand that the armored spearheads had reached the Baltic at Wismar and Lübeck on May 2. The Danish peninsula was sealed off.

Montgomery had just won the race. By six hours the Danes had been saved from Soviet occupation. By air a force was sent in to hold Copenhagen, where Russian parachutists had already been dropped. Fast-moving columns occupied the country. The Danes rejoiced at their freedom and at their escape from Soviet liberators.

By then the fighting in Europe was done. The German armies disintegrated. Capitulation followed capitulation. A million Italians surrendered to Field Marshal Alexander. Mussolini died in ignominy, strung up on a meathook beside Clara Petacci. Italy had been the Cinderella of the Allied fronts, Alexander having suffered successive depletions of his forces. It was of particular satisfaction to Churchill that the first capitulation should have been on the Mediterranean Front. It was the vindication of his and British strategy, which had tied down fifty-five German divisions in the Italian peninsula. Victory here had sprung from the handful of tanks, urgently needed for Britain's home defense, that by his insistence were sent out to Africa back in the dark days of 1940.

In Berlin, Hitler on his funeral pyre made his exit with Eva Braun, bride of a few days. The twilight of disaster was falling on the Germans. The end came at Lüneburg, on the blasted heath, where Montgomery received the emissaries of capitulation with his historic queries: "Who are these men? What do they want?" [10]

Congratulations were exchanged all around. Through Mrs. Churchill, then visiting Moscow, Churchill sent Stalin a warm message of heartfelt greetings on splendid victories. Stalin was no less cordial in his reply. Both expressed their confidence in the continued cooperation between their two peoples. President Truman testified to his appreciation of Britain's contribution to final victory. The Prime Minister responded with an expression of his sense of debt to Eisenhower.

> Let me tell you what Gen. Eisenhower has meant to us. In him we have a man who set unity of the Allied armies above all nationalistic thoughts. In his headquarters unity and strategy were the only reigning spirits. . . . At no time has the principle of alliance between noble races been carried and maintained at so high a pitch.[11]

It was the Prime Minister's voice that fittingly gave the signal for the celebrations of VE-Day, the eighth day of the month of May in the year 1945. After five and a half years of fighting the guns had ceased to fire in Europe, the last bomb had been dropped, and the last rocket had fallen. It was five years almost to the day since Winston Churchill had become Prime Minister. The voice that in the month of May, 1940, had given the historic summons to labor with blood, tears, and sweat, now announced the fulfillment of the appointed task and the destruction of the soul-destroying tyranny of the Nazis.

It was at three o'clock in the afternoon that he came to the microphone to make the announcement for which the country had been waiting. His voice had been heard throughout the course of the war, radiating strength when times were bad, never faltering even in the days when Britain had stood alone. On VE-Day that voice did not always ring so true. He had steeled himself against disaster, but the time of rejoicing found out his weak points and there were moments when the voice was heard to quaver with emotion. The listening world caught his phrases:

> The cease-fire began yesterday to be sounded all along the front.
> The German war is therefore at an end.
> The evil-doers are now prostrate before us.
> We may allow ourselves a brief period of rejoicing but Japan remains unsubdued.
> Advance Britannia! Long live the cause of freedom! God Save the King!

In 1918 the armistice had come upon the nation almost unawares. In 1945 it was otherwise. The people had made ready to greet it. As the Prime Minister drove across to the House of Commons there was a press of crowds in Whitehall. He passed down a cheering avenue. As he entered the House of Commons, members rose to him. A deep-throated cheer rumbled out on all sides. Members waved papers in salute. He was deeply moved.

He read out the formal announcement. Then, putting off his glasses and laying aside his notes, he offered his humble thanks to members who had sustained him and his Ministers in the long struggle. Only a few sentences were needed, but his voice quavered as he spoke. He was barely able to complete what he had to say.

He paused for a moment to recover himself and master his emotion. Members waited in silence. He resumed to move a resolution in the very words that had been used at the close of the war against the Kaiser's Germany twenty-seven years before:

> *That this House do now attend at the Church of St. Margaret, Westminster, to give humble and reverent thanks to Almighty God for our deliverance from the threat of German domination.*

Mr. Speaker led the way to the church that stands in the shadow of Westminster Abbey. Churchill followed with Arthur Greenwood at his side. Ministers of the Crown came after them and the faithful Commons. The gathering crowds cheered as the procession wound its way across the street, through the churchyard, and into the ancient church.

London gave itself up to rejoicing that May evening. Twice Churchill appeared before the multitudes thronging Whitehall, delighting in the delight with which they greeted him. Members of the Government were on either side of him as he stood on the balcony of the Ministry of Health, made gay with flags.

"God bless you all," he said, "this is your victory. In all our long history we have never seen a greater day than this."

Then a voice was heard: "For he's a jolly good fellow." The crowd took it up. The burly figure of Ernest Bevin was seen beating time as they sang. Then they raised three tremendous cheers for victory.

Later, after dark, the floodlighting was turned on. In the glare of the lights Churchill was again seen on the balcony. He conducted the crowds as they sang "Land of Hope and Glory," ringing out the words to Elgar's melody: "God, who made thee mighty, make thee mightier yet."

He spoke briefly of what had been accomplished. In this ancient land, he said, the British were the first to draw the sword against Germany.

"After a while we were left alone for a year. Were we downhearted?"

The crowd gave him its answer in a mighty, deep-throated roar.

So passed the night of victory day. It gave him moments of exquisite satisfaction. He, with the people, was savoring the rewards of all their effort. He could look back on a job magnificently done. But, as his eyes turned from the cheering London crowds before him, he was filled with forebodings about the future. There was Japan to conquer in the East. And, nearer home, were the Russians.

Victory brought extended responsibilities. The fruits of victory must not be lost. Britain had begun the war to make the world safe from the "Narzees." Now they were gone and the new shadow of the Soviets loomed over ancient lands. How would Europe benefit from the defeat of Hitlerites if the totalitarian police-government of Russia were to dominate the Continent?

CHAPTER THREE

LETTING IN THE RUSSIANS

MAY–JUNE, 1945

WITH victory won, the Prime Minister discovered that the unity which had made it possible began quickly to fail. At home the politicians were eager to return to the delights of the party game. The famous coalition was dissolved. Tories and Socialists gave themselves up to the political spree of a general election, with results that I leave for the succeeding chapter.

Abroad, his apprehensions concerning the Russians were intensified by differences with the Americans. As far as his preoccupations with affairs at home permitted, the Prime Minister's concern in the weeks between VE-Day and the final conference of the war at Potsdam was the future of the Anglo-American alliance. In this his hopes and fears for the future were centered. In peace, no less than in war, unity in effort between the English-speaking peoples of Britain and America was for him a paramount necessity. "If we are divided," he had once laid it down, "all will fail. If we are together, nothing is impossible." [1]

Never were relations so uneasy. There were times when Churchill was sorely tried, but he did not waver in his determination at all costs to carry the wartime association into the days of peace. The two countries, with their common faith in democracy, should strive together, with policy concerted, to preserve the free world against Soviet domination. It was a vision of what in the future was to be realized. In the early summer of 1945 he was thinking ahead of opinion in Washington.

The Americans had not yet come to a realization of the true nature of Soviet communism and the world designs of the Kremlin. President Truman drew counsel from those who looked on international affairs through the Roosevelt spectacles. The military staffs clung to the notion that Stalin must not be offended till the Japanese were beaten. In the State Department it was held that the good will of Russia was essential for the structure of world peace. There was a general determination not to be induced into a line-up against the Russians.

With such advisers around him, Truman was not disposed to hurry forward the summit conference with Stalin for which Churchill was pressing. He did not wish to commit himself too soon or too far. The future was uncertain, the line to follow not easy to find and, besides, there was the unknown factor of the atom bomb. Word had reached him that the scientists had made such progress that the first A-bomb was nearly ready for testing.[2] Was a world-shaking weapon to be added to the United States armory? Very probably it was. It gave him the comfortable assurance that he would be able to negotiate with Stalin from a position of unchallengeable superiority. He saw no reason to be perturbed by the Russians and their machinations.

In Downing Street other and quite different reckonings prevailed. The Prime Minister, two thousand miles closer to the Continent and its uncertainties, was acutely conscious of the advance of communism. In his eyes the "Soviet menace had already replaced the Nazi foe." [3] When the forces of the West had melted away, and when the American troops had been withdrawn from the Continent, what then was to stand between the remaining democracies of Europe and the Red armies? Time was on Stalin's side, and so Churchill pressed for a meeting of the Big Three and a showdown with the Soviets.

Meanwhile, he ordered such action as was within his competence to check the melting away of Allied strength.[4] He issued directives that all reductions of Bomber Command and of the Metropolitan Air Force should be stopped. The number of squadrons was not to be reduced without orders from the War Cabinet. He gave instructions for a "steady on" in Army demobilization. German aircraft in serviceable condition were to be preserved. Being informed that the Germans were destroying their aircraft and equipment, he asked Eisenhower that this should be stopped: "We may have great need of these things some day." Montgomery received a standstill order regarding the destruction of German weapons and equipment in case they might be needed by the Western Allies.

Peace was not a week old before the maneuverings of Marshal Tito caused concern. His ambition was to seize the city of Trieste and to push Yugoslavia's frontier southward into Italy. Churchill was gratified to receive a message from President Truman recommending that a stand be taken against Tito's land-grabbing. A firm line against Tito would, the President suggested, effectively check similar encroachments elsewhere.[5]

Overjoyed at this evidence of the President's intentions, Churchill sent his prompt and enthusiastic approval. He was encouraged to conclude that the Americans were moving toward his own views concerning affairs in Europe, and he cabled back pledging support for any action to prevent the fruits of victory being cast away. Would it not be as well, he suggested, for a standstill order to be given for United States forces in Europe? British demobilization would be similarly checked.

This reply produced a distinctly adverse effect in Washington. Truman's proposal for a strong stand against Tito, even if it meant fighting, was his own idea, unprompted by his advisers. General Marshall was definitely opposed to any military clash. The President was recommended to consider the advantages of settling the Trieste dispute by negotiation.

To Churchill's disappointment a colder tone marked the ensuing messages from Washington. There would be no fighting unless Tito attacked, nor was any support forthcoming for the proposal of a standstill order for American troops. He concluded that there had been a reaction of some violence in Washington following Truman's first bold cable. It is not to be doubted that the reaction was heightened by his own bold reply. Since the days when the Prime Minister had begun to press for military action in the Balkans, Washington had come to look askance at his political aims.

Determined to arouse the White House to the dangers of the European situation, he amplified his views in the cable in which he coined the famous phrase "the Iron Curtain." His challenging words have a ringing call about them even when read these many years later.

> I am profoundly concerned about the European situation. . . .
> In a very short space our armed power will have vanished. . . .
> What is to happen about Russia?
> The Iron Curtain is drawn down upon their front. We do not know what is going on behind.
> Germany is ruined and prostrate. It would be open to the Russians in a very short time to advance to the waters of the North Sea and the Atlantic.
> A settlement with Russia before our strength has gone seems to me to dwarf all other matters.[6]

The Prime Minister had intended to rouse the Presidential advisers in Washington. He succeeded in alarming them, and putting them on their guard against what were conceived to be his designs to obtain American backing for British influence in Europe. The "Iron Curtain" cable served to check, not to advance his purpose.

On one point the President was convinced—the time had come to arrange for a summit conference. Already the proposal had been made that he should travel to the Continent by way of England. "If you will entertain the idea of coming over here," wrote Churchill, "His Majesty will send you the most cordial invitation and you will have a great reception from the British nation." [7]

Truman rejected the suggestion. In doing so he made the blunt statement that he preferred that the two of them should make their way separately to the conference with Stalin so as to avoid the appearance of "ganging up." Churchill accepted the decision with regret. The terms in which it was communicated surprised him. He failed to understand how any meeting he might have with the President could be referred to in so disparaging a phrase as "ganging up." It was overlooked in Washington that Britain and the United States, united by the bond of their common democratic faith, were facing the opposition of the Soviets on deep issues of principle. And in those differences the Americans had not the detached place of mediators, as it pleased them to think, but were as fully committed as Great Britain. [8]

On the choice of a meeting place, Churchill was emphatic that it should not be within the Russian zone of Germany. Twice already the British and Americans had traveled far to meet Stalin. Several visits had been made to Russia. The appropriate scene for a victory meeting of the powers was battle-scarred London, "the greatest city in the world." He would not push his preference to the point of insistence, but was ready to accept the best point outside Russian-occupied territory to which Stalin could be induced to travel.

Ultimately the choice fell on Berlin. The city was within the Russian zone but was subject to common occupation by the three powers. A place for the meeting was found in the Potsdam Palace, once the home of the German Crown Prince.

These arrangements were not long agreed before the Prime Minister was outraged by a proposal from Washington. So zealously was the placating of the Russian pursued that it was conceived President Truman should confer with Stalin somewhere in Europe, before the Prime Minister joined them for the summit conference. It was sought to ground this idea on the fact that Truman lacked Churchill's advantage of having met Stalin previously, but as he also lacked the personal acquaintance of Churchill the explanation rang hollow.

The suggestion was made not by letter but was put forward at a per-

sonal interview by the messenger Truman sent over to Downing Street
—Joseph E. Davies, who before the war had been Ambassador to
Moscow.[9]

As a preliminary to Mr. Davies's mission, Averell Harriman, then on
his way back to Moscow, called at Downing Street. He and Churchill
met on cordial terms for they had a common understanding about Soviet
designs. Harriman had observed how the Communists everywhere in
Europe were seeking to undermine the influence of the Western Allies.

The President's special envoy to London held very different views
about the Russians. As Ambassador, Davies was known for his marked
sympathy for the men of the Kremlin, of whose regime he had written
a book in flattering terms. In a series of three interviews, Davies spent
eight hours with the Prime Minister, beginning with a meeting at Chequers that went on until four-thirty in the morning and was resumed
six hours later with the Prime Minister still abed.

Davies proved himself to be an ill-chosen envoy. He was so lacking
in awareness that he had no realization the proposal he was charged to
make would be taken as an affront by the proudest man in Europe.
However it was phrased, it was no light matter to have to suggest to the
Prime Minister that the other two leaders should begin to confer without him. When it had been made Davies found the Prime Minister to
be "emotional." It is to be imagined that his emotions reached the white
heat of indignation.

Appreciating so little the nature of the offense he had given, Davies
found it necessary to discover a reason in politics for the "most unfavorable" reaction he had produced. It was, he concluded, the general
election. If Churchill were to be by-passed by Truman it might give a
chance to his opponents to denigrate him in the eyes of hostile electors.
Davies had no realization of the simple truth that Churchill had been
hurt, deeming himself slighted as a man, as Prime Minister, and as
elected leader of the British people.

It was Davies's further task to convey that Truman was intending
at the summit talks to stand by Roosevelt's commitments. He was to
recommend that it would be an advantage if the Prime Minister would
modify his criticisms and mistrust of the Russians. On this subject he
provoked some further markedly unfavorable reactions.

The Prime Minister had reached conclusions from day-to-day contact
with the Russians, and he had reason to consider his views to be better
grounded than those of an ex-embassador whose official contact with
Moscow had ended in 1938. He stated his opinions in language that
Davies considered "vehement" and "violent." Like an interrupter in a
House of Commons debate, Davies served to rouse the Prime Minister

to the full flood of declamation. Churchill expressed the full measure of his detestation of Soviet methods, "Gestapo methods," more horrible than communism itself. Red Army propagandists were descending upon liberated Europe like locusts.

It was the turn of Joseph E. Davies to be outraged. This was language such as Hitler or Goebbels might have used. He could not credit that it represented the considered judgment of the Prime Minister of Great Britan. His report stated:

> I said to him that frankly, as I listened to him inveigh so violently against the threat of Soviet domination and the spread of communism in Europe, and disclose such a lack of confidence in the professions of good faith in Soviet leadership, I wondered whether he, the Prime Minister, was willing to declare to the world that he and Britain had made a mistake in not supporting Hitler.

In the rambling discussions over differences with the Russians, Davies gave further offense, for he attempted to play the mediator between the British leader and the Soviet dictator. This attitude of detachment had been trying when adopted by Roosevelt at Yalta. Assumed by Davies it was intolerable. Churchill made proper protest. These disputes with the Russians did not concern Britain alone. The British were not the sole repositories of the principles of the Atlantic Charter. The United States was equally involved and committed.

From his eight hours of discussions Davies left for home with two main impressions. The first was that he had discovered the principal reason why the Russians were unreasonable in their dealings with the West; it arose from the fact that they had become aware of Churchill's hostile opinions concerning them, which provoked them into aggressiveness. This was a very notable discovery. The second impression was that, for all his denunciation of the men of the Kremlin, the Prime Minister was now prepared to conform at Potsdam with American policy.

With commendation of his own embassy, Davies represented that he had been successful in paving the way for British cooperation at Potsdam. It might otherwise have been reported that Churchill, despite Mr. Davies, was still determined to maintain a common front at Potsdam with the President. This was reassuring in Washington, for his recent speeches in Parliament had fostered the idea in the White House that, if his wishes were not met, the Prime Minister was willing "to go it alone." [10]

From the Davies mission no meeting of minds could have resulted. What was to be regretted was that Churchill's views would reach Truman through so distorting a medium. They would be given no chance of making any impact upon the Presidential mind.

Davies went back to America with a written statement of Churchill's views. He bore an uncompromising and emphatic negative to the proposal that the Prime Minister should join Truman and Stalin a few days after their preliminary talks. The message ran:

> It must be understood that the representatives of His Majesty's Government would not be able to attend any meeting except as equal partners from its opening. This would be undoubtedly regrettable. The Prime Minister does not see there is any need to raise an issue so wounding to Britain, to the British Empire and the Commonwealth of Nations.[11]

In language no less plain and forcible, Churchill gave a reminder to the Americans of their responsibilities in resistance to communism and the police state.

> The Prime Minister cannot readily bring himself to accept the idea that the position of the United States is that Britain and Soviet Russia are just two foreign powers, six of one and half a dozen of the other, with whom the troubles of the late war have to be adjusted. The great principles for which Britain and the United States have suffered and triumphed are not mere matters of the balance of power; they in fact involve the salvation of the world.

These were plain words indeed. They were not addressed personally to the President but were headed: "Notes by the Prime Minister on Mr. Davies's message." It was as if Churchill were concerned not to identify Truman personally with all the communications Davies had made. As, however, Truman considered that his envoy had carried out his instructions with "exceptional skill," it seems that this was a superfluous distinction.

Churchill wrote that he had striven for friendship with the Russians and he would so persevere to the end. But there were the lands of Europe that had been overrun by the Russians, for whose peoples—Poles, Hungarians, Czechs, Rumanians, Austrians, and the rest—freedom and independence must be assured.

> The Prime Minister [ran the message] cannot feel it would be wise to dismiss all these topics in the desire to placate the imperialistic demands of Soviet-Communist Russia.

Forceful as were the expressions, it is not to be supposed that they produced any immediate effect on White House opinion. The American Staffs were still pleading for patience with the Russians, for fear that a crackdown would endanger Russian entry into the war in the Far East.[12]

The major problem still remained—to withdraw or not to withdraw the Allied armies within the zones in Germany. Churchill employed every argument against immediately yielding ground to the Russians. At least, he urged, the Big Three should hold their meeting before Eisenhower was instructed to draw back his armies. He contended in vain. In whatever form his contention was put forward, it was rejected in Washington. Truman and his advisers were not prepared to depart from the agreement to which Roosevelt had been a party. To delay withdrawal until the Big Three met in July would impair relations with the Soviets.[13]

At last, on June 12, there came a message from Truman, proposing that immediate orders be given for the Allied withdrawal. Churchill read it with dismay. In his own words, "This struck a knell in my breast." But, dreading the consequences as he did, he yet felt himself compelled to acquiesce and order Montgomery to conform with the movements of Eisenhower's forces.[14]

In Washington the Prime Minister's compliance caused surprise. It was, according to Admiral Leahy, entirely unexpected. It was so unlike him to give way that they concluded his health must be failing. In fact, there was no such reason.

"I had no choice but to submit," he wrote afterward in his memoirs.[15]

He saw no alternative, as he conceived it, if the alliance with the Americans were to be maintained. And, greatly though he deplored the decision, it was preferable to bear the consequence in partnership than to risk a break in that alliance. At all costs the British and Americans must remain together to face the hazards before them.

So it came about that orders went out for the Anglo-American armies to withdraw.

CHAPTER FOUR

SO STALIN WON THE PEACE

JUNE 21, 1945

T HE twenty-first day of June of the year 1945 was the day of fate for postwar Europe. The Anglo-American forces faced about and marched westward on a front of 400 miles to a depth, in its greatest extent, of 120 miles. As they moved back the Russians, moving in, gained the strategic and political advantage of being positioned in the heart of Europe.

In Washington no doubt was felt that Winston Churchill had been misguided in seeking to delay giving ground to the Russians.[1] The President's advisers were satisfied that their decision was the right one. They felt confirmed in the soundness of their own judgment—gratifying self-satisfaction. They did not seek to avoid the responsibility for the consequences. It was theirs, acknowledged, undisputed, undivided.

So fateful were those consequences for the world, then and thereafter, that it is necessary to probe further, to reconsider the circumstances in some detail, even though it may entail recapitulation of what has gone before.

There was once a leader in English politics who bested his opponents. It was said of him that he found the Whigs bathing and ran off with their clothes. In similar fashion Stalin bested the West by running off with the spoils of war.

When the Red armies moved in, the future of Europe had been decided. Not the Potsdam conference that was almost superfluous, not the peace conference that never met,* not the proposals and protests of foreign ministers; neither one nor other of the processes of diplomacy determined the shape of things to come. The simple fact of possession was decisive. For Stalin it was ten points of the law. When the curtain came down he was the man in possession of East Germany, Austria, the Balkans, Poland, and the Baltic States. Czechoslovakia was soon to be Sovietized. Greece, thanks to Churchill's intervention, escaped the Soviet net.

The Russians jumped their claims. The leaders of the West observed protocol. They honored their pledged word, they sought no territorial gains. In Sovietized lands reproachful eyes watched the consequence of their impeccable rectitude.

Already, as the war was being won, the Anglo-Americans lost the peace to Stalin and the price was paid by Balts, Poles, Germans, and those others in the Balkans of the multitudes who forfeited their freedom.

Had such consequence flowed from a peace conference at which the leaders of the West suffered so calamitous a diplomatic defeat, they would have had to bear the world's censure. Do they escape blame because Stalin worsted them in the preliminary encounters? History will require an answer of them.

Their responsibility is not to be evaded. They could have given another shape to Europe, forestalling the Russians here, reducing Soviet regimentation there. They had the opportunities. Action, save in Greece and Denmark, was not taken.

For the default, responsibility is to be differently apportioned. For the President's advisers there was a lack of awareness of what was impending. They had their eyes fixed elsewhere, on the Far East.

For the Prime Minister the case was otherwise. An abundant knowledge was his. His lack was the power to provide against the perils he foresaw. Only in conjunction with the United States could action have been taken. Seeking to obtain the cooperation in turn of Roosevelt and Truman, he suffered a failure in persuasion. That is the measure of his responsibility for the loss of the peace.

While the two Presidents had a lack of awareness of the realities about the Russians, the Prime Minister had a lack of awareness of the realities about the Presidents and their advisers, of the utter incompatibility between their policy and his, and of the dead weight of opinion opposed to him in Washington. He had no realization of the inadequacy of the

---

* The long-drawn-out wrangles of Foreign Ministers in Paris and New York are not to be accepted as constituting a peace conference, certainly not in the sense contemplated by Churchill and Roosevelt, following the pattern of Versailles in 1919 or of Vienna after the Napoleonic Wars.

methods he employed to bring the Americans around to his view of Europe's peril.

For long enough before the Yalta conference he had been conscious of the need to keep ahead of the Russians in the liberation of Europe. He had sought Roosevelt's support. His approaches were unavailing. He asked for joint discussions on political matters when they were fore-gathering for Yalta. Roosevelt refused. Always the Prime Minister's appeals met with a refusal.

His messages to Washington became more importunate as, with the war nearing its end, the need became more urgent. Time and again, with rousing phrase, his cables conveyed his warnings. But mere words, however well they were chosen, were powerless to achieve his purpose. The blast of trumpets had sufficed at Jericho. The walls of Washington were built of stronger stuff. Against them the force of mere words was directed in vain.

The cables continued with mounting emphasis. Surely his warnings and the pressure of the events must carry conviction in the White House? They did not. Still he cabled on. He failed to realize that times had changed and that no longer was Roosevelt responsive to messages, not at least to such messages from his voluminous correspondent, the "Former Naval Person."

As the war had moved on, the professionals had taken control. There was an extended circle of advisers around the President. In the early days Churchill and F.D.R. could settle matters between themselves, but the Washington Staffs got wise to the danger of allowing them to go off together for a strategic spree. The professionals formed a protective barrier around the White House. Harry Hopkins was only one of those to prompt his chief against merely falling in line with the Prime Minister and the policy of Britain.

From the time of the third Washington conference, and the differences over Mediterranean strategy, the advisers were on their guard against suggestions from Downing Street aimed, as they apprehended, to promote British political designs. The time came when the mere sniff of European politics was enough to raise the alarm. The Prime Minister talked politics over strategy in the Balkans. His messages on Berlin and Germany were stuffed with politics. He remained unconscious of the effect he was producing. Each cable strengthened opposition. The more emphatic his phrases the more solid the core of American resistance.[2]

Halifax, from his post as Ambassador, could sense the mounting feeling. He sent a warning to Downing Street. It was phrased too diplomatically to be effective. Halifax, like the Prime Minister, suffered a failure in persuasion, for otherwise the Prime Minister, made conscious of the prevailing winds in Washington, would have trimmed his sails and changed the method of his advocacy.

While Churchill, with his eyes on Europe, was urging measures to forestall the Russians, the military leaders in Washington, turning their vision on the Far East, concentrated their purpose on the defeat of the Japanese. Roosevelt's good-neighbor policy toward the Russians accorded with the purpose of his Staffs. Long before Yalta they had been pressing for an agreement with Stalin for his participation in the war in the Far East. This, they estimated, might last for two further years. In their reckoning the most important factor the President had to bear in mind in his dealings abroad was to secure Stalin's cooperation.

The generals' reckoning influenced State Department thinking. There was a solidity of conviction. At Yalta, according to Stettinius, "immense pressure was put on the President by our military leaders to bring Russia into the Far Eastern war." The Staffs ganged up against the President. Roosevelt, it seems, was inclined to hang back—immense pressure would not otherwise have been required.[3]

Truman was subjected to similar persuasion. Stettinius drew attention to Soviet breaches of faith in the Balkans. The military leaders prayed patience. A crackdown, as they termed it, would endanger Russian aid to beat the Japanese.

In Europe the advisers were set against any moves that could divert military resources from the Far East. Eisenhower's refusals to be implicated in political adventures conformed with Washington requirements.

Such was the dead weight of opinion ranged against the Prime Minister. Had he been aware of its strength and its extent he would scarcely have been satisfied to go on dispatching cabled warnings that were no more effective than peanuts against the Empire State Building. Personal messages addressed to the President were wasted on a syndicate. And the influence of the syndicate of Staffs and advisers was at its peak during the Presidential hiatus of Roosevelt's decline and Truman's novitiate. That was the critical period for Europe.

To have produced the effect he sought, Churchill would have needed to oppose syndicate against syndicate in a top-level conference at Washington. There, with Staffs and colleagues, he could have attempted by a supreme effort to have roused the President to the peril in which Europe and the rest of the free world stood from Russian communism, and to the need for concerting British and American policy against Stalin's designs. He had complete realization of the dangers ahead. His certitude of calamity filled him with foreboding. Should he not, therefore, have made formal demand for a conference with an authority not to be denied?

The suggestions he did make for joint talks on political affairs were consistently evaded—the President was too occupied by the pressure of business, he was electioneering, the Secretary of State was not available. Always Washington side-stepped. There was no penetrating the protective barrier of the advisers. Like relatives ringed round a dying Croesus, fearful that he may will his riches elsewhere, they guarded the failing Roosevelt and Truman, the newcomer, from the contaminating influence from across the Atlantic. They were resolved that there must be no departure from let's-be-friends-with-the-Russians.

With protested loyalty they insisted, during the hiatus, on the faithful execution of the Roosevelt policy, that is their own policy for which they had secured his support and to which they continued to assign the authority of his name. Opportunity was denied to the Prime Minister to develop his arguments in the presence of the new President. There was no underestimating the effect of his powerful advocacy. The idea was continuously fostered that any "ganging up" between Prime Minister and President would infuriate the Russians. During the critical period Churchill was kept the Atlantic's distance away from the White House.

The insistence of the American military hierarchy prevailed against the cabled warnings from Downing Street. The affairs of the Continent were determined in the light of United States requirements. Presidents, Staffs and advisers decided matters as seemed best for their country. They miscalculated. Not all men are born equal in political understanding. The misfortunes that followed fell upon the liberated peoples. They had to pay the price of the miscalculations—Balts, Germans, Poles, Hungarians, and the peoples of the Balkans no longer living in the free world.

Is Winston Churchill to bear history's censure because he did not press for the adoption of his policy, even to the point of a rupture between Great Britain and the United States? His was a lamentable dilemma. Facing it he had no doubt where his course lay. Unilateral action by Britain could not have checked the Russians. Only in cooperation had British and Americans the strength to oppose Stalin and counter Soviet designs.

Throughout his dealings with Washington, Churchill had bowed to the one overwhelming necessity—preserving the Anglo-American alliance. The friendship of the President was paramount and always Churchill had put an end to differences and arguments before that friendship could be impaired. Never did he waver in his feelings toward Roosevelt, or in the faith he reposed in the greatest friends the world had to offer to Great Britain. All considerations must give way before the imperious necessity overriding all others—the continuing partnership of the English-speaking peoples on which the salvation of the free world must depend.

It was in this spirit that he approached the last wartime conference of the Big Three. By the time preparations for Potsdam had been made, voting in the British general election had been completed, but the secret of the ballot boxes was not to be made known until after the conference had opened. Churchill took advantage of the break in affairs to spend a week's holiday at Hendaye, on the frontier of Spain. There he occupied himself with painting, putting the world's business from his mind. The sunny hours were disturbed only by an occasional prod of curiosity about the riddle of the unopened ballot boxes and the verdict of the electors.

CHAPTER FIVE

TO THE POLLS

MAY–JUNE, 1945

THE famous Coalition Government was dissolved on May 23, 1945, after an existence of thirteen days beyond five years. As head of a new administration known as the Caretaker Government, Winston Churchill thereupon engaged with his former Socialist colleagues in the turmoil of a general election.

Then in his seventy-first year, Churchill had already fought fifteen elections in his political career of forty-five years. Now, for the first time, he took the field as head of the Conservative Party, leading his battalions into the electoral fray. The future depended upon the results of the polls—the survival of his new Ministry, and his own chance of continuing to direct in time of peace the affairs of the people he had led onward to victory. His heart was set on gaining the opportunity to carry his work to its conclusion by garnering the fruits of the people's endeavors and sacrifices in the testing years of war.

It is sad to have to record the animosities that developed between wartime associates who were sundered by the exigencies of party politics, and to recall the rather puerile vilification in which they engaged, under the supposition that they were thereby recommending themselves to the free and independent electors. It was pathetic and it was ill-contrived, for no men who had cooperated for five years with such loyalty and to such good purpose, could have sunk so low in each other's estimation in a few brief weeks. However, the party leaders and their forces consider that mudslinging and vilification are expected of them by voters. And the free and independent voters humor their leaders by seeming to accept and even to applaud their efforts.

As is the usual practice on such occasions, both parties sought to make capital out of the timing of the election and the breakup of the coalition.

Churchill was slightly handicapped in these preliminary encounters by the opinions he had expressed some months earlier (October, 1944), when electoral arrangements had come up for discussion in the House. He had then pronounced that once Hitler had been beaten no delay should be permitted in taking the verdict of the country. With Parliament ten years old, no person under thirty had had the opportunity of voting in a general election. It would be a serious constitutional lapse not to hold the election at the earliest moment possible.*

Six months later, and Hitler disposed of, the matter appeared in a different light with the problems of a liberated and distracted Europe to be faced. Since the electors had gone five years beyond their time, it might not, after all, be so unreasonable to ask them to wait a few months longer.

For Churchill, in defiance of the weight of the disapprobation he had expressed in October, was now proposing to continue in office as head of the coalition for so long a term as a further eighteen months. That was the time, by his reckoning, it might take to defeat the Japanese. It would also provide the House with the opportunity for passing those measures of social reform which members of all parties were pledged to put into operation, on the basis of the Beveridge plan for developing the welfare state. To give the appearance of propriety to such a prolongation of Parliament's life, Churchill was ready to hold a referendum to secure the people's endorsement—or rejection, though he did not contemplate a refusal—of this course.

It was generally appreciated that the leader who had brought them safely to the beginning of peace in Europe ought not to be deprived of the opportunity of disposing of the Japanese. The Socialists were conscious of this feeling, conscious, too, that by flouting it they might antagonize a section of the electorate. Nevertheless, there was no liking for delay.

Politicians of all parties were spoiling for the fight so long denied them. Tories complained indignantly that the electoral truce was working to their disadvantage. Socialists, estimating the flow of the electoral tide, were eager to engage their opponents and gain the spoils they were

* The duration of a Parliament is normally limited to a maximum of five years, if it has not previously been dissolved. However, this rule was suspended during both world wars.

convinced the polls would accord them. Nor were they inclined to resign the Beveridge plan to a coalition government, when the kudos and prestige to be gained therefrom might be won for Socialists alone. Having evaluated the chances they resolved to take the risk and reject the eighteen-month proposition.

Through their leader, Clement Attlee, they declined the referendum. It was, they declared, with democratic rectitude that might work to their advantage, a device that smelled of Hitlerism. To avoid the semblance of responsibility for breaking up the coalition before the job against Japan was done, they expressed their readiness to go on in double harness until the autumn.

Churchill, for his part, found ground for rejecting this half-and-half proposal. Already the odor of parliamentary dissolution was in the air. Let the break, he pronounced, be made forthwith.

Honors in the preliminary exchanges were easy. For what it was worth, the Tories were able to represent that their rivals had broken up the coalition. The Socialists had secured a case to support the time-honored complaint that the election was badly timed—there never was an election yet which was not badly timed, according to the reckoning of the party that did not fix it.

At a later date regrets were voiced that the leader who had seen the country through to victory was deprived of the chance of putting his signature to the declarations from Potsdam. Had the Socialist proposal been accepted, Churchill would have been in office both for the conclusion of the Potsdam conference and the end of the war with Japan. He chose otherwise.

At noon on May 23, Winston Churchill tendered his resignation to the King and, four hours later, he kissed hands upon reappointment as Prime Minister. The Caretaker Government was formed. This stopgap administration was made up for the most part of Conservatives, though it was designated National and though Churchill had not confined his choice to members of his own party but had drawn upon "men of good will of any party or no party, willing to serve." There were forty members either in the Cabinet of sixteen (the War Cabinet was superseded) or "of Cabinet rank." Of the latter, twenty-six were Conservatives, eight non-party, four Liberal National, one Liberal (Gwilym Lloyd George), and one not an M.P. (Sir Walter Monckton, the new Solicitor General). Among the upper sixteen were R. A. Butler, who left the Board of Education to fill Ernest Bevin's place as Labor Minister, and Brendan Bracken, promoted from Minister of Information to the Admiralty. The honored name of Rosebery was once more to be found in the Cabinet list, the son of the former Liberal Prime Minister taking office as Secretary for Scotland.

Among the others of Cabinet rank, interest was focused on the choice for the new post of Minister of National Insurance of Leslie Hore Belisha, once numbered among the critics, who had made his peace with Churchill. Men of promise among the younger Conservatives were given junior posts, as were two women M.P.s—Miss Florence Horsbrugh (Parliamentary Secretary, Ministry of Food) and Mrs. Cazalet Keir (Under-Secretary, Board of Education), whose motion on equal pay for women had caused the coalition to sustain its solitary defeat in the division lobbies. For three weeks Ministers faced the Socialist Opposition in the House while essential business was disposed of. Then the cry of: Who goes home? was raised for the last time in the first Parliament of His Majesty, King George VI. Members, those of them who were standing for election, hurried off to their constituencies, leaving to the free and independent electors the decision: Who goes back?

There is no need, nor would this be the place, to recapitulate the events of the election in any detail. In the books, democracy at the polls appears to be a majestic feature of Britain's constitutional existence. In reality it falls short of the constitutional ideal, when misrepresentation does duty for argument and sustained noise drowns the voice of reason. The election of 1945 went the way of its predecessors without being conspicuously better or worse. There was a spate of oratory, or what passes for such, from 1,683 candidates nominated in 617 constituencies for 640 seats.

Candidates concentrated their attention on the issue of free enterprise versus state socialism. Tories sought to make the electors' flesh creep over the hidden menaces of socialism, and the Labour speakers to charm the voters with siren songs of national planning and nationalization. It was passing strange that in the year 1945 any vast degree of menace or merit could be imparted to the nationalization of the coal mines and of the Bank of England, but to this theme thousands of speeches were devoted.

Of the outcome of a straight fight between Toryism and Socialism, the Labour leaders had no fears. But of the result of a contest against the Tories plus the War Minister who had led the nation to victory, and who was held in universal esteem, they had no such confidence. To what extent would the electorate be influenced by the prestige of the Prime Minister? That was the unknown factor. With astuteness and persistence Labour speakers sought to destroy the magic residing in the name of Churchill, by concealing the figure of the leader of the nation united in war beneath the cloak and trappings of the Conservative Party boss.

Churchill went into the fight in splendid spirit. There were some in his ranks, among them Anthony Eden, his chief lieutenant, who were dubious about the outcome. Churchill had no doubts. How, indeed, could doubts have been his? His services were on the record, acclaimed by the free peoples of the world. How could the honest voters of his own country fail to reward him with the tokens of their confidence and approbation?

With every appearance of zest he hurled himself into the melee. But though his enthusiasm was to be applauded, his judgment was to be deplored. With reckless disregard of the consequences he cast away his advantages. His strength was his prestige as the nation's leader. That was the role in which he had fulfilled himself and it was one he was loath to resign.

"I was deeply distressed," he made confession in his memoirs, "at the prospect of sinking from a national to a party leader."

It was an instinctive preference. It was also sound political tactics. It should have been his purpose to remain above the dust of conflict, an Olympian figure, proclaiming the nation's high resolves and responsibilities. The purely partisan stuff, the trumpetings and bludgeonings, could be remitted to the faithful followers. Such petty business was not for him to undertake. Nor should he have descended to personal attacks on the wartime colleagues with whom he had recently parted company. With lofty unconcern at their departure, he might have chided them in sorrow rather than in anger, for choosing the partisan instead of the patriot path. By these means he might have won the suffrages of some of the middle men (and women) in politics, the floating voters, the uncommitted, wavering mass who decide the fate of governments.

Flinging such prudent considerations to the winds, Churchill took the opposite course, running full-tilt at the Socialists. His old colleagues were assailed with an extravagance of denunciation. The party spirit can work strange transformations, but a miraculous wizardry would have been needed to transform the mild-mannered Clement Attlee into the head of a British Gestapo on the Nazi model as Churchill depicted him.

The "Gestapo" speech with which he opened the campaign by radio was a blunder that must have cost the Prime Minister countless votes. The words came over the air in the familiar tones that had not long before been proclaiming the tyranny of the "Narzees." Now it was heard foretelling a tyranny for Britain.

> I declare to you from the bottom of my heart that no socialist system can be established without a political police. . . . No socialist government conducting the entire life and industry of the country could afford to allow free, sharp, or violently worded ex-

pressions of public discontent. . . . They would have to fall back on some form of Gestapo. . . .

For Churchill, the national figure, to have attempted to make the electors' flesh creep was a mistake. To have tried and to have failed was a blunder—and whose flesh was made to creep by the Gestapo fancy, so obviously inapplicable to a party of which Attlee was the head?

The party managers had provided an admirable poster for the billboards—Churchill's familiar face, looking down with an almost benign smile. Attached were the simple words: "Help him finish the job—Vote National." It served better than the leader's partisan oratings. The other side of the picture was presented by the Socialist propagandists, who designed a poster to beat Churchill by appeal to his own past. A vast medicine bottle bore the label: "National Eyewash—Tory mixture as before. Don't judge by the labels, remember what Churchill said." Below were quotations from a speech he delivered to his electors of Dundee in the year 1908 during his Liberal phase. He had then denounced the Tories with searing coruscation:

> We know what to expect when the Tories return to power—a party of vested interests, banded together in a formidable confederation—the trickery of tariff juggles; the tyranny of a well-fed party machine; sentiment by the basketful; patriotism and imperialism by the imperial pint; dear food for the million; cheap labor for the millionaire.

Churchill the Liberal was an engaging witness against Churchill the Tory. There was also Churchill of a later vintage to quote from copiously against the failure of the prewar Tories to arm the country against Hitler. The early Churchill was rumbustious stuff. The later Churchill was deadly in its effect. Churchill, in the thirties had arraigned Neville Chamberlain and his Tory followers before the bar of opinion and the verdict of the electors was at length to be given.

It looked at the outset that the campaign was to be pretty heavy going, but some light relief was found in Professor Harold Laski. In retrospect, we can sympathize with this electoral victim. It is a hard fate that drags a man out of the comfortable obscurity of a university chair to be elevated into a national bogey. But the electors must have their figure of fun and, since no one else offered, Harold Laski had to serve.

Though he was Chairman of the Labour Party National Executive, Laski, with professorial coyness, had resisted attempts to involve him as a candidate, in the hurly-burly of the election, preferring to scent the noise of battle from afar. But he obtruded himself in matters that had arisen between the Prime Minister and Clement Attlee.

The Potsdam conference was due to open on July 17, and, in view of the uncertainties of the political future, the Prime Minister proposed that Attlee should accompany him to Potsdam as a member of the British delegation. Thereupon Laski attempted to enter a caveat. Since the three-power conference would be deciding matters which had not been debated by his Executive, or by his party, then the party, he pontificated, could not be committed by the Potsdam decisions. Should Mr. Attlee attend at Potsdam, it was essential that it should be in the sole role of observer.

So far as the Potsdam proceedings were concerned the matter was soon disposed of. Churchill, in his formal invitation, wrote that his idea was that Clement Attlee should come along as friend and counselor to "help us on all subjects on which we have been so long agreed." For him to go as mute observer would be derogatory to his position as leader of his party.

Attlee replied that he accepted the invitation in agreement with his principal colleagues in the House. "There was never any suggestion," he remarked, "that I should go as mere observer." Attlee ignored the Professor and continued to ignore the Professor.

Press and politicians leaped at the Professor. Privately they were grateful to him for his intervention; it gave them a personal target for their polemics. He was an electoral godsend, above all to the *Daily Express,* whose columns became consecrated to Laski and his committee of twenty-seven dictators. After some days of it, one began to wonder whether the Conservative election campaign was being conducted by Winston Churchill from 10 Downing Street or by Beaverbrook's boys from their back room in Shoe Lane. It was monstrously diverting and, if it didn't win votes, it was good for circulations.

Churchill himself sought to make capital out of the Laski episode. He pointed out that the Labour Party leaders had not disowned the Professor, and that the Laski instruction to Attlee to go to Potsdam solely as observer had not been withdrawn. This, he submitted, showed that Laski was the leader of forces too strong for Attlee to challenge. It was to be concluded that the Socialist Executive would have far-reaching powers over Socialist Ministers of the Crown and that, furthermore, secrets of state would be divulged by Socialist Ministers to the committee of twenty-seven, an unconstitutional and undemocratic body.

To this Clement Attlee retorted with some heat. The insinuation that Labour Ministers had so little respect for their oaths as Privy Councilors that they would reveal Cabinet and military secrets to outsiders was one that Churchill knew from his experience to be "vile and false." He had expected the Prime Minister ("who has old-fashioned ideas about what is permissible in elections") to allow himself a deal of latitude in his attacks, but he had never thought that he would have descended to "such depths of misrepresentation and ingratitude toward men who had shown him such loyalty and consideration."

The Prime Minister passed a succession of strenuous electoral days. There was the party to lead, the speeches to prepare (he delivered four out of the ten broadcasts allocated to the Conservatives), the tasks of Prime Minister and Defense Minister to be discharged, and those of the Foreign Office in addition. Anthony Eden, a sick man, had been ordered to rest and Churchill deputized for him. In his new constituency of Woodford, Churchill had as his opponent a Northampton farmer, formerly a shoe manufacturer, Mr. A. Hancock, standing as Independent.

The last days of the campaign were devoted by the Prime Minister to a whirlwind tour from Aylesbury through the Midlands to Manchester, from Lancashire to Yorkshire, and northward to Glasgow and Edinburgh. He traveled more than a thousand miles and made more than forty speeches. A train was his headquarters and a special car served as his office for the discharge of his divers duties. The tour, the most spectacular electoral undertaking since the days of the revered Gladstone's Midlothian campaign of 1879, was marked by scenes of a royal progress. Everywhere the great War Minister was received by prodigious crowds and for the most part the welcome given him was of exuberant enthusiasm. To his personal popularity with the people the demonstrations were unequivocal in their testimony. As political pointers they were illusory. Back in London, Churchill made evening tours of the constituencies, where the crowds were repeated, though the cordiality of the reception was disturbed by hecklers and rowdies. The final mass meeting at Walthamstow Stadium, where a crowd of 20,000 gathered two nights before the poll, was the climax of the tour.

One warning Churchill gave at all his meetings—that he could not continue in office unless his party were returned by a substantial majority. It was a necessary correction. The suggestion had been put abroad that whatever the result of the voting he would still be at the head of affairs.

Polling took place on July 5, and the ballot boxes were then put in storage for three weeks. The interval was to provide time for the votes from the Services to be collected. It was not found possible to provide for the cases of personnel serving in Australia and New Zealand, but otherwise planes of RAF Transport Command took out papers and election addresses to the far-flung commands. They brought back the ballots from Europe and the Near East, from Africa and America, from the

Atlantic outposts, the Azores and Iceland, from India, and even from the front in Burma.

The ballot boxes still preserved their secret when the Prime Minister, accompanied by Anthony Eden and Clement Attlee, traveled to Potsdam for the summit conference.

CHAPTER SIX

TERMINAL AT POTSDAM
JULY 16–25, 1945

O NE July day—it was the sixteenth of the month—Winston Churchill stood amidst the debris that bore the name of Berlin. It was a victor's visit to the capital city of the vanquished. Around were the signs, eloquent testimony of defeat—battle-scarred walls, rubble where once government buildings had proudly stood, a chaos of devastation. London had no scars to display such as those. Trudging past him, as he paused amidst the ruins, was the mournful procession of the homeless, the march of the defeated, their belongings upon their backs. Always they moved toward the West, away from the Russian conquerors from the East.

No scene could have told more tragically of the fate of the vanquished than this landscape of the waste land. A man surveying it could think:

> . . . we are in rats' alley
> Where the dead men lost their bones.[1]

There stood the Reich Chancellery where once Hitler had loosed his words to applauding followers, and there the air-raid shelter where life had left his bones. Churchill walked down the steps and marked the spot where he had perished by his own hand. Coming up, he was shown where the business was completed, with the burning of the Fuehrer's body and that of his bride in death, Eva Braun. As he gazed at the place of immolation Churchill was satisfied to think that Hitler had done his conquerors the service they would otherwise have had to render to him with the other gallows-men of Nuremberg.[2]

The spectacle of the chaos that had been the capital of the Reich gave him no victor's thrill of elation. He was too moved by his sense of compassion for the people in their agony of defeat and for the pilgrims trudging westward. "My hate," he confessed, "died with their surrender."

Another visitor that day to the ruins of the Wilhelmstrasse was President Truman. He, too, looked on the remains of the Chancellery, reflecting on the days when Hitler harangued his Nazis. He found the moral for the occasion.

"That," he observed, "is what happens when a man overreaches himself." [3]

There were no buildings in the desolation of Berlin to offer a meeting place for the Big Three. Their conference hall was provided by the spacious apartments at Potsdam of the Cecilienhof, the palace that had been the country home of Wilhelm, the last Crown Prince. Standing in the wooded grounds above the Gribnitz Lake, the brown stone building was made bright by the red geraniums which the Russians had planted in the inner courtyard. The delegations were housed in the residences of Babelsberg, Germany's former film colony. Number 23 Ringstrasse provided the Prime Minister and his team with ample comfort, so different from the cramped quarters at Yalta.

Stalin's arrival was delayed for twenty-four hours by a heart attack. It removed the President's problem of whom to greet first. After the Joseph Davies contretemps it was providential.

Prime Minister and President were eager to meet. Although in each other's company at Roosevelt gatherings, they had not talked together, save by transocean telephone. Each was concerned to receive a good impression of the other. Both were gratified. Churchill found Truman to be gay and sparkling in manner, with an obvious power of decision, a person of character and ability. Truman conceived an immediate liking for the man who welcomed him in so rare and open a fashion: "I did not feel I was meeting a stranger." [4]

When they lunched together, Churchill spoke of the plight to which Britain had temporarily been reduced by her wartime efforts. This having been sympathetically received, he spoke of the matter so important to him of preserving into the peace the wartime association and the machinery for cooperation between the two countries. The Combined Chiefs of Staff, he urged, should continue their existence at least until the world had calmed down.

For length of its proceedings, the Potsdam conference held the record for the summit conferences of the war, with sixteen days (July 17-August

2) of discursive debate. In achievement it ranked low, with scarcely a major decision to its credit. Terminal was the code name and terminal it was, for Winston Churchill, marking the close of his wartime services.[5]

According to his American friends he was less well-prepared than at former meetings. On several matters they noted gaps in his knowledge, in contrast with their former experience when they found him usually to be a move or two ahead. Truman had worked hard to brief himself on every subject likely to arise. Voted to the chair, he was not handicapped either by unfamiliarity with the problems or the novelty of his position. His insistence was for the execution of the agreements into which Roosevelt had entered.[6]

Following the pattern of Yalta, Truman permitted no prior discussions to take place with the British. Not even the semblance of teaming-up was permitted to arouse the touchy Russians. All Churchill's admonitions to Washington had been in vain. Truman insisted and persisted in equality of treatment between Britain and Russia, just two powers, six of one and half a dozen of the other. Churchill had sought a showdown with the Russians over breaches of Yalta. It was denied him. But despite the handicap of American aloofness he strove with resolution (and eloquence) to obtain Russian compliance with the Yalta agreements.

Poland was foremost of the broken covenants. Section VI of the Yalta protocol provided that Poland's frontiers would be determined at the peace settlement. Even before Potsdam the Russians had transferred tracts of East Prussia to the Poles. So, when the question of Germany's future came up, Churchill put the question: "What is Germany?" To this Stalin replied: "What is left of Germany." Thereby the issue was raised that persisted throughout the Potsdam proceedings.[7]

The President might rule that for purposes of the conference Germany was the 1937 Germany. That was no more than a verbal fiction. Stalin might defer to adverse opinion and equivocate. He had not given the Poles a German zone; he had merely allowed them to "assume the necessary functions of government therein." That was superfluous casuistry. Churchill, with cogency, might contest the consequences point by point. Stalin offered no retraction. He said flatly that the arrangements he had made could not be changed.

"Are we through?" he asked, as if to close the debate.

"Hardly through," Churchill replied, "but it might be of advantage to pass on to more agreeable topics."

The impasse remained unresolved. Nothing, it was recognized, short of military action was going to cancel out the *fait accompli*.

It was during these discussions that Churchill raised the religious rights of Roman Catholics in Poland. Stalin reflected a moment, stroking his mustache, and then posed his famous question. Speaking in a hard, even tone he asked: "How many divisions has the Pope?"

On the Prime Minister's suggestion, Ministers of the Polish Provisional Government were summoned to Potsdam. Both he and Anthony Eden pleaded with them, urging them to be reasonable over their demands for territory and to be democratic, in the Western sense, in the conduct of their political affairs. Free elections and free speech were vital; they hoped the Poles would follow the British example and be proud of it. The Polish leader, Beirut, made appropriate responses with becoming professions in democratic ideas. Beyond this nothing resulted.[8]

On Yugoslavia, Churchill made complaint that Tito was not complying with Yalta. Stalin—it was prior to Tito's break with Moscow—championed the Yugoslavs, declining to permit the discussions to proceed unless they were present to answer for themselves. Eden remarked that the decision at Yalta was taken without Yugoslav attendance.

As the wrangle proceeded, Truman came in with a sharp intervention. He had not traveled to Europe to hold a police-court hearing on grievances. He wished to deal with the problems the three heads of government had met to settle, otherwise he would pack and go home.[9]

Churchill suggested that the United States' interest might be in the carrying out of the Yalta agreements. The President considered it better to pass on to other matters. In this fashion he allowed to fizzle out the incident of "uncontrolled land-grabbing" that a few weeks earlier he had denounced as a process of blackmail or intimidation.

Over the liberated lands of Rumania, Bulgaria and Hungary, a common line was established against the Russians. At Yalta it had been agreed that democratic governments should be set up under inter-Allied supervision. The Russians had proceeded with their own arrangements, and now sought recognition for the governments they had established. The President declined to accord recognition to these puppet regimes. When the Prime Minister backed up the President, Stalin sharply declared that their attitude precluded the conference from reaching a decision.

Churchill drew attention to the position of Allied missions in these countries. In Bucharest they were penned up as if they were under internment.

"All fairy tales," commented Stalin.

Churchill mildly replied that it was open to statesmen, if they so wished, to call each other's statements fairy tales, but he was satisfied about the accuracy of his information. To end the exchanges, which were becoming heated, Truman proposed referring these questions to the Foreign Ministers for consideration.[10]

According to Truman's account this dispute provoked the bitterest debate of the conference. It may well be so. It was also notable for enabling the President to testify beside the Prime Minister in support of the common democratic faith of Britain and the United States, making a common plea for the observance of the Yalta agreements in which they had an identical interest.[11]

On the future of Italian colonies in Africa, Stalin presented a claim for "some territory of the defeated states." The Soviet Union, he demanded, should be named trustee of one of the African colonies.[12]

The matter, ruled Truman, was one for the peace conference, but it could be discussed. Thereupon, the Prime Minister, speaking with a passion that impressed his American listeners, made indignant protest.

"Britain," he declared, "expects no gain out of this war; we have suffered terrible losses. We have come out of the war a great debtor. But in spite of our heavy losses we make no territorial claims—no Königsberg, no Baltic states, nothing. We therefore approach the question of colonies with complete rectitude. Great Britain has, of course, great interests in the Mediterranean. Any marked change in the *status quo* will need long and anxious consideration. But if there are claimants they should put forward their claims."

Stalin wanted to know whether that meeting was to decide whether Italy was to lose her colonies; if so, it could be decided what states should exercise trusteeship.

"I had not considered the possibility of the Soviet Union desiring to acquire a large tract in the African shore," responded the Prime Minister. "It will have to be considered in relation to many other problems and belongs properly to the peace conference."

The President remitted the problem to the Foreign Ministers for further discussion.

Potsdam was the inconclusive conference. Session after session the debates proceeded, with Churchill challenging the Russians. The temperature would rise, an impasse would be reached, and the chairman would take the easy way out by remitting the question to the Foreign Ministers. So frequently did he revert to the device that Stalin made the comment that with so much passed down to the lower level there would be little left for them to do at the top.[13]

On its social side Potsdam did not fall short of its predecessors. At the state banquets hospitality was lavish and toasting on a scale to impress the new member of the trio. "Stalin's dinner was a wow," Truman wrote home, "with caviar and vodka, watermelon and champagne. There was a toast every five minutes." He ate little and drank less, but made his own contribution to the entertainment that produced the battle of music.[14]

When he was host at dinner he arranged a program to which a pianist in the Services, Sergeant Eugene List, contributed some well-rendered Chopin. Stalin, not to be outdone, summoned prize-winning violinists from Moscow. The strains of Chopin, Liszt, and Tschaikovsky were continued as the vodka flowed.[15]

To a man who is ready to pass the night in talk the rapt attention of the music devotee is an impediment to the exercise of his natural functions. By one o'clock in the morning Churchill's appetite for the classics was exhausted.

"When are we going home?" he whispered to Truman.

The President signified that as a higher devotee he was content to go on enjoying himself and to await his host's pleasure.

"I'm going home now," growled Churchill.

Instead he sat it out, with the glowerings of the non-appreciative listener. It was one-thirty when the musical session ended.

For his turn as host, Churchill arranged for the attendance of the string band of the Royal Air Force. It was after 2 A.M. when he allowed his musicians to sign off. I have not been privileged to share the secrets of the program, but will wager a piccolo against a full orchestra that the classics were imperfectly represented. I should like to think that the guests were regaled with some of the more hearty items in Britain's national repertoire—some nautical ditties, dulcet airs from the Old Kent Road, and maybe, for the benefit of the President, Sousa in his more subtle moments.

"Winston, I found, wasn't very fond of music, at least my kind of music."

This reflection from Mr. Truman comes intriguingly to my mind as I think of those musical evenings. Was it, I wonder, a poignant memory of the roistering hours with the band of the RAF that wrung from him this recollection?

At last came the time when the secrets of the ballot boxes were to be revealed. Discussion of the world's future had to be interrupted for a time while the results of the general election were made known.[16]

At his dinner party Churchill gave the toast: "The Leader of the Opposition, whoever he may be." The company, Clement Attlee with the rest, laughed and cheered as the glasses were raised.

The ninth conference session was brought to a close with Churchill's announcement that he was going home for the poll declarations.

"What a pity," said Stalin.

"I hope to be back," was the parting comment. The following after-noon the Prime Minister was in Downing Street.

CHAPTER SEVEN

THE FALL

JULY–AUGUST, 1945

WINSTON CHURCHILL returned home from Potsdam with no forebodings of defeat. He accepted the assurances of the party managers that when the counting was done he would be returned to power, though with a much reduced majority. Anthony Eden had his doubts and there was a duke, with keen percipience, who foretold disaster for the Tories. But it was generally agreed that Churchill, confirmed in office as Prime Minister, would rejoin Stalin and Truman at Potsdam.

Churchill's sleep that night was troubled. He woke before the dawn with what he described as a feeling almost of physical pain. An obsession of defeat possessed him. He slept again. At nine he woke. The news conformed with his alarm. First results of the poll were consistently unfavorable. So they continued. By noon the verdict was unmistakable—the Socialists would have a majority. By the afternoon it was conclusive and calamitous—the Tories had been overwhelmed.[1]

For the second time in his career, Churchill's fate had been determined by an electoral landslide. In 1906 the Conservatives had been trounced and the young Churchill held office with the triumphant Liberals. In 1945 the Socialists were victorious by a vote scarcely less sweeping. From the stricken field the Tories returned with no more than 197 Members of Parliament, outnumbered almost two to one by 393 Socialists. In the old House of Commons it was the Conservatives who had enjoyed a two-to-one ascendancy.

In contemplating the electoral future, Churchill had resolved that, were the party to suffer defeat, he would remain in office, as was his right, until the new Parliament met, and then accept his dismissal from the House of Commons. This would have permitted him to return to Potsdam to complete the business of the conference. So humiliating, however, was the adverse vote that he felt himself unable to stay at the head of a government under suspended sentence. That evening, with the familiar cigar between his lips, he was seen driving to Buckingham Palace. To the onlookers he gave the greeting of the V-sign. In a brief audience he tendered his resignation to King George VI. The Caretaker Government had gone down, the briefest administration of modern times. The next day Clement Attlee, as new Prime Minister, with Ernest Bevin as Foreign Secretary, took the plane for Germany. Of the three who had met at Yalta, Stalin alone remained at Potsdam.

The news of Winston Churchill's dismissal was widely deplored. Even among political opponents, fiercely eager to replace his Ministry, there was a spasm of sympathy. Among the mass of the people there was a sharp stab of regret. A buttress had gone from the fabric of the state. The future was unknown, uncertain, but plainly hazardous. The familiar figure would no longer be there, conveying by his sturdy presence the sense of security from which confidence had been drawn in the dark days. You could almost feel a pause in affairs as the national mind adjusted itself to the supplanting of "Good old Winnie."

His dismissal was a test of his magnanimity. He had borne the burden of the war. His hopes and his expectations had been concentrated on victory and the people's mandate for the continuance of his services. His disappointment was bitter, and the hurt grievous, that the people should in this manner have requited him for his labors. Of these feelings he gave no sign as he went about his duties as Member of Parliament and Leader of His Majesty's Opposition. No protest or complaint escaped him. His account, in his memoirs, dismisses his defeat in a page of type, ending with his message to the people in which he gave the briefest utterance to his regret he had not been permitted to finish the work against Japan. For this all plans and preparations had been made and the result might come "quicker than heretofore they had been entitled to expect"—a reference, which could not generally be understood, to the new weapon of the atom bomb.

"It only remains for me," he concluded, "to express to the British people, for whom I have acted in these perilous years, my profound gratitude for the unflinching, unswerving support which they have given me during my task, and for the many expressions of kindness which they have shown toward their servant."

In terser fashion Mrs. Churchill pronounced that the defeat might be a blessing in disguise. To which he rejoined: "At the moment it seems quite effectively disguised." We may endorse his wife's sounder view. It was providential that there was to be a break. After all, he was in his seventy-first year and his health, strong though his constitution was, had shown that he could not indefinitely continue to sustain the strains of national leadership. And there were his memoirs to prepare for publication. Caesar might dictate his commentaries in his tent; the Churchillian records required more careful and leisured compilation.[2]

Regarded as an isolated incident in the human tragi-comedy there is a certain fitness about Winston Churchill's fall. He had been called in, it seemed, for the sole, specific purpose of his wartime leadership. As Hitler fired the first shots, he was summoned to office. When Hitler perished, the people were satisfied that his task was done. The circle of his wartime service was rounded off by the voters with the neat precision of the shears of fate.

He suffered a sharp and poignant pang. Had he deserved no better than this from the countrymen he had proudly served? But the dismissal that was wounding to his feelings was the preservation alike of his health and of his reputation.

There have been leaders who remained upon the stage too long for their good fame. Lloyd George's reputation was injured by the years of his peacetime premiership. Churchill escaped the slow decline of an epilogue. Almost before the plaudits of the election campaign had died away he was hustled summarily from office.

After the fall came the inquest into the causes. There was world-wide surprise that the great War Minister had gone down in defeat. Abroad it was incomprehensible, and to many at home it was baffling.

It was from a misreading of the public mind that the seeming mystery arose. It was not on Winston Churchill and the conduct of the war that the electors had given their verdict. Their judgment was passed on the mismanagement before the war that had all but involved the nation in defeat. None knew better than the fighting men how little Britain had had to fight with. They united and their womenfolk joined with them in voting against the rulers who had not prepared against Hitler. The Conservatives had been in office before the war. The voters passed a mass censure on the Conservative Party.

Winston Churchill, the back-bencher of the thirties, critic of Baldwin and Chamberlain, proved the ruin of Churchill the leader of the forties. The speeches of Churchill, the critic of appeasement, swung him into office when the war came. Opinion first molded by those speeches swept him out of office when the war was over, for he had succeeded in the party leadership to the men whom he had denounced. What he had done in the war was brushed aside by the voters as an incidental feature, not relevant to the matter at hand.

The electors, the men of the Services and their womenfolk, had their scores to settle. Blame for all the omissions of the years before the war was laid upon the party which had been preponderant in the House and in the Ministry. The nation had not been prepared for war—blame the Tories! The Empire had been neglected—blame the Tories! Labour might have clamored for collective security while opposing the means to make security secure. But Labour had not been in office. The party in power must take the knock when things go wrong, and in this case things had gone wrong at the very points where the electors had reason to suppose the Conservatives should have been one hundred per cent right.

By tradition and their own claims the Tories have been the party of Empire and a strong Britain. The Empire and Britain's defenses had been neglected in the prewar years. Conservative explanations were not accepted. There had been a revulsion of feeling over appeasement and Munich. Britain's weakness had nearly brought about her defeat and for this unpreparedness scapegoats must be found. You could hear on all hands the opinion that the Conservative Party had been false to its trust and to its faith. It was a reproach against the party that it stood for big business, for wealth and privilege—and big business and privilege were never so little esteemed in Britain as in 1945.

There were the reasons for the landslide that ended the Churchill premiership. His conduct of the election campaign, for which, as the defeated leader, he had to bear the displeasure of the critical, had no influence on the change of government. Other tactics might have reduced the adverse vote; they could not conceivably have reversed it. He had concentrated, apart from the personal attacks on his opponents, on the problems of the peace abroad. The electors, with narrower vision, were concerned with affairs around them and results at home—homes to live in, jobs to work at, and social security.

Here it is proper to take passing note of the social changes that flowed from Churchill's wartime Government. They amounted to a transformation in the nation's life. Almost unnoticed in the peril of the times a vast step had been taken in the process of social equalization.

With the peace there came a realization of the financial upheaval the war had produced in this, the most highly taxed country in the world. The incomes of the wealthy had been drastically reduced. The Prime Minister's salary of £10,000, for example, was cut by taxation to an actual income of £3,168. Even a millionaire found it difficult to draw £5,000 a year out of income. At the other end of the scale, the lot of the lower classes had been so improved that destitution and starvation, by no means uncommon in the hungry thirties, had been abolished. Everywhere equality had been imposed—equality in food and clothing, equality in service, equality in sacrifice. The financial spadework had been done and the state of public opinion had been created for the advance to the welfare state that was to be taken by the Attlee Government.

In the interval that followed before the new Parliament met there was much speculation as to how Churchill and the Tories would comport themselves. They had declared their emphatic and uncompromising hostility to socialism. Were they, in the House, to press their opposition to the limit, national feelings would soon be aflame. In the House of Lords, the Conservative peers would be in a position to veto Socialist legislation. In the days of Churchill's youth, the Tory Lords, in this partisan fashion, had manhandled Liberal legislation, so that it became a reproach that the Upper House was not the watchdog of the Constitution, but only "Mr. Balfour's poodle"—Balfour being the Tory leader of those days. Were these tactics to be repeated and Socialist legislation emasculated, then a crisis would arise.[3]

When Parliament met the Conservative leaders took the earliest opportunity of letting it be known that there would be no factious opposition to the Government's measures. These had been put before the electorate and the Labour Government could claim the possession of a mandate for carrying them out. Said Churchill: "We do not propose to join issue immediately about the legislative proposals. . . . The national ownership of the Bank of England does not in my opinion raise any matter of principle. It may be helpful for me to express the opinion as Leader of the Opposition that foreign countries need not be alarmed— British credit will be resolutely upheld." As to the nationalization of the coal mines: "If that is really the best way of securing a larger supply of coal at a cheaper price and at an earlier moment than is now in view, I, for one, shall approach the plan in a sympathetic spirit. It is by results that the policy must be judged."

There came world-shattering news before Parliament met, with the dropping of the first atomic bombs and the capitulation of the Japanese. These events followed swiftly on the decision taken by President Truman at Potsdam to which Churchill had been an assenting party.

CHAPTER EIGHT

A-BOMB DECISION

JULY-AUGUST, 1945

S CARCELY had Winston Churchill left office as Prime Minister than the world was startled into apprehensiveness by the use of the new and awesome weapon of the atom bomb against the cities of Hiroshima and Nagasaki. Thereby the war with Japan was brought to a summary close.

Had Churchill deferred his resignation by no more than nineteen days, he would have been privileged to announce the achievement of final victory. The interval was too brief for there to be any doubting that it was under his leadership that the Allied plans were agreed and the final decisions taken.

This cooperation in responsibility applied, in particular, to the employment of the A-bomb. The Americans had taken over the industrial processes that transformed the theorizings of the scientists into the most destructive instrument of war evolved by man. It was American airmen who delivered the bombs on the target of the Japanese cities. But the decision that the bomb should be used was one for which Winston Churchill, in the last weeks of his premiership, was responsible no less than President Truman.

There were to follow protests on moral grounds against the use of this thunderbolt of destruction, but Churchill made no pretense of deferring to these opinions. He proclaimed himself thankful that the Allies and not their enemies had won the race of the laboratories. For, during the latter stages of their work, the research team had been urged to press on with all possible speed by reports that the Germans were ahead in the atom race. Herein the Intelligence reports were misleading, grossly exaggerating the progress that had been made in Germany.[1]

It was by a prodigy of effort that the Americans brought the Manhattan Project to the point of success. British scientists had supplied much of the key data on which the research proceeded. But it was American money to the tune of two billion dollars, and American manpower to the total of 125,000 workers, under expert direction, that made the final achievement possible.

By the spring of 1945, the research team was confident it was on the verge of success. One of Truman's first acts as President was to set up a committee to advise on the crucial question: If the know-how is solved, is the A-bomb to be used against the enemy? [2]

The war in Europe was over before this became a matter of practical politics, but the Japanese had still to be defeated. On July 1, 1945, the committee recommended that the bomb be used against the Japanese as soon as possible. It was the first step toward Hiroshima and Nagasaki. The recommendation was the unanimous verdict of a committee of which Secretary Stimson was chairman, and which was formed by leading American figures in the government and scientific fields.

It was considered that the stage had been reached when Great Britain's assent should be obtained. At Quebec, in 1943, President Roosevelt and Winston Churchill had agreed that neither country should employ the A-bomb (if evolved) against a third party without the assent of the other. Accordingly the formal question was put and on July 4 the British Government's consent was formally given. Responsibility for what was to be done was shared by the partners in the alliance.[3]

Expectation was agog when President Truman set off for Potsdam. The time was near when the bomb was to be put to the test. Already in the deserts of New Mexico, in the Alamogordo reservation, preparations to this end were far advanced. On the voyage over, Truman awaited word of the results.[4]

At Potsdam, Churchill was taken into the secret. He was excited by the prospects, eagerly questioning the President about details of the work. His interest, according to the Secretary of State, James Byrnes, was tremendous, and he "foresaw more clearly than many others the possibilities presented by the release of atomic energy." [5]

At last, on July 16, there came the signal of success. The sands of Alamogordo had been illuminated by the gigantic flashlight of the first man-contrived detonation of the atom.

BABIES SATISFACTORILY BORN.

It was the code message announcing that the test had been made and that the bomb would blast. Truman was given the cable. It was the fulfillment of his hopes. The most secret enterprise of the war had succeeded. The United States, reflected Truman, had in its possession an explosive force of unparalleled power.

Winston Churchill was informed. Secretary Stimson arrived at Potsdam by plane with details of what had occurred in the New Mexican desert. The power of the explosion measured up to the highest estimates. The A-bomb was a weapon of revolutionary power. Churchill listened for the first time to a description of the scene—of the column of flame and smoke that ascended to the heavens, shooting up to the fringe of the atmosphere, of the devastation that was wrought below, everything within a one-mile circle suffering destruction. A vast crater, four hundred yards in radius, had been torn out of the desert, and this was glazed with a green glass, for the sand had melted and then solidified again.

A council of war followed. The blast in the desert had transformed the strategy of the war in the Far East. A revaluation was imperative. The Prime Minister joined the President, who had with him General Marshall and Admiral Leahy. From that conference originated the arrangements for the employment of the bomb against the Japanese.[6]

There was no formal decision to use the bomb. That was never in issue. There was, according to Churchill, unanimous, automatic, unquestioned agreement around that conference table that the bomb should be employed. Truman had never had any doubt about it. His military advisers were unanimous in their support. Churchill never heard the slightest suggestion that any other course should be taken. He himself had no hesitation. The moral issues that were afterward to be raised by those who protested against the "barbarism," the "crime," and the "mass murder" of Hiroshima were not debated. Had they been raised they would have been ruled out as irrelevant.[7]

To employ the A-bomb was a matter of military necessity.* The strategic argument was simple and compelling. The fanatical Japanese, prepared for death rather than dishonor, might cause the loss of a million lives to the Americans—"and half that number of British for we were resolved to share the agony." [8]

* I take no account of the disclosures that have been made concerning Japanese peace approaches to the United States and the contention that the bombs on Hiroshima and Nagasaki were superfluous barbarities against an enemy already bent on capitulation. These are matters affecting the President and his advisers, but not the Prime Minister, who was imperfectly informed concerning them.

Even greater losses would be suffered by the Japanese themselves. These lives might be saved by the terrifying intimidation of this weapon against which there could be no protection and no reply. Humanitarian influences seemed to support what strategy required. So far as the reckoning in human suffering was computed, it seemed almost to be doing a service to the Japanese, no less than to the Allies, to end the war "in one or two violent shocks" of atomic devastation.

From his war memoirs you may note how Churchill's imagination was fired by the prospect now opened up. His vision ("fair and bright indeed") was concentrated on the swift curtailment of what he had foreseen as a protracted and bloody struggle. Moreover, there would no longer be need for the cooperation of the Russian armies, and that was a circumstance promising a happier prospect for Europe, for no longer would Stalin need to be cajoled by concessions.

Truman's mind did not range so far. He was occupied with the practical consideration of how the arrangements could be made to produce the greatest psychological results upon the Japanese. The laws of war must be strictly conformed with and military targets picked for the first A-bomb assaults. Kyoto was originally in the list of targets but was eliminated on the ground that it was a cultural and religious shrine. So four cities were named, headed by Hiroshima, strategic headquarters of the forces defending southern Japan.

A more ticklish problem was what to do about the Russians. Truman was resolved that Stalin must be told. When was the disclosure to be made—forthwith, or at the close of the Potsdam conference? Churchill was against delay:

> If it were done when 'tis done, then 'twere well
> It were done quickly. . . .

It was so decided. Stalin would be informed that a new form of bomb, something quite out of the ordinary, had been evolved, that was going to have decisive effects on the Japanese.[9] Accordingly, when the conference discussions had been ended on the afternoon of July 24, Truman walked around the circular table to where Stalin was seated amidst his entourage. Truman's words were repeated by the interpreter. Stalin registered delight at what he had heard, but not surprise. Certainly he gave no hint that he had been impressed by the nature of the disclosure made to him.

It was a brief encounter. "How did it go?" asked Churchill as they were about to drive away. Truman replied that Stalin had asked no questions. He had displayed no unusual interest, remarking merely that he was glad to receive the news and hoped that "good use" would be made of the bomb against the Japanese.

Nor, at the next meeting, did Stalin bring up the subject by asking for further information. Had he failed to grasp the import of the discovery? More probably, as Byrnes surmised, the Generalissimo followed the example of his own reserve. The Russians kept quiet about the secrets of their military developments and thought it improper to question their Allies.

The formality of a last-minute appeal was observed, the Japanese being called on to avoid further bloodshed by capitulation. This was in the form of an ultimatum in the names of the President of the United States, the President of the National Government of China, and the Prime Minister of Great Britain. Bearing the date July 26, it was the last public declaration of Churchill's premiership. It called for surrender as an alternative to the complete destruction of the Japanese forces and the utter devastation of the Japanese homeland.

No mention was made of the new weapon. Complete secrecy was enjoined, for doubt still lingered about the effectiveness of the bomb. In New Mexico it had been exploded from a pylon, but it did not necessarily follow that it would function when dropped from the air.

There was hope among the Americans, according to Secretary Stimson, that the Japanese would forestall the impending calamity by offering to yield. Two days later, however, their Premier made the reply that the Allied ultimatum was "unworthy of public notice." Accordingly the arrangements for the dropping of the first bomb, under orders issued to General Spaatz, Commanding General of the U.S. Strategic Air Forces, were suffered to proceed.[10]

By that time the Potsdam conference had been wound up. In its concluding stages Clement Attlee had replaced Winston Churchill as the leading British representative, but the change in premiership brought no reversal of British policy as regards the bomb. The former decision was not called in question and Attlee, had the responsibility rested with him, would have decided as Churchill had done.[11]

The President, on his way home, called at Plymouth where he met King George VI, who was eager to know all about the bomb, of which he had been informed by Churchill. Contrary to Admiral Leahy, who was utterly skeptical, the King was completely confident of the results that would be achieved.[12]

News came on the fourth day of the President's homeward trip. He was at lunch aboard the *Augusta* when a cable was handed to him: "Big bomb dropped," it read. "Success even more conspicuous than earlier test."

The President, deeply stirred, greeted the occasion with another of his penetrating comments. "This," he said, "is the greatest thing in history. It's time for us to get home." [13]

Later that day there was issued from 10 Downing Street a statement on the bomb that Winston Churchill had drawn up before leaving office, in readiness for the occasion. It was a comprehensive and factual account of the cooperation between Great Britain and the United States that had wrested from nature this secret of the universe. No technical information was given—that was not Churchill's purpose. He was concerned solely to tell the tale of the progress of research. Two points he emphasized—the contribution made by British scientists in the earlier stages, which, as I have already indicated, came as a stimulus to the American physicists when their spirits were flagging; and the stupendous efforts made by the Americans in the later stages, when immense industrial plants were required. Acknowledgment was also made to the contribution of the Canadian Government, in providing raw material for the project as a whole and also the facilities for work on one section undertaken in Canada by the three countries in partnership.

> The smoothness with which the arrangements for cooperation were carried into effect [proceeded Churchill] is a happy augury for our future relations.
> By God's mercy British and American science outpaced all German efforts. These were on a considerable scale, but far behind. Every effort was made by our Intelligence Service and by the Air Force to locate in Germany anything resembling the plants being built in the United States. In the winter of 1942-3 most gallant attacks were made in Norway upon stores of what is called "heavy water," an element in one of the possible processes. The second attack was completely successful.

The statement concluded with Churchill's tribute to Roosevelt for having authorized the spending of enormous sums of money on what, in the early stages, had been a heart-shaking risk. "This stands to the everlasting honor of President Roosevelt and his advisers."

Events moved to their swift conclusion. Three days later the second bomb was dropped on Nagasaki. Within twenty-four hours the Japanese Government offered to surrender, in compliance with the ultimatum issued by President Truman, Prime Minister Churchill, and Generalissimo Chiang Kai-shek. On August 14—the pressure of destruction having been maintained by the bombing of Tokyo—Japan's complete and final surrender was tendered and accepted. Six days before the end the Russians hurried out their declaration of war. They had no time to fight, but exacted the full terms in payment for their belligerency.

Winston Churchill was in his place in the House of Commons as Leader of the Opposition when Parliament took cognizance of the final success. Three months earlier he had moved an address of congratulation to the King on the end of the war in Europe. Now (August 15) he, as Opposition Leader, seconded the address on victory over Japan:

> Our cause has been carried to complete success. Total war has ended in absolute victory. Once again the British Commonwealth and Empire emerges safe, undiminished, and united from a mortal struggle. Monstrous tyrannies that menaced our life have been beaten to the ground in ruin.

On the following day, August 16, the old Prime Minister and the new delivered in the House their winding-up-the-war speeches. By that time public expression had been given to the sense of uneasiness, alarm, and reprobation which in their varying degree had been aroused among people whose feelings had been moved by accounts of the sufferings of the victims of the first A-bombs in Hiroshima and Nagasaki. Churchill made answer to them:

> There are those who consider that the atomic bomb should never have been used at all. I cannot associate myself with such ideas. Six years of total war have convinced most people that had the Germans or Japanese discovered this new weapon they would have used it upon us to our complete destruction with the utmost alacrity. I am surprised that very worthy people—but people who in most cases had no intention of proceeding to the Japanese Front themselves—should adopt the position that rather than throw this bomb we should have sacrificed a million American and 250,000 British lives in the desperate battles of an invasion of Japan. Future generations will judge this dire decision. I believe if they find themselves dwelling in a happier world, from which war has been banished, and where freedom reigns, they will not condemn those who struggled for their benefit amid the horrors and miseries of this grim and ferocious struggle.
>
> The bomb brought peace, but man alone can keep that peace. I am in entire agreement with President Truman that the secret of this bomb shall, so far as possible, not be turned over at the present time to any other country. This is in no desire or wish for arbitrary power, but for the common safety of the world.

At that date it was calculated that the United States was likely to remain for four years in a position of unchallengeable supremacy by virtue of the A-bomb. This expectation was defeated by spies and traitors in the Allied camp. The Russians were let into the secret and produced their own, posing, thereby, problems that were to confront Winston Churchill in his later term as Prime Minister.

BOOK FIVE

ALLIES IN THE COLD WAR

CHAPTER ONE

FULTON—A LINE FOR THE WEST

MARCH, 1946

IN or out of office was of no matter. Churchill's was the leadership
that the free peoples were to follow on either side of the Atlantic. At
Fulton, Missouri, nine months after his dismissal from office, he set
before them the policy that was to guide them in their relations with
Soviet Russia.

The Fulton speech rounded off the contributions of the Churchill
premiership, yielding him at last the concerting of policy between Britain and the United States for which as Prime Minister he had pleaded
in vain.

Before Fulton, illusions had persisted in the West. There had been
an emotional upsurge for the Russians—the Communists referred to it
contemptuously as the "Red haze"—product of the wartime admiration
of the courage and achievements of the Red armies. The Fulton speech
puffed the "Red haze" away. Illusions faded. The democracies were
roused in time against the peril in which they were placed to take the
steps needed to protect themselves against an aggressive Stalinism.

The significance of Fulton and the service Churchill then rendered
have been pretty well forgotten as the tide of events has rolled on. For
so long have we been accustomed to the idea of a line-up in the West
that an effort of recollection is needed to re-create the climate of opinion
in the early days of peace.

With the Germans vanquished, the peoples of the West looked for an era of tranquillity. They in no way shared Churchill's apprehensions over "Soviet maneuverings," for they had not undergone his experience of dealing with Stalin. In their easygoing amiability they accepted the Russians as fellow travelers in a world freed from Nazis, Fascists, and dictators. In the general election the Socialist leaders had fostered the notion that under a Labour Government relations with Moscow would improve, for the left would then be speaking to the left.

From his desk at the Foreign Office Ernest Bevin looked in vain for the realization of those expectations, but despite a succession of rebuffs his hopes persisted. In Washington the Secretary of State, James Byrnes, was content to drift along and there was no break in the Roosevelt notion of hoping for the best from the Russians. There were few who felt like Senator Vandenberg that it was time for a firm line to be taken to disabuse the Soviet leaders of the idea that the Americans could be forever "shoved around like a fourth-rate power by contemptuous dictators in the Kremlin." [1]

The British electors had set Churchill free from the responsibilities of office, but they could not relieve him of his anxieties for the future in a Europe dominated by the Soviets. While still in office he had cabled to Stalin in an attempt to find the means to stave off the dangers he foresaw from conflict between the communist and the noncommunist worlds:

> There is not much comfort in looking to a future where you and the countries you dominate, plus the Communist Parties in many other states, are all drawn up on one side, and those who rally to the English-speaking nations and their associates or dominions are on the other. It is quite obvious that their quarrel would tear the world to pieces, and that all of us leading men on either side who had anything to do with that would be shamed before history. [2]

It was a vain approach. Stalin disdained history's shame. When the new Parliament met in the autumn of 1945, Churchill gave a covert warning to the Russians against the course they were taking. He paid his tribute to Stalin, "that truly great man," and went on to use a phrase that set reflective minds pondering. It was, he declared, inconceivable that Britain would follow an anti-Russian policy. "Nothing but a long period of very marked injuries and antagonisms, which we all hope may be averted, could develop again any such mood in this land." There was a hint of things to come, but his words gained no general attention.

By the time the peace was six months old, Churchill had come to the conclusion that it was time to "speak out in arresting terms about the plight of the world." [3] An invitation from across the Atlantic offered an opportunity. It was from Westminster College, Fulton, in President Truman's home state of Missouri, the college proposing to confer on him the honor of a degree. There was the chance, denied him during his premiership, to rouse the American people and their leaders to the realization of the plain fact that the salvation of the world depended on the acceptance by the United States of the continuance in peace of the wartime association with Britain.

Traveling to Missouri by way of Washington, Churchill was the President's guest, which underlined the significance of the ideas he was about to communicate to the world. It also provided the opportunity for consultation. As Prime Minister he had never failed to obtain Presidential approbation for any speech he was to deliver on American soil.[4] On this occasion Truman emphasized his approval by traveling the one thousand miles to be present to introduce the speaker to his audience.

Over 40,000 persons flocked into Fulton, of which the population at that time was no more than 7,000. For the most part they had to be content to listen in at overflow meetings. With other listeners throughout the United States they could note the boisterous cheering with which Westminster College greeted the visitor.

"The Sinews of Peace" speech was the title Churchill himself gave to his address, and he opened with a passage riveting attention on the main purpose he had in view. He was going to sound a warning about the Russians, but warning would count for little unless it led to action. Action could be effective only if taken in concert with the United States. He went straight to the point:

> The United States stands at this time at the pinnacle of world power. It is a solemn moment for the American democracy. For with primacy in power is also joined an awe-inspiring accountability to the future. If you look around you, you must feel not only the sense of duty done but also you must feel anxiety lest you fall below the level of achievement. Opportunity is here, now, clear and shining for both our countries.

What in the existing world situation was the "over-all strategic concept"? It was to shield the common people against the two giant marauders of war and tyranny. There was the role for the United Nations Organization to fulfill. But there was need to ensure that Britain and the United States did not cast away the solid assurances of national armaments, those essential means for self-preservation, before the new temple of the United Nations was made secure.

A passage on the atomic bomb followed, and the sharing of secrets that were still the exclusive possession of the West. At that time there was a proposal that the atom bomb should be placed under control of the United Nations. The suggestion had even been made that certain atomic information should be turned over to the Russians, a proposition that Secretary of State Byrnes was understood to support, to the alarm of members of the Senate Atomic Energy Committee, Vandenberg among them, who made a sharp protest to the President.[5]

The passage on the atomic bomb has the appearance of having been incorporated as an afterthought in the body of the address, an addition resulting from the talks Churchill had with the President.

> It would be wrong and imprudent [Churchill declared] to entrust the secret knowledge or experience of the atomic bomb, which the United States, Great Britain, and Canada share, to the world organization. It would be criminal madness to cast it adrift in this agitated and un-united world. No one in this country has slept less well in their beds because this knowledge, and the method and the raw materials to apply it, are at present largely retained in American hands. I do not believe we should have slept so soundly had the position been reversed and if some Communist or neo-Fascist state monopolized, for the time being, these dread agencies. The fear of them alone might easily have been used to enforce totalitarian systems upon the free democratic world, with consequences appalling to human imagination. God has willed that this shall not be, and we have at least a breathing space to set our house in order before this peril is encountered.

Churchill passed on to the crux of what he had crossed the Atlantic to say and to proclaim the need for the continued fraternal association of the English-speaking peoples. There was need, in peace, as well as in wartime, to preserve "the intimate relationship between our military advisers leading to the interchange of officers and cadets and weapons, with the continuance of facilities for mutual security by the joint use of all naval and air force bases all over the world." Such measures were needed for the preservation of the temple of peace and to prevent the Dark Ages returning to the world on the gleaming wings of science.

There followed words of grave warning against the peril to freedom from an aggressive communism. In his messages to the White House, sent while he was still Prime Minister, he had coined the phrase "the Iron Curtain." Now in this public address to the people of Fulton and their fellow citizens he gave to it a wider circulation.

> Beware, I say, time may be short. . . . A shadow has fallen upon the scenes so lately lighted by the Allied victory. Nobody knows

what Soviet Russia and its Communist international organization intends to do in the immediate future, or what are the limits, if any, to their expansive and proselytizing tendencies. . . .

From Stettin in the Baltic to Trieste in the Adriatic, an iron curtain has descended across the Continent. Behind that line lie all the capitals of the ancient states of central and eastern Europe. Warsaw, Berlin, Prague, Vienna, Budapest, Belgrade, Bucharest, and Sofia, all these famous cities and the populations around them lie in what I must call the Soviet sphere, and all are subject, in one form or another, not only to Soviet influence but to a very high and, in many cases, increasing measure of control from Moscow. Athens alone— Greece with its immortal glories—is free to decide its future at an election under British, American, and French observation.

The Russian-dominated Polish Government has been encouraged to make enormous and wrongful inroads upon Germany, and mass expulsions of millions of Germans on a scale grievous and undreamed-of are now taking place. The Communist parties, which were very small in all these eastern states of Europe, have been raised to pre-eminence and power far beyond their numbers and are seeking everywhere to obtain totalitarian control. Police governments are prevailing in nearly every case, and so far, except in Czechoslovakia, there is no true democracy. Whatever conclusions may be drawn from these facts—and facts they are—this is certainly not the Liberated Europe we fought to build up. Nor is it one which contains the essentials of permanent peace.

In a great number of countries, far from the Russian frontiers and throughout the world, Communist fifth columns are established and work in complete unity and absolute obedience to the directions they receive from the Communist center. Except in the British Commonwealth and in the United States, where communism is in its infancy, the Communist parties, or fifth columns, constitute a growing challenge and peril to Christian civilization. These are somber facts for anyone to have to recite on the morrow of a victory gained by so much splendid comradeship in arms and in the cause of freedom and democracy. But we should be most unwise not to face them squarely while time remains. . . . I do not believe that Soviet Russia desires war. What the Russians desire is the fruits of war and the indefinite expansion of their power and doctrines.

The address ended, as it began, with a call for the English-speaking peoples to unite in the defense of their freedom and their way of life.

If the population of the English-speaking Commonwealths be added to the United States, with cooperation in the air, in the sea, all over the globe, in science and in industry and in moral force, there will be no quivering, precarious balance of power to offer its temptation to ambition or adventure. On the contrary there will be an overwhelming assurance of security.

The Fulton speech provoked the sensations of a nine days' wonder. As with all statements of new truth that call men from their previous errors, it provoked the outcries that attend the painful process of national re-thinking. So far ahead was Churchill of prevailing opinion that he caused surprise and indignation on both sides of the Atlantic and he was reproved for his 'imprudence' and 'irresponsibility.' In America, Eleanor Roosevelt, in her syndicated column, expressed the fear that an Anglo-American alliance might provoke inconvenient counter-alliances in other parts of the world. A joint statement by three Democratic Senators (Pepper, Kilgore and Glen Taylor) described the speech as "shocking." Henry Wallace, then Secretary of Commerce, agreed. "Mr. Churchill," he said, "is not speaking for the American people and their government."

At home in Britain, Mr. Warbey asked in the House if the Prime Minister would confirm that the Government "entirely disapproves of the tone and temper of the speech." Clement Attlee replied that the Government was not called upon to express any opinion on a speech delivered in another country by a private individual.

A motion of protest, backed by the signatures of a hundred M.P.s, appeared on the Order Paper of the House of Commons. It was not proceeded with.

In Russia there was an outcry. Stalin gave a denunciatory interview to *Pravda,* which Moscow radio broadcast eight days after Fulton. Churchill's speech, averred the Generalissimo, was a "dangerous act, calculated to sow the seeds of discord among Allied governments and hamper their cooperation." Churchill was accused of rudeness, lack of tact, shameless libel, blatant distortion of facts. Like Hitler, he was letting war loose by a racial theory. He and his friends considered that the English-speaking nations, because they were the only "fully valuable nations," should rule the rest of mankind.

By midsummer the breakdown in collaboration between East and West was patent for all to see. Ernest Bevin, in a foreign affairs debate, presented a somber indictment of the men of the Kremlin for the treatment accorded to the Western Allies and the campaign of vilification conducted by the Soviet propaganda machine. In the space of three months the forebodings of the "Sinews of Peace" address had been borne out, "outpaced and overpassed" by events. The language of Fulton had become the policy of the Government of the United Kingdom and of the Administration of the United States.

It was too late to undo what had been done when the Russians had been admitted far into central Europe. There could be no penetration of the Iron Curtain. But Churchill's call had been made in time to arrest further yielding to Soviet pressure before it was too late. Fulton was followed by the Marshall Plan and the setting up of NATO. The course Churchill had taken in his premiership had been justified. He had declined to "go it alone," to commit Britain in isolation to resistance to Stalinism. Now Fulton had accorded him the reward for his patience and persistence. The peoples of Britain and the United States marched once again in step, strengthened by the union of hearts for which he pleaded, "based upon conviction and common ideals." Fulton crowned the work of Churchill's wartime premiership.

CHAPTER TWO

LEADING THE OPPOSITION

1945-1951

OR THE six years that followed his dismissal from office, Winston
Churchill was the leader of His Majesty's Opposition. It was not
the ideal position for the exercise of his talents. On the great occasion
he did all that could be required of him in leading the attack against
the Socialists and their policies. He made the rousing speeches, he denounced the schemes of nationalization with an exuberance of phrase.
But not for him the day-by-day attendance at debates and the endurance,
hour-by-hour, of the reiterations of parliamentary oratory. To profit from
the mistakes of the party in power, the Opposition Leader need always
to be at hand to exploit the situation as it may arise. Having participated
in the councils of the Allied leaders in war, Churchill had little patience
with the outpourings of the back-bencher. Other men's speeches had
never been greatly to his taste. There were frequent periods of absence
from his place in the House as he traveled about the world to contribute
to the conduct of affairs, for though out of office, he was recognized
abroad as the leading statesman of his country.

After his defeat at the polls there had been much speculation over the
course he would follow. He was closely watched, but he gave no sign
of the heart-searing chagrin he felt at his political defeat in the hour of
national triumph. *Serenitas, dignitas*—the Roman qualities were his. It
might have been otherwise. Like Achilles he might have withdrawn dis-
dainfully to his tent. He felt the temptation, he confessed it, to retire

gracefully "in an odor of civic freedoms." It was expected of him. There was pity for the great man in decline. One M.P. presented to the House a picture of Churchill as a noble stag dying with the curs at his throat, a scene depicted with becoming pathos. Churchill rejected the offered role. His duty was to remain in politics. His purpose was "to try to prevent the great position we won in the war from being cast away by folly and worse than folly on the morrow of victory."

When the guns had ceased to fire and the last bomb had been dropped, the people in their relief looked forward to the return of the old days and the easier ways before the dictators came. Churchill had a surer sense of the realities. In one of his first surveys of affairs in the new House of Commons he voiced his apprehensions about the future. "I must tell the House," he said, "speaking from my own knowledge, that the world outlook is in several respects less promising today than it seemed after the capitulation of 1918 and the Treaty of Versailles in 1919." It was no time for the national watchdog to relax.

Looking back on his leadership of the Opposition in the years of the Socialist Parliament, he claimed: "In all the main issues of foreign policy, we of the Opposition supported, sustained, and even pointed the course which the Foreign Secretary has pursued." The record bore out the claim.

It was Churchill who provided the Government with a solution of their problem in Palestine. It was he, in his Fulton speech, who formulated Allied policy toward Soviet Russia. It was he who, in his address at Zurich, gave the states of western Europe the lead to defense through unity, and his were the ideas that found their practical embodiment in the Atlantic Pact.

In home affairs, during the years of transition to the new order of socialism, Churchill played the part of national shock-absorber, bearing in his own solid person the first impact of change. He was a steadying and stabilizing influence, reducing the risks of rancor and the clash of classes when it was sought to divide the nation between the "vermin," as Aneurin Bevan termed the Tories, and the not so verminous. In the days when national bankruptcy seemed to be the imminent fruit of victory, his robust optimism tempered the depressions if not the rigor of austerity under the Socialist Chancellor of the Exchequer, Stafford Cripps.

The patriot statesman was also the party leader. When national circumstances were no obstacle, he embroiled himself in the fray (and fun) of party politics.

Graceful "odor of civil freedoms"—it was far from that. The vigorous septuagenarian displayed a vitality youth might envy. His varied achievements in the First World War, the burden of leadership in the Second, had not exhausted his energies. The Leader of His Majesty's Opposition found the time and strength to continue his missions abroad, on both sides of the Atlantic.

In the autumn of 1945 he was in Flanders to receive the honors of Brussels and Louvain. Early in 1946 he traveled to the United States to set the world's ears tingling with his Fulton speech. In May he addressed the States-General of the Netherlands. In September he delivered at Zurich the address in which for western Europe he pointed the way to survival. The years that followed were marked by further journeys in furtherance of his designs to achieve the unity of Europe. In 1948 he traveled to Oslo to receive a doctorate from the university and to address the Norwegian legislature. At Strasbourg in August, 1949, he was received with acclamation as the "first citizen of Europe" at the foundation meeting of the Council of Europe.

Amidst the pressure of affairs, he found the time to labor as chronicler of the history he had helped to make. It was with characteristic jest that he referred to his writings when a Socialist member in the House was seeking to make party capital out of the past. Churchill advised him to leave the past to history—especially as he would be writing that history himself.

Like Caesar before him he relied for assistance in the compilation of his war memoirs upon a team of amanuenses. Sheet by sheet and galley proof by galley proof he subjected his copy to sixfold revision, to the distraction and dismay of his printers. The first volume, *The Gathering Storm,* was published in October, 1948. The sixth, carrying events down to his fall from power, appeared in 1954. By then the record ran to nearly three million words. Never since Macaulay has history been read with such enthusiasm. Of the first volume, a record printing of 205,000 copies in Britain sold out within a few hours. For *Their Finest Hour,* the first British printing was 276,000. It sold as speedily as its predecessor.

A statesman-author must have his diversions from great affairs. Churchill found them on the farm—he was proud of his prize-winning Shorthorns at Chartwell—and on the turf. He registered his colors—chocolate, pink sleeves and cap—in the summer of 1949, and with his colt Colonist II won the Ribblesdale Stakes at Ascot and the Lime Tree Stakes at Windsor. As painter he received in February, 1949, the unique distinction of a diploma as Honorary Royal Academician Extraordinary; in the following May, six of his canvases were hung at Burlington House.

It was a Socialist Parliament that met in 1945. The nationalization of banks, mines and railroads was the subject most frequently debated. To this topic the Leader of the Opposition devoted a succession of vigorous denunciations, infinitely varied in their attack, but constant in their main objection: nationalization must fail because as a means of conducting business it was inefficient. It involved replacing the profit motive with the loss motive and, with its mounting thousands of civil servants, must reduce Britain to beggary and destitution. In Victorian days there had been anxiety about the submerged tenth; socialism was no longer a plan for helping the submerged tenth, but of submerging the other nine-tenths down to their level. Hagridden by Socialist doctrinaires the country, he submitted, was hampered and hobbled in its struggle for survival. The Government, for the sake of party fads and cast-iron Socialist dogmas, was impeding the national recovery:

> All enterprise is baffled and fettered. The interference of Government departments with daily life is more severe and galling. More forms have to be filled up, more officials consulted. Whole spheres of potential activity are frozen, rigid and numb, because this Government has to prove its socialist sincerity, instead of showing how they can get the country alive and on the move again.

With the launching of the National Health scheme, the Beveridge plan was put into operation. Here Churchill was not prepared to surrender to his opponents the patent rights in social reform. He protested against Socialist boastings:

> They dilate upon the National Insurance scheme, family allowances, improved education, welfare foods, food subsidies, and so forth. They point to the benefits flowing to the people and particularly to the housewives and children from these schemes. But there are facts which, up till quite recently, they have tried to hide. The first is that all these schemes were devised and set in motion in days before the Socialists came into power. They all date from the National Coalition Government of which I was the head.
>
> I have worked at national insurance schemes almost all my life and am responsible for some of the largest measures ever passed, both under Mr. Asquith as Prime Minister, and under Mr. Baldwin. The main principles of the new health schemes were hammered out in the coalition days before the party and personal malignancy of Mr. Bevan plunged health policy into its present confusion.

The 1945 Parliament brought to a close Churchill's long campaign on India. Under Lord Mountbatten, last of the Viceroys, the final arrangements were pushed through to hand over power to the Indian people. At midnight on August 14, 1947, King George VI ceased to be Emperor of India and the two new states of India and Pakistan came into being. In the closing stages of the negotiations between the Viceroy and the Indians, Churchill spoke with foreboding of the handing over of the government to Mr. Nehru with consequences that might darken ("and redden") the coming years.

When all was complete, negotiations ended and the necessary bill presented for Parliamentary approval, he announced his acquiescence. What had been done reflected credit not only on the Viceroy but on the Prime Minister who had appointed him. The day of the British "Raj" was ended. It was the end, too, of the Indian campaign which Churchill had sustained over the years.

After India, Burma. Here a personal note was struck in protest against the abandonment of what under his father had been gained, for it was during Lord Randolph Churchill's occupancy of the India Office that Burma was annexed to the Crown in 1885. As soon as he became aware of the Socialist determination to sever Burma from the Empire, Churchill rose in emphatic protest.

> It was said in the days of the administration of Lord Chatham [he recalled] that one had to get up very early in the morning in order not to miss the gains and accessions of territory which were then characteristic of our fortunes. The no less memorable administration of the Right Honorable Gentleman opposite is distinguished for the opposite set of experiences. The British Empire seems to be running off almost as fast as the American loan. The steady and remorseless process of divesting ourselves of what has been gained by so many generations of toil, administration and sacrifice continues. . . . The haste is appalling. "Scuttle" is the word, and the only word, that can be applied. What, spread over a number of years, would be a healthy constitutional process, and might easily have given the Burmese people an opportunity for continuing their association with our congregation of nations, has been cast aside.

Clement Attlee's handling of negotiations for the revision of the treaty with Egypt drew another indignant protest from the Opposition Leader. On the eve of the abortive discussions in May, 1946, Attlee announced the Government's decision to withdraw all British sea, land and air forces from Egypt. Churchill asked how the Suez Canal was to be defended if there were to be no troops on the spot?

When he spoke of Britain's diplomatic and administrative links with Egypt over sixty years, the Communist Piratin interpolated, "That is long enough." Churchill turned on him in angry reproof. "Things are built up with great labor," he exclaimed, "and cast away with great shame and folly."

On India and Burma and other aspects of Operation "Scuttle" (in his derisive, despairing phrase), Churchill spoke without influence on events.

On Palestine his speeches had their effect on Government policy and the development of affairs. Zionists had been heartened by the pledges they had received from leading Socialists during the 1945 election for the setting up of a Jewish national state, but with the Socialists in office, months drifted by and election pledges were unredeemed. By terrorist tactics Jewish fanatics sought to extort the fulfillment of their expectations. It was found necessary to guard Ernest Bevin against the peril of the assassin's bullet. Outrage followed outrage in Palestine, tension mounted between Jew and Arab. While schemes for a settlement were canvassed and rejected, British forces had the responsibility for maintaining law and order. British soldiers were kidnaped and tortured; British lives were lost. A settlement seemed no nearer. As the holder of the mandate, Britain had to bear the world's reproaches for the consequences to the Holy Land of a policy of drift, and in particular the reproaches of Jewish-inspired opinion in the United States.

On the eve of the summer recess in August, 1946, the House debated the Palestine impasse. A few days previously terrorists of the Irgun Zvai Leumi had blown up a wing of the King David Hotel in Jerusalem used as British military headquarters, killing ninety-one persons and injuring forty-five others. Public opinion was gravely shocked. Two principal Ministers, Stafford Cripps and Herbert Morrison, made the Government's defense, but it was the Leader of the Opposition who presented a policy to meet the occasion.

Churchill spoke, as he reminded his fellow members, with the authority of one who, as Colonial Secretary in 1922, had defined, with the authority of Cabinet and Parliament, the interpretation to be placed upon British obligations when the mandate for Palestine was accepted from the League of Nations. These obligations, with the delicate balancing of the opposing claims of Jew and Arab, had been faithfully fulfilled during the years that followed.

Churchill paused in his survey to dispose of the picture Stafford Cripps had given of the previous twenty-five years as having been the most unhappy Palestine had known. "I imagine," he said, "it would hardly be possible to state the opposite of truth more compendiously." It was the neglect of Ministers to fulfill their election pledges that, said Churchill, was at the root of the current difficulties, which had been accentuated by the attempt of the Government to make Palestine contribute to a solution of the problem in Egypt. He went on:

> Take stock around the world at the present moment. We declare ourselves ready to abandon the mighty Empire and Continent of India with all the work we have done in the last two hundred years. We scuttle from Egypt, which we twice successfully defended from foreign massacre and pillage. We scuttle from it, we abandon the Canal zone about which our treaty rights were and still are indefeasible. But now, apparently, the one place where we are at all

costs and at all inconveniences to hold on and fight it out to the death is Palestine, and, if necessary, with the Arabs of Palestine. For what reason? Not, all the world will say, for the faithful discharge of our long mission but because we have need, having been driven out of Egypt, to secure a satisfactory strategic base in the Near East from which to pursue our Imperial aims.

I wish to look forward before I conclude. I will not go so far in criticizing and in censuring without proposing positive action, with all the responsibility and the exposure to counterattack which one incurs when one proposes definite and serious action. Here is the action—action this day.

I think the Government should say that if the United States will not come and share the burden of the Zionist cause, as defined or as agreed, we should now give notice that we will return our mandate to the U.N.O. and that we will evacuate Palestine within a specified period. At the same time, we should inform Egypt that we stand by our treaty rights and will, by all means, maintain our position in the Canal zone. Those are the two positive proposals which I submit, most respectfully, to the House. In so far as the Government may have hampered themselves in any way from adopting these simple policies, they are culpable in the last degree, and the whole Empire and the Commonwealth will be the sufferers from their mismanagement.

It is a matter of history that on May 15, 1948, the British mandate in Palestine was terminated, whereupon the independent Jewish State of Israel was proclaimed. There had been an inevitable delay before the Ministers brought themselves to the unpalatable pitch of accepting the proposals of their opponent. Under Churchill's lead they at length found the way to the ultimate settlement of one of the more troublous of Britain's problem. On Egypt also they were moved to second thoughts.

The passing of the years and the anxieties of the times had not extinguished Churchill the jester. Having sat as a young man among the parliamentary wits, he enlivened the 1945 House of Commons with repartee that recalled the days when speakers put art as well as noise into their abuse. Opponents massed vociferously on the opposite benches gave him opportunity enough for scoring off the parliamentary heckler, until, by experience and the advice of their leaders, Socialist back-benchers ceased to offer themselves so readily as targets for the picador of debate. *Hansard* preserves gems of Churchillian wit during the Socialist Parliament.

During one Churchill speech, Piratin, the Communist, was inspired to cry out, "Shame." Quickly came the retort, "The Honorable Member is a good judge of shame."

Herbert Morrison interjected a question in the course of another Churchill speech, and his followers considered that his query did not receive due reply. "Answer," they shouted at Churchill. "There is nothing to answer," he retorted, which was received with bursts of laughter. "I always notice," he commented, "that the party opposite indulge in laughter which resembles the crackling of thorns under a pot whenever they are confronted with any mental proposition which their intelligence forces them to resent or reject."

During exchanges in debate, Hartley Shawcross shook his head to indicate dissent from one of Churchill's assertions. "The Attorney General," remarked the Opposition Leader, "shakes his head; he would shake it at almost anything. He has now started shaking his head at Bolshevism, of which he was such an admirer only two years ago." Later Sir Hartley ventured on a muttered interruption. "What," asked Churchill, "did the Attorney General say?"

Sir Hartley: "I said, 'Rubbish.' "

Mr. Churchill: "That may be what the Right Honorable and learned gentleman has in his head, but it does not carry conviction."

Some further exchanges were added to the acerbities of debate between Churchill and "Nye" Bevan. When the Welshman offered it as his opinion that the Tories were lower than vermin, Churchill recalled that this was the man who had been a burden to the war effort. It might have been thought that on becoming Minister of Health he would have tried to turn over a new leaf and redeem his past.

> Instead, he has chosen the very moment of bringing the National Health Service into being to speak of at least half his fellow countrymen as lower than vermin and to give vent to the "burning hatred" with which his mind is seared. We speak of the Minister of Health, but ought we not rather to say Minister of Disease, for is not morbid hatred a form of disease, moral disease, in a highly infectious form? Indeed I can think of no better step to signalize the inauguration of the National Health Service than that the man who so obviously needs psychiatrical attention should be among the first of its patients.

There was an occasion when he proffered words of sympathy to Herbert Morrison, reckoned at the time to be losing ground in the race for the succession to Clement Attlee as Socialist leader. Said Churchill with affability:

> There are moments when I am sorry for the Lord President of the Council, a man outpassed at the moment by his competitors, outdated even by his prejudices, scrambling along trying to regain

popularity on an obsolete issue and on an ever-ebbing tide. I hope he will not mind my quoting or adapting some lines, although they are of a martial character, about his position:

> Crippses to the right of him,
> Daltons to the left of him,
> Bevans behind him,
> Volleyed and thundered.

In this lighter vein of Churchillian banter was the retort to Hugh Gaitskell, then Minister of Fuel, who as a measure of economy in the 1947 fuel crisis recommended people take fewer baths on the grounds that it did not make much difference to health and as for appearance— "most of that is underneath and nobody sees it." Said Churchill:

> When Ministers of the Crown speak like this on behalf of His Majesty's Government, the Prime Minister and his friends have no need to wonder why they are getting increasingly into bad odor. I had even asked myself, when meditating on these points, whether you, Mr. Speaker, would admit the word "lousy" as a parliamentary expression in referring to the administration, provided of course, it was not intended in a contemptuous sense but purely as one of factual narration.

For an essay in irony there was a celebrated passage in the attack on the criminal justice bill. This measure contained provisions for amending the law of murder so that the death penalty would have been retained in certain cases of homicide but would have been excluded in other, and the greater number, of instances. Under the measure (it did not find its way to the statute book) the most frequent type of murder, as Churchill pointed out, would not have carried penalty of death unless three persons were concerned in the perpetration of the crime. The systematic administration of poison would have been punishable by hanging, but if murder were committed by a single dose, the death sentence would not have been incurred.

> The Government in fact—that is what we are asked to agree to— say to all and sundry and ask us to say to all and sundry: If you decide to kill your wife because, after cold, calculated and deliberate consideration you come to the conclusion that you will live more agreeably alone or with another woman, or because you will benefit under the terms of her will, you have a variety of methods at your disposal without endangering your life, even if found guilty. You can strangle her, or hold her head in the gas oven until she expires. You can stab her, you can cut her throat, or dash her brains out, each of which will be quicker. If you can arrange the procedure,

you can set her on fire, push her off the station in front of an on-
coming train, or push her through the porthole of a ship. Or more
easily you can drown her in the bath. There is a reciprocal set of
cases which arise on the part of the weaker sex. But whatever you do,
say the Government, you must be careful to invite not more than
one confederate; otherwise your immunity will be gone.

The statesman's aim is to serve his country. For this he must have
place and power. So he must play the politician and stoop to conquer
at the polls. Churchill, throughout the Socialist Parliament, conformed
with his conception of a patriot's duty—"that everyone, without distinction of party, should do his utmost to rescue our native land from the
dangers, privations, and misfortunes in which she is now plunged." But,
when the national interest was not involved, he lost no occasion to dis-
credit his opponents. In speech after speech he denounced the Socialists
for reducing the country to a critical plight by their mismanagement
and misrule.

The immediate and visible effects of his assaults were not encouraging.
By-election followed by-election and Tory hopes were dashed. With mo-
notonous regularity the Socialists retained their seats. Never in recent
times had any Government enjoyed such a record of freedom from electoral defeat. There was grumbling and muttering enough in the queues,
at scarcity and restrictions, at rationing of bread, shortage of coal, rising
prices and unremitted taxes. But when it came to the test of the ballot
box, the Conservatives and their leader could find no evidence that the
pendulum had begun to swing against the Socialist Party.

By the time the Parliament had passed half its span, the country was
faced with imminent bankruptcy. The American loan had run out, the
gold reserves were nearing exhaustion. Only by the timely assistance of
Marshall Plan aid was Britain saved from unemployment that would
have put 1,500,000 on the public dole. It was the time of Cripps and
austerity—"strength through misery," as Churchill termed it. The House
had met in 1945 preoccupied with the application of Socialism to the
major industries. By 1947, under the pressure of the economic crisis, it
was concerned with means for ensuring Britain's survival in the postwar world.

At this parliamentary halfway stage, Churchill devoted a political
broadcast to stating the case for the immediate election of a new Parliament, one that could start fresh in the light of the prevailing circumstances. "We need a Parliament which . . . will allow the laws of supply and demand to play their part. We need a Parliament which will
restore the natural and normal incentives to every honorable personal
effort and thrift."

Churchill's case was formidable in its presentation. But his opponents on the Treasury Bench were not dismayed, for the electors gave no sign of clamoring for their dismissal. By-elections continued to result in the Government's favor.

As the term of Parliament began to run out, however, there was some falling off in the Socialist vote. Public opinion polls showed a decline in Government popularity. For a space, after the devaluation of the pound in 1949, the Tories rose a point or two above the Socialists in the estimates of popularity. With the dissolution of Parliament in February, 1950, Churchill and his party saw reason for facing the country with restrained but not unfounded expectations.

The general-election campaign provided few surprises. It was a demure contest. Both sides were content to take a verdict on the experience of the previous five years. There was argument enough about the past, but a general diffidence to embark on discussion of the problems of the future. The electors, in their wisdom, had to make the decision, as Churchill defined it: "Whether to have a new plunge into Socialist representation or whether by a strong effort to regain freedom, initiative and opportunity to restore the British way of life."

On this occasion, his opening broadcast of the campaign was less emphatic in its note than five years before. There was no repetition of the "Gestapo" charge against the Socialists. Among the Socialists, too, there was a toning down of extremism. "Nye" Bevan, not entirely, it was surmised, by his own personal preference, restrained his natural talent for vituperation.

It was Churchill's eighteenth contested election, and his thirteenth general-election campaign. At seventy-five he was the oldest candidate in the Opposition forces, but his zest for the fray belied his years. North, south and west he traveled. Welshmen heard his voice in Cardiff and Scotsmen in Edinburgh. He addressed a meeting in his old constituency of Oldham. He spoke to large audiences in Leeds and Manchester. He traveled west to Plymouth to support the candidacy of his son Randolph.

Despite these activities, he had by public statement to expose a whispering campaign that sought to rob the Tories of the enormous asset of their great leader. His death was reported by slanderous tongues and he found it necessary to make a categorical denial that his demise had taken place, in circumstances that were being hushed up till the election was over. He had no difficulty in establishing that he was still very much alive.

On the eve of the voting, prophets and opinion tests were agreed that Clement Attlee and Winston Churchill were running neck and neck, not that much reliance was placed in electoral prophets after their signal and conclusive error over Harry Truman's fate in the American Presidential campaign a few months previously. On the night of polling day, prophecy seemed to have been proved false once again. On the strength of the results in the towns, the Socialists went to their late beds with the apparent assurance of a comfortable though reduced majority in the new House. The next day came the dramatic reversal of fortunes. It was neck and neck, with the Socialists winning in a photo finish by the margin of seven seats over all other parties. The Liberals, their candidates decimated, still came near to holding the balance of power in the new House of Commons. The Communists were extinguished.

In greater detail, the Socialists with a little more than thirteen million votes returned 315 members out of 617 candidates. The Tories with twelve and a half million votes had 298 M.P.s out of 620 candidates. Only 9 of the 475 Liberals were elected, by two and a half million votes. The Communists, contesting 100 seats, lost the lot. There were only 91,684 Communist voters. Their friends and fellow travelers were ignominiously rejected. The country could congratulate itself on having made a complete recovery from its "Red haze" infection of five years previously.

Neither Winston Churchill nor Clement Attlee was given much cause for self-congratulation. So closely did the result conform with the pre-campaign estimates of a month before that the two leaders, in the privacy of their chambers, might well have reflected that all their oratory had gone for nought. The electors had apparently made up their minds beforehand, and all the wooing by addresses, speeches, broadcasts and personal canvass had induced few of them to change their allegiance.

Churchill had the greater cause for satisfaction with the outcome. The prize had just eluded him, but he had reduced his opponents pretty well to impotence. As he put it on meeting the new House: "I like the appearance of these benches better than what we had to look at during the last four and a half years. It is refreshing to feel, at any rate, that this is a Parliament where half the nation will not be able to ride roughshod over the other half and so sweep away in a session what has been carefully constructed by generations of toil."

It was the deadest of dead heats in a hundred years. The electors had voted a standstill order in politics. The party leaders might deplore the parliamentary deadlock but it was seen that there were advantages for the country. With controversial legislation ruled out, the parties were free to give their attention to the dangers threatening from beyond the Iron Curtain in a world where safety was seen to rest, in Churchill's phrase, "on the somber balancing power of the atom bomb."

CHAPTER THREE

COUNSELOR TO THE FREE PEOPLES

1946–1950

For the second time his countrymen were refusing him executive office, but no period had been put to the national service of Winston Churchill. It is remarkable to note the extent to which he was responsible for guiding the course of the free peoples in the years of peril after the war when the shadows of an aggressive Stalinism were lengthening over Europe. Relieved of the responsibilities for his country's government, he was free to brood over the world's affairs and the measures needed to preserve the democratic way of life. He was counselor in chief to the free peoples. He pointed the way for them to follow, the path of their salvation, his thoughts moving ahead of public opinion and of the measures of Ministers in office. He drew, at times, the startled censure of less percipient minds, but ultimately his counsel was found to be acceptable and his suggestions became the policy for the West.

At Fulton he had called for the closest cooperation between Britain and the United States. At Zurich, later in 1946, he presented his proposals for the building up, nearer home, of an association of peoples in a United States of Europe, a conception which after the First World War had been pressed by the French statesman, Aristide Briand. In those days Europe had not been impressed. In the forties, under the urgent stimulus of danger, the idea was for a while given wide support. In August, 1949, the first session was held at Strasbourg of the Council of Europe and the European Consultative Assembly, creations that sprang from proposals Churchill had put forward.

There was nothing neutral about the reception the Swiss gave to the British war leader when he made his visit to Zurich on September 19, 1946. Flowers were thrown upon him as he drove through the streets in his open car. Cheering students, attired in brightly colored medieval costumes, complete with jackboots and rapiers, greeted him in the Great Hall of the University where he attended to receive an illuminated address, token of Swiss admiration for the defender of freedom. He used the occasion to call upon the peoples of Europe to take action to save themselves by their own exertions from the return of the Dark Ages with all their cruelty and squalor. They had the means, he declared, to transform the scene and make Europe, or the greater part of it, as free as Switzerland. What was this sovereign remedy?

> It is to re-create the European family, or as much of it as we can, and provide it with a structure under which it can dwell in safety and in freedom. We must build a kind of United States of Europe. In this way only will hundreds of millions of toilers be able to regain the simple joys and hopes which make life worth living. . . .

Germany must be deprived of power to rearm and make war again. Those guilty of war crimes must be punished. But when this had been done there must be an end to retribution. The world could not afford to drag forward across the years that were to come hatreds and revenges which had sprung from the injuries of the past. He called on the French and Germans to rise above their ancient quarrels:

> And now, I am going to say something that will astonish you. The first step in the re-creation of the European family must be a partnership between France and Germany. In this way only can France recover the moral and cultural leadership of Europe. There can be no revival of Europe without a spiritually great France and a spiritually great Germany.

Four months after the Zurich speech the formation was announced in England of the United Europe Committee of twenty members, representing, in addition to the churches and other interests, all political parties except the Communists. Churchill was chairman. In France, a corresponding organization was developed.

The next milestone was the Congress of Europe at The Hague (May 7–10, 1948), sponsored by the British and French United Europe movements and other international bodies with similar aims. Churchill, as *président d'honneur,* addressed over 700 delegates representing 23 countries. The British delegation of 148 members included 64 Members of Parliament, 27 of them Labour M.P.s.

During the preparatory stages of the Congress, Churchill had written to Attlee seeking his cooperation. The Prime Minister replied frigidly that it was undesirable for the Government to take any official action in the matter.

Despite Socialist hesitations, the United Europe movement made headway. In May, 1949, representatives of ten nations (Britain, France, Denmark, Italy, Ireland, Luxembourg, the Netherlands, Norway, Sweden and Belgium) met under the chairmanship of Ernest Bevin to sign the statute of the Council of Europe. In August the Council of Europe and the European Consultative Assembly were brought into existence. Churchill, as a representative of His Majesty's Opposition, attended the inaugural meeting. There were those who wished to nominate him for election as president of the Assembly, but before the opening session in the Great Hall of Strasbourg University, he made it known that he preferred to sit as an ordinary member. So he took his place in the alphabetical order of his name, between M. van Cauwelaert (Belgium) and Senator Cingolani (Italy). The ovation he received on entering the assembly was an unforgettable tribute to the "first citizen of Europe."

Edouard Herriot, the veteran French statesman, in his opening speech offered the Assembly's homage "to one to whom every free man owes so deep a debt. . . . In many moments of deep tragedy he bore on his shoulders the whole weight of a world crying for help. From his mind sprang the movement which brought us together here."

As the months passed antagonism was mounting between the Soviets and the free peoples. Under Churchill's inspiration the states of western Europe pushed ahead their plans for defense. What place was West Germany to take among the Western nations? In 1946 in his Zurich speech he had pleaded for the bringing back of the German people into the European circle, but he had not then been prepared to go further. Under the pressure of events in the Cold War he was brought to revise his opinion and to advocate the inclusion of armed German forces among the defenders of the Western security. Again his thoughts were in advance of current opinion. Again he bore—be it said with fortitude— remonstrance and reproof from Ministers of the Crown. And again, in the result, he had the satisfaction of contributing a proposal that found its place as the accepted policy of the Western powers.

His suggestion was made in March, 1950, in an early debate on the defense budget in the new Parliament. The decision, he said, to form a front in Europe against invasion by Soviet Russia and the satellite states was at once grave and imperative. The American view that western Europe was indefensible had been changed by the formation of a Western Alliance and the North Atlantic Treaty. He went on:

So long a front cannot be defended without the active aid of western Germany. Germany is at present disarmed and forbidden to keep any military force but beyond the eastern frontier lies the enormous military array of the Soviet and the satellite states, far exceeding in troops, armor and air power all that the other Allies have got. We are unable to offer to the Germans any assurance that they may not be overrun by a Soviet or satellite invasion. This mighty array of Russian armies and their satellites lies like a fearful cloud over the German people and the Allies cannot give any direct protection. Their cities and homes may be overrun by the Eastern deluge and no doubt all Germans who have been prominent in resisting Communism, or are working for the reconciliation with the Western democracies, would pay the forfeit.

We have no guarantee to give except to engage in a general way which, after wrecking what is left of European civilization would no doubt end in the ultimate defeat of the Soviets, but may begin with the Communist enslavement of western Germany and perhaps not only of western Germany. I say without hesitation that the effective defense of European freedom cannot be achieved if a German contribution is excluded from the thoughts of those who are responsible. To remain as we now are for a long period of time is certainly not the best way to prevent the measureless horrors of a third world war.

This idea of rearming the Germans took all parties by surprise. The Prime Minister made an immediate and emphatic protest; it was, he said, irresponsible and injudicious. The Foreign Secretary declared his opposition: "All of us are against it. I repeat, all of us are against it. It is a frightful decision to take. We have set our face against the rearming of Germany and that, I am afraid, we must adhere to."

Churchill offered a correction. He had not proposed the rearming of Germany, but that there should be a contribution to Western defense. There should be Germans serving with the British, Americans and French on honorable terms of friendship, standing in the line as part of a system of defense.

Ernest Bevin did not consider the distinction made effective, practical difference. To talk about arming Germany in any form would set the clock back in bringing France and Germany together for a considerable time. He was not prepared to take any such step.

In a foreign affairs debate on March 28, Churchill defended himself against his critics and delivered a compelling speech, releasing the results of his broodings on the fate of a Europe menaced with the catastrophe of an atomic war. He began by repudiating the Prime Minister's reproof and the accusation of irresponsibility.

My feeling is, and I hope the Prime Minister will allow me to say so, that I am as good a judge of these matters as he is. Certainly I should not like to be responsible for not stating my true and faithful belief and counsel to the House, as I have done several times in the past when it was not particularly popular to do so. I remember that during the last Parliament, not to go too far back, I made a speech at Fulton which became the object of a motion of censure. Shortly afterward, the policy I had advocated was adopted on both sides of the Atlantic and by all parties in this House. So I shall not feel myself utterly extinguished by the Prime Minister's censure.

For the unity and restoration of Europe the assistance of the Germans, he declared, was essential. France and Britain, both sorely distressed, should combine together and, thus joined, have the power to raise Germany, even more shattered, to equal rank and equal association with them. Then these three countries, helping each other, conscious of their future united greatness, forgetting ancient feuds and the horrible deeds and tragedies of the past, could make the core and nucleus upon which all the other countries of Europe, bond or free, could rally and combine. Thus would Europe be enabled to live again. He passed on to relations with Russia and found reason for the belief that there was still time, if wisely used, to ward off a third world war, which, if it came, would be catastrophic in its results.

Another world war would begin by both sides suffering as the first step what they dread most. Western Europe would be overrun and communized, with liquidation of the outstanding noncommunist personnel of all classes, of which I understand, in respect of several countries, elaborate lists have already been prepared—and which are, no doubt, kept up to date in those countries by the Communist groups and parties in their midst. That is one side.

At the same time, Soviet cities, air fields, oil fields and railway junctions would be annihilated, with possible complete disruption of Kremlin control over the enormous populations who are ruled from Moscow. These fearful cataclysms would be simultaneous, and neither side could at present, or for several years to come, prevent them. Moralists may find it a melancholy thought that peace can find no nobler foundations than mutual terror. But for my part I shall be content if these foundations are solid, because they will give us the extra time and the new breathing space for the supreme effort which has to be made for a world settlement.

Churchill's speech set before the House the dominating preoccupation of the times. The main issue of the 1950 election had been socialism. The paramount concern of the 1950 Parliament was national defense.

After initial doubts and hesitations the Government set about the task of rearmament. The substance of manpower was added to the defense skeleton of western Europe. Montgomery was sent to the Continent to direct building up the forces of resistance against aggression from the East. As the conflict in Korea underlined the urgency of affairs, Eisenhower was brought from his academic backwater to take up his old duties as coordinator of the efforts of the free nations.

It had been a general expectation that the 1950 Parliament, after a few months' life, would be dissolved and the electors would be given the opportunity to end the political deadlock. Expectations were not so quickly realized. The year 1950 ran its course and the Socialist Government continued in office, maintained by a minimum of votes, precariously surviving a series of critical divisions. The majority was sufficient to secure the carrying of legislation for the nationalization of the iron and steel industry. Churchill made repeated endeavors to induce the Ministers to abandon a policy that was damaging both to national unity and to the efficiency of this vital industry in times of national danger. His protests were unavailing against the uncompromising leftists.

As the year 1951 opened, it appeared that another general election could not be delayed by many months. The readings of the barometer of public opinion suggested that the electoral pendulum was swinging to the right. It was predicted that before the year was out Winston Churchill would have returned to Downing Street as Prime Minister.

CHAPTER FOUR

THE THIRD TERM

1951–1952

O N October 26, 1951, Winston Churchill drove to Buckingham Palace to receive the King's mandate to form an administration. He thus became Prime Minister for the third time a few weeks before his seventy-seventh birthday. The circumstances were vastly different from those in which he had first become Prime Minister twelve years previously. Then, with the nation at war, he had accepted the leadership in the hour of Britain's greatest peril. In 1951 peace prevailed, uneasily perhaps, but outside Korea undisturbed. Then Churchill had been the leader of a nation united as rarely before, backed by a House of Commons in which all parties had dropped their differences to support the famous coalition. Now he had the backing of no more than half the nation, and the support of only fractionally more than half the members of the House of Commons.

Leader of a party and of half the House—it was not the position of his hopes, but of this he gave little sign. He spoke and conducted himself as he had done before. His was to be no partisan premiership. The years had not dimmed his pugnacity. He would still, if prodded into it, lay about him in the party fray, but this was not the role he designed for himself. Half the electorate only might have voted for him, but he spoke for the nation.

The result of the general election had fallen below his hopes and his expectations. During the final months of the dead-heat Parliament, opinion had been swinging away from the Socialists. The predictions of the prophets had grown more encouraging for the Tories, whose spirits rose still further with the split in the ranks of their opponents betokened by the resignation from office of Aneurin Bevan, Minister of Health. Bevan, the Tories felt, was delivering the enemy into their hands, and there was gloating over the rift in the left brought about by the maneuverings of the Welshman. For Clement Attlee, precariously surviving, it was the last heavily falling straw that was to be supported by his much-tested back. When in the late summer of 1951 the cloud of a new financial crisis appeared on the horizon, Attlee decided that the time had come to solve his pressing problems by an appeal to the electorate. In a broadcast on the evening of September 19, he announced that he was seeking a renewal of confidence from the country.

The Conservatives were the first in the field with their electoral manifesto, a document written for them by their leader and bearing the Churchill imprint in its phrasing. Lively in language, in promises it was restrained. It opened with the declaration of the nation's need for a period of stable government, during which "national interests must be held far above party feuds," with a government not biased by privilege or interest, cramped by doctrinal prejudice or inflamed by the passions of class warfare.

"We," declared Churchill, "seek to proclaim a theme rather than write a prospectus. Many years ago I used a phrase 'bring the rear guard in.' This meant basic standards of life and labor, the duty of the strong to help the weak. That policy is adopted by all parties today. Now we have the new Socialist doctrine. It is no longer 'bring the rear guard in,' it is 'keep the vanguard back.' "

It was scarcely a stimulating election. The rival policies were too well-known to arouse intensity of feeling or exaggerated expectations. Labour's program for pushing ahead with nationalization had no longer the appeal of the songs the sirens sang. The Tory program for canceling nationalization of the iron and steel and road transport industries did not fire the voters with rapture. There was much speaking on foreign affairs but much less interest among the electors, whose main concern was with the cost of living and rising prices.

Each party found a bogey on the other side with which to make the electors' flesh creep. The Tories concentrated on the machinations of "Nye" Bevan, so that Attlee was driven to defend his party's *enfant terrible* against the charge that he was a Communist.

The Socialists, to blacken their opponents, attacked Churchill as a warmonger. This was not overtly stated by the party leaders, but was conveyed by implication. Bevan's version of the old taunt was adroit.

"I don't think," he said, "Winston Churchill wants war. The trouble with him is that he does not know how to avoid it. He does not talk the language of the twentieth century but of the nineteenth. He is still fighting Blenheim all over again."

Churchill made reply to this "false and ungrateful charge" when delivering his final speech of the election campaign, at Plymouth on behalf of the candidacy of his son Randolph. That he had remained in public life, he said, was because, rightly or wrongly, but sincerely, he believed he might be able to make an important contribution to the prevention of a third world war and to bringing nearer that lasting peace settlement that the masses of people of every race and in every land desired. "I pray indeed," he declared, "that I may have this opportunity. It is the last prize I seek to win."

Polling took place on October 25 and returns that night showed it was to be again close. The Socialists were relieved and the Tories chagrined to find that the swing away from the left had not been as pronounced as had been forecast. On the following day the returns in the rural constituencies sent up the Conservative lead. By the afternoon the Socialists were slightly outnumbered. By the evening the Conservatives had a majority, not as many as twenty seats, but still a majority. When all the returns were in, the state of parties was such that, with 321 seats, the Conservatives and their associates led the Socialists by a majority of twenty-five. Six Liberals alone had survived. Not one of the ten Communist candidates had escaped defeat. Had the election been determined by total votes cast instead of by seats gained, the Socialists would have been the winners by the narrowest of margins—less than one per cent of the 28 million votes cast. The party scores were:

Socialists	13,948,000	48.77%
Conservatives	13,724,000	47.98%
Liberal	730,551	2.55%

The Communists received the contemptuous backing of 21,000 voters.

Without waiting to receive his *congé* from the new House, Clement Attlee immediately made way for his successor. Churchill lost no time in taking over. Election day had been October 25. On the 26th the old Prime Minister went out and the new came in. On the 27th the names of the principals of the new Ministry were made known. The choice of men underlined Churchill's intention to subordinate the party and to emphasize the national aspect of his leadership.

Non-party men were selected for some of the principal posts—Lord Simonds as Lord Chancellor, Lord Ismay (Commonwealth Relations), Lord Leathers (Transport, Fuel and Power), and Lord Cherwell (Paymaster General). A National Liberal, John Maclay, was made Minister of Transport and Gwilym Lloyd George (Liberal and Conservative) took over the problems of the Ministry of Food.

Churchill wished to bring in the Independent Liberals but Clement Davies felt unable to accept the offer of Cabinet office.

However, the Liberals, "deeply concerned at the possible effect of the narrow majority on the House in the conduct of British policy both in home and international affairs," offered support to the new Government "in measures clearly conceived in the interest of the country as a whole."

Place was found for the old-guard Conservatives. Anthony Eden returned, inevitably, to the Foreign Office; Lord Woolton became President of the Council, and Lord Salisbury, Lord Privy Seal; R. A. Butler was sent to wrestle with the financial and economic problems at the Exchequer. Harold Macmillan was given a testing opportunity as Minister of Housing. Captain Crookshank, in addition to taking the Ministry of Health, was to lead the House of Commons, for Anthony Eden felt himself unable to undertake that duty in addition to the heavy responsibilities of the Foreign Office.

A peacetime innovation in Cabinet-making was the appointment of Ministers—"overlords" the critics called them—to supervise the activities of groups of Ministries. Lord Woolton was to coordinate food and agriculture; Lord Leathers was to range over the wide field of fuel and power; Lord Cherwell (formerly Professor Lindemann of Oxford) was to watch over scientific research and, particularly, atomic energy, research and production.

Churchill himself, following his own wartime precedent, was Minister of Defense, with the three Service Ministers answerable to him. Clement Attlee deplored the arrangement. Either defense would suffer because of competing claims for the Prime Minister's attention, or he would neglect his wider responsibilities because of his interest in defense. Churchill acknowledged the heaviness of the burdens.

"But," he said, "I do feel that I must, at any rate at the outset, master the situation in the sphere of defense." The arrangement did not long continue, for on his visit to America early in the following year, a Minister of Defense was found in Lord Alexander, who relinquished his office as Governor-General of Canada to join the Ministry.

With the names of the personnel, the Prime Minister made an announcement testifying to the earnestness of the new Government's intentions on economy. During the period of rearmament, Cabinet Ministers would have £1,000 a year lopped off their £5,000 salaries. The Prime Minister himself would suffer a reduction from £10,000 to £7,000, a saving, as the critics noted, that would have a greater effect on his surtax than on his personal income.

The new Parliament was opened in November with a King's Speech that the Leader of the Opposition described as the "thinnest" he had ever known. Attlee mistook, or misrepresented, his successor's intentions. By design, contentious partisan legislation was ruled out. Only one controversial measure, the canceling of steel nationalization was promised.

Outlining his policy in his opening speech to the new House, Churchill said, "What the nation needs is several years of good, steady administration. What the House needs is a period of tolerant and constructive debating on the merits of the question before us, without every speech on either side being dictated by the passions of one election or preparations for another." Churchill had succeeded to an anxious inheritance. For six years the Attlee Government had faced the aggressive Stalinism of the Russians. Some measures had been concerted with Washington to hold the Communists in check. In Churchill's view the peak of peril was passed. "I cannot," he told the House, "conceive that the danger is now as great as it was at the time of the Berlin airlift crisis." Three years had passed since then. The North Atlantic Treaty Organization had been given the backing of a defense force. It was a measure of the anxieties of those days that the Socialist Government had found it necessary to set about the rearming of Britain at a cost of £4,700,000,000.

Under the restrictive influence of finance, this program had of necessity to be slowed down. Britain's straitened resources would not run to expenditure on the scale that had been planned. One of the first decisions the Prime Minister had to take was to spread the rearmament over a longer term of years. He was very conscious of the burdens falling upon the British people, no more than six years emerged from the World War that for the time had bankrupted them. So, he devoted his premiership in its final phase to easing the tension in the world and lessening the bill for arms that was crippling the peoples of all nations.

The first move toward the goal of a new understanding between East and West must be made not with the Russians, but with the American allies. So Churchill resumed his task at the point he had broken off in 1945 by seeking the opportunity for concerting policy with President Truman. No longer were obstacles placed in the way of a meeting. By November the preliminaries had been concluded and it was announced that the Prime Minister, with the Foreign Secretary and other Ministers, had arranged to cross for talks with the President in the new year.

Following closely on the rigorous economy demanded by the country's finances, the Washington visit was inevitably looked on as a begging mission, with another American loan as its objective. This was a supposition entertained at home, so there was no reason for surprise that it was credited on the American side of the Atlantic, particularly in circles not well disposed toward Britain. The Prime Minister, it was suggested, was coming cap in hand for dollars.

With proper pride Churchill repudiated this notion in a broadcast to the nation three days before Christmas. "We are," he said, "resolved to make this island solvent, able to earn its living and pay its way. Without this foundation we cannot keep our people alive. If we cannot earn our living by the united exertions of our strength, our genius, our craftsmanship, our industry, there will be no time to emigrate the redundant millions for whom no food is grown at home. We have no assurance that anyone else is going to keep the British lion as a pet."

Before leaving for America, Churchill engaged in consultations to inform himself of opinion on the Continent. Adenauer, the German Chancellor, made a visit to London. In mid-December the Prime Minister and Foreign Secretary traveled to Paris to meet their opposite numbers of the French Government. "We wanted," said Churchill later, "our French friends to feel that we meant to be good friends and allies and that we welcomed the measures the French have taken to bring Germany into the new European system."

There was a final Cabinet meeting at which Walter Gifford, the United States Ambassador, was present for two hours, and then Churchill and his party sailed for New York on the *Queen Mary*. Landing on January 5, they traveled on by air to Washington to be greeted by the President and members of the administration. Preliminary talks were held aboard the Presidential yacht, *Williamsburg,* and there followed formal discussions at the White House, four meetings taking place in two days.

Collaboration for peace was the over-all topic, otherwise described as preparations to resist aggression. The agenda included such topics as air bases in Britain for the United States; enlisting the support of West Germany in European defense; the North Atlantic Treaty Organization; the standardization of rifles and ammunition; the question of the Atlantic Command; affairs of the Middle East (Persian oil and Egyptian treaty) and of the Far East; and the supply of scarce materials—steel for the United Kingdom, aluminum and tin for the United States.

Discussions in Washington were interrupted so that Churchill and his colleagues might travel north for a meeting with Louis St. Laurent, the Canadian Prime Minister. At a banquet in his honor at Ottawa, the Prime Minister gave an assurance to the Commonwealth that no steps would be omitted to restore the stability of Britain's finances.

Back in Washington, Churchill was delighted to be made a member of the Society of Cincinnati, an organization of men descended from officers who served under George Washington in the Revolution. He qualified for membership through his mother, for Jennie Jerome was great-granddaughter of Rueben Murrary, who had served in Washington's Continental Army. The wheel had indeed turned full circle when the successor of the Prime Minister who lost the American colonies for Britain was admitted to the fraternity formed in honor of officers of the insurgent Americans who achieved their independence.

Washington's Presidential successor and members of the Truman administration were present at the installation. Churchill relished both the honor paid to him and the irony of the occasion.

The following day (January 17), for the third time in his career, he addressed a joint session of the United States Congress. He began by expressing his appreciation of the honor done to him by the Congress, unique for one who was not an American citizen. He went on:

> I have not come here to ask you for money to make life more comfortable or easier for us in Britain. Our standards of life are our own business and we can only keep our self-respect and independence by looking after them ourselves. I have come here to ask of you not gold but steel, not favors but equipment; that is why so many of our requests have been so well and generously met.

He spoke of the change in the world scene since last he had addressed the Congress. It was astounding. Former allies had become foes, former foes allies; conquered countries had been liberated, liberated countries enslaved by communism. Russia, eight years previously our brave ally, had cast away the good will and admiration her valiant soldiers had gained for her. It was not the fault of the Western powers that a great gulf had developed. It had taken a long succession of unceasing and deliberate words and acts of hostility to convince the free peoples they had another danger to face, and were confronted by a new form of tyranny and aggression as dangerous and hateful as that which had been overthrown.

> You have been wisely resolute, Members of the Congress, in confronting Chinese Communist aggression. We take our stand at your side. We are grateful to the U.S.A. for bearing nine-tenths, or more, of the burden in Korea which the United Nations have morally assumed. I am very glad that whatever diplomatic divergencies there may be from time to time about procedure, you do not allow the Chinese anti-Communists on Formosa to be invaded and massacred from the mainland. We welcome your patience in the armistice negotiations. Our two nations are agreed that if the truce we

seek is reached only to be broken, our response will be prompt, resolute and effective.

It was in Europe that Britain's greatest dangers lay. Rapid progress was being made toward European unity and as a forerunner of a United Europe there was the European army. This could never achieve its necessary strength without the inclusion of Germany.

The sooner strong enough force can be assembled in Europe under a united command, the more effective will be the deterrent against a third world war. The sooner, also, will our sense of security, and the fact of our security be seen to reside in valiant, resolute and well-armed manhood rather than in the awful secrets science has wrested from nature. These secrets are at present, it must be recognized, supreme deterrents against a third world war and the most effective guarantee of victory in it. If I may say this—Members of the Congress, be careful above all things not to let go of the atomic weapon until you are sure and more than sure that other means of preserving peace are in your hands. . . .

Under the pressure and menace of Communist aggression, the fraternal association of the United States with Britain and the British Commonwealth and the new unity growing up in Europe—nowhere more hopeful than between France and Germany—all these harmonies are being brought forward, perhaps by several generations. If this proves true, and it has certainly proved true to date, the architects in the Kremlin may be found to have built a far better world structure than they had planned.

Thus he found compensations for the stresses suffered in the cold war.

The Washington discussions ended with a formal agreement for the exchange of metal supplies, steel, tin and aluminum, essential for the manufacture of arms. But the visit had produced greater results in political understanding. Relations across the Atlantic had fallen from their wartime cordiality. Under the Prime Minister's influence there was a renewal of good will. When President and Prime Minister shook hands at parting, they were sensible of a rekindling of warmer feelings between the old allies.

Churchill went home by way of New York, where he stayed a couple of days as guest of his old friend Bernard Baruch. He had planned a ceremonial drive to the City Hall, but a severe cold caused him to forgo the pleasure of the welcome Broadway gives to distinguished visitors. He was, however, able to receive the Mayor, Vincent Impellitteri, and accept from him the city's Medal of Honor.

Homecoming recalled the old days of the war. Always it seemed, a mission to Washington must touch off a political storm on his return.

When he had set out, on this occasion, speculation had been concentrated on his financial intentions. Back at Westminster he found that, finance forgotten, his critics were clamoring against his Far East policy and the backing he had given to the Americans.

His report on his negotiations did not satisfy his critics. He was told that under pressure from the Americans he had bought the agreement on steel at the price of consenting to undertake further responsibilities against the Chinese Communists. The Socialists fastened on the phrase in his address to the Congress agreeing that were a truce in Korea to be broken "our response would be prompt, resolute and effective." They introduced a motion of criticism, not of the policy of the Government as it had been expounded by Anthony Eden—this was no more than the continuance of their own—but of the Prime Minister himself, regretting his "failure to give adequate expression to this policy in the course of his recent visit to the United States."

Clement Attlee contrasted the terms of the Prime Minister's address to the Congress and his speech to the House on January 30. Everyone had been struck by the difference of tone and he quoted the comment passed in *The New York Times:*

> Prime Minister Churchill gave a good demonstration of how to say the same thing in two different ways. . . . Like a good salesman with different customers he displayed his wares to their best advantage first in Washington and then in London.

The question Attlee posed was whether they were the same wares. It might have been good salesmanship but it was not good statesmanship. The result had been grave disquietude. The Prime Minister had gone out of his way to deal with the most difficult point of the whole question of a Far East settlement in order to say what all were agreed on—that the people under Chiang Kai-shek should not be left to be massacred. The obvious interpretation of those words, the whole slant of them, was support for the Chiang Kai-shek regime to defend Formosa. The general reaction was that the Prime Minister's address was a backing of the Chiang Kai-shek Government, and any such backing was fatal to a settlement in the Far East.

The attack was pressed by Herbert Morrison, who had been Foreign Minister under Attlee. He charged the Prime Minister with causing confusion and doubt on both sides of the Atlantic by his vaguely expressed commitments. He had flung a wrench in the works at a time a truce was being negotiated; his provocative statements would arouse Chinese suspicions. Churchill responded to the stimulus of attack. Since succeeding to office it had been necessary for him to acquaint himself with the proceedings and papers of his predecessors. These, he found, had left Socialist ex-Ministers grievously exposed and he savored the "sport of having the engineer hoist with his own petard."

"I am complimented," he began, "by the fact that the Opposition vote of censure should concentrate its gravamen on me." It was not the first time he had been singled out by the Socialists in their wrath, and once again he twitted them over the motion they had once introduced condemning his Fulton speech.

Now the Socialist Opposition had adopted a position of protestation that there should be any war with China. Yet he had a recollection that the Chinese had gone into Korea fifteen months previously and that the Chinese Communists and their North Korean allies had killed and wounded more than 100,000 Americans and nearly 3,000 of Britain's own men. Their own losses had been estimated at over 1,250,000 killed and wounded.

"However, apparently, according to the mentality of the Socialist Party, which only five months ago supported this devastating struggle in Korea, nothing matters unless we call it war. Unless it is called war the high condition of moral idealism of the Socialist movement is in no way impaired. Thousands of men may fall, whole areas of Korea may be devastated, 35,000 dead may be picked up in front of a single American division, our own men may have killed many times their own number in deadly fighting, but whatever happens it must not be called war. . . .

"Since we have been in office the truce negotiations begun eight months ago have continued and the slaughter of the Chinese has abated. A comparative calm exists on the blood-soaked front. The Socialist Party can turn their energies, I have no doubt with a measure of relief, from being war-wagers to calling other people warmongers."

In his first speech on returning from America he had made it plain that he was opposed to action that would involve Britain, her allies or the United Nations in a war in China. He again drew the attention of the House to the statement of General Omar Bradley, "We would be fighting the wrong nation in the wrong war in the wrong place."

This by way of prelude. Churchill advanced to the hoisting of Herbert Morrison. "On several occasions in the last year," he said, "the U.S.A. asked the British Government what military action they would agree to if certain things happened. Questions were addressed to the late Socialist Government and to this Government. The first occasion was last year before the truce negotiations had begun. The then Foreign Secretary [Herbert Morrison] replied to an enquiry that the Government had decided that in the event of heavy air attacks from bases in China upon

U.N. forces in Korea, they would associate themselves with action not confined to Korea."

Socialist ex-Ministers were in the pit Herbert Morrison had ineptly dug for them. Morrison suffered the further humiliation of hearing his rival in the party, Aneurin Bevan, rise in his defense and attempt to silence the Prime Minister on a point of parliamentary procedure. It was ineffective and Churchill proceeded, jubilantly: "I do not understand why there should be all this fear on the benches opposite. . . . There was agreement—and I am entitled to inform Parliament of the fact—between the U.S. Government and the late Socialist administration that in certain circumstances or contingencies action would be taken not confined to Korea. I am stating the facts fairly and I will show how very little ground there is for the gentlemen opposite to make their slanderous allegations against us that we wish to plunge into war."

There had been a second agreement in September when the Socialist Government gave its consent to limited action. "In both cases," added Churchill, "we consider our predecessors were right, and in my view justified the words I used to the United States Congress, namely, 'prompt, resolute, effective.' "

As to Formosa, even Clement Attlee had agreed with what had been said to the Congress. "Well, it was the only thing one could say about Formosa which could be agreed on both sides of this House, on both sides of Congress and indeed on both sides of the Atlantic. I thought it was a good selection, almost a bull's-eye."

You may imagine how Churchill beamed as he paid this tribute to his own sagacity.

Aneurin Bevan tried to save the face of the Socialist leaders by charging the Prime Minister with having made a "lying summary," but this impressed no one. The Prime Minister's disclosure was unanswerable. He made a further revelation on atomic-bomb research that came as a surprise to all sides of the House, not least to the Socialist back-benchers.

"I was not aware till I took office," he said, "that not only had the Socialist Government made the atom bomb a matter of research, but that they had created at the expense of scores of millions of pounds the necessary plant for its regular production. This weapon will be tested during the present year by agreement with the Australian Government at some suitable place on that continent. This achievement is certainly a real advantage to us, and when I informed the Americans at Washington of the position which had been reached quite a new atmosphere was created on this subject. . . .

"The Conservatives, then in opposition, would certainly have supported the Government on this matter as we did on so many other measures of our defense. Nevertheless the Socialists had preferred to conceal this vast operation and its finances from the knowledge of the House, not even obtaining a vote on the principle involved, while at the same time, with Machiavellian art, keeping open the advantage of accusing their opponents of being warmongers. Clement Attlee is in the position of one who did good by stealth and blushed to find it fame. Before the whole story passes from life into history he will have to do a good deal of blushing in the explanations he will have to make to his followers."

Rarely had Churchill attacked his opponents with such relish, and with such effect. The Socialists would in the future have need for greater wariness in the launching of their attacks. Charges of warmongering would ring hollow.

The third term as Prime Minister could not match the luster of the first. The country was in no mood for heroics. After the exhaustions of the war and the changes under socialism the people were prepared to accept the humdrum in politics. The Government, with no more than a bare majority, proposed no measures to disturb their tranquillity. They were satisfied to leave it so.

Return to normal was the keynote—and the removal of controls. The identity card was scrapped, the ration book followed it into limbo, the humble sausage was decontrolled in common with other domestic necessities. There was some unscrambling of the eggs of socialism in iron and steel and in transport. Over larger issues Ministers availed themselves of the advantages of the open mind; in their legislation they claimed the privilege of the second thought. The ministerial machine came slowly into operation. There was some muttering of discontent that the resolute direction of wartime was lacking.

Was the Old Man suffering the effects of political exhaustion, had his energies been sapped by the second war? He soon established that it was otherwise, and that over matters to which his mind was bent there was no infirmity in his purpose, or falling off in his powers. Men who rise to the height of great occasions can fall below the level of their best in dealing with matters of less pith and moment. The Prime Minister gave the impression that he was less than one hundred per cent concerned with the run of day-by-day politics and domestic affairs.

It was on the larger issues of the world in the turmoil of the Cold War and the awesome potentialities of the atom bomb that he brought to bear the full resources of his mind. Here the old Churchill was manifest. His purpose was plain, his handling sure and decisive. He had avowed his intention of crowning his work as architect of victory by laying the foundations of enduring peace. It was to the realization of his hopes of a lasting settlement—"the last prize I seek to win"—that he devoted his attention, his patience, and his endeavors. One Nobel Prize was accorded him, for literature. Could he not qualify for another and gain the award by his work for peace?

The conferment of the literature prize was announced in terms that were particularly acceptable (October 15, 1953). It was awarded for "his mastery in historical and biographical presentations and for his brilliant oratory, in which he has always stood forth as the defender of eternal human values." Churchill's pride in accepting the honor was heightened by the fact that it was, as he put it, the first he had received that was international in character. It linked him with other British men of letters, with Rudyard Kipling and Bernard Shaw. Both of them he had known well. He considered that his thought was more in accord with Kipling than with Shaw. "Although," he added, "Rudyard Kipling never thought much of me, whereas Bernard Shaw often expressed himself in the most flattering terms."

The times were not encouraging, at the start of his third premiership, for the laborer of peace. Behind the Iron Curtain the leaders of Soviet Russia had all the appearances of squaring up for war. In the United States opinion was exacerbated, mounting under the priming of Senator Joseph McCarthy, to the peak of hostility against the Communists, suspicious and strident.

The Prime Minister accepted the conditions as a challenge. He committed himself to the pursuit of peace through strength. Atomic research was pressed forward under his eager direction so that Britain, whose pioneer work had made a major contribution to evolving the atom bomb, should not lag behind Americans and Russians. Britain was placed on terms with the leaders by the detonation of an atomic weapon at the Woomera Range in the South Australian desert in October, 1952.

The new premiership was little more than three months old when the death of the King raised a succession of new problems that for a time diverted the Prime Minister's attention from the urgencies of affairs abroad.

CHAPTER FIVE

SERVANT OF THE YOUNG QUEEN

(1952–1953)

O N a February day Winston Churchill was one of the central figures in an historic scene at London airport. Elizabeth of Windsor was returning home, Princess no longer but Queen of the Realm. Her father, King George VI, had died while she was across the seas in Kenya staying with her husband at a hunting lodge in the forests. She had succeeded to the throne while engaged in the treetops watching the wildlife of Africa. Immediately she boarded the waiting plane to begin the 4,400-mile homeward flight.

Leaders of the three parties in the state, the Prime Minister among them, were present at the airport to make their first act of homage to the young Sovereign. She stepped down from the aircraft a grave, slight figure. The line of black-coated statesmen bowed deeply in obeisance. For a moment she paused to acknowledge the greeting and then passed on to complete the formalities of her accession.

The scene takes its place among the vignettes of history, unforgettable moments of drama and poignancy. It recalled that other occasion, one hundred fifteen years before, when last a Princess had succeeded to the throne of her ancestors—Victoria, the eighteen-year-old Queen. A girlish figure, hastily clad in a dressing gown, she had been roused from her sleep to receive from the kneeling Archbishop the tidings that she was Sovereign of England. And, through the mists of the centuries, there emerged the picture of another Elizabeth receiving the news from the grave members of the Council that Mary, her sister, was dead and that she reigned in her stead. The messengers of state who had ridden that day through Hertford's leafy lanes to the palace of Hatfield were heralds of the Elizabethan Age. Was the accession of Elizabeth of Windsor to mark the opening of a second Elizabethan Age with glories of equal luster?

It was on the sixth day of February, 1952, that it fell to Winston Churchill to make to the House of Commons the announcement that King George had passed peacefully as he slept. Frail since the operation he had undergone for the removal of a lung, his life for months past had hung by a thread. He had enjoyed a day's shooting on his Norfolk estates, and had retired for the night in good spirits, looking forward to further sport the following day. In the morning, when tea was brought to his room, he could not be roused. He was fifty-six years old and was in the sixteenth year of his reign.

In the end, as Churchill related, death came to him as a friend. After a day of sunshine and sport and after a goodnight to those who loved him best, he fell asleep and so passed on.

The Prime Minister summoned his Cabinet and the constitutional arrangements for the accession of the new Queen were put in hand. They were simple in their formality. At five o'clock in the afternoon Churchill was present with his fellow Ministers at the Accession Council, the assembly of the nobles of the realm presided over by the Lord President of the Council. Thereafter Members of Parliament met to take their individual oath of allegiance to their new Sovereign.

The close association that had prevailed between King George and his Prime Minister during the war added to Winston Churchill's sense of loss. The King's confidence in his First Minister had been kindled during those days of crisis.

At the outset there had been more distant feelings. The King, we are told, had not looked with favor on the part Churchill had played during his brother's abdication. Halifax, not Churchill, (as I have related) would have been the royal preference when a successor to Neville Chamberlain had to be found. It was not long before there was a change in the estimation of the qualities of the Minister, with his matchless capacity for leadership in the days when Britain stood alone. The King, like the men around him, was soon speaking of "Winston." The Minister's weekly visit to the Palace to report on the progress of events was discontinued. Instead His Majesty, to save his Minister expending time and energy, made the journey to Downing Street.

No Minister saw so much of the Monarch. "I made certain," said Churchill, "he was kept informed of every secret matter. The care and thoroughness with which he mastered the immense daily flow of state papers made a deep mark on my mind."

In his broadcast, Churchill paid a moving tribute to the Sovereign who had been greatly loved by his peoples. "The simple dignity of his life, his manly virtues, his sense of duty, his gay charm and happy nature, his example as a husband and a father in his own family circle, his courage in war and peace, all these were aspects of his character which won the glint of admiration, now here, now there, from the innumerable eyes whose gaze falls upon the throne. His conduct may well serve as a model and a guide to constitutional sovereigns throughout the world today and also in future generations."

The people's hearts went out to two women in their bereavement—to Queen Mary, to whom there was the consolation of knowing how well her son had done his duty; and to Elizabeth, his consort and widow. "Their marriage," Churchill said, "was a love match with no idea of regal pomp or splendor. Indeed [until his brother's abdication] there seemed to be before them only the arduous life of royal personages denied so many of the activities of ordinary folk, and having to give so much in ceremonial public service."

He spoke finally of the fair and youthful figure, Princess, wife and mother who had become Queen. She was the heir to all their traditional glories—"never greater than in her father's day—and to all the perplexities and dangers of the time—never greater in peace than now. She comes to the throne when tormented mankind stands uncertainly poised between world catastrophe and the golden age. That it should be a golden age of arts and letters we can only hope."

Royalist and romantic, Winston Churchill was profoundly stirred by the situation of the young woman who in the midst of her grief ascended to the lonely eminence of the throne. He was now to end his career as he had begun, as a servant of the Queen. He was present when, with modest dignity, she made her accession declaration to her Council, her solemnly offered pledge to follow the shining example of service and devotion of her father.

When the House met for the first time to transact business in the new reign, Churchill moved the motion of tribute to the late King; of sympathy to his widow, the Queen Mother; and of loyalty to his daughter, the new Sovereign. There was none by length of service so qualified to undertake the task. Alone among Members of Parliament he had served as Minister under her father, her grandfather George V, and her great-grandfather Edward VII. He had even been a member of the last Parliament of her great-great-grandmother, Queen Victoria of illustrious memory. It was a record of service without parallel.

Early in the new reign, the Prime Minister raised with the Queen the question of the name she was to bear—Windsor or Mountbatten. Her grandfather, King George V, had determined and directed that "henceforth our House and Family shall be styled and known as the House and Family of Windsor." His intention was that the dynasty should forever remain the House of Windsor.

By her marriage, however, the Queen was wife to a man who on becoming a naturalized British subject had adopted the surname of Mountbatten, that of his uncle, the last Viceroy of India. As a private person and commoner Elizabeth would have been known as "Mrs. Mountbatten," and members of the family urged that Mountbatten should remain her name, that of her children, and of the Royal House.

This course was not favored by the Queen's advisers. On the official and insistent advice of the Prime Minister she formally announced the change of her name and that of her children (but not of Philip, her husband) to Windsor. The Mountbattens were left with the minor satisfaction that for the limited period from February 6 to April 9, 1952, the Queen reigned under her married name. She remains, however, on the roll of monarchs as the fourth Sovereign of the House of Windsor.*

Coronation year brought a change at last in the title of the Queen's Minister. He had opened his career as Lieutenant Churchill. He had appeared for a time as Colonel Churchill. But since he left the trenches in the First World War it was as plain Mr. Winston Churchill that he was known, save that as Privy Councilor he was entitled to place Right Honorable before the name and to follow it with the letters O.M. and C.H. in his right as holder of the Order of Merit and as Companion of Honour.

On St. George's Day in 1953, the Queen marked his devoted service to his Sovereign and his country by the conferment of the Order of the Garter, the highest order of chivalry of the realm. Eight years before, he had been offered the honor on his resignation after the war, but in view of the circumstances of his defeat at the polls he had then declined to accept it. Nor would he take the earldom that could have been his; for that title would have entailed his departure to the House of Lords. The inducement of a peerage could not have persuaded him to leave the scene of his life's work, with its extremes of defeat and triumph, in the Commons.

---

* The Queen's wishes were met to a limited extent in 1960 when she issued a declaration that, in future generations, any of her descendants not bearing the title of Prince or Royal Highness should as their surname be known as Mountbatten-Windsor. This could apply only to descendants of her sons in the second generation.

In 1953 there was no reason for him to reject the mark of the young Sovereign's approbation and he received the insignia of Knight Companion at her hands in a brief ceremony at Windsor Castle. Only five commoners had been recipients of the Garter since the century began. It was a further satisfaction to him to revive the ancestral "Sir Winston" after a lapse of over 250 years. The first of that name was Member of Parliament in the seventeenth century, one of the officials in the household of King Charles II, from whom he received a knighthood. It was that Sir Winston Churchill who was father of the military genius John Churchill, Duke of Marlborough.

On Coronation Day (June 2), Sir Winston took his place in the procession of Prime Ministers from Buckingham Palace to Westminster Abbey. There were ten horse-drawn carriages for the First Ministers of Her Majesty's Dominions, with mounted escorts. With Lady Churchill at his side, Sir Winston rode in the first, attended by an escort of the Queen's Own Hussars. From his privileged place within the Abbey he was a spectator of the pomp and solemn splendors of the ancient rite of the crowning and sacring of the Queen.

The clock of time was put back and the colors of the age of chivalry blazed anew as resplendent peers, officers of state in gorgeous apparel, and heralds displaying like peacocks were grouped before the High Altar. There Elizabeth was acknowledged as the undoubted sovereign, "rightful inheritor of the Crown of this realm." There she pledged her solemn oath to her people. There, having been anointed, token of investment in her holy office, she received the Crown, whereupon the trumpets sounded a fanfare and the guns fired in loud salute. London was a city of pageantry and procession on that day of national festivity and rejoicing. It was brought to a close with a BBC program which made her subjects throughout her dominions participators in the ceremonies of the occasion. Her broadcast address was preceded by speeches by her Prime Ministers. It was Sir Winston who introduced Her Majesty to listeners:

> We have had a day which the oldest are proud to have lived to see and which the youngest will remember all their lives. It is my duty and honor to lead you to its culmination.
>
> The splendors of this 2nd of June glow in our minds. Now, as night falls, you will hear the voice of our Sovereign, herself crowned in the Abbey and enthroned forever in our hearts. Here at the summit of our world-wide community is the lady whom we respect because she is our Queen and whom we love because she is herself. Gracious and noble are words familiar to us all in courtly phrasing. Tonight they have a new ring, because we know they are true about

560 / ALLIES IN COLD WAR

the gleaming figure whom Providence has brought to us, and brought to us in times when the present is hard and the future veiled.

It is our dearest hope that the Queen shall be happy and our resolve unswerving that her reign will be as glorious as her devoted subjects can make it.

Then Queen Elizabeth was heard in words of simple sincerity, repeating the pledges of dedicated service that she had given to her peoples at her crowning. Throughout the memorable ceremonies she had been sustained, she said, by the thoughts and prayers of those spread far and wide throughout every continent.

As this day draws to its close, I know that my abiding memory will be not only of the solemnity and beauty of the ceremony, but the inspiration of your loyalty and affection. I thank you all from a full heart.

The final words were an echo of those of the first Elizabeth on her last appearance before her faithful Commons: "Though God had raised me high, yet this I account the glory of my Crown, that I have reigned with your loves." There were times during that day of rejoicing when thoughts went back to Gloriana, last monarch of the Tudor line, a sovereign to whom Sir Winston, had he been born three centuries before, would have lost his heart, as witness this declaration of his admiration: "She had a capacity for inspiring devotion that is, perhaps, unparalleled in British sovereigns. By contrast she knew how to win popular acclaim. In a sense her relationship with her subjects was one long flirtation. She gave to her country the love she never entirely reposed in any one man, and her people responded with a loyalty that almost amounted to worship. It is not for nothing that she has come down to history as Good Queen Bess."

It would not be idle to suppose that when Sir Winston dwelt on Gloriana and the glories of her reign, he permitted himself, for once, the solace of a sigh at the regret he was not a young man embarking on a career to add to the renown of the reign of Queen Bess the Second.

CHAPTER SIX

TOWARD THE SUMMIT

(1953-1955)

THE year 1953 opened with Sir Winston Churchill, the evergreen septuagenarian of the Treasury Bench, pursuing his course in pursuit of peace and the means to relieve the anxieties of the troubled peoples of East and West.

In March there came the news from Russia that was recognized as a turning point in the world's affairs—the death of Marshal Stalin. Sir Winston, oldest of the trio, had been left sole survivor of the Big Three who had planned and achieved the overthrow of Hitlerism.

It was time for a new look at Russia, Sir Winston pronounced, and he prepared for the steps toward a meeting between the leaders. But time that had brought the "new look" in Russia was moving against him. Not even the most robust of septuagenarians can forever continue to bid defiance to the years.

As the first moves were arranged he was struck down by illness. With characteristic spirit he rallied his forces against the attack and, after an interval, was able to resume his place in the House. But the warning was not to be ignored.

He remained in office long enough to be hailed as an octogenarian, one of the select band, along with Gladstone and Palmerston, who conducted Britain's government despite the burden of eighty years. The final period of his premiership is presented in its successive phases.

I. THE NEW LOOK

There were two changes that marked the leadership of East and West in the year 1953. In Russia death closed the dictatorship of the Master of the Kremlin. In the United States, the electors terminated the long Democratic ascendancy and sent Dwight Eisenhower to the White House, its first Republican occupant since Herbert Hoover twenty years previously. Under Eisenhower there was no reason to apprehend an American relapse into isolationism that would expose Europe to subjugation by the Soviet; a change in the Presidency would mean little difference in the policy to be pursued abroad. But in Russia the consequences that might flow from the passing of Stalin were limitless and incalculable. Was there to be a hardening or a relaxation in hostility to the West?

Churchill's judgment had not been at fault over Russia in the past. He had had no illusions about the designs of Stalin, that man in whom the extremes of ruthlessness and ambition had joined, who with Hitler vanquished had dreamed of dominating the world, and who in pursuit of his aim had reduced a third of Europe to the level of satellites of the Soviet. Evaluating the chances now that Stalin was gone, Sir Winston found reason to hope for better things. Malenkov had not long been installed as figurehead in the Kremlin before Churchill began to probe the possibilities of peeping, in the dress jargon of the times, at the "new look" in Russia.

The suggestion was put forward to the House of Commons (May 11, 1953) in a speech which embodied what its author termed a few thoughts that made for peace and that would help a gentle breeze blow upon this weary earth. The supreme event that had recently marked the course of foreign affairs was the change of attitude and even of mind that had taken place in the Soviet domain, and particularly in the Kremlin, since Stalin's death. The new Soviet Government had given encouragement by a series of amicable gestures of leaving off doing things that the other side had not been doing to them. He recalled the friendly telegram he had sent to Stalin eight years previously seeking the means of ending divergencies between communist and non-communist states that might tear the world to pieces.

> I feel [Sir Winston went on] exactly the same about it today. I must make it plain that, in spite of all the uncertainties and the confusion in which world affairs are plunged, I believe that a conference at the highest level should take place between the Allied powers without delay. This conference should not be overhung by

ponderous or rigid agenda, or led into morasses or jungles of technical details, zealously contested by hordes of experts and officials, drawn up in vast, cumbersome array. The conference should be confined to the smallest number of powers and persons possible. . . .

They might be attracted as President Eisenhower has shown himself to be and as *Pravda* does not challenge, by the idea of bidding the weary, toiling masses of mankind enter upon the best spell of good fortune, fair play, well-being, leisure and harmless happiness that has ever been within their reach or even within their dreams. If there is not at the summit of things the will to win the greatest prize ever offered to mankind, a doom-laden responsibility will fall upon those who now possess the power to decide.

The speech was immediately welcomed by Clement Attlee for its tone and its approach to the world's most pressing problem. It set the policy which the democratic powers were to adopt. It marked a turning point, as the Fulton speech had done seven years earlier. It was Fulton in reverse and again it was ahead of opinion.

Across the Atlantic acceptance came slowly. The immediate reaction was one of incredulous misgiving. What now was afoot in Europe? Were the British going to "gang up" with the Russians? The President might have a better appreciation of affairs than his countrymen but, with McCarthy on the rampage, he had need to be wary. He felt himself unable to do more than appeal to the Russians to contribute to the relief of world tension and the removal of a life of perpetual fear. The Secretary of State, John Foster Dulles, voiced American mistrust in expressing doubt whether a high-level conference with the Soviet leaders could yield results as long as the Soviet bloc of countries was promoting a war of aggression in Korea and Indochina and as long as they refused independence to Austria.

The difference between the British and American points of view might be no more than a matter of emphasis, but plainly there were adjustments to be made. Once again the Prime Minister prepared to cross the Atlantic to confer with a third President of the Republic. Arrangements were planned for a meeting to take place, before midsummer, in Bermuda. Churchill looked forward with the liveliest expectations to a conference at which "we may take a definite step forward to a meeting of far greater import."

II. STRICKEN BY A STROKE

The Coronation, its ceremonial and the associated business, added to the burdens of the premiership. The week following the Queen's crowning, Sir Winston presided over the Commonwealth Conference of Prime Ministers. Five plenary sessions were held and many less formal discussions on the diverse problems of the British family of nations in their domestic and their foreign relations. The Prime Minister had also taken over responsibility for the day-to-day conduct of affairs of the Foreign Office in the absence of Anthony Eden, then recuperating from the operation he had undergone in the United States.

Arrangements, meanwhile, had been pushed ahead for the Bermuda conference. It was to open on July 8, and the Prime Minister was to make the crossing in the battleship *Vanguard*. Then, as the plans were completed, Sir Winston was stricken by illness, sudden and incapacitating.

The public announcement was made from 10 Downing Street on June 27 that Sir Winston, on the advice of his doctors, was to rest for a month. The Bermuda meeting was accordingly postponed, a temporary deferment only, as his friend the President remarked in a letter of sympathy. Whether this assumption was well-grounded was questioned by those accurately informed about Sir Winston's condition. Semi-inspired statements suggested that he was not physically ill, but suffering merely from fatigue brought on by a long period of particularly heavy work. The facts of the case, not made known at the time, were more serious.

Sir Winston had suffered a seizure, involving paralysis of his left side. For a man in his seventy-ninth year the implications were disquieting. There was the inevitable anxiety that a second and more incapacitating seizure might follow the first. No indication of this reached the public beyond the hint conveyed in the fact that in addition to Lord Moran, his personal physician, the patient had been attended by Sir Russell Brain, the eminent neurologist.

Politically the indisposition was particularly ill-timed. Not merely the Prime Minister, but Anthony Eden, second in command and successor designate, was absent from the political scene, recovering from the effects of his major operation. Stopgap improvisations were hastily contrived. Sir Winston was hurried off to his country home in Kent, where only the most pressing of official papers would be submitted to him. R. A. Butler, Chancellor of the Exchequer, was nominated to preside over meetings of the Cabinet and shared with the Leader of the House, Captain Crookshank, responsibility for statements on Government policy. Lord Salisbury was sent to take charge of the Foreign Office. In this manner affairs were conducted until Parliament rose in August for the recess. By that time the ministerial invalids had progressed toward recovery.

For his years, Sir Winston's return to health and strength was remarkable. Under the devoted care of his wife and attendants, he had progressed sufficiently by September to attend the St. Leger race meeting as the guest of the Queen. He traveled north to Scotland to stay with Her Majesty at Balmoral, and he rounded off his convalescence by a few days at Beaverbrook's villa near Nice. During the length of his absence from Westminster he did not cease to hold and exercise the responsibilities belonging to his office. On every decision of policy his advice was given. For a man far advanced into the seventies it was a characteristic display of the sovereignty of willpower over bodily disability. The Churchill spirit was adamantine, his determination proof against age. Nevertheless, the shock left its mark.

Sir Winston made his return to public life at the Conservative Party conference at Margate in October. There was wide curiosity as to how he would acquit himself. His continued absence from the scene had not passed without speculation about his capacity to continue in office. There were those who knew how serious had been the attack and others who, not knowing, hinted at the worst. Like his fellow convalescent from the Foreign Office, the Prime Minister was given an affectionate demonstration on his recovery. The speech he delivered established that his powers as orator were unimpaired and that he had returned fighting fit.

It was, he recalled, five months since he had last spoken in public, the first time in his political life that he had kept silence for so long. He gave a review, at half-term, of the achievements of his administration. For the Government, he said that there was no intention of plunging into an early election. Of himself, he indicated that he had no immediate thought of retiring.

"If I stay, for the time being, bearing the burden at my age, it is not because of love for power or office," he declared. "I have had an ample share of both. If I stay it is because I have the feeling that I may, through things that have happened, have an influence on what I care about above all else—the heralding of a sure and lasting peace."

III. THE LAST MISSION

During his weeks of convalescence events contributed little toward the realization of his hopes for high-level talks with the Russians. In place of the abandoned Bermuda conference, a meeting was held at Washington at which Salisbury had frank talks with Eisenhower, but he was unable to remove the President's objections to a meeting, at that stage, with the Russians. Churchill deeply regretted that his incapacity had prevented him from urging upon the President his convictions for an immediate top-level conference with Malenkov. American opposition was strengthened by Russian insistence on the inclusion of the Chinese Communists in a five-power conference. To this the President was implacably opposed.

All that could be agreed at Washington was a meeting of foreign ministers to discuss the specific and limited subjects of the future of Germany and the conclusion of a treaty of peace with Austria. Thereafter there was correspondence with the Russians, proposals submitted and counterproposals made. A fall in the temperature of American opinion was necessary before progress could be hoped for.

It was at this stage that Winston Churchill's purpose had a decisive influence on the course of events. American opinion lagged behind his forward policy. There was disquiet over events in the Far East; civil war in Indochina, with the Russians backing Vietminh against Vietnam loyalists; tension over China, and the risk of incidents, with glowering forces on either side of the Formosa straits. The Americans grew restive over the lukewarm sentiments in London. There were powerful influences in the United States working for a showdown with communism in the Far East.

British support could have involved the powers in a conflict to preserve the stake of the free world in a free Formosa. Under wiser direction, British influence was brought to bear to reduce, not to enlarge, the field of conflict.

In this final phase of his premiership Sir Winston was represented as working in close harmony with his Foreign Secretary.* Twenty years had passed since Anthony Eden had first won Churchill's admiration for his stand against Neville Chamberlain and appeasement of the dictators. As a member of the famous coalition team, Eden had grown in Churchill's esteem. It was on Eden's judgment of men and affairs that Churchill came to rely as most nearly matching his own. It was Eden whose name he submitted to King George when, during the hazards of his wartime missions, he was invited to advise the Sovereign on the succession.

The two men were linked by family ties when, in 1952, Eden married

---

* A conception of the relations between the two men rather different from that prevailing at the time was suggested by Sir Anthony Eden in his memoirs, *Full Circle*. He wrote: "The long era of crown prince was established [in 1942], a position not necessarily enviable in politics. Perhaps this experience helped to dampen my exhilaration when the time came to succeed. . . ." From this passage the impression emerges that like other heirs apparent, Eden at times had chafed over the delay in the succession to his inheritance. We learn further that his expectations from top level discussions with the Russians did not reach to the pitch of robust optimism conveyed by Sir Winston's speeches.

Clarissa Spencer-Churchill, Sir Winston's niece. A few months previously Sir Winston had demonstrated the depth of his regard for the younger man. When his illness incapacitated him, he was urged by his medical advisers to relinquish the burdens of the premiership. At that time Eden, also, was a sick man, convalescing abroad, and would not then have been able to undertake the responsibility of forming a Ministry. Sir Winston found here a compelling reason for continuing in office against his doctors' advice in his determination that Eden should not be cheated of the succession.

Prime Minister and Foreign Secretary strove to bring West Germany into the North Atlantic defense organization, laboring with patience to overcome the objections of the French. "It is," said Churchill in defense of his policy, "of major consequence to the cause we serve to range the mighty German race and nation with the free world instead of allowing it by infiltration or territorial bribery, by actual force, or by our own tragic memories, to be amalgamated with the satellite states to carry the doctrine and control of Moscow into world supremacy. Earnestly as I desire to come to a peaceful arrangement for coexistence with Russia, I should regard it as an act of insanity to drive the German people into the hands of the Kremlin and tilt into Communist tyranny the destiny of mankind."

Here there was accord across the Atlantic. It was when the problem of Indochina had to be faced under the complication of French reverses that divergencies in policy began to strain Anglo-American cooperation. The rebels, with Communist support, were preparing to invest the capital of Vietnam. A conference of the nations was summoned at Geneva. The Americans favored all-out military aid for the French, involving operations that might have to be illimitably extended.

The last weekend in April, 1954, was the critical time. The Prime Minister at Chequers received Eden's report. Ministers were summoned to a Sunday conference with the Service Chiefs. Eden went to Geneva to exert Britain's influence and his own skill as negotiator to compose the differences by negotiation as an alternative to action that must extend the field of hostilities. The opposing forces faced each other but were not committed. The steadying influence of Britain prevailed.

In America, Eden was denounced for truckling to the Soviets. When the Indochina settlement was eventually reached by French Premier M. Mendes-France there was an outcry in the press about a second Munich. Eden was depicted in a famous cartoon in *Time* magazine with a Neville Chamberlain umbrella. He and Churchill were reproached for looking "alarmingly like appeasers." It appeared that a settlement had been reached over Indochina at the cost of a breach in the good relations between Britain and the United States.

To put these matters right Sir Winston decided it was time for talks in Washington. He accepted with alacrity an invitation to spend a weekend in America as guest, with Eden, of the President. From the tone of hostile opinion in the American press, the British Ministers had reason to expect a lively reception. The newspapers wrote of tension. Eden's phrases in the House of Commons were said to hint at British views that Americans were over-hasty and excitable in their dealings with the Russians. A gulf had developed and the Americans had found that "we simply cannot pull our Allies with us any further."

The British visitors were gratified to find that the barkings of the Press stopped short of the doors of the White House. None of the missions to Washington was more agreeable or more fruitful. During four and a half days of hard work, all subjects of major current importance were discussed. "We talked," Sir Winston afterward reported, "with perfect frankness and in full friendship with each other. We dispelled some misunderstandings, even some nightmares, from the minds of our American friends about the direction of our policies. I think we convinced them that we have changed none of our ultimate joint objectives and that there is, at any rate, some wisdom in the means by which we are proposing to reach them."

The agreement that was reached on many points did not extend to a meeting at the top level with the Russians, although "there was no slamming of the door, no slamming down on the plan."

Sir Winston submitted himself in person to examination by critics of the press. Attending a luncheon given by the National Press Club, he replied to a variety of questions. On the crucial point of relations with Russia he made a statement that was quoted throughout the United States and contributed to a change in the American outlook:

> I am of opinion that we ought to have a really good try for peaceful coexistence. I am anxious that the real mood of the Russian people should be known. I have a great feeling—I may be quite wrong, but it is in my fingertips—that there must be a wish among the mass of the Russian people to have a better time and more fun. Nothing is more likely to bring about a modification of the rigid Russian system than contacts between the Russian people and the Western world—cultural contacts and trade contacts. I would like to make sure that the Russian people would feel that they might gain far more from a quarter of a century of peaceful development in their own country than they would be pushing matters to a point

where we would all be led into a situation which baffles the human imagination in its terror, but which I am sure, would leave us victorious—victorious on a heap of ruins.

The phrase "peaceful coexistence" was one that had been coined by Eden and it found acceptance in Washington, the President himself adopting it. It was in the peaceful coexistence of communist and non-communist countries, Eisenhower said, that the hope of the world lay.

From Washington the British Ministers flew on to Canada. A visit of thirty hours was passed in discussions with St. Laurent and other Canadian Ministers. Sir Winston, as a member of the Canadian Privy Council, was invited to sit at the Canadian cabinet table. Returning to New York, he and Eden boarded the Queen Elizabeth and arrived in London on July 6. He had been on his travels for eleven days, a considerable achievement for a man of seventy-nine recently recovered from a paralysis. This was the last of his missions overseas. It was fruitful in results. Misunderstandings had been removed, relations repaired, and a contribution made in the adjustment of American opinion toward Churchill's policy for peace.

In the account he gave to the House of Commons of the visit and its results, Churchill dwelt with satisfaction on the six-point declaration reaffirming the fundamentals on which the policies of the two governments were based.

I would ask you to bear in mind this declaration of our basic unity in days when newspapers are so full of bickerings and disagreements. Disagreement is much more easy to express and much more exciting to the reader than agreement. The highest common factor of opinion is not a fertile ground for lively epigrams and sharp antitheses. I should not myself fear even the accusation of platitude in such a statement if it sought only the greatest good of the greatest number. . . . I was thrilled by the wish of the President to bring our two countries so directly together in a new declaration or charter, and to revive and renew the comradeship and brotherhood which joined the English-speaking world together.

Despite hesitancy in the United States, Churchill did not permit his approach to the Russians to fail by default. On his way home he sent a personal telegram to Molotov with the suggestion for a friendly meeting, informal, without agenda or specified objectives, as the first step to a wider conference. Receiving an encouraging reply, he secured Cabinet approval for submiting the proposal of a meeting at Berne or Stockholm between himself and Eden on the one side and Malenkov and Molotov on the other. In the result, however, the Prime Minister's invitation was not sent, his approach being superseded by other moves in the diplomatic field.

The major purpose was for the time obscured while the Russians devoted their ingenuity to obstructing the ratification of the European Defense Community Treaty, with the associated plan for the inclusion of German contingents in the European defense force. French anxieties, grounded on Germany of the future rather than Russia of the present, were with difficulty overcome. Eden's patient endeavors had finally to be backed by a pledge of continued British aid on the Continent.

Churchill and the Cabinet, to relieve France's fears, committed Britain to the maintenance of a force of 100,000 men in Europe. It was an undertaking that no British Prime Minister had previously been prepared to contemplate. Churchill and Eden ended Britain's centuries-old isolation behind the Channel ditch. British troops would be permanently stationed in Europe in peace for the first time since Mary Tudor lost Calais.

This formidable departure from British traditional policy was acclaimed as a contribution to the security of western Europe or, as Eisenhower called it, one of the greatest diplomatic achievements of our time. Sir Winston gave full credit to Eden for what had been achieved. For the policy, he told Conservatives in conference at Blackpool, the Cabinet, which was consulted at every stage, bore full responsibility. But the initiative had sprung from the Foreign Secretary. Without his knowledge, tact and skill this monument and milestone could never have been passed.

Unknown to his hearers Sir Winston was addressing Conservatives gathered for their annual conference on the last occasion. There was no hint that in six months' time he would have handed over the leadership. In November he was present in London's Guildhall to make his last speech as Minister of the Crown to guests gathered to do honor to the new Lord Mayor. As he rose from his place among the notables, did his thoughts turn back for a moment to the past? Were there flashbacks of historic gatherings at which he had been present? Did he think of his predecessors on the roll whom he had seen rise within those walls—Baldwin, MacDonald, Lloyd George, Asquith and Campbell-Bannerman? Did he remember the night when Lloyd George had delivered the famous Guildhall warning to the Kaiser over Agadir? Did he think how he—it was almost forty years since—had first attended the banquet as Minister of the Crown, then President of the Board of Trade, a young fellow stepping into history? There was no sign that evening that it was a farewell appearance. There was a musing quality about the speech he made, the reflective comments of a veteran statesman brooding on the fortunes of mankind. His note was one of optimism as he surveyed the possibilities ahead, declaring:

> If the human race wishes to have a prolonged and indefinite period of material prosperity, they have only got to behave in a peaceful and helpful way toward one another. Science will then do for them all that they can wish and more than they can dream. If it is, of course, their wish to be quarrelsome and bite one another all the time, there is no doubt they can kill each other in a quicker and more wholesale manner than ever before. The choice is theirs and ours. Man is becoming increasingly master of his own fate and increasingly uncertain of what it is going to be.
>
> Nothing is final. Change is unceasing and it is very likely that mankind will have a lot more to learn before they come to their journey's end. For myself, I am an optimist—it does not seem to be of much use being anything else. I cannot believe that the human race will not find its way through the problems that confront it.

IV. OCTOGENARIAN

On the last day of November, 1954, there were birthday celebrations without precedent. Winston Churchill was eighty. There was never a human birthday like it in the world before. The homage paid to Queen Victoria on her Jubilee Days could alone compare with the tributes of respect, admiration and affection showered upon Sir Winston.

The political hatchet was buried while members of all parties united to greet the greatest living Englishman. The Queen and members of the Royal Family offered him their presents and well-wishers in the thousands sent their contributions to the birthday fund. Messages of congratulation poured in from all the corners of the world, from kings and queens, from parliaments and assemblies. New York hailed "an immortal," Paris the "incarnation of the spirit of a nation," Rome the "last titan of our great Victorian England." Eton, even, was moved to acknowledge the "greatest of old Harrovians."

In Westminster's historic hall, around which the whirl of ten centuries of history had revolved, men and women of all parties gathered to pay honor to the Prime Minister and to admit him, in happy phrase, as Freeman of British history. The V-sign was tapped out in Morse code on a drum as Sir Winston and Lady Churchill entered from St. Stephen's entrance to descend the staircase and be seated between the Lord Chancellor and the Speaker of the House of Commons. The playing of the Elgar march that provides the tune for "Land of Hope and Glory" was drowned by cheers and handclaps. Mr. Speaker, in brief and appropriate words, led the speeches.

It was remarked at the time that by common accord the speakers, with skillful touch, skimmed lightly over the surface, avoiding the deeper emotions of the occasion. It is not possible now to read without the passing reverence of a sigh the phrases that served to express their admiration, but that masked their affection for the man for whom these celebrations could not be other than greetings near the close of an illustrious career, prelude to the voice of history.

Clement Attlee saluted the great parliamentarian, "the last of the great orators who can touch the heights," with a Shakespearean greeting: "I come not to bury Caesar but to praise him—Caesar indeed, for you have not only carried on war but written your own commentaries." Mr. Attlee made the presentation of Parliament's gift—the portrait by Graham Sutherland. The painting had aroused a note of controversy to which Sir Winston lightly alluded in his acceptance of a remarkable example of modern art, one that "combined force and candor."

D. R. Grenfell, the senior of the House, presented, in a book suitably illuminated, the signatures of fellow members of the House of Commons. Lord Salisbury remarked on the privilege of knowing in the flesh one whom later generations would meet only in the pages of history.

The Prime Minister had sat in characteristic House of Commons pose, his hands flat upon his knees, listening to his opponent's magnanimous appraisal of a variegated career, reflecting on the effect on his own controversial value as a politician. No one, he said, when it came to his turn to speak, had ever received such a mark of honor before. There had been nothing like it in British political history. Indeed he doubted whether any of the modern democracies abroad had ever shown such a degree of kindness and generosity to a party politician not yet retired, who at any time might be involved in controversy. He was overpowered by the two emotions of pride and humility. Who would not be proud to have all this happen to him, and never was he more sure of how far it went beyond his deserts.

It was a special pleasure to have heard Mr. Attlee's description of his speeches in the war as having been the expression not only of Parliament but of the whole nation—and then followed the classic passage: "I have never accepted what many have said, that I inspired the nation. Their will was resolute and remorseless. It was the nation and the race dwelling round the globe that had the lion's heart. I had the luck to be called upon to give the roar." He had found the matchless phrase to describe one aspect of his own achievement.

At another gathering in the Royal Gallery of the House of Lords, Sir

Winston was offered, at the hands of Sir Anthony Eden, a gift from past and present Conservative, Unionist, and National Liberal members of both Houses of Parliament. It was a pair of silver jugs, once the property of General Charles Churchill, brother of the great Marlborough and son of the first Sir Winston Churchill. From the Queen and the Duke of Edinburgh, the Queen Mother, Princess Margaret and other members of the Royal Family, he received a set of silver wine-coasters, engraved with the ciphers of the royal donors. From Buckingham Palace he returned to Downing Street. In response to repeated calls from the crowd he came to the first-floor window of Number Ten to stand giving his famous victory sign.

There was some pother at that time—it was not allowed to disturb the harmony of the celebrations—over a passage in a speech he delivered before his constituents at Woodford. Recalling the time in 1945 when the Germans were surrendering by the hundreds of thousands, he spoke of having sent Montgomery a telegram directing him carefully to collect the surrendered arms so that "they could easily be issued again to German soldiers whom we should have to work with if the Soviet advance continued."

It was a disclosure that testified to the Prime Minister's concern over Russian intentions as the war was won. But why, it was asked, should he have recalled such an episode from the past at a moment when he was seeking to reach an accommodation with Russia's new leaders. There was a critical leading article in *The Times,* some expression of critical opinion by others, and much spirited defense of Sir Winston. But a mystery prevailed. Where was the telegram? What precisely were its terms? Prolonged search both by Churchill and Montgomery failed to discover it. In the end Churchill, in the unusual role of penitent, made a personal statement in the House, formally expressing regret for a statement he had made relying on his memory. He had failed to observe the rule "verify your quotations," and his memory had played him false.

"I am now nearing the end of my journey: I hope I still have some service to render." The closing words of his birthday speech in Westminster Hall had raised speculation and rumor that there would be a change at Number Ten before the year was out. Sir Winston, falsifying prediction for yet another time, was still in office when the bells tolled for 1954.

V. STRATEGY OF THE H-BOMB

The year that opened in January, 1955, was to be marked by great events. The signs of improvement in affairs were slight. Europe's uncertainties were unrelieved. France still delayed sanction of the plan for European defense. Summit talks with the Russians were still delayed. In the Far East the rumblings over Formosa grew more disturbing. In mid-January President Eisenhower found it necessary to seek authority from Congress to take military action that might be needed to repel any Chinese Communist aggression and to ensure the security of Formosa and the Pescadores. The Chinese People's Republic reaffirmed its intention to take Formosa. Fighting was intensified. Were hostilities over the Far East to be extended, with Russia and the United States engaged on either side, involving the world in a third and atomic war?

While the gloom in the Far East was unrelieved, the Russians changed their leader. Malenkov was dismissed and, more fortunate than fallen leaders in Stalin's days, was permitted to serve in subordinate place. Marshal Bulganin reigned in his stead, with Marshal Zhukov advanced to be Minister of Defense. What did these changes portend? Bulganin's protest that the United States was following a dangerous road over Formosa was scarcely to be accepted as reassuring.

It was during these unquiet days that Churchill reached the decision that his resignation from office could not be longer deferred. He devoted the labors of his last weeks in office to the dual purposes of his policy, peace through strength. From his place in Downing Street he brought his powerful and steadying influence to bear and Anthony Eden, in a succession of meetings, pursued his labors for a settlement. The Churchill-Eden combination was powerful in the cause of peace. By the spring there was a lowering of tension. The Formosa crisis passed. The contestants hesitated and drew back from the hostilities in which they had threatened to embroil themselves, deterred, it may be, by the catastrophic consequences of employing the weapons they had fashioned, by the awesome potentialities of the hydrogen bomb.

Atomic warfare was one of Sir Winston's major preoccupations in his last spell of office. It was with surprise that he had learned of the development of the H-bomb by the Americans. He was, as he confessed later, astounded by the official account of the results of the explosion of the first hydrogen bomb in the Pacific in 1952, when the test island in the Eniwetok Atoll was obliterated and a vast cavity torn in the floor of the ocean. The immensity of the destruction that was wrought made all previous defense plans immediately out of date. There followed the revelation of the destructiveness of atomic dust.

Sir Winston was dismayed at the lack of first-hand information from the American ally, information that could not be passed on under ban of the McMahon Act. Included in the British delegation for the 1954 mission to Washington were Lord Cherwell, the Prime Minister's adviser on scientific affairs, and Sir Edwin Plowden, head of the British Atomic Energy Authority. There were discussions with the Americans on atomic developments, but they were restricted in their scope by the McMahon Act limitations.

Further disclosures followed on the immensity of the forces released by the H-bomb, 600 to 700 times as great as the weapon used against the Japanese at Hiroshima. There was world alarm at the potentialities. Men looked into the abyss of annihilation and recoiled at the prospect.

In February, 1955, came the announcement that the British Government had decided to develop and produce the hydrogen bomb. A White Paper set out the Government's intentions in the language of a Government department no longer restricted in sobriety—unprecedented destruction, large tracts devastated, many more uninhabitable, essential services and communications put out of action, water and power supplies disrupted, public morale most severely tested.

The Cabinet's decision to keep Britain up with the leaders in the perfection of the instruments for mankind's annihilation was justified as a duty that had to be undertaken. "We have to prepare for the risk of a world war and so prevent it." It was one of the last major decisions to which, as Prime Minister, Sir Winston Churchill contributed. It was generally received as an unpalatable but unavoidable necessity. There were protests from pacifists and humanitarians, men and women opposed to Britain producing atom bombs or any of the paraphernalia of war.

Sir Winston rose in the House on March 1 to seek approval for the Government's decision. It was a remarkable parliamentary occasion. The speaker was a living link between the Victorian and the atomic ages. Fifty years before, when the machine gun was a novelty among military weapons, he had given to the House a forecast of what world war would entail—"the wars of peoples will be more terrible than those of kings." Twice he had seen his forecasts terribly fulfilled. Now, in his eightieth year, he stood at the dispatch-box to discourse on the strategy of the new warfare, with atomic artillery that would reduce all weapons of the past to the level of popgun toys in the children's nursery. Global war, in his stark phrase, would result for the participants in mutual annihilation.

Between the atomic bomb of the last war and the hydrogen bomb of the next there was an immense gulf. With all its terrors the atomic bomb had not carried man beyond the scope of human control. But, with the hydrogen bomb developed by the Americans, the entire foundations of human affairs had been revolutionized. Mankind had been placed in a situation both measureless and laden with doom.

The Prime Minister paused to strike the dispatch-box before him. He went on:

It is now a fact that a quantity of plutonium, perhaps less than would fill the box, here, on this table—and it is quite a safe thing to store—would suffice to produce weapons which would give indisputable world domination to any great power which was the only one to have it. There is no defense, no absolute defense against the hydrogen bomb. Nor is any method in sight by which any country could be guaranteed against the devastating injury which even a score of them might inflict in wide regions.

The potentiality of destruction extended beyond the direct effect of blast and heat. There was to be considered the consequences of a "fall-out" of wind-borne radioactive particles. These had an immediate and direct effect on human beings in the path of such a cloud. There was also the indirect effect through animals, grass and vegetables, which would pass on the contagion to human beings through their food. Many who escaped the direct effects of the explosion would be confronted with poisoning, or starvation, or both. "Imagination," declared the Prime Minister, "stands appalled."

From the very magnitude of the perils, Churchill derived some measure of consolation. On this he based his policy for the future—defense by deterrent.

The broad effect of the latest development is to spread almost indefinitely the area of mortal danger. This would certainly increase the deterrent in Soviet Russia by putting her enormous spaces and scattered population on a basis of equality, or near-equality with our small, densely populated island and with western Europe. I cannot regard this development as adding to our danger. On the contrary, to this form of attack continents are as vulnerable as islands. Hitherto crowded countries like the United States and western Europe have had this outstanding vulnerability to carry. But the hydrogen bomb, with its vast range of distribution, and even wider area of contamination, would be effective against populations so widely dispersed as to have made them feel, hitherto, that they were not in danger at all.

Major war of the future must differ from anything we have known in the past in one significant respect: Each side at the outset will suffer what it dreads most—in fact the loss of everything we have ever known. The deterrents will grow continually in value. In the past the aggressor was tempted by the hope of scoring an early advantage. In future he may be deterred by the knowledge that the other side has the certain power to inflict swift, inescapable and crushing retaliation.

There outlined were the general principles, the broad strategy of the future war of atoms. But, this was no speech of generalities. Sir Winston spoke in frank and utter realism, directly of and to the Russians. For the present they were outdistanced in invention by the United States. It would take them three or four years, perhaps, to make good the leeway. The only country then able to deliver a full-scale nuclear attack with hydrogen bombs, at a few hours' notice, was the United States. It was, of course, conceivable that the Russians, fearing a nuclear attack before they had caught up with the United States of America, might attempt to bridge the gap by a surprise attack with such nuclear weapons as they possessed already. It would involve immediate retaliation on a far larger scale. To the Russians he would say:

> Although you might kill millions of our people and cause widespread havoc by surprise attack, we can within a few hours certainly deliver several, indeed many times the weight of nuclear material that you have used and continue retaliation on that scale. We have already hundreds of bases for attacks from all angles and made a study of suitable targets.

This was the plainest of plain speaking. Never in time of peace had a Prime Minister from his place in the House of Commons addressed a warning so outspoken and of such dread import to the government of another people.

The development of the H-bomb had given a new urgency to the need for talks at the summit. Many months had passed since the Prime Minister had first roused public expectations. He had been sick but was now recovered—why the delay? From time to time there had been speculation. Odd tales were whispered in the clubs and were fostered in Opposition circles. The Old Man was bent on going to see the Russians but his Cabinet would not let him; under Salisbury's lead they had threatened to quit office in a body were he to insist. So rumor ran to be bent to political ends.

Then, the gossips suggested that while Churchill was willy Eisenhower was nilly, and Prime Minister had had perforce to yield to President. It was the line of criticism taken by Aneurin Bevan in the H-bomb debate. The Welshman contrived a backhanded compliment to lead off his attack. The difficulty of the Prime Minister in making a speech to the House, he said, arose out of his extraordinary capacity for presentation. The mediocrity of his thinking was concealed by the majesty of his language. His deeds did not match his great words. If he believed the statements he had presented to the House, then why had he not insisted on talks at the summit with the Russian leaders as the first approach to an understanding?

> It may be [declared Bevan] that he would like to do it but that the

United States won't permit him. That is a somber thing to say, it is a wicked thing to believe, but we have now reached the situation in Britain where we can, in a few short years, run the risk of the extinction of British civilization. We cannot reach the potential enemy in time to arrive at an accommodation because we are now at the mercy of the United States.

This brought Churchill to his feet to make indignant protest:

It is absolutely wrong to suggest that the course we have followed has been at the direction of the United States. I would like to have seen a top-level conference of the three powers shortly after Mr. Malenkov took power to see, as I said, "Is there a new look?" I wanted to do that and my colleagues agreed. I had charge of the Foreign Office owing to the Foreign Secretary's illness. I proposed to go over and see the President and hoped to arrange with him to invite a three-power conference. However, I was struck down by a very sudden illness which paralyzed me completely physically. I had to put it all off and it was not found possible to persuade the President to join in that process.

I have also considered the possibility of a dual meeting at some neutral place like Stockholm. While I was thinking about these matters—because I really have not been a ditherer on the subject—I have tried my very utmost. I would not retain the headship of our Government on a subject of this kind if they were not acting in what I thought was a sincere and honorable mood.

This statement was the first disclosure in public of the severe nature of the attack that Sir Winston had suffered eighteen months previously.

The matter of Russia was not allowed to rest there. Bevan's criticisms offered the Socialists an easy line to hunt. A formal motion was introduced in the House deploring the Government's delay and demanding immediate steps for a three-power conference between the heads of governments. Clement Attlee called for a greater sense of urgency in pressing forward in an effort to relieve world tension. At present it seemed to be bogged down.

This motion drew a vigorous rejoinder from the Prime Minister. He gave an account in detail of his patient and continuing attempts to meet the Russians in a two-power, three-power or four-power meeting. It was a survey of his stewardship. It was also, though this was not then realized, his last major pronouncement on foreign affairs.

Month by month Sir Winston chronicled his approaches on both sides of the Atlantic from the time of his first suggestion in May, 1953, after Stalin's death. The more these matters were considered in detail, the more, he claimed, it appeared that the Government had been untiring, in no way lukewarm or dithering, in pursuing its purpose across one obstacle after another. Malenkov had gone and new forces ruled in Russia. The new look he had proposed to explore in 1953 had been succeeded by another new look. So far the new look had not raised any extravagant hopes of improvement:

> Although I do not pretend to measure what the recent changes in the Soviet oligarchy imply, I do not feel that they should discourage us from further endeavors. One thing stands in my mind above all others—the increasing understanding and friendship with our ally, the United States.

The brake that the American administration was supposed to be applying on British action had been a frequent target for Socialist marksmen. It had been suggested that, ignoring the United States, Britain should "go to it" alone, a fatuity that Sir Winston had deplored. Now he closed his speech with an appeal for understanding of President Eisenhower's position.

> My feeling is that the wish of America for peace grows stronger at the same pace as their capacity for war. They give great consideration to our views. They show marked respect for our experience of the European scene. But this very attention which they pay to what we advise is accompanied by serious irritation of their public opinion at anything they take to be unfair criticism. When there are criticisms that the President has not come over here or has not come to an international conference, it must be remembered that he cannot move about as freely as ordinary heads of state move. No President has ever had the knowledge and experience of Europe and of the very urgent group of problems now confronting it as is possessed by President Eisenhower. I hope that nothing will be said on this side of the Atlantic which will arouse new inhibitions in the American mind against the freedom of his personal movements.

Progress toward a world settlement was held up by the French. Were they, victims twice in one generation of German aggression, to nullify the labors that had gone to the construction of the new structure for the defense of western Europe? In a letter of January 10, 1955, Sir Winston addressed himself to Mendes-France with words of praise and warning. The leadership of Mendes-France had given an impression that had not been sustained since the days of Clemenceau. But delay in completing ratification of the London agreements was an impediment to progress with the Russians. Weakness made no appeal to the Soviets. To mix up the process of ratification with what might follow afterward would be to dilute both firmness and conciliation. Sir Winston wrote:

I and my colleagues are wholeheartedly resolved that there shall be no meeting or invitation in any circumstances that we can foresee between the four powers . . . until the London-Paris agreements have been ratified by all signatories. In this we are in the closest accord with the United States. . . . I fear that an indefinite process of delay may well lead to adoption of other solutions [of Western defense] which are certainly being studied on both sides of the Atlantic. . . . I should be bound, whether as Prime Minister, or as a private member, to support the policy known as the "empty chair," although this may involve large changes in the infrastructure of NATO, both military and political. . . . Having, ever since 1910, worked and fought with and for France, for whose people I have a deep affection, I should feel the utmost sorrow to see her isolated and losing her influence with the rest of the free world. I hope that it will fall to you to save your country from this evil turn of fortune.

When the final debates took place in Paris, Mendes-France was no longer in office, but Sir Winston's letter was read and it had its influence on the votes for ratification. Did Mendes-France and his colleagues note the implications of the phrase, "I should feel bound whether as Prime Minister or *as a private member*"? It was a hint that Sir Winston had already made his decision to retire from office at no distant date. But of this no public indication was given at that time.

CHAPTER SEVEN

THE DEPARTURE

1955

A s THE weeks of 1955 passed by and Sir Winston added to his parliamentary technique the practiced skill of an octogenarian, speculation about his retirement began rather to fade. Certainly, they said, he would now see the Parliament out. Maybe, they thought, he might lead his party in the next election and see the following Parliament in. After all, the grand old Gladstone had formed his fourth administration when he was eighty-two, so why not Churchill? The years and the exhausting strains of two world wars had, of course, taken their toll, but he was still as outstanding in debate, the phrases came rolling out as sonorous as ever and in the cut and thrust of debate his repartee had lost none of its barbs.

The impromptus of the speaker in Parliament or the law courts are the sure measure of the quickness of a man's mind. With the prepared speech there is never the certainty that the lofty passage or the telling phrase may not be the result of some other inspiration. Presidential speeches have had their compilers. Follow Churchill's course through the debates, mark the unfailing readiness in riposte, and there is no doubt about the fertility of his wit and the swift working of his brain.

In his final phase, Churchillisms were coined at question time as readily as ever. The House waited in expectation as, with the blandness of Mr. Pickwick, he disposed of the parliamentary picadors. He curbed the loquacious, as when a member asking this and that and the other thing was advised: "Try one at a time." He brushed aside the persistent, as when a member, by his question, suggested this fact and that fact, he observed: "The Honorable Gentleman seems more desirous of imparting information than receiving it. Anyhow, I have nothing to give him."

Occasionally they scored against him as when some members began to boo and the Prime Minister inquired if it were in order to boo a member of the House. "What else," asked a Labour member, "can you say to a goose?"

The parliamentary feud with "Nye" Bevan was continued, though the Welshman's acerbity seemed to be less sharp than in the past. There was the occasion when the example of the Member for Ebbw Vale was used to point an argument. "I thought it would be a good thing," said the Prime Minister, "to have diplomatic representation, but if you recognize anyone it does not mean that you like him. We all, for instance, recognize the Right Honorable Gentleman, the Member for Ebbw Vale."

The Churchill brilliancies are scattered at random in *Hansard's* pages and, as quotation here cannot indefinitely continue, I select the following as an example of the readiness of Sir Winston's wit. The budget was under debate. Dalton, the former Chancellor of the Exchequer, continued the work of "debunking" Butler that had been begun by the Socialist ex-Chancellor, Gaitskell. Obviously, Dalton said, Gaitskell had got under the Prime Minister's skin, for Sir Winston, in a speech at Glasgow, had referred to this "old-school-tie careerist."

"It was not correctly reported," interjected Sir Winston. "I said, 'This old-school-tie, left-wing careerist.' "

"That amendment," Dalton resumed, continuing his quotation, "will be helpful to emphasize a comment I shall make in a moment. 'This old-school-tie, left-wing careerist may rightly claim to have been the worst Chancellor since Mr. Dalton.' In these days we tend to be too polite in our political exchanges and I welcome the robust abuse of the Prime Minister, hoping that he will not resent counterattack. 'The worst Chancellor since Mr. Dalton'—that may be a matter for argument."

Sir Winston (blandly): "May I assure the Right Honorable Gentleman that I did not attempt to set myself up as a judge of the competition between himself and the Right Honorable Gentleman."

For these lighter leavenings of the heavy dough of debate, members were in Sir Winston's debt. When he resumed his place after his absence through illness in 1953, Woodrow Wyatt rose to inquire: "May I ask the Prime Minister whether he is aware that the House of Commons is a duller place without him?" But even to the display of his wit and wisdom there had to be a period.

One Saturday morning in March, newspaper readers * were startled to learn that the great Churchill was at last to step aside in favor of his successor designate, the Foreign Secretary. The wits had made play over Sir Anthony's supposedly deferred hopes, and friends, according to the current gibe, had been heard to remark: "You know, Winston, if you don't retire soon Anthony will be too old for the job." The Saturday report was received with reserve. Was it no more than the latest variation on a time-worn rumor? But there was corroborative detail. The occasion of the parting between Sovereign and Prime Minister was indicated, and there were predictions about an election after the resignation.

There followed a period of uncertainty about the Prime Minister's intentions. Those in the know were not forthcoming, and those who were not looked in vain to the Treasury Bench for signs and portents. Once Sir Winston had been asked if he would give an assurance that he was not on a slippery slope to "another place" (the circumlocution used in the Commons for the House of Lords), and he replied: "Provided the term 'another place' is used in a strictly parliamentary sense, I will gladly give the assurance required." Now, sphinxlike and bland, he gave no indication that he was or was not moving on. So matters passed in suspense up to the last, and beyond the point that affairs could be followed by the majority of readers of the morning newspapers.

For almost the only time in his long career Winston Churchill, on his resignation, failed to achieve maximum display in the headlines. Fleet Street had been silenced by a strike. For a month the mammoth presses were idle. When the day of change in Downing Street arrived the *Daily Worker* alone of the London press appeared to blazon the news of the resignation in a banner across its front page.

It was on March 31 that Sir Winston Churchill rose in his place on the front bench to give his last replies as Prime Minister. A question on Formosa gave him the opportunity to commend the work of his successor. "No one has worked harder," he said, "indeed I doubt if anyone in the whole world has worked as hard as my Right Honorable friend, the Foreign Secretary, to steer this matter out of the danger area."

His final words to questioners were these: "I think the closer the contacts between the United States and Europe the better." It was an appropriate valediction. To establish and improve those contacts in the cause first of victory, then of lasting peace, had been a major purpose of his terms as First Minister of the Crown.

On the night of Monday, April 4, there was an occasion without

* The report appeared exclusively, I believe, in the *Daily Express* which was credited, with Lord Beaverbrook's inspiration, for one of the Fleet Street scoops of the century.

precedent at 10 Downing Street. To do honor to her Minister, Queen Elizabeth attended as guest at a dinner given by Sir Winston and Lady Churchill. The leading members of the Cabinet and of the famous coalition were present, many of the leaders-in-arms during the war, some close associates, and, a graceful recognition, Mrs. Neville Chamberlain, widow of the last of the five Prime Ministers under whom Churchill held office. Sir Winston proposed the health of Her Majesty and of the Duke of Edinburgh.

The Queen then rose to raise her glass to the toast of Sir Winston Churchill. It was something, she said, that probably few of her predecessors had had the opportunity of doing—proposing the health of her Prime Minister.

The crowds that gathered outside were witnesses of the parting scene— the veteran Minister escorting the Queen to her car, Sir Winston's deep bow of homage, Lady Churchill's graceful curtsey. For a moment Sir Winston stood alone in the doorway. The crowd raised a cheer with a hesitancy that conveyed appreciation of the sadness of this leave-taking.

On Tuesday, April 5, 1955, the formalities were concluded. Before lunch Sir Winston took leave of his Cabinet colleagues. In the afternoon the familiar figure was seen to arrive at Buckingham Palace. Three-quarters of an hour later he re-entered his car. In audience of the Queen he had tendered his resignation as Prime Minister and First Lord of the Treasury, "which Her Majesty was graciously pleased to accept." It was the time-honored, laconic formula. Gladstone, on the completion of his long service, was pained that Queen Victoria expressed no sense of regret at his last audience. No such omission had marked the leave-taking of Sir Winston Churchill with Victoria's great-great-granddaughter. Back at Number Ten, Ministers not of Cabinet rank shook hands with their late chief.

On Wednesday Sir Anthony Eden kissed hands on his appointment as First Lord of the Treasury. Sir Winston, having taken tea with the staff, made his exit from Number Ten. The waiting crowds were rewarded by the sight of the Churchill tokens—Rufus the poodle, the budgerigar, and the cigar. With a final, emphatic display of the V-sign, Sir Winston was driven away. He was glimpsed again in Kent as he passed through the gates at Chartwell. "Come into the grounds all of you and see my goldfish," was his invitation. It was one of the asides of history.

Back in the center of things they had been acclaiming him—in the House of Commons, in the Lords, and in countries across the seas. In the House the loss of the great front-bencher was thought to be compensated for by the gain of the greatest back-bencher of all time. In the Lords, the Conservative Prime Minister was seen to be one of the greatest of all liberals. Overseas, in the Commonwealth, in France and Flanders, and in the United States there was an outpouring of tribute. Eisenhower, in the rose gardens of the White House, spoke movingly of "his very old and very dear friend." The newspapers across the Atlantic spread themselves to mark the occasion. The *Herald Tribune* devoted twenty-nine columns to his career. In London, alone, there was no marshaling of type; Fleet Street was still under the interdict of the strike.

Having left the stage, Sir Winston did not hover embarrassingly in the wings. He slipped away for a change to Sicily and Syracuse. In the new House of Commons, to which his Essex constitutents took pride in returning him, he was glimpsed for a moment as he completed the brief formality of taking his seat. New members were disappointed in their hopes of hearing the great man in debate.

A little later in the year there took place the summit talks to which the labors of his third term had been the prelude. With a self-abnegation rare among holders of supreme power, he had stepped aside as the arrangements for the four-power meeting at Geneva were being completed. The French had ratified the plan for Europe's defense and the inclusion of the West Germans. The last obstacle had been removed. The way to the summit talks was open. Then, as the last steps were to be taken on this Mount Everest of his hopes, Churchill had relinquished office.

Late in the summer Sir Winston drove once more into Downing Street. He walked to the door of Number Ten. The clicking cameras caught the familiar figure as he stepped across the threshold. It was the record of a moment of exquisite poignancy. The old Prime Minister was calling upon the new. The successor who had attended the conference at Geneva was to render an account of what had been accomplished to the man whose patience and persistence had made Geneva possible. We can imagine with what satisfaction Sir Winston learned of the progress made toward a settlement of the world's problems. We can imagine, too, he felt a sharp thrust of regret that he had not been privileged to join in person in the harvest of his labors. At the moment of victory in the war he had been deposed as he was leading the British team at Potsdam. Now, ten years afterward, he had withdrawn himself from the scene as the fruits of this final premiership were to be gathered.

The summit meeting at Geneva fell short of Churchill's expectations. Other summits were to follow, other hopes in their turn to be disappointed, for summits alone cannot produce world settlements. There can be no easy path to the Everest of universal peace. The forward course has always been distinguished by many a "backward streaming curve." Looking now at his last term in office, the free nations can appreciate their debt to the statesman under whose leadership the hazards of the fifties were survived. Without Winston Churchill's steadying influence the guns might have started to fire again. He won his fame as architect of victory. He crowned his work by preserving the world's peace.

CHAPTER EIGHT

IN HONORED RETIREMENT

CHURCHILL's resignation ended his public career. The break was final and complete. He attempted no further intervention in Britain's affairs. He had finished his stint and was content. But though he had left the stage, he could not avoid the limelight as it played on his goings and comings.

He remained a personage and the photographers, as attentive as ever, never missed a chance to picture him boarding airliners, or walking down the gangway when his ship made port. He did not shirk the part of Winston Churchill, the public figure.

There had been much speculation as to how he would spend his days. In what fashion should a man conduct himself on stepping down from the highest place, on yielding the burdens of great affairs? Should he become the elder statesman, offering oracular pronouncements from afar to the embarrassment of his successors and to the detriment of his own fame? Or should he withdraw completely to a Sabine or Kentish farm and lapse into the emptiness of senectitude? Neither course was his. Characteristically he chose to remain a parliamentarian—Churchill M.P. Above all he was a House of Commons man. There he had proved himself. It was the support of the House that had sustained him through the darkest days. Never, not under the greatest stresses of the war, had he forgotten that his position and authority derived from the House of Commons. So it was as a House of Commons man that he chose to remain till for the last time the call went out to him: "Who goes home?"

The Right Honorable member for Woodford remained a silent observer of debates to which he did not himself contribute. He was satisfied to register his opinion in the division lobby. His place, in which he became the distinguished ornament of the Chamber, was the corner seat on the Front Bench below the gangway—adjacent to the Ministers of the Crown, but not of them. In times of crisis—in the early days of his retirement—members looked to him for a sign, but they looked in vain. He maintained a benevolent detachment. To this well-preserved aloofness there was one conspicuous exception. During the unfortunate Suez affair, when the Eden government were under heavy fire at home and abroad, Sir Winston was prominent in associating himself with Sir Anthony and his Ministers. This was taken as a sign and was widely reported. It had a marked and steadying influence on opinion. Many anxious minds drew comfort from the conclusion that Old Winnie backed the Government— and if he supported them it must be all right. When the operation ended in fiasco, he gave no indication in public of his judgment on the wisdom of what had been done or on the manner of its execution. Others were ready enough to assign him condemnatory opinions, though for this they had no warrant. To simple minds the contrast was too obvious to be missed—pointing, it seemed, to a no less obvious conclusion. When Churchill had been in control operations succeeded; under Eden they failed. *Post hoc propter hoc*—the conclusion might have been unjustified but that some should draw it was inevitable.

He cut himself off from affairs, but he passed into no secluded retirement. Throughout his years scarcely a day passed that the newspapers in one continent or another bore no reference to him. When he was not on view in person someone or other was recalling the part he had played. And there were the memoirs—Alanbrooke, Montgomery, Kennedy, and the rest. In a succession of installments in the newspapers they carried the tale before the public on both sides of the Atlantic. The Churchill legend grew and the figure of the war leader grew the greater by reason of the attacks upon his leadership.

From the Alanbrooke diaries and from the recollections of Sir John Kennedy we learned how interfering, how infuriating and above all how dominating had been Winston Churchill, defense minister. The service authors, releasing their pent-up feelings of wartime frustration, dwelt on the difficulties of working under Churchill. Emphasis on their contributions to the conduct of affairs seemed to reduce the measure of what Churchill had achieved. Beaverbrook—with whom Churchill stood only a little lower than his lifelong friend Bonar Law—rallied to the defense of his old leader. The generals were put in their places in the Beaver-brook press. It was most loyally done, but in truth the public had been able to draw their own conclusions. Churchill had pushed the service chiefs around? "Bully for him," said the man in the street. So the Church-ill legend grew. So did the people's affection.

Reading in the quietness of his study, Churchill had material enough to divert his idle hours. Did he resent the disclosures and denigrations? Never a whit, I will warrant. He had never wished his critics to be mealy-mouthed. Mercy in controversy he had neither sought nor shown, malice he had never borne.

In 1958 he made his own last bow as author with the publication of his *History of the English-Speaking Peoples*. Twenty years had passed since the writing of this magnificently told tale, with publication twice delayed —first by the episode of fighting Hitler and then by writing his own memoirs of the history he had made.

The work, appearing in its successive parts, was acclaimed. The pro-fessional historians joined in applauding its merits—in the grand style; sparkling; success with a gigantic theme; shot through with the timeless quality of genius. It was, of course, Churchillian. It was even acceptable as history. The verdict of the professionals was offered without envy, with approbation almost unqualified and unstinted. For the author it was eminently gratifying. In the line of prime ministers, one alone had won such renown as author—Benjamin Disraeli, Earl of Beaconsfield—and it was through the more popular medium of novels that Dizzy had scored his success as a writer.

As you read the third volume of the *History*, you will come across a passage in which a famous figure in English history is thus described:

> His policy was a projection on a vast screen of his own aggressive, dominating personality. In the teeth of disfavour and obstruction he had made his way to the foremost place in Parliament and now at last fortune, courage and the confidence of his countrymen had given him a stage on which his gifts could be displayed. . . . To call into life and action the depressed and languid spirit of England, to weld her resources of wealth and manhood into a single instrument of war . . . to conquer and command and never to count the cost whether in blood or gold—this spirit he infused into every rank of his countrymen.

Does this arresting figure seem familiar? No, it is not Churchill! The description is of the great Sir William Pitt, under whom England was led through her other finest hours in the eighteenth century. The words were written in 1939—before Hitler attacked—at a time when Churchill was out of favor, his advice rejected. In those days of frustration he had found inspiration from one of the leaders of the heroic past that moved him to pen this portrait which was also, unwittingly, a self-portrait. Even then, some months before the call came to him, he had fitted himself in his imagination for the role that was to be his, and he was thus qualified for the burdens he was to bear. It was a remarkable forecast to have described in that passage the qualities and methods that were to be his.

Old times came crowding back upon him (November 1958) when he stood face to face in Paris with General de Gaulle. They had not met for fourteen years. They had been together as staunch allies, they had had their differences that were acrimoniously pressed. There had been times when they had not found it possible to exchange speech. That day differences were wiped out and the amity of allies alone remained as Sir Winston Churchill was admitted to the proud fellowship of the Companions of the Liberation.

Under the plane trees in a Paris garden, the leaders of Britain and Free France were once again in complete harmony. They faced each other. De Gaulle bent to affix the bronze medal of the Companions, embossed with a sword and superimposed with the Cross of Lorraine.

"Sir Winston," he said, "we acknowledge you as our Companion for the Liberation of France in honor and by victory."

There was a brief pause and the two men regarded each other, Churchill looking up with a smile. Then, bending himself once more, De Gaulle gave the accolade in approved fashion, the faint brush of a kiss on either cheek. It was intensely moving for the little assembly which was privileged to witness it—two hundred Companions, British and French Ministers, and the leaders of the services. They remained standing as the band played the general salute. Words were needless to bring out the poignancy of that brief ceremony, but a public ceremony is not complete without its speeches. They were made in a crystal-lit salon of the Hotel Matignon, De Gaulle's home and office, where Sir Winston met his new Companions. From De Gaulle came the warmly offered assurance that France realized what she owed to Churchill. "I wish him to know this too —he who has just had the honor to decorate him values and admires him today more than ever."

Sir Winston gave expression to his confidence in a future in which Britain and France continued to be linked with their ally across the Atlantic. "Then," he said, "we have cause not only for confidence but for high hope—high and enduring hope." And he rounded off his speech, as so often he had done before, with a vigorous *"Vive La France!"*

Sir Winston's eighty-seventh birthday brought him bulging mailbags of greetings from admirers the world over. Queen Elizabeth, touring Sierra Leone, sent her good wishes and so, too, did President Kennedy voicing, as he wrote, the deep admiration and respect of his fellow Americans.

At Westminster it was made a parliamentary occasion. The Commons rose to him as his Pickwickian figure was seen to advance into the Chamber. As he made his way to his place below the gangway they cheered him and waved their order papers. Even members of the public in the gallery were permitted to add their voices to the salutations, an unprecedented departure from the rigidly enforced rule of silence for parliamentary onlookers.

Nor did the speaker of the House protest when the rules of debate were set aside by Sir David Eccles (minister for education) who, without license sought, observed "I am sure all members of this House wish to give their good wishes to the member for Woodford."

Members accorded their endorsement with a deep-throated cheer. Then, braving the speaker's displeasure for his breach of parliamentary proprieties, the leader of the opposition rose. "As a supplement to that," said Mr. Gaitskell, using the time-honored phrase of the parliamentary questioner, "may I ask the Right Honorable gentleman if he appreciates the pride and pleasure we all feel on his eighty-seventh birthday and of his presence amongst us on this historic occasion?"

A brief pause and the House was hushed. Then the familiar figure, a little bowed now by the weight of years, stood slowly up. They cheered him loudly but cut short their greeting to listen to him. And the voice that in the famous days had roused the House to the fiercest transports of feeling in times of disaster and in the exaltation of triumph, was once more heard. They would have been delighted had he committed a major infringement of the rules, but, mindful as ever of the requirements, he permitted himself no more than seven words.

"I am very grateful to you all," he said. He spoke in a low voice but was clearly heard. In the years to come, perhaps fifty years from now, some octogenarian M.P. will be boasting in the smoking room: "I was privileged to hear the last speech in the House made by Sir Winston Churchill."

A little later Sir Harold Macmillan, taking his seat on the treasury bench, received a wave and a smile from below the gangway. "Perhaps," said the Prime Minister, "I might be allowed to add my tribute to the greatest of all my predecessors."

The years went serenely by. Sir Winston smiled indulgently as Max Beaverbrook, five years his junior, made his birthday boast—"I have destroyed forever the foolish maxim that the good die young." Sir Winston could have claimed the same, but Beaverbrook said it first.

Milestones flitted by on his parliamentary journey—his fortieth year of unbroken membership of the House of Commons, sixty-three years since first he became M.P.—still the member for Woodford made his way to his corner seat. Then, with infinite regret, he reached the decision that the time had come to close the account. Not again would he seek the suffrages of the Essex electors who had done their loyal duty by him on the occasion of a dozen elections.

The Mother of Parliaments has borne the loss of innumerable of her illustrious sons. This one would still remain at hand to follow her proceedings, seated perhaps in Another Place. But would he after all still be there and survive to the close of the term of his final Parliament? For unexpectedly, out of the blue sky of the Mediterranean there came tidings of alarm in the summer of 1962.

He was staying at Monte Carlo, a man of 87, when he fractured a leg in the mischance of a fall. A spasm of apprehension followed the announcements on the world's radio stations. They patched him up and the R.A.F. flew him home. His resilience was remarkable, "positively Churchillian." But how could the Old Man, even with his determination and his will to live, hope to get the better of a fracture in the neck of the femur? With his limb encased in plaster from hip to ankle he was brought back to London. Irrepressible as ever he made the V-sign to onlookers who glimpsed him on his way.

That same evening, unaffected by his journey, he was in the operating theatre. World-wide attention focussed on the Middlesex Hospital. By post, telegraph and cable messages of goodwill came pouring in. The bulletins told of daily progress, followed by reports of the patient sitting up, dining on chicken and reading what the newspapers had to say about him. They had him out of bed as soon as could be, but signs of phlebitis and bronchial infection appeared. It was as many had feared. With this ominous portent there could have been few to give him an outsider's chance of pulling through. But the patient knew better than to doubt. What was a broken leg to him? He had survived far worse than that and, unconquerable yet, he refused to yield. Slowly he fought back. His son told of a father smoking a cigar, sipping his brandy and "wiggling his toes." His temper returned with his strength. He was fractious, eager to be gone.

Amazingly, he became involved from his hospital bed in politics once more and his views hit the headlines on the controversy of the moment. His old friend Monty (Field Marshal Lord Montgomery) embroiled him in the argument over the Common Market. What Winston Churchill thought once again became an oracular pronouncement.

By then he had recovered enough to become positively rebellious. He demanded to go home. To humour his family and his doctors he condescended to stay a day or two longer. At last, on the fifty-sixth morning since he was borne in, the hospital doors opened and the figure few had expected to see again emerged before them.

The London street that August day presented the unforgettable vignette of a multitude united in a tumult of cheering. Since early in the morning a crowd had been gathering to welcome him as he set out for home—Londoners assembled to greet him as he was restored to them. As he came into view they roared a testament of their delight and affection, a united thundering cheer from the thousand throats of an assembly that packed the street so that no vehicle could move. His eyes, eager as ever, looked out on the people crammed between the buildings on either side of the street.

"Good old Winnie!" was the cry. As he heard the words, the outpouring of the people's delight, he rejoiced with them. No actor in his farewell performance ever contrived so marvellous a curtain as Sir Winston passing homeward on that August day in the late evening of his career. Was it not worth the discomfort of a broken leg to have evoked a demonstration so eloquent of their affection? They marvelled at him and at his prodigious spirit. They told one another of the hazards he had survived. One spoke of the bullets of the Cuban revolutionaries that had gone whistling past him, or of the pursuing Boer. Another told of the spears of the Dervishes and of the attacks of the frenzied tribesmen on India's northwestern frontier. He had survived planes that were wrecked. He had survived the shells and bombs of two world wars. Three times when prime minister he had carried on through pneumonia. Even a stroke in his final term had not disabled him. Somehow he had prevailed and they were amazed by his pluck and his luck. Providence surely had watched over him since destiny had need of him.

So the talk ran on amongst the crowd that August morning. That this man had been under the care of providence many felt assured. But time at last must put a period even to such long-sustained favour. Defer it as he may, man in his mortality moves to the predestined, inevitable end. Already we number Winston Churchill amongst the immortals of our race, but only when he has crossed the river can he be joined with the company of his peers.

There must come a day—may it be far distant—when other and vaster crowds, assembled on a longer route, will stand tongue-tied as he is borne to the last resting-place of the happy warrior. Ponderous silence will then serve to attest the grief of his passing. Till that sad parting is brought upon us we may be glad to think that on his home-coming from hospital Londoners turned out to testify to their feelings whilst still he had eyes to see, ears to hear, and the human satisfaction to appreciate the outpouring of their admiration and affection. The man who, in their direst peril, had been exalted in freedom's cause to give them the inspiration of leadership in their finest hour—his fame and the memory of those times will serve down the ages to kindle the Churchill spirit in generations to come in the lands of the free.

AUTHORITIES AND SOURCES

The principal authority for the period of the Second World War is Sir Winston Churchill's own account of events in his six volumes of memoirs. These contain the chief documents and an extensive selection of his directives. As a writer of the history he helped to make, Sir Winston had facilities few historians have enjoyed. His memoirs carry their own seal of authority, but even he is not to be relied upon for a complete and impartial record of affairs. No writer is completely objective, least of all one who has been a leading actor in what he describes. Sir Winston's bias lead him to make omissions, not to absolve himself of responsibility or in the interests of his own reputation—in this respect he is scarcely to be impugned. But he wrote under the compelling influence of his devotion to the Anglo-American alliance. It was the cardinal point of his policy as Prime Minister. It was his guiding light as historian. Accordingly, he was disposed to minimize differences between British and Americans. Authors on the American side of the Atlantic, perhaps less devoted to the cause, have been more outspoken, more critical and more revealing. Without seeking to provoke or perpetuate differences, I have used American and other sources to make good omissions in Churchill's narrative.

The main supplementary sources on the American side are the White House papers of Harry Hopkins, edited by Robert Sherwood, a chronicle of events viewed from the standpoint of President Roosevelt and Hopkins, his confidant, adviser, and unofficial minister extraordinary.

For the last months of the war former President Truman covered the ground in his memoirs. This book is of a different order of excellence from Churchill's, whether considered as a contribution to history or literature. Truman's opening months of responsibility belonged to the period before the tide of opinion had turned, and when good fellowship with the Russians was still pursued in Washington. He had the advantage of writing after McCarthyism had swung American opinion to the opposite pole of politics. Only this, I think, can explain certain omissions and the nature of some of the entries in *Year of Decisions*.

There have been of late two principal contributions from the military standpoint to the Churchill story. First in point of time was Sir John Kennedy's *The Business of War*. Admiration for Churchill did not serve to silence Sir John's natural talent for criticism, and as the recipient of the confidence and complaints of Sir John Dill, during his term as C.I.G.S., Kennedy found cause to express the soldier's case against the statesman-strategist.

Covering the later period are the diaries of Lord Alanbrooke (formerly Alan Brooke) enshrined in the narrative setting provided by Sir Arthur Bryant's expert pen. Alanbrooke the diarist is less piquant than Kennedy, but fuller, and as a day-by-day record his writings have a quality with which reminiscences written at a later date cannot compare.

The two commanders, Eisenhower and Montgomery, proved disappointing as authors. Eisenhower was full, frank, and correct, but for the most part lacking in atmosphere and in the personal touch. Montgomery wrote with the terseness but not with the indiscretion of his public speeches, and his interest was in campaigns, not in persons, save in an autobiographical sense.

Sidelights on the Chiefs of Staff were provided by Sir Leslie Hollis, one-time Chief Staff Officer to the Minister of Defense. There must be an interesting story to tell of his special place as author. His first contribution to history appeared in 1956 under the title of *One Marine's Tale*. In 1959 the tale was retold in *War at the Top*, on the title page of which appeared the name of James Leasor as co-author. Hollis had been emended and vastly extended. At the head of the list of those to whom the co-authors acknowledged their indebtedness was the name of Lord Beaverbrook. They were fortunate in their cooperator. Beaverbrook placed much unpublished information at their disposal, made them privy to his differences with Churchill over the issue of the Second Front, and enabled them to state that his departure from the Churchill Cabinet in 1942 was occasioned by political differences and not by his health as was put about at the time. It was, so far as I am aware, the first appearance in print of an account of the episode that for a time deprived Churchill of the services of Beaverbrook, whose contribution to national affairs, *War at the Top*, will I suppose remain the sole account until he himself has carried his memoirs down to the period of the Second World War.

Another military author of whom mention must be made is Sir Edward Spears, whose *Assignment to Catastrophe* gave, from the inside post of liaison officer, a lively account of the fall of France and of

Winston Churchill's efforts to avert the disaster of that capitulation.

A special place is occupied by Henry Feis's encyclopedic *Churchill, Roosevelt, Stalin,* based on published works, supplemented by information made available in Washington by the State Department.

Here follows an enumeration of the many publications on which I have drawn and to whose authors I make my acknowledgment of profound gratitude:

ALANBROOKE, Field Marshal, Viscount, K.G., O.M., Chief of the Imperial General Staff 1941–46: Diaries and Autobiographical Notes—a study in two volumes by Sir Arthur Byrant—*Turn of the Tide, 1939–43; Triumph in the West, 1943–46.*

AMERY, the Rt. Hon., L.S., C.H., Assistant Secretary War Cabinet 1917, Secretary for War 1917–18, First Lord 1921–22, Dominions Secretary 1924–29: *My Political Life, 1896–1940,* in three volumes.

BEAVERBROOK, the Rt. Hon. Lord, Minister of Information 1918, Minister of Aircraft Production 1940–42, Minister of Supply 1941–42, Lord Privy Seal 1943–45: *Politicians and the War, 1914–16,* in two volumes; *Men and Power, 1917–18.*

BERTIN, Leonard: *Atom Harvest.*

BOOTHBY, Robert, Under-Secretary, Ministry of Food, 1940–41: *I Fight to Live.*

BRYANT, Sir Arthur: *Turn of the Tide* and *Triumph in the West*—see Alanbrooke.

BUTCHER, Captain Harry C., naval aide to Gen. Eisenhower, 1942–45: *Three Years with Eisenhower.*

BYRNES, James F., U.S. Secretary of State, 1945–47: *Speaking Frankly.*

CARTLAND, Barbara: *Ronald Cartland, by his sister,* with a preface by Winston Churchill; *The Isthmus Years,* an autobiographical study of the years between the two world wars.

CHATFIELD, Admiral of the Fleet, Lord, G.C.B., O.M., Minister of Defense 1939–40: *It Might Happen Again,* autobiography, volume II.

CHURCHILL, the Rt. Hon. Sir Winston, K.G., O.M., C.H.: Memoirs of the Second World War in six volumes—*The Gathering Storm; Their Finest Hour; The Grand Alliance; The Hinge of Fate; Closing the Ring; Triumph and Tragedy.* Speeches in nine volumes compiled successively by Randolph Churchill and Charles Eade.

CLARK, Gen. Mark, deputy to Gen. Eisenhower and later Commander 5th Army: *Calculated Risk.*

COLLIER, Basil: *Leader of the Few,* the authorized biography of Air Chief Marshal Lord Dowding, G.C.B., G.C.V.O., C.M.G.

COWLES, Virginia: *Winston Churchill, The Era and the Man.*

CUDLIPP, Hugh: *Publish and Be Damned,* the astonishing story of the *Daily Mirror.*

CUNNINGHAM OF HYNDHOPE, G.C.B., O.M., D.S.O., Viscount, Admiral of the Fleet: Autobiography, *A Sailor's Odyssey.*

DALTON, Hugh, Minister of Economic Warfare 1940–42, Board of Trade 1942–45, Chancellor of Exchequer 1945–47: *The Fateful Years,* memoirs 1931–45.

DE GAULLE, Charles: War memoirs, volume I, *The Call to Honor,* 1940–42.

DOMBROWSKI, Roman: *Mussolini—Twilight and Fall,* translated with a preface by H. C. Stevens.

DRIBERG, Tom: *Beaverbrook, a study in power and frustration.*

DUFF COOPER, Viscount Norwich, Secretary for War 1935–37, First Lord 1937–38, Minister of Information 1940–41, Ambassador to France 1953: *Old Men Forget,* an autobiography.

EADE, Charles: Editor, *Churchill, by his contemporaries.*

EDEN, Guy: *Portrait of Churchill,* with an introduction by the Rt. Hon. Anthony Eden.

EISENHOWER, General of the Army Dwight D., C. in C. Allied Forces 1942–45. President United States 1953–61. *Crusade in Europe.*

EVANS, Trevor: *Bevin.*

FEILING, Keith: *The Life of Neville Chamberlain.*

FEIS, Herbert: *Churchill, Roosevelt, Stalin, the war they waged and the peace they sought.*

FERMI, Laura: *Atoms in the Family, my life with Enrico Fermi, designer of the first atomic pile.*

GREER, Thomas H.: *What Roosevelt Thought, his social and political ideas.*

GUEDELLA, Philip: *Mr. Churchill, a portrait.*

GUNTHER, John: *Roosevelt in retrospect, a profile in history.*

HALIFAX, The Earl of, K.G., Viceroy of India 1926–31, Foreign Secretary 1938–40, Ambassador to Washington 1941–46; *Fullness of Days.*

HATCH, Alden P.: *Franklin D. Roosevelt, an informal biography.*

HERBERT, Sir A. P.: *Independent Member.*

HIGGINS, Trumbull: *Winston Churchill and the Second Front, 1940–43.*

HOLLIS, Gen. Sir Leslie, K.C.B., K.B.E., Assistant Secretary to the War Cabinet; *One Marine's Tale,* foreword by Lord Ismay, C.H., G.C.B., D.S.O.

HOPKINS, Harry L.: *Roosevelt and Hopkins,* an intimate history by Robert Sherwood, Volume I 1930–42, Volume II 1942–45.

HULL, Cordell, U.S. Secretary of State 1933–44: *Memoirs,* in two volumes.

KENNEDY, Major General Sir John, G.C.M.G., K.C.V.O., K.B.E., C.B., M.C., Director Military Operations 1940–43, Assistant C.I.G.S. 1943–45: *The Business of War,* edited with a preface by Bernard Fergusson.

LEAHY, Admiral of the Fleet William D.: *I Was There,* the personal story of the Chief of Staff to Presidents Roosevelt and Truman.

LEASOR, James: *War at the Top,* based on the experiences of Gen. Sir Leslie Hollis, Assistant Secretary to the War Cabinet and Chiefs of Staff.

LESLIE, Anita: *The Fabulous Leonard Jerome.*

MACNALTY, Sir Arthur Salusbury, K.C.B.: *The Three Churchills.*

MARCHANT, Sir James, K.B.E.: Editor, *Winston Spencer Churchill, Servant of Crown and Commonwealth,* a tribute by various hands on his 80th birthday.

MONTGOMERY OF ALAMEIN, Field Marshal the Viscount, K.G., Commander 8th Army 1942–43, C. in C. 21st Army Group 1944–45: *Memoirs.*

MORGAN, Lt. Gen. Sir Frederick, K.C.B., Chief of Staff Allied Commander (designate) 1943–44: *Overture to Overlord.*

MORRIS-JONES, Sir Henry: *Doctor in the Whips' Room.*

MORTON, H. V.: *Atlantic Meeting,* an account of Mr. Churchill's voyage in H.M.S. *Prince of Wales* in August, 1941, and the conference with President Roosevelt which resulted in the Atlantic Charter.

MUGGERIDGE, Malcolm: *Ciano's Diary, 1939–43,* edited with an introduction, foreword by Sumner Welles.

NEL, Elizabeth: *Mr. Churchill's Secretary.*

NICOLSON, Harold, Parliamentary Secretary Ministry of Information 1940–41: *King George V, his life and reign.*

OWEN, Frank: *Tempestuous Journey,* biography of Lord Lloyd George.

ROOSEVELT, Eleanor: *On My Own.*

SALTER, Sir Arthur, Chancellor of the Duchy 1945: *Personality in Politics.*

SAMUEL, Rt. Hon. Viscount, G.C.B., G.B.E., Cabinet Minister in successive Governments, 1909–15: *Memoirs.*

SHERWOOD, Robert: *Roosevelt and Hopkins*—see Hopkins.

SIMON, Viscount, G.C.S.I., G.C.V.O., successively Solicitor General and Attorney General 1910–15, Home Secretary 1915–16, Foreign Secretary, 1931–35, Home Secretary 1935–37, Chancellor of the Exchequer 1937–40, Lord Chancellor 1940–45: *Retrospect.*

SPEARS, Major General Sir Edward, K.B.E., C.B., M.C., head of Mission to Paris 1917–20, Prime Minister's personal representative with French Premier 1940: *Assignment to Catastrophe,* in two volumes—I. *Prelude to Dunkirk;* II. *The Fall of France.*

STETTINIUS, Edward R., Jr., U.S. Secretary of State 1945: *Roosevelt and the Russians, the Yalta Conference,* edited by Walter Johnson.

STIMSON, Henry L., U.S. Secretary of War 1940–45, and MCGEORGE BUNDY: *On Active Service in Peace and War.*

TEMPLEWOOD, Viscount (Sir Samuel Hoare), D.C.L., LL.D., LITT.D., Secretary for Air 1922–24, Secretary for India 1931–35, First Lord 1936–37, Home Secretary 1937–39, Lord Privy Seal 1940, Air Minister 1940: *Nine Troubled Years.*

TRUMAN, Harry S., President United States 1945–53: *Year of Decisions.*

VANDENBERG, Arthur Hendrick, U.S. Senator: *The Private Papers,* edited by Arthur H. Vandenberg, Jr., with the collaboration of Joe Alex Morris.

VANSITTART, Lord, Permanent Under-Secretary Foreign Office 1930–38, Chief Diplomatic Adviser 1938–41: *The Mist Procession,* autobiography.

WHEELER-BENNETT, John: *King George VI.*

WILLIAMS, Francis, adviser on public relations to Mr. Attlee as Prime Minister: *Ernest Bevin, portrait of a great Englishman,* with a foreword by the Rt. Hon. Clement Attlee, O.M., C.H.

WILMOT, Chester: *The Struggle for Europe.*

WILSON OF LIBYA, Field Marshal, Lord, G.C.B., G.B.E., D.S.O.: *Eight Years Overseas,* foreword by General of the Army D. D. Eisenhower.

WINANT, John G., U.S. Ambassador to Britain: *A letter from Grosvenor Square, the account of a stewardship.*

WINGATE, Sir Ronald, Bt., C.B., C.M.G., C.I.E., O.B.E., served in Second World War with Joint Planning Staff: *Not in the Limelight.*

WINTERTON, Earl, P.C., Chancellor of the Duchy 1937–39, Paymaster General 1939: *Orders of the Day.*

WRENCH, Sir John Evelyn: *Geoffrey Dawson and Our Times,* with a foreword by the Rt. Hon. the Earl of Halifax, K.G., O.M.

KEY TO REFERENCES

The reference *World War* is to Churchill's six-volume memoirs.
Speeches refers to the nine-volume compilation.

BOOK ONE

Chapter I   THE ADMIRALTY AGAIN

1. World War, I.
2. Duff Cooper; Amery, III.
3. World War, I.
4. Amery, III.
5. Spears, I.
6. Feiling; Cowles.
7. World War, I.
8. World War, I.
9. World War, I; Spears, I.
10. Spears, I.

Chapter II   PRIME MINISTER

1. Amery, III; Spears, I.
2. Spears, I; Amery, III.
3. World War, I.
4. Wheeler-Bennett; Feiling 441: Chamberlain's first impulse for Halifax.
5. Amery, III; World War, I.
6. Templewood; Duff Cooper.
7. World War, I.

Chapter III   DAYS OF DISASTER

1. Spears, I.
2. Among others, I have no doubt, I at my desk in Fleet Street was given this information.
3. World War, II.
4. Guedella, *The Duke.*

5. World War, II.
6. World War, II.
7. Dowding.
8. World War, II; Spears, I.

Chapter IV　　　　　FOR FALLING FRANCE

1. Cordell Hull, I; World War, II.
2. Briare Conference: World War, II; Spears, II, including a memorable description of the apparition of the Prime Minister asking, "Uh ay ma bain?"
3. World War, II.
4. Defeatist move: World War, II.
5. Tours Conference: World War, II; Spears, II.
6. World War, II.
7. World War, II; Alanbrooke.
8. Spears, II; de Gaulle.
9. World War, II.
10. De Gaulle; World War, II: "I was not the prime mover: my first reaction was unfavorable."
11. De Gaulle.
12. Spears, II.
13. Spears, II, quoting Reynaud.
14. Wrench.
15. Wheeler-Bennett. Some months later the King, in his diary, expressed thankfulness that the capitulation of France was not long delayed.

Chapter V　　　　　RUNNING THE WAR

1. Owen: "useless to join with present lot" and Lloyd George's reasons.
2. World War, II, for Churchill's account of his position as Defense Minister; see also 1942 White Paper "The Organization of Joint Planning."
3. World War, I.
4. Eisenhower: "a virtual member of the British Chiefs of Staff."
5. Contemporary memoirs contain numerous references to Churchill's late hours. See Alanbrooke: "harrowing, exhausting hours"; Kennedy.
6. Kennedy.
7. P.M.'s "heavy guns": Cunningham.
8. Alanbrooke; Montgomery; see also Sir Roger Keyes, quoted paper.

Chapter VI　　　　　BRITAIN ALONE

1. World War, II.
2. World War, II; Spears, II.
3. Cowles.
4. Action against French Fleet: World War, II.

Chapter VII　　　　　INVADERS FOILED

1. World War, II; Wilmot.
2. Eden.

3. World War, II.
4. World War, II.
5. World War, II.

Chapter VIII   ORATOR OF FREE MEN

1. A description of Churchill composing is given by Elizabeth Nel in her fascinating *Mr. Churchill's Secretary.*
2. World War, II.
3. De Gaulle.
4. World War, II.
5. Hopkins.
6. World War, III.
7. Hopkins.

Chapter IX   BATTLE OF THE MEDITERRANEAN

1. World War, II.
2. Mediterranean decision: World War, II; Cunningham.
3. Wilmot.
4. World War, II; see also Sir Ivone Kirkpatrick quoted in *The Sunday Times,* June 4, 1950.
5. Hitler's phrase for Lavel quoted in World War, II.
6. World War, II.
7. World War, II.
8. World War, II.
9. World War, II.

Chapter X   DEFEATS IN THE BALKANS

1. World War, III.
2. Kennedy.
3. World War, III.
4. "Greater part of the Nile Army": World War, III.
5. Hitler's directive quoted in World War, III.
6. Kennedy: "We know now he was right."
7. World War, III.
8. World War, III.
9. Letter to Roosevelt: World War, III.
10. Kennedy.
11. Wilson.
12. Alanbrooke.
13. Kennedy, who asserts "the most that can be claimed is that some (German) forces were diverted."
14. Alanbrooke's diary under date November 11, 1940. The narrative text by Arthur Bryant makes the concession of "delayed the start."
15. Hitler, March 27, 1941, quoted from Nuremberg documents by Wilmot.
16. Wilson.
17. Kennedy.
18. World War, III; and see Leasor.

19. World War, iii.
20. Hopkins.
21. World War, iii: Dill's memorandum and the reply.
22. World War, iii.
23. Kennedy, giving the text of the Churchill directive.
24. World War, iii.
25. Kennedy.
26. Kennedy. A full account of Dill's difficulties is given.
27. The text of Dill's letter is given by Kennedy.

BOOK TWO

Chapter I   RUSSIA AN ALLY

The opening of the war against Russia is the subject of two chapters in World War, iii.

1. The Sunday at Chequers: World War, iii.
2. World War, ii. This forecast bears the date June 27, 1940.
3. Wilson; World War, iii.
4. World War, iii.
5. World War, iii.
6. World War, iii.
7. World War, iii.
8. World War, iii.
9. Feiling.
10. World War, iii.
11. World War, iii.
12. Kennedy: "Dill regards the Russians as foul; they ratted on us."
13. World War, iii.
14. Kennedy.
15. World War, iii; Hopkins.
16. World War, iii.

Chapter II ATLANTIC MEETING—ATLANTIC CHARTER

Sir Winston's account of the conference is given in World War, iii. See also the account by H. V. Morton, one of the two correspondents of the British press.

1. Hopkins; Kennedy.
2. Hopkins.
3. Hopkins.
4. World War, iii.
5. Hopkins; World War, iii.
6. Hopkins; World War, iii.
7. Hopkins.
8. Hopkins.
9. Hopkins.

Chapter III   STRATEGY—BOMBS—ATOMS

1. World War, III: "It will not be possible in the rising temper of the British
   people against our inactivity to resist such demands indefinitely."
2. Kennedy; Sweden: Kennedy; World War, III; Leasor.
3. Alanbrooke.
4. Kennedy.
5. Dill's exhaustion: Kennedy; Leasor; Brooke's acceptance: Alanbrooke.
6. Kennedy.
7. World War, III; for Mountbatten's appointment, see Leasor.
8. World War, III, giving terms of Churchill directive.
9. World War, III.
10. World War, I.
11. World War, III.
12. "Sagging morale of the American team": report by H. D. Smyth to U.S. War
    Department quoted by Dr. J. G. Feinberg to whose *The Atom Story* I
    am indebted for details of research work in the United States.
13. World War, IV.

Chapter IV   AMERICA IN THE SAME BOAT

1. World War, III.
2. World War, III.
3. World War, III.
4. World War, III.
5. World War, III: "Several times expressed his pleasure."

Chapter V   ARCADIA

The main sources are World War, III, and Hopkins.

1. World War, III.
2. Hopkins.
3. Eisenhower.
4. Hopkins: Churchill exploded at expressions.
5. Roosevelt always particularly favorable to this operation: Hopkins.
6. Hopkins; World War, III.
7. Hopkins.
8. Hopkins; Eisenhower.
9. Hopkins.
10. Hopkins; World War, III.
11. World War, III.

Chapter VI   THE CRITICS

1. See Mr. McGovern's speech, House of Commons, January 28.
2. World War, IV.
3. Capt. McEwen, Commons Debate.
4. Eden.
5. Alanbrooke.
6. Williams; and see Evans.
7. World War, IV.

Chapter VII   CABINET CHANGES

1. For Churchill's view of Cripps, see World War, IV.
2. Leasor.
3. World War, IV.
4. Cudlipp.

Chapter VIII   DIFFERENCES OVER INDIA

Churchill's account of the Cripps mission is given in World War, IV.

1. Hopkins.
2. World War, IV: "I reacted so strongly and at such length."
3. Hopkins: "In the entire war no proposals from the President were more wrathfully received."
4. World War, IV.
5. President's letter to Hopkins, World War, IV; "act of madness," World War, IV.
6. World War, IV.
7. Vandenberg.
8. Madagascar expedition: World War, IV; objections to operation; Alanbrooke.
9. Kennedy: "No doubt he had been right."
10. De Gaulle.
11. World War, III.
12. De Gaulle.
13. Kennedy.
14. Kennedy.
15. Kennedy.

Chapter IX   SECOND FRONT—THE DEBATE

1. Hopkins.
2. Eisenhower.
3. Hopkins.
4. Stimson: "it was the 'proper and orthodox' line to follow."
5. U.S. memorandum and Churchill's comments: World War, IV.
6. Alanbrooke.
7. Hopkins.
8. Hopkins.
9. Hopkins.
10. World War, IV.
11. Alanbrooke.
12. Hopkins.
13. Hopkins.
14. World War, IV; Hopkins.
15. World War, IV.
16. Stimson; Hopkins.
17. World War, IV; Alanbrooke.
18. Alanbrooke.
19. World War, IV.
20. World War, IV.

21. See also directives, World War, iv.
22. World War, iv.
23. Hopkins.
24. World War, iv.
25. World War, iv.
26. World War, iv.
27. Stimson; Alanbrooke.
28. Stimson.
29. Stimson.
30. World War, iv; Stimson.
31. Alanbrooke: he was "very upset," a reference to Sir Winston's dislike of what had been agreed in his absence by Chiefs of Staff.
32. Stimson.
33. Hopkins.
34. World War, iv; Alanbrooke; Hopkins.
35. World War, iv; Hopkins; Alanbrooke.

Chapter XI　　　SECOND FRONT—THE DECISION

1. Hopkins.
2. Clark.
3. Eisenhower.
4. Kennedy; World War, iv.
5. Stimson. He attributes the strength of his own decisive opinions to Marshall, who was a shade less uncompromising in his views.
6. Stimson.
7. Hopkins.
8. Hopkins.
9. Butcher.
10. Alanbrooke.
11. Hopkins.
12. Clark.
13. Eisenhower.
14. Stimson.
15. Cables to Roosevelt, July 14 and July 27, 1942: World War, iv.
16. Cable to Prime Minister, July 28: World War, iv.
17. The figures are taken from Eisenhower.
18. Alanbrooke.
19. Leahy.

Chapter XII　　　CHANGES TO SAVE EGYPT

1. Alanbrooke.
2. Alanbrooke.
3. Speech to Commons, November 11, 1942.
4. World War, iv.
5. Alanbrooke.
6. World War, iv.
7. Alanbrooke.
8. Montgomery; Alanbrooke.
9. World War, iv; Alanbrooke.

Chapter XIII   FACING UP TO STALIN

1. Feis; Hopkins; World War, IV.
2. The Kremlin meetings are chronicled by Churchill in World War, IV, and by Alanbrooke.
3. Alanbrooke.
4. Alanbrooke.
5. World War, IV.
6. Alanbrooke.
7. Alanbrooke.

BOOK THREE

Chapter I   TORCH FOR AFRICA

1. World War, IV; Kennedy.
2. Kennedy, quoting Gen. Macready of the British mission in Washington.
3. World War, IV: Churchill's views in a letter written to Harry Hopkins that was not sent.
4. World War, IV.
5. Roosevelt cable, August 30: World War, IV.
6. Speech in secret session of Commons, December 10, 1942.
7. Eisenhower, on French sentiment, message to Roosevelt quoted by Hopkins; "Kingpin," see World War, IV.
8. Eisenhower's reputation: Hopkins.
9. Churchill letter of November 17: World War, IV.
10. Alanbrooke.
11. Cable to Roosevelt, November 24: World War, IV.
12. World War, IV.
13. Hopkins.
14. Alanbrooke.
15. Hopkins.
16. World War, IV.
17. Hopkins.
18. Churchill report to War Cabinet, January 20, 1943: World War, IV; also for Bevin: World War, IV.
19. World War, IV; Alanbrooke.
20. Alanbrooke.
21. The alarms of the Algiers visit are amusingly described by Butcher.
22. Stalin, messages of February 16 and March 15, 1943: World War, IV.
23. Speeches, IV.

Chapter II   PLANNING THE WELFARE STATE

1. World War, IV.

Chapter III   TRAVELS OF A STRATEGIST

1. Hopkins.
2. The conference proceedings are described by Churchill, World War, IV, and by Alanbrooke; for Stilwell see Hopkins.

3. Speeches, IV.
4. World War, IV; Dill's jest: Leahy.
5. Hopkins; Bertin; World War, IV.
6. Butcher.
7. Eisenhower.
8. Alanbrooke.

Chapter IV　　　　　　　　CONFLICTS AT QUEBEC

1. World War, v.
2. Roosevelt cable of July 26, 1943: World War, v; Churchill's memorandum, World War, v.
3. Roosevelt cable, July 30: World War, v, with Churchill's comment.
4. Hopkins.
5. Hopkins.
6. World War, v.
7. World War, v.
8. "They went to Quebec determined to make their ideas prevail by all means at their disposal": U.S. War Department official history, quoted by Alanbrooke; and see Vandenberg.
9. Stimson gives a completely frank account of his actions, together with the documents.
10. World War, v; Alanbrooke; Stimson, 231.
11. World War, v.
12. Hopkins.
13. Alanbrooke; Kennedy.
14. This amusing incident is described by both Churchill, World War, v, and Alanbrooke.
15. Stimson; Bertin.
16. See statement by Herbert Morrison, House of Commons, April 8, 1954.

Chapter V　　　　　　　　THIRD FRONT OPENED

1. World War, v.
2. World War, v.
3. World War, v.
4. World War, v.
5. World War, v.
6. World War, v.

Chapter VI　　　　　　　　TRIUMVIRS AT TEHERAN

1. World War, v.
2. World War, v.
3. World War, v.
4. World War, v.
5. World War, v.
6. World War, v.
7. Roosevelt letter of March 18, 1942: World War, IV.
8. Hopkins.

9. World War, v.
10. World War, v; Leasor.
11. Leasor.
12. World War, v.
13. World War, v.
14. World War, v; see also Hopkins, with an explanation of Marshall's position; acceptance of British commander: Hopkins.
15. Memorandum by British Chiefs of Staff, November 25, 1943, with phrases from the Churchill mint: World War, v.
16. Hopkins: "Americans and Russians would form a united front."
17. Leasor; Hopkins.
18. Hopkins; Leasor.
19. Hopkins.
20. Leasor, quoting Elliott Roosevelt, "as he saw it."
21. Hopkins.
22. Hopkins.
23. World War, v.
24. World War, v.
25. From Frances Perkins' *The Roosevelt I Knew,* quoted by Cowles.
26. World War, v.
27. World War, v; Hopkins.
28. World War, v; Hopkins.
29. World War, v; Hopkins.
30. Hopkins.
31. World War, v.
32. World War, v; Hopkins.
33. Hopkins.
34. Elliott Roosevelt quoted by Leasor.
35. World War, v; Hopkins: "Roosevelt felt impelled to revenge."
36. Leahy.
37. Hopkins; Leahy.
38. Hopkins; World War, v.
39. See Alanbrooke. The Prime Minister's health had evidently become a matter of major concern with the C.I.G.S.
40. See World War, v, and Alanbrooke for an account of this controversy. Churchill and Alanbrooke discuss the matter at length. Cunningham disposed of it in a page.
41. Churchill's minute, January 24, 1944: World War, v.
42. World War, v.
43. Alanbrooke.
44. Churchill's health: Alanbrooke.
45. World War, v. The conclusion of the controversy is stated differently by Alanbrooke.

Chapter VII   D-DAY AND AFTER

1. World War, v; Eisenhower; Montgomery.
2. Cable of March 11, 1944: World War, v.
3. World War, v.
4. World War, v. For an extended account of deception plans see Wingate.

5. Eisenhower.
6. Eisenhower.
7. Montgomery; Churchill's recollection, World War, v.
8. World War, v; Eisenhower.
9. Hollis.
10. World War, vi; see also Montgomery; for the consequences see Clark.
11. World War, vi.
12. World War, vi; Kennedy.
13. Hopkins; Alanbrooke; Montgomery.
14. For Roosevelt's health: Hopkins.
15. World War, vi.
16. World War, vi.

Chapter VIII   LIBERATION FEUDS

1. Minute to Foreign Office, May 4, 1944: World War, vi.
2. Eden's proposal and Churchill's cable to Roosevelt: World War, vi.
3. Exchange of views between Prime Minister and President: World War, vi.
4. Smuts' cables: World War, vi.
5. Roosevelt cable, September 28, 1944: World War, vi.
6. World War, vi.
7. Hopkins.

Chapter IX   BARGAIN-MAKING IN MOSCOW

1. Feis, quoting State Department memorandum.
2. World War, iv; explanatory memorandum of October 11, 1944: World War, vi.
3. Letter to Roosevelt: World War, vi.
4. Stalin's messages, Roosevelt's cable, "humbling submissions": World War, vi.
5. Letter to Smuts, December 3, 1944: World War, vi.
6. World War, vi, with President's reply; for Montgomery criticisms, see Montgomery; Alanbrooke.
7. Letter to Eden: World War, vi.
8. Vandenberg.
9. Hopkins; Eisenhower.
10. World War, vi.

Chapter X   UNDER FIRE IN GREECE

1. Minute to Foreign Secretary, November 7, 1944, and cable to Gen. Wilson, November 8: World War, vi.
2. Telegram to Gen. Scobie, December 5, 1944, World War, vi.
3. World War, vi.
4. Hopkins; Roosevelt cable, December 13, 1944: World War, vi.
5. World War, vi.
6. Account of mission to Athens, World War, vi; see also Nel.

Chapter XI   SUMMIT AT YALTA

1. Leahy; for small nations, Hopkins.
2. Stettinius.

3. Hopkins; Stettinius.
4. Hopkins.
5. Stettinius; World War, IV.
6. Roosevelt; Hopkins.
7. For the strategic consequences see Clark.
8. Hopkins; Byrnes.
9. Roosevelt the mediator: Stettinius.
10. The Yalta proceedings are reported at length by Stettinius, the Yalta Conference being the main international occasion of his term as Secretary of State. Also, World War, IV; Hopkins; Byrnes.
11. Hopkins; Leahy; World War, VI.
12. Pressure on President and account of pre-Yalta discussions: Stettinius; Hopkins.
13. World War, VI; Stettinius.
14. Byrnes.
15. World War, VI; Hopkins; Byrnes; Stettinius.
16. World War, VI.
17. Feis.
18. Leahy.

BOOK FOUR

Chapter I   HIATUS UNDER ROOSEVELT

1. Owen.
2. Gunther.
3. World War, VI.
4. World War, VI.
5. Telegram of March 13, 1945, with Washington reply: World War, VI.
6. World War, VI.
7. World War, VI.
8. World War, VI.
9. Stalin's cable, April 7, 1945: World War, VI.
10. World War, VI; Eisenhower.
11. Montgomery.
12. Cable from Eisenhower, March 30, 1945: World War, VI.
13. Montgomery.
14. Aim of military plans: Eisenhower; Montgomery's view: Montgomery.
15. Churchill's reactions: World War, VI.
16. Stalin's comment: World War, VI.
17. Message to Roosevelt, April 1, 1945: World War, VI.
18. Cable to Eisenhower: World War, VI.
19. Eisenhower; Montgomery; Feis, quoting Omar Bradley's *A Soldier's Story*.
20. World War, VI.
21. World War, VI.
22. Leahy.
23. Stalin's cable of April 3, 1945: World War, VI.
24. World War, VI.

25. The two last cables to pass between Prime Minister and President: World War, VI.
26. World War, VI; see Truman.

Chapter II   HIATUS TO VE-DAY

1. Message to Eden: World War, VI.
2. Cable to Truman, April 18, 1945: World War, VI; Feis.
3. Feis.
4. Cable of April 30: World War, VI.
5. Feis, for State Department's advice; Harriman's warning: Feis.
6. Eisenhower's view and Churchill's appeal: World War, VI.
7. Churchill's views on zones: World War, VI; "I never suggested going back on our word," World War, VI; see Truman; and see Eisenhower with the curious comment, "I always thought the Allies could have secured agreement to occupy more of Germany than they did."
8. World War, VI.
9. Churchill's anxieties over Denmark, see cables to Eden, World War, VI, and Montgomery.
10. Montgomery.
11. Tribute to Eisenhower: World War, VI.

Chapter III   LETTING IN THE RUSSIANS

1. Harvard speech, September 6, 1943: Speeches, IV.
2. Influence of A-bomb: Feis.
3. Soviet menace: World War, VI.
4. Demobilization slow-down: World War, VI; Montgomery.
5. World War, VI; and see Leahy and Truman.
6. Iron Curtain cable, May 12, 1945: World War, VI.
7. Churchill's cable, World War, VI, with Truman's reply. Truman in his account omits the essential and contentious passages in Churchill.
8. Churchill surprise at "ganging up": World War, VI.
9. Churchill's restrained account of Davies mission: World War, VI; also, Leahy, Truman.
10. Leahy.
11. Churchill's note: World War, VI.
12. Stettinius.
13. World War, VI.
14. World War, VI.
15. Leahy.

Chapter IV   SO STALIN WON THE PEACE

1. Leahy.
2. See cabled warning from Halifax: World War, VI.
3. Stettinius.

Chapter V   TO THE POLLS

The files of the British national newspapers, notably *The Times, Daily Telegraph,* and *Daily Express,* provide the materials for this chapter, together with the succinct record of *Keesing's Archives.* Cudlipp gives the aspect of affairs from the left-wing *Daily Mirror.* There is also the more substantial *The British General Election of 1950,* by H. G. Nicholas.

Chapter VI   TERMINAL AT POTSDAM

1. T. S. Eliot, *The Waste Land.*
2. World War, vi.
3. Truman.
4. Truman; World War, vi.
5. World War, vi; Truman; see also Leahy and Byrnes.
6. Leahy.
7. Truman.
8. World War, vi.
9. Truman.
10. Truman; Byrnes.
11. Truman.
12. Truman; Byrnes.
13. Truman.
14. Truman.
15. The musical interlude is divertingly described by Leahy; Truman.
16. World War, vi; Truman.

Chapter VII   THE FALL

1. World War, vi.
2. World War, vi.
3. "Balfour's Poodle"—Lloyd George's phrase in a speech in 1908.

Chapter VIII   A-BOMB DECISION

1. British Government statement after bombing of Japan, August 6, 1945: Truman; Byrnes; Stimson.
2. Truman; Byrnes; Stimson.
3. World War, vi.
4. Truman.
5. Byrnes.
6. World War, vi; Truman.
7. "Never a moment's discussion": World War, vi; Truman.
8. World War, vi; Truman; Stimson.
9. World War, vi; Truman; Byrnes.
10. Truman; Stimson.
11. See *The Observer,* September 6, 1959: "The Hiroshima Choice."
12. Byrnes.
13. Byrnes; Truman.

BOOK FIVE

Chapter I   FULTON—A LINE FOR THE WEST

1. Vandenberg.
2. The dispatch of this cable was not made known until some years later in the Edinburgh speech (February 15, 1950), during the general-election campaign.
3. New York speech, March 15, 1946.
4. Hopkins: not only was there consultation over the American speeches but he often consulted Roosevelt by telephone over his war speeches to the House of Commons.
5. Truman; also Vandenberg. The reader will note the difference in emphasis between the two accounts—Truman placed the responsibility in Byrnes, whereas Vandenberg's anxieties extended to President as well as Secretary of State.

INDEX

THE AUTHOR AND HIS BOOK

CHARLES LEWIS BROAD, *journalist, author and fruit farmer, was born in 1900 in the village of Marston, Oxford, England, and makes his home at Podkin Farm, High Halden, in the county of Kent. He was educated at Perse Grammar School, Cambridge, and began his writing career at the age of nineteen when he joined the staff of one of the oldest newspapers in England, The Hertfordshire Mercury. After serving his apprenticeship he moved to Fleet Street, London's newspaper row, and eventually joined the staff of one of the city's leading newspapers, the Daily Telegraph. He became night editor of The Daily Telegraph, and later joined the Norman Kark magazine chain where he served as Editor-in-Chief for two years. As a newspaperman and author he has written many millions of words—mostly in longhand—and he estimates that more than one million have been on Sir Winston Churchill, whose activities he first began covering while a reporter in London. His various books on Churchill have been the result of twenty-five years of research into this controversial figure in British politics, and his works have been translated into many languages, including French, German, Italian, Spanish, Czechoslovakian and Danish—"but never into Russian," he adds. Since 1948 he has lived on his farm, growing fruit and writing— "and it always seems to be about Churchill." His other books include* The Bernard Shaw Dictionary *(A & C Black, 1929);* Trunk Crimes Past and Present *(Hutchinson, 1934);* The Way of the Dictators *(in collaboration with Leonard Russell; Hutchinson, 1935);* Crowning the King *(Hutchinson, 1937);* A B C of the Coronation *(Hutchinson, 1937);* Crisis Year (1938) In Story and Picture *(Hutchinson, 1939);* Ming the Panda *(Hutchinson, 1939);* Pets of Pets Corner *(Hutchinson, 1939);* Winston Churchill: Man of War *(Hutchinson, 1940);* The Innocence of Edith Thompson: A Study in Old Bailey Justice *(Hutchinson, 1952);* Queens, Crowns and Coronations *(Hutchinson, 1952);* The Friendships and Follies of Oscar Wilde *(Hutchinson, 1954);* Sir Anthony Eden: the